P9-AQS-015

FLANDRE
Boulonnais
ARTOIS   HAINAUT
              Cambrésis
Picardie   *Thiérache*

Cotentin   *Caux*   *Bray*
Bessin   *Vexin*
Normandie
Avranchin   Ile-de-France   Champagne   Lorraine
              PERCHE   BRIE   BARROIS
Bretagne   Alsace
        Maine   BEAUCE   *Gâtinais*   *Vosges*
              Orléanais
Nantais Anjou   SOLOGNE
        TOURAINE   Bourgogne Franche-
                  NIVERNAIS   Comté
VENDÉE Poitou BERRY   *Morvan*
                  Bourbonnais
AUNIS   MARCHE   *Bresse*
                Limagne *Beaujolais* *Dombes*
   ANGOUMOIS   FOREZ
   SAINTONGE Limousin *Lyonnais* Savoie
Médoc   Auvergne
Bordelais PÉRIGORD   *Velay*
        Guyenne   *Aubrac* *Vivarais* Dauphiné *Briançonnais*
        Bazadois   GÉVAUDAN   *Diois*
Landes *Agenais* Quercy   *Gapençais*
   Condomois *Rouergue* *Barronies*
              Causses *Cévennes* COMTAT
Chalosse ARMAGNAC   Provence
Labourd Gascogne   Languedoc
PAYS BASQUE
   BÉARN COMMINGES
        BIGORRE
        Couserans FOIX
              Roussillon
              Cerdagne

Historical Regions

PEASANTS INTO FRENCHMEN

EUGEN WEBER

PEASANTS INTO FRENCHMEN

The Modernization of Rural France
1870–1914

STANFORD UNIVERSITY PRESS
Stanford, California
1976

Stanford University Press
Stanford, California
© 1976 by the Board of Trustees of the
Leland Stanford Junior University
Printed in the United States of America
ISBN 0-8047-0898-3   LC 75-7486

309. 263
W 373p

Pour Jacqueline
encore et toujours

CONTENTS

MAPS

INTRODUCTION

IN 1948, under the arcades of the Odéon Theater, where in those days one could pick up remaindered books for a few francs (or read them on the spot, standing up for hours on end), I bought a copy of Roger Thabault's *Mon village*. The book, now much the worse for wear, is still with me. It was my first intimation (I only read André Siegfried's great dissertation later) that a profound sea-change had taken place in Thabault's little village of Mazières, in the Gâtinais, and in many other villages of the French countryside during the period that his pages covered—1848–1914—and that this change was more than political history as I knew it, though it intertwined with political history.

Thabault traced the evolution of a commune—bourg, villages, hamlets, scattered farms—a commune in which life had followed the same pattern since long before the Revolution and changed only, but then radically, in the half-century before 1914. Material conditions, mentalities, political awareness, all underwent massive alterations, a sort of precipitation process wholly different from the rather gradual evolutions or sporadic changes that accumulate to make what we describe as a period of history. Historical change rushing in headlong carried Mazières not from one historical period to another, but into a new age of mankind—an altogether different form of civilization.[1]

It was all very interesting, but I was then concerned with other things. The story Thabault told colored my view of French history but did not really change it. The history I thought and taught and wrote about went on chiefly in cities; the countryside and the little towns were a mere appendage of that history, following, echoing, or simply standing by to watch what was going on, but scarcely relevant on their own account.

Twenty years later I discovered another book that described in its own way the same profound sea-change. I really do not know how I came by it, for this one was not a historian's work either. Written by a folklorist, *Civilisation traditionnelle et genres de vie* was almost contemporary to *Mon village*. On quite a different plane, more broadly argued, it talked about the decay and the dis-appearance of France's traditional rites and lore. These, said its author, André Varagnac, had always altered as far back as we can see to tell. But until the nineteenth century others had always emerged in their stead. The novelty now was that the renewal process ceased: traditions died, and they were not re-placed; there was no longer any spontaneous innovation in the countryside.[2] A whole mentality was dying—had died—out. Coincidence? Varagnac, too, situated the crucial changes in the last quarter of the nineteenth century.

By now, I was ready to go further. I had begun to sense in my work in political and intellectual history—the sort that we write about and teach, the urban sort—that I was ignoring a vast dimension of reality. What happened in small towns and in the countryside? Was Varagnac right? Was there a culture or rather several cultures that carried on beside the official one we knew and studied, and that at some point gave up or were integrated with the larger whole? If so, how did this happen?

I went back to Thabault. It was not the first time I had reread him; but when one looks for different things, one *sees* different things. Thabault's hero, in a manner of speaking, the pivot of the modifications that he etches, was the village school. All French historians knew that much, to be sure. But Thabault focuses on the school in a particular context: the passage from relative isola-tion and a relatively closed economy to union with the outside world through roads, railroads, and a money economy. The school was important because con-ditions changed, because it served new conditions, and the conditions that it *helped* to change were no longer local ones but national; they were urban, they were modern.

What a discovery! After a quarter of a century spent studying French his-tory, I was inventing for myself what any textbook could have told me. And yet perhaps that is essentially what the study of history is: the rereading of the past, so to speak, in the beginning because one wants to discover it for oneself and assimilate it, and later because what one looks for (hence sees) in familiar territory may be quite different from what one has discerned be-fore or learned from others. So it was with me. Looking for answers to the questions that Varagnac had helped suggest drove me to discover a new France in the nineteenth-century countryside, a France where many did not speak French or know (let alone use) the metric system, where *pistoles* and *écus* were better known than francs, where roads were few and markets distant, and where a subsistence economy reflected the most common prudence. This book is about how all this changed, and about how mentalities altered in the process; in a word, about how undeveloped France was integrated into the modern world and the official culture—of Paris, of the cities.

And it is about peasants. Gordon Wright has said, no one can say it better, how dangerous it is to venture into such quicksands: "Rural France is almost infinitely diverse, and almost any generalization about the peasantry becomes partially false as soon as it is formulated." And yet he adds, and I must echo him: "A nagging curiosity about general trends ... led me to persist in trying to see the problem in the large."[3]

La Rochefoucauld remarked that one can know things well only when one knows them in detail, yet detail is infinite, hence our knowledge is fated to remain superficial and imperfect. It is a convenient argument for a book like this, in which inferences of a general nature are drawn from documentation that is necessarily partial and incomplete in the first instance. Besides, given my working hypothesis that very significant portions of rural France continued to live in a world of their own until near the end of the nineteenth century, I have deliberately focused on the areas that served my interests best—the west, center, south, and southwest—and on the 40 or 50 years before 1914. And finally, because my purpose from the start was to be not exhaustive but suggestive, the documentation reflects that approach.

The period covered, which is roughly the period encompassed by Thabault, has remained oddly unexplored—from my point of view. Among secondary sources, those from which I learned the most, and the most directly, have been the path-breaking articles of Guy Thuillier and Alain Corbin's massive unpublished dissertation on the Limousin during the middle third of the nineteenth century. The other great studies that cast light on life in the countryside deal with earlier periods (Le Roy Ladurie, Pierre Goubert, Paul Bois) or with the first half of the nineteenth century (Maurice Agulhon, Jean Vidalenc, Philippe Vigier) or with the twentieth century (Gordon Wright, Henri Mendras). From the mid-twentieth century on, indeed, there has been a wealth of sociological investigation, but most of it extends back only sketchily for introductory purposes. There are numbers of monographs, many of them distinguished and sensitive, but few of them linger long on the years I am most concerned with; and those that do (André Siegfried, Georges Dupeux) are chiefly interested in politics. As my pages make clear, my principal interest lies in ways of life and thought—a more elusive quarry. Doubly elusive when documentation is hard to find, still harder to pin down.

Special problems arise when one tries to understand the evolution of conditions and mentalities among the inarticulate masses, inarticulate, that is, on those particular levels that provide most of the records on which historians rely. Most of the subjects of historical investigation have been literate and articulate themselves; many have left clear and often deliberate records or have been described by witnesses who were well acquainted with them. The acts, thoughts, and words of the illiterate (and most of my subjects were illiterate, or as nearly so as makes no difference) remain largely unrecorded. Such records as exist are the work of outsiders who observed and recorded what they saw for purposes of their own. Police, bureaucrats, folklorists, priests, teachers, agronomists, and men of letters looked on, even probed, but whether critical or sympathetic they cannot tell us what went on as true participants. My rule with this kind of evidence has been to try to indicate its sources and context, so that readers can take any possible prejudice (or at least orientation) into account; and to rely most freely on evidence that appears to be purely incidental to the main purpose of the witness or better still, contrary to his or her apparent interest.

Moreover, the illiterate are not in fact inarticulate; they can and do express their feelings and their minds in several ways. Sociologists, ethnologists, geographers, and most recently demographic historians have shown us new and different means of interpreting evidence, with the result that our fund of facts has turned out to be far richer than we previously believed. I have tried to learn from their work, though I have not followed the lead of any one discipline. A particularly fruitful source of evidence, especially in a work whose principal aim is to explore and suggest, is to be found in the songs, dances, proverbs, tales, and pictures of the country folk—in the whole broad realm of *arts et traditions populaires*. I have tapped this source repeatedly to discover what the rural people used, or said, or did, how these changed or came to be abandoned, and what replaced them.

But even research on traditional lines on the social history of the years 1880–1914 presents special problems. There are serious gaps in the Archives Nationales for the crucial half-century before 1914.[4] This is matched by a corresponding poverty in the departmental archives, which are rich in material right through the Second Empire and emaciated thereafter until the years after World War I. There is considerable documentation even so, and I have mined it for a dozen prefectures. Other archives yielded much information as well: of the Ministère de la Guerre, of the Musée des Arts et Traditions Populaires, of the Institut National de Recherche et de Documentation Pédagogique. So did the rich secondary materials in the Bibliothèque Nationale. To the directors and staffs of these institutions, and of the departmental archives of Allier, Ariège, Cantal, Finistère, Gers, Gironde, Haute-Vienne, Lot, Puy-de-Dôme, Pyrénées-Orientales, Vosges, and Yonne, I owe my thanks for helpfulness beyond the call of duty.

Other thanks are also in order: to the University of California and the National Endowment for the Humanities for a grant of leave and subsidies that made the enterprise possible and helped me to carry it through; to Mr. Robert Rockwell and Mlles. N. Grangé and M. Revel for resourceful research assistance; to Mrs. Claire Pirone for typing and retyping the manuscript with unflagging zeal.

Several French colleagues and research scholars have lent precious materials and advice. Among them are M. J. M. Dumont at Epinal, Mlle. L. Bouyssou at Aurillac, and above all M. Henri Polge at Auch, a man of inspiriting erudition and suggestions. Professor Tanguy Daniel, now teaching in Brest, allowed me to draw on his manuscript survey of *pardons* and pilgrimages in the diocese of Quimper; Professor Alain Corbin permitted me to read, and learn from, his monumental and fascinating dissertation on migration in the Limousin; and M. André Varagnac shared generously both his recollections and his personal archives with me. Closer to home, Charles Tilly contributed truly constructive criticism. My thanks to all of them. Nor must I forget (I would not want to do so!) the first occasion I had to air my views on this subject, provided by the University of Southwestern Louisiana's 1971 Symposium of French-American Studies;[5] and the two friends, Professors Amos Simpson and Vaughan Baker, whose urgings once upon an enthusiastic Louisiana night convinced me that the theme that had intrigued me for some years was worth pursuing.

I might have read much more, talked to more people, attempted a more comprehensive survey. But in the end the study would still have been incomplete, its conclusions still tentative like those of this book. Let this inquiry be taken for what it is, then: a venture in putting some flesh on the bare bones of general facts that we know already in a general way, and a suggestion of the work still to be done.

> For there is good news yet to hear and fine things to be seen,
> Before we go to Paradise by way of Kensal Green.

PART I

THE WAY THINGS WERE

Chapter One

A COUNTRY OF SAVAGES

Il y aurait de bons courriers à faire de France et de pays que nous
croyons connus; l'étrange n'est pas toujours au pays étranger; on
ferait d'immenses découvertes chez soi; on obtiendrait de singuliers
résultats si l'on savait regarder le pays habituel d'un regard in-
habitué; regarder la France comme si on n'en était pas.
                                                    —CHARLES PÉGUY

"YOU DON'T NEED to go to America to see savages," mused a Parisian as he
strolled through the Burgundian countryside of the 1840's. "Here are the
Redskins of Fenimore Cooper." Thus Balzac, in his *Paysans* (1844). Indeed,
there is a great deal of evidence to suggest that vast parts of nineteenth-
century France were inhabited by savages. Louis Chevalier has told us how
this label was pinned on the urban poor—classe laborieuse, classe dangereuse
—around mid-century. But it can as readily be applied, and for a longer period
of time, to sections of the rural population—equally strange and little known,
equally hard-working though perhaps less dangerous for being less concentrated.

In 1831, to reach no further back, the prefect of Ariège described the population of his Pyrenean valleys as savage "and as brutal as the bears it breeds."
In 1840, an army staff officer found the Morvandiaux of Fours "uttering cries as
savage as the beasts themselves." Officials, soldiers—who else would venture
into the wild countryside, especially the lost regions south of the Loire? In
1843, an infantry battalion marching through the marshy Landes northeast
of Dax discovered still more savages: poor, backward, wild.[1] The whole region was savage: wastelands, marshes, moors, heath. In 1832, when Georges
(later Baron) Haussmann visited the district of Houeillès in the southwest
corner of Lot-et-Garonne, he found no road or landmark, and the highway
inspector who guided him had to use a compass.[2] These were only the *petites
landes*; in the Landes proper, as the proverb had it, birds crossing the moors
had to carry their own food. Before 1857, when the planting of stands of pine
ushered in the dawn of a new era (but only a dim dawn as yet), references
to savagery abound, applied equally to the landscape, the conditions, and the
population. Pilgrims en route to Santiago de Compostela feared to cross the
Landes because they found there "neither bread nor wine nor fish nor fountain."[3] Indeed, Taine declared that he preferred the desert. When Edouard

Feret published his massive *Statistique générale du département de la Gironde* in 1874, the draining of marshy Médoc was still within living memory, and many Bordelais remembered the fevers and stagnant waters that justified its original name—*in medio aquae*. As for the great moors to the south of Bordeaux, they still stood unimproved—savage, waterless, the home of pellagra and fever among a population as wild as its environment.[4]

From Bordeaux to Bayonne all was wilderness. Savagery also from the Ile-d'Yeu, off the Atlantic coast, to the Drôme in the east, where in 1857 a colonel expressed the hope that railways might improve the lot of "populations two or three centuries behind their fellows" and eliminate "the savage instincts born of isolation and of misery."[5] The burghers of Tulle called peasants *peccata* (sins), and a Corrèze priest, offspring of a humble family of that prefecture but banished to a rural parish, noted with contempt: "the peasant is just that, sin, original sin, still persistent and visible in all its naïve brutality."[6] This observation, recorded by Joseph Roux, was probably jotted down at the beginning of the Third Republic, but it reflects a consensus that runs through the first three-quarters of the century. "The countryman shows, in his every feature, the face of misery and woe: his eyes are uncertain, timid, his face expressionless, his gait slow and clumsy; his long hair falling over his shoulders gives him a somber air" (Haute-Vienne, 1822). Terrible ignorance, superstition, dirt (Morbihan, 1822). Lazy, greedy, avaricious, and suspicious (Landes, 1843). Foulness, rags, miserable savagery (Loire-Inférieure, 1850). "Vulgar, hardly civilized, their nature meek but wild" (Loire, 1862).[7] No wonder that in 1865 a Limousin landowner had recourse to terms not unlike those La Bruyère had used 200 years before: "animals with two feet, hardly resembling a man. [The peasant's] clothes are filthy; under his thick skin one cannot see the blood flow. The wild, dull gaze betrays no flicker of thought in the brain of this being, morally and physically atrophied."[8]

The popular risings of December 1851 produced their own crop of references: savage horde, a land of savages, barbarians.[9] One does well to remember that to hurl the abusive expression *sauvage* at someone was considered slanderous and could lead to a fine or even a prison sentence if a case came to court.[10] Yet the litany goes on: in the early 1860's the savagery is waning in Nièvre, but it persists into the 1870's in Sarthe, where the "savage" moorland people live like "troglodytes" and sleep near the fire in their huts "on stalks of briar like cats on wood shavings."[11] It persists in Brittany, too, where the children entering school "are like those of countries where civilization has not penetrated: savage, dirty, and don't understand a word of the language" (1880).[12] And a musical folklorist ranging the west from Vendée to the Pyrenees compared the local folk to children and savages who, happily, like all primitive peoples, showed a pronounced taste for rhythm.[13] As late as 1903, the theme of rural savagery was still being sounded by a professional travel writer, who on a visit to the Limousin, just north of Brive, was struck by the wild character of the region and the "huttes de sauvages" in which the people lived.[14] What a relief after the wildness of the interminable chestnut groves to reach a township, however small. Civilization is urban (civic, civil, civilian, civilized), and so of course is urbanity; just as polity, politeness, politics, and police spring from *polis*—the city again.

Civilization is what the peasants lacked. In 1850 the Gramont Law making the ill-treatment of domestic animals a misdemeanor was inspired by the wish to "civilize people" and children.[15] The 1850's, in fact, never hesitated to make that point. A Beauce priest felt that his parishioners' greatest need was to become civilized.[16] In Haute-Loire, the boatmen of the Allier River showed a strikingly higher "degree of civilization," thanks to the "more civilized nations" they met on the way to Paris. So did the men of Saint-Didier, where commercial relations with Saint-Etienne had made for "a more advanced civilization."[17] In Morvan, by contrast, an 1857 guidebook noted that the villages were "hardly touched by civilization"; military surveys exposed the same state of affairs in Lot and Aveyron.[18]

Between the 1860's and the 1880's we find repeated references in the reports of primary school inspectors to the progress of civilization and the role of the schools in civilizing the populations in whose midst they operated. What did such reports mean to contemporaries? We shall examine the question in detail in due course. Right now let us suggest that they reflected the prevailing belief that areas and groups of some importance were uncivilized, that is, unintegrated into, unassimilated to French civilization: poor, backward, ignorant, savage, barbarous, wild, living like beasts with their beasts. They had to be taught manners, morals, literacy, a knowledge of French, and of France, a sense of the legal and institutional structure beyond their immediate community. Léon Gambetta put all this in a nutshell in 1871: the peasants were "intellectually several centuries behind the enlightened part of the country"; there was "an enormous distance between them and us ... between those who speak our language and those many of our compatriots [who], cruel as it is to say so, can no more than stammer in it"; material property had to "become the means of their moral progress," that is, of their civilization.[19] The peasant had to be integrated into the national society, economy, and culture: the culture of the city and of the City par excellence, Paris.

Progress reports mark the campaign to do so: in the Morbihan of 1880 civilization had yet to penetrate the savage interior and make it similar to the rest of France; but in Ardèche, "softer and politer habits are replacing rude, coarse, and savage ways," and in the Atlantic West the old customs were being "swept out by civilization."[20] Until the final success of the campaign, the countryman would continue to be, in the words of two southwestern observers, a rough and incomplete draft of the truly civilized man.[21]

Incomplete, of course, in terms of a model to which he did not conform, and for good reason: he knew nothing of it. A cultural and political aboriginal, like to beasts and children, and one whom even sympathetic observers found decidedly odd. In 1830 Stendhal spoke of that deadly triangle between Bordeaux, Bayonne, and Valence, where "people believe in witches, don't know how to read, and don't speak French." And Flaubert, walking around Rosporden fair in 1846 like a tourist through some exotic bazaar, noted of the peasants around him: "suspicious, anxious, bewildered by everything he sees and doesn't understand, he makes great haste to leave the town."[22] However keen his vision, Flaubert made the great mistake of judging the peasant by the way he behaved in town, a place that he came to only when he had to. "Because he finds only people who assume a superior and mocking air with him," explained an observer in Bourbonnais, the peasant was always ill at ease and constrained in town, and superficial observers took this as evidence of "savagery and dissimulation." In effect the savagery *was* dissimulation, enhanced by surliness. This would be worse in an area like Brittany, where the peasant could not be sure who among the townsmen (apart from small tradesmen and artisans) spoke his language.[23] As we shall see, French-speakers there and elsewhere needed interpreters, which did not make for easier communication or mutual understanding.

Ill at ease in urban settings, the peasant made his urban observers ill at ease; their opinion of him was the mirror image of his mistrust of them. Writing in the 1860's, one observer of the southwestern peasants—who, he was sure, hated and feared him—could not hide his own fear of them, or his contempt. And a squire near Nantes could not help noticing the way the peasants looked at him, "full of hatred and suspicion."[24] "Ignorant, full of prejudices," wrote an officer, speaking of the population near Le Mans, "they have no scruples in craft or in deceit." Ignorance, apathy, slackness, sloth, inertia, a brutal, grasping, dissembling, and hypocritical nature, are variously attributed to malice, poverty, and undernourishment.[25] We shall hear more of this later. At any rate, what could one expect? The peasant did not reason; he was selfish and superstitious. He was insensitive to beauty, indifferent to his surroundings. He was envious and detested anyone who tried to better himself.[26]

City dwellers, who often (as in the colonial cities of Brittany) did not understand the rural language, despised the peasants, exaggerated their savagery, insisted on the more picturesque—hence backward—aspects of their activities, and sometimes compared them unfavorably with other colonized peoples in North Africa and the New World.[27] In nineteenth-century Brest it was not unusual to hear the surrounding countryside described as "the bush": *brousse* or *cambrousse*. But colonial parallels were little needed when the armory of prejudice was so well stocked: "Les pommes de terre pour les cochons, les épluchures pour les Bretons."[28]

In the mid-eighteenth century, the famous *Encyclopédie* had expressed the established view: "Many people see little difference between this class of men and the animals they use to farm our lands; this manner of thinking is very old and it is likely that it will endure a very long time." It did. During the Revolution, writes Jules Bois, the urban national guard in the Maine had the most profound contempt for the rural barbarians of their region and even carried back necklaces of ears and noses from their incursions into the rebellious countryside. Nineteenth-century historians of the Vendée, in their turn, denied that country people could have any purpose or ideas apart from those suggested by outside sources.[29] This theme, which recurred time and again in discussions of popular culture, perpetuated the notion of the mindless dolt whose thinking was inconsequential, if indeed he thought at all.

Early-nineteenth-century folklorists were criticized for showing interest in the "low class of the population" or for recording patois unworthy of attention, let alone respect. The Republicans of 1871, with the obvious intent of demeaning the majority of the national assembly, had called them "rurals."[30] The rurals themselves agreed: it was demeaning to be a rural. To walk like a peasant or eat like a peasant was a sin that the little manuals of etiquette the peddlers sold condemned out of hand. Others used the notion of race in this same context. In Languedoc the unprivileged classes were regarded and regarded themselves as an inferior species: country girls, small, black, and wizened, were "of another race" than town girls. One result of this belief in a difference *in kind* was that well into the nineteenth century village midwives kneaded babies' skulls in an effort "more symbolic than real" to give the little round heads of peasant babies the elongated skull that was associated with the more intelligent city folk.[31] And just as the superiority assumed by strangers became a superiority attributed to strangers, so the pejorative judgments of strangers were incorporated into language, and hence inevitably into thought.

In Lower Brittany the word *pémôr* (originally used to describe a clodhopper) came to apply first to all peasants of that area, then to the Breton language itself. Terms like *pem* and *beda* followed the same route, originally signifying a clod, then a recruit, and finally any peasant of Lower Brittany. Similarly, in Franche-Comté the term for cow dung, *bouz*, gave rise to *bouzon* for peasant. *Croquants*, bumpkins, clodhoppers, *culs-terreux*—the list we began some pages back is far from complete. But as if all this was not enough, the word peasant itself became a term of contempt, to be rejected as an insult or accepted as an expression of humility, but in either case to be shed for a more honorable label at the first opportunity. And indeed an English traveler of the 1890's found the word falling into disuse: "just as soon as he can, the peasant becomes a *cultivateur!*"[32]

The peasant was ashamed to be a peasant; he was ashamed to be uncivilized; he agreed with his judges that there was something valuable and vastly superior that he lacked, that French civilization and notably anything from Paris were clearly superior and clearly desirable: hence the vogue of the *articles de Paris*. Bretons twitted those who sought to ape a refined tone for

speaking with "a little Paris voice." But they also spoke admiringly of someone of a noble, easy, relaxed, smart bearing as being "on a French footing."[33]
The ambiguity is clear and is a recurring phenomenon. We shall meet it again.
But for the peasant to know himself uncouth, he had first to become aware
of a model for couthness. And we shall see that in many places this took some
time. Meanwhile, Paris and indeed France remained vague, faraway places for
all too many—like the peasants of Ariège in the 1850's who imagined the
Louvre to be a fantastic, fairytale palace, and the members of the imperial
family to be some sort of storybook characters. No different, after all, from
the city people for whom peasants remained "almost as unknown as the red
Indian to the tourist on a stagecoach between New York and Boston."[34]

We often read that farmers and peasants together constituted about 50 percent of France's working population in 1870, 45 percent in 1900, and 35 percent in 1930. What, we may well ask, is comprehended in the terms peasants
and farmers? Were peasants a homogeneous professional group in any of
those periods? Did the terms farmers and peasants describe similar realities
at the various dates? In other words, when we talk of rural France and
the rural populations in 1850, 1880, 1900, and after, are we talking of similar
kinds of people, of similar frames of mind and similar shares in national
life (differing only in statistical weight)? Or are we talking of a two-way
evolution on the theory—as we were told long ago—that no one can ever step
in the same river twice, not only because the river will have changed, but
because the person will have changed too?

This sort of question begs its answer, but a precise answer is difficult to
formulate. Just how difficult, the rest of this book will show. One reason for
the difficulty, among many, is that French ethnographers and anthropologists
(not uniquely to be sure, but perhaps more than their counterparts elsewhere)
have until recently eagerly studied exotic peoples while much neglecting their
own; and the sociologists seem to have progressed straight from their early
studies of primitive societies to the study of urban and industrial ones, dis-
missing the peasant realities around or just behind them.

Typically, the distinguished sociologist Maurice Halbwachs made a survey
of life-styles in 1907 that covered 87 households, 33 of peasants, 54 of urban
workers, but referred specifically only to the urban group (and even then
concentrated mostly on five families of Paris workers) when he presented his
data in 1939.[35] In this he was no different from the rest of his contemporaries,
for whom Parisian life and national life were leagues apart, and only the
former counted. Thus, Ferdinand Buisson's great pedagogical dictionary of
the 1880's, bible of a generation of schoolteachers, includes neither *patois*, nor
idiome, nor *dialecte*. Similarly, at the turn of the century the great debate in
and around the university turned on whether the teaching of Latin and Greek
should take precedence over French, completely ignoring the problems posed

by and the lessons to be drawn from the still-current conflict between French and local speech. Among the spate of surveys that marked the fin-de-siècle and the early twentieth century, none looked beyond Paris and what went on there. And this without reservations, confident that the views and aspirations of a tiny minority taking itself for *all* did indeed represent all.[36]

Perhaps that is why Haussmann, writing his memoirs in retirement, could refer to "our country, the most 'one' in the whole world," when France was still very far from one, and when he himself had been in a good position to see this with his own eyes in the administrative posts he had held through the July Monarchy and the Second Empire, before his fateful appointment to Paris.[37] The myth was stronger than the reality.

Yet the reality was inescapable. And the reality was diversity. One reason believers in the essential unity of France ignored this most obvious fact may have been that they took that unity for granted. But as the century advanced the division between country and town began to attract comment. The economist Adolphe Blanqui, who traveled a great deal through darkest France, partly on official missions of exploration, partly to prepare a survey of rural populations that unfortunately never saw the light of day, was one of the first to insist on it. In his preliminary findings, published in 1851, Blanqui noted: "Two different peoples living on the same land a life so different that they seem foreign to each other, though united by the bonds of the most imperious centralization that ever existed." In the countryside, barbarism and misery were still the norm "despite the civilizing movement taking over neighboring towns." In the high Alps and parts of Var and Isère, a simple wheelbarrow would be as extraordinary a sight as a locomotive. "Village and city represent ... two completely opposite ways of life." Comfort and well-being were found only in a few "oases."[38] And while towns were becoming more alike, country people continued to show a remarkable diversity from one region to another and even from one province to the next.

Diversity had not bothered earlier centuries very much. It seemed part of the nature of things, whether from place to place or between one social group and another. But the Revolution had brought with it the concept of national unity as an integral and integrating ideal at all levels, and the ideal of oneness stirred concern about its shortcomings. Diversity became imperfection, injustice, failure, something to be noted and to be remedied. The contrast Blanqui drew between administrative unity and deep differences in conditions and attitudes became a source of malaise.

In 1845 Benjamin Disraeli had published *Sybil* with its perceptive reference to the two nations "between whom there is no intercourse and no sympathy; who are as ignorant of each other's habits, thoughts and feelings as if they were dwellers in different zones, or inhabitants of different planets; who are formed by a different breeding, are fed by a different food, are ordered by different manners, are not governed by the same laws." Disraeli was referring to the rich and the poor ("the Privileged and the People"), and to the reforms needed to knit a people together. His ideas, or very similar ones, were discussed and sometimes applied at the urban level. But they applied as aptly to France's rural situation—a situation noticed only rarely and by those few whose interest drew them to subjects that the dominant center deemed unimportant.

Blanqui had found occasion to remark that urban and rural civilization had always moved at a different pace, "but nowhere is the distance separating them greater than in France." In the first history of peasants as such, published in 1856, the journalist Eugène Bonnemère predicted the hardening of social lines, culminating in two distinct races, city dwellers and countryfolk, living in mutual ignorance, and in two distinct Frances, different and hostile, that of the country and that of the towns.[39] And if Gambetta, speaking at Belleville in 1875, felt the need to deny the antagonism between country and town ("two Frances opposed one to the other"), it must have been there when he spoke.[40] As late as 1893 Henri Baudrillart still spoke of the deep division between cities, "which have their life apart," and the countryside.[41] At the same time, it is worth noting that he had reference here to the relatively backward Haute-Garonne, not to the French countryside as a whole, suggesting that changes had taken place elsewhere in the meantime, and that different regions evolved at a different pace.

Such time lags and the disparities that ensued from different rates of change are crucial aspects of our story. Most of it deals with regional diversities that have attracted little notice in generalizations made from an urban point of view. If Disraeli concerned himself with rich and poor, it may have been in part because regional differences were of less account in England than in France. Comparing France and England in the 1860's, Léonce de Lavergne found little difference between rural and urban salaries in England, between the Londoner's way of life and that of the Cumberland man.[42] His statistical approach may be disputed, and his impressions too. But it is certain, as he claimed, that nowhere in England could one find anything approaching the distance that separated the departments of Nord and Seine-Inférieure, say, from Lozère and Landes. Nor, indeed, could one have found the kind of tribute that the country paid to the capital, and the countryside grudgingly to cities in general. "You have voted millions to embellish the cities," complained a deputy of Nord in 1861; "you have voted fine monuments and we, we are still in the mud up to our knees."[43]

In July 1789, after news of the fall of the Bastille, mountain peasants of the Saint-Romain region in Mâconnais revolted and carried their spontaneous jacquerie into the plains, which remembered this always as the time of the brigands. The rebels caused great damage—pillaging and burning—until finally put down by the urban militias of Mâcon, Cluny, and Tournus. Many were hanged at the gates of Cluny or in the town square of Tournus. Tradition says that those who escaped this summary justice were crucified by mobs on Cluny common. True or false, tradition is revealing: it gives us the venting of popular wrath on men whom some might regard as popular heroes. And the countryside between Igé and Cluny preserves the equivocal memory in Brigands' Roads, Brigands' Crosses, and other tributes to the well-established hostility between mountain and plain, country and town. Writing about the same period, Richard Cobb talks of the soldiers who marched out of Paris and other urban centers to enforce the economic policies of 1793 and 1794 (that is, to gather provisions), behaving just as if they were in enemy territory: "Indeed, many of these urban soldiers said that they were in enemy territory." The feeling was mutual, and it persisted.[44]

Country and town, bourg and hamlet, were complementary, but still incompletely so, and hostile. For the peasant, the bourgeois, however humble, was the inhabitant of the bourg, envied and distrusted. The girls who lived on isolated farms or in tiny hamlets traditionally preferred to marry artisans; witness the many Gascon tales warning the peasant maid against marrying a "bourgeois" like the village baker or hairdresser, or the equally numerous songs in which a farmer or a shepherd is spurned in favor of a miller or a baker.[45] When the song is of peasant origin it may predict the grief that awaits the girl, the beatings and the moldy bread (no different really from what could be expected on a farm), but the tone is one of rivalry and resentment. This becomes more acute when the rival belongs to a real urban community. A song of Lower Dauphiné tells of a peasant lad who tangles with a Lyon silk weaver and thrashes him, then meets a maiden he likes and wants to impress with his feat:[46]

> Had I but known how to tell her my tale!
> Peasants are every bit as good as gents!

Of course they were not. And the advantages all urban dwellers seemed to have over them prompted thoughts of revenge. All city people were gents—bourgeois, messieurs—and their hateful superiority contributed to the ambiguity of the peasants' reactions to them and to their influence. Emile Souvestre, who was persuaded of the hatred peasants felt for the bourgeoisie, tells of how, in the peasant siege of Pontivy in Vendée during the Hundred Days, the women who accompanied the *chouans* carried sacks for the loot they hoped to gain. One had two: the smaller for the money she could find, the bigger to carry off gents' heads.[47] Several stories of this ilk have circulated, but none has been authenticated so far. They reflect not only the fears of city people, but their accurate perception of how their country neighbors felt about them. Messieurs were many, but the feelings they provoked were the same. In Savoy in 1870, after news of the fall of the Second Empire reached the villages, peasants were reported to have cried, "A bas les messieurs! Vive la République!"[48]

Nor, as we have seen, did the hostility reflect a clear-cut sense of class divisions. On the contrary, the evidence suggests that peasants distrusted anything with the taint of the town. Around Limoges in the 1840's, young Republicans of the middle classes preached the doctrines of Pierre Leroux, Saint-Simon, Cabet, and Fourier to the local workers, and converted some of them. But neither the burghers nor the workers of the town could get through to the rural masses. Socialist militants trying to indoctrinate the peasantry in patois got a few leagues from town, as far as their legs could carry them in one day, but seem to have had little or no impact.[49]

The troubles that shook France between 1848 and 1851 showed that neither class nor political interests could override traditional hostilities and fears. When the peasants of Ajain marched on their county town, Guéret, in 1848, the local workers' club was torn between sympathy for the insurgents and fear of seeing them enter the town. Finally, workingmen, firemen, national guard, all "betrayed" the peasants and stood with their fellow townsmen. Again, after December 2, 1851, when the peasants marched on towns throughout the south of the Limousin, the townsmen stood against them. In the Drôme, at Crest, whose burghers had sucked the surrounding country dry with their usury, the peasants came down out of the mountains as poor, wild mountaineers have done through history, to pillage the bourgeois of the plains. But "the barbarian army" (as a leader of the municipal resistance called them) found neither help nor sympathy among the workers of Crest, by all accounts a pretty unruly lot themselves in other circumstances.[50]

We shall encounter these events again when we examine the political evolution of the countryside in detail. My point right now is that age-old hostilities had changed little, that social tensions remained in their archaic pattern, and that what has sometimes been taken as evidence of class war in the countryside was often the extension of an understandable feud between country and town. From Balzac to Zola, via Maeterlinck, the Abbé Roux, and many others, the peasant appears as a dark, mysterious, hostile, and menacing figure, and is described as such. When he is not a noble savage, as he was for George Sand, he is simply a savage.

Those who express regret at the passing of the level-headed, vigorous, hardworking countryman of yore have no idea what he was really like—no more, in many cases, than his contemporaries had. As Philip Gaskell observes, of the Scottish Highlander in roughly the same period: "He lived not in picturesque, rural felicity, but in conditions of penury and squalor that can only be fairly compared with those of a famine area in contemporary India, and that were tolerable only because they were traditional and familiar."[51]

In August 1840, when the Conseil Général of Loiret considered a series of questions submitted by the Minister of the Interior, their answer to one question was terse: "Is poverty hereditary in a great many families? Yes." So rare was the incidence of peasant wealth that when a villager managed to grow rich his success was likely to be attributed to trafficking with the devil or to criminal activity. In 1856 one Catherine Raoux of Ally (Cantal) was caught stealing from the mill where she worked, her employers having been alerted by her "acquisition of a pair of shoes, an umbrella, and two handkerchiefs in quick succession, and the purchase of these items in cash."[52] Proverbs and songs reflect the situation: "When one has nothing, one has nothing to lose," says the Limousin; and "A patched coat lasts longer than a new one." The tale of Hansel and Gretel, abandoned in the woods by parents too poor to feed them, is told in Auvergne about little Jean and Jeannette. The best known *bourrée* of Auvergne and one of the gayest has a swain wondering how to get married on practically nothing. He has five *sous*, his love has four, they will buy one spoon, they will buy one bowl, and eat their soup together. Further west, omnipresent misery struts through peasant shanties as it does through the peasants' lives, robbing them of everything, in due course of their lives.[53]

One evidence of poverty, often cited by contemporaries, was the sale of women's hair. This was particularly widespread in the center and the west, where the hair of countrywomen was periodically harvested to be exchanged in the market for a length of cloth, a couple of kerchiefs, or simply a few centimes. The midsummer fair at Limoges was especially dedicated to this trade, attracting buyers from as far as Paris; so did another important center, Treignac, in Corrèze. The practice waned as prosperity spread after the 1880's, and as Chinese competition drove the market down, a development that saw the value of a kilogram of hair drop from 100 francs in the early 1880's to only 50 in 1902.[54] By 1888 a Corrézien could rejoice that more and more peasant women refused to sell their hair, and that only "shepherdesses and poor servants" still traded it for a few yards of calico. But the practice declined slowly, and it persisted in most of the Limousin and Brittany, the poorest and most backward of French regions, until at least 1914.[55]

Extreme poverty could and did persist, of course, even in areas that were not poor: the Allier valley, Lauragais, Beauce, Berry. As an army officer remarked in 1850, after traveling from Clermont to Billom along the Allier valley: "The country itself is rich, the farmers are miserable." The situation was entirely normal, as the passing reflection of an Ariège tax collector on the life of a poor farmer attests: "His occupation allows him to live miserably, like all the working class."[56] What did this mean? Many lacked a table, a cupboard, even a chair, bedded down on straw or fern, had practically no clothes. From Yonne this police report on a search of a shoemaker's household: "No bed, no linen, no shirts, just nothing, absolutely nothing!" From the stony mountains of Puy, an equally dismal report by a local squire describing the huts, or rather the lairs, where men and beasts huddled together around a feeble fire built of peat and smoking heavily. Only the grandsire had a chair; the father squatted on a stone, the children on the peat blocks that would provide the next day's fuel. All slept on dried leaves.[57] Shepherds and other landless peasants lived even harder. The gendarmes of Lahorre described the cabin of a Pyrenean shepherd (1888): about one meter high, dry stones, earth roof, a little straw to lie on; a small heap of potatoes; a sack containing half a loaf, fat, and salt. The man carried his wealth on him: a box with three or four matches and nothing else. As a bourrée of the Foix country had it:

> Shepherds' life,
> Life of rich fare:
> Skimmed milk in the morning,
> Curdled milk at night.

Most shepherds were able to keep body and soul together, but how they managed to exist, they and the many other landless denizens of the countryside, remains an enigma.[58]

Of course they worked—when they could—and those who worked, worked very hard indeed. It has been suggested that new methods of farming, notably the shift from the biannual to the triannual rotation of crops, created a peasant without leisure. Again, we shall see that new methods of cultivation progressed at rates that varied greatly; and so did access to leisure. But I should think that peasants had enough to do even under the old system. What observers in fact noted was the result of the peasant's new opportunities to improve his lot at the cost of immense effort and with no certainty of success—more simply, the novelty of hope. Peasants in Upper Quercy began work at dawn, ended late at night, often went to work their own plot by moonlight after having worked another's land by day. "No more rest and no more ease!" lamented a landowner near Nantes in 1856. "Everyone scrimps, ... works without care for rest or food, ... to buy a plot of land from some neighbor ruined by usury."[59]

The more ambitious you were, the harder you worked. Benoît Malon's father, employed on a Forez farm, was free to work his potato patch and his kitchen garden on Sunday after church. He died at thirty-three of pleurisy, which he contracted as he hurried to get to his freshly planted potatoes.[60] As late as 1908 in the marshlands of the Vendée a man farming four hectares with only a spade (thus able to work no more than four ares a day) left home at five in the morning, returned at seven in the evening, and never saw his children.* Hard labor without chains—to which one remained bound by necessity and from which only death could bring release.

That the release was often yearned for is attested by the Alpine adage: "heyrouss com'un crébat"—happy as a carcass. Malon's grandmother entreated the little boy to accompany her in death; his mother envied him because she believed he would die young. There is a Berry song in which a woman dreams of escape, but every hope proves false: perhaps when she is married she will

---

* René Dumont, *Voyages en France d'un agronome*, p. 305. One hectare = 10,000 square meters = 2.47 acres. One are = 100 square meters = 119.60 square yards.

work in the fields no more; but marriage comes and still she works; pregnancy is no better, children are no help, so she yearns for death, and death at last sets her free. No wonder the Bourbonnais peasant holds life as nothing: "La vie, oné rien de tout." A life of labor is easily dispensed with.[61]

So much misery. So much fear. Of menaces known and unknown; and of the known, above all wolves, mad dogs, and fires. Forests were still vast and fearsome around mid-century.

In Mâconnais the wolves disappeared in the 1840's, and in Orléanais one could cross the forest without risk of attack by 1850. But elsewhere wolves ran freely in packs through forests and mountain regions until close to the end of the century. The last wolf in Châteauroux forest was killed in 1877. In Brittany they were attacking animals into the early 1880's, and in 1882 Maupassant recorded that in Lower Brittany sheep were put out to graze with cows to provide "la part du loup." Wolves were hunted in the Morvan into the 1890's (as were boars, which devastated the fields) and in the Vosges, Brittany, the Charentes and Périgord. In 1883, 1,316 wolves were killed in France or, rather, official bounties were paid for that many heads; in 1890, 461 were killed, in 1900 only 115. Bounty, gun, and poison were gaining the upper hand. Forests were shrinking, roads made wolves' lairs more accessible, and the noisy new railroads and highways frightened off the beasts.[62] But the tales told over winter evenings and the persistence of the increasingly vague but still menacing image of the wolf show better than mere statistics the grip the animal had on the popular imagination. Evil-omened spots were linked with wolves, like the notorious Carroi de Marlou or Mareloup in Sancerrois, where witches' sabbats were rumored into the twentieth century; and so were the activities of the terrifying *meneurs de loups*, who could set the beasts on one. For city dwellers the wolf was a storybook character, seldom closer than a tale from Jules Verne or the Comtesse de Ségur. But for people over great portions of France he was a howling in the night, a disquieting presence not far off, a hazard or even an interdiction of certain winter paths, and worst of all, a source of the dreaded rabies.

I have found little information about the incidence of rabies, but rabid dogs were not unusual and with news of one in the neighborhood fear spread very fast. An incantation to the moon used in Charente and Poitou asked first of all for protection against mad dogs[63]—more dangerous seemingly than snakes.* Since the farm dogs were typically half-wild themselves (they would

---

* But the peasant of Bourbonnais feared both, judging by his traditional prayer for protection "against evil beasts": "Saint-Hubert glorieux, de trois choses me défende: / Des chiens fous, des loups fous, / Des verpis [vipers] et des serpents." A medical report estimated that in Lozère 25 persons died of bites by rabid animals, mostly dogs, between 1849 and 1866. Not so many, it would seem, until we remember that some of those bitten survived after cauterization of the wound or amputation, and that others were smothered to death by their terrified families, then buried with no further inquiries on the part of local authorities. (Frantz Brunet, *Dictionnaire du parler bourbonnais*, p. 247; *L'Aubrac*, 4: 157–58.)

not have been much use had they not been aggressive), mad dogs were not always easy to spot and could easily bite several persons before being identified. It is not surprising that Pasteur became such a national hero.

Fires, by contrast, are well documented.* Police and judicial files offer an endless recital of fires, accidental and deliberate, attributed to envy, resentment, spite, greed, or, sometimes, lightning. Anyone and everyone might have been the culprit: an eight-year-old child working on a farm; an unbalanced or jealous spouse; a neighbor, rival, or servant; a tramp (though the matches of passing vagabonds were taken into custody when they dossed down in the barn); an owner hoping to cash in on insurance. Some contraband matches tended to burst into flames at the slightest friction. More often, no matches were to be had, and the constant fetching and carrying of embers between neighbors led easily to accidents.[64]

Fires were sometimes catastrophic. Two such conflagrations occurred in 1857 alone, one destroying 114 dwellings in the little village of Fresne-sur-Apance (Haute-Marne), and the other consuming all 17 houses in the hamlet of Fretterans in Bresse, leaving 100 persons destitute. Considering that the means of fighting fires were primitive at best and most of the time were practically useless, it is small wonder that people were easily aroused to panic. In October 1861, as the result of a series of fires around Nérac (Lot-et-Garonne), a wave of fear spread through the department and neighboring cantons of Gers, a fear so deep, thought the imperial prosecutor, as to invite comparison with the Great Fear of 1789: armed patrols, shots fired in the night, people barricading themselves in their homes, beggars and tramps arrested or run out of villages, even a "mass levy" on the rumor that clerical and legitimist bands were setting the fires in retaliation for the Emperor's papal policies. Such notions proved contagious, and one poor man set fire to a mill "because he heard it said that it was the thing to do, and that he would be richly rewarded." Finally, the alarm abated just as it had swelled, like other waves of panic in anxious times.[65]

The greatest fire hazard lay in the thatched roofs that covered so many structures. "If covered with straw," went the Gascon saying, "don't let fire come near it."[66] Authorities and insurance companies waged bitter campaigns against thatch. But many factors worked against change, above all the cost of a suitable substitute until improved transportation made slate or tile more readily available. Furthermore, in the mountains and other areas the thatch nicely insulated the huts so that food could be stocked in quantity. More important, perhaps, the walls and timberwork of the peasants' huts were too weak for heavier covering and had to be strengthened, if not totally rebuilt. This helps explain

---

*Emile Duché calls this the favorite crime of the lower orders (*Le Crime d'incendie*, Paris, 1913, p. 33). And Gabriel Tarde notes: "A la campagne, incendier la grange de son ennemi, quand on sait qu'elle n'est pas assurée, est le moyen de vengeance le plus souvent et le plus impunément employé" (*Essais et mélanges sociologiques*, Lyon, 1895, p. 121).

the obstinate resistance to outside pressure where building and roofing materials were not easily come by.* And it almost certainly explains the strange thatched roof rebellion that shook the Angevin countryside in 1854, when the prefect of Maine-et-Loire, eager to eliminate the source of too many fires, decreed that all thatch had to be replaced by slate or tile. Many peasants too poor to bear the cost of a new roof, let alone the cost of rebuilding their houses in stone rather than clay and wood, resisted the order and were evicted. They marched on Angers, several thousand strong, and the army had to intervene and disperse them. The prefect was replaced, the decree rescinded, and thatched roofs allowed to disappear more gradually. The relatively prosperous farmers who carried insurance were finally forced into compliance under a concerted attack by insurance companies in the 1860's and after. But the final slide to oblivion came when the threshing machine began to replace the ancient flail. The straw used for roofs had to be flailed; mechanical threshers broke the straw and made it useless. Insurance rates had made thatch impractical for the prosperous; machines made it almost impossible for the poor.[67]

Hunger and the fear of it were a more constant dread even than fire, the ubiquitous presence at many a hearth, the principal problem of many a province. The anxiety of providing daily bread or mush or bran for oneself and one's family was greater in some places, like Maurienne, than in others. But everywhere it shaped behavior, attitudes, and decisions.

In 1773 a royal official at Foix remarked that the poor "keep more fasts than the Church orders." The nineteenth century had its share of *disettes*: 1812, 1817, 1837, 1853, and especially the great hunger of 1846–47. In Ariège families ate grass, hungry peasants were "eager to get into prison," mendicancy was chronic, armies of beggars descended into the plains, and to the end of the century, travelers were beset by legions of children seeking alms.[68]

Songs and sayings record the wisdom of dearth: "Year of beechnut, year of famine; year of acorns, year of naught." "Bare arse goes along, empty belly goes no more." "Never mind about rags so long as there is food." "Full of cabbage, full of turnips, as long as one is full." And the importance of conserving precious bread: "Hard bread makes a safe house." Warm bread could mean ruin; one ate too much of it. Stale bread encouraged frugality.[69] As Cobb emphasizes, the problems of subsistence—that is, of a minimum substantially below subsistence-level—persisted well into the nineteenth century. Hungry peasants facing a grain shortage behaved as their forefathers had: blockading

---

* Yet in Yonne thatch seems to have been abandoned quite early. See Justice of the Peace, Saint-Florentin, to Prefect, March 31, 1857, in Archives Départementales, Yonne III M[1] 228, inveighing against the continued use of waterholes: "Ces mares ont eu, je le sais, leur raison d'être; elles étaient un mal nécessaire quand toutes les maisons étaient construites en bois, couvertes en chaume et présentaient ainsi des alimens faciles aux ravages du feu. Mais, grâce au bien-être qui se répand dans les campagnes, grâce aux incendies eux-mêmes . . . le chaume a disparu presque partout." But, then, Saint-Florentin is in the plains of northeastern Yonne and not subject to the harsh conditions of the areas further south.

or plundering convoys of grain. From the 1830's on, to the end of the Second Empire, ministers, prefects, and sub-prefects kept an anxious eye on crops; and police chiefs reported monthly and sometimes weekly on the state of crops in their area and of grain supplies in general. As the prefect of Loiret recognized in October 1856, distress and want were inevitable "in this season." One could only congratulate oneself if an extreme calamity was avoided. A year when want did not stir up trouble was cause for official comment. In 1854 government measures, public works and aid in Maine-et-Loire kept the countryside calm through a hungry winter and a hungrier spring. "For the first time ... a calamitous year will have passed without sedition and almost without muttering," boasted the local prefect.[70]

Even at this late date, a rigorous winter, a barren spring, a crop failure, could still cause misery and grain riots that called for public works, subsidies, charitable initiatives, and police action. Slowly—but only very slowly—roads and railroads were getting the better of the situation. In 1847 the Orléans Company was ready to proclaim its "glorious satisfaction that the lands along its railway have been spared [not hunger, but] the scenes of disorder that food shortages have caused elsewhere." The directors of the company rejoiced too soon, but the point would be made by others with better reason: Lavergne in 1855, glad that new rail links could stave off a disette even when the price of wheat was high; J. A. Barral in 1884, relieved that with the railway the Limousin was no longer exposed to frequent famines.[71]

Though provisioning the populace was a continuing problem to the very end of the Empire, there were fewer and fewer food riots, evidence of a growing success in solving subsistence problems. In 1868, a bad year, turbulence marked the hungry months of spring and summer, when the grain from the previous harvest ran out before the new harvest had been brought in. Soaring prices, along with rumors of hoarding and speculation, set off food riots from Manche to Ardèche and Tarn. Serious disturbances broke out at Gaillac and Albi, and magistrates in Toulouse reported the tensest situation in 15 years.[72] But this seems to have been the last old-fashioned food crisis. Increased productivity and improved communications together banished the fear of hunger from the public to the private sphere, from the general to the particular level. Dearth, which had ruled social life for thousands of years, became an exceptional event. For clear evidence of how dearth left its impress on society we can look at the most intimate of indexes: between 1836 and 1860 we see a statistically significant correlation between the price of grain and the marriage rate (-0.61); between 1876 and 1900 the correlation disappears (-0.04).[73]

Something else, though hard to define, began to disappear about that time: the habitual peasant resignation. The militant Louise Michel remembered what an old woman in her native village had said, recalling a year when profiteers threw the region into famine: "Of course the poor people have to resign themselves to the things they can't prevent!"[74] Endure what you can—

not help, submit to what is inevitable. "Quequ'vous voulez, faut ben durer," says the peasant of Bourbonnais; and *durer* means both to endure and to keep going. The peasant knows that he who bears, lasts. There is nothing to be done about a dry summer or a hard winter, about a sudden storm, about injustice or fate except wait, bend, and perhaps pray. The poor will always be poor, and always oppressed and exploited, teaches the wisdom of ages. All they can do is remember and act accordingly. "The scraggier the beast, the more the flies will sting it." "Poor people's bread always burns in the oven." "A swineherd in this world, a swineherd in the next." "Hard times for the poor are as inevitable as ease for the rich." "The poor man's cock sings winter is long; the miller's cock answers it will soon be over." Accept your condition and endure: "Don't try to fart higher than your arse." "Dragged arse creeps along, high arse perishes." Do not expect help: "There is more pity shown to a clod than to an orphan." And watch out, for pride, no matter how little, goes before a fall: "Who has no trouble must expect it." "Swim well, drown well." "One never knows what death one will die." "You think the eggs are on the fire when only shells are left." "When you've got a good soup made, the devil comes and shits in it." Never say "fountain I'll not drink your water." You may have to do so, even if you have pissed in it.[75] A stoic pessimism.

One accepted what had always been, tried to learn from experience, adjusted to circumstances instead of trying to change them. The assumption of an eternal order with limited alternatives—the ordre éternel des champs? Or just narrow horizons, ignorance, inertia? Something of both, I think, and rooted in perceptions that altered only as the century grew old. The Limousin farmer worked all year but, however hard he tried, he could not feed his tribe. That is the way it had always been. Yet, in his hovel, the crofter thought himself well enough off "because he has known nothing better." That was in 1817. In 1907 an old farmhand recalled for Jules Renard his life in earlier days: he had never slept in a bed before he married, had tasted no wine, and had first eaten meat only because a horse had died (which the employees feasted on for 15 straight days, eating it to the last hoof). "Didn't you dare ask for better?" "We never thought of it." By 1907 the peasants had learned better. They had learned to ask. And as the century turned, some found reason to rue the passing of resignation: "No one is resigned these days; the utopia of the right to happiness has replaced the utopia of the right to work."[76]

The right to work was utopia indeed. The need to work was not. In the northern hemisphere, at any rate, man seemed as naturally born to work as the bird was to fly. The word *travail* seems to have shed its original sense of torture and pain in the sixteenth century, taking on the meaning of two older words that referred to work, *labourer* and *ouvrer*, though it retained shreds of its origins to the eighteenth century (suggesting fatigue, anxiety, or pain, as in the old-fashioned English travail). For the privileged few, the word also embodied the idea that manual labor was demeaning; the ascetics of Port

Royal, for example, could find no better way to mortify themselves than to work in the fields or carve clogs. But in the countryside, where work appeared to be a necessary part of life and where most knew no other way to keep body and soul together, work became a virtue, perhaps the greatest virtue to be found in man or wife.

Good and bad work could be described by a broad vocabulary with many nuances. The good worker was noble, hardy, brave, courageous, valiant. Comparisons for bad work were significantly drawn from nonrural professions or from despised strangers. One who bungled his work was a cobbler; one who puttered around was a horse-dealer; one who promised to do something and then did not do it was an apothecary. All this varied with local fancy and experience: the apothecary was more often an extortioner than a liar; the horse trader was more often a chiseler than a pottering *bricoleur*. But in Franche-Comté, for instance, the chiseler was an *argonnier*, a peddler from the Argonne, a bit of a crook like most peddlers. My purpose here is not to discuss nicknames, but to point to the scorn that was attached to bad work. Perhaps the most striking example of the association of the two can be found in the evolution of the word *fainéant*, which from its original sense of idle or lazy grew increasingly pejorative and insulting, to the point where, in 1906, we find a trade union leader ludicrously calling on striking workers to go after the scabs with the cry "Go beat up the idlers who are working!"[77]

Of course, men worked because they had to. "Man works and scrimps," reasoned the prefect of Haute-Vienne in 1858, "produces and saves, only under the pressure of present need or the fear of need to come. Were the inferior classes to be delivered by charity from this vigorous stimulant and cushioned from this salutary threat, ... it would simply end the great motivation for work." There was virtue in "mediocrity," in poverty, in need, because they forced men to work, to obey "the divine law of labor," to keep busy and, hence, to keep out of trouble.[78]

Clearly the prefect of Haute-Vienne could envisage no means of relief from present need or need to come other than drudgery or charity. In 1858 necessity still ruled life, and its hold would relax very slowly. As it relaxed, we hear more references to work as an obligation, a duty to society and to God. Mandatory labor requires increasing justification and defense as it becomes less truly mandatory. Or, rather, as need becomes less ponderous and the obligation to work less stringent. Once it was clear which way the wind was blowing, there was a veritable chorus of comment from outside observers (prefects and other officials, authors of statistics and reports, teachers, priests, and travelers), all in praise of sobriety and the simple life, and deprecating what was most often described as luxury, which is to say, the tendency to live above one's station, trying to eat, dress, act, and even relax as the upper classes did.

The earliest references to this regrettable trend were aimed not at the peasants but at the urban workers, too quick to "adopt the ways of the idle class."

Though untypically early, 1848 may serve as a symbolic landmark of the rot
spreading in the countryside. We find a Limousin priest chiding his flock for
frittering their time away at pubs and fairs and wearing clothes "not of your
condition." Four years later, a landowner of Bourbonnais echoed the criticism:
"Too much leisure, too many holidays *despite* the opposition of the Church,
too much going to fairs to satisfy idle curiosity, above all perhaps too little
abstemiousness—the more the peasant grows, the more he consumes."[79] What
good was greater productivity if its results served mainly to bring the peasant
up from the low-water mark of traditional shortage to a subsistence level? A
middle class growing rich on the expansion of the market exalted virtues external to the market and to an industrial economy. Like dogs in an anachronistic manger, they wanted to see the poor as producers for the market (low
prices), not as consumers (higher prices). Thus consumption (extravagance)
was deprecated, and the traditional values of sobriety, economy, and industry
were extolled.

Few critics were as clear or as explicit as this about the reasons for the disapproval. But the trickle of criticism became a regular flow after the late 1860's,
when conditions perceptibly improved. Most of it reflected simple outrage at
the lower classes' unheard-of behavior. Too many women dressed like their
betters, too many working men indulged in luxury and intemperance—turned
to pipes, cards, kerchiefs or cravats, often even books (preferably something
ribald or the *Petit Albert*), expected to wear hats, boots, and broadcloth suits,
grew accustomed to high living, dressed their wives and children in finery,
and drank more than was good for them.[80] As the earliest and most visible
evidence of improvement, dress drew the most criticism. The numerous teachers' monographs on village life in 1889 refer to the growing extravagance and
suggestiveness of girls' attire and sometimes hint at some deeper motivation.
Clothes, suggested a teacher in the Meurthe, were used as a status symbol,
designed to demonstrate an equality of rank that did not in fact exist. But the
often-noted "unbridled longing" for material possessions was really no more
than the simple perception of new possibilities, the satisfaction of newly discovered wants. "What used to be superfluous has become indispensable; we
suffer deprivations of things our ancestors never heard of." Was this development entirely bad? Even some teachers who condemned it in one breath could
see the progress that it reflected. A teacher in the Vosges, after expressing the
ritual regrets over the growing luxury, expenditure of money, and drinking,
admitted these were coupled with comforts that none could have imagined
a few short years before: "Our grandfathers would find it difficult to recognize
their village, and wouldn't believe our natty youth to be of the same race as
themselves."[81]

By the 1890's Baudrillart had to marvel at the luxury and rising standard of
living of the lower classes of rural Provence, who were fed, lodged, and dressed
pretty much as bourgeois and property owners *used to be*.[82] This last gives

us a clue, for by this time the standards of mid-century had so changed that what had once constituted a comfortable living was now felt to be a relatively spare and spartan existence. Théron de Montaugé saw the point clearly as early as 1869: the more the general well-being improved, the higher the poverty line.

If poverty is defined in the most basic terms as the inability to satisfy one's needs, there could be little sense of deprivation so long as the perceived needs were sharply limited and the aspiration for something more abnormal. "The absence of an unknown good," Calemard de Lafayette told the agricultural society of Puy in 1854, "cannot constitute a need, or, consequently, become a deprivation." Or as Théron de Montaugé put it in 1869: "Poverty is measured by comparisons. One cannot feel deprived of possessions and pleasures one is unaware of."[83]

This is what urbanization—or more precisely, the spread of urban values through the countryside—was going to change. New expectations, and new frustrations when they were not met; desires that became needs; the fading of the ages-old resignation and passivity. How these changes came to pass, and how slowly they passed—that is what this book is all about.

Chapter Two

THE MAD BELIEFS

There is a Superstition in avoiding Superstition.
—FRANCIS BACON

"DO NOT BELIEVE in witches," warned a widely used elementary textbook of 1895. "...People who say they can steal or work harm by muttering certain words, those who claim to know the future, are madmen or thieves. Do not believe in ghosts, in specters, in spirits, in phantoms....Do not imagine one can avoid harm or accidents with...amulets, talismans, fetishes, such as... herbs gathered on St. John's Eve."[1] If Ernest Lavisse warned against such beliefs, it must have been because they were widespread. Others agreed. "For the least little reason, the peasant thought a spell had been cast on his cattle or his field. He bought talismans and wore them around his neck like a scapulary,...medallions, magic rings,...a piece of hangman's rope,...saw the devil's hand in anything out of the way and ran to a sorcerer."[2]

In 1880 Emile Littré thought that the word *charme* was being used less in its primitive sense of spell, and that even the reciting or singing of incantatory spells was on the wane. But spells and prayers for protection against devils or storms, snakes or mad dogs, seemed in no hurry to disappear. As late as 1908 we find the belief current that a hunter's gun would be charmed if he shot at a cross and drew blood from it. In 1892 an agricultural commission visiting Roquefort in the Landes was shocked at the hold of superstition there: the small farmers did not want beehives because they brought bad luck; branches of fern to ward off the evil eye hung from the roof of every sheepfold. The Bourbonnais had long believed in the efficacy of the *marcou*, the eldest of seven sons born consecutively, who was supposed to be able to heal scrofula by simply touching the victim before sunrise on the night of Saint John. Marcous drew great crowds in Bourbonnais until the end of the century and were paid for their help in kind. They continued to be called on still later in Beauce.[3] Well into the twentieth century, in Berry, everything was of fearsome or fantastic portent: the buzzing of insects announced a ghostly hunt; the ribbons of mist above the marshes were mysterious drivers of clouds; newly pruned elms, shadows, or haze turned into sinister fancies. The moonlight was crowded with goblins, sprites, elves, imps, wraiths, will-o'-the-wisps, werewolves, leprechauns, trolls, bogeymen, White Ladies, ghostly huntsmen, and occasionally even giants, offspring of the prodigious creatures who had left the looming menhirs and dolmens where they now stood. Fairy rings marked places where wood sylphs trod. The pack of the Black Huntsman bayed in the wind. Penitent souls roamed the fields or waited at the crossroads: forest guards or gamekeepers to whom Saint Peter closed his gates, as he did to bailiffs; or priests condemned to wander until they said every last mass they had been paid to say during their lifetime and had left unsaid.[4]

Many local spirits had been helpful, playful, and occasionally mischievous beings until the Church spread the notion that they were evil. They could turn dangerous if surprised, but peasant tales also contain fairies who build castles, open roads, and repair broken tools. In early-nineteenth-century Nivernais, when a plow broke a peasant could still invoke the fairies' aid and leave 12 *sols* by their rock to pay for it. In any case, they were a familiar part of life. So much so that in the Morvan Mélusine was known as La Mère Louisine.

Interwoven with current experience, the supernatural was adapted to it and sometimes in a very purposeful way, as in 1842 when robbers in a village of the Doubs valley disguised themselves as devils to cover their foray into the night to rob a cattle dealer. Breton fairies seem to have worn the same gray canvas that salt smugglers wore, and dwelt in the same cliffside caves. In the Alps, too, mid-century smugglers used local superstitions to explain their mysterious lights and keep the curious at a respectful distance. In Yonne, the Puisaye long remembered the sinister Birettes, who in the guise of werewolves, covered with skins, howling and dragging long chains, devastated fields and gardens into the 1880's. And various mythical ogres (probably derived from Uigurs and Hungarians) personified the devastating brigands of living memory.[5]

Superstitions survived for a long time.* In the Limousin of the 1880's, though the peasants' dread of ghosts and werewolves had dwindled, they still feared the effects of the stranger's evil eye on the cattle in their stable, and still scared easily at night; people sang on the way to and from a *veillée*—"probably to scare off spirits." In the 1860's Prosper Mérimée noted the peasants' belief that

---

* Around 1890, says René Nelli, mysterious noises and other unexplained phenomena previously blamed on various "elemental" spirits like the spirit of air or of water came to be attributed to the dead when spiritualism, very popular at that time, invaded popular belief (*Languedoc, Comté de Foix, Roussillon*, pp. 198–99). If so (and certainly urban intellectuals were fascinated by all aspects of occultism), there is here a pretty clear case of the influence of urban on popular culture. About the same time Catholic schools were spreading or confirming newly heightened suspicions about active diabolic intervention: the devil's connection with dancing, the devil presiding over masonic meetings, freemasons and other anti-clericals worshiping the devil, and the like. See Henri Ellenberger, "Le Monde fantastique dans le folklore de la Vienne," *Nouvelle revue des traditions populaires*, Jan. 1950; and for illustrations, Eugen Weber, *Satan franc-maçon* (1964).

the levels and other surveying equipment used by engineers in the building of canals and railroads caused droughts. In 1895 the inhabitants of Plounéour-Trez in Finistère found a siren dying on their beach and gave her a Christian burial, only to have the priest disinter the corpse and throw it in the sea. When, in the trenches of the First World War, a Vendean soldier told of his father's seeing a *guérou*—in this case a man changed into a sheep at night and back again at dawn—his fellows from Mayenne doubted not that there was such a thing, but that the father could still have seen one: "These are things from the olden days. It is a good 60–70 years since they have been seen."[6]

For all that, the old folktales still had sufficient force as late as 1906 to frighten the twelve-year-old brother of Jacques Duclos, who thought he saw something in the yard in the dark of the night and "came in trembling with fear, to be sick forthwith." The dark was literally fearful. Revealingly, in Languedoc the ghosts and other spirits that were cloaked in obscurity were known by the generic name "frights" (*poûs* or *pooüs*) and, as a Tarn proverb declared, "But for the frights, the priests would die of hunger." Perhaps, like the wolves with another modern invention, the spirits could be dispersed only by electrification. But it does seem that as old people died, imps and trolls and fairies deserted the countryside.[7]

Sorcerers held fast. "Kings and priests pass away," mused Emile Souvestre after 1848, "but witches survive." Cases of witchcraft appear in the courts at least into the 1870's, some serious, as when in 1863 an Ardennes brickmaker had a sorcerer murdered for having cast a spell on his brick kilns; or when a young couple of Solognots were executed in 1887 for murdering the wife's mother on a sorcerer's advice, then burning the corpse to eliminate her evil spirit. Less tragically, in 1883 the priest of Neung-sur-Beuvron (Loir-et-Cher) recorded the encounter between one of his flock and a coven of witches at a sabbat—who fled at the sign of the cross. Everyone could be a witch; anyone might be one, especially strangers and those who lived on the fringes of the community, like shepherds. Above all, though, the sorcerer was a person who had books, or notes taken from books, with esoteric formulas and incantations. *Grimoires* (from grammar, in this case something learned and obscure) were still sold in Bourbonnais in 1908, in their characteristic sextodecimo format with colored paper bindings and illustrations. Country people would ask the small-town bookseller for *livres de sorcelage*, especially those whose magic was strongest: "O voudro avouère tout ceusse que sont les pu forts!"[8] The most powerful books were popular corruptions of the medieval science of Albertus Magnus: *Le Grand* and *Le Petit Albert*. Copies of these works were rare, sorcerers were proud to own one, and, of course, the Big was more powerful than the Little. People were "terrorized" by those known to have a copy—though ownership had its hazards, since one could not die until it had been passed on to someone else. In the mid-twentieth century in the Tarn a man remembered his parents' warning never to accept a *Grand Albert*, "because you will never be able to get rid of it." The prediction had a way of turning out to be self-fulfilling. In 1951 at Rezay (Cher) a family found a copy of the dread work in the loft and tried to burn it. Damp and moldy, it would not catch fire—from which miraculous preservation the conclusion was drawn that it must not be touched again.[9] On the other hand a book of spells brought good luck. Even today the Morvandiaux will say of a man for whom things work out well, "He has the *Petit Albert* in his pocket!"[*]

Priests, perhaps because they had even more books than sorcerers, were more powerful still.[†] In the 1850's a Limousin priest reclaimed his parish from the slough of indifference and Protestantism into which it had fallen by patient argument and hard campaigning, but also by miracles and healings that reinforced his reputation for wisdom. Priests could bring rain or fine weather; and through the nineteenth century, curés were required to participate in the rites designed to secure these—at least in the dioceses of Autun and Nevers. At Viglain (Loiret) the priest got "20 fleeces and 20 measures of wheat," worth about 60 francs of the day, for "reading the Lord's Passion every single Sunday and in case of a storm both day and night to assure nature's bounty." In 1880 the surplice of a priest near Arleuf in the Nièvre burst into flames as he was performing his rites of sympathetic magic. Of Bourbonnais, where faith in tarot cards ran strong in the early 1900's, a folklorist noted: "In many parishes people are certain that their priest carries the great tarot game in his long sleeves, and that he knows how to tell fortunes from it. It is for this reason that many country people attribute so much knowledge and learning to him."[10]

A priest could cast a charm on storms and defy hail. He could throw his hat over his parish to protect it (symbolically covering it) or cast a shoe against the storm cloud to drive it off (symbolically kicking it away). Some priests were "good for hail," many were not. Though priests who refused to use their powers to drive off a storm or make one break risked a beating, people understood that a young priest might not be wise enough to know these secrets and generally sought an older, experienced man for their parish. At the same time,

---

[*]Augustin Dubois, *Les Anciens Livres de colportage*, pp. 4–5. In 1919 Dubois found a copy of the *Admirables secrets du Grand Albert*, some 150 years old, and could not get the owners to part with it: "It's sacred." See also H.-F. Buffet, *En Bretagne morbihannaise*, pp. 110–11; and especially Louis Ogès and F. M. Déguignet, "Contes et légendes populaires," pp. 104–7, on the wandering mountebanks of 19th-century Brittany who claimed that their science (often based on the *Grand Albert*) was stronger than the power of the old saints, and sold formulas for every sort of human ill or desire (e.g., the grass of happiness, the black cat of wealth, the secret of how to make a million by burning a goat at a crossroads).

† In Lower Brittany, where the great magic book was known as the Agrippa, all priests were thought to possess a copy, which had miraculously appeared on their nighttable the day after their ordination. Many tales were told of the disasters that had beset servants and other layfolk who had peeked into these texts or tried to use them. But the tradition also acknowledges a secularization (perhaps a democratization?) of magic. During the Revolution, the story goes, many priests emigrated and their Agrippas fell into the hands of laymen sufficiently schooled to use them, thence to their descendants, so that simple farmers came to own magic books. (See Claude Seignolle, *Les Evangiles du diable*, Paris, 1967, pp. 200, 204–5.)

it was important to beware of a curé who had "the gift" but whose powers had been worn down, so that his masses had no force (ses messes, alles ont pus de force). Masses and other religious rites played a role in several kinds of magic, designed to bless, to exorcise, to heal, to put an end to a torment or bring one on (messes de tormentation). The most effective measure, if one could bring it off, was said to be the triangular mass (messes en pied de chèvre) in which the priests of three churches forming a triangle all recited the mass at roughly the same time. Most priests were reluctant to lend themselves to such practices, but they generally could be maneuvered into taking part in them unwittingly. In any case, just touching a priest or his vestments was often sufficient to bring results; and of course the higher his rank, the greater his power. In 1881 the new inspector general of primary education in Lozère was shaken to find "the supreme importance [the people in the region of Mende] attached to contact with the robe of a prelate on circuit for healing the sick."[11]

Most peasant cottages kept a reserve of holy water brought from church on Easter eve or Candlemas in a special basin or pitcher to use as a protection for buildings and crops, and in an emergency, to baptize a stillborn child or sprinkle a corpse. An English wayfarer through the *causses* of Quercy in 1894 was intrigued to see bottles of holy water placed on top of chimneys as protection against lightning. Crosses, often woven of straw and wreathed with flowers, or palm leaves (or their local substitutes), or both, surmounted the door, after having been passed three times through the flames of the midsummer pyre or been blessed on Palm Sunday. These too were a capital defense against lightning, as well as against more intangible evils. And where, as in most places, hatred of the lord's hunting survived in tales of satanic riders— red, black, damned *gayère*—that passed at night and that charcoal burners had special cause to fear, the priest made a point of going out to bless their lonely huts.[12]

Prominent in the uncertain ground between religion and magic stood fountains, wells, springs, and bells. We shall meet the watering places presently, when we turn to religious practices; for now let us say simply that in general they played a crucial role for people who found it difficult to understand and dominate their bodies, minds, and physical surroundings. The fame of various spots waxed or waned, a few were even forgotten, but miraculous fountains as such retained their popularity throughout the nineteenth century. Some must have looked like Japanese temple groves, with votive rags, ribbons, and articles of clothing draped over them and over all the surrounding growth. And some clearly benefited from the growing prosperity of their devotees, reflected in more convenient installations or monumental decorations such as those contrived in Brittany. This cult of "good" fountains (which is still to be found) declined at least in the center, the west, and the southwest after the turn of the century, and most notably in the First World War years. Only local residents and old people still used them after that. As an old woman told an inquiring visitor to the healing springs at Sanguinet (Landes), "Since the war began, no more rags on the bushes; the war stops everything."[13]

It did not stop the ringing of church bells against storms. The *carillon de tonnerre* was banned by civil and ecclesiastical authorities in the eighteenth century and condemned by all public powers throughout the nineteenth. In Gers prefectoral decrees followed one another, in 1813, 1839, and 1855, and so did the official requests for still more decrees, indicating how ineffective all the decrees were. An official ecclesiastical survey of the 500 Gers parishes in 1840 found the practice in all but 14. Another, carried out in 1956, showed that in 194 of the 337 parishes responding, the custom had been abandoned, but that 143 still sounded the bells whenever storms threatened or broke.[14]

One important reason why priests and public powers opposed the practice was that it threatened the life of the ringer. In 1783 alone lightning struck 386 belfries in France and killed 121 bell ringers. With lightning rods the massacre diminished, but not in isolated departments like Ardèche, where one bell ringer was killed by lightning at Balbiac in 1874 and another at Grospierres the following year. Yet in 1878, when the bell ringer in a parish near Largentière refused to do his duty in a storm, two drunks took his place "and saved the fields from the hail" that devastated neighboring parishes. Like the bell in Montmorillon (Vienne), which was still rung before the First World War and perhaps after, many church bells spelled out what their major purpose was: "+ A FULGURIBUS ET TEMPESTATE LIBERA NOS DOMINE + 1743 +"[15]

Throughout Mâconnais and Bourbonnais, as in other regions, mayors hesitated to enforce the official injunctions against bell ringing, well knowing that their people would turn against them as readily as they turned against priests who tried to prevent the practice. In the 1890's Edward Harrison Barker referred to the ringing as an old custom that was dying out, yet he encountered it in the Drôme Valley as he passed through. And Henri Polge tells us that in 1908, in order to get back at the regular bell ringer who had refused to ring the church bells on July 14, the municipal council of Ligardes appointed a second man, specially charged with ringing "in case of danger from hail."[16] The ringing bells brought comfort to those who heard them, allayed anxiety, made them feel less helpless. They gave people something to do (or to think they were doing) when there was nothing they could do. The logic behind the pealing—that evil might be frightened away—made sense even if it did not work. Impotence devised its own defenses.

The strategy of impotence (that is, magic) was based on a primitive unity of objects and beings—that "obscure and profound unity" Baudelaire sang of in his *Correspondances*:

> Nature is a temple wherein living columns
> Will sometimes let slip a confused utterance;
> Man crosses it, with great hosts of symbols
> Casting upon him a familiar glance.

Modern thought isolated and segregated objects and beings. Objective units (the tree, the bell, the storm) had served as substitutes for subjective conceptions of vaster wholes formed on anthropomorphic lines and hence susceptible of symbolic manipulation. A linear vision of space and time replaced the maze of privileged places (trees, rocks, springs) and moments (solstice or All-Saints) that concentrated in themselves the very forces of life. Modern man could no longer communicate with the world by proceeding through ritual form to magic essence. Experience now taught, and school taught too, that magic specificity and totalism were misleading. They would be replaced by abstractions far, far removed from limited everyday experience. But only when everyday experience ceased to be so limited.

Is the supernatural that "life behind" to which the Auvergnat Pascal referred—*la vie de derrière*—where men seek refuge from the visible life before them? Or is it simply a reflection of the conditions of that prosaic world, a collection of suggested solutions for the problems of everyday life? Lightning came to be tamed, cattle healed, health improved; remedies were found for snakebite and for rabies; weather bulletins proved more reliable than astrological formulas or ancient spells; and fields were fattened by chemicals; but old practices survived, and especially where marriage, childbirth, and death were concerned. Fountains that promised love or marriage lasted longer than those with healing waters; fertility rites and funeral customs persisted beyond the First World War.[17] Those parts of life that are the most difficult to dominate, that are the most contingency-prone, retained their magic aspects the longest.

Chapter Three

THE KING'S FOOT

The invention of a barbarous age, to set off wretched matter with lame meter.
—JOHN MILTON

IN THE mid-nineteenth century one Charles Gille wrote a carpenter's song, "My Plane," whose last verse alluded to the metric system that the Revolution had introduced:[1]

> Challenging routine and hatred,
> Taking its stand on useful things,
> The measure of the Republic
> Has overthrown the foot of kings.

Actually kings proved easier to overthrow than the measures associated with them. A law of 1837 had made the metric system the only legal measure of the land, effective January 1, 1840. But its fate, like that of the *franc germinal* introduced in 1803, remained uncertain for several generations. Public archives and private transactions alike bear witness that ancient measures survived and thrived into the twentieth century, above all in the poorest and most isolated areas, where life and work were slow to enter the broader national market.[2]

There, as in the old regime, people proved reluctant to abandon measures based on familiar experience for abstract ones with universal pretensions. Land measures mostly related to the day's work (*journal* or *morgen*) or to the kind of labor (*hommée, bêchée, fauchée*). The journal and the hommée represented the amount of land a man could work in a day, and were thus sometimes equivalent to the size of the average field. These workday units varied according to regional differences in ground, tools, and methods of cultivation. In Lorraine the *jour* or *journal* was 20.44 ares, or 10 *omées* (hommées) of 2.04 ares each; in the Bassigny region of Haute-Marne many rectangular fields averaged 25.85 ares, and that was what the old *journal* was there. In Sarthe, the hommée was 33 ares and the *journal* 44; and in the Landes, where on the eve of the First World War the *journal* was still the standard measure, it was equivalent to 42 ares in poor land but only 35 in good land. Other systems of weights and measures were based on kinds of harnesses (*attélée, bovée, jouguée*); quantities of grain (*boisselée*, from *boisseau*, or bushel, *seterée* from *setier*); or familiar objects, such as the cord and the rod.[3] All naturally varied from place to place; the rod, for instance, was much longer in northern than in southern France.* In lower Vivarais, where in the days of President Grévy (1879–87) wine was still measured by the setier, eight setiers made a mule-load.[4] Similarly, the donkey-load (*saumade*) became a local unit of measurement in places where the roads, uncertain at best, could only be negotiated by donkeys in winter.

The enormous diversity of measures and of systems of measurement is less striking than the persistence, indeed the insistence, with which the state officialdom ignored their existence—except in its effort to stamp them out. The difficulty of converting one set of measures to another argued in favor of a single system that would replace them all. So did the variance in weights and measures of the same name, which meant that buyers were easily cheated. Suggestively, the number of trials for the unlawful possession of false weights and measures dropped markedly in the 1860's. But the old measures were deep-rooted, and though "all of the peoples of Europe admired and envied" the French system of weights and measures, at least nine-tenths of the French people still ignored it, grumbled a teacher in 1861.[5]

The official agricultural survey of 1866–67 emphasized the awkwardness of the great variety of local measures and concluded with a list of priorities that reflected how much remained to be done: (1) to rigorously impose the use of legal measures; (2) to standardize the weights and measures used in markets; (3) to establish official weighers, measurers, and gaugers in the countryside.[6]

Homogenization crept on at a snail's pace, and partly for the reason that an army officer reconnoitering the Isère in 1843 had given for its backwardness: commercial relations were limited to one city (Grenoble) and its immediate surroundings; beyond, they were almost nonexistent. Homogenization went fastest where the proximity of a city encouraged trade, as at Luynes near Tours, whose peasants soon learned to consult the *mercuriales* (market price-bul-

---

* Archives de la Guerre, MR 1212 (Isère, 1843), gives a long list of measures in current use in Isère, including *journal, seterée, fosserée, bicherée, le faucheur, l'hommée, la quarterée, la coupe, la couperée,* and *la pugnière.* Some equivalents are provided as well, which further indicate their variety:

le pied de France de 12		l'aune de tisserand à	
pouces	.3248 meters	Mens	1.486 meters
l'aune de Paris	1.188 "	la toise de Paris	1.949 "
l'aune de tisserand à		le boisseau	12.70 liters
Grenoble	1.307 "	le quartal à Grenoble	18.33 "
l'aune de tisserand à		le bichet à Voiron	19.21 "
Voiron	1.345 "	la bichette à Bourgoin	22.96 "

It also remarks in passing: "Les habitants de la campagne se servent encore dans leurs trafics des chiffres romains."

letins) and set their prices by them.* In the Pas-de-Calais, between Boulogne and Calais, though some of the older usages survived, the metric system was in fairly general use by 1874. In the center, west, southwest, and south, by contrast, measures and coins remained what they had always been to the end of the century. In Tarn in 1893 Henri Baudrillart found the decimal system in its infancy, the hectare unknown, and measures varying even from one parish to another. A few years later a priest could aver that the metric system was nonexistent in nearby Corrèze.[7]

Passive resistance scotched official initiatives. The prefects of Ardèche constantly complained that they could not get the new weights and measures adopted in the county seat, Privas, and the village mayors excused their own inaction on the inaction of Privas. When a prefect pushed local police into nabbing violators in the markets at Privas, the peasants took their produce to Aubenas, where surveillance was not so tight; the merchants of Privas promptly complained, and the prefect then turned his attention to Aubenas, which showed little inclination to comply with his orders. So fathom and foot, ell and bushel, quart, pound, and ounce, *poids de marc* and *poids de table* persisted into the twentieth century. In the early 1900's in Bourbonnais, though the hectare was "half-heartedly employed at the *notaire*'s by force of law," people still went by rod and acre, ell and boisselée. Milestones showed kilometers, but the countryside knew only leagues; iron sold by the inch and the line. The king's foot that Gille had spurned was still in general use, and ironmongers, who were bound by law to use official units, hid measuring sticks in the back of their shops that showed the *pouce*, *ligne*, and *pied* their clients would recognize. In 1895 Father Gorse lamented that in his "bas pays de Limosin" the peasant counted by *pistola*, *louis*, and *escu*; measured land in *eminade*, *sesteirada*, and *quarterounada*, and canvas in *auna* and *miéchauna*; sold wood *ei ciclhe*, pigs *ei quintau*, drinks in *mié-quart* and *pinta*. "The roads have crossed almost all our villages, our villagers have passed through military service and our children through school, but the metric system hasn't passed into custom yet. In a century perhaps."[8] Gorse was wrong; it had taken a century to come about, but the peasant's integration into the modern world was forcing him to learn and use its terms.

In 1884 J. A. Barral noted that in the Limousin sharecroppers were adopting the metric system because they had to settle with the owners, whose schooling had led them to adopt it.[9] The growing number of notarized papers, bills of lading, and legal or business formalities were making the exceptional familiar. In the early twentieth century Bourbonnais wines still went by the *poinçon* (which varied from 218 liters near the Loire to 200 liters around Saulcet). But the liter had displaced the *demi-setier* and the *chopine*, perhaps because pubs were closely supervised by the police. A host of disparate forces

---

* Archives de la Guerre, MR 2262 (1873). Even there, though, wood was sold not by the *stère* or the *corde*, but by a local measure, the *cent de cotrets*, a bundle 1.10 m around.

worked against the old measures. They had reigned through the nineteenth century. By the twentieth they were hard put to survive.

The same was true of coins and currency. The law of 7 Germinal, year 11 of the Republic (March 28, 1803) was a crucial act, creating the stable currency on which the French economy and French savings throve for the next 120 years. But the franc it created had to compete with earlier currencies almost to the time of its first devaluation in the 1920's. A big landowner in the Pas-de-Calais—a notable of his district and mayor of his village—kept his accounts in *écus* until 1837, in *sols* until 1849 (as a substitute for the centime, not as a term for the five-centime piece), and in *livres* and francs interchangeably, as if they were one and the same thing, all the way to 1877.[10]

In 1830 Bretons touchy about their backwardness thought that the low-denomination *liard* appropriate to poor regions was to be found only in their lands. But liards (once worth about three centimes, then generally one) circulated freely in Burgundy, Aisne, and Allier, and no doubt elsewhere at least until their official demonetization in the middle of the 1850's. In the Moulinois the farmers of Yzeure found thousands of Roman bronze coins in their fields, cleaned them, and used them variously as one liard, two liards, one sou, and *double* sous. Tradesmen accepted them, as they did the silver Roman coins found there, which were used as 50-centime or one-franc pieces. This practice too waned in the mid-1850's with the passing of copper coinage. Around Laon the appearance of shiny new one-, two-, and five-centime pieces bearing the effigy of Napoleon III confused a lot of people, who took them for five- and ten-franc gold pieces.[11] Clearly the old denominations were still holding their own.

The new Emperor was firmly in the saddle when the mayor of a village in Aunis drew up a document dividing his capital among his children and keeping for himself an income that included "une rente de 25 livres tournois au capital de 500 livres aussi tournois."[12] In the 1860's we find schoolteachers in Savoy reckoning in liards, and peddlers in the southwest making change in *pistoles* (five-franc silver pieces). And in the Breton's vocabulary we find 14th-century *blancs*, obsolete crowns (*écus*), and *réaux*, a survival from the Spanish occupation of the dim past. The people of Lower Brittany, we are told, always figured amounts up to five francs in réals and spoke of 12 five-franc pieces as 20 écus. As late as 1917 around Quimper one said four *réaux* for a franc and asked 60 écus for a cow worth 180 francs. That is, if one was not using the Breton language, which had its own denominations and terms:[13]

12 diners (deniers)	= 1 gwenneg (sou)	= 5 centimes
5 gwenneg	= 1 réal	= 25 centimes
4 réaux	= 1 lur (livre)	= 1 franc
3 lur	= 1 skoet (écu)	= 3 francs

Novelists recognized the persistence of such terms. The Three Musketeers were not the only ones to count in écus and pistoles. Jules Simon's *L'Ouvrière*,

126545

published in 1863 and reissued through the 1890's, uses these terms for servants' wages. In 1880 a knowledgeable if sentimental chronicler of rural life had a farmer marrying a girl who brought him a herd and 500 pistoles. In 1893 an English traveler through Upper Quercy found peasants and dealers at the Figeac fair transacting their business in pistoles and écus. And in Corrèze Father Gorse still insisted in 1895 that 110 francs was *ounze pistolas*.[14]

To further complicate matters, the kinds of coins that were accepted as écus or pistoles varied according to local practice. When cash was scarce, one took what came to hand, as with the Roman coins of Allier. In addition, their value differed appreciably from place to place: the pistole was sometimes worth five francs, sometimes ten; the écu was sometimes worth five francs, sometimes three. The pistole of eighteenth-century Brittany had been equivalent to the gold louis. But after the appearance of the 20-franc gold *napoléon* in 1803, the louis sometimes referred to the napoléon and sometimes (as in Sologne Bourbonnaise) to 24 francs. All this was little felt in an old-fashioned subsistence economy with a multitude of isolated local markets. But once money and goods began to circulate more widely, it made for dire confusion.

The use of unofficial currencies was repeatedly prohibited. In 1896 the police superintendent of Brassac reported lots of foreign sous circulating in his corner of the Puy-de-Dôme. But people in Haute-Loire, nearby, would not accept them any more. As strange coins ceased to be a medium of exchange, shops and markets experienced a temporary shortage of coins, and there was a brief currency crisis. But within a few months the sub-prefect of Riom felt the trouble was over, except for the parish priests, who were finding masses of the worthless coins in their poor-boxes and offertories. This must have been the real turning point. At the end of the century Cantal cheese prices were still quoted in pistoles, réals were still bandied about the marketplaces of Finistère and Morbihan, and six liards continued to make one and a half sous in the Bourbonnais countryside. Even on the eve of the war a farm laborer in Vendée could still be found hiring out for anything from 30 pistoles to 150 écus. But even in the remotest places the franc had become solidly established —perhaps because, at last, there were more francs around. As Pierre Bourdieu remarks of the Béarnais village he studied, where in 1962 many still remembered how rare cash was before 1914: "People aren't richer, but money circulates more."[15]

It is obvious that the persistence of the old coins reflected a scarcity of the new. And not of the new alone, but of currency in general. For a long time money itself was relatively rare and unfamiliar. While traveling through Ariège in 1836, Paul de Musset had given a ragged child some copper coins and noted the amazement with which the waif looked at them, as if he had never seen coins before. As late as 1861 a minister confirmed that in Ariège the rural populations very rarely handled money, which was extremely scarce. "Pénurie de numéraire," reported the general prosecutor of Limoges in 1848.

"The first and foremost thing lacking" in the Vosges, commented an observer in 1866, was cash. These were the times when a sou was really a sou. "For a sharecropper who gets paid for his labor in kind," Armand Audiganne wrote of Périgord in 1867, "who sells nothing or almost nothing, a sou is really something." Criminal records show how little cash people had on them, like the man knifed near Landerneau in June 1870 and left for dead, who though he carried a watch had only one franc and some coppers in his wallet. "On paye le docteur quand les cochons se vendent bien," observed a Comminges teacher in 1886. And only then. If then.[16] Cash was scarce, precious; every bit of it counted; even a few centimes unexpectedly added to the budget could cause anxious concern. The inability of peasant households to meet their cash needs is reflected in the vast numbers of official arrangements that were never carried out: the pension promised to old parents that was never paid, or the nominal sum an unmarried son was supposed to get for contributing his share to the family farm that he never got. Passing through Vic-sur-Cère in the 1890's, a small spa only a few miles from Aurillac, Jean Ajalbert found the servants at the inn "little used to tips," knotting into their handkerchiefs any small coins a visitor might leave them.[17]

All this was but one indication of an enduring autarky in the countryside—a self-sufficient life in which until around 1870 many peasants bought only iron and salt, paid for all else in kind and were paid the same way, husbanded their money for taxes or hoarded it to acquire land. In the southwest in 1853 observers noted that since few bought grain for consumption, its price mattered little. In Brie, as we can see from a local vintner's ledger, the winegrowers were self-sufficient to the end of the Second Empire and beyond. Pepper, salt, a little salted cod, and a few pairs of clogs were the sum total of their cash purchases. In Bresse at the close of the century, money came out of hiding in the autumn at Saint Martin's day (November 11), when the family bought basic stocks like sugar and salt and paid the taxes and the rent it owed. The rest of the time "money was almost unknown in the hamlets." Barter continued to play a significant role. Near Saint-Gaudens, in Haute-Garonne, the peasants brought their highland wheat to the markets of the plain and exchanged one measure of wheat for two measures of corn. The muleteers of Gévaudan carried on an active trade between the grainlands of Velay and the Vivarais wine country, exchanging wheat, beans, peas, barley, and the famous lentils of the Puy for goatskins of Ardèche wine. As roads replaced trails, wagons took over from mules, but the scale of this trade diminished only in the 1880's, when the lowland vineyards were devastated by the deadly Phylloxera. In 1902 in impoverished Corrèze the women of the Monédières still came down to the markets and fairs of Treignac to exchange their hair for "cloth or other articles." All over the Limousin at that time, and until the war at least, most village artisans accepted payment in services or in kind (potatoes, chestnuts, sometimes even the raw materials they needed).[18]

André Armengaud has noted, as Audiganne has of Périgord, that the agricultural workers of nineteenth-century Aquitaine were seldom paid in cash. Similarly, in Henri Bachelin's Limousin a miller's servant got two *doubles* of grain, a dress, an apron, and one pair of clogs a year. In Lower Dauphiné migrant harvesters were paid in kind until 1910 or so. So were shepherds in Aubrac. In some regions, like Bresse, the farmer seldom hired any help at all. When extra hands were needed, as at harvest or haymaking time, neighbors relied on one another. In other regions, like the Landes, where currency was scarce until the First World War, sharecroppers continued to be paid and to make their purchases in kind. In most places, though, wages were paid in both cash and kind in varying proportions, as in Brittany, where a farmhand might receive 50 skoed, six ells of linen, and three pairs of clogs a year.[19]

Perhaps, as René Nelli suggests, payment in kind was considered more honorable than a cash "salary" as a sort of symbolic participation in property. Thus, in Roussillon and Languedoc, where for a long time landowners paid for work and services in kind, the crews and masters of coastal fishing boats shared in the catch but paid extra hands in cash as if they were mere town workingmen, and accordingly despised. A simpler explanation might be that in a system where barter was king, cash could be hard to use, and the most basic of consumer goods difficult to buy. This could be why, in 1856, landowners in Agenais were unable to persuade their servants to accept salaries. As the market economy spread and necessities could be purchased in cash, this changed. In the Minervois, until the turn of the century, the pay of hired hands was based on a share of the harvest. A farmworker's yearly wage might typically have consisted of 300 to 550 francs in cash, 500 liters of wine, 800 liters of wheat, 10 liters of oil, 20 liters of beans, and between 200 and 400 bundles of vine-shoots to keep his fire burning. But a 1906 study on vineyard workers noted that more and more frequently the employer "instead of furnishing goods, which he no longer produced," paid his employees in cash—except, significantly, for wine.[20]

Until this came to pass, money continued to be in short supply. Its scarcity helps explain the references found in so many sources to the peasants' meanness, stinginess, and avarice. "Love of lucre ... blind absolute passion for money." "Money is their idol. To it they sacrifice everything ... and live more miserably than slaves in the colonies." "This great anti-social lie, thrift, has led to avarice."[21] Both thrift and avarice were natural reactions to a dearth of money (itself reflecting lasting backwardness), which is as inconceivable to us as it was to all these urban observers, for whom coins were quite literally the currency of everyday existence. But the peasant knew very well how rare money was and hence how much the harder to come by. As the Vivarais proverb has it:[22]

> He who has money is content.
> He can pay with it. Better hang on to it.

Venality, rapacity, are natural to men—arising out of need, as the impulse to gorge arises out of want. Limousin peasant stories attribute a sense of justice to birds, cunning to animals (among which the fox is master), and greed to men—above all a vast love of gold. Peasants were seldom heroes of the tales they told, which were mostly about castles and palaces, princes and kings, with little attention paid to the humble life. But when the peasant showed himself, what he most revealed was an incredible lust for riches, for silver and gold—essentially for cash.[23]

Cash needs reflected aspects of life that went far beyond salt and taxes. There was first of all the hunger for land, sharpened by the fact that social standing was measured by the size of the family holding. Noneconomic considerations —duty, pride, prestige—presided over the desire to preserve and increase one's patrimony; over the dowry without which few girls could find a husband and no clans an alliance; over the practice in certain regions of settling on one heir for the family holding (*faire un aîné*), which required the chosen one to compensate or buy out the other heirs. All this made important calls on capital, and often as not—as we shall see—resulted in properties encumbered with mortgages and usurious loans.[24]

L'argent—money—or rather the lack of it, reigned over the countryside as much as or even more than it ruled in the towns. Usurers, notaries, the village bloodsuckers Balzac has painted, were part of a landscape all peasants knew well. There were few peasant families that did not drag along, like fetters, generations-old debts they could not cast off. Since credit was scarce, usury was rampant. This stemmed in part from archaic banking structures and credit institutions ill-adapted to local situations. The peasants' hunger for land has come under heavy fire. But what could be done with savings besides buying land? So long as money remained scarce, opportunities for investing what there was of it, or even of saving profitably, remained scarce as well.

The famous woolen sock had few alternatives. The first ordinary savings bank had been founded in Paris in 1818. Its successors were few until the 1830's and, of course, were restricted to the towns. In the mid-nineteenth century most savings depositors seem to have been soldiers and domestics. In 1874 French urban savers had access to only 1,142 savings offices compared with 5,000 in England at that date, and even then they were open only one or two days a week. In the countryside, county seats and the *chef-lieux d'arrondissement* were served, but 1,775 towns had no facilities at all. There were a mere 16 savings banks and 164 branches to serve the residents of 34,039 rural communes. To take one rural department as an example, in the Tarn the first two savings banks were founded in 1835, followed by two in 1857, three in 1861–62, one in 1868, and one in 1879. But the real rise in deposits came only after 1870. In 1860 depositors numbered 4,102, and deposits amounted to 1.5 million francs. By 1870 the figures had risen to 17,469 depositors with savings of more than six million francs. The figures doubled again by 1880 and once more by 1900.

The proportion of depositors in the total population was negligible until about 1866. The ratio rose steeply in 1875–80, and then climbed almost as fast in the last quarter of the century: 52.8 : 1,000 in 1875; 103.5 : 1,000 in 1880; 184.7 : 1,000 in 1900.[25]

In 1881 the Caisse Nationale d'Epargne was founded. Essentially a postal savings bank, its facilities contributed mightily to the shift from mattresses and woolen socks to interest-bearing bank books. Between 1882 and 1890 deposits soared ninefold, and by the end of 1897 they had increased almost as much again.[26] Whatever else all this suggests, it clearly shows that both investment and credit structures remained primitive and archaic until the last quarter of the century. And the awkward effects of the money shortage were most strongly felt in poorer regions like the Limousin. It is not that the problem went unrecognized. In a poem that was probably written in 1848, a winegrower from Deux-Sèvres, Claude Durand, had spelled it out for all to hear:[27]

> N'écoute plus cette aristocratie
> Qui convertit tes sueurs en écu;
> Quand tu voudras, usure et tyrannie
> Dans un seul jour tout aura disparu.
>
> . . .
>
> Dans tout hameau des banques agricoles
> Existeront pour toi, bon paysan,
> Gratis aussi on aura des écoles,
> Et de l'argent à deux pour cent.

But money at 2 percent was even more utopian than free schools. And agricultural banks took their time in appearing, and longer by far in serving the interests of the good peasant.

The Crédit Foncier, founded in 1852, was "ill-adapted to small and middling properties" and could not help the rural public. It accepted only first mortgages and insisted on complicated formalities and paperwork that were bound to be discouraging to simple applicants. In any case, many peasants had no title deeds for property they might offer as collateral, or at least none acceptable to official institutions. Additionally and hardly surprisingly, the Crédit Foncier was stoutly opposed by the usurers, notaries, and small loansharks who dominated the local situation. By the 1860's its operations focused largely on urban real estate. Its offspring, the Crédit Agricole, was little better. In 1909 we find the prefect of Haute-Vienne lamenting that peasants made so little use of it: "They know only imperfectly the remarkable instrument of liberation at their disposal." That was true, but was it at their disposal? Or was it, like its predecessor, largely a source of loans to towns and to the minority of prosperous and knowledgeable farmers in a position to use its services?[28]

The chief source of credit remained the usurer. "When resources fail," the sub-prefect of Brive-la-Gaillarde (a prosperous town in a prosperous district) wrote in 1852, "the farmer begs and the owner has recourse to usury." What begging was for the poorest classes, usury was for the less poor, who might well end up destitute in turn. Most historians of early- and mid-nineteenth century France insist on the crucial role of the peasants' burden of debt. Contemporary accounts do too. "Usury is the malady that undermines the countryside," noted an army officer in Haute-Vienne (1845). "Far from all supervision, cut off from the outside," explained the prefect of Basses-Alpes in 1856, "most of the people of our district are the prey of petty tyrants who make money out of everything." Usury, the plague of poor regions, was one of the calamities of the Lauragais, declared M. F. Pariset in 1867.[29] Nineteenth-century economists were less concerned about the evils of usurious credit than local officials or notables: "To give credit is to give time," explained Frédéric Bastiat. "To give up time to another is to give up a precious thing to him." The conclusion is obvious. Balzac's Cérizet lends 10 francs on Tuesday and expects 12 back on Sunday morning; at 20 percent a week, he doubles his investment in five weeks.

The usurer gained power as well as money. His hold on his debtors was immense. It could be, and was, used for political ends.* But more often creditors demanded all sorts of extras, forcing their victims to pay for drinks, meals, and legal costs, subjecting them to various kinds of exploitation and humiliation the more maddening for people to whom every cent, every piece of bread or jug of milk counted. Many have denounced the evils of usury, the accumulating payments that could easily drive the interest rate to 25 and 30 percent. But no one has made a study of the psychological strain that rural moneylenders, most often peasants themselves, imposed on their debtors.

Clearly, the revolt against usury was one of the great themes of 1848–52. It may also have done its share to spread anti-Semitism in the rural areas. Certainly, the strong identification of the Jew and the usurer was a significant feature of the nationalist politics of the Third Republic. Yet, apart from the cities, where the equivalence seems to have been firmly established in working-class myth, and Alsace and Lorraine, where Jews were hated even more than forest guards,[30] I have not found any reference to Jewish usury.† Most lenders

---

* For example, in 1850 the tax collector of Ariège processed a request for tax relief from a villager—by his account a *rentier* and a man of considerable means who, having endowed his children, used his spare capital for usury. The man's commune, Sabarat, was alleged to be "very bad, crimson red, from mayor to garde champêtre," thanks largely "to the intimidation he exercises with his usury on all the working class." Whether true or not, the allegations suggest real possibilities. (Archives Départementales, Ariège 5M3, 1850.)

† But the seeds of anti-Semitic sentiment were planted in rural communities where no Jews existed, let alone Jewish usurers, by the Church, whether in catechism or during the Easter services on Maundy Thursday and Good Friday. Dieudonné Dergny, *Images, coutumes et croyances,* 1: 330–42, gives a variety of ways in which during the Tenebrae services the congregation upbraided and reviled those held responsible for the death of Jesus. At Las Illas (probably Les Ilhes, Aude) men and youths executed the Jews (lous facous del Jouéus) by striking the stalls and church pavement with sticks. Elsewhere members of the congregation set up a din with rattles and heavy stamping, extinguished candles (representing Jews), or burned Jews in effigy, in fires lit in the cemetery or (in Alsace) communal pyres. According to Charles Beauquier, in Franche-Comté at

were, as already suggested, local men—various notables, including landowners, well-to-do farmers, millers, innkeepers, and artisans; priests, who sometimes had a host of debtors;[31] and of course the *notaires* who invested both their clients' money and their own—and certainly not all charged usurious rates. But whatever their social or economic position, the moneylenders—and usury—continued to be an integral part of the rural economy and a major source of rural anxiety until the money shortage eased and interest rates fell in the 1890's. Final liberation came only from the profits peasants made during the war of 1914–18.[32]

All this suggests that the shift to a money economy was telescoped in a number of regions into a fairly short period that fell roughly in the last third of the nineteenth century. The start of the process coincides roughly with the beginnings of the Third Republic. That was when, very slowly, country people learned the gestures involved in handling coins, weighing them in the hand, testing how they rang on stone, and so on, before passing on to the intricacies of paper money.[33] Though little used in the countryside before the war, paper money too had seen a tremendous jump in circulation between 1887 and 1895. It had been a stranger to great parts of France at the end of the Second Empire, and by 1887 the amount in circulation had scarcely doubled. In the following eight years, however, the quantity increased sixfold. The pace slackened thereafter, and by 1913 it had taken 26 years for the volume to increase tenfold. The triumph of paper money came only after the First World War, but its advances in the preceding quarter century had been significant.[34]

Whatever indicator we turn to, therefore, the 1880's and the quarter century that followed them appear as a watershed in this as in other respects. The circulation and the use of money, the accumulation and the reliance on savings, the payment of wages in cash, eventually the circulation figures of paper currency, all testify to it. The traditional economy was clearly giving way. Cash in the traditional economy was saved with great effort as a reserve and as a sort of insurance, like grain in a barn. Its uses were as limited as its quantity. Once the subsistence stage had passed—once the closed circle in which it did not matter what coins one used, and most of the time one did not use any, broke open—money became of great consequence, not only as the means of exchange, but as the means of measuring everything, a universal language that all understood and all now wanted to speak.

How near and yet how far away the time when people said "un sou c'est un sou," and meant what they were saying!

---

the end of the century the faithful went to Maundy Thursday service armed with a wooden mallet. "At a certain passage of the service, the priest throws his book to the ground, and then everyone strikes repeated blows on the stalls and on the chairs. This is called *tuer les Juifs*." (*Traditions populaires*, p. 44.)

Chapter Four

ALONE WITH ONE'S FELLOWS

C'est donc à bon droit que les Anciens tenaient l'étranger à
distance. C'est celui qui a d'autres moeurs, et dont on ne
peut savoir ce qu'il va faire.
—BERTRAND DE JOUVENEL

AT THE END of the eighteenth century, when the intendant of Gascony wanted to have roads constructed so as to connect the area with neighboring provinces, the people of Auch, bourgeois and common folk alike, protested: "We
have all we need to live well. Our neighbors will come to take what they lack,
and we have no need of what they can offer us." This sort of attitude lasted
through much of the nineteenth century. But not all of it. As a country doctor
observed shortly before the First World War, "a profound moral evolution"
had taken place over the past 25 years: "The race [was] becoming separated
from this land it loved so much."[1]

The stubborn survival of local and domestic autarky is closely linked to the
survivals described in Chapter 3; and once again the watershed of change
seems situated around the 1880's. In 1794 Saint-Just had shrewdly pointed to
the connection between private selfishness and local isolation, linking geographical and political detachment from national affairs. Departments and
parishes, he complained, lived in autarky. Everyone kept his own commodities for himself; all output and produce were shut up at home. In 1827 an
officer riding through the western Puy-de-Dôme, in the area of the highway
from Limoges to Clermont, noted a life-style that was largely self-sufficient,
including the weaving of wool shorn from the local sheep, "whereby the inhabitants are not forced to look to neighboring towns for their garb." In a
passing reference to the whole great center of France at mid-century, Adolphe
Blanqui spoke of it as *sui generis*, separated from the rest of the country by
difficulty of access and long-standing isolation, "living its own life, having an
appearance apart and traits distinct from the great national physiognomy."
Naturally its inhabitants "have preserved ... their original character in face of
the general movement toward assimilation that civilization generates throughout the rest of France." Commenting on the effect of the grain shortages troubling many places in the hard winter of 1847, the prefect of Yonne, much

closer to Paris and to civilization, remarked that since everyone there grew his own supplies and journeymen were generally paid in grain, no one really noticed the state of the market.[2] As long as communications remained primitive and few, no market other than the local one mattered. Peasants grew what they needed or learned to need only what they could grow, kept what they could store, and sold what they could as best they could. Economists inveighed against "the narrow spirit that makes every family, every locality, every *pays*, live on its own resources asking nothing of trade." But the farms and villages of areas like the Savoy of 1864 and the still-isolated Lauragais of 1867, remained wholly self-sufficient—each "a sort of oasis."[3]

Only decent roads and railroads could alter this, and as we shall see, much of France had neither till after 1880.[4] Until then, villages and hamlets in Savoy or Lot remained "inaccessible ... turned in upon themselves," and the mentality this created survived well beyond the fact.* Toward 1905 the old women of the lower Limousin kept on spinning the local wool even though sartorial self-sufficiency had by this time been abandoned. Yet the ideal farm (even in villages near urban Brive) continued to grow all its own provisions. Even after the First World War peasants tried to buy as little as possible and "faire de tout pour que ça marche." Predictably enough, the mentality and the practices it bred survived longest in areas whose isolation was slowest to be disturbed: the west, the center, the southwest, and the Pyrenees.[5]

Material self-sufficiency has always been a model rather than a reality. And the more significant aspects of self-sufficiency in the peasants' universe were psychological rather than material. Paul Bois has shown that involvement in the market in pre-Revolutionary Sarthe did not necessarily mean integration in the urban world. Even in the wild vastnesses of the Puy-de-Dôme, some communities made coarse linen for sale at Clermont or Riom, and bought the flax they needed in the markets there.[6] Where such economic and human interchanges occurred, and especially when they involved temporary migrations, new ways trickled in a whit faster than elsewhere; but even then their adoption was slow and highly selective. Indeed, all societies at all times have adopted new techniques, or practices, or tastes. The question is, in what degree, at what rate, and how long did they remain the masters of what to leave or take. A society can apparently maintain its cultural isolation even if it has regular economic relations with other societies. Guatemalan peasant traders of the 1930's spent a good part of their lives buying and selling in a wide circle of markets, yet seem to have remained insulated from the influences of the

---

* Inspector Pujos, "Recueil des monographies" (St.-Caprain, Francoulès). In Haute-Savoie only the very end of the nineteenth century would break the isolation of places like Contamines and the Montjoye valley, which the railway reached in 1898 (Jean Chardonnet, *Annales de géographie*, 1938, p. 632). See also Archives Nationales, F^{17}9265 (Loire-Inf., May 4, 1880), which refers to the *natures primitives* of the inhabitants; long deprived of means of communication, they knew only the nearest bourg. On the sea coast of the department, and especially in the north (arrondissements of Châteaubriant and St.-Nazaire), "poverty, illiteracy, and isolation go hand in hand."

many local cultures through which they passed—their commercial life separate from their local culture. This applies to a fair number of local cultures, none in a position to overpower others. But the peasant can hold his own even against the strong culture of the city, as long as conditions force or enable his community to do so. Thus, we are told that, before the didactic campaigns of the Communist regime, Bulgarian peasants who bought and sold in cities carried few or no changes back into their villages. Tacit consent kept rural and city worlds apart. Even in town, peasants talked mostly to other peasants, not participants in urban life but spectators of it.[7]

This sharp division is easier to conceive of if one remembers the immense cultural distance between the peasants' universe and that of the city dwellers. Draft boards in Dordogne just before the July Revolution found many young recruits who did not know their surnames and could only mutter their parents' Christian names. Quérigut in Ariège had not seen a prelate in 120 years when the Bishop of Pamiers and the departmental prefect decided to visit it in 1847. The inhabitants worked for days rolling stones to make a trail passable for "the intrepid travelers," and the exceptional event was marked by 1,200 confirmations. The same utter isolation characterized Nièvre, Allier, and Vendée in the 1840's. In 1843, when an army battalion halted at Beaulieu (Corrèze), it found a population to whom soldiers were as strange as little Dorothy was to the city folk of Oz. "Military uniform, ways, and character [were] absolutely unknown," so that all turned out to marvel as at a circus (probably also unknown), and one local notable mistook the impressive-looking drum major for the colonel of the regiment. Officers were amazed that the populace of Lozère and Aveyron had "no idea of the outside world"—no more than the woman of Oléron off the Atlantic coast, who asked a sergeant major what people in the interior could find to eat when the sea was so far away.[8]

Isolation made for ignorance, indifference, for rumors that spread like wildfire in contrast to the stubbornly slow assimilation of current events.* It also

---

* When, in August 1914, the people of Champeaux and the Millevaches plateau of Corrèze heard the church bells sounded to announce the declaration of war, they were wholly perplexed since no storm appeared to be brewing. The news of war was greeted with depression and talk of the possibility of hiding in the woods to avoid mobilization (René Bonnet, *Enfance limousine*, pp. 27–29). Similarly, at Malleval (Drôme) mobilization in 1914 came as a "profound surprise." Yet though no one seemed to have the time to read the papers (it was haymaking season), the order to have horses ready for requisition by July 31 had "begun to affect opinion" (J. J. Becker, "L'Appel de guerre en Dauphiné, *Mouvement social*, 1964, especially p. 34). The fact is, the peasant took his news selectively, paying attention solely to what affected him—and drawing his own conclusions. Thus in 1830 and 1848 the political news was quick enough to penetrate upland Ariège, but what the people seized on was the possibility this seemingly offered of reclaiming some of the grazing, hunting, and wood-gathering rights that local landowners had been steadily closing off. For them, political revolution meant an opportunity to return to traditional ways. The indifference to national events is nowhere more strikingly illustrated than in Maurice Barrès, *Oeuvre*, 6: 228. Observing how little impact the German occupation had on the Lorraine countryside in 1908, he wrote: "Dans ces communes placées en dehors du chemin de fer et qui n'ont pas de douaniers ni d'employés de gare, c'est absolument comme si l'annexion n'existait pas."

made for local solidarity, which was reinforced by mutual aid—a practice that may have arisen out of sheer necessity in the absence of other alternatives but that had generally become ritualized by tradition. Villages accepted their local madmen and beggars, but those foreign to the parts were feared and rejected. Both local wisdom and local vocabulary stressed the importance of mutual aid and disapproved of those who refused to live up to the traditional demands— as in the pejorative Provençal attribute *gouste soulet* (goûte seul), meaning a lone eater, one who does not share.[9]

Sharing might go a long way, as in the solitary settlements of the resin workers of the Landes where, noted a visitor in 1911, "life was carried on almost in common," even to sharing any letter a neighbor might receive—or any visitor. This of course applied to all places where letters and visitors were things to wonder at, events among the few that broke the monotony of every-day routine. As a gendarme at Lourdes explained in 1858, "anything out of the ordinary is rare and causes interest when it occurs.... Curiosity suddenly urged from its fast feeds a long time [on the occurrence], since its menu rarely varies." This is exactly what Emile Guillaumin would say about life in his Bourbonnais half a century later, and J. H. Ricard about the people of the lonely Landes he visited about the same time. It explains the interest a stranger aroused, the hospitality he (at times) enjoyed and also the suspicion he invari-ably encountered.[10]

On this score the evidence, particularly rich, reflects the shock and incom-prehension of travelers unable to see why a countryman—their countryman as a rule—should react so negatively to what seemed to them natural activities or requests. A staff captain reconnoitering the road from Nantes to Vannes in 1822 regretted that he could report no positive information, having been unable to elicit any from the inhabitants "because of their suspicion of those who ask them questions, if [the questioners] are unknown to them." Under the Second Empire we hear the same song in Lot ("jaloux des étrangers"), and we are told things were even worse across the Lot River, in Aveyron. In 1877 at Plélan (Ille-et-Vilaine) the people were "ignorant and suspicious." And on the eve of war, still, the Périgourdin appeared "suspicious and close with strangers."[11]

But the clue comes very early, if one is willing to pick it up: the peasants of the Puy-de-Dôme, said an officer in 1827, were unwilling to furnish infor-mation for fear it would be used against them.[12] In Aveyron the natives either refused to provide any information at all or gave misleading answers because they inevitably took a questing stranger for a fiscal agent or some other gov-ernment representative.* Their suspicion was such, complained an 1836 report

---

* Similarly, in a notorious court case in Ardèche in 1842 all witnesses swore, despite con-vincing evidence to the contrary, that they had seen nothing. Their testimony gave rise to the saying "Sous dé Lonas, ei rèn vis" (I'm from Lonas, and I've seen naught), later applied also to the village of Lussas, whose inhabitants reenacted the comedy some years later (Pierre Charrié, *Folklore du Bas-Vivarais*, p. 248).

on Lozère and Aveyron, that often you could not even get anything at an inn. In 1840 an officer described the inhabitants of the area around Clamecy as stupid, for they could never give him a straight answer when he asked where the roads led. In the Mézenc area near Saint-Agrève any stranger in city clothes could only be there to serve a writ or collect taxes. "The peasant is extremely suspicious, a stranger can expect no help from him even for money, and the most insignificant questions seldom receive an answer." The writer of this particular report was taken for a sorcerer when he drew a plan of Castelnau in Lot-et-Garonne, was arrested by a group of armed men, and was released only after a deal of tribulations. Did the hostile yokels really take him for a sorcerer? Half a century later an artist sketching near Sarlat would be asked by an anxious peasant why he should take an interest in his house: "Is it for the Revenue you are working?"[13]

In Brittany the natives, as they were still described until the Third Republic, appeared amenable enough but unforthcoming. "They do not speak French, and do not want to speak French, and you cannot get any information out of them," reported one officer from Morbihan in 1873. Even in the Dinan countryside of Côtes-du-Nord, where only French was spoken, the natives "greet strangers with suspicion and nearly always refuse to give them whatever information they may need" (1877). As late as the 1890's an English traveler in the Tarn valley was repeatedly taken for some sort of spy and asked for his papers. He found people between Albi and Saint-Affrique and especially between Arthès and Millau exceedingly rude, treating all strangers with suspicion. Suspicious and closed with strangers, open and frank only with his peers, was the way a local scholar described his fellow Périgourdins, yet "only speak his language and acquaintance is made." But this was easier said than done. No wonder, since the difficulties of communication were so great, that all strangers French or English remained "foreigners."[14]

"The least of our villages," wrote a local historian of the Var, "considers itself a pays in its language, legends, customs, ways."[15] The awkward and untranslatable term pays has the fundamental significance of "native land" and applies more properly to local than to national territory. It is in this sense that most Frenchmen use it, applying it to greater or to smaller regions, sometimes a province, sometimes a limited valley or plain, as well as to fellow countrymen sharing this limited fatherland. The pays may be an administrative division (but infrequently); an entire region (Périgord, Marche, or Quercy); or simply (and most often) a parish or village. Ramuz explains that the canton of Vaud is also and foremost pays de Vaud, however small, because it is a whole unto itself and if need be self-sufficient. Above all, the pays is an entity whose members have something in common—experience, language, a way of life—that makes them different from others. That may be why journeymen-guilds used the term for all fellows of their societies. The notion of common belonging and fraternity, which makes the offspring of the same pays call each other pays as well, was transferred from the local to the professional group, so that members of the same guild were also pays within a restricted entity. The sense was clear. That was why, too, most Frenchmen for a long time did not think to describe France as their pays—until what they were taught came to coincide with experience.[16]

For a long time, that experience verified differences rather than similarities. "Each land its war; each pays its aspect; each village its tongue; each place its speech; each house its ways," runs a southwestern song.[17] "Change village, change language," says a Limousin proverb.[18] Two regions like Languedoc (Haute-Garonne, Ariège, Tarn, Tarn-et-Garonne) and Gascony (Gers, Lot-et-Garonne, Gironde) were distinguished by rare human and commercial interchanges; by linguistic differences that made Gascon and Languedocean mutually unintelligible; by separate political tendencies, agricultural implements, even breeds of cattle. Gascony looked to Bordeaux, Languedoc to Toulouse. Distance made little difference. Auch is 77 kilometers from Toulouse, 186 from Bordeaux, but of 11 post roads radiating from Toulouse in the 1840's only one went to Gers and, even today, only one railway line runs west out of Toulouse. In Brittany the names of Léon, Cornouaille, and Trégorrois were as familiar as the departments incorporating them, and differed far more from each other than Côtes-du-Nord did from Finistère. Real hostility existed between Lower and Upper Brittany, a division based on the Celtic speech of the west and the French dialect of the east. Bretons and Gallos disliked and despised each other, insulted each other and each other's womenfolk, and stood together only in their hearty dislike of the French—notably the Normans, who returned the aversion with interest. In 1873 Breton pilgrims to Mont Saint-Michel were threatened and insulted by Normans, and fighting was only narrowly averted.[19]

At Chitry (Nièvre) in 1902 Jules Renard was struck by the dislike for strangers, the reluctance to accept them, the ease with which they could be "excluded." There were people, he noted, "who pale at the idea of sleeping in the cemetery beside someone from outside the pays." Most villages had regionally valid nicknames. Most villagers had them too. But whereas those of the villagers focused on particularities inside the community, reflecting a familiarity with the background and actions they described, the nicknames given to resident strangers focused on the place of origin (e.g., Le Savoyard) and were usually in French, like the names of the new settlers themselves, whatever the local forms might be. A subtle but natural way of stressing strangeness.[20]

And it is true that pays can differ measurably from each other, sometimes over small distances (as mountain valleys very often do), in the quality of their water, the taste of their nuts, or the fineness of their sheep's-wool, as in the Campan valley of Bigorre. "When one passes from Maine-et-Loire into Loire-Inférieure," wrote a school inspector in 1880, "one finds everything changed, from the looks of the land to those of the people. Dwellings lack the air of comfort and ease they have in Anjou; the country people dress differently and with less care, look dirtier; the general impression is altogether poorer."[21] Differences such as these, or some of them, were the reflection of circumstances and changed with circumstances. The good lands of Loire-Inférieure would be developed as soon as road and rail made their exploitation profitable. The savage backwardness of inland Brittany would give way before fertilizers and prosperity. The prevalent beggary at Nîmes was considered a natural consequence of the city's southern clime, until Gard prohibited begging and eliminated it, just as Rhône had in Lyon. Elsewhere, we observe that the miners of Saint-Etienne were notoriously ill-kempt and lived in ill-kept homes, while those at Rive-de-Gier, not far away, were conspicuously clean and lived in neat, clean houses; in Saint-Etienne we hear the women worked, at Rive-de-Gier (in 1860) "never"—presumably because opportunities for employment were lacking.[22]

More fundamental differences could pass away as well, like the kind of natural division the olive (or rather the range of its growth) had set between Upper and Lower Provence. Similarly, the chestnut, a vital element in the diet and life of some regions, had given those places a peculiar vocabulary, awareness, and taste that set them apart from others, until the chestnut's hold decayed. Other differences were written in physical conditions: the ravines and gorges that ripped through Auvergne and Velay, cutting up the soil, dispersing the hamlets and cottages, and making for an especially strong individualism or localism. But village particularisms seem to go beyond that sort of thing, ruling even where (outside the parish) one could look for a spouse. At Chanzeaux in Anjou, Laurence Wylie tells us, people traditionally married to the west: always into the Mauges, never in Saumurois. When you go to the veillée, advised the local wisdom in the Doubs, do not go farther than the barrier of Cerneux-Monnot—that is, where the clear air of the mountain country gives way to the lowland atmosphere. In the Ardèche-Vivarais the mountain people (Padgels) mixed with the people on the lower slopes (Royols), but never intermarried: "Fillo que mounto et vatcho que descen, touto lo vido s'en repen," says the proverb. Further to the north, on the other hand: "Femmes du Puy, hommes de Lyon, Ont toujours fait bonne maison."[23]

But regional orientations were remote abstractions compared with the traditional relations between neighboring parishes. "Every valley," wrote an economist in 1837 about the central Pyrenees, "is still a little world that differs from the neighboring world as Mercury does from Uranus. Every village is a clan, a sort of state with its own patriotism." Villages hated each other from time immemorial, and all hated the gentlemen of the bourgeoisie—by definition strangers and outsiders. We have already encountered the suspicion and "repulsion" evoked by "city dogs," not least the artisans and traders of the bourg. Rare trips to town showed city folk to be contemptuous and rude.[24] So one replied in kind. The Basques despised all outsiders. In the masquerades regularly put on in Basque villages, the peasant actors divided into two troupes, Reds and Blacks, differentiated by their roles and by the nature of their costumes. The Reds, who represented the natives, good and noble, wore rich local garb. The Blacks, rascals and ragamuffins, represented a variety of foreign charlatans—bohemians, tinkers, knife-grinders, doctors, apothecaries, often a stray Parisian notaire or two. The Blacks were identified by the strange clothes they wore (hats or caps instead of the native beret, shoes or boots instead of espadrilles), and spoke gibberish meant to represent Béarnais, French, or the Auvergnat dialect. Always ridiculous, they could appear dangerous as well.[25]

It is not surprising the peasant looked askance on strangers, often welcomed with pitchforks as in the Couserans, when all he saw seemed either despicable (because poor and rootless) or dishonest, or like as not both. Strangeness, in any case, was disconcerting—as in the English word strange, which carries both meanings in one. Breton slang expressed the same feeling when the word *fuistic*, meaning alien, came to be used in the sense of funny and odd, because strangers of course are strange. Spasmodic acquaintance only increased contempt. The vocabulary of nineteenth-century Mâconnais shows an incredible variety of such nomadic strangers, most of them pejoratively described: *romanichels, bohémiens, sarrasins, égyptiens* (whence Mâcon's rue d'Egypte), *polacres, bougres, broutchoux* (traveling hemp-carders), and not least *magniens*, a patois term for snail, applied both to tinkers and to the mountain men of Auvergne and Bugey, who came down every winter to seek a living in fatter Burgundy. In 1876 the building of a road and bridge over the Cher, in Henri Norre's lonely Allier village, brought in many "foreign workers... nomads"—masons, stonecutters, laborers. Though the young Norre worked with them through the winter, he found them repugnant (vicious, debauched), and they in turn, eating and drinking in their own canteens, had little intercourse with the local people.[26] Was it fear of vagrants or simply of foreigners that made so many set their dogs on wandering working men? One world could only with the greatest difficulty trust members of another.*

At the end of the nineteenth century, Father Gorse still saw each Corrèze hamlet as a small republic with its own peculiar usages. Half a century later we find the folklorist Arnold Van Gennep describing the villages of the past in close to the same terms: "Each a little citadel, morally and psychically independent."[27] These citadels, these republics, had fought in the past over lands or privileges or pasture rights. The memory of ancient feuds lived on in traditional enmities or alliances whose sources had long since been forgotten. Thus in 1819 a tiny village in the Couserans reacted violently to a projected

---

* Emile Guillaumin, *Paysans par eux-mêmes*, p. 32, quotes a farmworker writing in September 1909 about the plain of Limagne where "les gens sont à demi-sauvages. Si un ouvrier se risque aux abords d'une ferme, on lâche le chien et l'on crie de loin qu'il n'y a rien à faire. 'Quonet con donc qu'l'étrangé que s'prommeno para tché?' "

administrative reform: "If our parish is joined to that of Salsein, we risk being murdered, beaten, and maltreated by those of Salsein, and especially during the night."[28] Isolation encouraged persistent mutual distrust. In turn, stereotypes arising out of this distrust (concerning one's own village and its neighbors) reinforced isolation, endogamy or selective exogamy, and existing orientations, that is, the rivalries and the psychic distance between one village and another. Norre recalled that in the Allier of his youth, the patron saint's day apart, "we had nothing to do with people from neighboring communes." In Sologne the people of La Marolle were known as Les Etrangers, because a man from a neighboring parish once said to his wife, "Tu m'ennuies, je m'en vont à l'étranger," and had promptly taken himself off to La Marolle; and the people of Cerdon were known as Les Retourneux, because they turned back all strangers from their village that they might return whence they had come. All this helps to explain the distrust and caution with which peasants treated not only the unfamiliar, but everyone who was not part of their community.[29]

Anyone who came from beyond the familiar radius of ten or fifteen miles, said Guillaumin of the peasant as late as the 1930's, was still a "foreigner." It is a natural prejudice that proverbs reinforced: "Lying is easy when you are from far away." But they taught also that it was not safe to go too far from home: "Women and chickens get lost when they go too far." "In strange lands small cows can eat large beeves." It was unsafe above all to marry away from home. A Franc-Comtois asked his village priest to help him decide between two girls, one from his town, the other from another pays. "Ah," said the priest, "dung here, dung there, take it in your pays, you'll save on transport." More to the point, perhaps, as the Basque proverb has it, "Who goes far to marry is either fooling or fooled." The youth who married in a neighboring village married an *étrangère* he could not really know. So, it is said in Tarn-et-Garonne, "Prends la fille de ton voisin, Que tu vois passer chaque matin."[30]

"Mistrust," wrote a priest at the close of the century, "is the outstanding trait of the peasants' character. The peasant does not trust anyone, not even himself."[31] This was both true and false. It was true that rural defenses remained high and the rural mentality a distinctly separate one. But the observation reflects, too, a natural vexation at being unable to penetrate the closed world of the village society, and the kind of judgment this inevitably evoked from those condemned to watch it from the outside.

Chapter Five

FROM JUSTICE, LORD, DELIVER US!

*La jhustic', moun amit, é coum' les arentèles: O prend reinq' les
mussets, le tuon peurc' la toèle.*

—SAINTONGE PROVERB

ONE SOLID REASON for the peasant's abiding suspicion of all comers lay in the devastating intrusions of the alien law and its representatives into his world. Adolphe Blanqui, very far from a radical, called lawmen the true scourge of rural populations. The rural populations evidently agreed. In the Limousin the farmer's evening prayers would long include the tag line "Deliver us from all evil and from justice." The same formula survived in Charente into the 1930's: "My God, deliver us from all ill and from justice!"[1]

When asked what was meant by justice, the peasant's answer inevitably included some reference to "the cornered hats" or "the blue coats": not just the gendarmes, but all those in their train, from the bailiff and the tax collector (still known as the tithe collector in Confolentais) to the lowliest forest guard and gamekeeper. All that had to do with "justice" was a cause for fear. The countryside was full of *lieux-dits* with ominous names like La Potence, La Justice, and Le Gibet, all synonymous. Breton fishermen called a certain bird *sergent* after the bailiff—sergent de justice—because it stole sardines from other, smaller birds. Similarly, the notorious brigands who haunted the Morlaix-Lannion road in the seventeenth and eighteenth centuries got their name from the official collector of tithes and tolls. The royal archer, predecessor of the gendarme, survived in Burgundian lore as a bugbear, and in the description of a naughty child: wicked as an archer. Mâconnais tales of the nineteenth century even present jurors as doomed to eternal remorse, ashamed to face the light of day and hiding their faces from any passing stranger.[2]

The man of law was not necessarily an officer of the court or the state. He could be that special kind of businessman described by the French term homme d'affaires—a retired bailiff, some clerk of the court who had sold his commission, a lawyer without clients, or a onetime law student who had chosen to drop by the way, cultivating (as Blanqui at mid-century put it) at the same time his little garden and his little cases, with moneylending and land speculation thrown in. Whatever he was, he could only be bad: "Process servers are rascals, lawyers are lickspittles, attorneys are thieves."[3] It was a proverb that other peasants would have readily shared with their fellows in Upper Brittany, where legend had it that even Saint Ives, patron of lawyers, had been forced to slip into heaven when Saint Peter was not looking and had managed to remain there only because no bailiff could be found to serve him with an eviction notice.*

The countryman, so often illiterate, always believed himself diddled by the educated or semi-educated men with whom he had to deal—and he very often was. The legal costs of settling an inheritance might amount to three-quarters of the estate. Loans were surrounded by a vast and intricate array of legal fees, which were generally inflated by clever manipulation. The same was often true of land sales. Court costs alone, even of the most modest proportions, could appear astronomical to men and women who hoarded every copper. And paper, official documents, few as they were compared with what we must contend with, baffled and overwhelmed the simple man. Negligence on the part of mayors or their assistants could lead to the loss of a birth certificate, and to a costly but unavoidable verification of civil status on the eve of a marriage. Through ignorance or inertia a would-be seller could find himself faced with a demand for a deed of property that he had never dreamed existed. No wonder that in 1848 so many peasants would have loved to massacre magistrates and their like![4]

These, the bailiffs, the tax collectors, the gendarmes, were the principal intermediaries between the country people and the wider community of the nation. For the peasants of Ille-et-Vilaine, as a passing officer found reason to deplore in 1875, France was taxes. Or as a country doctor put it, France was "the agents of the state."[5]

Little as they were loved, the agents of the state had their work cut out for them. Rural crime was far more prevalent in the nineteenth century than has been generally conceded to date, a vaster problem certainly than I can fully cover here. The War Ministry Archives fairly bulge with reports of thefts, rapes, robberies, fires set in vengeance or out of spite, infanticides, parricides, and suicides; with fights, scuffles, brawls, frays, even pitched battles between poachers and gendarmes, poachers and gamekeepers, smugglers and customs men, peasants and forest guards, rival villages, youth gangs, and conscripts; and with countless homicides, premeditated murders, and attempted murders, by pistol, revolver, gun, rifle, fowling piece, knife, dagger, ax, club, staff, cudgel, hammer, adze, rock, compass, iron bar, or by a sharp weapon or blunt instrument that defied further description, or quite simply by foot or fist.[6]

Still, criminal records can mislead the student and make him take the ex-

---

* Roger Devigne, *Le Légendaire de France* (Paris, 1942), pp. 76–77. Devigne also cites this familiar proverb: Sanctus Yvo erat Brito, / Advocatus et non latro, / Res miranda populo. (Old Saint Ives he was a Breton, / Man of law and yet no thief, / Wondrous thing beyond belief.)

ceptional for the commonplace. Figures are not very revealing when we know
that statistics continued to be poor until the century was nearly gone, and that
much slipped through the official net besides.

The judgment of contemporaries is no more trustworthy, but it is suggestive.
Their attention, as we might expect, was focused on what went on in towns,
at first because that was where civilized life was centered, later because that
was where the dire side of modern civilization showed itself. In 1833 A. M.
Guerry saw cities as improving men's behavior and restricting their ability to
escape justice. But by 1891 Emile Levasseur, in his massive study of French

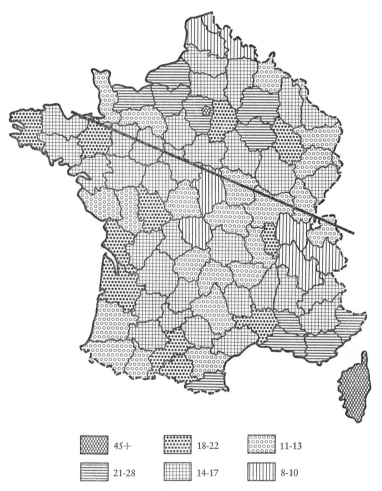

45+	18-22	11-13	
21-28	14-17	8-10	

Map 1. Crime rate by number of persons charged per 100,000 population,
1831–1880. National average: 17. The diagonal roughly separates the most
undeveloped areas from the developed areas. SOURCE: Emile Levasseur, *La
Population française*, 2: 461.

populations, was insisting on the temptations cities held for criminals, and the opportunities they offered them. Perhaps, as a fin-de-siècle sociologist equably remarked, urban life favored evildoers as much as it hindered them.[7] All the same, Levasseur's findings reflected the experience of the latter half of the century. Whereas in the 1840's some 60 percent of all the accused criminals lived in rural parishes, in the early 1880's over 50 percent were urban. Given the slow rise of the urban population (roughly from a quarter to a third of the total population between 1851 and 1881), its share of crime had grown markedly in two score years. During the 1880's and 1890's criminals were (proportionately) more than twice as numerous in towns as in the country.[8]

They also, on the whole, committed different crimes. Crimes against property, notably theft, were more frequent in cities than in the countryside. Homicide, on the other hand, was more of a rural crime. In 1880 there were 11 murders per million population in the countryside against 9.3 in towns; by 1887 the gap had widened, to become 11.1 to 8.6. In general, crimes against persons, especially assault (and battery), accounted for a great proportion of rural criminality.* But certain offenses against property were also characteristic: arson, vandalism, poaching, and trespass. Unfortunately we have no rigorous analyses of court records to give us a view of rural crime in its specific details. Obviously, when we find offenses like *bris de clôture* increasing sixfold and the destruction of crops increasing fourfold in the half-century before 1880, we know that these crimes scarcely refer to towns. But it does seem that as the statistics on crime in general increased, those categories of offenses most typical of rural areas (hunting, fishing, poaching) fell steadily: 275.5 per 100,000 population in 1854, 74.9 in 1874, 50.2 in 1900, 43.7 in 1912, 24.3 in 1921.[9]

Experts do not agree on the way criminality as such developed. Some look at the declining figures of major crimes coming to assizes, others at the steady advance in the number of offenses tried in correctional courts. One might hazard a guess that since the crime *rate* for the country as a whole remained fairly steady for a century after 1850 while the proportion of older people in the population grew, and since the aged as a group are less disposed to crime, the younger criminals were having to sin harder to keep statistics up. *A fortiori*, this is particularly true where crimes of violence are concerned. Such

---

* Emile Durkheim, *Le Suicide* (1912 ed.), p. 403; Denis Szabo, *Crimes et villes*, pp. 62, 121. Some 50 years before, Guerry had contrasted the thievish north and northeastern parts of France with the brutal violent Midi: the richer the area, the more crimes against property. He had proposed that the border between the two coincided with the limits of olive culture, but had stressed at the same time the variety of internal differences, which "despite the regularity of our new administrative divisions still forces us to recognize within the kingdom something like distinct nations, each with its own language, mores, practices, and traditional prejudices" (A. M. Guerry de Champneuf, *Essai sur la statistique morale de la France*, Paris, 1833, p. 40). In 1880 "crimes against persons" still exceeded crimes against property in seven departments: Savoy, Hautes- and Basses-Alpes, Aveyron, Lozère, Pyrénées-Orientales, and Corsica (Gabriel Tarde, *La Criminalité comparée*, p. 155).

crimes, as we have noted, were relatively more numerous in rural communities. Given that the population of rural communities tended to stagnate or to decrease during the century after 1850, while the proportion of aged increased, the countryside's contribution to crime statistics, especially those most characteristic of its violent past, ought to have decreased as well. It would be interesting to see if the data bear out this hypothesis.

Crimes connected in one way or another with sex are hardest of all to estimate. The most accessible figures are on the crimes stemming from unwanted pregnancies; the bulk of them concern the towns and most often involve domestics, that is, poor girls in trouble living away from home, where concealment might have been arranged. At any rate, abortion and infanticide seem to have been common enough in the countryside, at least in regions where large families were more of a hindrance than a help. These practices too reflected at the least a matter-of-fact attitude to life, and sometimes what we would have to say was a total disregard for life, as in the case of a mother who helped her daughter kill her unwanted child, boil it, and feed it to the pigs; or that of a twenty-two-year-old girl who gave birth to her child alone, dismembered it, burned some of the pieces, and threw the rest into the cesspit.[10] But this can be no more than the tip of the iceberg. In the absence of substantial data, all one can hope for is a general impression, rough and approximate. My general impression is that violence was a fact of everyday life, and that it receded only slowly, and then selectively: it persisted within the family long after intervillage fights all but disappeared. Cases of assault and battery appear to have increased, as in the rest of France; and so did the self-inflicted violence of suicide.

Like much of the violence, many "crimes" reflected a world where the conditions of life remained primitive. On Brittany's rocky shores, just as the flotsam of shipwrecked vessels was fair game, so were the survivors who made it to shore. Scavengers quickly deprived them of anything they might have on them—watches, money, or rings. Shipwrecking or what was left of it, like smuggling or brigandage (often related trades), contributed resources that complemented the economy of scarcity.[11] It also bore witness to the survival of conditions we more often connect with the Ancien Regime, which, after all, was not very far away. Those isolated regions that the prefect of Nantes alluded to in 1812, "where the power of magistrates is weak and that of inertia almost invincible," were still to be found under the July Monarchy. Roads were not safe; forests were even more dangerous. Breton peasant stories are full of the adventures of men, women, and children who take refuge for the night only to find they have fallen into the hands of robbers.[12]

The answer lay in viable communications. In the North African Ansarine region the brigands who had long harassed the area were finally dislodged in the twentieth century, "when the trail from Mateur to Tébourba ... was turned into a passable road." But in nineteenth-century France few roads crossed the forests, moors, or mountain wastes, and brigands found safe haven there. In 1840 Breton beggar bands—*truands* from the Breton *truhe* (pity) or possibly from *tryan* (vagabond)—were still supposed to follow a single leader, Coesre (Caesar?), and to meet annually on the Pré-à-Gueux, near Kerospec. In 1858 Princess Bacciochi had them driven out of Colpo (Morbihan), on what is now the route from Locminé to Vannes; but they set up quarters in other parts and only the twentieth century saw an end to their organized crime. In 1844 the military reports still spoke of outlaws taking refuge in the wilds of Gévaudan, as they had done a generation or two before. In 1853 the commanding general at Bourges reported a criminal who remained beyond the reach of the law "in the vast perimeter of forests between the departments of Nièvre, Saône-et-Loire, and Côte-d'Or"; and the Minister of Justice appealed to the Minister of War to help clear the area around Gouloux in Nièvre's arrondissement of Château-Chinon.* The forests still stretch over the area today much as they did a century ago, but they are crossed by roads. Gouloux itself, released from the close embrace of the forests, is now a crossroads on the east-west road from Burgundy to the Loire.

Brigandage persisted longest in Corsica; and in its most remote and least developed areas, at least, the island bore little or no resemblance to the rest of France.† Still, it is interesting to find the sub-prefect of Bastia boasting in 1896 that bandits had disappeared from his arrondissement: "The ease of travel, the low mountains, the ever more numerous farmlands, would prevent an armed band from hiding for long from the gendarmerie." Yet, Corte and Sartène continued to be infested with bandits: "armed robbery, plunder, robber bands, stealing, pillaging, holding up travelers," read the reports. Gangs ruled the countryside, levied taxes, condemned people to death and carried out their verdicts. But then, as the sub-prefect of Sartène explained in 1908, his arrondissement was the most mountainous, the poorest, and the wildest section of the island.[13]

In Corsica, as elsewhere, but more than elsewhere, conditions had to change before their criminal expression could change. But policing had to become more efficient as well. There had to be more policemen; and more efficient policemen than the local grocer or tobacconist, schoolmaster or shopkeeper,

---

*Jean Cuisenier, *L'Ansarine*, p. 24; H.-F. Buffet, *En Bretagne morbihannaise*, p. 235; Archives de la Guerre, MR 1274 (1844), G⁸1 (Jan. 25, 1853). Some authorities recognized that besides making policing easier, roads would create employment and, by improving conditions, would lessen crime. In 1833 the sub-prefect of Die (Drôme) wrote to his superior, pressing for a road so the timber of Vercors could be exploited. This "mettrait fin aux habitudes de dévastion et de fraude qui sont malheureusement trop communes chez les habitants du Vercors et qui les mettent sans cesse aux prises avec la justice correctionnelle. La facilité de se procurer des moyens d'existence par une industrie légitime les ramènerait à des sentiments plus honnêtes." The road, and the benefits it was supposed to bring, would have to wait for half a century. (Georges Jarré, "L'Etablissement des routes," p. 243.)

† "La Corse se meut sous la Constitution de 1875 avec une âme du XIVe siècle italien," remarked a French jurist in 1887 (quoted in Madeleine-Rose Marin-Muracciole, *L'Honneur des femmes en Corse du XIIIe siècle à nos jours*, Paris, 1964, p. 2).

who often doubled as part-time officers. If they had the time, that is: the man who served as police chief in Brienon (Yonne) in 1855 did not; he resigned in that year to tend to his several profitable businesses. And they had to speak the local language, unlike the commissaire Flaubert found at Pont-l'Abbé in 1846, who had to use the local gamekeeper as interpreter.[14]

Even the makeshift services of a *garde champêtre* were wanting in some number of places. In 1856 one-quarter of the communes with rural territory had none; and many of the others would have been better off without them. But the Second Empire did preside over a great expansion of the forces of law and order, installing police superintendents in rural areas* and increasing the number of gendarmerie brigades whose special province was the country-side. One result of this expanded police power was a steep rise in the quantity of reports and charges drawn up annually by the gendarmes; by 1880 these numbered some 189,000, nearly quadruple the yearly average of 56,000 in the 1840's.[15] Another result was a similarly steep decline in the activities of such anachronistic criminals as highwaymen and brigand gangs.

Brigandage in fact was soon stamped out in all save the most isolated places, but smuggling, which played a real part in many a local economy, espe-cially around the periphery of the nation, proved much hardier. And under-standably so, since all recognized the smuggler's usefulness and few thought his work a crime. Indeed, he was regarded with much favor. The legendary fame of Mandrin, the eighteenth-century bandit, undoubtedly grew out of this view, but also from the general feeling that avoiding tolls and taxes, though clearly illegal, was not necessarily immoral. For that matter, members of the Basque clergy explicitly taught that since indirect taxes were contrary to canonical and social justice, smuggling was not a sin. Their flock certainly agreed. Something of the same lesson was taught in a vastly popular children's novel of the 1830's, which went into a fifteenth reprinting in 1889. It pre-sented smugglers in the friendliest light, and even had the hero and the local mayor lending them a helping hand against customs guards without a second thought. But then, as military observers explained, for the inhabitants of the Pyrenees at least, smuggling was their only resource, the only trade they had, part of local customs.[16] In time the mountain men found new resources, and smuggling ceased to be the chief occupation in even the poorer valleys. But the state monopoly of match production created a new crime: the making and sale of contraband matches, the resource of poor people, catering to poor people, to the turn of the century at the very least.[17]

The strongest evidence of archaic survivals, among the most ancient and certainly the most violent, comes from the records of the affrays between vil-lages, which continued in some places to the First World War, but whose golden age seems to have ended with the stricter police methods of the Second

---

*Though they were spread thin compared with the urban areas. In 1860 Hautes-Alpes and Lozère had seven commissaires de canton each against 70 in Nord and 19 in Lyon (Howard C. Payne, *Police State*, pp. 213, 246).

Empire. The *Statistique du département du Lot*, published in 1831, refers to "the bellicose temperament of Quercy-men," apparent "in those wars that break out between parishes and that give rise to real battles." And this was no exaggeration; the Lot archives contain a very fat file on the subject—bloody scenes, combats, disorders, serious wounds, treaties of peace, and rumors of war—with the local national guard playing its part, sometimes fighting other national guards or gendarmes, sometimes intervening to restore order. Similarly in Provence we hear of two villages near Nice whose inhabitants agreed to settle their differences in pitched battles with no recourse to the law whatever happened, only to become enmeshed in endless litigation when they ignored their mutual promises.[18]

When traditional warfare of this sort died down, the tradition lived on in clashes between gangs, generally youthful, representing rival wards of the same village, rival hamlets of the same parish, or rival villages of the same district. A typical instance among many occurred at Plogastel-Saint-Germain in Finistère, where in March 1866 the canton's draft board met for the annual drawing of lots that would show who would perform seven years' military service and who would escape duty. When the contingent of draft-age youths from Plozévet arrived, everyone else fell on them, and the tiny village square of Plogastel became the scene of "a frightful struggle" in which more than 300 participants of all ages, using staves, stones, and cudgels, gouging and biting, fought themselves out, the authorities finding it impossible to separate them. Before it was over, all had been wounded more or less lightly, though none complained: "vieille rancune qui vient de se traduire par une rixe nouvelle."

What happened was this. The lads of Plozévet, marching *en corps* behind their banner, were determined to march around the village cross—a practice started in 1848 that was supposed to ensure "good" draft numbers—and the rest of the youths were just as determined that they should not. In previous years the mayor of Plogastel, who knew what to expect, had managed to keep the peace by insisting on general disarmament and seeing that all conscripts who came into town were barehanded. In 1866, however, the gendarmes had pooh-poohed his fears of trouble, and everyone had been allowed to keep the cudgels that the Breton peasant seldom laid aside. The copious correspondence this affair gave rise to is revealing: we find superstition at work, and moreover, surrounding a practice of very recent origin (traditions become immemorial not because they are old, but because memory is fallible); a long-standing hostility between rival hamlets; a natural recourse to violence; and the irrelevance of outside authorities to local practices (no one offered resistance to the gendarmes or soldiers who sought to intervene; they just ignored them). "Try to understand the ways of the peasant young," the mayor of Plogastel wrote to the prefect, "and their need for violent contrasts to their agricultural labors."[19]

The mountains of Auvergne, where miners fished with dynamite and gangs of toughs roamed the countryside, seem to have been another center of violence—endless brawls and scuffles, between men who wielded ax or pick as easily as knife or gun, tended to end in stabbings, shootings, and other forms of massacre reminiscent of the American frontier. The slightest squabble could end in murder and mayhem: men were shot or battered to death "following an argument," blows were exchanged, shots fired, picks brandished, because of "a futile discussion," "a futile wrangle," for "the most futile motive." A son shot at his mother, killing his young sister; two lads hunting together fell out over a jay, and one shot the other. And so it went.[20] One wonders whether in a stark world this was not a form of relaxation, of rough entertainment, among the few available. But the frequency with which judgments for *coups et blessures* show violence occurring without apparent cause also suggests the pent-up anger and resentment of the hopeless, which too long contained finally broke out in a blind violence that offered some relief.[21]

Thefts were among the most common and revealing breaches of the law. Most of them were pathetically small, like the two sous that were taken as booty from an old woman in a forest near Lombez (Gers); or the jersey, knife, and 50 centimes extracted from an old man of Saint-Cernin (Cantal); or the rich haul of the housebreaker of the Lectoure region who made off with a net, a pruning knife, a candle, a towel, and one piece of bread. One guesses that the "injures et voies de fait relative au partage d'un morceau de lard volé," noted at Sainte-Menehould (Marne) in the year XIII, were reproduced under subsequent regimes. There are several instances of girls who seem to have been tempted, or anyway were alleged to have been tempted, by kerchiefs. A typical case involved a young girl in the employ of an ironing-woman at Elne (Pyrénées-Orientales), who was accused of stealing a small cambric handkerchief worth one franc; her vehement denials availed her no more than a suspended sentence.[22] Petty and pitiful, cases such as these bear witness to a world of small possessions and great need.

The police were less welcome when they intervened to establish or restore a public order alien to the populations. Some felt their liberty increasingly restricted—more so, complained the men of Tarascon (Ariège) in 1848, than before 1789.[23] Historical memory may have been faulty, or the representatives of public order thicker under foot. Whatever the case, two jurisdictions in particular created endless trouble: hunting and forests. Each deserves a study of its own. And each testifies to the fact that the country people did not allow their traditional practices to be upset easily.

"Our populations, as you know," wrote the sub-prefect of Châteaulin in the summer of 1853, "hold the figure of the gendarme sacred." Yet the same file where this implausible assertion appears shows that gendarmes were frequently attacked when they interfered with local gambling, drinking, and poaching habits or with the accepted behavior for pilgrimages or fairs, especially when the interference was pressed so far as arrest or confiscation. Indeed, in Ariège the attempt to arrest local men could set off what were described as "insurrections."[24] But Ariège, like most of the Pyrenees, was of a particularly inflammable mood because of the incessant friction over forest rights.

The legislation introduced in the late years of the Restoration limiting access to the forests fed violent hatreds wherever free range had been a way of life and the forest's resources indispensable to even a marginal living. The Forest Code of 1827 gave broad powers to the French administration and the rather surly foresters, rangers, and guards it recruited among populations plagued by underemployment. This authority was used at the expense of the local population to preserve great stands of trees and foster reforestation, largely for the sake of a wooden navy that would no longer exist when the new plantations reached maturity. The peasants knew little and cared less about such Colbertian aims. They knew only that arbitrary and incomprehensible decisions meant that their animals could no longer graze, and that they could no longer gather kindling or firewood, as they had done as far back as memory could stretch. Maurice Agulhon has recorded the bitter conflicts to which this gave rise in Provence. From the Restoration right through the Second Empire, the records show similar, and similarly violent, reactions from Burgundy and Dauphiné to Anjou, Gascony, and the Pyrenees. The number of offenses soared: not only trespass, pilfering, and theft, but acts of vengeance against guards and against the prohibited forests and plantations themselves. The poor rose in wrath (as they did in Gers in 1828 or in Cantal in 1839) and cut down thousands of trees; and army or national guard units had to intervene to quell riot after riot. Strange rumors ran wild, such as the one in 1851 that spread through the villages on the outskirts of the Ombrée forest in Anjou with the false news that the people could gather wood at will; within a day, some 2,000 bundles had been carried off. The rural court files tally huge numbers of crimes and misdemeanors connected with forestry, and the number continued to run high for years, tapering off only after the 1850's, when such offenses began to be treated with greater leniency. But the preceding period left its mark on popular thought, and many a folk legend doomed the forest guard to eternal damnation, condemned after death to haunt the forests he used to patrol.

In Ariège, however, the conflict maintained its intensity well after it died down in other areas. There, large-scale violence had erupted as early as 1829, when the Demoiselles—bands of peasants disguised in long shirts and bonnets, often with blackened faces, armed sometimes with guns but mostly with woodsmen's axes—ranged the countryside to strike suddenly and by night against gendarmes, forest guards, jails, and restrictive landowners. The War of the Demoiselles (as it has been called) reflected the resentment of people to whom the law, almost any law but forest legislation particularly, appeared alien and destructive. Their sense of injustice was overwhelming. In 1848 the General Council of Ariège explained that the peasants had come to hate the forests themselves, and hoped that if they ravaged them enough they would get rid of their oppressors. That same summer the chief government prosecutor in Toulouse, reporting the forest fires that were being set in his jurisdiction and the raids to mutilate the trees, recognized that "the rural populations of these areas are imbued with the idea that they have been unjustly despoiled of property rights they have held from time immemorial." They said as much in one of their songs—one of many:

Nous boulen exulp aquesto montagno,	They want to steal our mountain,
He que noste ben,	Which is our good estate,
Et que nous apparten. . . .	And which belongs to us. . . .

The situation was aggravated by the overbearing and corrupt nature of the personnel who were entrusted with enforcing the law. Many of the reports of mayors and other officials over the period 1843–59 speak of foresters and forest agents who were strange to the region, ignorant of local practices and rights, let alone needs, and worse yet ill-paid and hence usually corrupt, crushing the local people with their exactions. No wonder that smoldering resentment flared into open rebellion over and over: in 1829–30, 1842, 1848, and again, though less intensely, 1870–71. In 1879 the sub-prefect of Prades (Pyrénées-Orientales) noted with relief that friction had diminished and that disturbances were *fewer*. Though Michel Chevalier records the persistence of savage battles, notably one in 1895 over a proposed government fir plantation at Guzet, court records do suggest a gradual acceptance of the new conditions.[25] In the arrondissement of Saint-Palais (Basses-Pyrénées) *délits forestiers* numbered 145 in 1856—far, far ahead of the next-most-common categories of offenses, theft (46) and begging (32). But they fell sharply thereafter, to 29 in 1866, 32 in 1880, and a mere seven in 1905.[26] A draining of the population, new sources of revenue, and, quite simply, time had finally turned past injustice into present usage.

The right to hunt was another source of friction. In Gers a huge set-to at a village festival, in which two gendarmes were seriously manhandled and for which 15 men were eventually imprisoned, was attributed in the first instance to popular resentment over the imposition of a higher fee on hunting permits.* The measure was patently undemocratic, cutting into the food sup-

---

* The rioting took place at the little village of Aujan near Mirande (1973 pop. 144), where on June 24, 1850, the fête patronale had drawn more than 4,000 visitors from 30 neighboring communes. Those arrested all belonged to the "classes infimes de la société," and their "revolt" was termed "inconceivable," the more so since the accused did not know one another. (Archives Nationales, BB 30 370; Agen, July–Oct. 1850.) In 1851 the general prosecutor at Aix-en-Provence wrote of the great discontent at the 25-franc fee set on hunting permits ("Let it be lowered to 10 francs, and they will pay!"), and of the frequent clashes between "honest landowners shooting on their own land" and gendarmes enforcing an unpopular law (*ibid.*; Aix-en-Provence, Nov. 11, 1851). Hunting permits, introduced in 1844 partly to combat poaching, could only be obtained from the departmental prefecture, after an application on *papier timbré*: an accumulation of costs and complications. After 1861 they were delivered at the sub-prefecture. By the 1890's nearly 400,000 permits were issued annually. See Pierre Dufrénoy, *Histoire du droit de chasse et du droit de pêche dans l'ancien droit français* (Paris, 1896), especially p. 8.

ply and into a major source of revenue or pleasure of all but the wealthiest peasants, and it made for constant trouble. Not thefts but hunting offenses were the commonest cases brought before the rural courts of the Second Empire. At Bazas (Gironde) the year 1856 saw 45 hunting violations against 43 thefts; the year 1867, 92 against 41. Similarly, at Châteaulin (Finistère), 1856, 86 against 71; 1867, 95 against 72. The number of cases seems to have fallen with the easier laws of the Third Republic: at Bazas from 92 in 1867 to 53 in 1909 (no figures are available for the 1880's); at Châteaulin from 95 in 1867 to 52 in 1880 and 31 in 1906.[27]

Legislation of course created crime: such other familiar practices as begging, drunkenness, gleaning, gathering wood, and peddling without a permit also became offenses. Modernization created crime too. Conscription brought with it failure to report, desertion, and self-mutilation to escape the draft—all criminal offenses. The use of traditional weights and measures became illegal. New hygienic regulations governing the practice of medicine or midwifery, the sale of drugs, and the control of contagious diseases in cattle and humans found their reflection in police records and in courts.* Improved diet encouraged the enterprising not only to sell adulterated milk, but to circumvent the controls placed on pepper (1907) and mustard (1913) as well. The introduction of postage stamps was followed by a law (1849) making the re-use of cancelled stamps a crime. Here we find a particularly striking example of how novelties became the ordinary. The civil court records of Sainte-Menehould list 18 offenses on this score in the 1850's, four in the 1860's, four in the 1870's, and two in the 1880's, the last in 1886. The court of Bazas (Gironde) tried 12 such offenses in 1856, none in 1867, one in 1880, and none thereafter. Among the first four transgressions two were committed by girls who were released for obviously not knowing what the stamps were all about ("these little images," one of the accused called them). Railways also brought regulations and infractions thereof. At Bazas these rose from two in 1867 to 19 in 1909. At Châteaulin in 1886 an eleven-year-old boy was fined for throwing an apple on the right-of-way of the Nantes-Landerneau railroad.[28]

But if modernization could create new crimes, or at least legislate them into being, it also worked to eliminate or alter the old ones. Thus, at Châteaulin the number of offenses for *coups et blessures* almost tripled between 1856 and 1906,[29] but far from indicating a rising tide of violence, this change was due to a greater readiness to lodge complaints for actions long taken for granted. The nature of the charges clearly changed. One finds fewer brawls, and more and more complaints by women, especially wives, for whom the

---

* It is well to remember that not all laws were enforced as stringently in the countryside as in the cities. Thus a law of 1873 had made public drunkenness a minor offense and if repeated, a misdemeanor. Yet records suggest that the law was rarely applied in rural areas. One commentator, in 1875 (Dr. Lunier, quoted in Emile Levasseur, *La Population française*, 2: 439), attributed this laxity to the influence of publicans, who were often village councilmen or mayors. I would attribute it rather to a combination of local attitudes and small police forces. See F. Dubief, *La Question du vagabondage*, pp. 251–52.

occasional or regular thrashing had once been a matter of course. Certainly, the consideration of legal costs helped to stay many an eager hand. The little boy who threw an apple on the tracks was fined only one franc; but with legal costs his parents paid nearly 50 francs in all. Beating one's wife might cost as little as five francs, beating a strange woman four times as much; and a good fight between men could bring some days in prison with work left undone and wages unearned—plus fines, of course. But these costs were at the low end of the scale. In any given case the costs could climb as high as 20 or 30 francs (10–15 days' wages), an astronomic sum for families with only a tiny income. If more people—and especially women—lodged complaints around the turn of the century, it must have been only in part because the mores of their little world had changed; the family budget must also have allowed it. Wives and children continued to be beaten, to be sure, but more of them seem to have revolted. By 1906 one even finds the Châteaulin court handing down a judgment on the specific charge of ill-treating children.

Offenses against minors, mostly sexual, were common enough; they are a running theme through the legal files from one year to another. But at the turn of the century a new note sounds. At Sainte-Menehould, for the first time in the records, the court held that the abuse of a young child was a crime: the earliest judgment was brought in 1900; another followed in 1902, two in 1905, one in 1913. At Saint-Palais (Basses-Pyrénées) nine cases of this sort came to court in the year 1905 alone. And Châteaulin followed suit, as we have seen, in 1906. They did so under a law passed in 1874 for the protection of children. It had taken a quarter of a century or more for urban values and urban legislation to penetrate the more isolated parts of the countryside. It would have taken longer at an earlier time. Now—tentatively, reluctantly, but relentlessly nevertheless—all parts of rural France were being drawn into the modern world.

And yet a measure of just how long the old order, or disorder, took to pass can be found in the persistence of beggars and of begging vagrants as one of the major social problems of the nineteenth century. *Extinction de la mendicité* was a separate rubric requiring specific mention in the weekly and monthly reports local officials submitted to their superiors.

The *Cahiers* of 1789 are full of complaints against vagabond beggars, of references to the fear they spread and the extortions they extracted in the name of charity. Misery (especially the misery of strangers) did not evoke sympathy, only unease and fear. The Revolution and the Empire set thousands adrift who had little hope of haven. Even when the worst had settled into normal want, poor regions like Brittany went through horrifying famines. In 1814, a priest tells us, the starving poor gathered in hordes of several thousand on the beach at Cesson (Côtes-du-Nord) looking for shellfish, which they devoured raw so great was their hunger. Physically weakened to the point where they could not even cope with a cooking fire, several still tried to carry something back to their families, only to fall along the roadside and die. Other hordes of starving peasants swarmed into the towns and tried to intimidate the city folk into charity, but the burghers barricaded themselves behind their doors and left the starving yokels to die in the streets or to be driven out by the military.[30]

Mass suffering of this order was exceptional, or would become so. Indigency was not: *indigence, vie précaire, mendicité* are a triple and recurrent theme.* In Loir-et-Cher begging was the only obvious recourse when "the scourge of indigence" struck the rural proletariat. In regions like Beauce even poor laborers generally managed to tread the fine line between poverty and destitution. But in the Perche, explained an agricultural survey of 1848, begging was as chronic as penury; people were so used to it that they did not feel the least shame about it. There was the precarious economic situation, always on the point of collapse. There was the unexpected disaster, like a fire or flood, which sent its victims begging by the roadside. There was, quite simply, perpetual want, under whose merciless rule beggars, permanent or occasional, were unavoidable. During the hard winter of 1847 the prefect of Cantal reported that the poor had to resort to begging. That was their only hope; and, after all, those who begged from door to door found bread.[31]

The city poor, of course, had certain forms of organized charity to fall back on. Beggars accordingly crowded into cities whenever they could, and especially at times of famine, attracted by these resources: the concentration of private charity, the *bureaux de bienfaisance*, the food and alms that the rich and pious distributed on regular days and hours. This may be why a city like Toulouse was full of beggars through the 1840's and 1850's. "One couldn't take a step [complained the *Annuaire de la Haute-Garonne* in 1848] without being assailed, importuned, and often insulted by these wretches who laid bare to all eyes their sores, fictitious or real. They even invaded our homes, and one could rid oneself of their importunities only by yielding them alms."[32]

Many of these wretches came from Ariège, especially from the mountainous areas, where begging was an ancient tradition, every winter precipitating a seasonal migration into the more fertile plains or even further afield. Solidly anchored in custom and an essential part of the normal subsistence pattern, such begging migrations endured to the very end of the Second Empire, even though conditions had by then improved. As the prefect of Ardèche correctly observed, the migrations persisted because of the sheer inability to break with established habits. Some of those who went down into the "good country"

---

* Of course, not all poor people begged. In May 1829 the mayor of Moulins reported that almost a third of the people in his area were indigents (4,574 in a population of 14,195), but that only 200 of these were habitual beggars (L.-J. Allary, *Moulins, 1831–36*, p. 24). "Many suffer in silence" (Archives Départementales, Cantal 110 M1, Feb. 8, 1847). But in Creuse, according to an official report in 1854, there was one beggar for every 56 inhabitants (Alain Corbin, "Limousins migrants," p. 654).

while snow covered their barren lands were not even poor, and many of the migrants were encouraged by village authorities, who could have ended the flow by the simple expedient of withholding the passports that were essential for travel.* A testimonial to the beggars' enterprise was an annual Beggars' Fair, the *fera de Montmerle*, held every summer near the hamlet of Charguerand (Allier); the war of 1870 seems to have marked its end. At Montmerle the begging folk of Bourbonnais sold the rags, used clothes, and linens, household goods and junk that they had gathered from as far afield as Roanne and Renaison in Loire (many even took along a donkey to carry their haul).[33]

Few beggars were this organized, to be sure, but most traveled far afield. In Maine-et-Loire we hear that in 1865 most of them came "from the depths of Brittany"; and indeed the peninsula always had a rich crop of indigents. The sponsor of a traditional marriage feast in Cornouaille or Morbihan, which into the late nineteenth century included a special dinner and dance for the poor, had to count on an attendance of 200 or more at the event. Not all of these, presumably, were regular beggars; but it is hard to draw the line between regular and occasional beggary. In the Aube of the late nineteenth century, when hard times struck, whole families turned to charity, with the young, the old, and the sick begging for bread from door to door; these were clearly not professional beggars on the order of the familiar *abonnés* with their regular rounds. But in the ports of Brittany, cannery workers and fishermen worked when they could, and begged or sent their children to beg when they could not. Similarly, in Cotentin at the turn of the century, Paul Mayer tells us, some villages survived only by sending their children to beg for bread and sous among the farms, and their women to beg for firewood. "There is no humiliation in it. All know it is the only means to avoid starvation. And farmers feel that alms cost them less than raising [their workers'] wages." Still, they would also have had to accommodate the vagrant beggars who passed through, many (noted a Breton report of 1890) coming from some nearby marriage or feast. Occasional or chronic, begging was clearly, as a police superintendent remarks, "anchored in local custom." All poor regions bred and exported beggars, as Savoy did right through the early decades of the Third Republic, a plague that left authorities completely helpless.[34]

In the towns, where there was generally some representative of the police and where, in any case, neighbors provided reassurance and if need be support, beggars could be kept within certain limits. But in the country, wrote a commissaire in Gers in 1876, "they are real tyrants and many deliberately make themselves feared by their threats."[35]

---

* Archives Nationales, F¹cIII Ariège 7 (Mar. 1857), F¹cIII Ardèche 11 (Apr. 1859); André Armengaud, *Les Populations de l'est-Aquitain*, p. 291. Perhaps they chose not to interfere because, as the prefect of Puy-de-Dôme remarked in 1843, villages like Saint-Jean-des-Ollière, in the Livradois, whose inhabitants regularly went off to beg with false certificates testifying that their homes had burned down, paid their taxes very punctually (see André G. Manry, *Histoire de l'Auvergne*, Toulouse, 1974, p. 398).

More fear. By Jules Méline's estimate, there were around 400,000 beggars and tramps in 1905 (over 1 percent of the total population). "Battalions of the famished, a real scourge for our countryside," the swarms of vagabonds created a feeling of insecurity that contributed to a rural exodus, especially of the bourgeoisie, fearful for their safety.[36] These are more than the reactionary fantasies of a conservative politician. Méline knew his Vosges. But other evidence corroborates his views. Court records show that beggars often menaced those who refused them alms, generally quite humble people, or women who could ill defend themselves. Fences torn down, fruit trees or crops maliciously damaged, fields flooded, fires set from spite—the authorities received such reports over and over. Into the twentieth century the Cantal archives swelled with circulars and reports: beggars and vagabonds enter isolated houses and farms, demand food and drink, sometimes even money (though this seems somewhat doubtful), threaten reprisals, vengeance . . . all the southwest invaded every spring by lame and crippled beggars . . . the country people complain; they are afraid.[37] A writer in 1894 observed that in Bresse and Savoy houses tended to be crowded into hamlets—as they did along the Saône, or between Mâcon and Nantua—partly for fear of beggars. In Bresse they said of families that took an isolated house: "There are people who are not afraid to be murdered."[38]

Arrests on charges of vagrancy and begging rose from 2,500 in 1830 to 20,000 in 1890, and 50,000 in 1899. But law enforcement, mostly urban, did not diminish anxiety; it merely reflected it. In the Sainte-Menehould district only 16 vagrants had been charged in the 1843–75 period; 35 were rounded up in 1876–1910. At Saint-Palais, where vagrancy was a worse sore, arrests nearly doubled between 1856 and 1880, from 13 to 24. The year 1905 saw 36 cases brought before the court. By then the high tide of vagabondage was beginning to recede, reflecting the economic upturn. The incidence of vagrancy seems to have paralleled bad times, so that depressed prices put many people on the road who would not have otherwise moved about.[39] Emile Durkheim pointed out, in his study of suicide (whose rate also rose markedly in the 1890's),* that in economic crises the specifically economic effects are less significant than the disruptions of the collective order: the ruptures in the balance of society and life that set men and women adrift from their moorings. This could well apply to vagrancy, too, though more straightforwardly material explanations might suffice. At any rate, while the beggars and tramps roamed, and while the memory of their roaming lingered on, the idle, loitering figure of the vagrant cast a dark shadow over the countryside.

Yet one should keep in mind that not all pressure was physical. The whole

---

* *Le Suicide* (1912 ed.), p. 271. It would be misleading to make too much of the coincidence. In fact, the suicide rate had been rising steadily through the century. It declined slightly in 1896–1905, then rose again. By 1913, in a time of great prosperity, the rate had passed its pre-1896 peak (Maurice Halbwachs, *Les Causes du suicide*, p. 92).

weight of traditional morality argued against turning away the stranger or the poor.* Many popular tales taught that reward came to those who fed the hungry or sheltered the weary traveler. Fear of supernatural retribution, especially if predicted by a desperate or unscrupulous supplicant, must have been more effective than a brandished cudgel. At the same time, charity (which often meant hospitality) to strangers and especially to the poor reflected more than fear of supernatural or criminal retribution. It attested to the social function of the wayfarer, who repaid hospitality by carrying news and telling what he had learned on his travels. Beggars, and part-time beggars like rag-and-bone merchants, hawkers, peddlers, knife-grinders, were also gatherers and dispensers of information, as were others who trod the roads: millers and tailors, carters and showmen.[40] In Lower Brittany especially, as Emile Souvestre noted, "the beggar is also the bard, the news carrier and commercial traveler of this wholly patriarchal civilization."[41]

But the two useful functions that begging may have performed—supplementing an uncertain subsistence in an economy in which catastrophes were frequent and remedies rare, providing a loose communications network— were outdated. Beggary survived, as we have seen, but it ceased to be endemic. What is perhaps more important, it was no longer taken for granted. It became an anomaly. Beggars themselves grew ashamed to beg. The Vergougnans of the Pyrénées-Orientales wore a mask so as not to be recognized when they came to the door. And when, in Roussillon and in Hérault, the crisis of 1907 brought back misery of a kind unknown by most for over a generation, a local doctor saw the new beggars wearing masks too.[42]

Indigence continued. But now it wore a mask. That was not only new in itself; it was indicative of the modern attitude toward grinding poverty.

---

* Charity could be a source of social prestige; conversely, stinginess could tell against one. In Aubrac one candidate for the elections of 1898 seems to have tried to denigrate an opponent by getting local tramps to complain of the man's ill-treatment of them (*L'Aubrac*, 2: 186).

Chapter Six

A WEALTH OF TONGUES

"Parlez français," says the master to the pupil. "Monsieur, je parle
comme je save et comme je poude." The villager forgets a little of
his mother tongue at school, and learns only a parody of French.
—ABBÉ M. M. GORSE

IN 1863, ACCORDING to official figures, 8,381 of France's 37,510 communes
spoke no French: about a quarter of the country's population. The Ministry
of Public Instruction found that 448,328 of the 4,018,427 schoolchildren (ages
seven to thirteen) spoke no French at all, and that another 1,490,269 spoke or
understood it but could not write it, suggesting an indifferent grasp of the
tongue. In 24 of the country's 89 departments, more than half the communes
did not speak French, and in six others a significant proportion of the communes were in the same position (see Map 3). In short, French was a foreign
language for a substantial number of Frenchmen, including almost half the
children who would reach adulthood in the last quarter of the century.

The manuscript from which these figures are drawn (see Appendix table,
pp. 498–501) is the last statistical survey I have found on the awkward subject
of patois, as the various languages, idioms, dialects, and jargons of the French
provinces were generally described. Some of the data are suspect on their face,
but one would want to accept them with caution in any event, since the Ministry of Public Instruction had every reason to exaggerate success and to conceal
failure. Apart from the internal evidence, other official statements show that
the survey in fact underestimated the situation.

Thus in Bouches-du-Rhône, Cantal, Haute-Savoie, and Vaucluse the schools
reported that more than 10 percent of their pupils did not speak French, a
strange discrepancy when all around them that tongue was supposed to be in
general use. Still more odd, in Hérault more than a quarter of the children
did not speak French, in Lozère an even higher percentage did not, and in
Dordogne fully a third did not—but all three departments were "French-
speaking." Yet a third of the children suggests at least a third of their elders
and, sure enough, the *Etat de l'instruction primaire* for 1864 reported patois
"in general use" in Dordogne and, despite the schools' efforts, "as indestructible
as the air breathed in each locality."[1]

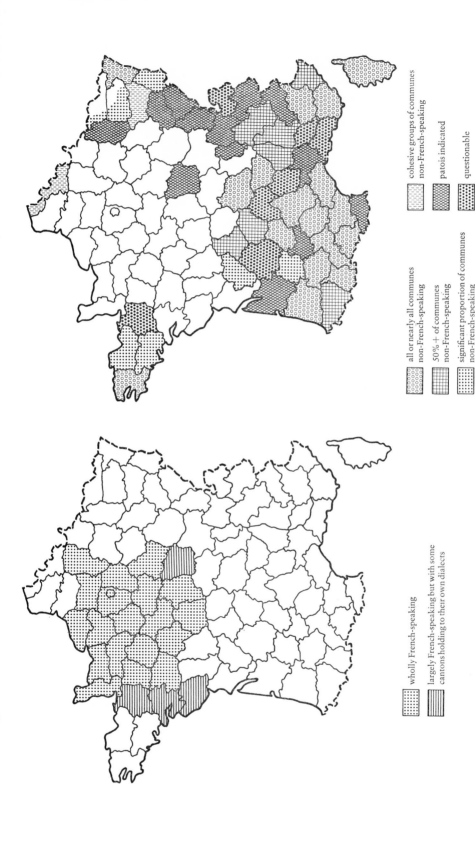

Map 2. French-speaking departments, 1835. SOURCE: Abel Hugo, *La France pittoresque* (Paris, 1835), 1: 16.

    wholly French-speaking

    largely French-speaking but with some
    cantons holding to their own dialects

Map 3. Patois-speaking communes, 1863. SOURCE: Archives Nationales, F¹⁷* 3160, Ministère de l'instruction publique, "Statistique:

    all or nearly all communes
    non-French-speaking

    50% + of communes
    non-French-speaking

    significant proportion of communes
    non-French-speaking

    cohesive groups of communes
    non-French-speaking

    patois indicated

    questionable

Other figures in the survey conflict with outside evidence. In Loire-Inférieure French seems to have the department to itself. And yet as late as 1889 a linguist insisted that throughout the inland sections of the department, people spoke Vendéen or Poitevin patois, and that at Batz (a small Celtic enclave near Le Croisic) they still spoke Breton. Not a grave oversight, perhaps, but enough to shake one's confidence. Nièvre too seems wholly French-speaking in the 1863 statistics. Yet the *Etat de l'instruction primaire* remarked with some pride that in Morvan (the eastern part of the department), "over two-thirds of the children know French," which even if true means that about one-third did not. In Cantal, of the 1,124 men in the conscript class of 1864, 529 were French-speaking, and the other 595 spoke French badly (340) or not at all (255). In cantons like Montsalvy in the southeast, contiguous to the wilder parts of Aveyron, and Laroquebrou to the west, bordering the narrow gorges of the Cère, the proportion of French speakers ranged between one in five and one in three; yet the survey of 1863 showed French in general use in all of Cantal's 259 communes.[2]

In several departments some schools were conducted in local speech to teach what none could otherwise understand: Alpes-Maritimes, Ardèche, Bas-Rhin, Basses-Pyrénées, Corsica, Côtes-du-Nord, Finistère, Haut-Rhin, Meurthe, Morbihan, Moselle, and Nord. In Basses-Pyrénées, the survey reported that 875 schools taught exclusively in French and only 62 used Basque or Béarnais in whole or part; yet a general inspector's report of 1877 indicated that only around Oloron were classes given in French. In the Pyrénées-Orientales, by the 1863 survey, nearly half the children did not speak French, yet there is no indication that any other tongue competed with the national idiom; 12 years later, in 1875, the truth came out: "Catalan is the only language used throughout the Roussillon." No wonder school inspectors complained that children read their French "like parrots"![3]

Other questions arise. Several departments included sizable areas where the local speech was alien to French: Flemish in Nord, Germanic dialects in Bas- and Haut-Rhin. But nearby regions were held to be wholly French-speaking, though they had a similar problem. In the Pas-de-Calais, for example, much of the countryside spoke Flemish, Artesien, or Picard through the 1890's. Teachers' reports submitted to a school exhibition in 1884 reveal that the department's northwest corner, especially the points between Boulogne and Saint-Omer and extending as far east as the hinterland of Béthune, accepted French slowly and with reluctance. At Bouvelinghem, Dohem, Haut-Loquin, Audincthun, and Alquines, French was "unfamiliar" or "almost unknown." The dialects of Boulogne, Artois, and Picardy reigned there, in some form, as they did at Enguinegatte, Fauquembergues, Aquin, Bléquin, Blendecques, Maisnil, and Argues.[4] Far to the south, Tarn-et-Garonne stood out as an island of French speech amid the dark waves of neighboring Oc departments. Perhaps the Protestant influences of Montauban contributed to that.

But the *Etat de l'instruction primaire* suggests otherwise. "Despite all efforts" it noted in 1864, "the French language spreads only with difficulty." One wishes one knew more. Perhaps as in Lozère, where more than a quarter of the schoolchildren knew no French and rather fewer than that knew it well, the situation was that one could hear it everywhere but nowhere was it spoken.[5] The Third Republic found a France in which French was a foreign language for half the citizens.

The French Crown had shown little concern with the linguistic conquest of the regions under its administration. Language was relevant merely as an instrument of rule. The Ordinance of Villers-Cotterêts in 1539, dealing with legal and judicial processes, was a step in the Crown's long march to establish its authority over a diversity of rivals. Its intent was not to make French the national tongue, but simply to make sure that the language of the King's court would be used in the quarters significant to his power. Yet this functional and limited act had effects beyond its immediate purpose, chiefly arising from its article III: "We wish henceforth that all awards, judgments, and all other proceedings whether of our sovereign courts or of other lower and inferior ones, whether registers, inquests, contracts, commissions, sentences, wills and other acts, writs, or processes of justice or related to it, should be pronounced, recorded, and delivered to the parties in the French mother tongue and not otherwise."

Along with the institution of a register in every parish to record each person's baptism ("to prove the time of majority"), marriage if it occurred, and death, this meant that within the dominions of the King of France, and shortly after in Savoy as well, every public act of life was sometimes transacted and always recorded in French.

Transacted only sometimes, because of course the King's "langage maternel françois" was not that of the majority of his subjects. The King's speech had precedence over those of his subjects, and all who engaged in public affairs were bound to use it or pay others to use it on their behalf. But linguistic unity hobbled far behind even the incomplete administrative unity of the Ancien Régime; nor does it seem to have been a policy goal. In the Treaty of the Pyrenees (1659), Louis XIV guaranteed his new subjects the right to use "the language they wished, whether French or Spanish, whether Flemish or others." The treaty was in French, Europe's new diplomatic language. But the King's subjects were slow to learn it. Jean Bart of Dunkirk, greatest of seventeenth-century French privateers, wrote his ship's logs in Flemish, and fumbled his rare brief reports to Louis XIV in a language he hardly knew. (But then the monarch himself was to be harangued in Picard during a royal process through the north.) All the same, French was spreading through the areas most accessible to Paris: Champagne, Burgundy, Normandy, the Loire valley. South of the Loire, La Fontaine found that French was not spoken beyond Montmorillon in Poitou; and Racine, at Uzès in darkest Gard, needed "an interpreter as much as a Muscovite would need one in Paris."[6]

Burghers of the bigger towns, men of law of course, nobles, and clerics became bilingual or multilingual. Universities and colleges continued to teach in Latin through the seventeenth century and, in many cases, to the mid-eighteenth century. So in a fashion did many rural schools, as we shall see in another chapter. It was only in the eighteenth century that the speech of Paris made headway among the rural populations of Oïl and in the Lyonnais. Everywhere else, it remained a preserve of city dwellers, adding still further to the growing gulf between city and village, and, in the city itself, creating a linguistic division between rich and poor.

Devoted as were the many academies, provincial counterparts of the Académie Française, to the propagation of the French language, they functioned in the midst of populations that knew little or no French. In 1726 the Academy of Marseilles held no public sittings because the public did not understand the language in which they were conducted.[7] Members of the academies themselves must have been rather like foreign students of French literature and language: approaching the culture of Paris as something strange to their own everyday speech and practice; they might write in French, but they thought in their own language.*

Still, the growing prestige of French was winning converts among the middle and upper classes. There was the increasing vogue and availability of theaters and opera houses: an influence comparable to that of twentieth-century cinema, with everyone eager to adopt the admired accents and turns of phrase used on the stage. There was the spread of educational establishments and their increasing interest in French, especially with respect to seventeenth-century authors. There were learned societies—(*sociétés de pensée*), lodges, clubs, drawing rooms, and reading rooms, along with an endless flood of works of literature and philosophy, fashion bulletins, newspapers, and periodicals—preferably from Paris. The whole notion of *comme il faut* focused on the capital, for language as for fashions, for manners as for ideas. By 1794 the prelate Henri Grégoire was ready to report to the Convention that three-quarters of the people of France knew *some* French, though admittedly not all of them could sustain a conversation in it, let alone speak or write it properly.[8]

Like the report of 1863, Grégoire's seems to have taken an optimistic view.

---

* Auguste Brun, *Parlers régionaux*, p. 87. And their French was sometimes closer to their everyday speech than to the French of Paris. J. Régné, *Situation économique et hospitalière du Vivarais à la veille de la Révolution* (Aubenas, 1914), cited in *Annales du Midi*, July–Oct. 1916, p. 523, published a memorandum from Blachère, sub-delegate of Aubenas, dated Dec. 10, 1786. It was remarked that Régné "a respecté la syntaxe et l'ortographie de Blachère, homme bien informé et de bon sens, mais qui écrivait un français patoisant, pratiqué dans les Cévennes par la bourgeoisie et la noblesse jusqu'au milieu du 19e siècle, le peuple ne parlant et ne comprenant guère que le patois. Le langage de Blachère parait, à l'Intendant, si différent de celui de Versailles, qu'il pre-scrit de 'mettre en français' les passages à conserver."

Many of the provincial assemblies discussing the *cahiers* of 1789 had encountered linguistic problems, and the great survey Grégoire set on foot revealed more areas where French was hardly spoken than places where it was known.[9]

This was serious. Linguistic diversity had been irrelevant to administrative unity. But it became significant when it was perceived as a threat to political—that is, ideological—unity. All citizens had to understand what the interests of the Republic were and what the Republic was up to, Barthélemy de Lanthemas told the Convention in December 1792. Otherwise, they could not participate, were not equipped to participate in it. A didactic and integrative regime needed an effective vehicle for information and propaganda; but it could hardly have one if the population did not know French. In November 1792, just a month before Lanthemas's speech, the Minister of Justice had set up an office to translate laws and decrees into the German, Italian, Catalan, Basque, and Lower Breton languages.[10]

This could be no more than an expedient. The ideal of the Revolution lay in uniformity and the extinction of particularisms. "Reaction . . . speaks Bas-Breton," insisted the Jacobins. "The unity of the Republic demands the unity of speech. . . . Speech must be one, like the Republic." Most agreed with Lanthemas that the various tongues "have no kind of distinction and are simply remnants of the barbarism of past ages." Grégoire put it best when he called for the elimination of "the diversity of primitive idioms that extended the infancy of reason and prolonged obsolescent prejudices." The Convention agreed with Grégoire. It acted to abolish dialects, and to replace them with the speech of the Republic, "the language of the Declaration of Rights." It decreed that throughout the Republic children must learn "to speak, read and write in the French language," and that everywhere "instruction should take place only in French."[11] All this was easier said than done. The policy foundered. If revolutionary patriotism spoke French, it often spoke it badly. And where the people did not speak French, revolutionaries who wanted to reach the people addressed them in their local tongue. What survived from the shipwreck was the principle.

A state unconcerned about linguistic diversity, a catholic cultural ideal largely indifferent to the problem, were replaced by an ideology that embraced unity as a positive good and recognized language as a significant factor in achieving it. As the Cahors Committee of Primary Education declared in 1834, "the political and administrative unity of the kingdom urgently requires the unity of language in all its parts."[12] In any case, the committee added, the southern dialects were inferior—a view that earlier ages had developed more discreetly, that the revolutionaries had trumpeted, and that didactic propaganda henceforth helped to spread.

Teaching the people French was an important facet in "civilizing" them, in their integration into a superior modern world. Félix Pécaut, apostle of progressive education under the Third Republic, expressed the Fabian view in 1880 that Basque would soon give way to "a higher level of civilization." And the literary critic Francisque Sarcey had even greater pretensions: the French, all the French, must come to speak the same language, "that of Voltaire and the Napoleonic Code; all must be able to read the same newspaper, published in Paris, which brings the ideas worked out in the great city." There can be no clearer expression of imperialistic sentiment: a white man's burden of Francophony, whose first conquests were to be right at home. That they were seen as conquests can be perceived in Henri Baudrillart's remark that Oc was "giving way to the ascendancy of the victor's speech." The local folk agreed: "French is for us a language imposed by right of conquest," declared the Marseillais historian François Mazuy. Yet the conquest was slow. Unity was still an aim and a source of concern a century after Grégoire; witness the fears expressed by the Minister of the Interior in 1891 that by continuing to preach in dialect priests "may endanger French unity." The French God has always been a jealous God. He can be worshiped only in French, as Anatole de Monzie made clear in his famous circular of 1925 defending "the one French language whose jealous cult can never have too many altars."[13]

By that time, if the jealous cult had not stamped out all competitors, it had at least persuaded many that such competitors had never really existed. As early as 1907 a laureate of the Academy had declared that popular speech and literary language developed from the same source: Old French. In 1966 the head of the Education Ministry's Service of Pedagogical Research spoke of the promotion of French over Latin in the schools as an affirmation of "the people's language."[14] By 1968, when Antoine Prost published his fine history of French education, *L'Enseignement en France, 1800–1967*, we look in vain for one whisper about the worst problem plaguing schoolteachers through the whole of the nineteenth century: that so many of their pupils did not speak French or spoke it poorly.

Perhaps the myth and the striving for linguistic unity stood as a consolation for a persistent diversity.* At any rate, until the First World War the langage maternel françois of Francis I was not that of most French citizens. As Arnold Van Gennep wrote in 1911, "for peasants and workers, the mother tongue is patois, the foreign speech is French."[15] The purpose of the following pages is to document this statement, to show where it most readily applied, to indicate how patois waned, and to suggest what the side effects of that waning were.

---

* "If we haven't always the same feelings, the same ideas, the same philosophies, the same opinions, the same faith, alas! let us at least have the same language!" (Ernest Prévost in *La Victoire*, quoted in *L'Eclair*, Sept. 28, 1925.)

Documentation is hard to find at best. But beyond that, many documents are deceptive—unintentionally as a rule—because they render in French what actually took place in another language. Even some local scholars sin in this way, reporting a song or phrase of their region in their own French. Particularly troublesome are the reports of priests, police, and gendarmes, where only the occasional hint intimates that the exchanges rendered in (often-stilted) French actually took place in a local tongue. The reader has to keep a sharp lookout. "He spoke patois and so did I," observes a Limousin priest, very much in passing. How else, indeed, could he have communicated with a villager in the early years of the Second Empire? A new sub-prefect posted to Saint-Flour in 1867 complained that though he could communicate with the village mayors in French, he could neither understand nor make himself understood by anyone else in his area (but, he added, "at my age I am not about to learn Auvergnat").[16] Policemen sometimes admitted they could not understand what they heard. In Gers they often were unable to follow the sermon in the church; and one police superintendent in 1875, reporting on a home search for contraband matches, noted: "It's true that I have great difficulty understanding the local speech." One wonders what Flaubert's police superintendent of Pont-Aven, who needed a translator to deal with his charges, wrote in his reports. The occasional clue appears when an officer of the law quotes some untranslatable local term.[17]

There is some indication that many of the accused and the witnesses called before the courts spoke patois—some translating what they could themselves, others having their testimony translated by sworn interpreters. As late as 1890 the Ariège assizes tried a man for homicide who spoke for himself in patois. But the hard evidence on this point is scanty. So are the true facts about what went on during the great *crise du Midi* in 1907. The copious testimony on events in Narbonne, Béziers, Perpignan, Agde, and other rebellious centers says not a word about the language that the rioters and their leaders used; silence the more revealing when witnesses stressed the social class or garb of their interlocutors or assailants.[18] I do not think the silence was deliberate; likely, the information was not considered pertinent. But it does mean one has to rely on rather restricted sources.

The reports of officers reconnoitering the French countryside from the Restoration through the Second Empire swarm with references to incomprehensible local speech. In predictable areas (Brittany, the Limousin, the southwest, the Pyrenees) the soldiers employed or called for interpreters, just as the doctors who were sent to Ariège during the cholera epidemic of 1854 had to do.[19] In Lozère and Cantal, remarked a distraught soldier, the speech was unintelligible. "As difficult as it is to make oneself understood, it is even more difficult to understand an answer." But that was in 1844. In 1858 the Virgin who appeared to Bernadette Soubirous needed no interpreter; but she did find it necessary to address the girl, at least in part, in the Pyrenean dialect of Lourdes, where her words are now engraved: "Que soy era immaculada concepcion." By the end of the Second Empire many country people understood French even if they did not speak it. But familiarity with French in the countryside was still cause for comment. And there were those like the old Auvergnat who, sent as a prisoner to Hesse, in 1870, had married and stayed on. When Jacques Duclos met him, in 1917, the old man got by in local Hessian dialect; after half a century, he still knew neither French nor German.[20]

This state of affairs did not change significantly until the Third Republic. In 1874 an officer reporting on the area near Azay-le-Rideau (Indre-et-Loire)

Map 4. Documented entrenched areas of patois under the Third Republic. SOURCES: Various documents cited in the text. Note that this map and others of the kind that follow are not to be taken as exhaustive.

found it worth mentioning that "all speak French," so that though the people used the patois of Touraine, he was able to make himself understood. In 1877, reporting on the itinerary of a convoy through Hautes-Pyrénées, an officer complained that since most of the inhabitants hardly understood any French, one was often forced to have recourse to an interpreter to get any information at all from them. That same year in Périgord another officer noted that while the residents of Périgueux could speak French, though they preferred patois, "it is almost impossible for the stranger to understand [the peasants] or to make himself understood." In 1879 a folklorist could still publish the parable of the prodigal son in 88 different patois. Walking through Lower Brittany in 1882, Maupassant found the linguistic situation little changed since Flaubert's visit two-score years before. Hospitality was as ready, but information was still hard to get, "for often during a whole week, while roaming through the villages, one does not meet a single person who knows a word of French."[21] And at the Paris Exposition of 1889 the operators of one of the attractions, the little narrow-gauge Decauville railroad, thought it worthwhile to print their warning posters in Breton and Provençal as well as French. Of course, anyone who could actually read Breton or Provençal could probably read French too.

This is where teachers and school inspectors, whom we shall meet again in a later chapter on education, furnish useful information (or sometimes helpful hints). The picture that we get from their reports is of shrinking but still significant areas where patois prevailed. In Tarn patois was still heard everywhere through the 1870's. This was the case as well throughout the Limousin, one of the most stubborn holdouts. In Haute-Vienne even the teachers used patois for business activities outside the school. There, noted an inspector in 1881, French was not the normal language for most inhabitants, and those that used it mangled it. French continued to be an uncertain thing for the inhabitants of several regions into the twentieth century, as we can see from a police report of 1910 on a union meeting noting that a labor leader from the Tarn addressed his audience "in bad French."[22]

In Lot-et-Garonne and Basses-Pyrénées (1880) the children spoke French only during school hours. "Mediocre results," reads Pécaut's report, "because the child, outside school, thinks and speaks in patois." Same song in the 1881 inspection reports, in those departments and in Aveyron and Alpes-Maritimes, where even at the junior high school of Cannes, "the difficulty is to get the students who think in patois talking in French." In Dordogne "the obstinate indifference to French" would probably not be overcome for another generation, in a school inspector's judgment. In Haute-Loire (1882) the child "studies a language that he never uses outside school, and that he finds very difficult to understand."[23] There, a tourist guide of 1886 advised travelers that patois was in general use. As it was in Ariège, where in 1887 we find a teacher having real problems with her little charges, who could speak nothing else.[24]

After the 1880's this kind of negative evidence runs out—which is what we might expect once Jules Ferry's school laws began to work. I shall argue that several factors besides the schools were working for French and against local speech. But that is not the point here; whatever the cause, the progress is evident. Any degree of schooling had always given its beneficiaries a notion of French, a touch of bilingualism, however slight. Bernadette Soubirous had used patois in recounting what the Virgin did and said, but when another little girl translated the account into French for the benefit of Sister Damien, Bernadette was able to "vigorously correct her mistakes." Similarly, when she was interrogated in French by the imperial prosecutor about her vision, she understood him well enough, though she answered in patois.[25]

There could be few occasions in the mid-nineteenth century for simple peasant girls like Bernadette to engage in even such primitive exchanges. The 1870's and 1880's created more of them. In non-French-speaking areas more and more people came to understand the national language, and in due course to speak it. In lower Auvergne the last of the old people who could not understand French died around 1880. In parts of upper Auvergne they survived a little longer. Only a few adults spoke French, noted the schoolteacher at Vic-le-Comte, 15 miles from Clermont, in 1899, but it was beginning to be used off and on by the young, who picked the habit up in the schools, "where patois is strictly forbidden." Bilingualism thus became almost general. The difficult schoolchildren of the early 1880's, raised wholly amid local speech, grew up in the 1890's to mouth only a faltering and literally fractured version of what they had been taught. "A lot of water will flow under the bridges before we get the peasant to speak French," wrote Father Gorse in 1895 of the Corrèze where he still preached and explained the scriptures in Limousin dialect. "The child uses it as long as the teacher keeps his eye on him; the soldier gets another taste of it in barracks; but once back in the village... *diga li que vingua!*"[26] The school inspector of Dordogne was right. There had to be another generation before French became the mother tongue for Frenchmen such as these. At the very least. More likely this was only generally true of the offspring born to those who were educated in the late 1880's and married in the 1890's. That was the generation that manned the trenches in 1914–18.

This slow, hesitant process, and the way its stages overlapped between different classes and generations (not to speak of regions), explains how travelers could still find themselves unable to communicate in French until the end of the century. "The Caussien—Bas Breton—Morvandial," remarked an English traveler in 1892, "will in these days shake their heads if interrogated in French." Jean Ajalbert described a more typical situation for that period: a man in Cantal who understood questions put in French but could not answer in the same language and had to fall back on patois. That was Edward Harrison Barker's experience in the Landes about that time, where many (especially the women) could not—or could barely—understand French, and spoke only a few mangled words. In Roussillon, too, Catalan remained the everyday speech, but there French was mostly understood. Barker wrote of another occasion, in 1893, when he asked his way of a shepherd boy in Dordogne and was not understood. But he added that this was a rare occurrence, especially among the young: "In the Haut-Quercy, where patois is the language of everybody, even in the towns, one soon learns the advantage of asking the young for the information that one may need."[27] School and military service were at work. Only women and the old escaped their influence. Hence the professional travel writer who in 1903 found himself in a village in the Ambazac Mountains, not far from Limoges, where he could neither make himself understood nor understand the women, who spoke only patois. He could not find his way until at last he encountered men who "spoke French pure."[*]

In the decade preceding 1914 such blank spots must have become exceptional indeed. As a 1911 survey of rural speech in Savoy indicates, the peasants now made a point of speaking to their children in French, something they had refused to do only a few years before, so that the child had less trouble at school learning the new language. The generation gap stands out: an old peasant addressed by a city man (un monsieur) answered in patois; a young one answered in French. The old peasant spoke patois to priest and teacher; the young one spoke to them in French. In workshops and factories patois was hardly heard at all; because so many of the workers were "foreign"—immigrants from Bresse and other provinces—French had to be used as a *lingua franca*. Increased mobility and social exchanges played their part in the spread of the national language, as they had in the spread of the national currency and measures. Industrialization also helped speed the process. In Vosges, for example, the installation of a cotton industry in the 1870's and its expansion after the 1880's all but wiped out the local dialect when country people moved into small industrial centers where French or an unfamiliar dialect obtained; they also worked alongside Alsatian immigrants, whose speech was different still. As a teacher noted: "The mixture of patois favors a common language."[28]

The war of 1914 saw the culmination of the process, though not its end. With vast numbers of refugees set in motion and soldiers from every part of the country serving together, millions were forced to use French on a daily rather than a sometime basis. Jacques Duclos, mobilized at Pau in 1915, met a Basque soldier who did not know a word of French, "but events would force him to learn it." At the start men were mustered into local units and so could rely on their familiar patois. But as the war went on, new units were set up with the survivors of decimated ones and old units were bolstered with recruits

---

[*] Ardouin-Dumazet, *Voyage en France*, 28: 43 (see also pp. 86, 171). Shortly before the war, as Frances M. Gostling and her husband motored down the Dordogne valley toward Saint-Privat and Argentat (Corrèze), they tried to ask their way in the villages, but were not always successful, "for the Auvergnat patois still pursues us." Impromptu guides were incomprehensible, their French "but indifferent." (*Auvergne and Its People*, New York, 1911, p. 264.)

from every corner of the country. Men had no choice but to speak French. And they did. Many continued to do so home on leave or after demobilization. It was a giant step. In Isère, Pierre Barral tells us, the old patois was completely abandoned by the young after 1918. In the Vosges it became increasingly rare, rather despised.* The situation in 1920 was just the reverse of what it had been in 1880: bilinguals were more awkward in patois than in French; the majority and, most important, the young were on the side of the national language.[29]

The same departments and regions keep coming up in this account, but scattered bits of evidence suggest that patois was spoken in many other areas. In Mâconnais, for example, patois was in general use until 1880 or so, and disappeared only after the First World War. The same seems to apply to the Vosges, the Jura, Dauphiné, and Franche-Comté. In Marche and Berry, villages continued to use Berrichon or Marchois at least until the turn of the century. Even in Normandy, at least some of the peasants apparently did not speak French as late as 1899, since we are told that in the Manche the school-teachers understood the "rustic patois" of their pupils.[30] I am inclined to ascribe the lack of references to problems in these other areas, all of the langue d'Oïl, to two things. First, these regions were quicker to adopt French and put up less resistance to what was taught in school than other parts of the country, so that teachers had few grounds for complaint on that score. And second, though the children in these regions too spoke their various patois at home and in the street, the structure and pronunciation of the Oïl tongues were fairly compatible with French, so that they had less trouble learning Parisian speech.

Three parts of France deserve particular mention because they spoke (or slowly ceased to speak) languages wholly different from French and resisted it the longest. The largest, though by no means the most resistant, was the realm of Oc from Gascony to Provence. "If a traveler through the French countryside wants to understand what is said around him," wrote one such traveler in 1852, "he has to stop [in Bourbonnais] on his progress south. Further on, he would hear only graceless sounds that would make no sense."[31] By that time, 1852, the graceless sounds reflected less the persistence of Provençal, which had long since begun to decay, than the efforts of southerners to adjust to French.

As French speech and culture spread through southern towns and along the highways in the early nineteenth century, the language developed regional forms—mixtures of local terms camouflaged as French and of French words adapted to local usage and pronunciation. Travelers from the outside complained that they could not understand this *baragouin*. Local polemicists

---

* Yet Auguste Brun asserts that the war had no influence on the use of Provençal: "Au contraire, le patois a servi de ralliement entre *pays*, au régiment, au front ou en captivité" (*La Langue française en Provence*, p. 165). But of course such a development does not necessarily rule out a spreading knowledge and use of French.

railed against the renegade Franciots who spoke it. Grammarians and lexicographers admonished and advised. Yet increasingly after the late 1820's the realm of Oc became the home not of two languages but of three: the local idiom, which was Provençal, Gascon, or some other tongue; French as taught in the schools; and the confused mixture of the two that scholars describe as français régional. In Auguste Brun's succinct definition, a language is a dialect that has made good, a patois is a debased dialect. By the 1850's Provençal was a patois: it had ceased to be written; it had become fragmented into local idioms; the upper classes no longer used it except to deal with the man on the street.[32]

In 1854 a group of young poets and intellectuals concerned for the preservation of the speech and literature of Oc founded the Félibrige, and in the following year they began publication of a yearly almanac, the *Armana provençau*, with an initial printing of 500 copies.[33] To revivify their native language, the Félibres sought to create a literature. But literature needs a reading public, and such a public was hard to find. The country people, when they learned to read, learned to read in French; they thus found reading "patois" difficult—the more so since French orthography is not designed to express the sounds of Oc. Furthermore, people who used forms of speech that were highly localized and in constant evolution found it hard to understand a literary language that was often archaic and incomprehensible, as Petrarch's Ciceronian Latin must have been to his contemporaries of the fourteenth century. At Toulon in 1873, according to François Beslay, "men of the people hardly understand the poems of Roumanille," the Félibre of Avignon.[34] Beslay was a prejudiced witness, but he was buttressed to some extent by the experiences related by the Félibres themselves: such as addressing country people in literary Provençal and being met with uncomprehending stares.

In fact, the Félibrige seems to have been a political reaction initiated on a plane several removes away from ordinary people, and from their concerns. Its populist ideals had originally been set forth in French, because French stood for liberalism and emancipation and because already in the 1840's fashion and school made French the favorite vehicle for poetic and political expression. In 1848 the eighteen-year-old poet Frédéric Mistral had composed an ode to liberty in French. But after 1848 and, even more, after December 2, 1851, he turned to his native Provençal to express the sentiments that had once seemed best said in French. But the circumstances that had first suggested using French were not changing; and the Félibrige fell between two stools. By the time its masterwork, *Mirèio*, appeared in 1859, the literate upper classes in the south had been Frenchified. Their reaction was reflected in the words of Monsieur de Pontmartin: "What a pity that this masterpiece should be written in the language of our servants!" Unfortunately the servants agreed.* Seeing

* It is worth noting that in the dedication to *Mirèio*, Mistral characterized himself as a peasant, and Lamartine, to whom the work was dedicated, was quick to accept him as such. The claim,

the rich, the noble, the intellectuals, the city people, businessmen, and civil servants abandoning dialect as a spoken language, the common man accepted their scorn for it even if he did not imitate their practice. He spoke patois at home; but beyond parochial limits patois was despised and useless, an irrelevant anachronism good perhaps for intellectual games but no use to peasant children.

Provençal, Gascon, and the multitude of local dialects continued to be spoken, of course, as they still were in Laurence Wylie's Roussillon. At the turn of the century street vendors from Bayonne and Périgueux to Marseille and the Alps still hawked their wares in the local dialect. But the regionalists could not revive or recreate a common popular speech because they could not deal with the causes of its decline.[35] And the same process was at work in other regions.

Shepherd Clough notes, in his fine *History of the Flemish Movement*, undeservedly forgotten today, that Flemish "reigned supreme in the rural sections of French Flanders," north and northeast of Hazebrouck. Though by 1930, when Clough's book was published, the supremacy was dubious, Flemish was not easily dethroned. The French Revolution, suspicious of dialects, does not seem to have attacked Flemish. And the survival of Latin in the drawing up of administrative acts, which were executed in French elsewhere, closed one avenue by which French had penetrated other regions.[36] It was mainly in the nineteenth century that the superior attractions of French sapped the cultural and literary activities without which a language cannot survive— except as a patois. The old literary and poetic societies (*chambres*) decayed, the traditional songwriters (*dichter*) died away. The chambre of Eecke celebrated *landjuweelen*—poetic contests—in 1835, 1861, and 1874. But in 1861, though the theme of the prize competition was given in Flemish, all the poetry entries bore French titles, and only four of the 16 songs submitted had Flemish titles.[37] A Belgian contemporary of Mistral, the poet-priest Guido Geselle, sparked a last effort to compete with the French influence, but this was the final flicker of the culture that had been.

Deprived of an intellectual and literary base, Flemish in France was condemned. It did not die an easy death, however. André Malraux's grandfather, a Dunkirk shipowner who died in 1909, did not speak French but Flemish. The Abbé Lemire, born near Hazebrouck but on the French side of the linguistic frontier, had to learn Flemish after 1876 in order to fulfill his pastoral duties. In the middle and late 1880's primary education was still hampered by

however, is difficult to take seriously. We may note, too, that though poets and songwriters produced works in Oc throughout the nineteenth century (see Jean Giron, *Vie des personnages célèbres de l'Aude*, Montpellier, 1940), very few of the works represented what could be called popular culture; in the main these writers presented a populist point of view. Significantly enough, when the winegrowers rebelled in 1907, the signs they hoisted (which are to be found in many village townhalls in Aude and Hérault) were written in Oc. But their leader, Marcelin Albert, wrote his mystical populist texts in French.

the general dominion of that tongue. Baudrillart, who visited and observed the region in his usual thorough way, was distressed to find himself speaking a little-understood language to people who answered in a patois he did not understand at all: "a painful feeling to find oneself a stranger in one's own country."[38]

The Third Republic, suspicious of regionalism in general, disliked it even more on this sensitive periphery. After 1877 this attitude was reinforced by the government's rigid anticlericalism. Like most linguistic minorities, the Flemish-speaking French had the support of the Catholic clergy. Sermons and catechism in Flemish raised political problems. A ministerial decree in 1890 prohibited religious instruction in the language, but though the prefect suspended mayors who failed to enforce the decree, the campaign proved ineffective, and in 1896 the Archbishop of Cambrai had to be asked to intervene. He refused, and the friction did not abate until 1905. After that, with the separation of church and state, the documents on the conflict peter out, though the practices to which the state objected continued. In the meantime, however, the teaching of the schools had been making itself felt, and so had the culturally destructive attractions of nearby industrial centers. Between the turn of the century and the First World War, this seems to have produced a generation of children who did not really know their mother tongue—which was no longer taught in any structured way—and who had an even poorer grasp of French.[39] The growing pains of modernity.

Last but not least, Lower Brittany. "The Breton people," wrote an agriculturalist in 1863, "forms, in the middle of the nation . . . , a population apart." Visiting Frenchmen felt this strongly. What one of them called the Chinese wall of Breton speech made communication hopeless, and strange things stranger still. Several times in 1846 the young Flaubert and his traveling companion, Maxime du Camp, found themselves lost and could not raise help. Thus between Audierne and Plogoff, "We lose our way. Deserted village; barking dogs; no one speaks French."[40]

All the same, French marched through the Breton peninsula, moving slowly but surely along the highways, then the railways, from Rennes and Nantes to Brest. It spread outward in growing circles from ports and naval installations like Brest, from administrative centers like Vannes, and generally inland from the coast. On the eve of the Revolution, Breton or Gallo was spoken in all but two of Brittany's seven dioceses.* By Ferry's time only two still held out. Everywhere else the situation had been reversed. The rivulets or inlets of French had become an advancing tide that nibbled at and washed over the still-resistant reefs. But on the tip of the peninsula over a million people clung to the Breton speech. In Finistère in 1881 four out of five women, one out of two

* The Dukes of Brittany had tried to colonize their gallo lands with lords and settlers from Lower Brittany, but the only result was to create small Breton-speaking islands, which shrank to practically nothing after 1870 (see Marie Drouart, L'Etat actuel du folklore, pp. 4–5).

conscripts, neither spoke nor understood the national language; further, there, as in great parts of Morbihan and Côtes-du-Nord, priests still preached in Breton. And even as the *Revue pédagogique* carried encouraging bulletins, it had to admit in 1894 that teachers appointed to posts in Brittany who did not speak Breton had to be given dictionaries.[41]

Just how much progress French really made, on its march through the Breton countryside, is hard to determine. Peasant girls came to town knowing no word of French, to work as maids. They took a little time to learn enough to communicate with their mistress and talk "enough for the needs of [their] service." Soon they could go to the market alone, and deal with the baker, the butcher, and the grocer, as Spanish and Portuguese maids would learn to do in Paris a century later. Peasant lads, primarily the sons of wealthier farmers, attended school in town for a year or two and picked up enough French to use in the market later.[42] Most young recruits, it was said, in two months "acquired a number of words sufficient to understand and make themselves understood."* Back in the village, though, those using French ("young men," revealingly) were mercilessly kidded back into line—even in Upper Brittany— and children knew that French, "good when one is at school," was better dropped outside where "on reprêche comme tout le monde."[48]

So even when French was taught, it was not spoken. In 1906 a couple of English travelers had repeated difficulties in making themselves understood in Lower Brittany: young people proved to have "some knowledge of French," or had "French that [was] not easy to understand." Was it as one commentator suggested, a question of the "stubbornness of the Cornouaillais, who though he knew the language of the rest of France, made it a point of honor" to speak only his own? Or was it that he spoke French so badly? A few months of winter schooling could not compete with a world where one heard only Breton, so even "if at one time he knew how to translate a few words of French, he's forgotten them quickly." What was left of the French vocabulary was often limited to "Donne-moi un p'tit sou, M'sieu!"[44]

Here, too, one must take a hard look at the statistics, especially when one comes across something like the following. To be registered as a sailor, a man had to know how to read and write. Here is the way the examination for the *inscription maritime* was administered at Audierne in the early twentieth century. "We show them a page of a book, they spell without understanding: they can read. We dictate a sentence, they cannot write it; we show them the

---

* *Revue pédagogique*, March 15, 1894, p. 218. Rigorous methods were used to achieve this. The commanding general of the 11th Army Corps once canceled all leaves for the entire 118th Infantry Regiment at Quimper because men had been found speaking Breton in barracks. Remarks Jean Choleau: "Le conscrit se trouve au milieu d'anciens qu'on a tout d'abord 'débretonnisés,' commandé par des sous-officiers qui reçu l'ordre de ne pas parler breton à leurs compatriotes, sous la coupe de jeunes officiers venus en Bretagne pour y faire des études de moeurs et qui, las de ne rien comprendre à notre race, passent sur le dos des soldats leur mauvaise humeur" ("La consommation de l'alcool et la natalité en Bretagne," *Réforme sociale*, June 16, 1908).

book and they painfully copy a line or two: they can write." Their French was like the village precentor's Latin: a song without meaning. As late as 1916 a soldier from Mellionnec (Côtes-du-Nord), François Laurent, was executed as a spy because he could not make himself understood in French.[45]

But Baudrillart, that excellent chronicler of French's imperial progress, had noted the Chinese wall beginning to crumble in 1885. Those who could not speak French, he said, felt ashamed. Perhaps not yet. More important, he noted that literary Breton was becoming the purview of the learned.[46] The gulf between literary language and everyday speech, in which the cultural revival of the south had foundered, was opening up in Brittany as well.

One has only to read the desperate plaints of local traditionalists against the shift to French speech, dress, and manners,[47] and browse through the Breton newspapers, especially the Catholic ones in 1894 and 1895, to realize that more and more parents and children were becoming committed to integration, to Frenchification, which stood for mobility, advancement, economic and social promotion, and escape from the restrictive bonds of home. One can sympathize with the fears of what this commitment implied, but also with the needs and yearnings it reflected. In any case, not sympathy but elucidation is the scholar's business. And so we turn to the question: what made patois recede?

We have already accepted that the schools and schoolteachers played a crucial role. None thinks to gainsay it. As Auguste Brun well put it, the inkwell and the pen worked for French.[48] He might have added, and worked only *in* French. Arithmetic, for example, was taught in French. Thus, even those who normally spoke in some other tongue could reckon sums only in French, the language in which they had learned the skill. And if the catechism was often a bastion of local dialect, Protestantism, which was an active movement in the countryside through the first two-thirds of the nineteenth century, and whose propaganda I have found from Yonne down to the Pyrenees, was a powerful instrument of Frenchification, spreading Calvin's language along with his heresy. We shall consider two other significant influences in due course: military service and the printed word. In the meantime, we may note what the veteran linguist Albert Dauzat had to say about his own Auvergnat village, Vinzelles, near the Dore: that French came in after the French Revolution and spread during the Second Empire "by newspaper and barracks even more than school."[49]

French could, and did, enter through such channels where the local language was relatively close to French. The teachers knew the difference this made. In places like the Doubs (1864), where the local tongue was used everywhere but French co-existed with it, the extirpation of the competing language was deemed less necessary "than in certain departments where the traveler who speaks only French cannot make himself understood in many villages."[50]

Even the wild Morvan, whose denizens in the eighteenth century were like "people of another continent," speaking a jargon that in the last years of the Empire remained unintelligible even to their neighbors—even the wild Morvan accepted French before the lands of the southwest. By the 1860's the local idiom had retreated to the fastnesses of the forests east of Château-Chinon: Planchez, Arleuf, Villapourçon. In the Morvan, as in more open country, the speech of the countryside did not wait upon the schools to give in to French: the patois of Burgundy, of Champagne, of Poitou, of Beauce and Perche were already fading in the 1860's and 1870's. Indeed, the success or failure of the schools simply reflected their linguistic environment, either predisposed to French or alien to it. This is quite clear on the linguistic frontier between Oc and Oïl, where Marche (north Creuse and northern Haute-Vienne) proved more open to French than the true Limousin only a few miles away. Even in poor regions like Perche the proportion of literate conscripts was far higher than in comparable areas of, say, the southwest. However backward, Oïl regions raised no particular obstacles to the advance of official culture. Thus French was being spoken "reasonably well" in the Moulins area in 1908, whereas Limousin speech held on in the Cher valley to the west.[51]

But above all, what worked first for and then against patois was the way of life in many rural quarters. It was in 1889 that Ernest Renan insisted that no work of science, philosophy, or political economy could be produced in patois. One hears a confirming echo of this at that very time from a village teacher in Lozère: of course everyone spoke patois, he wrote, but when a peasant wanted to discourse on politics or current events he was likely to try to impress his hearers by turning to (terrible) French. Politics (as opposed to village business) was done in French, and we shall see that national politics, which entered the unintegrated countryside just about this time, accompanied the national language. Official business was done in French too. Flemish and Corsican had begun to give way after the legislation that ordered people's everyday life was translated into the national language during the Second Empire. And Wylie has shown how, at Roussillon, a dispute over a bowling game caused men to shift from Provençal to French: another result of legislation, in this case requiring associations to submit for official use a copy of their statutes, naturally in the national language. Rules, regulations, and consequently litigation all were exclusively in the domain of French.[52]

So were dealings with officialdom. That had not always been the case before 1870. Indeed, as late as 1867 we find the new sub-prefect of Saint-Flour complaining to his superior, the prefect of Cantal, that all the officials in his jurisdiction were local men, which meant, among other things, that the villagers and peasants there, "always sure of being understood by them in their impossible gibberish," did their business in patois, and made no effort to learn or retain French, "quickly losing what the schools have taught them."[53] This free-and-easy exchange between citizen and officials ended after the Third Republic made the *certificat d'école* a prerequisite for even minor civil service jobs. The minor public servant became a man who had learned French, often with much pain, in the midst of populations who had not. The consequent sense of superiority on the part of such petty bureaucrats and its effects on relations between officials and the public can still be felt today.

One of the greatest enemies of patois was simply its own parochialism. The factors that worked against French in the old isolated world, self-sufficient in far more realms than mere subsistence, turned against local idioms as that world changed. Breton was useless beyond a certain area that had once seemed vast but that became increasingly limited in the perspective of the modern world. Nor was Breton one tongue, or Limousin, or the so-called langue d'Oc. Vannetais was incomprehensible to most other Bretons; men from Léon found it hard to understand those from Guingamp. The old dialectical world was fragmented in the extreme. Dialect might change from one valley to another, from high ground to low, from one riverbank to the next, if physical barriers made communications difficult.* In 1816 a man held up by thieves near Avallon in Yonne had been able to place their origin in a particular *pays* of Nièvre, by their speech and manner of dress. In 1844 an officer in Lot noted that "the natives found it very difficult to make themselves understood outside their own village." One of the arguments in a famous impersonation trial of the 1850's was that the accused, who came from Saint-Marcellin in Isère, could not have known the patois of Corps that she was said to have used because, though Corps was also in Isère, its patois was different from her own. And when, at the end of the century, pork butchers from southern Creuse went north for the fairs in the Creuse districts close to Berry, no one could easily understand their speech. "O y at pas d'besoin de feire trotter in chrétien," declared the Charentais, "pour queneutre de là voure i sort." If the wisdom of Saintonge said that you did not need to make a man trot around (like a horse at a fair) in order to know where he was from, it was because his speech would tell you.[54]

As time went on, and especially as more and more people moved about, the advantages of knowing French became increasingly obvious. Recognition of the fact spurred the decay of local speech. As we have noted, industrial development worked for the linguistic unification of the polyglot labor force that migrated to the cities. Market changes worked more slowly but to similar effect in the countryside. "Le français rapporte, le patois ne rapporte rien," was Arnold Van Gennep's response to a Savoy linguist who deplored the trend. Even children, especially children perhaps, had come to despise patois. When, on the eve of the First World War, the schools became somewhat more friendly to local dialects, it was the country people's turn to reject them.[55]

---

* This was the case in Ariège, where Massat and its valley spoke a Languedocien similar to that of Foix, and the rest of the Couserans spoke Gascon (J.-M. Servat, *Histoire de Massat*, pp. 50–51). As a long-suffering Picard philologist remarks: "Le patois, on le sait, varie parfois d'un village à l'autre, d'une famille à la voisine et, dans la même famille, d'une génération à la suivante" (Gaston Vasseur, *Lexique serrurier*, p. 17).

Knowing French had become a matter of pride for them, just as one's dialect had once been a matter of pride. For people who lived in coherent communities with their own life, patois retained its earliest sense of a language one did not understand. It was not they who spoke patois; it was everyone else, the strangers. And the language strangers spoke was part of their strangeness and their ridiculousness, something that was likely to be derided rather than imitated, let alone admired. Basque peasant farces, as we have seen, often used strange jargon for the Blacks, always with satirical intent: Latin or French for lawmen, Béarnais and Spanish for barbers, tinkers, vainglorious oddbodies or giants to be bested.[56] And later, when the prestige of French began to be recognized, most peasant communities still felt that its use was inappropriate in their midst and acted to discourage—chiefly by ridicule—those who tried to use it (clumsily as a rule) when a particular function or situation did not call for it.

French was a "langage de parure et de cérémonie"; and country people knew quite well the difference between exalted speech and their own usage. As a basketmaker recently explained to a folklorist to whom he told his tales: "Il y a bien des mots en *grandeur*, il y a bien des mots en *mayonnais* aussi."[57] One used French forms, which were considered more noble, to show respect.* A Gascon peasant speaking to a bourgeois would not use the homely *pay* and *may* in referring to the man's parents, but would say *boste péro, bosto méro*. The use of French could also emphasize quality. Gascon for hat is *capet*; but for a gentleman's top hat or a lady's bonnet one preferred *chapeau*. In lower Armagnac the shepherds called the strawberries that were theirs for the picking *arragne*; but in Auch and upper Armagnac, where strawberries did not grow wild but were cultivated as delicacies for a rich man's table, they were known as *frésos*.[58] Aimé Giron's novel of 1884, *La Béate*, about life in Velay, opens with a peasant couple visiting a convent. The man addresses the mother superior in French, a mark of respect. His wife would do so if she could, but she has no French. The mother superior, "a very distinguished woman," naturally speaks French. In the Loire country, where patois was still used in general conversation down to the Second World War, polite usage called for French. At a dance, for instance, a lad invited a girl to dance in French, and they preserved that formality through their early exchanges.[59]

The pulpit, too, so often represented as a fortress of patois, was often the chief stage for recitals in the honored language—as it was expected to be. There was nothing a popular audience liked so much, remarked a priest at the end of the century, as to be addressed in a tongue that was not its own but

---

* Or, on occasion, to try to gain a little respect, as when a peasant gave his children French names, taking his cue from the local squire. In that connection Albert Dauzat relates this anecdote. Around 1820 a priest espied a little girl at Vic-le-Comte and asked her for her name. "Mary," she answered. "Mary! But that is a young lady's name, not a name for a peasant. You must be called Miyette or Mayon." To which the little girl responded: "I'm as entitled to bear the Holy Virgin's name as any lady!" (*Glossaire étymologique*, pp. 18–19.)

was understood. For that matter, understanding was not always requisite. As early as the 1820's, we are told, the villagers of Morière near Avignon, who spoke no French, were resentful when the priest chose patois for the sermon at a first communion ceremony. "It struck us as common, trivial, grotesque, unworthy of so great a solemnity," Agricol Perdiguier remembered many years later.[60]

What language to use in church was a thorny problem for the clergy, though perhaps no thornier than the authorities' problem of what to do about a re-calcitrant priest. True, political orientation, as well as sympathy, may have been a factor in some cases, but my own impression is that in general the priest's resistance to calls for him to use the national language reflected rather than led local resistance. Priests, after all, were trained in French. They too thought French superior to the debased idioms of their charges. Many might have preferred it. Beyond mere suppositions, one finds cases—in Ardèche, Allier, the Limousin—where a priest simply declared that he had to preach in patois if he wanted his parishioners to understand him. Some priests had trouble mastering the local tongue but were forced to use it. Oblates sent out on preach-ing missions seem to have run up against that problem, too. Even the Ministère des Cultes recognized that there were parts of France where a priest might be forced to use local dialect. Father Lemire, we recall, had to learn Flemish in order to do his job. He might well have preferred to save himself the trouble. In any case, where there was a public for French it was catered to: people were given a choice of masses, with the sermon in French or patois as suited them.[61]

This practice fell off sharply at the turn of the century, in part under gov-ernment pressure, but mostly because this period witnessed the triumph of French. In 1901 La Semaine religieuse of Auch lamented the passing, in Armagnac, of the Gascon-language catechism and of homilies and sermons in Gascon, which had far outnumbered those in French through the whole of the nineteenth century. Thereafter, sermons in French, "which used to mark par-ticularly solemn occasions," became increasingly routine in that region.[62] In Brittany, by contrast, many priests refused to observe the government's ban in 1902 on Breton-language sermons and catechism; in Finistère alone 51 priests saw their salaries suspended.* It was only when—and where—French had ad-vanced sufficiently that the clergy turned to it. The Church reflected regional conditions; it did not create them.[63]

Once patois came to be widely scorned, its fate was sealed. It was increasingly rejected after the 1890's by the young and especially by girls and women, who

---

* M. Dumesnil, Des manifestations des ministres des cultes à l'encontre des autorités politiques (Paris, 1903), p. 16. In 1903 or thereabouts the term coucou became a Breton slang word for a seminarian or priest who was born in Lower Brittany but did not know Breton; such men were often assigned to a gallo parish, yet were still "foreigners," like a cuckoo in a wren's nest. By extension: any Breton born in a Breton-speaking region "who is ignorant of his native tongue" (Gaston Esnault, L'Imagination populaire, p. 117).

were to become strong carriers of a language that was seen as a badge of refinement and of emancipation. A similar scorn of patois grew among those who had improved their condition or were eager to do so. A perceptive officer of the Restoration had predicted: "Le discrédit du patois est l'effet naturel du progrès du luxe et de la civilisation des capitales ..., qui s'étendent peu à peu jusqu'à leurs extrémités."[64] The little by little was slower than some expected. At Lantenne (Doubs), an agricultural village 21 kilometers from Besançon, we are told that in 1896, 177 of 195 men and 163 of 197 women still spoke patois; during the 1914 war all the Lantenne boys at the front spoke only patois. Still, a century after the officer quoted, Auguste Brun could note: "One dresses as in town, one will speak as in town. New way of life, new way of speech."[65]

What did all this mean, what did it do, to the people involved?

Local tongues had not endured unchanged until the nineteenth century. They had evolved under the influence of fashion or need, or both, however isolated the regions where they were spoken. When, after the fourteenth and fifteenth centuries, local ruling classes ceased to treat the speech of Oc as a literary language, when the cities, lost for Oc but not yet won for France, ceased to act as unifying centers for rural speech, particularism took over. The more self-sufficient a region, the more likely it was to develop its own dialect. Relative wealth could work this way as easily as poverty and isolation. The rich Limagne, where every village was virtually self-sufficient, kept its own speech and ways longer than some poor mountain areas whose people were wont to move from place to place, and carried in the culture of the outside world.[66]

By 1848 many erstwhile languages had been let loose from all the disciplines that maintain a language, to become what the Revolutionaries called jargons: unfixed by writing, ignored by literature, without formal structure or grammar. That was when they caught the eye of intellectuals, poets, and linguists, who sought to regulate and revive them. But by then it was too late: conditions worked against the dialects, just as the official campaigns against them could succeed only when conditions were right.

The social function of language is to permit members of a society to understand each other. When the national society became more significant than the various local societies, national language was able at last to override its local rivals, and other particularisms as well. Yet what developed was not always truly national. Notably in the center and the south there developed a whole series of compromises between official or school French on one hand and the local speech on the other: buffers between patois and French, drawing on both, applying the structures and the accent of patois to French, changing the meaning of terms in order to use them in vernaculars that ran from Frenchified patois to *patoisant* French, a hodgepodge that its users accurately described as *carroun* (maslin), the mixture of wheat and rye the French call *méteil*. This regional or local French contained expressions that disconcerted strangers, but that all natives used naturally and considered to be French.[67] It characteristically included patois terms referring to activities and objects peculiar to the area—measures, games, and trades, and their articles of equipment. It performed, in a word, the crucial service of all vernaculars, which is to represent the local reality.[68]

The very aspect that made local French opaque to strangers made it luminous to those familiar with the experience it reflected, and placed it in a broad context of related meanings. In Forez, for instance, where nail-making was an important industry, the bellows (*la mantcha*, from the early models made in the shape of a haft or helve) appeared in locutions that made sense only to those familiar with their broader meaning. Sickness, for example, became "the haft is not doing well." Since bellows were made of leather and rats were their worst enemies, rat infestations were particularly dreaded, and rats play a greater part in Forez sayings and folklore than they do in that of other rat-infested regions.*

Other regions, other conditions. In the Morvan:[69]

South-southeast and west winds	Soulèr e drévan
Are two good lads;	Son deû bon anfan;
Dry and cold north winds	La biz e galarm
Are two bad gendarmes	Deû movê jandarm.

Where, as in much of the southwest, nuts were both eaten and made into oil (used not only for cooking but more important, for lighting), nuts on the tree that were to be picked for oil had one name, those that fell or were knocked off to be used for food had another.[70] Terms such as these would fall into disuse, along with the practices they mirrored, as did the vocabulary of pastoral life in the Pyrenees, very rich and old, expressing the detailed care lavished on sheep when wool brought good returns. When the poor-quality Pyrenean wool could no longer compete on the market with wool from other regions, and especially with imports, sheep came to be bred primarily for slaughter and the shepherd's vocabulary was lost along with his now-unnecessary skills.[71]

Because local vocabulary was firmly rooted in local practice, there were many blanks that had to be supplemented as the need arose, by borrowing from elsewhere. Thus, at Vinzelles in lower Auvergne, where cows drank their fill at the local brook, the village had no drinking trough and village speech no name for one. At need, the villagers used the term current in a neighboring town. This situation offered plenty of opportunities for the penetration of French as life-styles changed. Thus in Franche-Comté, where garden flowers

---

* Albert Boissier, "Essai sur l'histoire et l'industrie du clou forgé," pp. 71–72. Thus: "Go, go, miserable clod, / You've cast a rat-spell on my father's haft!" (Filo, filo, traino-malheu, / L'a trai lou rats à la mantcha de moun paire!)

were no doubt rare, as they were in many rural areas, most ornamentals carried French names. Similarly, horses, which were not in much use there, had most of their anatomy described in French.* Often a new word was adopted for a new form of a familiar object, as when *lampo* (the oil lamp and its offspring) edged out the old *caleu*. Sometimes the adoption of new words in French relegated old terms to an inferior function, as when Savoy's *pare* and *mare*, bending to *père* and *mère*, came to be used exclusively for animals.[72]

Of course, words related to agricultural and technical innovations, to changes in furniture, dress, and dwelling, to administration, and to newly identified maladies were borrowed from French. As were all the many terms related to moral and intellectual life. The patois of Auvergne had no words for poet, musician, painter, or artist. It had functional terms, to be sure, for men who made music with certain types of instrument or who made up songs, but it had no way—or need—to deal with art in the abstract. French supplied such words when the need arose, but those who found them relevant used French anyway. Some abstractions, though, were very relevant indeed; and so, little Janed of the Breton song, who is tired of service and wants her freedom, sings: "Mé' zo skuiz o servicha, La mé houl va *liberté*!" Altogether, the evolution of local speech looks less like decadence than like adaptation. All language is connected to the needs and interests of its speakers. As these changed language changed, more slowly, of course, but revealingly, and in good part responsively. Necessity created the expression. Waning need laid it away.[73]

This does not mean, however, that mentalities were quite unaffected in the meantime. On the contrary, the simple shift from a spoken language to one based on writing alone was an immense change. The stilted style of official reports bears witness to the awkwardness of the adjustments involved. The music of discourse, once spare or lyrical, become coldly didactic, swollen with the terminology of administrative French. The very notion of language, like the term, refers to speech not writing;[74] and oral style has little in common with its literate neighbor. The rhythm of the phrase in the spoken language models the idea and its nuances—repetitive, melodic structures frame the fleeting thought, punctuated with sonorities, with striking images, with inflections of sound that convey inflections of meaning.

When, in September 1846, the Virgin appeared to two young shepherds at La Salette, she addressed them first in what sounds like the formal French they could have heard in church, and dealt with themes they might well have heard in a sermon, complaining that people swore and worked on Sundays.

---

* Albert Dauzat, *Glossaire étymologique*, p. 4; Abbé Jean Garneret, *Un Village comtois*, p. 74. Even the word bouquet was borrowed from French. On the other hand, parasites, weeds, and wild herbs, like the trees in the farm orchard, bore local names. In Auvergne, too, weeds and a few local flowers had their own names, whereas potted geraniums and chrysanthemums bore French names. Likewise, the horse, more expensive (hence nobler) than other animals, was addressed in French (M.-A. Méraville, *Contes populaires de l'Auvergne*, Paris, 1970, pp. 266–67, 272).

When she turned to patois, however, predicting retribution and famine, the language became more lyrically rich, more "biblical" in a recognizably popular vein:

Let him who has wheat not sow it; the cattle shall eat it, and, if any should sprout, it will fall to dust in the threshing. There will come a great famine; before the famine comes, the little children under seven will be taken atrembling, will die in the arms of those who hold them, and the grownups will do penance by hunger. The grapes will rot and the nuts turn bad. If they reform their ways, the stones, the rocks will turn to wheat; and the potatoes will be restored by the earth itself.

Simple, concise ideas full of images, specific and based on local experience. That was the nature of rural speech, poor in abstract terms, rich in concrete ones, and in pejoratives.[75]

And then, of course, it was local. The way of life affects speech in its purely physical aspects. The breathing of people operating in different terrain affects the rhythm of their speech and their pronunciation. A doctor traveling through Ardèche in the 1870's noted the sonorous endings of the local patois, which made the voice carry further. A Corrézien today has similarly pointed to the preponderance of consonants in his native Occitan, which helped to make speech more audible so that it carried further in difficult natural circumstances. Audibility was also served by the hard "r" of the old pronunciation, abandoned in school and in Paris French but retained by actors whose voices must carry a long way. Modern French falls lightly on the ear. Popular speech is harsher, more abrupt, more perceptibly rhythmic. French, meant to be spoken in a relaxed manner with a relaxed body, has more open vowels and fewer diphthongs. The phonetic evolution from a wealth of rude diphthongs to more delicate sounds is clearly related to changing conditions; or, at least, to the triumph of values related to such conditions.[76]

Modern students of rural language have stressed how important body language—gestures and posture—is for the peasant. This, too, reflects a society where all share in a common fund of knowledge that makes much explanation superfluous. As Henri Mendras says, the peasant shows what he does or is about to do in forms of behavior that are wholly familiar to his fellows and so are easily interpreted by all of them. If one sees a man in such a place, at such and such a time, one can generally tell what he is up to. Deduction based on concrete observation is what counts, and speech adds little to this. It is used more often to conceal the true sense of an act or gesture than to express an attitude.[77]

Writing sets up a screen between practice and our inner selves, and so does the mentality that is based on it. This is perhaps why patois clung on longest where practice and thought were closest: "Quand il s'agit de la terre," wrote Emmanuel Labat in 1912, "on pense en patois."[78]

It would take time before one ceased to think in patois. The patoisant child knew birds, trees, and watercourses under their local names. The French names he learned at school were never attached to familiar things but remained detached, evoking a distant realm and abstract images. This tended to two results. In the first stage, newly bilingual people had difficulty understanding ideas conveyed or developed in French. A little girl of above-average intelligence and able to read well, might follow every turn of stories in Oc but stumble over French stories with language that departed from the patterns taught at school. French stories called for great effort: the individual words might be understood but not the sense of a phrase. Older persons, similarly limited to a schoolbook French, would mostly have the same problems interpreting, say, a news item. Intelligence is not enough to ensure mastering ideas in an alien medium. All the signs we read, whether they are letters, words, or simple images, are symbols whose reference is more or less familiar, hence more or less easily registered and comprehended. The peasant reader had to master not only the elusive French alphabet, orthography, and grammar, but also the references that these were meant to serve—that is, the symbols of an alien culture.

A word calls up an image, or a whole covey of images, and there can be serious problems of adjustment when a word familiar in one's own speech carries quite different connotations in another—as was the case, among others, with the word *rentier*, which in the south denoted not a man who drew a rent and lived on it, but a man who paid it. Even on the level of sheer practicality, difficulties of mental adjustment may arise when an object endowed with a particular gender or personality in one frame of mind has to be given another in translation. Gaston Bonheur cites a striking illustration of this problem involving the river Aude. In the local patois the river was treated, not as an object, but as a person. The article was accordingly never employed in referring to it: one went to Aude, or said that Aude was high, that Aude growls, and so forth. A whole mentality had to be bent for a small article to be added. Small wonder children and adults both had difficulty in coping with a language that was not only alien in itself but also represented an alien vision. A schoolteacher writing about teaching French in his rural school of Ariège remarked that people tended to think city children were cleverer or quicker on the uptake than rural children, when it was just that the city child heard French spoken all the time, and the country child heard it not at all. One might add that the entire frame of reference was also different.[79]

In the second stage, when French had become more fully assimilated, the effect could be more alienating still, because the novice passed from a point where words were close to the things they stood for, to one where they were far apart. French, which prizes abstract terms over concrete ones, abandons pointed reference and analogy for tenuousness. It refines language by eliminating the details that count so much in popular speech and the great variety of specific and descriptive terms that flourished in patois. It prefers to interpret rather than describe reality, to express ideas, not just to relate facts. Accordingly, it tends to lead its user to attribute less importance to the what of things, acts, or events and more importance to the why. A cultural equipment that makes words triumph over things may be appropriate to a society in which necessity and immediate experience play a secondary role, or which has learned to adjust its ideas to that way of thinking.[80] For simpler minds operating in a harsh, concrete world, such implicit values can only be confusing if not totally alienating.*

Language is one technique for mastering reality. Local dialects had mastered the everyday world of the peasants' experience, personified it in its details, coped with it. As urban speech edged those dialects out, the familiar became alien. New speech, new words, new forms did not permit the same easy, immediate participation in situations that time and habit had made familiar and that words had, so to speak, domesticated too. The new words were more abstract. The values and ideas they reflected were more distant. Intellectual effort was required to reestablish contact with objects and experiences. This need to readjust made for a certain timidity—the savagery that we hear about—not only in public expression but in the private acceptance of a new world that was very different from the old.

"Right now," said Father Gorse of his fin-de-siècle Corrèze, "the peasant has no language to serve him. Patois he has unlearned; he even lacks the words to express his thought. And when he uses them it is absurdly. He does not know what they stand for. The French into which he is brutally thrown ... makes him forget his Limousin language, but does not get through to him."[81]

Not all French peasants lived through such painful transitions, to be sure. And if, in certain parts of France, the transition did cause pain, it did so only for limited periods—though longer than in a land like the United States, where the adjustment was less long-drawn-out, more forcibly sudden. But the experience marked the minds of generations. Its high-water mark, around the end of the nineteenth century, was also a high point of political and social torment. And its products, like the daughters and sons of the American immigrants, would face the great challenge of the First World War with a resignation born of their condition, but also with the firm certitude of neophytes.

---

* Speaking of the alienation involved in the peasant's conversion to a new tongue that reflected none of his feelings or experience, Father Gorse wrote, "The peasant cannot say what he sees, what he feels. French lacks words for many of his implements, etc. How does one translate: *rilha, fulhas, pica-prat, pouda* ... ? How does one say: *estranujar, essirbar, foueirer, afournelar, abarjar, acounelar?* What does one call: *la fourna, lou rueul, lou palhassou, la palhasseta, lou tinau, lou pelau, la sesta, ...la coudieira, la barja, lou counoul, la bourouda, lou zalou?"* The problem would be settled only when the acts or objects described disappeared. (*Au bas pays de Limosin,* pp. 9–11.)

Chapter Seven

FRANCE, ONE AND INDIVISIBLE

Le grand précepte qu'il faut donner aux historiens, c'est de dis-
tinguer au lieu de confondre; car, à moins d'être varié, l'on n'est
point vrai. Mais malheureusement les esprits médiocres ont le
goût de l'uniformité.

—AUGUSTIN THIERRY

WHEN DID FRANCE become one? Surely we know that. Forty kings worked
hard at the task, but it was the Revolution that finished the work in the end:
abolished local particularisms, perfected a national unity stronger and more
compact than any other nation ever knew. By 1808, as Hippolyte Taine asserted in his preface to *The Origins of the Revolution in France*, "all of France's
traits" were "set and definitive."[1] This is pretty much what the schoolbooks
of the Third Republic taught: one people, one country, one government, one
nation, one fatherland.[2] This is what historical studies expounded and still
expound, an axiom most recently repeated by Albert Soboul: "The French
Revolution completed the nation which became one and indivisible."[3]

This national unity is perceived as the expression of a general will—the general will of the French to be French, to achieve a state that was somehow his-
torically foreordained (as expressed in the use of the term *re*unite when speaking of the annexation of various territories, which "realized unbeknownst to
them their true aspiration"). Long before the Revolution formulated and perfected the terms of the social contract, the inhabitants of the land called France
had achieved the spiritual unity that is the necessary precondition of nationhood: the "community of feelings and ideas concerning certain fundamental
problems, a certain identity in the way of conceiving the external world, of
classifying its objects, of ordering its values, in short a certain unity of spiritual orientation, a certain common spirit."[4] Few could put in words better than
Julien Benda this notion of nationhood *and* its abstract quality. We are talking about more than political or administrative structures; we are talking
about a unity of mind and feeling, implicit or explicit. The nation, in the
last resort and the most fundamental, is a cultural unit. It is in this respect
that it must be considered.

But the nation, as Alphonse Dupront has perceptively remarked, is "a solemn public power of little intimacy."[5] The French nation, like the kingdom,

had to become a patrie, a fatherland; the larger abstraction had to replace the immediate experience of a man's pays. The concept of the patrie, land of one's father, can mediate between private society (the family) and official society (the nation). And the concept was extended as the father's realm itself was extended beyond the natural limits of the pays or petite patrie to a broader, much more mobile world. The question is, how long did this process of extension take? How fast was a coincidence established, then perceived, acknowledged, assimilated, between pays, patrie, and France?

When, in 1860, an officer noted that the people of Puy-de-Dôme "possèdent à un très haut degré l'amour de leur pays," his concept of the pays was as limited as theirs. Some of these men, he reported, were forced to expatriate themselves to other parts of France and to seek "on foreign soil" the food their fatherland (patrie) denied them. Clearly pays and patrie were one, and everything beyond was still foreign soil. If, as Benda (and others) insist, being French is not a mere abstract acknowledgment, but rather a consciousness and an everyday experience, then these people who lived in the middle of France in 1860 were scarcely French.[6]

This is something one seldom finds acknowledged, and then only discreetly, in an undertone. Carlton Hayes, who described France as a nation of patriots, perceptively noted the survival of "centrifugal forces" in the 1920's—localism, provincialism—then explained, "The history of the development of national spirit in France [the spirit that he describes as a supreme national loyalty] has been the history of the overcoming of centrifugal forces in the life of the nation by centripetal forces."[7] The image "centrifugal," whether he intended it to or not, suggests a preordained unity. It assumes an existing "center" that is more than a base for conquests of opportunity; and it obscures the existence of societies for which the "center" remained largely unknown and irrelevant until it subjugated them—let alone assimilated them.* Traveling in the French Alps in 1846 Adolphe Blanqui had found "populations further from French influence than those of the Marquis Islands." Some 20 years

* The reigning myth is clearly accepted or asserted by Beatrice Hyslop (French Nationalism, p. 23), Hans Kohn (The Idea of Nationalism, New York, 1944, pp. 16–17), Franz Boas (Nationalism in Europe, New York, 1915, pp. 3–4, 8–9, and especially 11), Karl Deutsch (Nationalism and Social Communication, 1953 ed., p. 93), and Alphonse Dupront ("Du sentiment national," in Michel François, ed., La France et les français, p. 1465). As Augustin Thierry remarked a long, long time ago, since theory said that the nation was one, French history (and historical theory) must be one too (Considérations sur l'histoire de France, Paris, 1840, chap. 4). Yet he never ceased to insist that "c'est par des conquêtes successives qu'elle [France] a reculé ses frontières. Ces conquêtes ... avaient pour objet ... le gouvernement des pays subjugués" (Lettres sur l'histoire de la France, Paris, 1827, pp. 207–8). And then, "Partout où ils [the French] portèrent la conquête, sous un prétexte ou sous un autre, ils rencontrèrent une opposition nationale, l'opposition des souvenirs, des habitudes, et des moeurs" (ibid., p. 209). Hayes apparently had not read Thierry, or at least had not heeded him (see France, A Nation of Patriots, pp. 3–5, 15). Note that in his chapter 11, devoted to regionalism, he speaks of its "influential counter-teachings" (ibid., p. 293), testifying to the equally artificial and didactic nature of nationalism itself. As we have seen, regionalism was not a "survival" of something old, but a form of the new.

later, an English voyager at the other end of the country expressed very similar feelings. The people of the Landes, he wrote, "live on French soil, but cannot be called Frenchmen. They speak a language as unintelligible to a Frenchman as an Englishman; they have none of the national characteristics —little, perhaps, of the national blood." But holdouts and mere "superficial counter currents" are as nothing next to the transcendent reality of France's being molded into a nation. What matters, in Ernest Renan's words, is "the general line, the great facts that stem from it and that remain true even if all the details were to be wrong."[8]

There is a level on which this may be true. But it discounts detail and covers the intricate pattern of things as they were with a general mantle of things as they should be, as if a France become one and indivisible had thereby become uniform as well.[9] We might do better by following the precept of the old romantic Thierry, and distinguish rather than confuse the conditions under which national consciousness developed. We shall find that the process was more varied than is generally conceived, far slower and more complex than most historians would have it.

To begin with what is least disputed, but at the same time is little acknowledged, the state astride the revolutionary watershed—the kingdoms, Republic, and Empire called France—was at best loosely integrated. In 1751 Charles Pinot Duclos, permanent secretary to the French Academy and a former mayor of Dinan, published certain astute *Considérations sur les moeurs* in which he compared the difference between Paris and the provinces to that between separate peoples: those who lived a scant one hundred leagues from the capital were a hundred years removed from it in their manner of thought and action. This equation of time and space is one we should retain, for it can as appropriately be applied to nineteenth-century France as it can be applied to different continents today. It appealed to one of Duclos's Limousin readers, who found it just as relevant to conditions some 60 years later. It might have appealed to Arthur Young as well, who, on the eve of the Revolution, found that "that universal circulation of intelligence which in England transmits the least vibration of feeling or alarm, with electric sensibility, from one end of the kingdom to another . . . has no existence in France."[10]

When a new edition of Duclos appeared in 1828, it carried as a preface a *notice* by the critic La Harpe, written in 1799. In it La Harpe contended that in the period between 1760 and 1780 the difference Duclos had perceived had "become almost unnoticeable so far as concerns the large cities, which are here the only objects of comparison." This judgment, if we accept it, emphasizes less the growing cultural integration of the land than the deepening gulf between a few great urban centers and the rest of the country. The Revolution stressed the same fact. Separatist tendencies asserted themselves even before the Estates had met in 1789, and several regions might have echoed the contention of the Béarnais that their region was bound to France much as

Ireland was bound to England. Grégoire's correspondents noted sadly that "there is no patriotism in the countryside." Only "the more enlightened" could conceive the notion. Patriotism was an urban thought, a handle for an urban conquest of the rural world that looked at times like colonial exploitation.[11]

Certainly the Revolution and revolutionary agitation carried national politics and the national language into quarters they had not touched before. Clubs, appeals, speeches, gazettes, and broadsheets, propaganda of every sort, news eagerly awaited and discussed with passion by groups once oblivious to anything but their immediate world, a new terminology that had no counterpart in native speech, war, military service, troop movements, the political promotion of men of ever-lower status when their superiors had been eliminated by Terror and Counter-Terror, the pride of simple people bent on showing that they could handle their betters' tools—all these created a situation that invites comparison with the China of the 1960's, breaking down the peasants' isolation and crumbling traditional societies. In the ten years of Revolution, in the words of Auguste Brun, "a crack appeared in the block of peasant habits." But only a crack. Much of the block held fast.[12]

A school inspector tells us how Franche-Comté, whose character had resisted change as strongly as Brittany's, was "Frenchified" after 1833 and turned into "a natural frontier of solid military populations." A witness like Maurice Barrès testifies to Lorraine's attachment "to the memories of independence, glorious and not long past" in the 1840's. And *Les Olivettes de Lorraine* sings of the French as if they were unfriendly aliens:[13]

> Lou, lou, la, laissez-les passer,
> Les Français dans la Lorraine,
> Lou, lou, la, laissez-les passer,
> Ils auront du mal assez!

The France of local songs and speech was not the patrie but somewhere else, as in the Limousin soldiers' song "Soudart ve de la guerra," where the soldier has a French girlfriend, described as such over and over—*mia Francesa ... la tua Francesa*—until the last strophe:

> Adiou, adiou, mia Francesa,
> Que jamais pus nous reveiren.

If one's home happened to be in the south, then one could get to France by traveling toward Loire and Seine. Near Marmande in Lot-et-Garonne the road toward Virazeil (then north to Bergerac) was still remembered in the 1930's as "la côte-de-France"; and other lieux-dits of the same kind abound elsewhere. What is of interest here is not the particular names used, but the deep-seated sense of difference that gave rise to them. When the Dominican Emmanuel Labat passed through Marseille in 1706, he was struck by the residents' refusal to admit that they were French. Some 150 years later a historian from that city still spoke of "the Frenchman" and "the French" as if they were a race apart (and not a very nice one). The same at Toulon, where true natives seldom mixed with *regnicoles*, "whom they don't yet consider their compatriots, and whom they always designate as Franciaux."[14]

"Great love of their *pays* . . . , great scorn for the foreigners from the north," reported an officer from Tarascon in 1859. "The old hatreds are not completely dead," wrote another from the Marseille area in 1862.[15] And as late as 1875 a staff captain warned of the hazards of an army corps formed exclusively of Provençaux, or the presence of too many of them in any one unit.*

We have little information on unpatriotic attitudes in this period, not only because some took them for granted in certain circles and made no remark, and others (teachers, for example) preferred to ignore what they deplored, but also because such views became socially unacceptable and their holders chose to conceal them. Thus at Cogne near the Italian border the great local saint, Saint Besse, had the power to exempt lads from military service and was in fact invoked to that end for many a decade. But on the eve of the First World War, though people still sought his intercession, a visiting folklorist found few who were willing to admit that the practice continued, and some who flatly denied it.[16] Accordingly, one's sources are bound to be patchy and impressionistic, and one's argument simply tentative.

No one in the nineteenth century undertook any sort of broad survey of national consciousness and patriotism. And discussions of the subject in the early years of the twentieth century focused spottily on urban—mostly student —groups. Later ones, for that matter, do not seem all that thorough. The rather thin evidence I am able to marshal should suggest the need for more systematic study. Yet, as it stands, it shows a very incompletely integrated nation. Again, the center, the southwest, and the west were the notable holdouts. The Basques were said to have not one sympathy in common with the rest of France. "Closed to outside influences," deplored Félix Pécaut in 1880, they had so far been hardly touched by "the emancipating action of French genius." At the other end of the Pyrenees, where in 1844 the French were referred to as dogs, "French blood is still lightly grafted on the Spanish stock." It was quite clear, during the 1907 crisis, that the French conquest was readily

---

* Archives de la Guerre, MR 2269 (Marseille, Nov. 15, 1875). The good captain no doubt would have prided himself on his percipience if he could have foreseen that the Fifteenth Corps, recruited in Provence, would be accused of cowardice before the enemy at Morhange during the difficult days of August 1914. The charge and the ensuing scandal bore hard on southern soldiers; they were a little less French than other Frenchmen, a little less aggressive or reliable, it was said, exactly as the traditional Tartarin image made them out to be. (See *Le Matin*, Aug. 24, 1914; J. Bellendy, *La Légende du XVe Corps: L'Affaire de Dieuze*, Avignon, 1916; and Maurice Agulhon in Edouard Baratier, ed., *Histoire de la Provence*, pp. 519-21.) For all that, numerous streets in southern towns bear the name of the maligned Fifteenth.

recalled by many in the areas most affected—Gard, Hérault, and Aude, as well as Pyrénées-Orientales. The winegrowers, echoing the Béarnais charge, compared the south's position to that of exploited Ireland and denounced the "victorious barbarians who treated them as slaves." It was not the reality that counted, but the rival myths.[17]

Even where no local myths survived, the national myth did not have easy going. La patrie, noted Father Roux in his Corrèze parish, a "fine word... that thrills everyone except the peasant." In Velay, wrote a novelist quite incidentally in 1884, "the word patrie signifies nothing and stirs nothing. It exists no more in local speech than in local hearts." A few years later, when General Georges Boulanger stood for election at Dunkirk, his bilingual posters ended: "Vive la patrie. Leve het Vaterland!" This led to strife between Boulanger's Republican opponents and his irredentist Flemish supporters, who proceeded to put up a poster that boldly declared: "Flemish, that's what we are, not French. We have no other fatherland than Flanders; France is not our fatherland, it is the pump that has been sucking up our sweat for over 300 years."[18]

Expectably, it was Brittany that held out longest. In 1870 when, alone of all French provinces, Brittany organized a *levée en masse*, the news of the action gave rise to fears of separatist intentions. Léon Gambetta himself wrote to De Kératry, leader of the Breton forces, before the bloody battle of Le Mans: "I beg you to forget that you are Bretons, and to remember only that you are French." Other political factors were at work, of course, but Gambetta obviously thought that this point was worth emphasizing. So did the author of an important report on the Breton departments written ten years later, who placed the issue in historical perspective: "Brittany, which was not willingly joined to France [again the term used is reunited], which never wholeheartedly accepted its annexation, which still protests," had yet to be merged into the nation: "Frenchify Brittany as promptly as possible...; integrate western Brittany with the rest of France." This, said the writer, the rector of the Academy of Rennes, Baudoin, would be accomplished only through schooling. That was how Franche-Comté was conquered half a century earlier. And that was how Prussia set out to Germanize "our poor Alsace-Lorraine," and there, at least, the people knew colloquial German. The parallel with Alsace-Lorraine is revealing. But despite the spread of the schools in which Baudoin put his trust, we still find a Breton delegation in 1919 pleading with President Woodrow Wilson for "the right of national self-determination."[19]

Even the war of 1870 had not evoked a universally patriotic reaction, assertions to the contrary notwithstanding. Reaction to wars in France had always varied with their impact on local affairs—the further off the better—and with their success. The nineteenth century saw no great change in this respect. A good war aroused enthusiasm as long as it went well, made few demands in terms of taxes and recruitment, and furnished occasions for excitement and celebration. Thus the Crimean War was greeted, in the beginning at least, with a "military spirit," "warlike songs," "enthusiasm," and "a festive air," according to a newspaper in Franche-Comté.* But the newspapers of the period are uncertain sources, first because they expressed the kind of emotional response one would expect in the circumstances, and second because they tended to reflect urban attitudes—which in this case were somewhat ambivalent. The cities had their own way of seeing things, as can be seen from an editorial of *La Franche-Comté*: "Better get it over. Business has not been the same since 1866." And though, in the Doubs, for instance, all local papers of every imaginable tendency were unwavering through July 1870 in their warlike enthusiasm and national indignation, they also continued to publish the advertisements of companies that provided substitutes for reluctant recruits Such scenes as were reported in July and August 1870 almost certainly took place, suggesting that a "remarkable patriotic excitement" probably could be found in the little towns, where the local band often played the recruits out of town, old men, women, and girls escorted them to the next village, and people readily drank to La Patrie.[20] But, first of all, how many scenes to the contrary would have gotten into print? And second, how far beyond urban limits did such sentiments extend, even at the height of the war fever?

Arthur de Gobineau's iconoclastic views on the events of the period reflect strong prejudices, but also his personal experience of what he saw around him. By his account, the government tried hard to convince everyone that the French people as a whole were burning to drive back the invaders, but "the masses persisted in believing that it was not their business." George Sand in her country retreat recorded the contrast in July 1870 between Paris, "braying with enthusiasm," and the provinces, in which the overwhelming feelings were consternation and fear. In Ardèche: "little enthusiasm," "poor reception for conscripts," "general negative attitude." In the Limousin, though the bourgeoisie and the city workers were for the war, the peasants quickly turned against it, against recruitment and taxes. Riots broke out when the war continued: "Down with the Republic! Long live the Emperor! Long live Prussia!" By September, in the center, what people wanted was an end to war: "peace at any price." In more exposed regions, Soissonnais, Beauvaisis, Vexin, the villagers had stubbornly refused to join the local national guard. If Gobineau is to be believed, everyone in the 37 communes of his rural canton of

---

* "Everywhere local songs whose naivety betrays their authorship attest to the courage that animates these conscripts," wrote the prefect of Jura on May 23, 1854. "The people are infused with a wholly French spirit," observed the prefect of the Doubs on March 1, 1854. (See Roger Marlin, *L'Opinion franc-comtoise*, pp. 27–38.) On the other hand, around Largentière, the conscripts of Ardèche were singing quite different songs: "O petit roi de Prusse, / Viens donc me secourir, / Le général de France / Y veut me faire mourir; / J'ai cinq cent mille pièces / En bombes et canons / Je t'en ferai présent / A toi et à ta Nation." (Pierre Charrié, *Folklore du Bas-Vivarais*, p. 45.) It is not clear quite where the Prussians came in in a song of the 1850's, but Russia and Prussia could have been confused either in the locals' mind or in rendering the patois original into French. In any event, there is little doubt about the spirit of the words.

Chaumont-en-Vexin insisted that under no circumstances would they go to fight the Prussians. Indeed, French villagers even were known to refuse food to the French troops and to give it to the Germans, of whom they were more afraid. The peasants resented anyone and anything that threatened their security and homes, and perhaps most of all the *francs-tireurs* recruited in the towns, whose depredations they feared and whose foolhardy threats to resist the enemy provoked ever more hostile reactions. By September villagers fearful of German reprisals were denouncing the guerrillas to the enemy, leading enemy troops to their hideouts and places of ambush, or arresting them themselves and handing them over. Even if Gobineau stretched the truth for his own purposes, a recent doctoral dissertation supports the general impression of his account; and the officers who reconnoitered the countryside through the 1870's clearly despaired at the thought of what the army might expect in case of conflict.[21]

As Léonce de Vogüé made his way to Versailles after the preliminary peace settlement at Bordeaux, he noted the relief and happiness of the peasants in Périgord and the Limousin. It would take some time to teach the peasantry that Alsace and Lorraine mattered to them. Perhaps, as an Englishman suggested in the 1880's, the patriotic reaction was in direct proportion to the German presence, feeble where the Germans were far away, strong where they came close. It is certainly true that in some regions the German threat had virtually no effect on the tempo of life. From an Ain village, for example, we have a family journal that carefully noted the year's events, crops, prices, and conditions, yet made no mention of the war. Neither did the diary of a retired magistrate, who simply noted: "They say that the Republic has been proclaimed in Paris."*

But what of the evidence of out-and-out anti-patriotism? We find some cases that fit the bill, or come perilously close to it. Madame de Gobineau in Oise seemed more in fear of French looters than of the Prussians. And her husband did not hold too bad a memory of the German occupation. In Normandy Flaubert noted with disgust "the bourgeois' universal cry: 'Thank God! the Prussians are here!' " At Nancy it was the laborers who, when the town surrendered, cried: "Down with the French! Long live Prussia!" And when German troops were quartered in a girls' school at Bar-sur-Seine (Aube), they received constant visits from the children, who taught them the "Marseillaise" and even bought a German–French dictionary the better to communicate with the soldiers. Apathy, collaboration, or simple human nature

---

* Léonce de Vogüé, cited in Louis A.-M. de Vogüé, *Une Famille vivaroise*, p. 142; Philip G. Hamerton, *France and England*, pp. 75–76; René Dumont, *Voyages en France*, p. 183. Martin Nadaud, who was the prefect of Creuse in 1870–71, remarked of the general lack of enthusiasm: "One might have thought the country wasn't threatened.... No, France did not feel that tremor of patriotic wrath that carried our fathers to the borders in 1792; it didn't rise as one against the invader.... What apathy!" (*Discours et conférences*, 2: 27.) The general prosecutor at Rennes found the popular mood no better in his area: "apathie, insouciance, absence d'esprit public... du patriotisme... grande lassitude" (Archives Nationales, BB 30 390, Mar. 23, 1871).

uncomplicated by abstract considerations—in the end we have a mixed bag of evidence, and probably other instances can be adduced to show deep patriotic grief or, at least, shock, particularly among urban populations. Yet there is one impressive clue to how little impact the war had on the popular mind in the countryside, a Holmesian one of the negative dog's-not-barking variety: practically no folk songs have survived to preserve the memory of the *année terrible*, and no episode of 1870–71 seems to have so caught the popular imagination as to be preserved in legend.[22]

It was only human that time and a change of the political winds should persuade many in retrospect that conditions had been worse than they had in fact been, and that their patriotism had been of the deepest order; that being led to school as an eight-year-old by a Bavarian soldier had been a real humiliation; that one had done, seen, and felt things as the new national orthodoxy now demanded. In the event, most people seem to have seen war as a nuisance, to have greeted its end with relief.

What is more surprising is how quickly separatist movements grew in newly annexed territories. Savoy, which had voted to join France in the 1860's, had hardly been assimilated by 1870—as soldiers and officials, treated as carpetbaggers and smarting under the Savoyards' "unjust hatred for all that bears the French name," well knew. Men of Savoy fought bravely in 1870–71, but "apart from the departure of a few soldiers" the unexpected war, the rapid and still less expected defeat, had little effect on local life: "Everything took place as if in a far-off dream." When the dream turned to nightmare and a German occupation loomed, some Savoyard groups urged drastic measures: an occupation by Swiss troops, a separation from France, a declaration of neutral autonomy. At Bonneville in February 1871 the local Republican committee discussed the possibility of annexation to Switzerland. The historian Jacques Lovie has charted Gambetta's difficult struggle to persuade his own Republican supporters that the notion of France overbore any one regime, and so, though they might dislike a given regime, they could not just reject it and go their own way. Gambetta's efforts to instill this notion of a permanent fatherland that would be more than a target of opportunity may have succeeded in educating some; they left others untouched. Like the radical of Saint-Julien who was heard to shout in 1873: "Down with France! Down with the French! ... We hate the French. We have to make a revolution to get rid of them." Brought to court for insulting a gendarme ("I don't give a damn about you, you are French, I hate the French, I've never been French and never will be!"), the man was merely fined by sympathetic local judges. No hope for patriotism in this department, complained the prefect in 1874.[23] A subordinate saw things more clearly: it was too soon to expect the Savoyards to feel French.* We have seen that this could apply with equal justice

---

* The sub-prefect of Thonon wrote on June 2, 1873: "Somme toute, ces populations de nos campagnes, qui ne sont françaises que de date récente, et dont l'esprit s'est peu nourri des traditions qui font le patriotisme, demandent avant tout la tranquillité et se soumettent sans effort à

to regions beyond Savoy. There too, as the authors of a recent study of rural change in Maurienne perceived: "These people had not yet reached a national consciousness. . . . Submission to the state does not mean that they share in the common traditions and the common enterprise that define a nation."[24] Dependence without participation: here is an idea and a state of affairs that we shall encounter again.

The most reliable evidence I have found on patriotic sentiments is furnished by military authorities, either indirectly through conscription records or directly in the reconnaissance reports of officers. E. Le Roy Ladurie and a team of scholars have thoroughly explored the first source with the aid of computers. But their work only covers the period 1819–26, too early for my purpose. Just how closely their findings coincide with my more spotty ones, however, can be seen from Map 5, showing the departments where the Ladurie team found the greatest incidence of draft evasion and self-mutilation to avoid military service, e.g., cutting or biting off a finger, knocking out the front teeth (which were needed to bite the bullet). Le Roy Ladurie remarks that these departments tend to be grouped in Occitan France, where tax resistance was also greatest. He wonders whether this reflects "a certain lack of national integration of the Midi at this time," especially when compared with the departments of the northeast, which "present strong evidence of national integration." This is borne out by his map of volunteers for military service, which shows a fertile crescent of martial commitment running from Nord to the Doubs, very close to the results recorded in my Map 8.[25] It is further borne out by a map taken from Adolphe d'Angeville's statistical survey of France in the early 1830's (Map 6), which shows those departments where government agents encountered the greatest difficulties in collecting taxes. If patriotism and a sense of civil obligations go together, reluctance or refusal to discharge the latter testify to a slight sense of the former (and to the state's inability to impose both).

The evidence recorded in my own maps is drawn from the War Ministry's files of the military reconnaissances carried out between the Restoration and the fall of President MacMahon. It is of quite a different order from the exhaustive work of Le Roy Ladurie. For one thing, it is based on the subjective impressions of men, and men who were moreover often strange to the locality they were reporting on. For another, it depends on the luck of assignments and on what was preserved in the files. All available files have been read, but their contents by no means cover the country, far from it; and it is well to remember that the army made most of its reconnaissances in areas around garrison centers, along highways, and so on. But even thus limited, the results are suggestive.

tout gouvernement qui pourra la leur assurer" (quoted by Jacques Lovie, *La Savoie dans la vie française*, p. 555).

I have noted every statement that refers clearly to the local population's indifference to the interests of the army, open hostility to troops, or active avoidance of military service (Map 7); and likewise every reference to its patriotism or lack of patriotism (Map 8). All dubious or equivocal remarks have been set aside; and we shall see presently that the statements whose meaning could not be questioned reflect something more than "a certain lack of national integration." In the meantime, what emerges clearly is a sizable pocket of patriotism along the northern and northeastern borders; its contrary at the opposite, southwestern end of the country; and a disparate but important jumble south of a line running roughly from Saint-Malo to the Italian border, where negative attitudes to one's patriotic duties encounter negative attitudes to the patrie itself.

The army had a very matter-of-fact attitude to the population: were the people friendly, could one expect aid, could one expect trouble, what was the best way to handle them? Since the reports were not for publication, the officers could speak frankly, and their assessments generally reflected few illusions. The local population would feel no moral or patriotic grief about the loss of territory to Spain, wrote an officer in the Pyrenees: "Je ne les crois pas, en effet, assez français par le coeur" (1853). From another, at Ponts-de-Cé in Maine-et-Loire, where one could find good fighting men provided they could stay near home: "They are still Angevin, not French" (1859). The Corsican, of course, "has always borne the foreign yoke impatiently; it is not [our] conquest that binds him to France forever" (1860). In Hérault "the population is not very patriotic in general" and "little inclined to make sacrifices" (1862). "Like all the populations of central France," Allier's "has little patriotism" (1864).[26]

One did not need to trouble overmuch about such things, but should be prepared to take appropriate action. "There is no reason to apprehend the inhabitants...easy to hold down by fear" (Loiret, 1828). "The peasants of Brie are timorous and have little guile, and all resistance on their part would be easily put down" (Seine-et-Marne, 1860). Southerners possessed "a memory of their past liberties that makes them awkward," hard to handle, unwilling to take orders; "the deployment of force will nevertheless suffice to break these resistances" (Hérault, 1862). Double-check any information furnished by the natives because "most of them have kept wholly Italian sympathies. One shouldn't fear at need to assert oneself" (Nice, 1869). They did not mind soldiers in most parts of Auvergne, but "you can't expect help except by payment, requisition, or threats" (Puy-de-Dôme, 1873). The inhabitants would not refuse aid, "but rather out of fear than out of true patriotism" (Gironde, 1873). Same note a few months later at the very gates of Bordeaux: guides and informers should be tempted by gain or threatened with guns (Gironde, 1873).[27]

Defeat had made military men bitter. "Limoges people are both aggressive

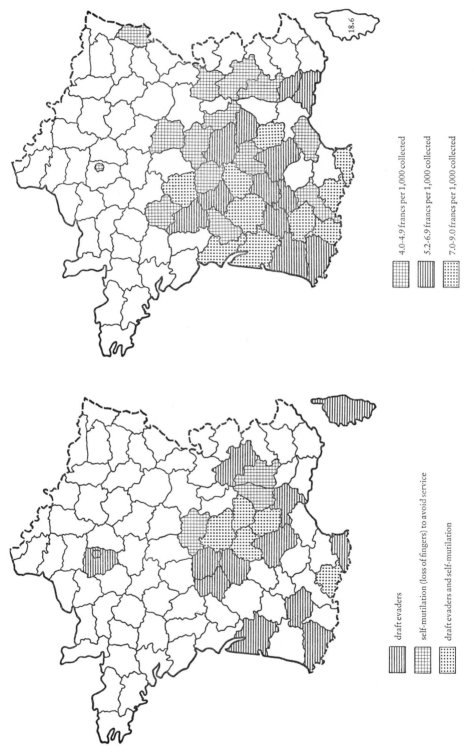

Map 5. Lack of patriotism as reflected in attempts to avoid military

Map 6. Lack of patriotism as reflected in the cost of collecting taxes,

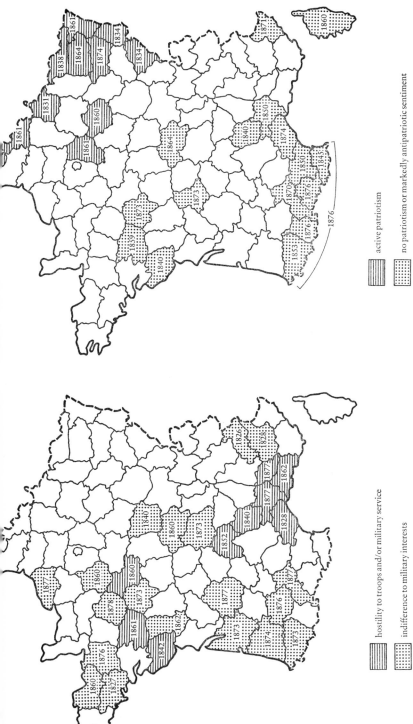

Map 7. Lack of patriotism as reflected in indifference or open hostility to the military, 1820's–1870's. SOURCE: Archives de la Guerre, *Mémoires et reconnaissances*, as cited in the text. NOTE: In every case the latest report has been shown.

hostility to troops and/or military service

indifference to military interests

Map 8. Areas of patriotic and nonpatriotic sentiment as observed by military officers, 1820's–1870's. SOURCE: See Map 7. NOTE: For reports on patriotic feeling I have used the earliest date; for those on antipatriotic sentiment, I show the latest.

active patriotism

no patriotism or markedly antipatriotic sentiment

and cowardly. All in town and country have very underdeveloped patriotic feelings." In case of combat in the region, one should count on no help from the population (Haute-Vienne, 1873). In the Indre valley, unfortunately, "military spirit and patriotism are little developed" (Indre-et-Loire, 1873). Further south, the spirit was still worse. The population "completely lacks patriotism": not only would it accept no sacrifice, it would not hesitate to make trouble (Hérault, 1874). Generally quite hostile to the army; troops could expect difficulties (Gard and Vaucluse, 1877).[28] Things had not changed radically since the days when conscription had been resisted with pitchforks or by flight to the hills. True, conditions now made such reactions difficult, but there had been little change in the mentalities that justified them.

There is a story told in a Peruvian novel about Indian peasants who thought that a war with Chile was being waged against a general of that name, and were nonplussed when told that Chile was one country and Peru another to which they belonged. To be sure, few French peasants could have been that uninformed, but one may still wonder what their image of their country was, how much they knew about the country to which they belonged.

For a start, their historical notions were usually vague and personalized. In Vivarais the stories told of evenings recognized four legendary periods: that of the giants, imps and elves; that of the Camisards; that of the Revolution; and finally, that of the "ferocious beast," probably a wolf, which scourged the countryside around 1812–16.[29] Fantasies based on fact coexisted with fantasies based on pure fancy, the whole jumbled and telescoped in time, food for entertainment or admonishment. The Breton peasants said that all the red monks' castles fell down in one night, and in truth, Philip the Fair had ordered all Templars arrested on the same day. The wars of the Catholic League took place, not in the sixteenth century, but simply in a time beyond the recall of the oldest grandfathers in the parish. So far as the Ermenonvillois knew, Henry IV, the best remembered of French Kings, was a contemporary of Jean-Jacques Rousseau. In Brittany, where most peasants had not heard of their own countryman Bertrand Du Guesclin, grand constable of France in the fourteenth century, one thought he might have been a Revolutionary general who beat the English. The historical memory of illiterate societies, brief and selective, grants personalities and events the accolade of remembrance only by attaching them to saws and common sayings. Thus, Henry IV survived in the Lower Limousin as a Henric-quatre—an old worn thing. Charette, the only Vendean leader remembered in Upper Brittany and along the Lower Loire until the schools revived to memory his anti-Revolutionary fellows, lived in such locutions as "Chouan like Charette," "brave like Charette," "patriot like Charette" (this last ironic). The Swedes, who ravaged Franche-Comté during the Thirty Years' War, survived in the Doubs as synonyms for brigands or symbols of wickedness (*chvède*); around Belfort, in the mid-nineteenth century, all ruins and destruction were still attributed to them.[30]

About the only historical event that served as a chronological milestone for all French people of the fin-de-siècle was the Revolution, the great dividing point that separated the present from the past. In Upper Brittany storytellers placed the departure of fairies at the time of the Revolution. But they were not quite sure when these events happened, and reference to them seems to have meant simply "a long time ago"—hence the placing of Du Guesclin about the time of the Revolution. Stories often begin with reference to a time when things were utterly different from the present; the Revolution sets the limits of that time.

Like all cataclysmic events, the legendary Revolution seems to have been portended by wondrous sights: great battles between cats, *chasses fantastiques* in the sky, statues that shed tears. Similar wonders were sometimes attached to Napoleon's name. But Napoleon's legend was one that he himself largely fostered after 1804, in history books, in army communiques, and in the arts. A favorite medium was the popular engraving, designed in some cases to indicate that he possessed almost supernatural powers (Napoleon crossing the bridge at Arcole, Napoleon touching the men stricken by the plague at Jaffa), in others to depict him as the pluperfect democrat, simple and good (Napoleon and the grenadier's mother, Napoleon and the sleeping sentinel).

Fed by the *Mémorial de Sainte-Hélène* (1823), stirred by the policy of Louis Philippe (who ordered Napoleon's statue repositioned atop the Vendôme column, had the Arc de Triomphe completed and opened, and enshrined Napoleon's ashes in the Invalides), and fanned by the songs of Béranger, the image of Napoleon-heir-of-the-Revolution inspired semipopular stories born of publicity rather than oral spontaneousness. Naturally, that image flourished in the 1860's under Napoleon III. But its *popular* vogue, such as it was, had waned by the end of the century; and what survived, significantly, was a strong memory of the great butcheries over which the Emperor had presided. In Champagne, Franche-Comté, and Upper and Lower Brittany the Te Deums that celebrated his victories turned into *tue-hommes* in peasant language, or *tud-éom* (Lower Brittany: "need men").[31]

> Te Deum,
> Il faut des hommes,
> Laudamus te,
> C'est pour les tuer.

We can be sure, at any rate, that not everybody in France at the end of the century knew Napoleon. J. E. M. Bodley, putting up at an inn by the Durance, close to the spot where Napoleon crossed the river on his way from Elba, asked an old woman if she had known elders who might have seen him there,

"Napoleon," she replied in her broad Provençal accent, "connais pas ce nom-là. Peut-être bien c'est un voyageur de commerce."*

I am inclined to think that the "awareness of great things done together," or suffered together, may well have been less widespread than we believe. In 1864 a school inspector in Lozère was incensed to find that at one school he visited not a single child could answer questions like "Are you English or Russian?" or "What country is the department of Lozère in?" Among most of these children, the inspector added bitterly, "thought doesn't go beyond the radius of the poor parish in which they live."† Every year, reported Bodley shortly before 1914, "there are recruits who had never heard of the Franco-German war" of 1870. He quoted a 1901 survey in which an average of six out of every ten recruits in a cavalry squadron had never heard of the war. A similar inquiry among recruits of 1906 revealed that 36 percent "were unaware that France was vanquished in 1870 and barely half knew of the annexation of Alsace-Lorraine." Indeed, only one man in four could explain why July 14 was a national holiday. A military novel of that period confirmed his findings: many privates did not know about the war of 1870 either, to say nothing of the Franco-Russian alliance closer to their day.[32] On the other hand, we may safely assume that when a Corrèze farmer whose barn was requisitioned in 1909 to billet an artillery troop on maneuvers asked if the soldiers were French or Prussians, he knew about the war, if only vaguely.‡

"The idea of the fatherland," wrote Joseph Fleurent in a revealing but unconvincing discussion of Alsatian patriotism, "is above all the love of one's country as state, then as a legal and economic structure." This is far from the idea most advocates of patrie had of the nation, or wanted others to have of it. But it is not far removed from the way the alien notion struck the peasant. As with the Indians of Peru, the only figures that represented national authority in their eyes were the recruiting sergeant, the tax collector, and the judge. A variety of evidence shows that Fleurent came closer to the truth

---

* *Cardinal Manning and Other Essays*, p. 184. See also Bodley, *France*, 2: 364, on villagers in Haute-Savoie who, in 1894, believed Napoleon III was still Emperor. In 1885 Hamerton noted that the French peasants had no sentiments for Alsace-Lorraine and were indifferent to its loss. They did not "really know what the word *France* means. . . . Why should they make sacrifices for the people of Alsatia, who were always as foreigners to them?" (*Round My House*, pp. 230–31.)

† *Instruction primaire*, 2: 71. The point was well taken—and was still valid around 1900, when peasants near Burg (Corrèze), nine or ten miles from Brive, did not know the names of villages less than two miles away, even those they could see on nearby slopes (André A. Meynier, "Deux hameaux limousins," pp. 369ff). Another writer, another area: "L'Etat c'était quelque chose de vague. On ne pensait guère plus loin que Villebon et certainement pas plus loin que Mâcon" (V. Dupont, *Quand Eve filait*, p. 118).

‡ Ernest Lavisse deplored the fact that at every examination session (*session de bac*) examiners found young men who knew nothing of the defeats of 1870 or of the new eastern borders of France, who forgot that Metz was in German hands or placed Nancy in German territory ("L'Enseignement de l'histoire," p. xxvi). So perhaps we should not insist on such ignorance as peculiar to the common people.

than, say, Julien Benda. And it is worth remembering that until the Second Empire some communes, too poor to buy a flag, lacked even that basic symbol of the nation-state. "No one has ever found the secret of forging a patrie without common ideas," insisted Pécaut in 1879. Before that mutuality could be achieved there would have to be more flags; and there would have to be more teachers. And teachers would have to inculcate (for it was not there) what Dupront's paean to France calls its religion: that (in Gambetta's words) "there is a moral entity to which [a man] must give all, sacrifice all, his life, his future, and that this entity ... is France."[33]

We shall examine in detail, in the chapter devoted to schools and what they taught, how the teacher carried out this injunction. Certainly he was not allowed to forget it. Indeed, he was regularly reminded by circulars and by assigned essay subjects in courses for teachers, such as this one in 1880: "On the teaching of national history and on the way it has been used to develop patriotic feelings."* Moreover, he seems to have put it to good use. Young François Jaffrenou, the future Breton patriot, born at Carnouet (Côtes-du-Nord) in 1879, was sent to school at Guingamp in 1889. In 1892, at the age of thirteen, he wrote a poem called "Long Live Our France!" bidding proud Frenchmen to march where the bugle called:[34]

> Ravagez cette fière Allemagne,
> Devastez-lui ses campagnes,
> Exterminez jusqu'au dernier
> Ces Allemands, soldats de papier.
> Crachez mitrailleuses, tonnez canons,
> Et marchez au son des clairons.

Exactly what Rector Baudoin had hoped for in 1880.

The cult of Joan of Arc spread too. In 1876 a third-year student teacher at the Limoges Normal School could not say two words about Joan. The case would surely not occur ten years later. The visitors' book at Joan's house in Domrémy shows 1,342 signatures in 1872, 2,128 in 1877. At this time the visitors came mostly from nearby departments (Vosges, Aude, Somme, Doubs, Marne, and Meurthe) and from Paris. There were many soldiers, but otherwise nobles and Parisians predominated. Travel was a luxury; Domrémy not yet a popular shrine. By 1893 things had changed: the numbers had increased, *noms à particule* had become of less account, there were more visitors from distant places—Sarthe, Deux-Sèvres, Nièvre. One cannot tell who they were,

---

* Archives Départementales, Gers, *Rapports d'inspection générale*, 1881. All the same, patriotism had its limits. In 1886, when the War Minister put forward a plan to make teachers subject to three years' military service like everyone else, the action drew heavy fire. During the ensuing parliamentary debates, one argument frequently heard against ending their exemption was that it would dry up the recruitment of teachers. In the end the law as passed in 1889 permitted them to serve only one year.

but the *Petit Lavisse* and its fellows may have had something to do with the new interest in Joan.[35]

What do I dare conclude from all this information? There is many a weary step, said Edmund Burke, before "a number of vague, loose individuals" form themselves into a mass that has a true political personality: people, nation.

In a lecture in 1882, Renan criticized the German concept of nationhood, as worked out by Herder, Fichte, and Humboldt, which contended that there were four basic elements of nationhood: language, tradition, race, and state. Renan proposed his own list instead: present consent, the desire to live together, common possession of a rich heritage of memories, and the will to exploit the inheritance one has received in joint tenancy. One can understand why Renan would reject the German principles of nationhood. It would be hard for a Breton to ignore the absence of common language; tradition might well be taken in a political sense where division, not community, was the rule; race was a dubious concept; and only state remained, but as an expression of power, not of organic growth. Still, Renan's own desiderata served no better. In 1882 consent might be assumed from indifference, but there could be little desire to live together with people who might as well have come from another world. The heritage of memories was not held in common, but differed according to region and to social stock—witness Renan's own assumptions. And there was no inheritance in joint tenancy. The Republic under which Renan formulated his idea had inherited a territorial unit but a cultural jigsaw. It was up to the Republic to turn the legal formulas into actual practice.

What Renan reflects is the assumptions and the serene conscience of his kind. But it matters little really if he is right or wrong. His France, like that of Barrès's Professor Bouteiller, is an *ensemble d'idées.* One is French, says Bouteiller, if one assimilates certain ideas, an abstract approach to something very concrete: being, feeling, however elusive these may be.[36]

There is something strange about the talk that swelled in the late nineteenth century, and that continues to this day, about being French. If the French were (are?) as French as we have been led to believe, why so much fuss? The fact is, the French fuss so much about the nation because it is a living problem, became one when they set the nation up as an ideal, remained one because they found they could not realize the ideal. The more abstractly the concept of France-as-nation is presented, the less one notes discrepancies between theory and practice. When one gets down to facts, things become awkward. Take, for example, Carlton Hayes's naive definition of nationality: "a group of people who speak either the same language or closely related dialects, who cherish common historical traditions, and who constitute or think they constitute a distinct cultural society."[37] This would never do for the France we have been talking about, because it simply does not fit French conditions. A lot of Frenchmen did not know that they belonged together until the long didactic campaigns of the later nineteenth century told them they did, and their own experience as conditions changed told them that this made sense.

Finally there was force. Finally, but also originally and throughout. In the end it was a republican of Toulouse, albeit a Gaullist, who told the truth in the clearest and bluntest terms: it was centralization, said Alexandre Sangui-netti, "which permitted the making of France despite the French, or in the midst of their indifference.... France is a deliberate political construction for whose creation the central power has never ceased to fight."[38] Commonplaces perhaps. But too often forgotten.

E. J. Hobsbawm recently asked whether the "nation" might be "an attempt to fill the void left by the dismantling of earlier community and social structures."[39] This actually reverses the order of events, at least in regard to France. In France the political nation of the Ancien Régime functioned side by side with traditional community and social structures. The ideological nation of the Revolution had to compete with these. It was not invented upon their dismantling; its invention implied their dismantling. It is interesting in this context to read the reflections of the sociologist Marcel Mauss on the injustice of cultural imperialism, of a Pan-German or Pan-Slav movement that attempts to impose a "dominant civilization on a composite society." It never occurs to Mauss, a humane and learned man, that his criticism could apply to France as well.*

All these difficulties arise, it seems to me, because the theory of nation and patrie is too rigid, hence too brittle. In other words, its generalizations are particularly liable to collapse under the weight of exceptions, which in this case do not prove the rule but crack it. All the familiar imagery of patriotism and nationhood is based on unity. To question the assumption of unity is like Psyche's holding a light over sleeping Amor. Amor has to go away. Unity vanishes. Perhaps salvation lies in an alternative formula, suggested appropriately enough by a folklorist, Arnold Van Gennep. In Van Gennep's view the nation is a complex of collective bodies, all in process of perpetual change and in a constantly varying relationship with one another.[40] The static view of the nation as a precise entity that having once been forged is thereafter stable or threatened by corruption is thus replaced by a Bergsonian model of continual interaction much closer to what actually went on.

---

* "La Nation," especially p. 40. Mauss shows the same blindness in a later passage when he refers to the linguistic attitudes and expansionism of others (pp. 62–66). We may note also his own understanding of the nation: "a materially and morally integrated society, with a stable permanent central power, with fixed frontiers, with inhabitants relatively at one morally, mentally, and culturally who consciously adhere to the State and to its laws." He clearly thinks that national integration involves the disappearance of every kind of subgroup: nation and citizen coming to face each other with no intermediaries between them (pp. 20, 24).

The purpose of my argument in this chapter is not to prove that the French were unpatriotic, but to demonstrate that they had no uniform conception of patriotism at the Revolution or at any other time in our period, and that patriotic feelings on the national level, far from instinctive, had to be learned. They were learned at different speeds in different places, mostly through the latter part of the nineteenth century. When, in 1881, the teacher of Castelnau (Lot) claimed that France was moving *toward* unity, he was right, of course. When he concluded from this that local history must be abolished, merged, lost in the history of the nation, of the one French people, he was premature. And wrong. But he was doing what he conceived to be his job. He and his fellows did their job so conscientiously, in fact, that until quite recently there has been little hint of anything else. And yet, within the nation, Castelnau and its like had, have, a history too.

Chapter Eight

THE WORKING OF THE LAND

Il ne faut pas regretter les choses, même les plus jolies, quand
un peu de misère et de fatigue humaine disparaît avec elles.
—RENÉ BAZIN

ALL THROUGH THE nineteenth century and into the first decades of the
twentieth the rural and agricultural populations were a majority in France.
On that everyone agrees. But the figures vary depending on how such populations are defined. The data most often cited are also the least enlightening.
Official definition classes as urban any locality with 2,000 or more inhabitants,
and on this standard, estimates that in 1851 three-quarters of the French population lived in rural areas, that by 1901 the proportion of rural to urban inhabitants had shifted to about 3 to 2, and that between 1921 and 1929 the urban
population gained a slight edge over the rural.[1] The difficulty, of course, is that
some localities with fewer than 2,000 inhabitants were essentially small towns,
and some with more than 2,000 remained largely rural. A bourg of Provence
or Languedoc, for example, would have had more urban characteristics than
a bourg of the same size in Lorraine. For this reason, such figures are useful
only in indicating and to some extent charting a general trend.

The same applies to more precise statistics. First, because they also vary;
witness the recent works of Theodore Zeldin and J.-M. Mayeur, who though
they agree that the agricultural sector of the French economy employed the
largest proportion of the population in the late nineteenth century, differ on
what the exact proportion was.[2] But no one disputes, at least, that in absolute
numbers the active agricultural population continued to grow through the
end of the century. As Table 1 shows, there were more people earning their
living in agriculture, fishing, and forestry in 1896 than in 1856 or 1876 (or in
fact ever before).[3] According to the table, they no longer constituted a majority of the working population, as they had during the Crimean War, but
taking into account the people catering to them in the small towns dotting
the countryside, the French population would still have been a predominantly
rural one.

All this is by way of saying, if it needs to be said, that we are talking about

TABLE I
Working Population of France by Sector, 1856, 1876, 1896, 1906

Sector	1856 No. of workers (*millions*)	1856 Pct. of working population	1876 No. of workers (*millions*)	1876 Pct. of working population	1896 No. of workers (*millions*)	1896 Pct. of working population	1906 No. of workers (*millions*)	1906 Pct. of working population
Primary: agriculture, forestry, and fishing	7.305	51.4%	7.995	49.3%	8.463	45.3%	8.845	43.2%
Secondary: manufactures and industry	4.418	31.1	4.469	27.6	5.452	29.2	5.936	29.0
Tertiary: services	2.493	17.5	3.754	23.1	4.749	25.5	5.701	26.1
Hard to categorize or unemployed	—	—	—	—	—	—	.239	1.7
TOTAL	14.216	100%	16.218	100%	18.664	100%	20.721	100%

SOURCE: Jean Bouvier in Georges Duby, ed., *Histoire de la France*, vol. 3: *Les Temps nouveaux de 1852 à nos jours* (1972), p. 17.

a great many souls; and even if this discussion focuses on only certain parts of the agricultural population, in the most truly rural and the least advanced areas, it nevertheless bears on the lives of a lot of French men and women. What concerns me here is the way in which their work and their methods of working changed, and what this portended for their way of life and their way of thinking.

I shall use statistics from time to time, but it is well to remember that the statistics of the period are at best suggestive indicators. As the prefect of Creuse declared in 1873, the statistical-gathering process was still being perfected and not very reliable. The coverage tended to be patchy. Productivity figures were not to be trusted because of incomplete returns and the unwillingness of the peasants to furnish precise data.[4] Even in great official enterprises like the censuses the benchmarks were shifted so frequently that their results are hard to use for comparative purposes over a number of years. Only studies in depth focused on particular localities, like those now available to historians of the early modern period, will provide the detailed information that we require. Until then—and even then, for there was infinite local variation—any conclusions are perforce speculative. A situation where information is clearly incomplete forces us to acknowledge what in other circumstances we might seek to avoid.

Nothing would ever be the same again after 1789, claims Ernest Labrousse in a 1970 collection on the economic history of pre-Revolutionary France. Yet what strikes one most forcibly about agriculture in the early half of the nineteenth century is how little anything actually changed: stubborn survival and indifference to the accidents occurring in the political sphere. *Pace* Labrousse, there seems to be general agreement that the rural economy changed little with the Revolution, that there was no radical modification of land structure or work techniques or productivity before the middle of the century. The farming methods of the July Monarchy, wrote an agronomist of the period, were comparable to those of the Algerian Arabs: "a little better than those of the Iroquois and the Tartars." About the same time (1836) an officer reconnoitering the area between Oloron and Navarrenx, in Béarn, simply copied out the report of an intendant of 1698, noting that nothing had changed, and that agriculture "seems to have been in its present state since a very ancient age."[5] Perhaps the Physiocratic ideas of the eighteenth century persisted so far into the nineteenth because they remained relevant to an enduring reality.*

The sociologist Robert Redfield makes a distinction between the peasant, for whom agriculture is a way of life, not a profit-making enterprise, and the farmer, who carries on agriculture as a business, looking on land as capital and commodity. In those terms, through much of the century, most Frenchmen who worked the land and many who owned it were peasants, maintaining the old ways, producing without worrying much about the market, relying above all on the natural productiveness of the land. It would be late in the century before a significant proportion of them tied their production to the needs of the market, because it would be late in the century before the market became significant and accessible to them. Thus, the weight of live animals slaughtered in the departments of the Limousin—Corrèze, Creuse, and Haute-Vienne—changed very little between 1840 and 1852; the number of cattle specially fattened for the market appears to have been negligible indeed.[6] The end of labor was to feed the laborer and his family, not to obtain cash. We observe, for example, that meat, the chief source of cash profits, was hardly exploited to that end. The network of trade and the mentality of the producer remained, in economic terms, at the archaic stage.

There is some argument about when all this changed. One view sees the

* Speaking of the economy of Vergigny (Yonne) after the Revolution, Georges Lizerand has noted: "La consistance générale de la propriété n'a pas changé.... Quant à l'économie rurale, aucune révolution ne s'est produite.... La structure foncière et même sociale de Vergigny n'a pas été modifiée radicalement." (*Un Siècle d'histoire d'une commune rurale*, pp. 20–21.) This is not to suggest that there had been no change at all, but only to draw attention to how relatively slight it was. Peasants as a whole did not own much more of the French soil under Charles X than they had owned under Louis XVI. But more of them owned *some*, and their numbers probably increased with time. In 1862, according to the Agricultural Survey, there were 1,812,000 peasant landowners who worked their own lands; 1,987,000 smallholders who supplemented their holdings by working another's lands as tenants, sharecroppers, or simply laborers; 588,000 tenant farmers or sharecroppers who owned no land; and nearly three million (2,965,000) landless farm servants and hired hands. Twenty years later, the situation was "slowly changing." For one thing, the first category, peasant landowners, had risen to 2,150,696, largely at the expense of the second. For another, landless and land-poor laborers were beginning to leave the land in increasing numbers. (Marcel Faure, *Les Paysans dans la société française*, Paris, 1966, pp. 15–17.)

1840's as *one* turning point, a period in which the areas of predominantly large-scale farming experienced their agricultural revolution. Such areas, however, as we know them, lie mainly in the north; and good portions of, say, Marne and Aisne only abandoned mixed farming and self-sufficiency for cash crops in the 1870's. But even if we were to accept the 1840's theory, it applies to only a limited portion of the country. Virtually all of the center, the south, and the west are excluded; and there the great survey of 1848 suggests that eighteenth-century advances accounted for whatever progress there was, and that methods of work on the whole remained those of the Ancien Régime. Michel Augé-Laribé, a man wholly knowledgeable about agricultural conditions in his country, insisted that between 1860 and 1880 peasants in poor regions, which were "more widespread than is usually recognized," were still close, in their life and methods, to the late Stone Age. It is a potent statement—and one that should give pause to anyone envisioning a rural France in the throes of modernization during the Second Empire.[7]

Progress there was. But, as in every other realm, it was slow, patchy, and only substantial enough to be apparent in very limited areas. Until about 1880 the peasant's life was little affected by it. In 1882, says Alain Corbin, the Limousin was little touched by agricultural changes, except those that affected cattle raising. The conditions of labor had not changed, productivity had hardly increased, most of the improvements in crops and fertilizer were still unknown, and most peasants still practiced a mixed farming designed to satisfy their own needs.[8]

The real changes in the rural economy came only in subsequent decades. This is confirmed by evidence from Lower Brittany, Lozère, Auvergne, and the Landes, in all of which the watershed between the old agriculture and the new (for the mass of peasants) seems to lie in the 20-odd years before 1914. This is when wooden plows were replaced by improved models, when manure and artificial fertilizers appeared in significant quantities, when tools and methods "so primitive that they deserve to figure in a museum of prehistory" gave way. In Dordogne the ancient symbiosis between the poor, birch-covered highlands and the more prosperous chestnut country below endured until 1900, with tribes of hill people coming down to work for the valley farmers, gathering chestnuts on a 50–50 basis. But by that time the closed economy had broken down. Easier communications and imports of foreign grain had turned poor mountain regions to dairy farming. And greater access to fertilizer was carrying others, like the area around Valensole, above the old subsistence levels.[9]

Rouergue and Quercy had traditionally been divided between the *pays fromental* of the Causse, the calcareous tableland where roads were good and dry and wheat grew in abundance, and the Ségala plateau, where every shower made roads impassable and only rye (*seigle*) could be grown. Roads came to the Ségala in the 1880's and 1890's, and with them there came liming, then chemical fertilizers, to drive back rye, the poor man's fare, for the nobler wheat. By 1910 the Ségala was only a place-name, and its people like the Caussiens ate white bread. In Bourbonnais poor holdings on barren lands with no roads had names like Brame-faim (Bellow hunger) and, in several places, Tout-y-faut (All's wanting). "Today," wrote a local folklorist in 1908, "as a result of agricultural improvements, two such domains have changed their character, and their name, to Rien n'y manque [Naught's wanting]!" A parallel evolution can be traced in Saintonge, rich in lieuxdits with similar implications: Poussepenilles (Rags and tatters), Brusse-misère (Wretched brush), Les Chiches (The niggards), Pain-perdu (Lost bread), Petit-gain (Little gain), Porte-fâche (Troublemaker), and a host of Tout-y-fauts and Toutlifauts, some of which, at a later date, received more innocuous names like Tour-Garnier and Beaumanoir.[10]

Any attempt to systematize the process or for that matter to provide a systematic account of it is bound to obscure how immensely varied was the reality. Any attempt at theoretical order turns genuine confusion, coexistence, interpenetration, into a picture more artificial and clearer than it really was. The reader is well advised who keeps this point in mind. Yet if we do not divide the organic jumble into (some of) its component parts, we may also miss what happened.

Daniel Faucher, in a discussion of such changes, has divided the "agricultural revolution" into four stages: the first is that of *fallow* or, rather, of its abolition, which he dates back to the eighteenth century. The second, the *biological* revolution, took place in the nineteenth century, with advances in root crops and the growing of fodder. Next, in the mid-nineteenth century, came the *chemical* revolution bringing improved soils, changes of crops (e.g., from rye to wheat) and increased yields. Then, finally, there followed in the late nineteenth century the *machine* revolution, which completed the process of modernization.[11] These categories are as good as any for those who want to see what actually took place. But the first thing one encounters is that, in general, Faucher's periodization anticipates events, presenting first steps, however significant, as if they had been the norm. Perhaps the exceptions to them were closer to the norm.

Certainly, population growth and land hunger in the eighteenth century led many to turn to less and less productive parts of mountain, moor, or forest, and even to encroach on rural roads. We hear about it in the Pyrenees; and in the Argonne under Napoleon I a man was brought to court for plowing up and planting a local road.[12] But in many parts the clearing of land for cultivation awaited the division of common lands in the late nineteenth century; and in any case did not become truly "revolutionary" until the ancient practice of letting fields lie fallow (every other year in the south, one year in three in the north) was abandoned, and the plots used as cropland.

Commons, which played a crucial role in the village economy as pasturage and as a fallback and resource for the poorer inhabitants, were slow to be abandoned. Burnbeating as a means of improving the soil was long used on moors and in forest clearings in Dauphiné, the Ardennes, the Breton interior, the Limousin. In Allier, until the 1880's, many fields (the worst, according to our informant, but a lot were in this category) were left uncultivated for two or three years to become covered with broom, which was torn out before clearing and used for domestic heating, family bread-ovens, and, of course, *balais*. In Upper Corrèze, until around 1880, when the commons at last began to be divided, landless peasants set fire to the briar heath, cleared a few acres, worked them for three or four years without any manure, then moved to another place. In Ardennes, almost to the present day, such lands were put through a 20-year cycle: burned off at the end of summer, to be planted in rye for two years; used next for two years for a vigorous growth of broom, which was cut for stable litter; and then left to revert to forest brush for 15 years or so, when the whole process was repeated. In 1835 attempts to suppress such practices provoked a popular outcry against proposals that "condemned the working population to hunger," which when ignored gave rise to the *sarteux* riots of 1837. As late as 1897, this *sartage* was still practiced in half the common forests (about 6,000 hectares) of the arrondissement of Rocroi.[13]

Clearly, this was not the most productive way of using land. But here, as in other instances, resistance to change was not a mere stubborn blindness, but rather a clinging to ways without which the economy of household and community fell apart. Thus in the Limousin, where land clearing for regular cultivation got going only at the turn of the century, the peasant continued to rely on the gorse and broom that grew on uncleared lands for stable litter as long as straw was used in paper manufacture and was more profitably sold for that purpose. Nor was private initiative easy even off the commons when it went contrary to custom, as in the Limousin, where fallow roads (*chemins de jachère*) were sowed over every other year so cereals could be grown. Tradition imposed a biennial rotation that all were forced to respect—whether they wanted to or not.[14]

Moreover, abandoning fallow required finding some other means of nourishing the soil. But what Faucher calls the chemical revolution came late in many regions. For a long time natural fertilizers played (or at least could have played) the most important role. In places where cattle were few or absent, such as the Moyenne Garonne, dovecotes were maintained to provide pigeon droppings (*colombine*), without which cash crops like hemp and tobacco could simply not be grown.* But through most of the country manure was

---

* Pierre Deffontaines, *Les Hommes et leurs travaux*, p. 54. The expense of this important item (even in 1830, 20 liters of colombine, or something over five gallons, cost five francs) goes a long way toward explaining why the lord's exclusive right to build and keep a dovecote particularly angered the peasants. But it was a burden they had to shoulder for years; only chemical fertilizers would kill the *pigeonnier*.

simply dung, and there, as a contemporary chorus deplored, its potential was largely overlooked. Some regions seem scarcely to have used manure before 1830 (Haute-Garonne). At that, they were 40 years ahead of the Limousin, where the use of dung and liquid manure to enrich the fields spread only after 1870. Equally important, when dungheaps were kept for this purpose they were generally ill-managed, their riches allowed to wash away and go to waste. Indifference and ignorance, combined with lack of means, lasted well into the Third Republic. It would be the greater number and weight of cattle that placed more manure at the peasant's fork. In most places this development, too, began in the 1880's.[15]

As the proverb puts it, "Who has hay has bread." Hay feeds cattle, cattle give manure, manure makes crops grow. But cattle continued to be small and scrawny, underbred, underfed, and overworked, their contribution to the dungheap not nearly as impressive as their numbers might suggest. Horses were no better. As an army officer reported in 1838: "There are plenty of horses, but one could not use them; they are almost all blind in one eye or in both, small, and sapless." Army officers cared less about livestock, but as we have noted, the existing figures paint a lean picture for the Limousin, today a major source of France's meat supply.[16] Similarly in the Morvan, the white Charolais breed appeared only after 1840. Chroniclers of the mid-century west agree on its *chétifs bestiaux*. In 1858 the peasants of Mayenne called on each other to help get enfeebled beasts to their feet so they could be led to drink. There was even a routine method of doing this, with the strongest man hauling on the animal's tail.[17] It would be a decade before specialization and select breeding would show results at the grass-roots level in these parts.*

True, urban meat consumption rose through the Restoration and the July Monarchy, and meat prices rose accordingly. This, along with a government policy that was designed to keep grain prices low, turned some farmers to cattle. However, many others remained outside the commercial network, oblivious to market conditions. More immediate considerations had to suggest new possibilities.

The first of these was, again, the need for more and richer manure. And that meant more fodder, the increased production of which depended on other forms of fertilizer, above all lime. Improving acid soils with lime was not a new method, but it was one that was limited to limestone regions or areas within easy range of limekilns. Elsewhere, lime was rare and was reserved for the building of churches and manors. When, for political reasons, the Vendée got highways in the 1840's, well before they would normally have been built, fields in the *bocage* could be limed and sowed with wheat "for the rich." But even then carted lime was still too high for many. Canals, then railways, brought cheap lime to the peasants along their paths. But beyond

---

* And even longer (after 1870) before the local nags would be replaced by black draft-horses capable of going to a trot.

their radius and that of the coastal ports, there were vast areas where the price of lime continued to be prohibitive until branch lines were constructed in the last third of the century.[18] Peasants consoled themselves with the thought that, as the proverb claimed, lime enriched the father but impoverished the son.* Nevertheless, a map of lime consumption in Creuse and Haute-Vienne at the turn of the century (indicating, as one might expect, highest consumption along railway lines and around railway stations) shows a clear coincidence between the use of lime and intensive and prosperous farming, often on land that had been barren shortly before.[19]

Communications were crucial in the history of fertilizer, which took its time to travel: like the slag that only began to be used in Bresse in 1890 and the guano that was first imported in 1840 but only reached Dordogne around 1870. Guano and the chemical fertilizers, when they were introduced, were bought with reluctance, partly because of scandals over the adulteration, cheating, and extortionate prices that had marked the trade of these products, partly because of their cost, and the cost of transport. Even in regions like Normandy they did not really spread until just before the First World War, and more generally, only after it.[20]

Change in equipment was also slow and halting. Traditional farm implements had changed little if at all since ancient days. The sixteenth-century agronomist Olivier de Serres, who recommended crop rotation, nevertheless felt Cato's warning worth repeating: "Do not change your plowshare, for every change carries with it the danger of loss." As long as subsistence remained marginal, the danger of loss ensured that his warning would be heeded. Wooden swing plows of the most ancient model were in general use south and west of the heavy northern soils at least into mid-century, and survived in some places even longer. The improved dombasle plow was adopted generally in Dordogne between 1840 and 1890, in Morbihan between 1850 and 1860, in Livradois in the 1860's, in Savoy in the 1870's. But coexistence was more typical. In the Alps the dombasle had settled into the alpine valleys by the late 1860's, but the medieval swing plow was preferred in mountain areas, where roads were few and bad, because it was light and could be easily carried. In Aveyron, where the dombasle also spread through the 1860's, and in Ariège, where the first dombasle appeared in 1837, the old *araire* survived through the century. In Corrèze the most widely used plow through most of the century was a form of the old wooden one, homemade of birch, with a metal-tipped share of beech or oak. Around 1885 this plow acquired an iron moldboard; around 1890 it was replaced by the dombasle. Finally, in 1920, there came the heavy brabant, named after the Belgian province where

---

* This had reference to the fact that by the 1870's some lands had been overlimed, almost to their ruination. Musset, who cites the proverb (*Le Bas-Maine*, pp. 331–32), notes the efforts in that area in the 1880's to break down the peasants' *résistance routinière* and get them to use less lime. Routine catches on quickly!

it had been developed, a metal plow with a forecarriage and, as a rule, a pair of plowshares.

There was a world of difference between Corrèze and Aisne, where the brabant was in general use as early as 1860. The conditions in Corrèze and other regions slow to make the transition simply did not encourage change. There was the quality of the soil: the lighter the soil, the lighter the plow that could work it. There were the physical features of the land: certain mountainous patches could not accommodate larger, heavier gear. As long as such land was worked for crops, the old portable plows were more appropriate. Indeed, in parts of the Midi, on steep slopes, for instance, where plowing was awkward, the hoe, *la charrue du pauvre*, reigned supreme. There, as the rustic said, *lou bigot* [hoe] *vau maï que l'araire*, and farmland was traditionally evaluated in terms of hoeing days (*journals de fossure*). There was, finally, the search—the need—for self-sufficiency. The peasants' tools were homemade. Passage from wooden plows to plows with iron parts meant relying on others. The peasant who had once made his gear at home had to turn to the village smith for a metal tip for his wooden share, then for much more with the dombasle. The brabant lay beyond even the smithy. Bought in the market, it meant a substantial investment of capital, not only for the equipment itself but for the animals to pull it, passage to a different stage of productivity.

No wonder accommodation to new gear was slow. In Savoy, where in the 1860's Tarentaise and Maurienne still used wooden Roman araires and other cantons medieval plows with a double moldboard, newer models were resisted for a time because they seemed so fragile and village artisans could not replace damaged parts, making repair costly. In some villages of Comminges in the mid-1880's the plow had only just appeared to ease the peasant's work, heretofore carried out with hand tools: a shovel equipped with moldboard (for stubble plowing), a spade and hoe for corn, and a wooden mallet to break up the clods. The plows came in, and then animal traction, so that where hardly half the peasants of Comminges had had a yoke of oxen in the 1850's by the late 1880's everyone had his pair.[21]

Comminges was poor; Touraine relatively wealthy. Yet there, too, improvements in equipment came late, beginning in the 1890's. This was true even beyond the poor *terres froides* of the plateaus, because the best lands had been so divided up that plows could not turn in the narrow strips. In the Varennes region, whose alluvial soil produced the best hemp in France, an old proverb indicates that the horse stayed in the stable, the plow stayed in the shed, and one worked with the spade. The rule continued to apply in this prosperous region as late as 1900 or so, when farmers still used a rake for harrowing.[22]

Humbler tools showed the same persistence as the plow, notably the sickle. Scythe and sickle coexisted in many regions, the scythe used for haymaking, the sickle for harvesting. The scythe was vastly more efficient: one could work much more quickly, two or three times as fast as with a sickle, and could crop close to the ground, thus saving straw and a lot of labor. Agricultural societies did all they could to boost scythes, both by featuring them in the shows and contests they organized and by sending harvesters out to resistant areas to show what the scythe could do. But the farm laborers, especially, opposed the scythe for excellent reasons: because their women, following after the harvesters, gleaned less straw and fewer fallen ears of corn, especially when rakes came in to supplement the scythe. So not only did the sickle continue in use into the twentieth century in the highlands and other places where the terrain made scything difficult, the struggle over its displacement lasted longer in the plains than mere considerations of efficiency would have decreed: until the 1870's in the plains of Gard; through the third quarter of the century in Indre-et-Loire and Indre, and even in the poorer regions of Champagne, like Brenne and Borschaut; to about 1890 in the canton of Foix, even though the scythe had been introduced there half a century earlier, around 1840.[23]

Moreover, certain varieties of grain, like the red wheat of Limagne, were easier to harvest using sickles. Though the scythe could cut faster, the sickle permitted a more uniform cut, with ears at the same level, so there was less loss of grain in threshing. With machines the peasant was able to harvest grain at its peak of ripeness, as he likes to do, without chancing the losses he faced with the scythe, but there were places where machines would not work well or where the peasant could not afford them. Hence in the Corrèze hills, until the First World War, meadows were cleared with scythes, but rye, oats, and buckwheat were harvested with sickles. "With a scythe," observed a Corrézien, "one would have lost grain, and it would have been difficult to gather the small conical sheaves that one set up to dry." Observe that the practical reason, here, rested on a traditional base. Sheaves were set up in a particular way, and it was hard to learn to do things otherwise. Above all, perhaps, the abundance of labor into the 1850's and in some places in the 1860's prolonged the life of the sickle: it may have meant hiring more harvesters and working them for far more days, but harvesters were plentiful and cheap. Furthermore, sickles demanded no great skill or strength, whereas it took a strong, fit man to wield the scythe. So, for example, we learn that in Gers women did the harvesting, with sickles, until 1885, and after that the work was done, with scythes, by men.[24]

In a way, the progress of the scythe was coterminous with that of machinery; both were appreciated as a way of saving labor or replacing it when the supply of farmworkers dried up. In certain areas, that is to say, the Loire valley, for example, sickles gave way only to mechanical mowers. The machine was a device to replace scarce labor, not to increase production. Mowers, reapers, harvesters, and combines made little sense to most farmers as long as local hands or gangs from poorer regions could do the work as well or more cheaply. The scarcity of labor, higher wages, and better working conditions, all relative of course, but clustering at the end of the century, help explain why harvesting machines were generally adopted before improved plows were—or seed drills. Thus in Aveyron, reported the Agricultural Survey, it was after 1900 and especially 1905, "when depopulation began to be seriously felt," that machines came in and "notions of productivity and of the importance of time penetrated the peasant's soul." And it was then, too, that "the mediocrity of life [was] replaced by a certain comfort."[25]

Still, one must be careful not to confuse appearance with use, let alone general use.* In 1867, J. A. Barral tells us, the owner of a prize-winning farm in Nord had bought a harvester but hardly used it. It was less satisfactory than the Flemish short-handled scythe with which his wheat was cut, but he kept it there "as a sort of warning for the workers who, this way, understand that one can do without them if one has to; and this sort of warning is very necessary these days." Conversely, as a teacher reported in 1886 from Salerm (Haute-Garonne), sharecroppers took the owner's plow into the fields along with their own wooden ones, but used it only if there was a chance of his turning up. Under the circumstances, it is not surprising that when the first reaper-binders appeared in Lower Dauphiné during the 10 to 15 years before 1914, they provoked the ire of the harvesters.[26]

It was not only their wages that machines affected, it was their way of life. Implements made at home, often individualized to fit the owner's needs and circumstances (for example, to accommodate a left-handed man),[27] had been replaced by village-crafted products, then by standardized gear brought from far away. The long accumulation of details discretely borrowed as suited the local situation had been precipitated into radical change, and no facet of family or village life was left unmarked by it. With reaper-binders came compressed bales of hay and straw too heavy for women to handle; so women, already nudged out by scythes, stayed more than ever out of the fields.† When haying, harvesting, and threshing had been done by hand, involving several weeks of backbreaking work each day from before sunrise past dark, it was natural to greet their flagging end with feasts and rejoicing. With machines, however, these tasks were no longer memorable trials, their completion less of an event. We shall see how, with machines, with production no longer regulated by custom, a mass of popular traditions and feasts were either abandoned altogether or became hollow rituals.[28]

---

* In the Jura, for example, the temporary meadows that altered the crop-rotation pattern of the mountainside dated back to the introduction of sainfoin in 1786, but they only became a general part of the Jura landscape in the 1880's ("Enquête sur . . . l'agriculture," Jura, Musée des Arts et Traditions Populaires archives).

† Women's roles also altered in regions that shifted from crops to cattle. With the men spending a good part of their time traveling to markets and fairs, women became dominant in the operation of the farm. (See "Enquête sur . . . l'agriculture," Calvados, Musée des Arts et Traditions Populaires archives.)

For all this, the grounds for the peasants' resistance to new methods were more often practical than social or psychological. For example, over a period of perhaps 15 years, from the 1880's to 1895, the people of Roger Thabault's Mazières fought hard against the introduction of new plows and persisted in using the sickle. Why? Sickles were appropriate to raftered fields, in which two plowed furrows formed a ridge that would be a nuisance for the scythe. The introduction of the dombasle or brabant would have eliminated the ridges and allowed the use of scythes. But their adoption involved profound changes all along the line, affecting not only equipment, but the drainage of the land. It was not traditions that prevented change; it was conditions and circumstances that had imposed traditional methods, and that would maintain them until they themselves could be changed.[29]

As Jean Cuisenier tells us, attached though the Tunisian peasants of Ansarine were to traditional methods, many passed without difficulty from their primitive araire to the improved *charrue vigneronne*. The tool was new, but they could use it with the same team (oxen or mules) as their older plow. It called for no additional investment in draft animals, hence necessitated no increase in land for their upkeep. Like the harrow, adopted with equal ease, the innovation fitted into tradition and made no demands for change on the existing order of things. In contrast, from *charrue vigneronne* to the all-metal brabant the distance was immense, and for most Ansarine fellahs insurmountable. To work a brabant in the *djebel*, one needed at least five pair of oxen, which had to be fed, cared for, and replaced. This supposed a much vaster farm, and more important, the knowhow to run it, a training and experience that few could have acquired on their limited holdings.[30]

In the end, then, which implements were used and how new ones were adopted depended on the possibilities of the land: the living standard it afforded and its potential for supporting improvements; the nature of individual plots and the demands they made (we have seen that in some cases novelties were inappropriate and no improvement); the structural characteristics of fields and the communal servitudes these may have imposed;[31] even the kind of crop, for corn was more labor-intensive than wheat, and root crops when they came cut not only into the pool of local labor but into the time the peasant had to make his own pitchforks and harrows.[32] And so on.

Land-tenure patterns were important too. Where sharecropping, itself testimony to poverty, was widespread—in the southwest, the center, and the southeast—its effects on agriculture were generally negative. The tenant, who most often held the land on verbal lease (or on a short-term written lease for as little as one year), was unsure of his tenure and unwilling to make improvements. The owner, equally unsure of his tenant and drawing little profit from his property, was not eager to invest in it either. Sheer poverty made sharecroppers conservative. At Saint-Germain-les-Belles (Haute-Vienne), where the average grain yield in mid-century was only five times the quantity of seed sowed, "implements are wretched, because they cannot buy good ones. Cattle are poor, because there are no studs." The sharecroppers farmed largely for their own consumption, not for the market. And "since they generally have to furnish the gear and keep it up, they avoid expense, keep that of their fathers, and endlessly repair it." In the Pyrenees we find references, in 1895-96, to delays in sowing due to old, ineffective tools, used because the landowners were unwilling to spend anything on new equipment. Hence "farmers stagnate in the old routines."[33] Altogether, sharecropping was typically where the old survivals resisted longest and in greatest numbers.* It was also the form of farming that diminished most rapidly between 1882 and 1929 in all departments where it had been a notable feature.

Mutatis mutandis, what has been said about sharecropping applies to tenant farms as well. In parts of Brittany a form of holding called *domaine congéable* went counter to any improvement, especially of buildings. It required that every building be repaired or reconstructed exactly as it had stood, which meant that even in 1907 thatched, mud-walled cabins were being rebuilt as they had always been; and new ones were mostly built on the old model. But even straightforward leases seem to have discouraged tenants from making improvements lest the owners be moved to raise their rent. Jean Vidalenc mentions that the great agricultural reformer Mathieu de Dombasle himself only got an ironclad 20-year lease at Roville thanks to the intervention of Charles X. The tenants' situation was no less precarious nearly a century later. The best they could do, wrote Paul Mayer, was to buy machinery and quality cattle. And indeed, cattle breeding could bring high returns, incomparably higher than those to be gained from cereals. But then this required real capital, as did developing and improving land. J. A. Barral's studies reveal the costs involved in building access roads, draining, clearing, and fertilizing new acres, buying equipment, and quite simply acquiring the economic and scientific knowledge necessary to do all this. The task was quite beyond the average peasant, let alone the poor one.[34]

"Today," said Barral in 1870, "to farm with profit, one has to know a lot."[35] Few did, even in the prosperous north.† And those tempted to innovate were

---

* On the other side, though, Musset saw sharecropping in Lower Maine not as a source of backwardness but, on the contrary, as the starting point of all improvements: "instrument of progress," "alliance of capital and labor." The resident owners (especially after 1852) initiated improvements in all fields, and their sharecroppers slowly followed their example; it was the tenant farmers and smallholders who stubbornly resisted, presumably for lack of capital to follow suit. (*Le Bas-Maine,* p. 327.) See also Comte de Tourdonnet, *Situation du métayage en France* (Paris, 1879–80), p. 99.

† Most significant, in this respect, is the absence of accounting or even of the sense of the need of it. For a few examples among many: "les cultivateurs de notre région ne se rendent compte qu'en gros et dans l'ensemble de l'état de leurs affairs" (Xavier Thiriat, *La Vallée de Cleurié,* p. 278); few keep accounts, even fewer figure their own labor as a production cost (M. F. Pariset, *Montagne Noire,* p. 168); of 250 households in the commune of Miremont, in Combrailles, only two or three were known to keep accounts (Archives Départementales, Puy-

often held back by social pressure. Landowners could not favor good incumbents because they were expected to treat their tenants just as neighboring landowners did. Ordinary villagers came under pressure from their fellows. This ranged from loud and repeated predictions of ruin and sterility to more forceful forms of disapproval.* In addition, material conditions bolstered natural conservatism, and preconceived ideas of the immutability of things worked against the possibilities of innovation and held off change effectively enough to make negative judgments self-fulfilling—at least for a while. As might be expected, those improvements that took place were suggested or imposed from the outside, and tended to catch on best where outsiders (by dint of proximity, residence, or economic control) were most numerous, most influential, and least isolated. Where this was not the case, and where the cohesion of peasant groups was greatest, resistance to innovation was greatest too.[36]

It is clear that such resistance reflected a correct estimate on the part of the peasants of their true situation. The modern improvements extolled by outsiders made perfectly good sense on the outsider's terms. For the peasants they could not be accepted freely, except as part of a broader complex of change that would replace the existing working complex. As Father Serge Bonnet noted, before the peasant of Lorraine had access to insurance for his crops and cattle, the parceling out of land, the common pasture, and the three-yearly crop rotation were forms of agricultural insurance. This is where the commons played an important role, as factors and indicators of local change. This is why the commons survived when dominant economic thought would have liked to see them abolished. Then, as private improvements increased, common lands came to mean less, and to matter to fewer people. In Lorraine the number of applicants seeking permission to clear and plant them shrank. In the Limousin advances in cattle-breeding similarly resulted in a decrease in the number of those interested in using common pastures. More important, the cost (but also the common interest now) of building local roads, then schools and other municipal installations, could be met only by selling off the commons.[37] The rich farmers (the term is relative) who sat on municipal councils wanted to sell or rent common lands, especially common forests, and use their revenue profitably. They could afford to buy their own coal. The poor peasants, whose budget depended on the right to cut or gather firewood, could not heat or feed themselves adequately without the proceeds of

de-Dôme F 0274, schoolteacher's report, 1899). Compare J. A. Barral, *Agriculture du Nord*, 1: 10, speaking of a sugarbeet factory at Masuy (Nord), where the head bookkeeper got 3,500 francs a year against 60 francs a month for laborers, 75 for overseers, and 110 for chief overseers: "Il faut savoir payer les bons employés, et la dépense faite pour la comptabilité est une des mieux placées . . . productive par les enseignements qu'elle fournit."

* Around 1835 a city man farming in Vendée planted rape-seed instead of the usual spring barley, food of the poor. His neighbors vented their anger at this by cutting down both his crop and his newly planted stand of walnut trees (Jules Michelet, *Journal*, Paris, 1959, 1: 165, quoted by J. J. Hémardinquer, *Pour une histoire de l'alimentation*, p. 269).

gleaning.* Deprived of these marginal resources, they migrated more willingly.

So the developments (schools, roads, economic advances) that facilitated emigration also created the situation that precipitated it, by eliminating the traditional means the peasant had used to make ends meet. Land not used to capacity was developed, and with development there came depopulation and a sort of social fallow. Soon, the innovative rich farmers would sorely miss the squeezed-out farmworkers at harvest and spring sowing, and would have to restrict their operations or invest in machinery. Soon, too, the last survivals would be put to rest without great opposition: a law of 1891 established total liberty for all to grow what they pleased in whatever way they pleased; *parcours* and common grazing lands were legally abolished in 1899; gleaning rights after harvest, even for the poor, lapsed around 1914.

At the turn of the century, there were fewer poor, the margin of subsistence was broader, poverty counted less heavily in the way resources were shared out. Fallow had shrunk by more than one-third between 1862 and 1882, by well over half in wild country like Haute-Loire. Meadows and grasslands devoted to fodder had nearly tripled in size. More fodder, more cattle; more cattle, more manure; more manure, more productive fields. Tillage was deeper, chemical fertilizer more abundant. The peasant grew more of everything, but where in the 1880's the rise in productivity had most affected poorer crops like rye, by 1912 rye had leveled off and the more noble wheat had forged ahead.[38] Quality improved along with quantity: tokens of prosperity and of a change in diet.

---

* The decay of gleaning, a practice most farmers and winegrowers had always resented, is a complex story, best followed in the pages of Paul Degrully, *Le Droit de glanage, grapillage, ratelage, chaumage et sarclage: Patrimoine des pauvres* (Paris, 1912), especially pp. 138–40. In the 1860's and 1870's the practice still yielded profits sufficient to provide girls with Sunday dresses and to prompt employers' complaints that journeymen's wives refused to be hired at harvest time, preferring to glean in the fields of the farmers for whom they would not work (see "Enquête sur . . . l'agriculture," Marne, Musée des Arts et Traditions Populaires archives), or that servant-girls left their regular jobs, preferring the pickings of *glanage* or *grapillage* to the "dur labeur du métier." By 1910 or so, in Berry at least, Degrully found only a few old women picking up some grain for their chickens.

Various factors contributed to the waning of the practice. The growing number of smallholders tended to harvest their crops with great care, and cut down much of what a hired harvester would have left; the increased use of scythes and rakes, then of machines more efficient than human hands, had similar effects; the gradual disappearance of local mills, easily accessible to the local poor, made it more difficult to dispose of gleanings or turn them into flour. Besides, quite simply, gleaning was hard work and when alternatives offered they were seized. Degrully tells us that peasant women preferred to sew at home for Paris stores, earning as much as 60 centimes for 12 or 14 hours' work. "As for the men, they have better things to do!"

Chapter Nine

GIVE US THIS DAY

Ce n'est pas le malheur, c'est le bonheur qui est contre nature.
La condition naturelle d'un homme comme d'un animal c'est
d'être assommé ou de mourir de faim.

—HIPPOLYTE TAINE

"As FA! mandja ta ma, garda l'aoutro per dema!" Many's the snuffling child
or the pinched adult who must have heard it: "You are hungry! Eat your
hand, keep the other for tomorrow!"[1] We have already seen how hunger had
its place at the peasant's board well into the nineteenth century. To pass from
hunger to subsistence and from subsistence to a degree of sufficiency is to make
the transition from the ancient to the modern world. In rural France real
hunger only disappeared, or minds only adjusted to its disappearance, as the
twentieth century was dawning.

But perhaps not all minds even then, for to this day there are those in
Franche-Comté who remember the older generation as being very stingy about
food and as giving children as little as possible to eat. That was how they had
been brought up in the last third of the nineteenth century, in a world that
still recalled and feared famine. From the Pyrenees to the Vosges, old peoples'
memories, sole archives of the poor, told of the calamities of the living past:
the requisitions of year II of the Revolution, the dearth of 1816, the hunger
of the 1840's, the years of hail and of grain rotten before it was ripe, the difficult
days of spring when reserves ran out, the shortages when bread was made of
barley or beans, and those when there was no bread.* The call for one's daily
bread remained an anxious prayer.

The proverbs remembered the lean years, continually reminding countrymen, if they should need reminding, of the belly's need to be filled with
anything as long as it was filled, or even half filled. Language remembered
them, too, rich with locutions that meant cutting things fine, eating just
enough to stay alive, giving a tailor barely the necessary cloth; and with

---

* The disettes of 1817, 1818, and 1848 and the terrible bread of the times were still discussed
at Cheylade in Cantal in the 1880's (Pierre Besson, *Un Pâtre du Cantal*, pp. 67–69). Memories
died even harder at Clessé in Mâconnais, where the famine of 1817, year of the great hailstorm
when nutshells had been ground up in an attempt to make bread, was still vivid in people's minds
in 1890 (Emile Violet, *Clessé*, pp. 114ff).

ritual phrases exhorting to economy: you've got to live hard, you've got to stretch things out, you mustn't eat everything at once. "A grasse cuisine, pauvreté voisine" and "Morceau avalé n'a plus de goût." Conclusion: better save it!²

It was easy to remember all this for, to mid-century, everyday life carried everyday reminders of past scarcity in present need. Conditions under Louis Philippe were not terribly different from those under his older cousins. Salt, for instance, staff of the staff of life, remained scarce and dear, and was treated like something precious long after the Revolution abolished the gabelles. It was stored in special boxes or in the seat of chairs carefully kept near the fire, and was sometimes replaced by a variety of wild sorrel known as salt grass. When Lamartine abolished the salt tax in 1848 and sorrel was no longer needed as a fallback, peasants—at least in Lamartine's own Mâconnais—called it Monsieur de Lamartine's grass. Projected new taxes on salt, when they were mooted, continued to stir the strongest resentment. For a good reason, too, as we can learn from the sub-prefect of Saint-Girons in 1862, who observed: "In the countryside, where the political news never penetrates, people paid heed to [the proposed tax] immediately. It is the only expense for peasants of this district."³

Money was scarce, we know; and money was paid out grudgingly for sustenance—for the *nécessaire*, as it was sometimes and revealingly called, should not exceed what was absolutely needed. And this was meager. In 1881 the Directeur des contributions directes in Haute-Loire wrote a report that echoed almost exactly the report filed by a predecessor 30 years earlier, which had estimated that 17 of 20 inhabitants were indigent or close to destitution: "The stranger could not imagine their manner of life, their black bread, their extreme deprivation of wine and meat, even pigs' meat,...their tendency to stint themselves of everything and utterly neglect their own well-being, their every moment's concern to save centime by centime. It is only in behaving thus and living close to misery each day that they can manage to escape it."⁴

Most people skirting misery daily sought to get by, or had to get by, with the bare minimum. This was sometimes bread or pancakes, always *la soupe*. The soupe, which could be gruel, porridge, any kind of hodge-podge boiled with water, or just water with salt or fat added, was the core and base of the peasant's diet. "*Soupe* makes the man, woman makes the *soupe*," declared the proverb; and making soupe was the woman's first task. To cook a meal was "faire la soupe"; "venir souper" was to come and eat; souper, of course, means the evening meal. Indeed, satiety was measured by it: "J'en ai soupé" means I've had enough. And it was sometimes even used for comparisons, as in Franche-Comté, where if you could not make anything good of something or someone, you said one could not make a good soupe of it or him. So soupe was basic, and a basic food was often the only dish: pottage of corn, millet, buckwheat, chestnuts, cabbage, turnips, or potatoes, with bread made of barley or rye, and water or milk for drinking. For a holiday, wine, cider, or meat was served if possible.[5]

In Côtes-du-Nord the peasant of means ate lard once a week and bread once a day. In Forez, where he grew up, Benoît Malon remembered that they ate rye bread soaked in salt water with a thimbleful of butter in it, morning, noon and night, with a piece of dry bread after and, on feast days, an apple or a piece of cheese. At about mid-century the peasants of Hautes-Alpes were said to be very happy just to have bread, "even hard and black, even a year old and all of rye." In Tarn, noted a traveler's guide of 1852, the poorer peasants greased their vegetable diet with a little lard in a small bag, which they plunged briefly in the cooking pot and used over and over for as long as it would last.[6] The potato, of course, was a crucial staple; a crop failure could condemn half the population to underfeeding or worse. As the Vivarais proverb had it, when there were potatoes, the rabble could get by: "Quant de tartoflas i a, Canalha s'en sauvara." Or as in the Berrichon song:

> A Givardon, dans un'maison
> Y s'nourront mal com'des cochons
> Durant l'année entière,
>   Eh ben!
> Y s'bourront d'pom's de terre
> Et vous m'entendez ben!
>
> Le p'tit qu'est dans son lit
> Qui baill', qui cri', qui fait la vie,
> Sa mère y dit: Veux-tu t'taire,
>   Eh ben!
> En l'bourrant d'pom's de terre.
>   . . .
> Deux amoureux dans l'coin du feu
> Deux amoureux dans l'coin du feu
> Y'parlont d'ieux affaires,
>   Eh ben!
> En s'bourrant d'pom's de terre. . . .

In the Morvan, it was potatoes, beans, groats, chestnuts where they were available, and beastly bread. In Velay potatoes were the common fare, and bread a luxury not eaten every day. So it goes on. Guy Thuillier quotes a report of 1844 concerning the peasants of Nièvre, who "in winter, having repaired their gear, will take to bed and spend their days in it, pressed against each other to keep warmer and to eat less. They weaken themselves deliberately . . . so as to refuse their body nourishment it doesn't seem to deserve since it remains inactive."[7]

Army reports show that such conditions still prevailed some 20 years later.

"Great frugality": potatoes, garlic, corncakes, seldom bread, meat on rare occasion for the better-off (Haute-Garonne, 1862). Rye bread, potatoes, milk and cheese, soup with some fat, on Sundays lard (Allier, 1864). They have barely begun to eat meat (Cher, 1862). Like an earlier report on Lot, which had attributed the natives' irritability to their diet, several saw undernourishment as the cause of apathy and sloth. One officer observed, economically: "They have many children, but they raise few."[8] Alain Plessis, who finds that the daily caloric intake improved during the Second Empire—rising from 2,480 per capita to 2,875—remarks that from this point of view and by today's criteria, the France of the late 1860's was just about to leave underdevelopment behind.* But only just about. And it is interesting to note that human and animal foods (potatoes, chestnuts, buckwheat) remained interchangeable for quite a while, so that when food was scarce, animals simply got less of it.[9] A spare vegetable diet facilitated transfers between beasts and men.

The increasingly numerous references to improved conditions as the century passed attest that real progress had indeed been made. At the same time they bear equal witness to the low standards of evaluation and to how far things still were from modern expectations. Consider, for example, the improving situation in the Limousin, where the changes in the early 1870's were said to have brought "affluence and well-being"—to the point where in 1874 the production of lands improved by fertilizers "more than suffices for the needs of the inhabitants who, during most of the year, subsist almost exclusively on chestnuts and potatoes." A few years later, a traveler in Valgorge, in southwest Ardèche, noted the frugal regime—soup made of chestnuts including spoiled and moldy ones, rye bread made of unsifted flour, and whatever pittance could be dredged up to go with these, possibly potatoes, curds, or whey, or milk or, mostly, water. In the Mâconnais of the 1890's the standard diet still consisted primarily of bread rubbed with garlic, potato pancakes (to save wheat), and buckwheat wafers (black and sticky).[10]

Yet things were certainly getting better. At Chermisey in the Vosges, where the old proverb said that you could starve even at harvest time, the farmer's weekday diet had changed very little by 1889, but Sunday would see a bit of beef simmering in the stew, and sometimes he might even manage a cup of coffee. "More perhaps than Henry IV had dreamed of," says the *instituteur*.[11] What we hear of now is lack of variety—little or no meat, a poor selection of fruit and fresh vegetables—and boring repetition. Hunger has passed, the

---

* Plessis is cited for the point he makes rather than for his figures. The 2,480 calories per day he mentions is not a bad average. In 1965, the 90 underdeveloped nations of the world had a woefully "low nutritional level" of 2,150 calories per capita per day (René Dumont, *Nous allons à la famine*, Paris, 1966, p. 72). But national averages provide no more than a general indication that further stresses the disparities between urban and rural consumption, the latter of a far lower order. As Bartolomé Bennassar and Joseph Goy conclude: "La campagne nourrit mal" ("Contributions à l'histoire de la consommation alimentaire," p. 417).

cereal-and-vegetable diet marches on.* At an inn near Béage (Ardèche) in 1904 Ardouin-Dumazet watched as the innkeeper's family took their evening meal. "The children sit near the fireplace, where the potatoes are boiling; the potatoes are poured into a basket to drain them, then put on the table. The father crushes them with his fist, grinds up some salt with a bottle, and everyone selects a piece and salts it from the table. A jug of milk for each, and dinner is over."[12] In 1908 day laborers in Cornouaille (who still lived "in indescribable misery") had lard only at feasts and lived off milk products, porridge, and potatoes. That same year Jules Renard described the standard peasant diet in Nièvre: bread, soup (water, salt, lard), salad, onions, radishes. Butter was too expensive; eggs could be sold, so they were not eaten; so could everything else one might be tempted to cook for a feast.[13]

The last point is important, because many have wondered about such penury in the midst of plenty. The peasants seemed to live surrounded by provender. Why should they lack, when so much lay at hand? The fact is that they sold it. Frogs, snails, mushrooms, plentiful in some regions, supplemented the peasants' diet, but were more often gathered for the market.† Still, the countryside loomed rich with edible herbs and leaves: there were larch shoots to chew, and leaves like young holly to brew, plus hawthorn, the "bread and cheese" of the English Lake District. Bilberries and huckleberries were found in Ardèche: shepherds ate them for lack of better fare; mountain villagers made jam of them (good against diarrhea), and even tried to make huckleberry wine. In Basses-Alpes after mid-century beechnuts once grilled and used as coffee were mostly prized for oil, and briar no longer provided a flour substitute. But the kernels of fir-cones (pignons), the wild fruit of mountain ash or cornel tree still supplemented diet. And when the Phylloxera struck a generation later, a good few winegrowers who, in Saintonge at least, had made piquette, not wine, their staple, learned to make do with distilled essence of hawthorn berries, laurel, rosemary, or even beets.[14] None of this went very far, or so we assume, for it is not part of the record. But the record we do have suggests a depressing tale.

The peasant, judged Father Gorse, saved for himself the very scum of his products. The finest potatoes or chestnuts were set aside for sale, the pig he slaughtered for his table was always the most miserable specimen, the butter his wife churned was hardly touched, eggs were for the market, as were the hens and any fish he caught.[15] Even wealthier peasants, a Tarn doctor tells us, sold their birds, rabbits, and eggs in the market and ate like the share-

---

* In 1900 Charles Beauquier found Easter to be the only day of the year when every peasant table in Franche-Comté saw butcher's meat and a sweet: "A Pâques courte messe et long dîner!" (*Traditions populaires*, p. 54.)

† Moreover, diet often depended less on the possibilities than on local custom. The Nièvre peasants, for example, virtually ignored such foods as honey and mushrooms until mid-century. (See Thuillier in J. J. Hémardinquer, *Pour une histoire de l'alimentation*, pp. 158–59, 162.)

cropper and the laborer—with a fuller plate perhaps, but that is all.* "The fatter the kitchen, the thinner the last will." Fish and game were "rare and costly" when the century opened and, though less rare as it advanced, they could still bring a reward. Hence the Morvandiau, whose rivers were full of trout and crayfish, seldom ate his catch. What he did not sell, he used as presents for the upper classes. By Paul Sébillot's account, even the Bretons along the coast ate only the cheapest shellfish and the abundant crabs, selling all the oysters and lobsters that they could. In the Aube of the 1880's, where the vegetable diet seldom varied, the peasants not only sold every bird or fish they bagged, but also sold some of the meat whenever they butchered a pig. What fish they knew was salted or pickled herring, "and many died without ever having tasted a sardine." Only what could not be disposed of or the bare minimum of luxury the peasant permitted himself went into the soupe.[16]

Bread, on the other hand, was jealously guarded—where it was eaten, that is. The prefect of Ariège, for instance, advised the Minister of the Interior that bread crises did not matter in his area because the people never ate the stuff. Whether for lack of means or for reasons of taste, the Pyrenean peasant to the end of the nineteenth century ate corn and oats as gruel rather than bread. In the Couserans a man who rose above his station was said to have moved from porridge to bread; and bread, at the end of the century still kept in a locked cupboard, was reserved for feasts. Yet in most places bread was the end of labor and the very core of the household. A child who wasted something was admonished: "One can see you don't know how the bread comes." And a young couple setting up their household "se mettent à leur pain." Unfortunately, as the proverb had it, when you were young you had teeth but no bread, when you were old you had bread but no teeth. You might lack bread in old age as well; but certainly teeth were crucial if you did have it.[17]

For the most part and for a long time, the peasants' bread was miserable stuff, though not so bad as the loaves of oats and barley that Vauban described, from which the bran had not been removed and which could be lifted up by the straws still sticking out of them. Most bread was homemade, and baking was not always a success; indeed the saying went that a good batch baked was

* Maurice Bastié, *Description ... du Tarn*, 2: 159–60. At mid-century, we hear that in Nièvre better-off peasants lived no differently than their poorest fellows (Adolphe de Bourgoing, "Mémoire en faveur des travailleurs," pp. 398, 401, 402). This is confirmed for a much later period by certain stories by Emile Guillaumin, notably "Le Beurre," in *Dialogues bourbonnais* (Moulins, 1899). Another Guillaumin story features a family dispute between the mother, who is determined to sell all she can in order to get "un p'tit d'argent," and her daughter and daughter-in-law, who complain that they raise everything and never enjoy it ("Au pays des ch'tits gas," in Frantz Brunet, *Dictionnaire du parler bourbonnais*, p. 56). Such sales provided cash for taxes, rents, and what had to be bought in the *boutiqua*: salt, pepper, matches, a bonnet, a small shawl, maybe a calico dress. It has been argued that poaching and fishing were a real resource for the peasants, but even there most evidence suggests that the bulk of their haul was eaten by the middle classes.

cent sous gained. But a "good batch" usually meant bread that was badly leavened, badly kneaded, sour, and prone to mold. Local lore suggested consolation: moldy bread brought luck. "Whoever eats moldy bread finds pennies," they said at Sablières (Ardèche). And at Loubaresse, nearby, it was held that if your bread turned moldy you could expect to become rich within the year. The countryside would have been an opulent place had this proved true. When in 1892 Margaret Betham-Edwards visited a prosperous farmer in the Pyrenees, she tasted "the bread made of wheaten and maize flour mixed, a heavy, clammy compound," and diplomatically commented: "It is said to be very wholesome and nutritious."[18]

Bread was baked in large batches to save on fuel: every two or three weeks where fuel was accessible; otherwise every six or twelve months. In the Romanche valley, between Grenoble and Briançon, Adolphe Blanqui found villages so short of fuel that they used dried cow dung to bake their bread and prepared the loaves only once a year. He himself saw in September a loaf he had helped begin in January. That sort of bread had to be cut with an axe, a hatchet, or an old sword, and you could not count yourself a man until you had the strength to cut your own bread when it was stale and hard. Sometimes, as in Saint-Véran (Hautes-Alpes) in 1854, once-yearly baking declined with the opening of a road or highway to the outside, and one shouldn't wonder. But fuel continued to be a major concern there and in other places—Maurienne, Oisans, Larzac, the coast of Brittany—and in these places children long gathered cow pies (*bois de vache, bois court*) that could be dried and saved for their mothers' infrequent bakings. At the end of the century Alfred de Foville found bread still being baked annually in Hautes-Alpes: stored in a dry place it could last for two or even three years. In any case, where timber stood some way away, the problem went beyond lack of fuel to the time it took to gather the cartloads of gorse or broom that went to feed the ovens— at least a whole day lost for other kinds of labor. So, where home-baking persisted, as in the Limousin through the First World War, bread was still made only every three or four weeks, to be mostly eaten past its prime and often riddled with rat holes. But then, as the proverb says, "A la faim, tout bon pain": to hunger all bread tastes good![19]

Even so, or perhaps precisely because of such circumstances, the black and indigestible bread, base of the daily diet, was an object of veneration, never cut into until the sign of the cross was carved on it with a knife; and the sharing of bread was the very essence of companionship. Up in the Cantal mountains, Pierre Besson remembered "a cult for it . . . no wastage . . . eating crusts." One man went to Murat every 15 days, brought back two sacks of round loaves baked in town, and resold them only for the sick. On meeting a neighbor on the road carrying a loaf, one asked him who was ill at home. Baker's bread was rare and delicate, a gift, a symbol of riches, as in the *quignon du jour de l'an*, the traditional New Year's gift that godparents at Lantenne

(Doubs) presented to their godchildren: "a nice, round loaf with a slit in it and a few *sous* inside."[20]

Intriguingly, despite the great prestige of white and baker's bread, acquired tastes kept the old coarse black loaf in fashion. The poor had eaten gruel and rye for centuries; a change even for the better took time to swallow.[21] Buckwheat, too, had advantages: it cost little to cultivate, its flowers drew bees (at a time when honey made up for lack of sugar), and surpluses could be sold as poultry feed or to distilleries. In Brittany, 120 pounds of barley cost 11 to 12 francs, and 150 pounds of wheat just 14 francs. Yet peasants ate only barley bread, explaining that though white bread would be no more expensive, they would eat it with too much pleasure and hence consume too much. It was a temptation that the poor and even the more fortunate did not want to subject themselves to. "In a good house, hard bread and dry wood," said the southern proverb.[22]

If such explanations (offered as well for the rejection of baker's bread) have the whiff of sour grapes, that does not detract from what they say about the mentality of those who advanced them. Scarcity furnished arguments that only plenty would contradict.* And reality was overtaking sour grapes. In even the poorer mountain areas of the Vosges guests were being offered good black bread by 1869. In the Limousin there were mills to sift the peasants' flour by 1888, permitting them to eat their rye free of bran. In Beaujolais, where in 1860 the rye bread was reportedly so sodden it would stick to a wall if you threw it, peasants were eating white baker's bread by 1894. In Nivernais, Thuillier tells us, from about 1880 the family oven began to give way to the baker's, partly because so many women insisted on relief from the task on their return from a life in the towns as nurses or servants, partly because lads on military service had outgrown the taste of stale bread. White bread became so common in certain parts of Brittany between the 1890's and 1914 that rye came to be despised. We hear of a baker at Pontrieux (Côtes-du-Nord) telling a customer that he did not make dogs' bread.[23]

---

* Even then, foodstuffs that did not conform with local beliefs about what was acceptable were rejected for some time. In Saintonge until the Phylloxera revolutionized economic life, and mentalities with it, milk and dairy products were despised. There were few cows, and their milk went only to babies and the sick. Goats, the poor man's cows elsewhere, were suspect: their milk was said to make children willful and malicious. (See Raymond Doussinet, *Les Travaux*, p. 62.) In Gers milk was thrown away throughout the nineteenth century (but not apparently before the Revolution, when it was used to make cheese), and butter began to be used only after the First World War. (Henri Polge, personal communication; see also Zacharie Baqué, *Le Département du Gers*, vol. 2; *Géographie humaine*, Auch, 1933, part 2, p. 39; and Baqué, *En Gascogne gersoise*, Paris, 1950.) But white bread gained acceptance fairly quickly, even in the southwest, where the poor had eaten corn for two centuries. Corn was a labor-intensive crop, but the poor had plenty of hands to give it the care it needed. As peasants left the land, however, the acreage planted in corn shrank. The great estates, which had paid their work forces in corn, were being broken up, and wheat culture was no longer their peculiar privilege. There was less corn, more wheat, and the consumption of cornbread fell steeply in the 1880's; pellagra, once rampant throughout southwestern France, declined as well. (See Daniel Faucher, "De quelques incidences,"

Gradually, ovens grew cold in farmhouse and village. Bakers, once called on only by those without grain or an oven and a few local notables, increasingly acquired customers, who usually paid for their wares in kind.[24] By the 1880's bakers could be found in most of the accessible parts of the countryside. More isolated regions—Franche-Comté, Dordogne, much of the Pyrenees—followed the trend as the century turned. Buying from the baker was more convenient.* By 1919 even the high mountains had been won over. At Bêne, near Tour-de-Carol, the ruins of an unfinished oven still stood a few years ago where the owner of Esteva's farm began to build one in that year and left it uncompleted: mute witness to one of the great revolutions of our century. By that time only 7 or 8 percent of the family budget went for bread, against nearly 40 percent in 1800 and 20 percent as late as 1850.[25]

The chestnut, at one time a staple as important to Corsica and great parts of the center, south center, and west as bread was to other parts of France, had experienced an even more rapid decline. In such areas chestnuts were "winter bread," base of the winter diet. They had played an even more important role until some areas had inched their way above the hunger level. Between Châteaubriant and Laval and in the Cévennes around Vigan, bread had become a part of the regular diet during the July Monarchy, but before that army officers had warned that troops without supplies risked being reduced to a chestnut diet, like the natives'. In the late nineteenth century Corsica, Vivarais, Cantal, Périgord, and Comminges still depended on them.[26] Backward isolation amounting to autonomy, great frugality bordering on want, here were the regions that were most resistant to assimilation and unification.

Between 1875 and 1900 the great chestnut forests began to be eaten up. While the Phylloxera ravaged the vines, great stands of chestnuts through the center were felled by disease (the so-called *maladie de l'encre*). The search for tannin,

---

p. 121; Roger Brunet, "Les Campagnes commingeoises," p. 216; and Archives Départementales, Gers M 2799, gendarmes Seissans, July 10, 1875; and on pellagra, Daphne A. Roe, *A Plague of Corn*, Ithaca, N.Y., 1973, chap. 6 and especially pp. 47–49.)

* Quantitatively, the change came fastest where, as in Bourbonnais, many landless laborers were unable to produce their own bread and had to get it from the baker. There is evidence in the Agricultural Survey of 1867 that bakers were spreading even by that date, notably a report that the regulation of commercial baking had become an issue in Lot because many families that used to bake their own bread now bought it (Archives Nationales, F¹¹2725, "Enquête agricole"). At Espère (Lot, pop. 400), still without a baker or an inn in 1881, two bread depots had been set up the year before at private farms where the products of the bakers of nearby Luzech were sold (Inspector Pujos, "Recueil des monographies"). In Brie bakers were still often paid in kind until the eve of the First World War, accepting 100 kg of flour for 100 kg of bread, or a 120-kg sack for 30–32 loaves weighing three kg each (*Bulletin folklorique de l'Ile-de-France*, 1942, p. 30). Interestingly enough, the use of tallies (two marked planks) continued with the sale of bakers' bread (reported in Morvan in the 1920's), indicating that illiteracy must have survived in some degree (Jean Drouillet, *Folklore du Nivernais et du Morvan*, 2: 85). Complaints about short weights were widespread and constant, to the point where the mayor of Limoges observed, in 1875: "In the country...a kilo means 750 grams" (Archives Départementales, Haute-Vienne M 1430, maire Limoges to préfet, July 5, 1875; see also Alain Corbin, "Limousins migrants," p. 69).

extracted from the bark, also ate up trees by the thousand tons. This sometimes had beneficial effects. The small tannin-processing plants that were set up in the heart of chestnut country (Ardèche, Dordogne) depended on the existence of railroads; and the railroads that permitted easier provisioning and opened possibilities of trade also made the chestnut less vital. In area after area the *arbre à pain* began to be gnawed away—in Savoy after 1888, in Ardèche after 1897, even in Périgord after 1900. French chestnut production fell from 757,000 metric tons in 1886 to 333,000 in 1901.[27]

The chestnut's diminished role in the peasants' diet marked a real improvement all around: easier access to provisions, more money with which to buy goods, entry into the market economy. So did the retreat of the walnut, a vital source of cooking and lighting oil until gas lamps and commercial salad oil came along. The demand for walnut wood for furniture and rifle stocks considerably thinned the walnut groves.*

For all this, eating well was something to be remarked and remembered— reward for special aid, as when men lent each other a hand with building a house in exchange for a feast ("C'est pas souvent que ça leur arrivait de bien manger!") or a *fête de gueule* to celebrate the prosperous end of a year's enterprise. A spread of this sort was among the very few available entertainments— a voluptuousness, as one peasant called it.[28]

A good meal was an event, a rising up to another level, a gent's repast ("in boin repet de mossieu": Vosges). And a good meal everywhere meant meat and wine, delicacies whose appearance glorified an occasion and made a dinner fit for a king: "Lou qui a pan, car e bî, lou Rei pot beni." The plain-living Pyrenean mountaineer, who drank only water and seldom ate meat of any sort, saw wine and butcher's meat once a year, on his local saint's day. "Pa, bî e car," with two or three families getting together to share a calf, turned such festivities into "supreme moments." Memory enshrined them. In the Pyrenees a big bear hunted down made a village feast that would be long remembered. At Aulus-les-Bains (Ariège) an event of the sort in the 1820's was still discussed 60 years later: "Those who shared in it talk about it still in the *veillées* and cite it as a memorable occurrence of their youth." Memories were long even in 1907, as Jules Renard's old peasant couple demonstrated: "The Philippes can enjoy one scraggy rabbit a year; but once, in 1876, it happened that they ate so well they will never forget it." Speech confirmed the exceptional nature of such occasions: Sunday clothes became meat-eating garb

---

* Railways again! In Savoy when this happened around 1914 veillées organized for the shelling of walnuts also disappeared (see "Enquête sur ... l'agriculture," Savoie, Musée des Arts et Traditions Populaires archives). In Haute-Loire the stones of local peaches had provided a primitive lighting oil used only for dinner or work, and cooking oil had come from nuts. At the end of the century several years of hard frost in the spring forced families to resort to the grocer, but otherwise the peasants had little use for retail oil for some time thereafter (O. Costérisant, *La Vie rurale*).

(les habits mangeant viande), and dressing up was to get dressed for meat or stew. Of course, quantity meant more than quality: "Tout fait ventre, pourvu que ça y entre." And the richer the better: "E pu gras meu vire" (the fatter it is, the better it goes down). In any case, a glutton's knife was sure to cut well, and so much the better: strong to eat, strong to work.[29]

Meat, for most, meant pork. If bread stood for plenty, bacon or lard was a symbol of wealth. The hog was the real patron saint of the countryside—Sent Pourquî in Gascony—a miraculous animal, every bit of which was good for something ("Porc penut, arré de perdut"; pig slaughtered, nothing wasted) and which almost everybody could afford to raise ("B'ei praube lou qui nou s'en pot pela û!"; poor indeed who can't skin one!). And in fact in Périgord, whose forests provided ample forage, to kill meant to kill a pig; "we have killed on such and such a day" meant that a feast would follow. Even so, there were some who could not afford to indulge themselves.* And for those who could, a single slaughtered pig a year, and never the fattest, would surely not go far. Most of the carcass was consumed after the slaughtering, in family or communal feasts. Bacon and lard had to be stretched a very long way indeed. One might treat oneself "sometimes" on Sundays to a little bacon and "savor it," like the peasants of Bort (Corrèze) "because they like it and they rarely eat it." As a Flemish doctor remarked of the Flemish countryside in 1859, almost all differences in living standards can be summed up in one fundamental distinction: the habitual use of lard and the habitual lack of lard.[30]

In Cornouaille, where by 1908 conditions had "much improved," the better off ate lard every day. Families in more backward communes, however, managed it only twice a week and then "only in good houses"—and of course "only a very small piece." As for day laborers, they saw lard only on feasts. Even in the rich Limagne country bacon was scarcely common fare. Not when a workman, boasting of having eaten a bit of lard at his employer's board, should feel impelled to flourish the rind so his listeners would believe him. As good a piece of evidence as any of the continuing rarity of meat is a tale from the 1880's in which four Breton lads from Langneux (Côtes-du-Nord) discuss what they would like to eat if they were King. "Beans and smoked lard, big as my big toe," says the first. "A sausage long as the way from Lamballe to Saint-Brieuc," declares the second. "The sea turned into suet and me in the middle with a wooden spoon," outbids the third. The fourth is speechless: "There is nothing left for me. You took all the good things."[31]

The third lad's fantasy, of a sea of suet, reminds us that the really festive meat, the *ne plus ultra* of a peasant's table, was butcher's meat—preferably beef. So rare was commercial meat indeed that in Lower Brittany a special traditional song was called for when it was served.[32] J. A. Barral, noting that

---

* Martin Nadaud lived in Paris a full year before he could get himself to try meat, which he had never had at home. In his first months there he had always traded his meat for cheese, despite his father's advice to eat meat when he could (*Mémoires de Léonard*, Bourganeuf, 1895, p. 53).

between 1860 and 1875 yearly meat consumption in the Limousin had risen about 20 pounds per person, hailed this considerable progress over the time not far back when even pork was a luxury served only at great feasts. But for all that, the retail sales of meat, our only indication of the consumption of meat above and beyond pork, were pitifully low, and the butcher was long merely a part-time operator primarily engaged in slaughtering for others. In Haute-Vienne hardly any butcher's meat was to be had in a small country town in 1861 and then only poor cuts at very high prices—obviously not destined for the general public. In the Vosges in 1869, we are told, only a very few wealthy farmers ate stew on Sundays. In Aunis around 1886 butchers customarily took ten pounds of meat to market and sometimes made no sale at all. Even in the prosperous region around Langres, in Haute-Marne, where by the 1880's the farmers of some means at least ate bacon every day, the butcher who passed through every Friday to supply the rectory and the chateau was seldom approached. Ordinary people patronized him only in case of illness or when expecting an important visitor, tried to hide the meat they bought "for fear of comments," and wondered at its excessive cost—*en voilà pour 27 sous!*—more than one franc.[38]

That the gargantuan meal we tend to associate with the nineteenth century was poles removed from what most people really ate is obvious. Less obvious, perhaps, but more significant was the difference between contemporary urban ideas of a normal diet and what was normal in the countryside. A gulf always existed between the eating habits of country folk and those of cities and larger country towns. But it may be, as Thuillier has suggested, that the gulf grew wider as the century drew on.*

At Bitche (Moselle) an officer filed a report in 1842 stressing the radical differences in the diet there, with the rich eating a variety of meat, fresh or smoked game, and even fish, the moderately well off dining on soup and stew, lard, and vegetables, and the poor making do "almost exclusively" with potatoes and curdled milk. Bread too was different; white was for the rich, rye for the poor. But in Paris, we are told, no one, of whatever station, would accept anything but first-quality white bread. When, in 1869, the municipal authorities distributed brown flour to local relief committees for bread for the needy, the program had to be halted because the poor took the tickets to be used for the brown bread and, reaching into their own pockets to make up the difference, used them to buy white loaves. The brown bread was left

---

* *Aspects de l'économie nivernaise*, p. 62. Yet Pierre Besson was moved to remark that the servants of the 1930's ate much better than the wealthiest bourgeois of the 1880's (*Un Pâtre du Cantal*, p. 62). In that connection, we may note Elicio Colin's work in picking out the first mention of various foodstuffs in the notarial records of Finistère: sugar, 1833; beer, 1851; cognac, 1866; chicory and rice, 1876; rum, 1880; tapioca, 1886; vermouth, curaçao, and kirsch, 1889; sardines in oil, 1892; absinthe, 1901 ("L'Evolution de l'économie rurale"). Obviously, this does not indicate the first local appearance of these items. But, at the other end of the scale, what would be the time lag between the first mention of these products and their use in nonaffluent quarters?

to molder.[34] Plainly, wealth was only one factor in a more complex whole: sauce for the rural goose did not satisfy the urban gander. And meat consumption makes the point.

Official statistics show that between 1840 and 1882 French meat consumption nearly doubled. But this was city food. The peasant who ate butcher's meat was a rare figure in the 1860's and 1870's, and the fortunate few were chiefly near the cities, especially Paris. Most of the time, we are told, it was the meat of sick, or worn, or useless animals that was sold to the village butcher-*cabaretier* for local use. In Paris, meanwhile, demand for meat among the poorer classes kept on growing. (It was met with horseflesh. The first slaughterhouses exclusively for horses appeared in Paris in 1866; within six years the capital boasted 150 such establishments.) By 1882 Parisians were averaging 79.31 kg of meat a year, and their brothers in other cities were not far behind at 60.39 kg. But the yearly per-capita consumption in the countryside was a paltry 21.89 kg.[35] The cities in short were carnivorous enclaves in a herbivorous land.*

In fact urban workers ate better than country ones, that is, more, but retained rural standards and even mealtimes until toward the end of the century.[36] This began to change sometime in the mid-1880's: less bread, more meat, more wine, at meals that increasingly followed the bourgeois pattern and even, at times, included dessert.† In the countryside, the change came much more slowly. Food shops opened in big country bourgs, especially after 1870. But in 1900 the peasant still ate just a quarter of the average meat ration of a city dweller, and only a fifth of what the Parisian consumed. Indeed, the great divide between vegetarian peasants and carnivorous townsmen survived to the Second World War.[37]

Still, the improvements cannot be gainsaid. In 1913 Emmanuel Labat recalled an old sharecropper in the Landes whose one wish was to see and touch a pig before he died. Now, exulted Labat, "the times have been accomplished, the old dreams realized: of land and meat. One cannot imagine how heavily this last weighed on the peasant's soul." A Breton geographer put it differently: the agricultural revolution was, above all, a revolution in diet. The coming

---

* "L'alimentation carnée du prolétaire agricole est, en 1852, cinq fois moindre que celle d'un citadin et égale à la moitié de celle d'un Français moyen," remarks G. Désert ("Viande et poisson," *Annales: E. S. C.*, 1975, p. 525). Discrepancies also show up at the regional level, with Brittany in 1885 eating half as much meat (10 kg per person) as the French rural average (Elie Gautier, *Dure Existence*, pp. 100–101). B. Bennassar shows that in Lower Normandy, where the meat consumption of country folk had risen from 9.7 kg per person per year in 1830 to 31 kg in 1892, local townsmen consumed nearly twice as much: 54 kg (*Annales: E. S. C.*, 1975, pp. 417–23).

† Using hospital and asylum statistics and toll taxes, Alain Corbin has demonstrated that dietary standards did not change significantly until the 1880's. His findings can be stated briefly as follows: 1830's undernourished; 1860's, less undernourished, increased quantities but the diet unchanged; 1880's, minimal undernourishment and much greater variety ("régime alimentaire bouleversé"), including not only eggs, cheese, noodles, sugar, jam, and coffee, but sometimes even pepper and sardines. ("Limousins migrants," pp. 82–92.)

of white bread and meat, with the First World War, marked the "decisive break" with the past. Views like these, putting aside production figures for a look at ways of life, cut closer to the bone of history.[38]

All evidence seems to agree on 1880–1900 as the period when once-hard-to-find novelties entered the countryside in some quantity, and many peasants became accustomed to buying them in shops: sugar, coffee, rape-seed or olive oil, macaroni, vermicelli. Café au lait replaced morning soup, and women welcomed "city ways" that meant less work.* Sugar, extremely rare for a long time even on wealthy farms and only used as a remedy for sickness, became more common. In Loire the best-man had traditionally carried some sugar to sweeten the wine of the girl he escorted at a village wedding. The custom, known as *sucrer sa cavalière*, lapsed in the mid-1880's as the sugarbowl began to be an expected table item on great occasions. But courting lads continued to carry a piece of sugar in their pockets and "gallantly offered it" to their sweethearts.[39]

Coffee, too, took its time to spread. In Corrèze coffee at weddings was still seemingly a novelty representing modern progress in the last years of the century, for the fact that it was served "almost everywhere when the wedding is of some importance" was considered worthy of remark. Around 1902 the new Breton craze for coffee, especially among women, gave rise to a repertory of satirical songs and sayings that lasted into the 1920's, when coffee-drinking presumably came to be a matter of course. In Vivarais, until the First World War, a visitor's ritual gift was a package of coffee, a kilo of sugar, or a loaf of white bread.† All these by then were in general use, but the persistent custom showed how recently they had still been a luxury—as in the case of the ninety-six-year-old man who was buried at Saint-Etienne-de-Lolm in the Gardon valley in 1903 and who to the very last had made his every meal solely of chestnuts. Yet again we note that this was now a matter to be mentioned in the newspapers. Even in the highlands of the Gard, Raymond Belbèze's coachman was remarking, by 1911: "*Les gens se font gourmands*; they have to have soup, stew, potatoes." The old marveled at the change they lived through,

---

* Pierre Barral, *Le Département de l'Isère*, p. 113. Gabriel Boscary has suggested that farm-wives fell into the habit of drinking coffee when their men were called to army service and they no longer had to serve cabbage soup at seven in the morning (*Evolution agricole*, p. 226; see also Elie Reynier, *Le Pays de Vivarais*, 2: 128). Evidence of the new well-being shows up in family ledgers, as Patrice Higonnet has noted. In his *Pont-de-Montvert* (p. 98), he cites one entry from July 1911 listing the "unusual delicacies" a farmer purchased: "a box of sugar, one tomato, 2 lbs. macaroni, and one piece of chocolate." Another farmer, in June 1913, recorded the purchase of "a box of sugar and a piece of chocolate." For all that, coffee and sugar were still rare in the Cévennes until 1914, and we hear of an eighteen-year-old girl from Corrèze, hired as a maid by a Toulouse family in 1909, who saw canned foods and *pâtes* for the first time (André Meynier, *A travers le Massif Central*, p. 370).

† Local monographs have noted that by 1878 sugar could be found everywhere in the upper regions of Vivarais, that in 1903 at Sécheras (Ardèche) many families drank coffee, and that in 1907 at Saint-Jean-le-Centenier the women could not do without coffee (Pierre Bozon, *Histoire*, p. 278; H. Labourasse, *Anciens us*, p. 7).

that in a Nièvre village, where there had been but one butcher, 1907 could see five: "People have become carnivorous!" As for Ragotte, when the butcher's wife gives her a piece of meat, she still does not know how to cook it.[40]

Doctor Labat noted the effect of the new, rich meat diet: a rising tide of arthritis, some cases of gout, the early onset of arteriosclerosis. "The social promotion of the Gascon peasant becomes complete as his pathology becomes bourgeois." Since undernourishment goes hand in hand with diminished fertility,[41] one is tempted to speculate that better food also made contraception more necessary. More food and better food might call for imitating the bourgeois in this respect as well. Meanwhile traditional dishes, abandoned by the peasants when conditions permitted, became the pasture of urban gastronomes. The rural people looked on them as symbols of the bad old days—dirty, complicated, too demanding of work and time.

One more symbol of change remains, and that is wine. A feast would be incomplete without it; and wine, like meat, was for the peasants one of the fruits of modernization, the gift of the Third Republic. When Adolphe Blanqui made his survey in 1850, three-fifths of the population were still strangers to wine consumption. Complaints of drunkenness abound, but that state was reached with brandy (*eau de vie*), not wine. Cheap, locally distilled alcohol was a product of the bad transport conditions and it fell out of favor as soon as communications improved. The other source of drunkenness was lack of familiarity with liquids drunk. The Bretons, for example, soon acquired a national reputation for sottishness. But sound observers attributed their proclivity to become tipsy less to the quantities they imbibed than to inexperience. The Breton peasants, Olivier Perrin noted in 1835, almost always drank water at home; even if they had cider, they kept it mostly for sale and drank it themselves only on very special occasions. Hence a pilgrimage or a trip to town inevitably led to trouble. Maxime du Camp confirmed this observation with his complaint that the drunks at a pilgrimage he attended were not even properly drunk. In effect the evidence suggests that into the 1860's most peasants drank little or no wine. In Nièvre they drank it maybe twice a year, at Carnival and at the end of the harvest. The same in the southwest, where in the 1850's wine was a luxury, rare and "highly valued by peasants as a dainty drink." According to the available resources, the peasants drank *piquette*, made by pouring water over the skins of grapes after their last pressing; cider, which was usually pretty bad, especially when it was prepared with the same presses that were used for oil; perry, made of pears; drinks fermented from wild cherries or berries; and rarely beer, more of a bourgeois drink.[42] And of course water.

Heavy habitual drinking was restricted to regions that lacked transport facilities, where casks were few and had to be emptied before they could be filled with a new year's crop. As we have seen, poor communications also accounted in large part for the production of grape or apple brandies, but even then (as with the calvados of the pays d'Auge) the "firewater" was reserved for feasts—until the end of the century, at any rate. For the same reason, much of the wine produced in some regions, such as Argenteuil (Val d'Oise) was locally consumed—and was hardly anything to write home about. But it was not that so much as the cost that put people off. As the police superintendent of Bessines (Haute-Vienne) reported in 1861: "Few customers, because drinks are dear."[43]

Moreover, the price was made all the dearer by the taxes imposed by the authorities, who took an exceedingly dim view of drinking, especially public drinking. The village public-house, a house like every other, distinguished only by a bunch of holly or juniper or a handful of straw (the *bouchon* that now signifies a tavern) had a bad press in official documents. Source of moral laxity, of political cabals, of plots and pranks against neighbors and public figures, the public-house of whatever name, tavern, pothouse, wine shop, was legislated, regulated, and policed (when there were police), yet could not be kept down. Sole consolation for routine misery, escape from impossible conditions in the home, chief village meeting-place (or tryst for different clans), nothing could take its place.[44] From indirect evidence, however, it appears that the reporting officials were concerned chiefly about conditions in the small towns, and that, for most of the century in most places, the rural population had neither the time, nor the means, nor for that matter, the stomach, for frequent tippling. They drank on holidays. The fact that most drinking songs were in French and were learned on army service suggests that there was little popular drinking locally, and that a good part of the credit for the generalization of wine should go to the establishment of universal military service in 1889. That is not to deny some credit, of course, to the liberalization of the wine trade after 1880, gift of the Third Republic to its faithful supporters.[45]

Just as facilities for public drinking increased, so did those for private consumption. By 1869 many could boast of a barrel of wine in their own cellar (*un tonneau en cave*) to tap routinely on feast days. Railroads brought wine to regions where the price had been prohibitive. By the 1890's on the plateaus of Aveyron, once-isolated peasants were drinking wine. In other poor regions, the Limousin and the Landes, haying and harvest time now brought wine with them, and getting drunk in company was not limited to great feast days.[46] And the same railways that carried the wine to the outlands allowed the land to be used for what it could do best—that is, specialization—which meant an end to wine so bad that the peasant claimed it took three men to get it down: the one who drank, the one who held him, and the one who made him drink.[47]

Chapter Ten

FROM 'SUBSISTANCE' TO 'HABITAT'

Oh happy, if he knew his happy State!
The Swain, who, free from Business and Debate;
Receives his easy Food from Nature's Hand,
And just Returns of cultivated Land!

. . .

Unvex'd with Quarrel, undisturb'd with Noise,
The Country King his peaceful Realm enjoys.

—VIRGIL

AT THE TIME of the French Revolution the great socioeconomic issue had been *subsistance*—how to feed the poor. By the 1840's, however, the focus of interest had begun to shift to *habitat*, their miserable quarters. Physical misery still flourished on all fronts, but with the food problem near solution, priorities could be readjusted in terms of relative need.

The national trend reflected mainly conditions in urban areas. But rural observers echoed it. Not food or lack of it, but bad living conditions accounted for the poor health of the countryside, insisted a student of rural hygiene in 1849. True, the food was very bad, but since it was equally bad in most places, the real fault lay with the unhealthy dwellings and disastrous habits of life.[1] Even the addition of wine as a dietary staple would be welcomed, not only as a nutrient in a deficient diet, but as a replacement for the polluted water most people had to drink.

The peasant got his water where he could. Water from springs, rills, rivulets, brooks, rivers, or streams was only as available as proximity made it. More often the peasant relied on a pond or well whose stagnant waters were used by the whole community for bathing, for laundry, and for steeping hemp, and where communal sewage generally oozed in when it did not flow. In 1856 at Saint-Ours (Puy-de-Dôme) 2,336 people had to draw all their water from 15 wells "fed more by the seepage from kitchen waste and manure than from neighboring lands, which in any case are covered with stagnant pools full of stinking vegetable matter." An army report in 1860 remarked on the difference between those who lived along the banks of the Allier River and used its clean waters and those who lived on the plateau between the Loire and the Allier, with only stagnant water to drink, a difference that was reflected in the physique of the recruits and the number of men rejected as unfit from the two regions. Henri Baudrillart spotted a similar disparity in Vendée in the 1880's, stressing the plight of the northern fenlands, where any kind of fresh water had to be fetched from three and even six kilometers away, and people consequently drank mostly muddy ditchwater. Sources befouled with worms and putrid matter, the absence of ducts and sewers, and the lack of clean water were a leitmotif of rural documentation—when observers thought to mention it, that is.[2]

Another was bad air. Piles of manure stood guard outside the doorways. "Stagnant waters contaminate the air," complained a staff captain in the Limousin in 1874. Not really surprising to find ague so common an ill among country people, "all of whom breathe in foul surroundings, live on putrid exhalations, amid the heaps of dung surrounding their abode." Hamlets and villages were wrapped in suffocating stinks, their streets turned into cesspools by great rills of foul stuff fed by liquid manure from stables, in which one had to flounder and be mired.[3]

One is tempted to relate the shortage of fresh water and the difficulty in obtaining it, so that in even the best of places fetching it was a laborious, time-consuming job, to the peasant's general unconcern with personal cleanliness. Certainly washing and cleanliness had no place in proverbs and folk sayings, except in negative forms like the saw advising that the broom and duster brought no gain:

> Lai r'messe et le torchon,
> ne raipotant ren ai lai mâson!

All they did was take up time. So did laundering; and the time had to be fit into a schedule of periods when doing the wash could bring the direst consequences—the Rogation Days, Holy Week, All Souls' Day, and Saint Sylvester's feastday (or rat's day, when the linen would be gnawed by rats). An enterprise calling for the most complex logistical preparations, laundering was not lightly undertaken, an occasion for women of the neighborhood to get together, to eat, drink (*riquiqui*, a mixture of brandy and sweet wine in Mâconnais), and fritter away precious time in useless socializing. In Aunis a family's yearly laundry was done all at once; this could mean up to 60 sheets and 70 shirts to be soaked in lees and ashes and boiled, a job for seven or eight women. There were no handkerchiefs, of course. Table linen was practically nonexistent, and personal effects were severely limited: male undergarments, especially drawers, began to be worn around 1885, principally by young men back from military service; female undergarments came into use still later; nightwear was unknown, and sleepers slept in all or some of their day clothes. As for these last, often as not they were threadbare, ragged patchworks, their only airing coming in the wear. That was all right, and the conventional wisdom reinforced it:

> Dins las pilhas
> Soun las bellas filhas;
> Dins lous pilhous
> Qu'ei lous bous garsous.

Handsome lads and lasses are brought up in rags![4] All this made frugality easier, and the six or twelve months' pile of dirty linen not nearly so daunting as it would be today. By 1914 the family wash was undertaken perhaps two or four times a year in relatively advanced areas like Mayenne, still only once a year in Morbihan. Either way, washdays were few and far between, helping to explain the magnitude of linen chests and trousseaus and the lasting quality of linens so seldom washed. Also the smell of garments, beds, and people. Also certain beliefs, for instance, in the danger of giving clean linen to sick people.*

If washing linens was rare, washing oneself was an exception too. In the Morvan, one way to protect oneself against sorcery was to wash one's hands in the morning—a rite that suggests such action was not in the ordinary course of things. Passing through the little town of Chaudesaigues near Saint-Flour, famous for its hot mineral springs, Ardouin-Dumazet was struck by the unusual cleanliness of the inhabitants. Here, he wrote, "in a region where one does not take baths, the use of ablutions is quite widespread." Chaudesaigues was clearly an exception. Even in towns, few made a habit of washing and bathing. Doctors decried the modesty that made washing particularly repugnant to women, which meant that only the immoral—*cocottes* of the better class—were likely to be clean. Indeed, as an old Aveyronnaise who had been hospitalized protested: "I'm over sixty-eight and *never* have I washed *there!*"[5] How many times had she washed at all? Perhaps before her marriage, like the young girls of Orléans, who visited a public bathhouse just once in their lives, on their wedding eve—"une formalité unique en son genre, comme le passage à la mairie et à l'église."†

Apparently, most people came to terms with this. Like the principal of a normal school who, in 1877, quite conscious of the fact that his charges bathed only in summer (and how often then?), was happy to say that "we have more or less managed to prevent all disagreeable effluvia arising from either their bodies or their clothing.... Thus we live constantly in the midst of our stu-

---

* Robert Hertz, *Sociologie religieuse*, p. 175; Archives Départementales, Haute-Vienne M 1047 (1873), Corrèze M 717 (1871). One rural mayor advised: "L'air pur, les aliments sains, les bains et les ablutions fréquentes, les vêtements souvent nettoyés, le linge et les habits propres." (*Conseils hygiéniques aux cultivateurs des campagnes, par un maire de campagne*, Paris, 1850, p. 5.) Unfortunately, such counsels of perfection could seldom be followed.

† Comte Baguenault de Puchesse, *Un Demi-siècle de souvenirs, 1860–1914* (Orléans, 1915), p. 121. Hannah Lynch quotes the prospectus of the very posh Collège Stanislas, a boys school in Paris, which told parents their son would be expected to wash his feet once a week and his body once a month. As for girls, most were educated by nuns, who "deem it an offense against modesty to wash oneself." During her own years in a French convent, she says, "nobody, to my knowledge, had a bath of any kind." Modesty prevented girls from washing even their necks, and when they washed their feet once a fortnight, a cloth was kept over them "to avoid the sight of nakedness." (*French Life in Town and Country*, New York, 1905, pp. 134–35.) This was not a problem in the countryside, where bare feet were more frequent than shod ones. Even there, though, many could have echoed the old woman's boast: "Water's never risen above my knee. Not that I like dirty people." (Raymond Doussinet, *Le Paysan santongeais*, p. 368.)

dents without being inconvenienced by their proximity." If this was the situation in the towns, what must it have been in regions where, as a traveler wrote on entering Lozère in 1894, all cleanliness ceased north of Ispagnac? Not very different from what so distressed Madame Romieu—that except where rivers lay nigh, everyone she knew took a perverse pride in seeing that no drop of water should ever touch the body. What was the need for washing? As they said in Saintonge: "Nous aut'pésants, jh'attrapons de bounes suées, o nous nettie le corps."[6]

Rutebeuf, the thirteenth-century poet, said that when a villein died even Hell would not have him because he smelled too bad. This remained true six centuries later. Draft boards could testify to the extraordinary filth (*saleté immonde*) in which countrymen wallowed. Unfriendly testimony, but corroborated by a variety of sources. The slovenliness and dirt of the peasants of Forez and Vivarais so disgusted Doctor Francus in 1890 that he let his outrage come through: everyone knows that our peasants take less care of themselves than the Swiss and English do of their animals. Along the road to Monastier, a few years later: "A single compartment: men and beasts live fraternally, until the ones eat the others."[7] Nor was the eating always in one direction, for fleas, lice, and other parasites abounded. About to go to bed, the Saintongeois announced: "I'm going to feed the fleas."* No wonder, with no opportunity to wash in the tiny, crowded outhouse, and little time to bathe in streams in a long workday. An old Christmas carol still sung in Auvergne in MacMahon's time rejoiced that the year's wine was so good even the women would drink too much of it and, hence, sleep so well they would not feel the fleabites in the night.[8]

No nineteenth-century Le Nain has left us scenes of people scratching, or mothers delousing their children's hair, but the pests were there for all that, and in the early twentieth century, too, as many travelers noted to their sorrow. And popular wisdom, in its contrarious way, developed theories designed to accommodate their omnivorous presence. Scabies, lice, parasites on children cleansed the blood. In some places, children without lice would be endowed with them: good for their health. And in a New Year's ditty along the Rhône valley in Ardèche, one wished a neighbor, "Good day and a good year, with lice by the handful" (Bouon jour et bouono annado, Embé pesouls à pougnado). Scurf and pimples, rashes and boils, suppurating sores of every sort—all let evil humors out and purified the body. Better avoid washing them. Better avoid washing altogether: "The dirtier the children, the better they grow" ("mais lous enfans soun sales, miel se fon"). At Bugeat (Corrèze) baths were still unknown in 1913, but the schoolchildren had advanced to the point where they washed once a week—on Sunday. Their parents cleaned

---

* Raymond Doussinet, *Le Paysan santongeais*, p. 83. Auvergnats announced bedtime more poetically: "To bed! / The straw is cold. / The lice are hungry. / The fleas are thirsty." (Marie-Aymée Méraville, *Contes populaires*, p. 282.) The patois rhymes.

their hands to go to mass or to a fair, or, sometimes, before entering the stable in a ritual meant to protect their cattle's health.[9]

But dirty children did not grow too well, or very healthy, whatever the proverb said. Ill-bred and ill-fed, the men and women of the first half of the nineteenth century produced offspring very much in their own sickly image, who would of course live (when they lived!) into the twentieth century. In 1830 the minimum height for army recruits was lowered to 1.540 meters (a little over 5′). An 1849 reference to "men remarkable by their height and strength," fit for elite units, makes clear that they are between 5′ 6″ and 5′ 8″ tall. A writer pointed out, in 1854, that many recruits needed a few months of solid regular feeding, including 340 grams of meat a day, before they could cope with the physical demands of service.[10] And of course these were the men who had met the army's standards. Until 1863 and after, when the general fitness of conscripts began to show measurable improvement, many men who should have seen service were rejected as physically unfit.*

Richard Cobb has found descriptions in the criminal records of the Revolution and the Ancien Régime that leave the impression of a France swarming "with a bizarre multitude of semi-cripples."[11] The same might be said of the nation for a long time past the days of the Directory and the Consulate, and not only of its criminal elements. In the rural areas especially, deformities were appallingly common. Birth defects, as often as not the result of an unaided delivery; accidents in which some limb would be left unset; the aftereffects of diseases and parasitical infections; and hereditary ills all saw to that. Since most women had no choice but to work even when heavy with child, many, feeling the first birth pangs, were forced to repair to a stable or loft to manage as best they could, much as in Bethlehem. The priest, as Chaix noted in his work on Hautes-Alpes, often collected baptismal and burial fees at one and the same time. Even if the newborn survived, the mother's exertions within a couple of days of birth threatened his health as they sapped hers: "Thus there is not a woman still recognizable after three years of marriage, and there are so many conscripts unfit for service."[12] Recruitment records show that in this respect as well, the toiling classes were kin to the criminal classes: ill-favored on every score. The blind and obviously crippled did not appear

---

* As many as 50 percent of those refused were rejected for *défaut de taille*. Consider these figures from Lot in 1830: Cahors district, 1,051 draftees, 212 *réformés*, 120 for stuntedness; Gourdon district, 598 draftees, 152 réformés, 75 for stuntedness; Figeac, 687 draftees, 203 réformés, 99 for stuntedness. Similarly, in 1847, on the plateaus of Haute-Vienne, more than half the conscripts were rejected for physical causes, half of them for their height. (J.-A. Delpon, *Statistique du département du Lot*, 1: 192; Alain Corbin, "Limousins migrants," p. 124.) According to Emile Durkheim, the number of conscripts rejected for height dropped from 92.8 per 1,000 in 1831 to 59.4 per 1,000 in 1860 (*Le Suicide*, p. 64), and F. Chamla finds a rapid increase in average height between 1863 and 1881 (*Bulletin de la Société Anthropologique de Paris*, 1964, pp. 201–78). The 340-gram meat ration of 1854 may seem ample, but in the 1840's, when the ration was only 295 grams, a contemporary source described it as "bones, fat, gristle, cell tissue, and sinews" (see J. J. Hémardinquer, *Pour une histoire de l'alimentation*, p. 70). A lot of what passed for meat was inedible.

before the recruiting councils; but otherwise their lists chronicle a sad tale of rural ills: deafness and eye sores, tapeworm and hernia, goiter and scrofula, stuntedness, twisted limbs, weakness of constitution, and "diverse maladies."

In 1860 one village near Grenoble had this to show to the army recruiters: goiter, 140; deaf or dumb, 13; lame, 13; myopia, 36; tapeworm, 19; scabies, 1; skin maladies, 86; scrofula, 15; epilepsy, 2; general weakness, 197; hunchback, 29; bone distortion, 2. In a total of 1,000, 553 men were disqualified, only 447 found fit for service. Here in the mountains, as in the Pyrenees, goiter was a relatively common complaint. Throughout the Second Empire the high incidence of "goiter and cretinism" prompted numerous studies and even official surveys. The quality of the water? Undernourishment? Intermarriage? The debate continued through the century. But goiter, and cretinism too, seem to have waned as roads broke down the isolation of these regions: modern ways and, in due course, outmarriage helped the biological destiny to fade away.[13]

But many of the "diverse maladies" were deadly. There was smallpox, of course, and the *mal de misère*—pellagra. There were great epidemics that did their worst among the country poor, like cholera, which killed 11,226 in Ariège in 1854: one soul out of 23, compared with one in 123 in Seine. There was croup; and there was diphtheria, whose appearance caused panic flights from stricken villages where, a report of 1877 tells us, the bells unendingly tolled death. There were endemic "fevers" of every sort, typhoid and more important malaria, which was so prevalent in some areas that quinine became a staple like salt or pepper. Dysentery was endemic, too, cutting great swathes through lands where the water was stagnant and putrid, and through homes where dirt lay everywhere. Hunger or dearth taught that everything that could be eaten should be. "One doesn't die of eating dirty." "To live long you must eat dirty." "You don't fatten hogs with clear water." "No wolf ever choked on a goat's hair."[14]

Anxiety seems to have caused a fair share of medical problems. Shortly before the First World War a doctor from Tarn-et-Garonne devoted a book to what he called peasant neurasthenia, which manifested itself in widespread insomnia and *réveil anxieux*, headaches, gastritis, dyspepsia, constipation (affecting about half his patients), and all sort of bilious troubles. The peasant, he said, went around constantly apprehensive, prey to diffuse or specific anxieties; but whatever the apparent concern of the moment, this anxiety had one fundamental cause—fear. Fear of the night, of thieves, of neighbors, of the dead, a deep, abiding fear that lay in wait for the peasant at every turn, and that far surpassed anything the city man might feel. Corroborative evidence is scanty. Widespread belief in the efficacy of the magical *nouement de l'aiguillette* (the tying of a knot that was supposed to produce impotence) suggests an equally widespread multitude of husbands unable to consummate their marriage. There are remarks about the growing number of mad people,

and figures that suggest a steady rise in the suicide rate (in the three departments Alain Corbin writes about, from 43 in the year 1845 to 96 in 1880).[15]
And there is this from Emile Guillaumin on his fellow peasants: "They were
always afraid, they didn't know of just what they were afraid, but they were
always afraid of something."* But sparse as the evidence is, the context of
insecurity in which so many peasants lived from birth to death, the brink-
manship that was played out over an entire lifetime, suggest plenty of reasons
why the doctor's assessment should be correct. Certainly it is something that
deserves further investigation.

Nervous or otherwise, ill health was a diffuse, poorly grasped concept in
the countryside. Peasants often confused illness and fatigue, and popular
speech today retains this point of view, describing someone who is unwell as
being a little, somewhat, quite, or very tired. Complaints were lumped into
vague categories: weaknesses (*naujas*); fevers (*fevres*); worms (*lous vermes*),
which could affect stomach, teeth, and eyes; pox of every sort from smallpox
to syphilitic eruptions; and even warts, which were variously attributed to the
weather, the ground, the air, magic, or conspiracy.†

Home remedies tended to the peculiar, like the prophylactic use of excrement
(animal or human), and to the sympathetic, like putting a toad in bed to
counter smallpox. A dose of powdered taenia was supposed to rid children of
tapeworm (or, alternatively, one could lay a thread spun by a virgin across
the victim's stomach). In the Jura a tallow candle boiled and melted in a
quart of red wine helped to treat a bad cold. Ear wax was good against colic
or, mixed with nut oil, a sovereign remedy for chilblains. In Poitou a purge
or bath taken between July 24 and August 26 exposed the adventurous to
catching the *canicule*, which could degenerate into jaundice, best treated by
eating roots soaked in urine or, as some suggested, by taking five pills made
of a she-goat's fecal matter in white wine twice a day for eight days. Remedies
for fevers were particularly abundant: grass bracelets prepared on Saint John's
Eve; infusions of mistletoe; dust scraped off of tombstones (matter from the
tomb of Saint Eutropius at Saintes was reputed to be particularly effective),

---

* Maurice Halbwachs notes the rising suicide rate in the countryside, pointing out that whereas
in 1866–69 there were almost twice as many suicides in towns (pop. 2,000+) as in the rural
areas, by 1905–11 urban suicides were only 20 percent more numerous, and by 1919–20 only
14 percent. But this convergence of urban and rural suicide rates is a function of modernization,
not of the anxiety that might have been characteristic of the hitherto isolated rural areas.

† During the cholera epidemic of 1833 "red women" were seen near Brest, "breathing death
over the valleys," and one beggar woman hauled into court maintained that she had spoken to
them (Emile Souvestre, *Les Derniers Bretons* [1854 ed.], 1: 15–16). In 1844, when the disease
broke out again, some believed that *cartouches* full of cholera were being thrown into the streets,
and one woman swore that she had seen a statue of the Virgin Mary cry just before the outbreak
of the plague (Paul Sébillot, *Le Folk-lore de France*, 4: 402; Bérenger-Féraud, *Superstitions*, 2:
433). In the Limousin the cholera outbreaks of 1832 and 1849 were attributed to poisoned wells,
and sometimes to wine poisoned by employees of the Contributions indirectes. At Limoges "the
lower classes [did] not believe in the malady" (Alain Corbin, "Limousins migrants," p. 135;
Archives Départementales, Haute-Vienne M 1055).

preferably taken in white wine; eggs beaten up with chimney soot (for intermittent fever); poultices of squashed earthworms (for malaria) or of spiders crushed to powder; decoctions of snakeskin or powdered viper (the water in which a viper had been boiled was good for rheumatism and so was eating celery); or infusions of carrot seeds in urine. This last, taken for eight or nine days, was also good for dropsy (*hystropisie, hypocrisie*).[16]

Doctor Francus recorded a case in the 1890's in which a peasant suffering from pneumonia drank a concoction of pig urine in guise of an infusion and died. Vaccination had a hard row to hoe right through the century, from Napoleon's day to that of Jules Grévy, when health officers still had to resort to subterfuges in order to vaccinate children without parental consent: "antipathie funeste," "invention diabolique," "maléfice," "a threat to life itself." Such prejudices were confirmed when children died, despite the haste that nurse or mother made to wash the youngster's arm with urine after vaccination.[17]

A very early report on the question of vaccination quotes the familiar argument that ailments are placed by God's will on earth and that to prevent them is thus to offend God.[18] In anxious people notions of this sort are calculated to increase anxiety. How far this particular argument may have affected peasant hearers is anyone's guess, but it surely reflects a general attitude. A way of life and a mentality in which nature and natural causes are paramount may well suggest that an attempt to heal—especially with the untraditional, that is unnatural, methods of medicine and science—is hubris, a form of pride that challenges the natural order of things and risks provoking nature's wrath. I am tempted to wonder whether some reason such as this may not be one factor behind the peasant's notorious reluctance to call a doctor except as a last resort. Were the fees of a village healer so much more reasonable?*

The dictionary translates *rebouteux* as bonesetter, a man who heals or pretends to heal fractures and dislocations. But *rebouteux* was also a generic term for a swarm of healers, charmers, midwives, old wives and village gossips, sorcerers and spellbinders, *toucheurs* and *toucheuses*, *panseurs* and *panseuses*, *médecins de plein vent et charlatans de bas étage* who successfully competed with physicians and, through most of the century, kept well ahead. Traveling mountebanks, impostors, and quacks, policed out of the cities, survived in the countryside, especially since rural regions had few profes-

---

* Hard to say. One can speculate that more of them would be paid in kind, whereas doctors expected cash (and sometimes got it!). Doctors also prescribed remedies that had to be bought in a shop. Here is Adolphe de Bourgoing in 1844: "6 F la visite d'un médecin! puis, les remèdes sont si chers, car ils leur sont vendus dix fois au-delà de leur valeur et en outre ne leur procurent aucun soulagement, car pour eux, pauvres hommes ignorants, timides et sans défense, ils sont falsifiés ou dénaturés; 6 F encore, c'est quinze jours de travail! le pain de deux semaines! Ils préfèrent mourir." ("Mémoire en faveur des travailleurs," p. 404.) Even at the end of the century, in Aude: "On le faisait pas venir souvent; quarante sous, on gagnait vingt sous par jour, il venait quand c'était désespéré" (Daniel Fabre and Jacques Lacroix, *La Vie quotidienne,* p. 298).

sionals to call on (16 doctors and 8 midwives per 100,000 inhabitants in Côtes-du-Nord in 1893), and those they had were hard to get and slow to arrive.[19] "After death, the doctor!" they said in Armagnac.* But, once again, prejudice reinforced material inhibitions. Since doctors were habitually called when sickness was past help, they were as much a symbol of death as the priest mumbling the last rites. Is it fair to cite urban evidence in this context? At Lille by 1876 nearly all parishes had *bureaux de bienfaisance* that provided the services of a *médecin des pauvres* free, on request. But the doctors declared that the workers feared their presence.[20] As an old man explains in Victor Hugo's *Les Misérables*: "Que voulez-vous, Monsieur, nous autres, pauvres gens, j'nous mourrons nous-mêmes."

Not only was the doctor seen as a messenger of death; many peasants were convinced that once they were dead he would take their corpses in charge for his own nefarious purposes. The belief that the doctor was eager to secure "Christian fat" (*graisse de chrétien*) stemmed from the days when grave-robbing was the only means of obtaining a body for dissection. At the end of the century, people still recalled that when a plump person died (like the priest of Gravières, Ardèche, in the spring of 1820), armed friends and relatives took turns standing guard over his grave for some period of time.[21]

Whatever the causes of the peasants' ill health or their reservations about modern healing techniques, one thing is clear: physically, the rural folk lagged behind the city dwellers. In 1844 the country child entered puberty a year or more later than his companion in the towns. The health and physique of rural recruits tended to be poorer than those of the urban recruits, despite the oft-deplored conditions in which many of the city lads lived. In the decade of 1860–69 the national average of conscripts found unfit for service was 16 percent. In that period, the figure for the Nevers district in Nièvre, where one-third of the population worked in factories, ironworks, foundries, and coal and iron mines, was 18 percent, not very far from the national average, whereas 31 percent were rejected in the bucolic district of Château-Chinon.[22] So much for the joys of country life, a life that in time came to seem even worse the longer an area remained untouched by the outside. In 1893, for example, though the conditions of life had greatly improved in many places, an English traveler found things essentially unchanged in Upper Quercy. The peasants, he said, "are dwarfed and very often deformed. Their almost exclusively vegetable diet, their excessive toil, and the habit of drinking half-putrid rainwater from cisterns which they rarely clean may possibly explain this physical degeneration."[23]

---

* Sometimes, after the doctor, death. Bourgoing tells us that if the doctor was sent for, his fee was bound to exhaust the household's meager savings, leaving no spare cash for the drugs he prescribed ("Mémoire," p. 404). But in fairness to the doctors, the remedies they prescribed were often used indiscriminately (mustard plasters might be swallowed rather than applied), and those who were persuaded that patients would ignore their advice were prone to leave them to their prejudices and their fate.

So if conditions improved, they did so haltingly, as always. A law of 1893 stated that any French citizen, ill and indigent, had the right to medical assistance at home or, if he could not be cared for there, then in the hospital. The law was seldom implemented, to be sure, but it was a promise of better days to come. At Eygurande in Corrèze certain maladies that had once been endemic all but disappeared precisely in this same year: intermittent fever, so common in the 1870's; smallpox, rare and then mild after the epidemic of 1870–71, thanks to vaccine; dysentery, now turned to diarrhea. Scrofula and puerperal fever had become far less frequent, and typhoid cases cropped up only sporadically. Even skin infections had thinned out, and rabies, glanders, and anthrax were just memories.[24]

The number of hospitals grew, and country people began to benefit from their existence (though in 1908 the belief was still current in Bourbonnais that the incurable poor who were sent to a hospital were dispatched at once with poisoned sugar-coated pills).* Terminology changed faster than basic ways. Where people had once said that garlic drove out the plague, they learned to say that it drove out microbes. But microbes were only the spirits of yore in a new guise, so that when some disease ravaged a woman's rabbit hutch, she put the pig in it "because his stink killed or discouraged microbes." People continued to be slow to call a doctor (and they are reluctant still: "He didn't ail much; he didn't need no doctor for to die.") During the 1914 war, with most doctors called up for military service, there was a recrudescence of healers and popular remedies. But the war also made great numbers of soldiers familiar with medical personnel and hospitals, hence readier to use them.[25] By that time material conditions had done much to ease and accelerate what change was taking place. That was the revolution in *habitat*.

A nineteenth-century traveler in Ariège expressed surprise one day when he saw a pretty young shepherdess emerge from a dirty hut that seemed "destined rather as a retreat for wild beasts." And the brothers Combes at mid-century, having mentioned a number of structures "that deserved the name of house" (though only just, to judge by their description), go on to "the sort of earthen huts" one finds only too often in the center of France, "dug in the ground and deprived of every comfort."[26]

Primitive cabins became fewer, but living conditions took a long time to

---

* Francis Pérot, *Folklore bourbonnais*, p. 19. Myths plunge their roots in experience. For a long time the hospital, an urban institution, scorned the rural poor. Here is Bourgoing again: "Il faut être riche ou protégé pour entrer à l'hôpital. Celui-là qui peut payer 1 F par jour, qui est appuyé par un administrateur ou recommandé à un médecin, *et qui dépose trente francs*, celui-là est admis à l'hôpital. . . . Celui que ne paye rien et qui n'a pas de *protections* ira mourir à la porte de l'hôpital. . . . Voilà ce qui est ignoré par beaucoup de monde." ("Mémoire," pp. 404–5.) Admittedly, this was in 1844. But such attitudes endured through at least another generation. In 1891 Emile Levasseur could still report that peasants regarded hospitals with profound repugnance, a feeling that hospital administrators did nothing to counteract, "quite the contrary" (*La Population française*, 3: 137).

improve. Many houses at the turn of the century were still very simple: four walls, sometimes a chimney, "rooms" if any simply plank divisions within the main structure, very few openings, and, rarely, a second story.[27] Even when buildings were larger, the purpose was more functional than self-indulgent. Comfort or anything smacking of "ease" was deliberately rejected. Privation, trouble, *se peiner*, were recognized as virtues almost divorced from practical ends. But practical ends were obviously important: "It isn't the cage that feeds the bird," they said in western France. Poor housing and golden coins in a woolen stocking often went together. In any case, a home that looked like a hovel discouraged the landlord, if there was one, from raising the rent, the tax collector from demanding higher taxes, the neighbors from becoming jealous. For such a very long time, passing for poor had been the only way to keep from being truly poor that habits long survived their causes.

Yet many were truly poor, or relatively so. A house mattered less than land, but it did matter. The peasant wanted to be "chez soi"; and in 1894, when 30 to 35 percent of the urban population owned their homes, 69 percent of the peasantry, in some regions over 80 percent, owned theirs.[28] But what homes? Having put his savings into a roof and walls, the peasant had little left to equip himself with any comfort, let alone with spaciousness. First things had to come first. In the west and the western Massif Central, cattle took precedence over people; oxen are bulky, and the houses were built to accommodate them and their winter feed. Horses, pastured in open field country to graze freely, trespassed less on human quarters. Around the Mediterranean, where equipment was relatively skimpy, animals relatively few, and human labor predominated, asses, mules, sheep, and goats took up less room, required less fodder, and made fewer demands on building space.

Houses built side by side, as in the Mediterranean villages, offered the economy of a common wall. Separate houses cost more to build; the means had to come from somewhere. Worst of all were the isolated holdings of *habitat dispersé*, whose occupants had no inkling that things could be better, an insight they might have gained living in concentration.* Village life increases sociability, imitativeness, eventually comfort and progress. Even in the bocage, a house beside the road was likely to show more traces of comfort than a croft lost among hedges at the end of a muddy track. So, the size and the shape of housing varied from region to region, as we might expect. But for a good long time certain essentials scarcely varied.

Most rural houses had the least possible number of openings. This is generally and quite rightly blamed on the door-and-window tax, introduced under the Directory and abolished only in 1917. But other factors help explain their absence. In building a structure every opening added to the structural

* François de Dainville, "Taudis ruraux," pp. 150–51, 156, 158. In 1940, when farmers from Thiérache in the north took refuge in Mayenne, the local peasants were amazed to hear of their spacious dwellings, and simply at the thought that each of these northerners owned his own house.

TABLE 2
Taxable Structures by Number of Windows and Doors,
1831–32, 1860, 1871, 1893

No. of openings	1831–32	1860	1871	1893
1	346,401	293,757	278,482	190,521
2	1,817,328	1,860,594	1,886,355	1,724,215
3	1,320,937	1,520,704	1,598,672	1,629,919
4	884,061	1,063,484	1,118,892	1,207,235
5	583,026	748,963	790,241	898,792
6+	1,846,398	2,505,052	2,776,264	3,583,043
TOTAL	6,798,151	7,992,554	8,448,906	9,233,725

SOURCE: Alfred de Foville, *Enquête sur les conditions de l'habitation en France* (Paris, 1894), 1: xli.

complications and to the cost: three or four openings cost more to build than only one or two. Beyond that, sun, light, air, drafts, and above all cold were feared and shunned. Houses were built to keep them out. Fuel was scarce and heating a constant problem, and when so many homes were literally homemade or put together by workmen of no particular skill, everything fitted badly, so that openings (window, door, chimney) were guaranteed to admit wind and cold.[29]

In the circumstances, countrymen showed little interest in talk that the window tax might be abolished, since (unlike salt) this largely affected only the better off. Most rural dwellings, remarked a Yonne report of 1852, derived virtually all their light from the doorway.[30] The interesting thing is how long this situation would persist. Dwellings with one or two openings, that is, with at most one window, accounted for one-third of the taxable structures in 1831–32, for one-quarter in 1871, for better than one-fifth in 1893 (see Table 2). Though many of these houses were of ancient vintage,* we must assume that they were in use since they were taxed, and more than one in five of them as the century ended had only one window or none at all.

Adolphe Blanqui, in his 1851 report, noted that dwellings in Hautes- and Basses-Alpes lacked effective fastenings at doors and windows.[31] The introduction of adequate clasps and latches is one of those infinitesimal events that have powerful effects on human comfort and, one dares say, happiness. Thus in Bresse, which is cold and misty, houses tended to face east. In Bresse a western orientation would have been preferable; but the west wind (*la traverse*) blows in sudden gusts that bang the shutters, blow open windows shakily fastened with a wooden bar, and fill the house with rain or wind. So, many avoided the southern or western orientation they would have pre-

---

*In 1966, 65 percent of the houses in the village of Chanzeaux had been built before 1871, and only 4 percent had been built since 1932 (Laurence Wylie, *Chanzeaux, a Village in Anjou,* p. 104).

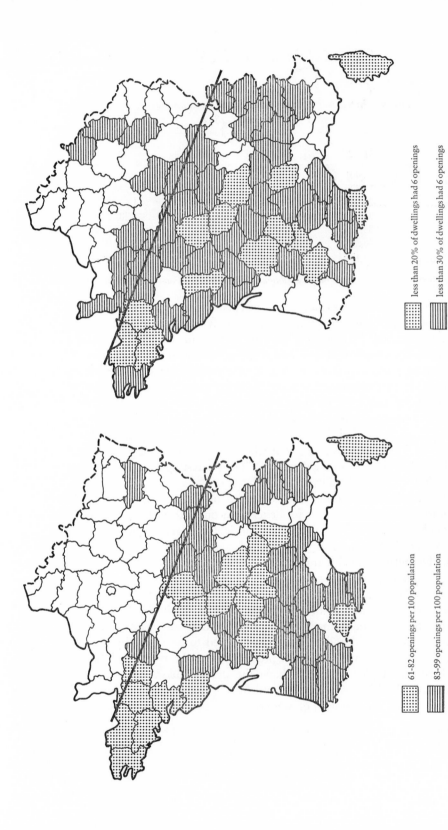

Map 9. Departments with fewest taxable windows and doors per 100 population, 1831. National average: 112 openings per 100 population. SOURCE: Adolphe d'Angeville, *Essai sur la statistique de la population française* (Paris, 1969 ed.), map 19.

61-82 openings per 100 population

83-99 openings per 100 population

Map 10. Departments with lowest percentage of houses with six or more windows and doors, 1876. National average in the six and under class: 3.06 openings. SOURCE: *Annuaire statistique de la France* (Paris, 1878), p. 195.

less than 20% of dwellings had 6 openings

less than 30% of dwellings had 6 openings

ferred, to avoid the troubles that would ensue. Then came bourgeois houses, whose windows, effectively secured by bolts and hasps, could afford to brave the *traverse*, and by the end of the century most of the common people were imitating them, and new buildings could face in whatever direction their owners fancied.

Meanwhile, the peasant's house had begun to take on a different look in other respects. Jacques Fauvet and Henri Mendras pinpoint the years between 1875 and 1910 as the period when roofs changed, cellars appeared (useful for the storage of potatoes and wine), second stories were built, and many old buildings were renovated, enlarged, or replaced.[32] The most dramatic change was in the roof, traditionally made of thatch or flimsy wood shingles. Thatch, which administrative regulation had not eliminated, was slowly driven out as slate and tile became available, especially mass-produced tile, which though cheaper and uglier than the traditional artisanware, was also very much lighter, and so made fewer demands on foundations and walls.[33] In the 1870's Edmond Bogros had thought the homes of the Morvandais as bad as the huts or wigwams of complete savages. But this was about to change. Even as he wrote, thatch, shingles, and wooden slats were giving way to "aristocratic slate and vividly colored tile." Improved transportation was making such novelties available; but in this instance the practical benefits of the novelties were quickly recognized. The new roofs, of course, provided greater safety, but beyond that, they left useful storage space for grain or rainwater where thatch had left none. In the "dry" country of Normandy, which has ample rainfall but not many sources of fresh water, so that people had to drink from dirty pools and ponds, this was an enormous improvement.[34]

Riding along the road from Châtellerault to Poitiers in 1877, an officer noted that the houses were of the same general, low-lying type but were built of different materials, the older ones being made of porous tuff, the more recent of free stone. In the Morvan the windowless house of timber was likewise edged out by stone between 1875 and 1915. The older structures built of stone and some of the new ones, too, were as miserable as the wooden ones, their granite poorly held together with clay mortar. They improved notably with the increasing availability of limestone from Auxois and Nivernais and of cement, which were introduced around 1875, expenses now "permitted [at least in the Morvan] by the important gains" that local wet nurses brought by hiring themselves out. Soon, with lime, hence with mortar more easily available throughout the countryside, stronger structures might even bear a second story. A second story was a step up in the social hierarchy— a sign of prosperity and success even if the builder left it empty and unused, as many "Parisians" returning home to Orne, Quercy, or Nivernais did. Where families moved upstairs, however, and made the top floor into a residential unit, they had to abandon the heavy furniture formerly used, and notably the large closed beds. Too bulky to follow their owners up the stairs, the old *lits clos* gave way to open beds, less prone to dust, more open to fresh air.[35]

The hygienic gain was unsuspected, the social advance was all. "The mere idea of having built a two-story house," wrote René Dumont about the Mayenne of our own century, "fills with pride a peasantry that long considered beyond its reach a type of building connected in its mind with the chateau and the *maison bourgeoise.*" And indeed progress meant access to upper-class facilities—*embourgeoisement.* By 1900 there were 171 lime and cement works in Nièvre. Stone mullions and lime for whitewash became available to more than bourgeois homes. The use of plaster and paint, long reserved for the better-off, made great strides. In 1879 Francus saw these flourishes as a common index of the degree of comfort a family had achieved. But the plastered-and-painted home was still out of the ordinary at this time in Ardèche, at least, standing out among the surrounding dark homes and attracting beggars and tourists: "If you don't want visits in the country, don't have a white-painted house."[36]

By the 1890's the improvement seems general. A teacher in Vic-le-Comte was struck by the contrast between the houses of 1899 and the hovels of 20–25 years before; the new houses were rectangular and symmetrical, with "large and numerous openings, giving free access to air and light." The increased spaciousness of the average home also impressed Alfred de Foville, who thought it "one of the most evident tendencies" in the housing of the time. The tight quarters built to save the cost of a wall or to keep out the chill were loosening up. As more and more peasants traveled about, they learned that there were many ways of building besides the one their fathers or neighbors used. Imitation of bourgeois building styles—which were themselves turning away from local tradition toward rationalistic cubic structures—and of railway architecture, as "pretty red-and-white brick stations" began to appear here and there, altered the looks of many a *bourgade,* then of the countryside as well. In 1903 Ardouin-Dumazet, noting the dwindling use of timber, lath, and clay in Sologne Bourbonnaise, remarked: "What is lost in picturesqueness is gained in health."[37]

Fundamental changes took place out of the sight of passing travelers, and one of the greatest concerned heat and light. These were related to total building structures, especially to the dearth of windows. A house with only one window would be too dark without the light coming through the opened door. Its inhabitants had to choose between semi-darkness, even in daylight hours, and the wind, cold, rain, or dust blowing over the threshold. In any case, the primitive fireplaces smoked heavily, and the best way out for smoke was also through the door.*

---

* Local sobriquets attest to the frequency with which homes were filled with smoke. In Ardèche alone the inhabitants of several villages were known as *lous fumas* or *lous foumous* (*les fumeurs; les enfumés*). (Pierre Charrié, *Folklore du Haut-Vivarais,* p. 34.)

The fireplace was the focus of the home—so much so that in houses with more than one room the room where the fire burned was called *la maison* (Bresse, Normandy) or was singled out with some special name such as *the* room or the heated room. In certain areas, notably Mâconnais and Bresse, central fireplaces with high chimneys raised in the roof (*cheminées sarrasines*), ancient in design and not very good at heating, were used through the nineteenth century. Thousands still survived in 1880, filling maison, *hutau*, or *chambre chauffure* with acrid smoke, making the winters even colder and more uncomfortable than they already were. Only gradually were the last of these supplanted by stoves, which were located either in the fireplace itself or in a small, separate *chambre de poële.*[38]

In these areas, as elsewhere, light from the fireplace was generally the only light after the sun went down. In some places tallow candles were used—cylinders of beef or mutton grease, with a cotton wick, that were hard to light, gave only a flickering yellowish flame, smoked and smelled unpleasant, and dripped badly, leaving dirty deposits on their candlesticks. For good reason they were used sparingly, primarily for meals and for the veillée. In most of the south and the center the dubious light came from ancient oil lamps propped on a tall stand or hung from a hook, which consisted of nothing more than a wick (sometimes made from the topknot of a cotton bonnet) burning in a small pool of nut or kale or rape-seed oil. At that, these *chaleux*, or *caleu, caleil*, or *chalei*, themselves appeared to guzzle too much fuel ("gormand m'in chaleuil," they said in Saintonge), and so were treated as a rich man's light. Used only when the nights were long, they were stored in a cupboard from spring to fall. "In September hang up your caleu," says the southwestern proverb, "in the month of March throw it away."[39]

The problem, as always, was cost. The first wax (stearin) candles appeared in northern France around 1840, but their price restricted them to middle-class households, which were already using oil lamps of modern design. The development of paraffin in 1850 paved the way for a revolution in private lighting, but the early paraffin lamps were dangerous, which inhibited their use until perfected models appeared in the 1870's and especially the middle 1880's. Even then, their cost, though small (about ten centimes a day), was too high so long as there was a plentiful supply of hemp oil to burn. Their generalization thus waited on the gradual extinction of the hemp fields toward the end of the century: in Allier and Mâconnais around 1880–90, in Nièvre around 1900, in Loire around 1910. By 1906 we hear that in Minervois the better-off were using a paraffin lamp in winter. But in summer the sun was the source of light for most: "If a laborer lights himself to bed with a candle, it is because he is not wholly broke." There is no question that the peasants heartily welcomed these innovations. In Brittany soon after 1888 we hear of big farms where hanging or standing lamps had driven out resin or tallow. In 1899 Foville exulted that in Lorraine, where evenings had once been spent in stables, with women doing their embroidery and men dipping hemp around a smoky *lumignon*—a poor, dim candle surrounded by bottles full of water to reflect its flame—the oil lamp now shone "with incomparable brilliance."[40]

Of course only in urban centers did one find the dazzling illumination that made the nineteenth century the age of the conquest of the dark. In city home and in city street there was gaslighting, then incandescent lamps with the invention of the gas mantle late in the century, and for the very rich, not long after, electricity as well. But around 1905 Daniel Halévy, visiting Ygrande in Allier (pop. in 1973 just over 1,000), found the municipal council just then introducing acetylene lamps, and commented: "Rural lighting is a major problem.... If peasants move to town it is to a great extent because there they find light."[41]

"Born in a stable," says the 1848 agricultural survey of the mountain man, "he spends his childhood and half his adult life there"—because it was the only place where he could find some shelter from the cold. But the house itself, sometimes divided from the stable by only a few planks, was not all that different. "As dirty in their interiors as they are in their persons, they and their beasts inhabit the same apartment." What the officer wrote about the Bretons in 1827 could be repeated almost word for word to the end of the century, at least in the Auvergne, Velay, and Vivarais. In the Charentes, too, by local testimony, many homes were *mardoux coume in nic de puput* (filthy as a hoopoe's nest). Squat one-room houses, with the bare beaten earth for a floor, lit by a small dormer and a door, "which remain open all the time," inhabited in common by the family and the domestic animals (Cantal, 1864), a single compartment, men and beasts together (Ardèche and Haute-Loire, 1895).[42]

Space was costly. It was natural for animals and men to share it. Their food and quarters were similar after all; and besides, the body heat of cattle or sheep was reason enough to prize their proximity. Less bulky beasts would wander in and out of the hut or cottage (except when winter kept them indoors too), and in Brittany, we are told, pigs often nibbled at the babies with whom they shared the floor. In the Moselle vineyard areas, farmer and family lived below ground, while animals and equipment "occupied the most salubrious and least humid quarters" (1858). In the Landes, where a book published in 1911 emphasized the improvements and comforts of new housing, the stable was still divided from the kitchen, the center of family life, by a plank partition with two openings through which the oxen poked their heads in order to be fed by hand twice a day by the farmer sitting by his stove. No wonder a country mayor had noted the wide use of aromatics to purify the air. But benzoin, juniper berries, and sugar on hot embers hid mephitic odors without dispelling them. They merely made the air thicker, heavier, and still less fit to breathe.[43]

These ill-heated, evil-smelling quarters were scantily furnished. Dark, damp, smoky, earthen-floored, humid, airless (but for the drafts), they were, said a report about the rather large parish of Saint-Ours, full of dusty rags and stinking objects. An inventory of the possessions of a seventy-nine-year-old widow who died at Jouy (Eure-et-Loir) in 1851 gives us an idea of what these rags and objects might have been: pothook; tongs and andirons; candlestick and two bad chairs; table, kneading trough, chest; three plates, three spoons, two forks, platter, pot; nine bad shirts, three corsets, three dresses; two blankets, one for bed and one for self; one feather mattress and one bolster; three sheets and one bad canvas bag.[44]

Even such skimpy possessions might be crowded in the narrow quarters that stunted building and yearning for warmth imposed. In 1849 we hear of a family of eight in Deux-Sèvres who lived in a single room 1.95 m high, 4.65 m wide, and 6.65 m deep, with one window measuring 85 cm by 55 cm and a door 1.87 m by 81 cm, and who shared three beds. These last were mere wooden boxes, fairly deep, equipped with a palliasse and a feather comforter and fully enclosed by a low canopy and thick curtains of green serge. Such beds were treasuries of dust and parasites, where children and old people lay together, sick or well, catching each other's ills and sharing the lice. No wonder, in this case, that three of the children were malformed.*

Perhaps this family was exceptionally poor, but the description 40 years later of the average dwelling in Auvergne sounds suspiciously similar. The single room was larger, but the same kind of enclosed beds stood around the walls, equipped with straw pallets to which rich people added one or two feather comforters and the poor another pallet filled with beech leaves (gathered in November).† There was at best one sheet per bed, for laundry as we have seen posed its own problems. In Creuse, Dordogne, Haute-Garonne, and Lot-et-Garonne, quite frequently in Burgundy and Lyonnais as well, even in dwellings with several rooms people lived six or eight to a room and used the least possible number of beds "to have fewer sheets to wash." The other furniture consisted typically of a table and benches, a massive cabinet for the plates, one or more troughs (one to be used for kneading), a coffer for salt in the fireplace, and, for the rich, a clock. With a stone feeding basin for the dog, this was the lot. And these were not poor people, at least compared with the cowherd and his helpers who, we are told, slept in the stable, where they were warm and had no complaints.[45]

---

* J.-Z. Amussat, *Quelques considérations sur l'hygiène*, p. 258. In feet, the room measured roughly 15¼ by 22 with a ceiling height of about 6⅓. Note that when offered the chance to move to more spacious quarters, the family hesitated in fear of a raise in rent, explaining that it was better to be lodged less well and come out ahead.

† This is confirmed by E. Harrison Barker's description of conditions in an Aveyron home: two beds without linen, nothing but a patchwork quilt over big bundles of dry corn leaves. "It is thus that many of the peasants of the Aveyron sleep." (*Wandering by Southern Waters*, p. 294.)

In fact a cabinet for the dishes and benches for the table were comforts of a fairly advanced kind. We do not find a single glass in the Widow Drouet's inventory given above; and except for the more prosperous households, which might have had a few glasses that would serve for all, people drank from the pot (in Bresse, for instance, until 1890–1900). Yet the widow owned forks where many had only spoons. Some households had a carved receptacle for wooden spoons hanging in the hearth or suspended from the ceiling. And in Finistère and other places richly carved spoons were ritual wedding gifts. Then there were knives, of course; but these the men carried in their pockets, the women in their pockets or hanging from their belts. In Finistère forks were rare until 1890 and did not become a routine utensil until the twentieth century, when table knives made their appearance too. Glasses, first seen under the Restoration, spread only after the Second Empire. Tableware itself was rare, consisting at most of several bowls. We are specifically told that in the Morvan and Upper Brittany people spooned their food out of the common pot until late in the century. The rest was eaten, as the French say, "sur le pouce," the thumb put to use to hold a piece of something on bread or pancake. In the Morvan, Brittany, and Franche-Comté tables sometimes had a saucer-shaped depression into which the gruel, porridge, or soup was directly ladled. Around Brioude (Haute-Loire), in the Laonnois, and perhaps at Orléans, however, people did not take their soup at the table at all: in winter they kept the bowl in their lap and sat as close as possible to the hearth; in summer they moved outside to eat, holding the bowl and squatting on the doorstep or just making their meal standing up.[46]

Charles Péguy remembered spooning his soup out of a little saucepan balanced on his knees. He remembered too the absence of all comfort, so that in later life, as he said to Daniel Halévy, he was never able to sit in an armchair without feeling ill at ease. Chairs were very rare, and armchairs rarer still, though little Péguy, whose mother mended chairs for a living, had a tiny one all of his own.[47] In most rural households the family head traditionally enjoyed the only chair, whether with arms or not, and everyone else sat on benches, stools, or anything handy they could find.

Students of Languedoc, the Morvan, and Mâconnais have all noted how the end of the nineteenth century brought a clear progress in household inventories, less rudimentary and also cleaner.[48] The rate of change varied, of course. Eugène Bougeatre puts the change in Vexin, closer to Paris, in the 1860's. There many of the richer peasants, after seeing the Paris Exhibitions of 1867 or 1878, were moved to buy ready-made furniture and crockery, though these were still used only on great occasions. In the Morvan, its poverty relieved by the gains of its fertile wet nurses, factory-made furniture began to appear in the late 1870's, and again the evidence suggests more for show than for use. In Loire, more out of the way, traditional chests or coffers began to be replaced by cupboards after the 1870's, then by wardrobes, eventually (from the 1900–

1910 period on) even by wardrobes with a mirror. In Finistère, on the other hand, closed beds with straw or oats-chaff mattresses went out only in the early twentieth century. All of this of course implied the end of the village artisans who had made the old chests, cupboards, and dressers. Their services had been in ever-smaller demand since the late eighteenth century, and their output practically ceased around 1900. After 1914 almost all household furniture came out of a factory.[49]

The truly revolutionary change lay less in the furniture itself than in the fact that peasants now realized that they could have homes like those of the workingmen and artisans they had seen in the bourg. It had never occurred to Henri Bachelin's typical villager that his cottage could or should be changed into a house, with round tables, varnished chairs, curtains at the windows and pictures on the walls. By the turn of the century this transformation was well under way, bringing the living patterns of country and small town a step closer.[50]

The really crucial changes happened around the hearth. The open fireplace as the only source of heat (not to say light) grew increasingly rare after 1865, replaced by stoves for heating and then for cooking as well. Dutch ovens (*cuisinières*) and spirit-stoves (*réchauds*) followed in time. As the kitchen hearth disappeared, the interior of the house and all it contained changed. Big cooking vessels were replaced by smaller ones; chairs and other furniture were spaced around, no longer focused on one spot in the room; the curtained bed could be dispensed with, even bedwarmers were gradually put away.[51] The ritual of lighting the fire altered, too. Matches became more prevalent, partly because hemp was less of a commonplace. Until the mid-nineteenth century no house was without its tinderbox, containing a flintstone, tinder (hemp fiber), and a file. The tinder had first to be fired with flint and file, then touched to a homemade match—a short stalk of hemp waste soaked in sulfur with which the broom wood or vine branches in the fireplace could be set ablaze. Then came the ready-made match, taxed in 1871, a state monopoly after 1872, with the contraband trade that this encouraged and the special hidey-hole in the chimney wall (*la poutire* in Mâconnais) for the matches purchased from the *chimicon*.[52] While matches were rare, households had always tried to keep a small pile of live embers going through the night to relight the fire in the morning. If these went out, someone took an old clog and went to appeal to neighbors for spare embers. This provided the opportunity for a chat, and Lorraine teachers remarked in 1889 that such sociability was waning because, with matches, relighting the fire no longer provided an occasion for a neighborly chat.[53]

The next crucial change in domestic life would come with electrification, which, mostly between the wars, altered the rhythm of work and leisure. Life and labor, regulated by daylight (for oil and gas lamps were used sparingly), came to be ruled by a personal choice. The fears that dwelt in darkness and in the mysteries of shadow dissolved. So did much of the dirt that had never really been seen in homes obscure and full of smoke. The taste for cleanliness and comfort had spread with means, with paint, with the imitation of the bourgeois's ways.[54] So the effects of electric light were, in some ways, symbolic of a whole new world that had settled in within the lifetime of those who learned to turn a switch.

Chapter Eleven

THE FAMILY

Marie-toi, ne te marie pas,   Will you marry, yea or nay?
Pour sur, tu t'en repentiras.   You'll regret it either way.

MARRIAGE WAS ONE of the great social occasions of traditional French society, a vast feast, with as many as 500 guests, for all of them one of the rare breaks in a routine of hard and weary work and frequent privation. But marriage was not just an occasion for socializing, for reaffirming bonds of friendship, kinship, and social obligation. It was an alliance that concerned far more than two individuals—two clans and the whole of the society they lived in were affected by their arrangements. Witness the traditional *donnages* practiced in Lorraine and elsewhere, at which the village youth group proclaimed who was to couple off with whom. Couplings were no private matter.[1]

"There are no friends in the countryside," writes Henri Mendras (that is, no strong relationships based on private choice), "only relatives or neighbors." Be it distant or vague, it was kinship that counted, the bond, in the absence of many others that we are trained to recognize today, that commanded association, visits, intercessions, favors: "We must sell to him, buy from him, deal with him, ... he is of the family."[2] Hence the attention weddings received, and the variety of ritual with which they were surrounded. The wedding was above all a business arrangement, both between families, which assessed the compatibility and worth of their proposed allies very carefully, and between two individuals who entered a partnership. Hence the preliminaries that, while using a variety of devices to avoid giving offense and making enemies in a narrow world where every gesture counted with people one would frequent all of one's life, made courting couples sound exceedingly businesslike.

Pierre Dupont's *Peasant's Serenade* has the courting hero marry Denise, beautiful as the day, but above all, "worth five dowries put together." Dupont was a petit bourgeois from Lyon, schooled and hence presumably romantic enough to pay mind to very secondary considerations. But beauty counted little when a wife was weighed. As peasant wisdom had it, land marries turds and money marries the ugly ("terre marie merde et l'argent marie peute gens").[3] More characteristic than Dupont's suitor would be the Vendean who woos his intended with food, and exchanges confidences with her about their respective worth: his oxen and his plow, her frantically reproductive chickens.[4]

> I li parlis de ma charrue et de mes boeufs,
> A m'disait que tot' ses poules pougnant doux oeufs.
> O faut donc bé, ma megnoune, nous marier tos deux.
> Faisons donc vite tielle besogne, si tu o voeux.

If the material claims proved true and there was no higher bid, the deal should have raised no problems. The families, of course, had the last word, and the first too, most often. One married a family, not a woman or a man. As the phrase goes, one married "into a family"—and when or before one did it, the families did the marrying.

A family might be almost the total population of a commune. Between 1876 and 1936 the number of communes with a population between 100 and 200 almost doubled, from 3,295 to 6,158; the number of those with populations below 100 increased fourfold, from 653 to 2,512. This helps explain the prevalence of sobriquets, essential to discriminate between so many households bearing the same name. "There is not a family in our villages," noted Father Gorse in 1895, "without its sobriquet."[5] Many were nicknames, of course, but many referred to houses. The Great House of earlier times had its humbler reflection, and Pierre Dupont might have been dubbed Pierre of the Mill or of the Gulch or of the Four-Acre-Farm, the better to tell him from his many cousins. The choice of a spouse was thus quite seriously limited, and the traditional and natural prejudice against marrying outside the community made the choice narrower still. The three-score years after 1876 are only relatively characteristic of earlier days, because they were the heyday of rural emigration. But the period does give a hint of what must have been, and what continued to be, though (as we shall see) increasingly mitigated by mobility and collapsing taboos. Yet, in such circumstances, intercourse among close relatives must have been rampant, leading to some number of mental and physical deficiencies, which may well have grown as the ablest and most enterprising left the village community for cities. Placide Rambaud has found that in Maurienne, because of the shrinking mountain population and the new opportunities to emigrate, inbreeding increased in the 30 years before the First World War, rising from 47.7 percent of marriages in 1884–1903 to 55.2 percent in 1913. The rate of intermarriage then fell again after the area opened up in 1914–18.[6]

Despite timid warnings ("When cousins marry the race goes to pot," they said in Hérault and the southwest), both family interests and deep-rooted prejudices encouraged the selection of a spouse as close to home as possible.[7] There was the pressure of laws and taxes that threatened family property and suggested the need for arrangements to maintain it or patch together again what had been put asunder. But there was also the intense cohesion that made families reluctant to admit into the protected and protective circle anyone who was not thoroughly known, and that made young people pleased to marry kin or neighbor whose comings and goings they had always seen. Marrying out was horrid. Entry into a strange household was a harrowing experience in itself. An in-law was accepted only in part, as well as with ill-grace:

> El o écri su lou cu di chi
> Qe jémâ janr n'o évu bï
> El o écri su lou tro di cu
> Qe jémâ bel mer n'éma bru.

Proverbs attest to it. Sons-in-law and daughters-in-law were marked strangers: "Janr è bru son jan d'ôtru," or "Tout genre et tout bru sont des gens d'autru." Hence: "A son-in-law's friendship is like the winter's sun"; or "My daughter's dead, farewell my son-in-law."* If marrying into a family one knew was such an ordeal, then marrying among strangers was decidedly worse. Where each community was a law to itself, in-laws unfamiliar with its customs, ways, and turns of speech felt and were made to feel even more like strangers.

Self-interest and traditional prejudice interpenetrated. Villagers resented all strangers who moved in, because their presence would weigh on the use of commons and encroach on the communal right to cut wood. And just as at Broye-les-Pesmes (Haute-Saône) potential buyers of land who came from the outside were intimidated and discouraged, so in most places spouses from outside the community were put off by every means, including violence.[8] Some of the numerous fights between the youth of neighboring villages were sparked by attempts to poach on local preserves; village girls seem to have joined in, and no doubt for similar motives: in a restricted marriage market, loss of one potential spouse threatened the prospects of either sex.

Of course, male activities were more visible (and audible). At Saint-Bueil (Isère) a locally composed song of the 1870's shed scorn on local girls who frequented lads of other villages, or even worse, the despised "Savoyaux." The song was adapted for use in other villages of the region, and girls who dared transgress the explicit prohibition had their faces blackened with shoe polish or, more often, soot. Obviously, at this stage other girls must have played a part in the proceedings. On a more solemn note, we find the village women of Sourribes, near Sisteron, greeting any strange bride at the entrance to the village with a monitory speech, after which they made her swear on the fattest book they had been able to lay their hands on—which was supposed to represent the Bible—that she would not try to be worth more than her fellows.

---

* Charles Perron, *Proverbes de la Franche-Comté*, p. 53; *Barbizier*, 1950, p. 358. To cut bread into tiny pieces was to cut it the way a mother-in-law would: "Vou fat da briq de bél-mer." More revealing, in the cemetery of Minot (Côte-d'Or) couples from families that owned separate tombs in the end rejoined their blood kin: husband and wife were separated in death (Françoise Zonabend, "Les Morts et les vivants," pp. 13–14).

Rather less, one would assume. In such circumstances, it was reasonable that (to use Martine Ségalen's term) socioprofessional endogamy should so long remain the predominant matrimonial model.[9]

Family interest and collective ideals remained crucial in determining what made a good husband or a good wife, suggestive and highly restrictive while their hold endured. "If you marry take a rake [used to gather hay], not a pitchfork [used to spread it]." "Beauty can't be eaten with a spoon." "There is no shoe so fine that it doesn't get down at the heel." "An ugly cat has pretty kittens." And an admonition rather seldom heeded: "To beat one's wife is to beat one's purse."*

But collective notions of the necessity of family solidarity did not prevent family feuds. Since every marriage was first and foremost a business arrangement turning on the bride's dowry—seen as a compensation for the woman's loss of rights to her family's land but also as an endowment that gave her claims on her new family's wealth—there could be endless conflicts; and there were indeed, arising out of this and out of inheritances. Proximity, which made for confidence (meaning no more than familiarity), also made for conflict. As an ex-country boy remembered of the Mantois, with some notable exceptions families did not see much of each other, divided as they often were "by interminable lawsuits concerning party rights, joint property, apportionment of land, and boundary disputes, which gave rise to secret grudges and tenacious hates." Intermittent violence and brutality, mutual exploitation or indifference, must have been as much a part of life inside the home as outside it. Meals were brief and silent, little occasion for communion: "few words are exchanged." Mutual interest seldom went beyond interest plain. Spouse, offspring, kin were not company or companions, but aids. When not of use, children and the elderly sick were simply a burden for the family, wrote Charles Perron about Broye-les-Pesmes: "One made for them the least sacrifices that one could." And "people and things were evaluated only in terms of their material worth."[10]

Children there were aplenty, at least for a good while, and so the loss of one was no particular blow, noted the Board of Hygiene of Haute-Vienne in its report for the decade ending in 1866. We are still in the age when from Forli's walls Caterina Sforza shouted to the besiegers who threatened to put to death six of her children they held hostage: "Fools! You've only to look to see that I can make others!" Infants and tots were expendable commodities.† Their upbringing, sporadically indulgent, left them great freedom to run around

---

* Perron, *Proverbes*, p. 53. A wedding song, very popular in the central Pyrenees, stipulated that the notary drawing up the marriage contract should write on his blue (official) paper that the husband must not beat his wife: "Bouto, noutari, sul papiè blu / Que non la bate pas, sigur. / Bouto, noutari, sul papié / Que non la bate pas jamès." (Robert Jalby, *Le Folklore du Languedoc*, p. 84.)

† Archives Départementales, Haute-Vienne M 1047, *Rapport du conseil départemental d'hygiène, 1865–1866*, p. 26. Nicole Castan has found no evidence in eighteenth-century Languedoc of any particular interest in or affection for children, at least among those lower classes "that

unsupervised once out of swaddling clothes, and thus to maim themselves. But there would be little pity: "To grow, one has to cry. Cry, you'll piss less!" As soon as their growth permitted, between five or six and eight, children would be put to work—guarding chickens or geese, lending a hand with cattle, fetching and carrying—before a regular task or hiring out, at ten or so, integrated them fully into the adult world.[11]

Women worked harder and they were less free. "It is for women to work for men. My wife, I've only taken her so that she can work." Worn out after having toiled right through the second or third birth, which was often managed largely unassisted, wives were beasts of burden seldom set to rest. Father Gorse has a searing chapter devoted to the slavery of women after marriage, never ending *besounhas* (a word that means both labor and trouble), never sitting down; and to the hostile suspicions that men entertained toward them. The Church's old-established view of women as potential vessels of sin and of temptation was steadfastly maintained. Women were forbidden to sing in church, and their periodic "uncleanness" was consecrated by a variety of rites.[12] Simple menfolk could find here confirmation of their engrained prejudice. And prejudice was rife and vocal.* Of a pretty girl one might well say she would make a good cow. But a good goat, a good mule, and a good woman made three spiteful sorry beasts. No saws or proverbs did women honor. All slighted or criticized them: "Gambling, wine, and women are three great destroyers." Or insisted on male supremacy: "Where the cock sings the hens are silent"; "The purse holds the crest" (only men hold the purse!). Or stressed the disillusions of marriage: "After courting, famine"; "If you want to break in the wolf, marry it."[13]

Women ate standing up, serving the men and completing their meal later on what was left. This may have been purely practical, though the serving process could not have been a big job; but other evidence suggests that it was one more symbol of the stubborn division of the sexes, *after* marriage. In Corrèze couples never walked side by side. If the man walked ahead, the

---

would be last to show signs of [such feelings]." Children, the newborn in particular, were treated "with as much indifference as in the past": they were referred to as "créatures," so that in the records their sex is not evident; their ages and birthdays were only vaguely noted, even by the mother ("6 or 8 months, 11 years old or 14"); the death of illegitimate children was welcomed. (See the discussion in André Abbiateci, ed., *Crimes et criminalité en France sous l'Ancien Régime*, Paris, 1971, pp. 96–97.) Much of this was still valid a century later, except that by then "créatures" were more obviously female. See Marguerite Audoux on her childhood as *pupille de l'assistance publique* in the care of Sologne farmers, for whom she guarded cattle: "non pas malheureuse: pire." "You're cold?—Work hard, you'll get warm. You're hungry?— There's a potato left in the dresser. . . . And then a slap here, a slap there, not out of cruelty— mais il faut bien dresser les enfants." (Interview quoted in Henry Poulaille, *Nouvel age littéraire*, Paris, 1930, p. 256.)

* Could the prejudice have been heightened by resentment born of enforced celibacy? On the whole, the poorer the region the lower the proportion of people that ever got married—under 50 percent in Hautes- and Basses-Alpes, Aveyron, Cantal, Côtes-du-Nord, Doubs, Finistère, Ille-et-Vilaine, Haute-Loire, Loire-Inférieure, Lozère, Manche, Morbihan, Hautes- and Basses-Pyrénées, and Haute-Saône right through the century.

woman followed behind at a distance of at least 30 or 35 steps; or it could have been vice versa. But even for Sunday mass, one left before the other: "Tirats, davoun, ou ieu?" (Will you go first, or me?) It was a division downward: in Marche, Berry, and the Maine the man tutoyered his wife, as he did his children, while she said *vous* to him.[14] As possessions went, women were not important; and one finds many prayers in which chestnuts, turnips, and cattle are to be saved by God or the saints ahead of womenfolk.*

True, the domestic economy of peasant households called for the services of both the sexes. The woman cooked and kept the house (badly, quite often), mended and patched the clothes as hastily as she could, and brought up the children. But she also spun yarn, and she cared for the cattle. "No woman, no cow, hence no milk, no cheese"; nor chicken or eggs and, given her spinning tasks, almost no linen. Inventories of bachelors and old widowers reflect the almost total absence of shirts and sheets. On the other hand, the man was irreplaceable, not only for the heavy work, but for his cash earning power; women were less easily hired and then at much lower rates.[15] So, men and women complemented each other in a working partnership. But they were not equals and, hence, seldom friends. The woman, reported a pastor from Ariège in 1861, was of course considered much less than a man. The birth of a male baby was greeted by gunshots and rejoicing. If a girl was born, "the father feels cruel disappointment.... He is almost humiliated." "Ce n'est qu'une créature," they said deprecatingly in Mayenne or Sarthe. Mothers rejoiced in boys for fear of their husband's anger at a girl. Too many daughters were "a calamity." This same attitude was noted in the Limousin and in many other places half a century later:[16]

> One daughter, no daughter;
> Two daughters, enough daughters;
> Three daughters, too many daughters;
> Four daughters and the mother—
> Five devils against the father!

The father was usually so embarrassed at a daughter's birth, he would try to have her baptized as quietly as possible (no bells in certain parts) and with no expense. "It's only a girl," people said—but "it is a fine boy." And Edmond Bogros tells the story of the father who was asked what his wife, recently delivered of a girl, "had turned out": "*Nout'foune?* Ye gods! She's turned out nothing at all." In Franche-Comté the same ill-omened owl that announced death appeared as the harbinger of a girl's birth when it hooted on the chimney of a pregnant woman. Nor did a man like to get his first New Year's wishes from a woman—for it was men who brought luck![17] Indeed, in

---

* G.-M. Coissac, *Mon Limousin*, p. 176, quotes an example: "Monsieur Sen Marsan, nostra boun foundatour, pregatz per nous nostre seinhour qu'il veuilla gardar nostras castanhas [chestnuts], nostras rabas [turnips], nostra femma."

Finistère as Olivier Perrin mentioned (but that was under the July Monarchy), in places where the old ways were preserved best, men wore no mourning when their wives died.*

The war of the sexes did not await the nineteenth—or the twentieth—century, and the oppression of the weaker by the stronger is easy to understand: it is the contrary that would have been artificial. There were good reasons for wanting male offspring: greater strength, hence more employable and more use in the farm's work. And, of course, when a son married, the family's property was likely to be increased rather than drained off in dowries. Thus the popular proverb: "Marry your son when you will, your daughter when you can." Yet, despite the man's superior strength, one somehow suspects that things did not go one way only, that women did not content themselves with picking on other women. There are many Breton stories, for example, about Yann and Chann (John and Jane), the husband conspicuously stupid, forever bungling things, the wife the bright one in the family, forever outwitting him. But women's intelligence did not have a good press in the countryside. For that matter, intelligence in general was not popular, and of clever children one said that they would not live long.[18]

Bullied husbands certainly existed, but though village farces maintained alive the odious image of husband-beating wives, I have come across no actual case of such an incident. If women did their menfolk violence, it was more likely to have been by stealth, as in the case of one Marie-Anne Nicolas, forty-two years old, who was sentenced to six months in jail by the district court of Châteaulin for having grabbed her husband by his *verge* while he was asleep, and thus dragged him around despite his screams, causing grave lesions in the urethral canal.[19]

In certain instances where the men were ordinarily away, fishing or hired out for months on end, women in fact managed the household or its funds. But this does not appear to have contributed much to their emancipation, because the men seem to have kept tight hold on home affairs, as circumstances permitted, giving detailed instructions on how their wages should be spent and even on the sale of cattle.[20] Real opportunity for women came with independent earnings in such jobs as domestic service or wet-nursing, though even then emancipation, once back on the home ground, must have been very relative. It also came with or just contemporary to education, despite a school program designed to reinforce women's traditional roles. There is no question that education was a progressive force, offering girls opportunities they had not had before, especially the possibility of escape and also of sharing the sort of

---

* Olivier Perrin and Alex Bouet, *Breiz Izel*, p. 279. The implicit lower value of the woman is suggested also in the disparate length of mourning in bourgeois circles: one year and six weeks for a widow, but only one year for a widower (Arnold Van Gennep, *Manuel de folklore*, 1.2: 805). Further, in many Ardèche villages a "more important" death knell was sounded for men—lasting longer than the peal for a woman and rung on the bigger bells (Pierre Charrié, *Folklore du Bas-Vivarais*, p. 64).

knowledge that had invested men with ancient superiorities. But the school, as always, was consciously more conservative than subversive of traditional patterns, teaching girls not skills that would emancipate them (nobody wanted that), but skills that would make them better wives, mothers, housekeepers— cleaner, more productive, able to sew, patch, mend, perhaps knit or embroider, cook a nourishing meal, and make a good moral home for present and future citizens. The different expectations of the sexes appear in schoolbooks, like this aside in a text for *petites classes*: "If one leaves one's village, one's native city, to travel a little afar, as you will certainly do, at least you, little boys."[21]

Unfortunately, the old routines in domestic life, diet, and upbringing prevailed much longer than was hoped. Between 1914 and 1918 country women may well have gained a new sense of autonomy and confidence, thanks to the initiatives and the responsibilities that they were forced to take, the jobs that they learned to do, the family allowances that they had to spend. And yet as late as 1937 the director of agricultural services in Lot could answer the agricultural survey in terms that fit the previous century: "The woman maintains her traditions, and her domestic virtues manifest themselves as a condition of slavery freely accepted."[22] Life on the farm had to be slavery. The only change now was that it was "freely accepted" because there was more of a choice. The pressure of parental authority and the once inescapable socioeconomic necessity that left no alternatives, or only bad ones, had relaxed or vanished. Now a woman accepted her slavery by choice—or by failure to attain emancipation. But emancipation was available and, equally important, women had become aware that it was available.

The dawning of such awareness had been gradual. Within certain limits, mountain girls had always sought the plain. Goats go up and girls go down, said the Pyrenean proverb. But to begin with, they sought the plain for much the same reason as their brothers did, because it held out the prospect of a less lean life, though with fewer chances of success than any male could expect. Girls went to fill the silk and textile mills of smaller industrial towns, walking ten miles or so from their village and living in miserable conditions in town through the week; others turned to part-time prostitution, especially in garrison towns; still others worked as seamstresses, milliners, nurses, and house servants. One and all for a long time worked to a single end: to gather a dowry, a *dot*. But school and print and growing opportunities in the last years of the nineteenth century made girls begin to have greater aspirations, and to feel that they now had a chance of realizing them. When girls got together, complained the village teacher of Clerjus in the Vosges in 1899, their talk was about how they loathed country life and farmwork, "their sole ideal" was "to marry a functionary, do nothing, and live in town." "Country girls await prince charming," agreed a country doctor in 1911, that is to say, a worker or artisan from town, better still a postman, a petty civil servant, or a noncommissioned officer. By now there were more such prince charmings; chance and choice were both greater. And we shall see that village womenfolk, working through swains or husbands, led and spurred the second wave of rural emigration to the towns.[23]

Meanwhile, it is well not to overestimate the degree of progress. Men were for work. Women were for breeding, and to be used as beasts of burden. Children were meant to pull their own weight in the strained economy of poor, penny-pinching households. In households living on short rations, wives and children, sometimes husbands too, would steal their own family's grain or wine to sell in the market or to *coquetiers* passing through.[24] Their feelings for each other must have been matter of fact at best, and hardly generous.* I am inclined, perhaps unjustly, to see the emphasis that schoolbooks placed on filial affection as part of a campaign to teach the rural folk urban sentiments that they had had little time or chance to acquire, to inculcate notions that were strange to them by insisting that they were natural and right.

There is no way of telling. Only the (perhaps misleading) evidence of bourgeois witnesses—doctors, landowners, and such—shocked by the fate of ailing peasants whisked into their graves because one must get back to work ("He is not good for anything anymore; he is costing us money; when will he be finished?"); and of aged peasants resented for taking precious time as they went to their tardy rest: "[The family members are] harsh on the dying as they are hard on themselves. [They] are not embarrassed to say in his hearing that he is dying and will kick the bucket anytime. His wife and his children mutter bitter words about wasted time. He is a burden and he feels it."[25] A sick man or an ailing woman was bad enough. An oldster dragging out his or her life was worse, a creature, or a nothing, like a female child, with not even the promise of some productivity to come—except perhaps when dead, *crevé.*†

The peasant, wrote a sympathetic witness in 1913, could not hide the relief he felt to see the end of those whom he called stragglers (*trainiaux*) or encumbrances (*embeurgnas*): "We inherit from the old man, but our old man is a sheer loss!" "Oh! it's nothing, it's an old man."[26] The old knew this, of course, and did their best to guard against being left at their children's dubious mercy. A host of proverbs warned, in almost identical terms, against the folly

---

* As evidence of how long it took for children to be granted any significant place in family or society, Pierre and M. C. Bourdieu cite the almost complete absence of pictures of children in peasant photograph albums and collections before 1939. By contrast, children have been a favorite subject since the Second World War, featured in half the pictures taken after 1945. ("Le Paysan et la photographie," p. 165.)

† Under the Second Empire, a school inspector in Aube deplored the fact that the countryside knew "practically no filial love or respect for [old] age." Every day furnished "thousands of examples" of offspring who, having secured their fortune, wished only for their father's death (quoted in Pierre Zind, *L'Enseignement religieux*, p. 176). Attitudes to death were matter-of-fact, when they were not lighthearted. Raymond Doussinet quotes a flippant formula, "Better him than us: if you blow into his arse, you'll keep him from croaking"; and a children's song, "Pied bot! ma grand-mère é morte, / Et mon grand-père otout. / Jh' hérit'rons d'sa thiulotte / Et d'son jhupon de d'sous." (*Le Paysan santongeais*, pp. 190–91.)

of divesting oneself of what one owns. "One should strip only to go to bed" (not even then, as we have seen!). "When father gives his son money, both laugh; when son gives father money, both cry." "A father can feed 12 children, yet 12 children won't feed their father."[27]

It is not clear whether such constant reference to fathers reflects their symbolic supremacy over the consort as representative of both parents, their dominant role in the forging of proverbs, a deeper resentment between father and children, or the mother's more modest expectations. Old women, of course, could still render services where decrepit males could not. At any rate, there is ample evidence of indifference to surviving parents; of resentment rising to hatred and even leading at times to parricide; of old people shuffled about from one child to another, taken in à charge because they had to be housed, yet "worse off than in the alms house" because of the constant changes and because there was no one to take care of them[28]—awkward parasites on short rations and less space, cursed as useless mouths by grudging son and perhaps vengeful daughter-in-law who wished them dead and sometimes drove them to it, maltreated, abandoned to hunger and disease.*

So, it was need and greed that bound the family. First how to make ends meet, then how to achieve a degree of security by acquiring capital and bits of land. Children, their numbers, whether great or small, and their inheritance rights, were a crucial factor in that equation. We hear a great deal about birth control, and certainly the 30 years before 1914 saw it spreading throughout the countryside. But for the poor and for those who clung to the old style of cultivation, children were still hands, hence wealth. The land-mincing machine, as Tocqueville called it—the equal division of inheritance between all offspring, established by the law of 1794—has been roundly blamed for inhibiting family size. But this applied only to property owners. It was not only the lack of skill or know-how that kept most peasants from contraceptive practices; it was the lack of need. The proof lies in the fact that in regions like the Moyenne Garonne, as Pierre Deffontaines has found, access to property in significant numbers coincided with a fall in birthrates (as well as with migration)—precisely when concern for the continuity of the family holding made family limitation relevant to need. Until this happened, Jules Renard's Philippe must have the last word: "I came into the world with my two arms," says Philippe. He marries and has four, and each child adds two more arms. "If no one in the family is crippled, it will never lack for arms and only risk having too many mouths."[29] The question, it seems, is what counts more, the child as mouth or the child as hand. For those who had little or no land to work or to leave behind them and whose chief commodity for sale was work,

* Balzac's Abbé Brossette notes: "The old people tremble to stay at home, for then they get no more food. Hence they go to the fields as long as their legs will carry them. If they lie down, they know very well that it is to die for lack of food" (Les Paysans, Paris, 1964 ed., p. 199).

children represented additional earning power, hence were properly produced in droves.

The size of the farms rented by tenants or sharecropped in the Lower Marche or the highlands of the Limousin was such, Alain Corbin tells us, that they required the labor of eight to twelve persons, possibly two or three households of people actually at work. There and in many other parts of France where the same situation existed, great importance was naturally attached to large families and to their need to stick together to survive.*

In a Limousin peasant poem, the titmouse criticizes the dove, because the dove is big, beautiful, and rich, yet produces only one or two offspring, whereas she herself, though small and weak, produces 15 or 16. "The head of family who works hard and who has many children," wrote Edouard Decoux-Lagoutte in 1888, "is almost sure in our countryside to acquire if not wealth at least honest comfort." And in 1894 Charles Dumont, walking through the Causses, amazed an innkeeper at Dargilau (Lozère) with tales of childless people. "How do they manage to earn any money then?" asked the host. Children, especially males of course, saved paying hired help; they were the *richesse du laboureur*, the farmer's wealth. So, in Corrèze at least, births continued as regularly as fecundity permitted. "How many great feasts a year?" asks a priest at catechism. "Four," answers a child. "Name them!" "Well, they are the day of the vote, the day of Carnival, the day we stick the pig, and the day my mother delivers."[30]

Where numerous progeny were seen as a source of comfort, premarital pregnancy was no dishonor, but proof of future fruitfulness. The sharecroppers of Lauragais welcomed more boys, illegitimate or not: "In ten years we shall be rich!" And in the Loire lowlands, official disapproval was mild and tolerant: "The case is very frequent." Boys and girls often married before the infant's birth. In any case the girl was not dishonored: "The little accident proves she is not a mule [i.e., sterile], which is a serious blemish." Married or not, women who had babies could contribute to household income by wet-nursing when, as in the case of Nièvre, the city baby market was easily accessible. And at the very least, a wife's fertility ensured a family's hold on a dowry that might have been reclaimed if she died childless.[31] Since sterility was always attributed to the woman, one need hardly wonder at the frenzied search for divine aid to conceive that fills the annals of popular superstitions.

As for contraception, a term I use not to indicate the use of any technical de-

---

* "Limousins migrants," pp. 352–53. According to Lucien Gachon, the Ambert region saw a rising use of birth control in 1880–1914, with the numbers of children falling in inverse proportion to the accumulation of wealth (see his paper in Jacques Fauvet and Henri Mendras, eds., *Les Paysans*, p. 397). It has been argued that a high-fertility strategy reflects a high child-mortality rate and will change as a fall in that rate makes the survival of an heir more likely. Certainly the rural France of the nineteenth century could show child-mortality rates comparable to those of the seventeenth century. But strategies differed according to regional and family labor needs, and this before any significant decline in the mortality rates.

vices, but simply to describe the deliberate limitation of progeny, it is hard to trace the spread of the idea, let alone the practice, among the lower orders of society. But the evidence—or rather reference without much specific evidence—suggests that this development took place side by side with the greater propensity toward savings, greater geographical and professional mobility, the abandonment of religious practice, the generalization of military service and of the experience of city ways, and the example of the lower middle classes, for whom, in the late nineteenth century, the single child became the family ideal.[32]

The demographic patterns of nineteenth-century France have been well studied by Etienne Van de Walle. Unfortunately, even his rich offerings leave a good deal obscure, notably, the differences in behavior between country and town, bourg and outlying areas. We can, of course, draw certain inferences from his work based on what we know about departments and their population; and when we do, we see that rural departments show a declining birthrate from the beginning of the century at least and perhaps before. Unhappily, we have no way of telling how the most rural districts performed in relation to the rest of their department, how isolation or poverty affected fertility. Nor, when we compare the rate at which births declined in departments that were obviously poorer, more isolated, more thoroughly rural, can we draw unequivocal conclusions. (See Maps 11–15, pp. 180–82.)

It is clear enough that the birthrate declines, the proportion of people getting married rises, and the age of first marriage drops in direct relation to economic activity, prosperity, and easier communications. The Breton peninsula, the south-central departments around Lozère, the mountainous regions—Alps and Pyrenees—and the western interior south of the Manche all clung longer to high birthrates, high rates of celibacy, and a preference for late marriages. On the other hand (and here the trouble starts), the wealthier departments of Nord and Pas-de-Calais shared these tendencies, whereas much of Languedoc, though more backward, began to marry more and to procreate less at dates that match or better the evolution of wealthier, more modern regions. To take another example, in 1831 girls born in Haute-Vienne were getting married six years earlier on the average than those born in Ille-et-Vilaine (at 21.7 and 27.6 years, respectively). Sixty-five years later, the difference was still close to five years (22.3 and 27.5).[33] Yet the Upper Limousin was poorer than Upper Brittany, and Rennes is a little closer to Paris than Limoges is. To note that the average age at first marriage was steadfastly and markedly higher in the west than in the Limousin does not make us any wiser, but does suggest the existence of regional orientations that outlasted changes in the economy or communications.

Once again, generalizations can by definition only hope to be generally correct, and correlations between one trend or local feature and another can be pushed only so far and no farther. Thus, in a seminal paper delivered in 1972,[34] Van de Walle made the suggestion that the departments with the highest per-capita income from the land were also those where birthrates declined first. In support of this he noted that in 1836 the per-capita land taxes paid in Seine and Calvados (where birthrates declined before 1800) were 10 francs and 11.90 francs, respectively, and the door-and-window tax figures were 2.40 francs and 1.10 francs. Meanwhile, the inhabitants of Finistère (where the birthrate declined only after 1890) paid only 4 francs in land tax and .50 francs in door-and-window tax. And it is true that poverty and high birthrates do seem to go together, and that the departments in which birthrates declined late in the century were generally (though, we have seen, not always) the poorest.

Yet an attempt to correlate economic conditions and birthrates during 1831–76 in those departments paying the lowest rates of door-and-window tax contributes little to our understanding. In Brittany, the western Pyrenees, and Lozère, low taxes (few windows) and high birthrates coincide. In more cases, though, we find a decline in birthrates with little or no improvement in housing; and some of these departments (Tarn-et-Garonne and Gers) had very low birthrates to begin with.

So one could procreate like the bourgeoisie without even aspiring to live like them. And if fertility figures sometimes confirm what we know already—drive yet another nail into the fortifications of enduring backwardness—they do not necessarily invalidate the impression that other areas, where the steady decline in fertility is supported by reliable statistics (Ariège, for instance), were perforce less backward. Discrepancies of this sort do nevertheless raise questions about the extent and meaning of what we generally describe as backwardness: the effective hold of isolation and poverty, which were always relative, and the way the peasants' indifference to the outside world actually worked, always highly selective, seldom ignoring what was perceived as being relevant to local need and possibility.* It seems that men—and sometimes women, too, perhaps—however poor and isolated they may have been, were not beyond devising or adopting means of their own for manipulating life.

There were, of course, well-established ways of limiting the population. Illegitimate children, like other socially marginal beings, had vastly higher

---

* Van de Walle's suggestion in an earlier paper ("Demographic Transition in France?," Population Association of America, Cincinnati, 1967) that linguistic differences seem to have played a major part in delaying the spread of birth control speaks to this point. It is true that his maps show fertility tending on the whole to decline more slowly in areas where local languages survived longest. But if the persistence of local speech proved an obstacle to the diffusion of ideas that found a freer course elsewhere, it was because the cultural structure of the region was different. And the mentalities this culture forged lived on, even while slowly assimilating new attitudes.

Interestingly enough, discrepancies in the two maps compared occur in the center and the south, as if there the impact of the national culture nibbling at local ways was harder to withstand. At the periphery, greater isolation (Lower Brittany) or contact with areas of similar culture across the borders (Basque and Catalan, Italian, Flemish, German) maintained what, from a French point of view, would look like cultural heterogeneity. See Ansley J. Coale, "The Decline of Fertility in Europe . . . ," in S. J. Behrman et al., *Fertility and Family Planning* (Ann Arbor, Mich., 1969), maps 1–3.

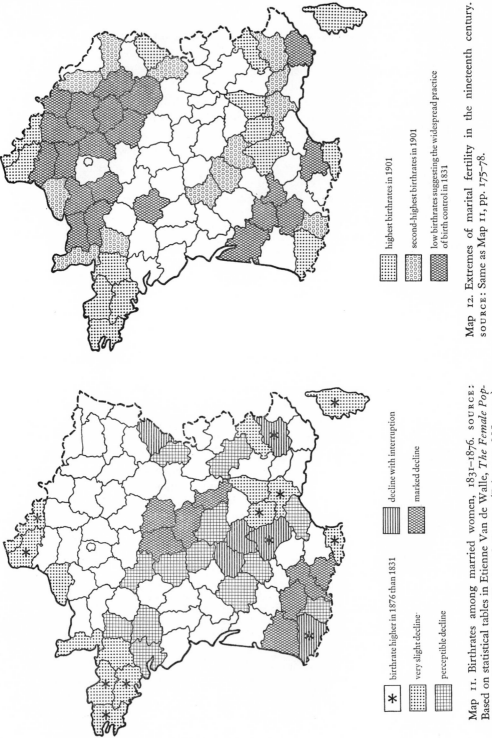

Map 11. Birthrates among married women, 1831–1876. SOURCE: Based on statistical tables in Etienne Van de Walle, *The Female Population of France in the Nineteenth Century* (Princeton, N.J., 1974).

* birthrate higher in 1876 than 1831

⫿ very slight decline·

⫶ perceptible decline

▨ decline with interruption

▦ marked decline

Map 12. Extremes of marital fertility in the nineteenth century. SOURCE: Same as Map 11, pp. 175–78.

▨ highest birthrates in 1901

⦾ second-highest birthrates in 1901

▨ low birthrates suggesting the widespread practice of birth control in 1831

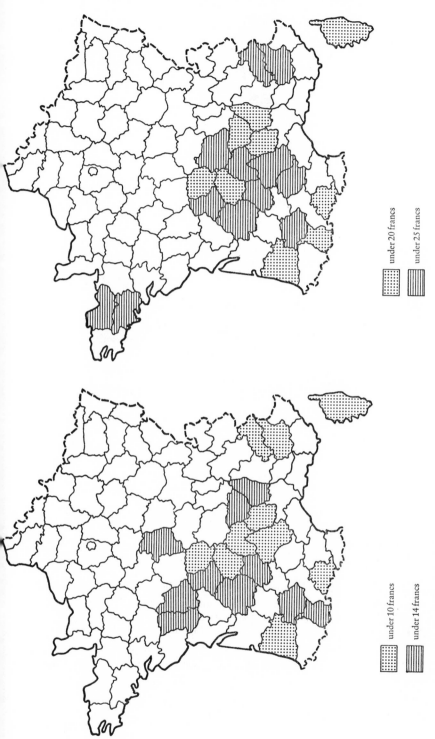

Map 13. Poorest departments by tax revenue per hectare, 1857. National average: 31 francs. SOURCE: Léonce de Lavergne, *Economie rurale de la France depuis 1789* (4th ed., Paris, 1877), pp. 463-64.

under 10 francs

under 14 francs

Map 14. Poorest departments by tax revenue per capita, 1857. National average: 46 francs. Population density accounts for the difference between this map and Map 13. SOURCE: Same as Map 13.

under 20 francs

under 25 francs

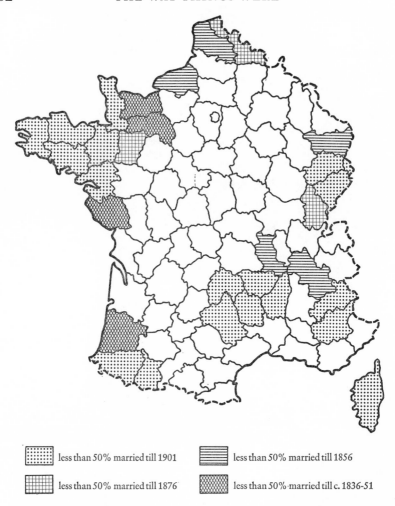

less than 50% married till 1901   less than 50% married till 1856

less than 50% married till 1876   less than 50% married till c. 1836-51

Map 15. Celibacy among women ages 15–49, 1836–1901. SOURCE: Based on statistical tables in Van de Walle (see Map 11, above).

death rates than children who were born in wedlock. Rural communities,
less emancipated than others from traditional controls and always anxious
to identify their members socially, had a lower rate of illegitimacy than the
cities. But still, an infant-mortality rate double the normal rate, which was
high enough, must have taken care of a good proportion of those most likely
to be a burden on the resources of the community.* Infanticide was a delib-

* In Nord, in 1853, the infant-mortality rate in towns was 149 per 1,000 for legitimate children, 288 per 1,000 for illegitimate ones; in the countryside the rates were 139 per 1,000 for
legitimate children and 324 per 1,000 for the illegitimate (A. Lesaëge, *L'Homme, la vie et la
mort dans le Nord au XIXe siècle*, Lille, 1972, p. 99). Thus, the difference between the death

erate way of getting rid of unwanted children, legitimate as well as illegitimate. Indeed, the imperial prosecutor at Agen in 1863 referred to it as an aid
to birth control or to redeeming failures in birth control, and noted that the
number of married women killing unwanted children was increasing because
so many wives were determined to limit the number of their offspring.[35] But
abandoning children was almost as effective, and more general. Malthus had
pointed out that a government wishing to limit population had only to increase the number of homes for "lost" children; and foundlings (three or four
a month in some small country towns) counted heavily in the statistics of
infant mortality.[36]

Other additions to the statistics came from the spreading practice of putting
babies out to nurse, a practice that took its victims not only among the infants
entrusted to wet nurses, but among the children of the nurses as well.* During the 1860's the mortality of infants given out to country nurses varied between one and two in three. But between 27 percent and 33 percent of the
babies abandoned by mothers who went to the city to sell their milk—especially Paris—also died.[37] Once a wet nurse had found a place, she sent her
own baby back home with a professional baby driver, who through drunkenness, incompetence, or downright dishonesty could lose it, exchange it, or
abandon it somewhere, to let it die of inanition. The child who escaped these
hazards stood a good chance of dying on arrival as a result of the trip (in 1857
in one Nièvre commune alone eight infants died in the space of ten days because of this), or of succumbing to a higher rate of accidents and illness than
that of its more fortunate fellows.[38] Fortunate, however, is a relative term, for
the natural children in such circumstances, since they were not the valuable
properties that the boarding children were, took second place on a scale whose
chief indicator was potential profits. As a grieving woman explained to the
priest who sought to console her at an infant's burial: "Unfortunately, it's not

---

rates of legitimate and illegitimate infants, a sufficiently impressive 93 percent at the urban level,
soared to 133 percent in the country where unwed mothers and their offspring were more readily
abandoned. True, illegitimacy seems to diminish in proportion to the agrarian character of communities (Placide Rambaud and Monique Vincienne, *Les Transformations d'une société rurale*,
p. 66), but note that as late as 1950–51 the mortality rate among illegitimate children was still
double the rate for others: 8.2 percent versus 4.3 percent. In the country, since no church bells
were rung for the christening of bastards, they were sometimes known as *sansonnets* (H. Labourasse, *Anciens us*, p. 25). Yet in some villages fruit trees were planted at their birth, especially
along roads, as for other children.

* Many of the wet-nursed babies were children of the affluent, but it is important to remember that numerous urban workers hired wet nurses too. Louis Borsendorff, the son of a working-
class couple, barely survived the ordeal. His mother returned to work the day after his birth,
handing him over to a nurse from Arpajon; nine months later, when the woman brought him
back, he was more dead than alive (*De l'instruction du pauvre*, p. 4). Borsendorff's mother had
ten children; seven died before age seven, and an eighth died in an accident at twenty. That
must have been fairly typical. "The Franco-Prussian War reduced infant mortality in France
during the war from 33 percent to 17 percent because actual or feared disruption ... caused
bourgeois mothers to suckle their own children" (Sanford Kanter, "Defeat 1871," p. 57, citing
the official report of a medical commission to the Minister of the Interior).

one of mine, but my *petit Paris* who brought me 20 francs a month, and so regularly paid! How am I going to replace him?"*

A less destructive means of population limitation and one employed for a long time was continence or, at least, celibacy. Even celibacy without continence was still reasonably effective, because it implied real efforts to prevent conception and because, when such efforts failed, the offspring was more likely to die, as we have seen. But celibacy as a major means of population control underwent a marked decline after the end of the eighteenth century and particularly (claims Paul Gemaehling) after 1861. At that date in only 21 French departments did the marriage rate among women fifteen to forty-nine years of age exceed 600 per 1,000, and these were grouped in two blocs: the one around Paris, the other in the southwest, between Deux-Sèvres and Tarn-et-Garonne. On the other hand, in 24 departments—in the west, east, south, and center and in the Pyrenees—less than half the women in this age group were married. Gemaehling gives no comparable figures for bachelors in 1861, though his map of their incidence in 1931 suggests a correspondence. But we do know that in the Ancien Régime celibacy was widely practiced, and we occasionally hear of families in which one brother or more abstained from marriage, often to live with the married one, who carried on "the house." But marriage became increasingly more common, and with more marriages the birthrate fell. Between 1861 and 1931 the proportion of married women increased by 12 percent, their fecundity fell by 43 percent. The highest birthrates were in areas where the marriage rates were lowest: the more one married, the less one reproduced.[39] In other words, where celibacy no longer held the line, some other method had to be used instead.†

One fairly widespread method of family limitation was for a young man to marry an older woman and thus deliberately shorten the child-bearing period. At Chaponost (Rhône) during the first half of the nineteenth century 27 percent of brides were over thirty at their first marriage, a fact that led one scholar to comment on "the surprising choice so many well-off peasants make of an aged wife." Writing in 1883, Armand Desprès claimed that young men between twenty-five and thirty-five married widows and older women more

---

* C. Monot, *De la mortalité*, p. 85. A law of December 1874 for the protection of infants required all parishes to keep a register of infants placed out with a wet nurse or withdrawn from one. But an 1879 survey carried out by justices of the peace shows a general lack of compliance (Archives Départementales, Vosges 42 M 2). Laws proved more effective in their negative aspects. Article 55 of the Civil Code required that the infant's birth be verified by the local registrar within three days. In certain places this was taken to mean that the baby had to be carried several miles to the mairie regardless of the weather, a belief that did its part to raise the infant-mortality figures.

† Similarly, in Brittany the marriage rate had climbed between 1890 and the early 1920's, but the birthrate had fallen nearly 20 percent. The greatest decline had taken place in the most prolific department—Finistère. In 1929 the young women of Léon had made plain their determination "de ne plus faire comme leurs mères." (Gilbert Le Guen, "D'une révolution manquée," p. 491.)

often in France than in any other country. In country towns, he said, it was "common" for men in their early twenties to marry middle-aged widows. By his account, in Normandy and from Hérault to the Dauphiné some 10 percent of marriages were between people unable to have children. Desprès gives no references that would bear him out. But a 1969 study tells us that in 1890–92 in Côtes-du-Nord, where the women's marriage rate was 14 percent below the national average, more than 50 percent of the married women were twenty-five or over, whereas in France as a whole 61 percent were under twenty-five. Popular proverbs vaunting the virtues of older women and crying down the young also lend credence to this contention: "Better a ripe head than one that needs maturing." "It's in old pots that one makes the best soup." "Young woman and warm bread are a household's ruin." "Young woman, green wood, and new bread soon make a house for sale." So does the Breton saying that a girl is marriageable at thirty, a man at twenty. Paul Sébillot, who quoted this saying in the 1880's, added that young men often married girls 15 years older because this meant less chance of having many children, and claimed that the wife was several years older than the husband in at least one-third of Breton marriages.[40]

In the end, though, positive action, if one may use the term, had to take precedence over the negatives. As early as 1791 a priest in faraway Dordogne was reporting that both peasants and upper classes limited their offspring, whether by poverty or by will. While bestiality was "almost extinct," he added, and sodomy more rare than it used to be, masturbation and deliberate chastity were current and so, one supposes, was what the church manuals described as onanism—coitus interruptus.[41]

Lacking other evidence of a privileged nature, we are left to draw what inferences we can from incidental data. In 1866 the Agricultural Survey found scarcely a four-child family left in Haute-Garonne; even families with three children were considered large. In 1869 Théron de Montaugé felt that "voluntary continence" was the poor man's only way of improving his position. Statistics, says André Armengaud, show this trend toward smaller families after 1870. In 1875 a chronicler of Blagnac (Haute-Garonne) found the peasants there lamenting any pregnancy beyond the first child and apparently trying to terminate such "accidents" by all and every means. As the local mayor put it, when one has had one child one should thereafter leave one's tools in the toolshed ("il faut déposer les outils au galetas").[42] It would not be long before medical men related continence and coitus interruptus to the marked growth in nervous and mental troubles. As birthrates went down, the rate of mental disturbances went up.[43]

It is hard to tell, though, whether in the end such practices frayed nerves worse than unwanted children did. A Vendean song certainly suggests that too many children were more of a desolation than continence:[44]

After one year, one child:
It's merriment and cheer;
After two years, two children:
It's only gloom, my dear;
After three years, three children:
It's devilish cruel;
One calls for bread,
The other calls for gruel,
The other to be suckled,
And the breasts are dry.

Rural teachers throughout the 1880's and 1890's constantly inveighed against the selfishness of those who refused to breed for France and deplored the shrinking size of families, the lower rate of births, the insistence on a single heir. They also noted a related phenomenon, namely that in a dwindling population, the number of households had increased. In Domptail (Vosges), lying in the rich plain between Meurthe and Moselle, the population had fallen from 1,056 in the year 1865 to 849 in 1880, but the number of family households had risen from 315 to 325. The extended family was dying. In Puy-de-Dôme, too, at Yronde and at Buron, in the Limagne, the average household by 1899 consisted of father, mother, and two children. If any grandparents survived, reported a schoolteacher, they usually lived apart, "in the old house."[45]

The peasants were discovering will and choice. In 1911 Emmanuel Labat described how they had learned birth control from the bourgeoisie and were now limiting their families to save money and avoid dividing property. And as he also noted, more and more were passing from sharecropping to owning their own land. This meant harder work, to pay for land or get more of it, and all the harder for having to get by without the hands that the more numerous family furnished. But mentality was changing once again: people sought less to rise in the world than to enjoy themselves. Now, said Labat, men and women sought "to live their life for their own sake," to enjoy what resources and what time they could, to expend less effort and take less risk.[46]

The peasant's workload was beginning to be eased as manufactured goods, chemicals, and modern tools became available; and where once there had hardly been any thought of relief or alternatives, other options now suggested themselves. As peasants began to understand and avail themselves of the opportunities for an easier life, recreation, or even escape, ad hoc moralists stepped forward to deplore what they felt showed a weakening of character or will. In fact, the changing ways of the countryside merely showed a greater possibility of choice and a growing will, when this was possible, *to* choose.*

* Thus the traditional distribution of weddings throughout the year had been affected by old-established taboos and necessities, and reflected the agricultural and religious calendars that made marriage extremely rare during harvest time, Advent, and Lent. By the 1890's the compensating

And one of the things inevitably affected was the traditional pattern of the family.

Exogamy increased, though at a painfully slow rate. At Albiez in Maurienne the rate of increase in exogamous unions through the eighteenth and nineteenth centuries, when approximately 84 marriages in every 100 were made at home, was almost imperceptible. From 16.1 percent in the eighteenth century, the figure climbed to only 16.8 percent in the nineteenth century, and was still only 21.1 percent in the first half of the twentieth century. But over the same 250-year period the proportion of spouses in such unions who came from places outside the canton changed significantly, rising from 6.7 percent in the eighteenth century and 9.9 percent in the nineteenth century to 35.8 percent by the mid-twentieth century. Meanwhile, in the less isolated community of Vraiville (Eure) the number of marriages that *seem* to have been concluded outside the village group more than doubled in the second half of the nineteenth century.[47]

As endogamy waned, so too did effective and perhaps affective family cohesion. In one village of Eure the turn of the century marked a clear break in the custom of founding marriages on a contract. In the decade 1883–92, 26 marriages were regulated by contract and only six were not; in the decade 1903–12 only six were regulated by contract and twenty were not. This reversal of proportions suggests that marriages now were founded less on family property, and were focused more on the couple and their own efforts.* At Vraiville about the only weddings without a contract in the past had been those of artisan families, in this case weavers, where matrimony united not property but workers. Now, the old age of landed-clan alliances was giving way to a new age in which marriage associated the working partners as individuals, rather than members of a clan. The family as the center of production had been maintained by necessities inherent in the mode of production to which it was bound. It disintegrated when and where the demands of production altered, or where the center of production shifted to factory, shop, or office, so that family cohesion seemed less important.[48]

Family solidarity, scarcely founded on affection, or on equality, was fostered by necessity, labor, coexistence in a self-sufficient economy, and isolation from society. The farm, the croft, the holding made their occupiers bond-slaves of the past, and of subsistence. In such circumstances, the home became the focus of all the family's tensions, but of tensions largely repressed. Cohesion lasted as long as questions remained unasked and alternatives unperceived, hence

---

peaks of marriages in January–February and October had been much reduced. Thereafter, at least in the Rhône countryside, Gilbert Garrier tells us, more young couples married when they pleased; and, he adds, bred when they pleased (*Paysans du Beaujolais*, 1: 472–73).

* In Languedoc, too, at the turn of the century, marriage contracts were often dispensed with. And according to Robert Jalby, those entering into them did so less to secure the bride's dowry against her new family than to ensure the future security of the young household (*Folklore du Languedoc*, p. 83).

more apparent to outside observers than real to those concerned. The strains of life expressed themselves in boredom and in aggressiveness, both accepted as inevitable. But the conflicts between the desires of the individual and the demands of the group that undermined the family's concord were offset by an interdependence that made it stand as a unit against all others, preserved its balance, and permitted it to survive. Only new possibilities, new means, radically new conditions, could upset this secular order and bring freedom from the subjection to tradition, to nature, to the needs of common labor, the lack of money, and the paucity of choice. These new conditions appeared only in the late nineteenth century.

Gradually, the family could be seen to have lost its protective role—in matters of public security, in health, in clothing, education, and social training. Its educational functions were preempted by the schools. Medical care, remedies, and cures, all once locally provided or homemade like clothing, came ever more from the outside. Above all, means of escaping the clan's constricting grip became more numerous, to the point where it took only a little initiative to get away from home—and, having done so, to survive.

As soon as opportunity and mobility beckoned, the old authorities began to disintegrate. The Second Empire echoed with complaints, not only that peasants no longer showed the proper obedience and deference to their betters, but that children likewise had ceased to give their parents their due. However exaggerated such reports, they are evidence of a novelty of historical proportions: the yoke of necessity was just beginning to break down, and parents and employers felt this keenly. The shrill complaints about the waning of parental authority were sometimes accompanied by explanations: sharecroppers' children, said an agronomic review, left their parents "as soon as they could" to better themselves. "Their old respect for paternal authority"—which no doubt bent itself to make them stay at home—had fallen victim to their desire to earn their way to independence.[49] But the desire would not have existed without the opportunity that suggested it!

"Children no longer respect their parents, peasants no longer respect their word," lamented Labat.[50] The cause in both instances was the same: alternatives, mobility, choice, the possibility of getting away. One had supported ailing elders because they symbolized continuity. When the belief in continuity began to fade, one was reduced to acting out of duty or affection, or even more unlikely, out of pure humanity. It is surely more than simple coincidence that at this very moment paternal authority was simultaneously sapped by a number of legislative measures that trespassed on what had once been considered the father's natural domain: protecting working children, requiring them to attend school, in one way or another ignoring the will or interest of the paterfamilias. In 1889 a law defined the conditions under which unworthy fathers could be stripped of their paternal rights. Other measures regulated or prohibited child labor (1874, 1892), punished parents who ill-treated their children (1898), introduced the possibility of judicial administration of a child's property (1910), limited the father's right of consent to his children's marriages (1896 and after), and protected illegitimate children (1896 and after). Above all, the schools provided a potent source of rival authority and values, as close to home as you could possibly get. And in those parts of France where, as in Brittany, a determined drive against local speech separated the French-speaking young from their Breton-speaking elders, the local tradition was left to seep away, and the young came to despise their elders as ignorant, when all they ignored was French. No wonder that the crisis of authority became an important subject of public debate, to the point where in 1914 the Catholic Semaines Sociales, so representative of *bien-pensant* opinion, selected it as the topic of their annual meeting.[51]

Naturally, trends growing out of socioeconomic changes would be hastened by these outside influences. Family dissensions became more apparent, and possibly more divisive. The young were readier to question, dissent, rebel, or even adopt different political positions from those of the family or the clan. One result of this, widely noted, was fewer family reunions: "Chacun chez soi, chacun pour soi," wrote a teacher of Mogeville (Meuse) in 1889. The young, especially young couples smarting under the subjection, restrictions, and frictions of large households where their elders dominated and sometimes bullied them, seized the first opportunity to gain some degree of independence. In the 1880's sons began to expect and to demand wages, and wages similar to those paid a hired hand. In the Limousin marriage under joint property rules triumphed over the older *régime dotal*. Fewer young couples continued to live with the parents, a condition that marriage contracts had sometimes specified. Fewer unmarried sons and daughters remained at home.[52] In Lauragais and the Montagne Noire, a good observer connected this development with the schools. Once young people knew how to count, said Pariset, they claimed their share of family holdings and, if the claim was rejected, they left. In Tarn-et-Garonne, driven by the "spirit of independence and insubordination," children escaped from the family as soon as they were old enough to hire themselves out, "leaving their parents in a difficult position to work their farm." This chiefly after 1900, when the fall-off in the rural population offered opportunities for such employment.[53]

In the center of France, where large families were needed to work relatively large holdings, isolation had long helped preserve family communities in which several couples lived and worked as one production unit. These closed or semi-closed domestic economies, based on strong family bonds, managed to hold out for a long time, but by 1897 we hear that even there "the father lacks authority to retain his children." Especially in Creuse, where the possibilities of emigration were well known, the young now went out at sixteen or seventeen to make their own way. Those who did not go to town in search of higher wages or simply of adventure hired themselves out as farmhands to earn cash. The "family republics" of Auvergne, some of them said to go back as far as the eighth century, slowly disintegrated. The last, near Thiers, was broken up in 1925.[54]

References now begin to appear to the influence of the young over the old, and to the old following the lead of the young. In the 1830's simply abandoning the belt for suspenders seems to have been taken as the most audacious act of independence and innovation on a young peasant's part.[55] By 1889 at Broye a man's wife no longer called him "our master," his children no longer addressed him in the third person.* In Allier, remarked a local scholar in 1911, the father's supremacy, which was the rule 20 years before, was now the exception. Children no longer accepted subordination, especially when they returned from military service, and absolutely insisted on equal rights. About the same time Labat referred to "the precocious, intense, rather ferocious individualism of the young."[56] One wonders whether this did not play some part in the trend to smaller families. The poor had lagged behind in limiting families, partly because they had no property and hence no worries about dividing it among too many heirs, but above all because (as we have seen) children meant income. In the Vendée bocage, as in many other places, children could be expected to begin work at ten years old or so, and to remit all their earnings to their father. "The poor peasant has every interest in having a big family."[57] But if the offspring could be expected to bolt rather than contribute to the family budget, what interest would the poor peasant have in bringing up a large brood? What, for that matter, was the interest of family continuity in the long run?

The new developments created a paradoxical situation. The combined trends toward small landownership and birth control changed the look of the rural population, making for the predominance of older people who owned house, land, and money, and were used to giving orders to their children, who were fewer than they had been, economically dependent, and as far as possible, indoctrinated to honor and obey the old.[58] The heads of households also now tended to live longer, and the gradual aging of this group (as well as its limited means) made for economic backwardness and reluctance to modernize. This in turn encouraged the departure of the most enterprising among the young, impatient for responsibility or independence—an emigration related not to technological improvements on the land but, on the contrary, to the resistance to such improvements by the masters of the land and to the obstacle their presence presented to vertical mobility. So on the one hand the entrenchment of the old drove off the young. On the other hand, the same situation (of course,

---

* Charles Perron, *Broye-les-Pesmes*. In Languedoc, too, a turn-of-the-century observer noted that a young bride no longer entered the household as a stranger and "almost a servant." Now the young husband appeared to prefer his bride to his parents. Nor was the husband any longer the uncontested head of the family: wives and husbands were beginning to share authority and even, *horribile dictu*, "the influence of the wife is dominant." (Quoted in Jalby, *Folklore*, p. 81.)

in its wider context) also permitted the emancipation of the young whether they stayed or left. The shrunken population and the shortage of young hands were crucial to the higher wages and job opportunities that allowed, indeed suggested, escape from what may in some ways have been a worsening situation.

All these trends reinforced each other. Continuity had been a factor of survival, hence a reinforcement of the family. In times when other social structures were weak the family mattered more, and its authority was more easily preserved or enforced. Furthermore, the more difficult the land and the less advanced the methods of cultivation, the more important it was that it should be cleared and worked with continuity. Raising the question of continuity anew at each generation could seriously threaten the family enterprise and, ultimately, the society in which it operated. The Napoleonic Code, reflecting abstract urban ideas and interests, showed a readiness to dispense with needs such as these, or to ignore them, in a manner quite alien to realities in much of the countryside. The Code was therefore ignored for a while in certain places, and ways were found to adjust its notions to local needs. On the other hand, when conditions of work and life had changed enough, the mincing machine of the Napoleonic Code became less dangerous, and in some ways convenient. Continuity now counted less and mobility counted more. A mechanism to make changes seemed much more suitable now that change had become a part of life. And the less continuity men now perceived around them, the less value they put on continuity.

If fewer grandparents or older relations lived in now-smaller households, this meant that fewer children would be brought up under their influence, hence that they would be more open to emancipation and freer to adapt to the culture of the schools. If endogamy crumbled, however slowly, this meant that the environment of home and neighborhood was more varied and less constrictive in the cultural suggestions that it made. Children, Ferdinand de Saussure once said, are the freer compared with preceding generations "to the extent that norms are less precisely established and unity less total in the communities where they learn to speak."[59] The turn of the century was, par excellence, a time when the status of local speech had become uncertain, and this development would be intensified with exogamous marriages that brought people of different speech, ways, and values under one roof, and that left the child freer to choose from the very first.

Societies that had been stable and homogeneous for centuries were coming under several stresses at once. In stable societies, changes—and there is never a time when changes do not take place—affect only details, not the general structure. But the late-nineteenth-century rural society of France was no longer stable; and it was gradually becoming less homogeneous. Every blow against the details of its organization placed its total system more and more at the mercy of modernity.

PART II

THE AGENCIES OF CHANGE

Chapter Twelve

ROADS, ROADS, AND STILL MORE ROADS

Les routes, les chemins de fer, ces grands moteurs de la civilisation.
— IMPERIAL PROSECUTOR, Agen, 1867

"ROADS, MORE ROADS and always roads," wrote the prefect of Loiret in September 1867, "this sums up the political economy of the countryside."[1] Until roads spread, many rural communities remained imprisoned in semi-isolation, limited participants in the economy and politics of the nation: France.

Historical geography is in large part the tale of men struggling against space, and of the efforts made to tame space by creating ever more efficient, more reliable means of communication. In the beginning space is the master; its distances run wild, overwhelming man. Gradually space is conquered, distances are tamed, brought to heel or, rather, increasingly to wheel. Space becomes manageable. This process was still in progress through much of the nineteenth century. Many who lived when the century ended remembered the days when familiar places were farther, vaster, and more daunting too. That was what Eugène Le Roy remarked in 1899: "All these lands now are full of roads and highways...but in the days I speak of [and they were not far off] the forest was a great deal bigger than it is today...and one could discern only two bad roads that skirted it."[2] Everything is in that passage: the novelty in 1899 of a land crisscrossed by new thoroughfares, the old untamed order of yesterday and its more chilling scale, the paucity of the old roads and their discouraging state.

Yet France did not lack roads. Arthur Young had found reason to admire these monuments to the enterprise of the central government, but he had also found them empty, silent, "a perfect desert," even at the gates of Paris. Young had attributed this to the absurdity and oppression of the government. But it was due rather to the layout of the roads. A system built to serve the government and the cities and lacking a supporting network of secondary thoroughfares had little to do with popular habit or need. Administrative highways, a historian of the center called them, made for troops to march on and for tax revenues to reach the treasury. Lucien Gachon has noted the lack of correspondence between rural habitat and highways, between local roads and main roads. Both Roger Thabault writing about Mazières and Ernest Lavisse remembering the Thiérache confirm this. Houses were independent of the roads, sited with no regard for them or indeed so as to avoid them: a countryside still living, as it had done for centuries, turned in upon itself.[3]

The road-building policies of the first half of the century did little to change this. Napoleon's roads had been built with an eye to strategic advantages; the Restoration tried to restore and complete the ravaged network it inherited; and Louis Philippe's ministers did the same, which was not very much, until the Duchesse de Berry's ill-fated rising in 1832 persuaded them to change their ways. A crash building program in eight departments endowed both the Atlantic west with a system of strategic roads and the Department of Roads and Bridges with the training for the more enterprising role it was to undertake after 1837.* The department's main task was rather less to build new roads than, by repairing, grading, and servicing the existing highways and building solid bridges, to make troop movements possible in all weathers. This meant that, though the highway network was not greatly expanded, its viability improved immensely. In 1824 of 33,536 km of national highways only about 42 percent to 44 percent needed no more than regular upkeep. By the late 1830's about 70 percent of 34,512 km had been made serviceable; by 1845 almost the entire system, some 36,000 km, stood ready to be used. This figure would not alter markedly until after the First World War (in which the network comprised roughly 38,000 km).[4]

What has to be remembered, however, is that the highway system was only a skeleton. The main roads, to which most of our statistics refer until the 1860's, stood in the same relation to France as the Nile to Egypt: fertilizing only a narrow strip along their course, becoming nationally relevant only in terms of their tributaries and of what irrigation could be based on them. There was little such expansion before the 1860's, and the construction of a far-reaching road network that encompassed the entire country was only taken in hand under the Third Republic.

The same was true of the first railway lines, which fanned out in the 1840's and especially the 1850's and left aside vast areas where the old way of life survived untouched. The railways took some time to make their mark; so that at Douai, in the industrial north, where a railway station was inaugurated in 1846, traffic for the first few years was so slight that the more enterprising among the bourgeoisie organized ballgames in it.[5]

* The departments in question were Sarthe, Mayenne, Ille-et-Vilaine, Maine-et-Loire, Loire-Inférieure, Vendée, Deux-Sèvres, and Charente-Inférieure (see Henri Cavaillès, La Route française, p. 203). As an officer pointed out: "Exécuter ainsi grand nombre de routes nouvelles, c'était offrir le travail à bien des bras inoccupés, et dès lors dangereux. . . . Unir par des routes nombreuses et faciles la Vendée à l'intérieur de la France, c'était aplanir les obstacles qui l'avaient jusque là tenue dans l'isolement, . . . c'était user par un frottement salutaire ce vieux type Vendéen qui perd chaque jour de son originalité." (Archives de la Guerre, MR 1234, Vendée, 1840.)

As railways spread, the network was seen (by a very few) to be designed, as the highway system was, to serve special interests, not the needs of ordinary people. Railroads, created by urban capital, went where the interests of capital and of urban industries took them, not where people actually lived. Indeed, railways played no small part in the underdevelopment of the countryside. Their heavy capital needs, and those of the urban improvements for which the Second Empire is famous, drained the budget for the country roads. From 2.2 million francs in 1853, the budget of the rural road section of the Public Works Department dropped off to an average of only 1.6 million over the next seven years. In 1855 the prefect of Cantal complained that the important stretch between Aurillac and Mauriac was going to pieces for lack of upkeep, "an object of terror for the travelers, abandoned by the traffic, no longer of our time." Yet repairs were not undertaken until 1864; the road was reopened to traffic in 1867, but things were not really in shape until 1874. We are reminded of the plaint of the deputy of Nord in 1861 summing up the situation: "You have voted millions to embellish the cities, you have voted fine monuments and we, we are still in the mud up to our knees." And in 1865 Marie-Thérèse Romieu noted what few city people bothered to regret, that the train glided by her village, but did so without stopping. In any case, the mesh of the railway network was much too wide to cover all the land: "How many villages only a few miles from the railway line are really more isolated today than in the days when the post chaise and the stagecoach crossed them or passed nearby!"[6]

Not that traffic was lacking. On the contrary, much traffic and a poor communications network were characteristic of the old society. The circulation was intense. Trails, paths, tracks, lanes, and causeways covered the countryside: rough roads where, as the peasants put it, the Good Lord did not often pass. They served private needs, going from village to village, from farm or hamlet to field, orchard, pasture, or bourg. They served professional pursuits, like the special trails followed by glassmakers, carriers or sellers of salt, potters; or those that led to forges, mines, quarries, and hemp fields; or those along which flax, hemp, linen, and yarn were taken to market. There were pilgrimage routes and procession trails (mostly along the crests), leading to a miraculous fountain or to the chapel of a healing saint; there were traditional walkways for marriage and funeral parties; there were tracks demarcating fields, or farms, or communes—and even drawing a border between dialects.[7]

Along these, and on the roads as well, people and goods traveled—first of all the local people. Agriculture has been called an involuntary transport industry.[8] The peasant is a carrier and a driver. In industry, the machine is stable, its raw materials mobile. Here the land is fixed: plows, harrows, cattle have to be taken to the land and then away again. This makes for a lot of movement, even before we count other comers and goers: local people setting out to see relatives or to make a pilgrimage; migrants going off to town or tramping in and out for haying or harvest; journeymen-artisans on their *tour de France*; basketmakers, knife grinders, tinkers, porters, and stevedores, tramps, vagabonds, bohemians, recruits on their way to join their units, veterans returning home, troops marching from one garrison to another, rag-and-bone merchants, Savoyard chimney sweeps, itinerant showmen and mountebanks, hawkers and peddlers from every part of France.

Yet amid such immense activity, most of the circulation was limited in scope. Goods and products were exchanged wherever possible between neighboring complementary regions, say, cattle and chestnuts traded for wine and grain; and the greater part of the tonnage moved only over small distances.[9] The peasant's world was compartmentalized into small areas defined by his interests. It lacked a general sense of the space around, restricted itself to certain confines and corridors, like that between the village and the market. His vision of space and scale was structured in terms of potential movement and of routines; he ignored nearby places that he skirted on his way to and fro, even forgot they existed if a change of routine put them off the frequented trail. As for travel outside familiar trails, it was not undertaken lightly. In the uplands of Lower Vivarais, even as late as the 1890's many had never gone beyond the few miles within which they followed their pasturing sheep: "Going any further would be to leave the *pays*—a big and difficult business."[10]

Travel beyond the limits of a good stiff hike was indeed a difficult and costly undertaking.* Young Georges Haussmann, posted from Poitiers to Yssingeaux in Haute-Loire in the 1830's, took six full days to make the 340 km to Le Puy and then a seventh to cover the remaining 28 km to Yssingeaux over the terrible Col de Pertuis. His arduous and costly route was typical of the problems encountered when one left major highways. But even straightforward trips were long until the Second Empire, and sometimes after that. By coach it took from daybreak to sunset to get from Gray to Besançon (44 km), and three days to go from Bar-sur-Seine to Paris (191 km). The packet boat that Frédéric Moreau took from Rouen to Paris (137 km) took two days; the *bateau-poste* of the Canal du Midi took five to cover the 224 km from Toulouse to Cette. The price of such a journey, on an average peasant's budget, must have been terrible. And to what end should it be undertaken? No wonder, when even short trips "represented a veritable expedition," that people rarely left their villages except for markets and fairs. The few who went to Paris, even once in a lifetime, were known as Parisiens, much as the pilgrim back from Mecca proudly bears his title for the rest of his life. And when one went somewhere, one generally walked. That could mean 66 km (or some 40 miles in one day), from Bourg to Troyes and back, to save the expense of overnight lodging.[11]

---

* The *Gazette universelle de Lyon* warned on August 7, 1827: "Le père de famille doit par précaution songer à son testament avant de monter en diligence" (Gilbert Garrier, *Paysans du Beaujolais*, 1: 224).

In 1880 the Collège de Saint-Flour presented no candidates for the Concours Général because, explained the principal, the expenses of a trip to Aurillac (74 km away) were beyond the parents' means. In most places conscripts and other travelers who had to make a trip were escorted some way beyond the village by the local people when they set off; proof that such ventures were still rare events. The France of the 1880's and 1890's remained vast. The time-space equation kept it so. When Maupassant and other Parisian Sunday fishermen took the stagecoach from Courbevoie to Asnières, 9 km away, that village was as far from the capital in time as Rouen (137 km) is today by train, or Nice (933 km) by plane: two hours. "Going to Toulouse is an expedition that counts in life," wrote a teacher from a village 56 km away, in 1886. And when, in 1887, an inspector of primary schools requested that the school-teacher of Legé visit him in Nantes, 40 km away, he added, "that is, if the weather permits such an expedition: for you must expect over four hours of a bad public coach ride, *in ordinary weather*, to come here and as much to return."[12]

Even near Paris, at Courgent in Mantois, in the last year of the nineteenth century "one travels only if one must." Those who went to market knew Mantes (13 km) or Houdan (12 km), but there were many even among the better-off who had seen Paris (60 km) once or not at all. Three-quarters of the children had never seen a train, and some had never been as far as the next village. As for the colonial wilds of Corsica at that time, draft boards had to hold their meetings where the few roads crossed each other so that the conscripts of three or four cantons could attend with only average trouble.[13]

Most of the nineteenth century was one consistent moan over the state of the local roads: they were nothing but ruts, sometimes four, five, and six feet deep, damp and miry. Peasants let the grass grow on them, stacked stones on them, drained off their fields in them, plowed over part of them, dug up mud from them to use on their own land, so that travelers were forced to tramp through adjoining fields, damaging the crops. Repairs, wailed a police superintendent in the Pyrenees in 1895, left them as bad as they were before, the potholes hardly filled: "The farmers have encroached on them or plowed over the whole road, leaving only one furrow."[14] Bad enough when the weather was fine, the rural roads became quite impossible in winter. With the first rains, the cattle broke them up, and that is how they stayed till summer; the inhabitants made tracks through the adjoining fields, but these rude substitutes did not permit wheeled traffic. At Saint-Maurice-la-Souterraine (Creuse), roads were so bad the villagers could hardly get their dead to the cemetery; even cattle had trouble making their way, let alone people.[15]

Floods, or simply bad weather, washed away roads, isolated villages. Not even mules, only people on foot could pass (Ardèche, 1857). Not even pedestrians could use the roads (Puy-de-Dôme, 1896), and that for a period of four years! "Terrible misery," the authorities reported. Many country communes, for instance, in Velay, Vivarais, Gévaudan, and the Alps, were used to five or six months of winter isolation. But country towns, too, small and not so small —Mauriac, Aurillac, Meulan—were cut off for days on end, with serious problems when food no longer appeared on the market; especially for the poor who bought their pittance from day to day. As Marcel Lachiver has noted in his study of Meulan: "It was not the railroads that most changed the countryside in the second half of the nineteenth century; it was the creation of roads that could be used in all seasons."[16]

And, one might add, the creation of bridges too. The old sacred awe of rivers and the fear of their murderous ire remained alive throughout the Second Empire. But rivers did not need to rage and ravage. Even at their most placid, many were hard to negotiate. In the Garonne valley, almost 300 km from Toulouse to Bordeaux, there was not a single bridge until the mid-nineteenth century. Fords were rare, dangerous and practicable only at low water. When bridges were attempted (at Agen, for instance) they were washed away—and, not surprisingly, there were many second thoughts about reconstructing them.

The most eloquent testimony about the state of roads comes from school inspectors, who as late as the 1870's often had to cover great stretches on horseback or on foot to check on village schools.* Their trials seem to have lessened after mid-century, or at least the records of such trials thin out at that time. But in a number of places the lack of roads or of adequate roads kept wheeled traffic at bay for a good time longer. In the large district of Prades (Pyrénées-Orientales) under the Second Empire, apart from one road opened to wheeled traffic, the territory had to be covered "over goat trails." Many bourgs in Forez and Vivarais had no real road until the 1870's. At Roche-en-Forez (Loire) the first road that a cart or carriage could use was built in 1875. At Saint-Pierreville (Ardèche) the first carts appeared in 1880. In Ariège some cantons remained roadless until the First World War. No carts, only mules and porters, reported a reconnaissance party surveying the area around Olette in the Pyrenees in the 1840's. At that, the mules made hard work of the narrow footpath, and the narrow footbridge one had to cross was often washed away.[17]

At the end of the century people in these areas remembered the first appearance of wheeled conveyances in local bourgs, which whole villages from

---

* Pierre Deffontaines, *Les Hommes et leurs travaux*, p. 399. In December 1838 a primary school inspector of Finistère at Guerlesquin, in the northeast corner of the department, was asked to make haste to Quimper. It took him three and a half days to cross the department on horseback, little more than 40 miles as the crow flies. His predecessor had died in 1836 from the hardships of his job (Louis Ogès, *Instruction primaire*, p. 31). But the primary school inspector of Bellac may have had it worse still, for he had to do his rounds on foot, and in an area, as he explained in a report in 1840, where the most abominable road was still considered passable. Indeed, the peasants even had a classification system for the degree of abominability: a road where the horse sank to its breast was *rabiat* (rabid), one where the rider sank to his eyes was *péri* (perishing), and one where rider and mount were swallowed without trace was *despérat*. All the local roads beyond Dompierre were rabiat or despérat! (Archives Départementales, Haute-Vienne T 113, Feb. 13, 1840.) See also Archives Départementales, Cantal IT 501 (1835 and after, 1853, 1878).

roundabout turned out to see: Burzet after the July Revolution; Largentière under the Second Empire; Saint-Etienne-de-Serres and Saint-Pierreville in the high country northwest of Privas only under MacMahon and Grévy. When Louis Napoleon was President, the largest share of the traffic in Privas was carried by mules rather than by carts or carriages. The same must have been true for rather longer in the isolated uplands of Lozère where, Patrice Higonnet tells us, wheeled vehicles had remained practically unknown until the middle of the century. There, as in the Pyrenees and in the Alps, packing—by mules, donkeys, horses, the backs of men and the heads of women—remained the fundamental means of transport.[18]

Even in the plains below, such roads as existed served only their immediate neighborhoods, so that these areas had to rely on animal transport for many products. "For the low country," went the Vivarais proverb, "the pack saddle. For the highlands the *saccol*."[19] The saccol, used to carry burdens in Ardèche, was a sort of sack that dangled from the head and was lined with straw to cushion the weight on head and shoulders. In the Pyrenees there was a whole array of carrying devices, ranging from the headpads of twisted straw or rag on which the women of Béarn carried everything, including a child's cradle, to hooded sacks something like the saccol (Campan valley), straps or thongs worn frontally (upper Ariège), a pole or yoke balanced on the shoulders (Cerdagne), and kangaroo pockets to carry babies in (Gavarnie, Bigorre, Campan). Even the notion of putting everything to use, or leaving no stone unturned, which the French express as *faire flèche de tout bois*, was translated in local terms as *de tout perràc cabadère* ("of every rag a headpad").[20]

Until 1860 or so, the peasant of Malarce or Lafigère (Ardèche) carried his chestnuts on his back to the market at Les Vans, four or five hours' walk on difficult mountain paths—50–60 kg for men, half as much for women. Later than that, until the Phylloxera killed the vineyards, the table grapes of Naves and of Gravières in southwestern Ardèche were sold at Villefort market in nearby Lozère, some 20 miles away: a four-hour trek with a load of 50 kg. In Ariège the charcoal burners who supplied the iron forges of Ax "carried 100-lb sacks for four or five hours, barefoot on difficult stony paths" and, on arrival, "hardly do they get a little bad quality bread." Back in the mountains behind Nice basic necessities had to come in by backpack, and local timber went out in long "processions," with every man carrying immensely heavy loads (140 kg—over 300 lbs—the official report tells us, but that sounds incredible). Hardly easier was the lot of the nail-makers of Haute-Loire, who had to get the iron for their nails at bigger centers like Firminy and bring it back in bars slung on their backs, 50 lbs at a time, once every week.[21]

How long did this go on? It is hard to say. Presumably until decent roads permitted the use of wheeled vehicles. But in the 1890's Henri Baudrillart found the men of the Cévennes still wearing the saccol and the women wearing its female cousin, the *chapsal* or *chasson*, which, he explained, was a round pad worn on the head to carry loads of between 60 and 80 lbs—obviously less heavy burdens than the men appear to have carried on their saccols. "All the women of the region are trained to this sort of carrying from their tenderest youth and work with it as easily as if they were merely wearing a hat." One had to fetch and carry. If possible with a mule or a donkey; but if not on foot. As the Forézien sang, bouncing his baby on his knee:[22]

> I'll take my donkey to Aurec.
> If there is no donkey, we'll go on foot.
> Hi colt! For tomorrow we'll go for salt.
> Hi mare! For tomorrow we'll go for grain.
> Hi horse! For tomorrow we'll go for wine.

The song went far beyond the singer's means, which might extend to a mule or donkey but were limited most often to his own back and legs.

In areas such as these muleteers remained prominent into the Second Empire, a tight-knit and traditionalist-minded group who wore pigtails well into the 1830's, a red wool bonnet (which they did not even remove in church) under a large hat, gold earrings, a red waistcoat and neckerchief, a white serge jacket studded with copper buttons, and green serge hose. Bedecked with pompoms, tinkling with bells, the pack-mules were as dazzling as the muleteers; and in many villages and small towns, in the Cévennes for instance, a mule train passing through was one of the few distractions of the time. It was also a nuisance, for muleteers were known to let their beasts graze in people's fields. They were also a notably rough and foul-mouthed crew; and any raucous child or adult was "a true pack-carter," or a muleteer.[23] Yet they could not be spared: their caravans conveyed necessities. A mule could carry three sacks of coal (240 lbs), twice as much as any family donkey; and five or six muleteers provisioned a whole valley. One assumes that consumption would have been slight: a few goatskins of wine, some sacks of wheat, oil, small packs of merchandise, iron bars.[24] Mules also carried Aubenas silk to Saint-Etienne, or wines of Roanne and Lower Vivarais to the Auvergne plateaus, as far as Mende or Le Puy. They declined only as roads and railroads advanced in the 1860's, to be replaced by carters: sign of a new order in transport.

Another sign was the steady fall in the country's mule population (almost all concentrated in the south): 1840—373,800; 1862—331,000; 1882—250,700; 1887—237,400. Even the number of animals exported to countries with worse roads than France's—Spain, Italy, Portugal, and Greece—fell from an average of 27,500 a year in the 1850's and 1860's to an average of 15,000 in the decade 1877–86. The number of donkeys also diminished slightly: 1840—413,500; 1862—396,200; 1886—382,100. On the other hand, the number of horses rose, along with the number of carriages and machines they pulled. Thus in Aveyron, while donkeys dropped from 3,265 in 1893 to 2,155 in 1907, horses increased from 11,473 to 14,500.[25]

The crux of all this lay in local roads, especially those the government described as *vicinal*, that is, recognized as necessary to the inhabitants of one or several communes to give them access to a market, a railway station, or some other neighborhood center. The improvement of these roads, which at the beginning of the Third Republic totaled ten times the mileage of the national highways, was recognized as a worthwhile expense as early as the July Monarchy. But when the Monarchy ended, more had been planned than done. It is hard to speak more precisely because credible figures are difficult to find. Even under the Second Empire, J. B. Proudhon had noted that whole categories were excluded from the statistics, and modern statisticians have found the same inadequacies in the later data, with traffic statistics referring primarily to the highway network, ignoring local roads altogether and, for a long time, all secondary roads as well. What evidence we have therefore would not fill a page. Théron de Montaugé, while praising the improvements achieved in Haute-Garonne under Louis Philippe, tells us that in 1866, out of 6,800 km of planned vicinal roads 5,000 remained unbuilt; and we learn from the agricultural survey of the same year that only one-third of 354,000 km of *vicinaux* were then in use, that work had begun on 68,000 km more, and that 168,000 km remained in the planning stage. Perhaps it was findings such as these, officially publicized at long last, that brought the decree of August 17, 1867, which sought to hasten the completion of vicinal roads, a decree widely welcomed by local authorities—more testimony to how much there was still left to do.[26]

This is what statistics often do not show: that, as an official report said of the roads in Nièvre in 1858, most of them were "projects or hopes." Evidence of goodwill, of political promises, and of real interest in giving work to the poor so as to keep them out of trouble, scores of road projects flowered every spring, anarchically dispersed and not getting much done. Moreover, the engineers worked like Penelope. In Ardèche, for example, roads begun in 1861 were still only a few kilometers long in the 1880's. The same at Eygurande (Corrèze), where in the 1890's many of the roads planned in 1836 were still unbuilt, and those that had been opened were "in a deplorable state." As Jacques Lovie says about Savoy, the secondary roads remained mediocre. In most rural parishes, the grip of poverty that went with isolation remained unbroken.[27]

The real change seems to have come after the law of 1881, which promoted the building of rural roads "recognized as being in the public interest." Coming when it did, this law would be the one most likely really to serve the interests of a public at last awake to the possibilities. When, in 1848, the municipal council of Chavignolles in Calvados had sought to provide the unemployed with work, it had a branch road built to the local nobleman's chateau.* After 1876, such roads would be built to small hamlets and outlying farms. In Cantal, though roads multiplied after 1860, the movement accelerated in 1880–1900, when local roads became more numerous and better: 16 vicinal roads in 1850, 103 in 1870, 130 in 1899. In 1929 76 percent of the local roads in Vendée had been built after 1881. In Finistère the isolation of the countryside was broken after 1870, the vicinal network completed in the decade before 1900.[28]

As a cul-de-sac, the Breton peninsula presented problems all its own. The first military network, finished as the eighteenth century ended, was built in straight lines, paying no heed to local circumstances or to relief. When it was done, the continental mass of the peninsula "remained as closed as before to the circulation of goods, men and ideas."[29] The old roads had to be rebuilt in the second half of the nineteenth century, even while the network of vicinal roads was being built, and the railways too.

The two main railroad lines reached Brest and Landerneau in 1865 and 1867, respectively, but they had no branches until 1881. Until these links were made and until narrow-gauge railways made tracks through the interior (1891 to 1914), bringing lime and chemicals, carrying out meat, butter, and fresh produce, most of the agriculture remained primitive. Even when all was done, the three departments of Lower Brittany had less roadway than the rest of France—Morbihan had only five-sixths as much as the national average, Finistère less than half as much—helping perpetuate their backwardness. What the General Council of Loire-Inférieure declared in 1841 remained true for a long time after: "The first of all fertilizers is the stone that paves our roads!"[30] Bad roads put the cost of fertilizer out of reach, doubling the price of every cartload of manure, and turned current ideas of agricultural progress to nonsense.† At the same time, there were many regions where the local materials were unsuitable for road work: shale or slaty rock, sandstone that crumbled easily, soft limestone, and even granites with high concentrations of feldspar, which weathered rapidly into fine clay and sand. In these

---

* On Chavignolles, see Gustave Flaubert, *Bouvard et Pécuchet* (New York, 1954), chap. 6. Marcel Gautier tells us that in the late 1830's at Mazières (Deux-Sèvres), familiar to us from the work of Roger Thabault, the Vicomtesse de Tusseau had her servants carry her from her chateau to the bourg, 3 km away, because the road was too bad for any other form of locomotion. In 1850 the road was still useless, even in summer. Real change came only after 1881. ("Quelques aspects de la circulation rurale en Vendée," *Bulletin du Groupe Poitevin d'Etudes Géographiques*, 1951, pp. 17–22.)

† Jacques Lovie, *La Savoie*, p. 206. Just north of Chambéry, it took three pair of oxen to pull half a cartload of manure up the slopes of the Chartreuse to Montagnole, only a few miles away. The 36 cubic feet of manure cost seven francs, their transport a little more than five francs. If one *journal* of land needed ten *demi-voitures* of fertilizer, the cost of such improvement would come to 120 francs—a prohibitive sum and vastly higher than the cost would have run in the plain or near a railroad.

regions the materials for the roadbed or the paving stone itself might well have to be hauled from far away. So, generally speaking, apart from the Paris area, the north, Bordeaux, and the Meuse, all or some road-building materials had to be imported.[31] Only rails could facilitate this, especially in totally hopeless areas like the Landes, where there were no roads at all, just trails. After the attempt to use camels had failed in the 1830's, the problem of the Landes stubbornly resisted solution until the area had railways (the Bordeaux–Bayonne line, 1855, but all other lines inland 1875–1900), which in turn encouraged and permitted the building of real roads.*

The rails brought a new life and everybody knew it, at least in little cities like Saint-Girons (Ariège) where, when the news came in 1861 that its line had been approved in Paris, the whole city celebrated with ringing bells, cannonfire, and impromptu parades. But though Saint-Girons had its station by 1866, Tarascon further to the east waited until 1877, and a branch from there to the roadless wastes of Ax took until 1888. When it got there, most of the traffic around Ax was still carried by donkeys and humans. So for a long time railways were (as Emile Coornaert called them) "a spinal column deprived of articulations in the countryside." If what he said was true of the busy Flanders, east and northeast of Lille, it was even truer of areas more isolated or more difficult. Auvergne and the Limousin remained little affected by the lonely rails that crossed rather than irrigated them until 1880. Main cities were connected to Paris, but not to each other, so that Clermont was linked to Lyon and Tulle only after 1877.[32]

In any case, the main lines needed branches, like the roads. A railway inspector, writing in the 1890's, judged that regions ten miles from a railway, or even less, gave it about one-tenth of the traffic that they would have given it had they been closer: "They close in on themselves to live off their own products instead of obeying the great law of exchange."[33] A law of 1865 intended to create cheap railway links "of local interest" showed results only after another law, this one of 1880, established the economic conditions that made such enterprises possible. The length of rail that stood at 19,746 km at the end of 1879 had jumped to 26,327 km by 1882. It would be 64,898 km in 1910, if one includes nearly 12,000 km of lines "of local interest" and nearly 10,000 km of *tortillards*—electric tramways and narrow-gauge railways giving villagers easy access to markets where they could buy and sell.[34]

Grass grew on some sections of the national roads as railways began to haul more of the long-distance freight (until bicycles and automobiles helped to revive them), but local roads, now seen as leading to and from the railway,

---

* Henri Cavaillès, "Problème de la circulation dans les Landes de Gascogne," *Annales de géographie*, 1933, pp. 561–82. In 1838 Etienne Arago had laughed at the idea that two parallel iron rods could endow the Landes with a new look. Some 40 years later Isaac Pereire could in turn laugh at Arago, boasting that the iron lines had bestowed a new department on France by turning wastes into living land (*La Question des chemins de fer*, Paris, 1879, p. 151).

flourished.[35] And so did communities with a railway station. Between 1866 and 1936 rural communes without a railway station in a zone 15 km on either side of the Paris-Lyon-Méditerranée line lost almost one-quarter of their population, while those with a station (excluding Paris) gained 1,645,373 inhabitants. More graphically, we can see what this meant to the little bourg of Amanlis (Ille-et-Vilaine), whose council rejected a narrow-gauge railway project in 1885 and only changed its mind in 1899; the line itself was not completed until 1903. By then livelier neighboring places like Châteaugiron and Janzé, with their stations, stores, doctors, and notaries, had attracted the villagers of the vicinity away from a bourg that was not that much closer than its competitors, which had in the meantime become more accessible by virtue of better vicinal roads. Where in the 1880's 15 percent to 20 percent of the communal population had attended church in neighboring parishes on Sundays, by 1925 the rector of Amanlis had lost more than one-third of his parishioners.[36]

It was not just that the railway was a pole of attraction; it was, at least for a while, a shifting pole. The road served the railway; but it served above all people who wanted to get to the railway or to get to what the rail centers could offer. This meant an extreme instability of road traffic, which, while rails unfolded, kept shifting to ever-closer railheads, no matter in what direction these might lie. Thus, in the Indre, Aigurande looked first to Châteauroux, 48 km to the north, which got a railway station in 1847; then to Argenton, 30 km west-northwest, reached by a line in 1864; next to La Châtre, 26 km east-northeast, linked in 1882; and then back north to Cluis, 10 km away, in 1903, three years before it got a station of its own.[37] This sort of thing, which must have been repeated elsewhere, meant that traditional orientations were abandoned, traditional hostilities or habits laid aside, in the pursuit of new or at least newly perceived possibilities. The peasants' so-called inertia had mostly been the refusal to respond to challenges or conditions that struck them as inappropriate or irrelevant. As soon as novelties began to speak to their own situation, the peasants hastened to respond.

So, roads and rail lines that were secondary in name but primary in fact brought the isolated patches of the countryside out of their autarky—cultural as well as economic—into the market economy and the modern world. The era of their building and the period of their completion were so close to the coming of the motor vehicle, which slowly replaced them after the 1920's, that their effects have not received all the attention they deserve.[38] But the conjunction of secondary lines and of the roads built to serve them resulted in a crash program of national integration of unparalleled scope and effectiveness; a program that could operate on this scale only because, for the first time, economic and technological conditions offered the possibility for radical cultural change. Before culture altered significantly, material circumstances had to alter; and the role of road and rail in this transformation was basic.

Where and as long as local roads were lacking, localism was bound to remain "narrow, ignorant, apathetic, cross-grained," as a Cantalien described it under Louis Philippe. The lack of local roads, he continued, "forces the farmer to consume all his produce, invites him to inertia, to laziness, to wastefulness." After the 1870's and 1880's the concert of complaints turns into one of joy: the valleys of the Massif Central were now opened to fairs and economic activity. In Dauphiné, Savoy, Bresse, and Franche-Comté, marshy or mountainous areas—Oisans, Dombes, Vercors—were finally joined to France by road and railway branches. The rugged Vercors, shortly before a world unto itself, "a true fortress ... deprived of communications with the surrounding country ... any exchange almost impossible," hence miserable and ignorant, swiftly developed new resources (especially cattle) and became one of the richest plateaus in the French Alps.[39] The area around Die also changed radically after 1880. The region had stayed almost self-sufficient. So long as mules were the only means of transport, there was no point in growing commercial crops for export, for instance fruit, to which its climate was well suited. Once roads and railroads breached the mountains and connected "this cell of the French Alps" to the life that flowed only some miles away, past the Drôme gorges in the Rhône valley's plains, buyers appeared for cattle, lavender, and in due course fruit from newly developed orchards; chemical fertilizer and superphosphates could reach the narrow valleys and help meet new demands; rye gave way to wheat; comfort replaced grinding poverty. The profound transformation can be dated to the railway's coming in 1894 and the years immediately following, when the peasants became used to it and learned how to handle the formalities involved in shipping and receiving merchandise. The outside world, which till then had had little bearing on their own, now came in with a rush: skills like writing invoices and bills of lading, counting, and schooling in general acquired concrete meaning as occasions to use them multiplied. It was a story that repeated itself elsewhere.[40]

As long as villages remained roadless, the peasants ignored general market conditions. Fruit and other produce could not be shipped for sale, so their possibilities were not worth exploiting. In Var figs were fed to local pigs; plums at Brignoles or Agen were kept for local consumption. The peasant sold what he could, when he could, at whatever price he could get. He lacked storage facilities and he needed cash. If, like most peasants, he carried his goods to market, he was very much at the mercy of the buyer. After hauling a load of chestnuts or charcoal on his back for four or five hours on difficult mountain paths, he was in no position to haggle much about what price he got, and the dealers knew it. In Ardèche, the canton of Valgorge and the Drobie river valley had been almost totally isolated for lack of roads and bridges. Mules could go as far as Deux-Aygues, but past that even men made their way through the valley with difficulty. A road had been planned since 1854. In 1875 it was still unbuilt. This meant that peasants driving a pig to market had 25 km to do on foot, one way, instead of the ten it would later be by road. Many fell victim to pleurisies as a result, and the official registers show that death rates jumped after the great annual fairs.[41] As late as 1900, the peasant of Beaumont in Ardèche still made two bundles of heather, carried one for two miles, then went back for the other, and did this all the way to Joyeuse, eight or ten miles away. From Beaumont to Joyeuse, from Genestelles to Antraigues, from Intres to Saint-Agrève, pigs were taken to market tied to a stretcher or a ladder, carried by four men who could hardly afford not to sell at any price once they arrived.* Roads that permitted carts, roads reinforced by railroads, would be an emancipation as important as political revolution, probably more important.

Schoolteachers in Lot, writing in 1881, exulted over the arrival of roads that brought with them prosperity and "civilization." Hillsides were being cleared, stagnant waters drained, and fallow plowed and sowed; new vineyards turned out wine; and the local people had "the special satisfaction... of seeing the merchants come to them to buy their diverse products." The same at Cabrespine in Lauragais, where chestnuts and olives grew in abundance, but where lack of roads meant only mule-back transport that halved the seller's profit. Then, a new road finished in 1870 meant that "today [in 1882] the buyers come seeking chestnuts at Cabrespine and pay them as high as they could be sold at Carcassonne in the old days"—not so long before. After the road opened, we hear that the houses looked clean and comfortable, that the farmer could afford to mix his rye with a little wheat, that he drank wine and bought a sack or two of millet every year, either for himself or to fatten his pig, which better fed in turn provided him with more meat. *This* was radical change.[42]

There was still much room for improvement. The 1880's were only a beginning. Along the Tarn valley, where at that time there was still no road, villages like Brousse in Rouergue had never seen a cart. Hoisting a barrel of wine up the steep ramps to the Ségala plateau on which the village stood took three pair of oxen. A major enterprise. There could not have been much wine drunk in Brousse. Or much white bread eaten. By 1904 Brousse was still isolated, but it had a road. Wheeled vehicles could reach it. What had happened was that in 1902 a secondary line between Rodez and Carmaux brought lime and fertilizer to the shale and slaty rocks of the plateau, increasing agricultural production tenfold within a few years.[43] Here was the Ségala shifting into the twentieth century, along with the rest of France!

The same was taking place in other areas: in the Rhône valley, which saw a great expansion of commercial agriculture and where fruit, fresh, dried, or

* Elie Reynier, "Voies de communication," pp. 202–5. Pierre Charrié, *Folklore du Bas-Vivarais*, p. 294, mentions this method of carrying heather as being employed in all Tanargue, each load weighing 80 kg. It would be interesting to trace the dates when wheelbarrows replaced stretchers. This seems to have occurred sometime in the second half of the century in Creuse, Allier, and Corrèze. But when? (See "Enquête sur...l'agriculture," Creuse 37, p. 13, in Musée des Arts et Traditions Populaires archives.)

candied, became a profitable export; in the Lot valley and on the Aubrac plateau, whose cattle and cheese were tapped only after 1908; in Corrèze, where the consumption of fertilizer increased 13 times and crop production 65 times between 1866 and 1906; in Brittany, where the whole face of agriculture was changed by the introduction of narrow-gauge lines between 1890 and 1914; in much of Isère and Dauphiné, whose isolated areas were gradually brought into the general swim during the three-score years after 1870.[44] Ardouin-Dumazet in 1904 was still close enough to this recent past to find it exciting: "The railway—infusion of life," we find him exclaiming. And he was right to add that where the locomotive passed (one should add, and where it stopped), economic activity grew tenfold.[*]

It is doubtful that all of this could have happened, or could have happened quite the way it did, but for a political conjunction in which the interests of capital and of the politicians who sought ways to please it coincided with a political situation that lent new weight to the votes (hence views) of rural populations. "I would vote for the devil, if he built us the Beaume road," declared an elector in the desolate Drobie valley.[45] He said this in the late 1870's, just when circumstances gave him a chance to do precisely that; and those soliciting his vote knew that it might go to them, or to the devils of the other side, depending on who could build a necessary bridge or get a much-needed stretch of roadway at last.

Hence the crucial importance of the Freycinet Plan, so called after the name of its inventor, the statesman Charles de Saulce de Freycinet, who devised it as a way of buoying up the sagging French economy of the late 1870's. His plan has been linked with school-building, as a political decision designed to bring "progressive" ideas to France's backward lands and carry Republican scripture into refractory territories or areas still untouched by its message.[46] This is to argue from effect to cause. Though its effects were cultural and political, the Freycinet Plan was an economic enterprise and undertaken for economic ends: to get a sluggish economy going, by pouring funds into it. It was what Marcel Marion, the conservative historian of financial policies, described as "setting aside all considerations of prudence and of measure": six billion francs to be spent in ten years, more than half of which was for

---

[*] Ardouin-Dumazet, *Voyage en France*, 32: 68. A report of December 31, 1861, in Archives Nationales, $F^{10}2342$ (Landes de Gascogne), notes that where new farm roads were built, permitting the replacement of the slow, cumbersome ox-carts, pine could be sold at five or six times the previous price, *but* that roads were built only near the railroad, and the rest of the area, east of the railway line, remained roadless. There the situation was not much changed from 1839, when an army report found most Landais living and dying with no knowledge whatever of the world beyond their vast solitudes, "drowned in winter and parched in summer" (Archives de la Guerre, MR 1231). Dominique Renouard gives one pause with the statement that secondary lines never carried important quantities, and indeed that some carried a mere 1,000 to 4,000 tons a year. But he agrees that they were of great social use in dragging the countryside out "of its primitive existence" (*Les Transports*, pp. 46–47). This is my point; and we must remember that statistics in no way reflect the full impact of a railway line.

building new railway lines. That was the program of 1879. Things did not quite turn out as planned. Instead of some 8,000 km of projected track, more than 16,000 km were built and better than nine billion francs were spent under electoral pressure. For the first time, millions flowed into the countryside, especially through those disinherited regions this study is about. A great deal of money went toward improving rivers, canals, and port installations; and substantial amounts were spent at last on the surfacing and building of vicinal roads.[47]

The Freycinet Plan, wrote a contemporary, was "launched like a display of fireworks set off to glorify the Republic." And though this was not (or does not seem to have been) its purpose, that was how it worked out. Coming on the heels of the crisis of May 16, 1877, and of President MacMahon's resignation in 1879, the plan affirmed that the new regime did not by any means signify depression, carried the regime's influence into the countryside, and consolidated its hold through the patronage involved in the building programs and the administration of the railway lines. In this connection, the extraordinary rise in numbers of railway employees is most relevant: 86,300 in 1861, 113,000 in 1866, 172,000 in 1876, and 222,800 in 1881, they numbered 308,000 in 1907, 355,600 in 1913, and 511,000 in 1922. An army of steady workers, looking forward to steady positions, was more effective than construction gangs in converting peasants to the modern world, for the road crews and railway builders came and went, a raucous foreign presence whose influence, however disruptive of the village youth, was but a passing one, unlikely to leave a lasting mark on a solid community. But the railway *station* offered steady jobs for steady people—in the long run an influence more subversive of traditional institutions.[48]

Two occupational groups—carters and bargemen engaged in long-distance transport—were mortally wounded by the railroads, and their decline inevitably affected many established ways of life. The stores, stables, inns, smithies, and cartwrights that catered to them were among the casualties. So were many of the peasants close to the highway zone, who relied on the horse manure dropped on the highways and who had geared their production to the carriage trade, especially fodder and oats, but also vegetables, poultry, and wines for the travelers.[49] Still, though there were many local and individual tragedies, road transport as a whole managed to adapt. River traffic did not.

Waterways were widely used in the nineteenth century, but they were slow and uncertain, subject to currents that could be very strong, or to low water that could hamper or stop passage. Some could be open anywhere from 300 days a year to only a few weeks. It is small wonder that a more reliable alternative and one that did not depend on seasons or on particular and limited skills would readily take their place.[50] So, how long river traffic survived depended only on the speed with which competing railway lines appeared to displace it.

The Rhône and Loire valleys were the first to succumb, assassinated, as a director of the Rhône steamship company put it, by the ministers of the Empire—and even by those of Louis Philippe. The Allier followed. In 1815 some 2,500 boats had plied the river, mostly carrying coal downstream to Paris. But by 1854 the Paris railway line had reached Arvant in the northwest corner of Haute-Loire, and the river trade collapsed in a few years. Meanwhile, property values in the arrondissement of Brioude (to which Arvant belongs) rose at an unprecedented rate now that local wine and timber could be sold more profitably.[51] Floating logs down the Yonne and then down the Seine to Paris had furnished the French capital with firewood since the sixteenth century, and the Morvan with an important source of revenue. Then came the rails—especially the secondary lines into northern Nièvre—and finally the opening of the Nivernais canal to heavy barges, permitting the transport of dressed lumber, which was more valuable and in greater demand; by around 1880 the *flottage* was dead.[52]

The southwest resisted longest. It was well provided with a communications network of rivers and canals, a system that railways would replace but would not markedly supplement. But save for the Garonne, to which a line between Toulouse and Bordeaux offered an alternative after 1856, the rivers gave way only slowly to the railroads: the Tarn between Montauban and Gaillac in 1884, the Vézère between the Lower Limousin and the Bordelais about the same time, the Dropt between Bordeaux and Eymet in 1899. Only a tenth of the boats that plied the Tarn in the 1860's were left a decade later. But rafts and logs still floated down the Aude in 1895, carrying the timber of the Pyrenees to Limoux and Carcassonne. And 94 boats still worked the Dordogne in 1900, carrying 16,049 tons of cheeses, coal, charcoal, firewood, and timber for casks and staves from Périgord into the Bordelais. There, too, however, the traffic that once filled the river after the autumn rains was drawing to its close. As an old Loire mariner declared in 1900, the skills of the river navigator were as dead as those of the men who made the stained-glass windows of the old cathedrals: "Our descendants will not guess that there was ever navigation on the river."[53]

They would not guess there had been so much industry either.

What is generally described broadly as industrial revolution made inroads in France very slowly, at least compared to its advance in other industrial countries of the West. Its progress, that is, the replacement of handicraft production by machine production, was marked most vividly by the decline and eventual disappearance of regional and rural industries.

These small, local enterprises, which were undertaken to boost the income of families unable to make ends meet by farming alone, have been called daughters of misery. As agricultural productivity improved, as more lands were cleared or salvaged from fallow, as root crops were introduced and demanded more attention, peasants had less time to spare for such pursuits. Home production, especially in the realms of food and clothing, fell from an estimated 6–7 percent of total industrial production under the July Monarchy to around 3.7 percent under the Second Empire and kept on falling.[54] Supplemental income could now be better sought in "modern industry"; and industrial products were proving relatively more accessible, driving home and local industry into ever-remoter vastnesses.

The first victims of this process were the oldest of the cottage industries—spinning and weaving. By 1847 and 1848, in those parts of France that had been penetrated by the products of the new textile mills cotton had driven out flax. Where once tens of thousands of women and children had spun flax there was now nothing but a starving trickle, and handweavers had been reduced to begging. But in remoter regions home-weaving survived as a village craft, and households continued to work hemp or flax or wool into coarse, durable cloth for their own use. Thus in the Vosges handlooms were still flourishing when the Franco-Prussian war broke out. By 1889 textile mills had killed them.[55] But there the influx of Alsatian immigrants to man the mills precipitated the process. Otherwise, it might have taken longer, as in Auvergne and Brittany, where the change waited on the coming of the railway.*

In 1860 the French planted 105,000 ha of flax and 180,000 ha of hemp. By 1938 only 6,000 ha of flax survived, and hemp was hardly grown at all.[56] Of course, factory goods were cheaper and more elegant. But before the peasant took them up, he had to obtain the cash to buy them. At another level, he had to learn to discriminate between the relative costs of home-produced and store-bought goods, and indeed to understand that things made at home or traded in the village also had a cost. Finally, he needed an accessible alternative to that essential by-product of the flax fields, linseed oil, which was used to light the lamp, to enrich the soup, and to mix a salad.

More variables perhaps than were involved with wool. There the adoption of factory products was a matter of means alone, which meant (at least, among other things) transport facilities that did not add to the price of goods shipped in from the towns. Savoy, for instance, had an old-established textile industry based entirely on local product and local handicrafts. Family herds supplied the wool, which was spun by hand, fulled in local mills turned by the local streams, and woven on family looms. The building of railways permitted the import of large quantities of low-priced woolens, which peasants found to be

---

* The last Breton weavers at Loudéac tried to hold out in 1890, but they were unable to do so for long. Though Brittany still had 15,000 weavers and spinners in 1896, they were relics of the past (Jean Delumeau, ed., *Histoire de la Bretagne*, p. 469). On the other hand, a survey carried out by the Lyon Chamber of Commerce in 1900 showed 47,406 handlooms in use in nearby rural areas of Rhône, Ain, Isère, Loire, Saône-et-Loire, and Vaucluse. Here was putting-out of the old sort, perpetuated because these part-time workers accepted rates that the *canuts* rejected (F. Dubief, *La Question du vagabondage*, p. 195).

of better quality and no more expensive than the old cloth. They had been thrifty and undemanding. New possibilities changed their mind. Savoy cloth —*drap de Savoie*—was condemned to death.[57]

But manufactured textiles can easily go with industrial backwardness. Transport difficulties protect the persistent past. Where and while such difficulties persisted and the economic dimension was fixed by life on foot, a multiplicity of manufacturing centers persisted as well. And the fact that peasant labor was cheap, or satisfied with small profits, permitted certain local manufacturers to compete successfully for a good long while. The crucial factor always would be the availability and the accessibility of alternatives. Thus, with the development of viticulture in Lower Languedoc, the small drapery centers of Hérault, Gard, and Aude collapsed. The weavers began leaving the little towns to work in the vineyards where salaries were higher, and the textile works closed down one after the other until, in 1884, the drapery manufacture of the southwest was practically dead.[58]

There was no clear divide between rural and industrial labor. When masons or roofers struck in Orléans, they went off to bring in the harvest. Small industrial enterprises, scattered through the country, relied on seasonal or part-time labor. Workers in these small brick works, tile works, tanneries, quarries, and mills tended to have their own garden, sometimes kept a field or vineyard. A tile mill employed four persons and one horse to knead the clay. A walnut-oil mill would take on ten or fifteen women and a cow. The sugarbeet refineries of Nord called for more hands when the heavy demands of harvest had been filled, then sent them back to the fields after winter. Well into the twentieth century some of the porcelain factories of the Limousin continued to use wood-burning kilns, and their employees worked both as porcelain makers and as woodcutters, switching from job to job according to the season.[59]

Guy Thuillier tells us that in Nièvre the miners no longer hired on as field-hands after 1870;* but in Haute-Loire, around Brioude, two-thirds of the miners were still farmer-owners, a situation that may have had "advantages from the point of view of public tranquility," but also created difficulties for the mine owners, who could "never control their enterprise." There and in neighboring parts of the Puy-de-Dôme, to the turn of the century, miners took off all the time they could, and especially Mondays, to work their plots of land. The same was true in such old-established industrial regions as the area around Thiers, renowned for its cutlery, where in 1894 the workers preferred "their

---

* And no longer saw social status in buying a piece of land after 1880–90 (*Aspects de l'économie nivernaise*, p. 343). Rolande Trempé tells us that at Carmaux, in Tarn, the struggle to turn peasant smallholders into a permanent work force took longer. Seasonal absenteeism, massive during sowing, haymaking, and harvest, affected from 10 percent to 50 percent of the labor force. In 1874 the mine directors bewailed the good crop that tied up their workers. Problems like these waned only after 1878, when the agricultural depression limited the choices (or temptations) of peasant-miners. (*Les Mineurs de Carmaux*, 1: 180–83, 190ff.)

liberty" (to work their fields) to higher wages, and the bosses had to resign themselves to this attitude. "This primitive industrial life," sighed the sub-prefect, "has its traditions that one must respect."[60]

Iron-mining, iron-smelting, and related industries, such as charcoal-making and woodcutting, were extraordinarily widespread. Timber meant charcoal, charcoal meant ironworks. Like brandy, charcoal grew out of transport diffi-culties. In the Ardennes, in the Grande Chartreuse, in Périgord and the Pyre-nees whole forests were felled for charcoal, which was made locally and shipped to forges or to cities. Small mines and forges dotted the countryside. In some hamlets of Périgord, "everyone had his mine!" The presence of ore close to the sandy surface, which could be scratched with a hoe or easily dug up, made for a forge every two or three miles along the shady valleys.* But though wood was abundant, it was consumed at a phenomenal rate. It took some 2,000 lbs of wood to make 1,000 bricks and some 1,600 lbs to produce about 1.3 cubic yds of lime. To cast 200 lbs of iron required 700 lbs of char-coal, or roughly 2 cubic yds of hardwood. One of these forges could produce 150 tons a year, but such an output consumed between 25 and 40 acres of forest.[61]

Not very surprisingly, these small charcoal-burning enterprises were hard-hit when improved transport brought coke into a competitive position. The free-trade treaties of the Second Empire finished their ruin. In 1859 Haute-Vienne had 42 furnaces, in 1861 only eight or ten. In the 1830's Dordogne had 37 blast furnaces and 88 ironworks. The small Crempse river valley alone was filled with small ironworks, their machines powered by the river's waters. By 1864 only 31 of these enterprises were still alive, 33 having shut down. In 1865 an official report showed the fires out in almost all the forges of Dordogne. By 1900 the department had become purely agricultural. An industry based on water power, on the charcoal of local forests, and on shallow iron mines could not compete with better-sited works, once coal became accessible.[62]

The story was the same in other places. The Privas iron mines entered a decline after 1870. Production fell from 144,000 tons in 1853 to 41,000 tons in 1893 and a mere 3,000 tons in 1910. In Ariège, the last furnaces faded away in the 1870's. They had been decaying for ten or twenty years like those of Périgord, and for similar reasons. With them there disappeared a whole in-dustrial, political, and social world. In Mayenne five ironworks that employed fewer than 1,000 workers and used local charcoal to smelt local ore mined by 100 or 200 men (in 1848) turned out 2,300 tons a year right through the Sec-ond Empire. The completion of the railroads finished them off at the begin-ning of the Third Republic, as it did those still holding out in Upper Brittany, as coke took the place of charcoal.[63]

---

* Pierre Deffontaines, L'Homme et la forêt, p. 85. Similarly, the peasants living near Alès, in the Cévennes, exploited the accessible pyrite of Saint-Julien-de-Valgalgues and sold the ferrous sulfate.

The ups and downs of industry that throve in isolation and withered with it are illustrated in the story of the ironworks of the Semouse valley in the Vosges. They had been numerous as the nineteenth century opened, using the Semouse when it was high and stopping work when its flow dried up, trading on the proximity of Franche-Comté and on the needs of the surrounding region, where wire mills prospered at mid-century. In 1859 and 1860 steam engines were installed, including "a gigantic machine...with a stone chimney nearly 30 meters high." Then, competition from foreign imports and from more malleable puddled irons began to create difficulties, compounded after the Prussian war by the new mild steels of Bessemer and Siemens. The metal refineries gave in. By 1899 only two ironworks survived, working the mild steels of the big mills of Lorraine, "where ore is abundant, coal cheap, and transport easy."[64] That said it all.

The nail-makers whom we have encountered carrying their iron bars home from market found themselves under suspended sentences as well. Their tools and materials had changed very little since Diderot (son of a cutler) had described them in five pages of *L'Encyclopédie.* A good man working 18 hours a day for six days a week (on the seventh he took his wares to market) could turn out 24,000 nails a week. Then came machines and, with them, the saying "ça tombe comme des clous," a wondering comment at how much they turned out. Trade outlets shrank to narrow local limits. Nevertheless, where the harsh terrain discouraged competition, in Savoy, Forez, and Bourbonnais, hand-crafted nails managed to withstand the offensive of the machine product. Around Oisans, in Isère, nail-making died by 1875. But in the Alps, at Bauges, for example, the last nail forge closed only in 1901, the year when the Annecy–Albertville rail link opened. The Morvandiaux's nail forge, fed by a dog-turned wheel, went out about then, too. In Forez it took the First World War to kill the hand-made nail in many villages. But every carriage road, like the one that linked Les Près in Drôme to the outer world in 1872, pressed back the pack-mules, permitted heavy materials to come in by road on carts, and changed house-building patterns. Masonry and slate replaced timber and thatch—and standard nails replaced the specially shaped local nails, bent individually to suit each local structure.[65] That was the typical unspectacular process of subversion: not one but several factors ushering in the new and wearing down the old.*

---

* Much the same could be said about a far more important industry—the salt industry of the western marshes. Traditional supplier of the whole coast as far north as Amiens, as far south as Tulle, and inland to Paris and Clermont, the western salt industry had remained astonishingly stable between 1700 and 1866 (even in its reluctance to give way to the metric system). Then came the railways, whose networks favored the spread of eastern and southern salt. With no rail link to the Orléans network, western salt found it increasingly difficult to reach even Caen, Orléans, and Poitiers. Between 1852 and 1866 its Paris sales fell from 9,600 tons to 103 tons a year. The bourgeois owners thereupon sold the land to their farmers and sharecroppers, leaving the salt-pans to nature's mercy. (Marcel Delafosse and Claude Laveau, "L'Evolution des marais

In the last ten or twenty years of the century, small industries based on local materials and on sales to an immediate clientele disappeared, lost importance, or simply stagnated. We find reports of regression coming in from everywhere. In the Limousin forges, paperworks using rags or the straw of rye, hatmakers, and weavers were all throwing in the sponge. In the Limagne in one community (a prosperous one) the local pottery, the wool-carding shop, and one of the two lime-kilns disappeared in the space of a few years. In the Pyrenees the espadrilles industry was slowly being broken by the competition of Toulouse, and local tanneries were helpless when faced with cheaper foreign leathers. In Cantal sabots, copper-smithing, cloth made of local wool, barely dragged along, and even fishnets were now woven by machines.[66] These industries had all been based on poor communications. When communications improved, they could not hold their own. Once this had happened, or while it was happening, the peasants could find nothing to replace them as a source of supplementary income. The part-time earnings that had helped maintain "the patriarchal life" and its archaic institutions were no longer to be had. The closing off of subsidiary activities encouraged migration to the cities, particularly by the young; left an aging population in the countryside; and led to the abandonment of the poorest lands and then of the less-poor ones. On the other hand, this situation reflected the penetration of modern market goods and helped encourage it.

One of the most important of these goods was wine, which as we have seen had only a limited market in the countryside during the first half of the nineteenth century. The railroads changed all that. But it was not just that they opened up new markets for the wine trade. They also permitted wine-producing regions to enter that trade. Until their coming, in Agenais and Armagnac for example, the further a village lay from a river, the more stills it had. Brandied wine was a more compact cargo than the sheer juice of the grape. The production and local consumption of brandy thus related to the access to a waterway, hence the ability to market a product that had to be hauled to the closest port on the Garonne, 10–15 leagues away: three or four days overland by ox cart. In 1830 the freight cost for such a trip was higher than the cost of sending a comparable amount of cargo from the Garonne ports to Paris. By 1862 the municipal council of Narbonne rejoiced that "the wine that passed through the copper [still] can now be put on sale since the coming of the railway." The same applied to the wine of regions like Auvergne, where at one time it had been so abundant and so cheap for lack of means of export that it was even used to mix mortar.[67]

The wines that benefited most were those of the Midi. By the late 1850's

<hr>

salants," pp. 256–59; A. Audiganne, *La Région du bas de la Loire*, pp. 2–12.) The old locution "C'est porter sel en Brouage," equivalent to carrying coals to Newcastle, died as the trade and the salt-pans of Brouage (Charente-Inférieure) died.

they were selling in Lyon for a fifth of what they had cost under Louis Philippe, and reaching out for the Paris market. Soon, predicted a railway engineer in 1863, the hogsheads "painfully transported in Indian files of little carts
pulled by the small oxen of the Tarn mountains will be carried at little cost
by railroad" to Cantal and the Limousin. He was right. In the southeast, too,
when a new line opened from Grenoble to Valence in 1864, the peasants of
Morette (Isère) gave up their poor local growths for better, cheaper Midi
wines, and grew walnuts instead, which they could export profitably over the
new rails.[68] This kind of thing happened more gradually in the center—in the
Limagne, where in mid-century half to two-thirds of the rich farmlands were
planted in grapes and where the wheel only turned with the century; and in
Vivarais, where even the country roads were covered with trellises until the
wines of the Rhône valley and regions further south came in by rail and road
around the 1890's.[69] Such places on the whole held out until the Phylloxera
had destroyed their vineyards in the 1880's or, further north, in the 1890's. But
the catastrophe past, few vineyards north of Périgord or west of Yonne were
replanted on the old scale. Lower Languedoc, on the other hand, which rails
had turned into a vast vine factory, destroying the old balance between agriculture and local manufactures, went through some manic-depressive phases
in which disaster followed on prosperity, before settling into the industrial
wine production that we know today.

My purpose is not to chronicle the growth of the wine industry or of any
other, but to suggest what the presence of viable and accessible roads and rails
did to people and to their way of life. It changed them radically. It opened
possibilities sometimes sighed for but never within reach. The turning wheels
on road and railway, even wheelbarrows, meant vastly greater carrying power,
more movement and faster movement, more productivity and more resources,
more choice or at least more freedom to choose. The peasant used to bad
roads began to resent and avoid them once he could compare them with
rather better ones. Man who, in a geographer's words, had always ignored
difficult terrain and stalked over it regardless, no longer did so once he had
learned that such effort could be avoided. Roads would be left to die, not because they were unusable but because they were at last recognized as hard. But
also roads, once something of a luxury, became a necessity. Roads and rails
brought men into the market, permitted them to drink wine or sell it profitably, or to develop crops that could not be marketed before, and to give up
growing others that could now be bought more cheaply. They also brought
ruin to local enterprises no longer protected by earlier isolation, to outdated
occupational groups like the riverboatmen, and to producers of mediocre local
goods or crops fated to be outmatched by specialized ones. They set people on
the move—because those people could get away more easily or because they
had to get away, because things were going better or worse, because oppor-

tunities beckoned somewhere else and could now, for the first time, be seized.* The move was not only in space, but in time and mind as well: roads and rails introduced new foods into the diet, new materials in the building of the house, new objects in its interior, new tools in the fields about it, new things to do on holidays, and new kinds of clothes to wear. They offered opportunities for enterprise and hence for social mobility that were not there before; the jobs that went with roads and railways alone were temptations that set many on the move.

Great motors of civilization, the imperial prosecutor of Agen had called the roads and railroads in 1867.† But what was needed before civilization could percolate to the rural masses were the humbler motors that the Freycinet Plan set within their reach.

Not only civilization, but national unity too. There could be no national unity before there was national circulation. The Pyrenees, Brittany, Flanders, and the Massif Central were either self-contained or part of entities to which the larger entity, France, was largely irrelevant. The railways closed down the mule passes of the Pyrenees and eventually (as the economy and the mentality they spread caught on) made those peaks a wall for France. On the other hand, railways breached the Chinese wall that fenced in Lower Brittany and helped homogenize the lands along their routes. It was more than a coincidence that the old Breton minstrels first disappeared along the new railways. Or that the building of a local railway line from Furnes to Poperinghe turned the Flemish peasants' ancient north-south trade across the Franco-Belgian border to a more purely French direction.

So roads, of stone or steel, welded the several parts into one. The postal service had a role in this as well. It too developed from an exceptional and costly service to a commonplace of everyday use. In the 1840's, when Benoît Malon's father died and his uncle sent a letter to say that he would take the boy, the arrival of the postman, in his smock with red-facings and a crossbelt embossed with a glittering shield of bronze, set the whole family astir. "It was the first letter mother ever received; in the six-household hamlet there weren't two letters a year; it cost twelve *sous*. The postman read it out."[70]

* And, finally, because third-class rail fares were more than halved between 1871 and 1910. This could lead to previously unheard-of ventures, as when, shortly before the First World War, René Bazin encountered a peasant family traveling in a third-class compartment somewhere in the Pyrenees: "Je n'avais jamais rencontré des paysans ... voyageant si loin de chez eux, sans idée de lucre ou de piété. Et ce paysan touriste, encore mal éveillé et traîné par le monde, m'apparut comme un symptôme, comme le prédécesseur inconscient des masses qu'allèchent le billet à prix réduit, l'aquarelle affichée dans les gares rurales et l'envie grandissante de goûter à tous les plaisirs des riches." (*En Province*, Paris, 1921, p. 208.)

† In this connection, we may note the words of Claude-Joseph Tissot, dean of the Faculty of Letters of the University of Dijon, who thought that the best remedy for the epidemic of "demonic possession" in the wilds of Savoy in 1865 would be the completion of the last 16 km of road between Thonon and Morzine—for "with goods and travelers, ideas would circulate that would advantageously modify the prejudices of the populace" ("Les Possédés de Morzine," *Revue moderne*, May 1865).

In 1848 the English system of the prepayment of letters by postage stamp was introduced (actually beginning 1849). Letters henceforth cost only four sous to send, one-third the cost of Malon's uncle's letter, and postal traffic gradually increased. We have seen already that in the 1850's the use of stamps remained unfamiliar to some, and indeed the total postal traffic remained negligible: 3.64 pieces per capita in 1834, 4.86 in 1844, 9.06 in 1854, 19.75 in 1874, 37.49 in 1884. These figures include periodicals sent by mail, a category that in those years had little meaning for peasants (as opposed to rural notables). For letter post alone the figure, rounded off, jumped from one letter in 1789 for every French man, woman, and child to two in 1830. Not much of a jump. The figure stood at five in 1860, at nine in 1869, at 14 in 1880, at 20 in 1890, at double that on the eve of the war, and there it reached a saturation point. So the sharpest changes in the rhythm of growth occurred expectably during the Third Republic, notably it seems in the quarter century or so before the war.[71]

In the remoter areas that most interest us, the pattern is roughly similar, though steadily behind France as a whole. Thus Corrèze and Creuse, which Alain Corbin has studied, bought about two and a half times as many stamps in 1888 as in 1845. But this still left these departments at about a third of the national average. Part of the trouble may have been the lack of post offices, least likely to appear in poor and difficult country, yet most needed there if such areas were to be reached or mail distributed. The large department of Aveyron, whose 305 communes were cut off from one another by numerous ravines that made distribution difficult, had 27 post offices in 1860, 43 in 1872, 78 in 1886, 110 in 1900, 145 in 1908. And there were villages like Mosset in Pyrénées-Orientales (which did not have a decent road to Prades, 10 km away, until 1882) that got their post offices in the twentieth century.[72] My guess is that in areas like these the real acceleration of postal traffic came after 1880 or even later, and that when, in 1910, Emmanuel Labat found a Gascon village that was adding a third postman because the two it had were "overloaded by newspapers and postcards young men and girls have got into the habit of sending each other," the situation he described was both rare and recent.[73]

It was nevertheless true that all postal activity was increasing. Postal orders (the salvation of a young boy in 1866, who used them to send home every five francs he earned as a peddler so he could not be robbed on the road) soared after they became exempt from stamp duty in 1879: 14.5 million francs' worth were delivered in 1881, 789 million in 1898. The optical telegraph (Chappe's semaphore) went out by 1852, leaving behind a description for those who gesticulate: that they have a telegraph in their stomach.[74] Between 1851 and 1855 all the prefectural seats were linked to Paris by telegraph lines, Mende and Bastia bringing up the rear. But lesser places were not connected until the 1870's, so that sub-prefects in Tarn and Ariège, for instance, learned how the Italian wars were going by couriers, who were outpaced by ordinary travelers. The number of telegraph offices tripled and more, as the railroads spread between the 1880's and the end of the century. As a result, by 1897 in the fairly typical southwestern department of Tarn, where in 1859 the sole bureau at Albi had handled just 663 telegrams, mostly official messages, the traffic had reached a modern figure, above 140,000. More and more links that helped to persuade people that the land was one.[75]

A number of Frenchmen have spoken of roads as having cemented national unity.[76] If this is true, and I think it is, the fallout of the Freycinet Plan did more to achieve this than the great highways of Monarchy and Empire, which cemented no more (though it was a great deal) than an administrative structure. If, as Maurice Bédel would have it, the roads "have forged the profound sensibility of France and, above all, its patriotic feelings," then it is in the latter part of the nineteenth century with macadam and steel rails that these feelings were hammered out.[77]

Communications are cumulative. It was Robert Louis Stevenson who persuaded the tribal chiefs of Samoa to cut a road through the wilderness, which later, in his memory, was called the Road of Gratitude. When it was opened in October 1894, a very good date from our point of view, this is what Stevenson said: "Our road is not built to last a thousand years, yet in a sense it is. When a road is once built, it is a strange thing how it collects traffic, how every year as it goes on, more and more people are found to walk thereon, and others are raised up to repair and perpetuate it, and keep it alive."[78]

Chapter Thirteen

KEEPING UP WITH YESTERDAY

Before the cherry orchard was sold everybody was worried and
upset, but as soon as it was all settled finally and once and for
all, everybody calmed down, and felt quite cheerful in fact.
—ANTON CHEKOV

THE STORY OF France's entry into the industrial age has generally been told
in terms of the numbers of engines moved by steam.* As a practical matter,
the spread of roads and railroads would be a sounder indicator, for it was they,
particularly the local roads and lines of the late century, that created a truly
national market in which the wares that the machines turned out could be
sold and bought. More, they were crucial in spreading the relative prosperity
that sustained that market. Until this happened, or rather until the effects of
a wide-reaching communication network made themselves felt, "industry" for
most Frenchmen was home and local. Its representative was the artisan. There
were more people engaged in artisanal production than in large-scale industry.
This was true in the 1860's, when they outnumbered all those engaged in industry, workers, managers, and proprietors alike, by almost three to one. It
remained true ten years later, when their number was still double that of
industrial workers.

Statistically, the artisanal enterprises of France consisted of small workshops
in which employee and master were practically balanced: about 1 : 1 in 1865,
about 1.5 : 1 in 1876, quite a long way from a modern situation.[1] France was
and continued to be a country of men and sometimes women who were their
own masters: *un pays de patrons.* Sometimes, in the countryside especially,

* One village in Nivernais was actually called La Machine, so great a sensation did the installation of a simple engine create in this distant countryside in 1836. However, though steam engines
multiplied through the first half of the century, they do not seem to have gotten bigger. As J. H.
Clapham first pointed out, the relationship between their number and the horsepower produced
suggests a great multiplication of small machines between 1830, when the average horsepower
per machine was 16, and 1848, when the figure was only 12.5 (*The Economic Development of
France and Germany, 1815–1914,* Cambridge, Eng., 1948, p. 62). Significantly, the average continued to fall: in 1870, it stood at 12.25. Then the trend began to reverse: 13 in 1880, 14.69 in
1890, 24 in 1900, nearly 35.5 by 1910. (Based on figures in J.-A. Lesourd and Claude Gérard,
Histoire économique, 2: 345.) Once again, the shift from small-scale industrial enterprise to a
"modern" model seems to have taken place in the ten to fifteen years before 1900.

they were no more than their own masters: small, independent artisans, owning their instruments of production and employing no help at all. It was these
men and their skilled helpers, or *compagnons,* who formed an interested public for political debate in towns and cities; and it was their like who both sustained the autarky of the village and helped to carry villagers out of it.

More literate than their fellows, better informed and also better able to earn
a decent living, the artisans were important carriers—capillary vessels through
which the national interest and national culture reached into the rural world.[2]
The police knew this; they had seen blacksmiths, shoemakers, hostelers, and
tavern-keepers furnish a fair share of the opponents to the various ruling
regimes. At the same time, the very existence of a rural artisanate was evidence of and support for self-sufficiency, however relative. The more numerous the rural artisans, the less thorough the national economic integration,
hence the less concern with national politics, which, acted out in an urban
world, had little obvious relation to self-contained rural life. The less the impact of national politics, the less chance there would be of organized opposition to urban interests and, hence, to the government.

The role of the rural artisan was thus highly ambiguous. His presence
helped keep his community apart from the national traffic. But it also helped
clarify—that is, teach the community—how it was linked to the nation, slowly
developing the formulas of political, that is adversary, relationships. An adversary relationship in politics requires the existence of a perceived connection,
like that between capital and labor in industry. There, interdependence soon
created tensions whose very acuteness testifies that the degree of integration
was advanced. At the rural level this sort of friction, with all its integrative
undertones, did not develop until around the First World War, contemporary
with a significant decline in the use and numbers of artisans. By then, their
job was done.

We shall attend to the political evolution before very long. My purpose now
is to see the artisans at work in their rural setting, and to trace how their
functions shrank as modern market goods replaced what they turned out.

Artisans were numerous in traditional society. In 1836, by Henri Polge's
count, Gers had 18,833 artisans (plus 3,591 apprentices) in a population of
312,882 (see Table 3). Even supposing that each person so categorized spent
some time working the land if at all possible, how many of these were full-
time jobs? Presumably, the categorization is based on the person's principal
source of income. But blacksmiths apart, few village artisans could earn a
living from the practice of one trade.[3] The butcher probably also kept a tavern
or did something else on the side. The miller or the smith might well have
done some barbering; indeed, any man with enough confidence and enough
capital to buy a razor was able to serve, or maim, his fellows that way. And
oil-pressing was clearly seasonal work. Strikingly, six trades accounted for
over half of Gers's artisans (and people making cloth and turning it to clothes

TABLE 3
Artisan Population of Gers, 1836

Occupation	No.	Occupation	No.	Occupation	No.
Weavers	3,300	Carpenters		Blacksmiths	216
Building and con-		(*menuisiers*)	654	Locksmiths	183
struction workers		Bakers	591	Saddlers	173
(*charpentiers*)	2,128	Sabotiers	371	Sawyers	150
Shoemakers	1,672	Tilemakers	366	Wagonners	
Dressmakers	1,586	Butchers	270	(*rouliers*)	148
Masons	1,561	Wool carders	256	Oil-pressers	132
Smiths		Lathe workers		Hatters	124
(*forgerons*)	1,151	(*tourneurs*)	244	Tanners	118
Millers	1,012	Stonecutters		Carriers	
Cartwrights	965	(*trasseurs*)	244	(*voituriers*)	111
Coopers	761	Quarrymen	243	Barbers	103

SOURCE: Henri Polge, "L'Artisanat dans le Gers sous le règne de Louis-Philippe," *Bulletin de la Société Archéologique du Gers*, 1969, pp. 217–18.

for over half of these), nine trades for over two-thirds, and 12 for over three-fourths. There were remarkably few butchers, and even if one includes the more numerous bakers, there was only one person employed in the food trade for every 363 inhabitants. As for barbers, they must have been mostly concentrated in the market towns: 103 of them for 466 communes is not very many. What we have here is a picture of an economy in which only a few products needed special skills, namely, clothes, footwear, houses, carts, metalwork, casks, grain meal.

One thing that scintillates by its absence is the store. What passed for the village store was, as a rule, merely some private home where a couple, perhaps only the wife, more or less informally sold this or that. The artisan acted as his own distributor. But he went in for trade, too; and most often this was selling refreshments, like Thomas Rouge, a cartwright and coffeehouse-keeper at Céret (Pyrénées-Orientales) who was denounced in 1861 for speaking disrespectfully of the Emperor; or Edouard Lejeune, a cabinetmaker from near Laon who set himself up to sell drink.[4] In trade an artisan could hope for greater gain, whether he sold just his own products or dealt in those of others as well. For trade was associated with gain that somehow went beyond the price charged for work done—and making money was an unusual skill, at once admired and resented. In the patois of Franche-Comté, the term *commerce* is used to describe complicated affairs, even disorder, an intricate confusion. And one presumes that the widespread association of trade with exceptional knowledge, ability, and intelligence was based on fact. Sayings reflected this general prejudice, along with the peasant's resentment of the seller's superior shrewdness. "A trader and a pig: you only know their worth when they are dead." "A hundred millers, a hundred weavers, a hundred tailors make three hundred thieves." "Seven tailors, seven shoemakers, seven millers, and seven students make twenty-one thieves and seven gluttons."[5]

Yet such men, though suspect because they took advantage or were supposed to do so, were also envied. They were men of affairs—they had a calling and a station. Girls preferred them. In Loire they were "highly regarded": "A girl feels that she rises in the world when instead of a humble peasant, she gets a cartwright. It is often the men of station (*les hommes d'état*) who matter in the village. They have the time to read the paper, and they know every new arrival in the place."[6]

As economic activity increased—more roads, more trade, more circulation, more consumption—and peasants found less time for making some of the things they used to make at home, the local artisans *seemed* to benefit. The number of artisans began to grow and so did the number of shopkeepers. At Mazières-en-Gâtine, the bare minimum of artisans (cartwright, mason, tile-maker, sabotier, blacksmith, baker, carpenter, sawyer) grew between 1841 and 1881, by which time the single sabotier had proliferated to two, supplemented by a shoemaker who also played the fiddle at village dances: proof that more people used more footwear, and even shoes. In 1841 the mason had employed three journeymen. In 1881 there were five masons and three journeymen. More roads, more carts: the single blacksmith had turned to three, one of whom employed three helpers, among them a locksmith. Cartwrights and a harness-maker appeared in 1886; so did three carpenters, indicating that household furnishings began to receive attention. There was more money to spend: six coffeehouses or inns now thrived where at mid-century there had been but two. Even on the shopkeeping front, the two "merchants" of 1841 had now become three grocers and haberdashers, two of whom had begun to stock ready-made work clothes around 1878–80. Even the labor costs of time seem finally to have become a common consideration, so that old Ragotte, in Nièvre, and her like began to realize it was not worth knitting woolen stockings, because wool cost 30 sous and the same pair bought in a store only 39.[7]

Down in Vivarais, another village in the 1880's had two blacksmiths, two harness-makers (this was mule country), three shoemakers, two tailors, one dyer (there was one at Mazières as well, newly established to dye the local cloth), four carpenters, and ten masons. The market economy that condemned artisans to decline and death in the long run began by increasing their numbers. Whether in Nord near Dunkirk, in the east near Langres, or in Comminges in the southwest, one family in every three or four drew some of its revenue from small-scale industry or shopkeeping. Even the small village in Bigorre where Jacques Duclos was born in 1896 had three mills, two taverns, one blacksmith, one wheelwright-smith, one nail-maker, who sold his nails to peasants in the mountains, and one housebuilder (Duclos's father), who doubled as an innkeeper while his wife worked as a seamstress.[8]

There were communities, it seems, where even the 1890's did not increase the very limited number of local artisans or see the appearance of stores. Such communities still depended on itinerant shoemakers, tinkers, tinmen, and other tradesmen, who, as in part of Mâconnais, supplemented the services of the local blacksmith, weaver, and nail-maker. Even there, however, each village had those lesser specialties that gave the poor a share in parish life and a means of subsistence: molecatchers, snake finders, and hemp-carders; *rebilhous*, who during the night cried out the hours and at midnight went to the cemetery to tell the time to the dead; *mataïres*, who killed the pig on your own premises; *cendrousos*, literally cinderellas, who collected ashes and sold them in the market for laundry use; porters who carried bastards by night to the nearest almshouse; reciters of the psalms of penitence (a bit feared as sorcerers); and professional mourners. And then there were those curious breeds to be found at least from the Limousin to Languedoc—the *ditzamondaïre*, who sucked the overfull breasts of mothers who had lost or weaned their babies; and the *tétaïres*, or milk-drawing men, who sucked on the nipple of a newly delivered woman to start the flow of milk when she had difficulty nursing, and left the house only when she had successfully suckled her child (they would be lodged, fed, and paid a handsome five-franc fee). These ways of integrating indigents into the community, by giving them a social function to fulfill, would fade along with more honorable crafts. In 1922 René Fage noted, of his own Limoges: "These little trades have disappeared."[9]

Much else had disappeared by then. The crude local earthenware that inspired the Gascon saying, "Stupid as an earthenware jug," had gone the way of most hand-potted kitchen items. At Bas (Haute-Loire), where pottery had been turned out at least since Roman times, the last local potter died in 1912. By 1929 the last potter in Loire closed shop at Pont-de-Vabres. The Breton tailors—marriage brokers, news carriers, story-tellers, the police gazette of Lower Brittany—began to disappear after 1875, as ready-mades spread and bourg shopkeepers began to sell fabrics and sewing articles. This also happened slowly, with ups before the downs. Growing prosperity meant richer costumes, and the late nineteenth century was Brittany's gaudiest age. But more of the latest stitches were the work of seamstresses, who resisted or adapted better than the male tailors, whose many social functions were being gnawed away. The sewing machine, first noted in Brittany in 1892, became a part of standard farm equipment after 1900. Another gift of the new regime: the women knew it well who listened as Jules Renard, running for mayor in his Nièvre village, soared into praise of the nineteenth century and of the Third Republic that had given them sewing machines.[10]

Two important institutions now entered their decline: the smithy and the village mill. Just as the public wash-house was the social center for village women, so was the smithy the meeting-place for village men, especially on rainy days. Indeed, Lucien Febvre has called it *le lavoir des hommes*, and has noted that the two decayed as village institutions more or less together. The smith was a notable figure. He had quite often done his *tour de France* as a compagnon. He was at the dead center of all comings and goings. Something of a magician, he was healer, dentist, and veterinarian, and often sold wine or a few groceries on the side. Interestingly, when a witness from the inner west spoke of the decay of smiths in the 1930's, he had reference not so much to their trade (for many had adjusted as tractors and automobiles replaced the horse) as to their other functions, and the sheer prestige they had enjoyed in consequence.[11]

If the smithy was the village social center, the mill was the social center of the countryside—a rustic, floury salon, as a Breton put it—and the miller the peasants' newspaper, because like smiths he saw so many people. In wine country, people would gather at the mill even when they had no business "to chat at the barrel's end" (*au cul des barriques*) as they sipped the year's wine, dropping in to learn how their neighbors' crops fared, to ask the hour of a train, or simply to hear the latest gossip. There and elsewhere, the miller's wife kept a kind of café and restaurant for her clients, and the son might do some barbering on the side.[12]

Windmills first, then water mills would die out gradually, leaving the country scattered with picturesque homes for summer visitors indifferent to mosquitoes. Sabots too were condemned to become tourist souvenirs. When shoes were a luxury, villagers lived in sabots—that is, when they wore them. A youth got his first pair at first communion. The importance of sabots in everyday routine is reflected in proverbs and locutions: sabot and strap go together; so do old sabots and embers; Carnival arrives with an unstrapped sabot; a prattler has a mouth like a sabot (wide-open).[13] Greater prosperity meant more sabots for all, then gradual evolution as the graceless heavy sabots came to be painted and elegantly shaped, "trying to look like shoes." The competition of shoes and even boots was driving back sabots, used ever less for any but dirty jobs. At Mazières five men made sabots in 1886, only two 20 years later, and these two also sold ready-made shoes, slippers, and hats. Meanwhile, the single shoemaker had turned to three, and two of them even employed workmen. They were soon to retreat in turn before the manufactured shoes, which by the eve of the war were bought by all—or almost all.[14]

By then, shops had gone far from their timid beginnings. Between 1836 and 1936 the proportion of shopkeepers in the total population in three rural cantons of Picardy doubled—which is not very much—but most of the change took place after mid-century and before the war: 1 : 62 inhabitants in 1836; 1 : 42 in 1872; 1 : 37 in 1911; 1 : 34 in 1936. The greatest increase was in the food trade: the ratio of grocers, butchers, and bakers was 1 : 138 in 1836; 1 : 73 in 1872; 1 : 53 in 1911; 1 : 51 in 1936. It is clear that by 1911 the great change was over. There was little left to alter in the following years. In Vendée, too, the money economy was altering the life-style: Thabault reported a dry goods dealer in Mazières in 1896; one, then two, hardware stores after 1898; in 1911 even a milliner. But, as in Picardy, the greatest change came in the food trades.

The town had one baker in 1886, five in 1906. The local railroad station, which received 9.4 tons of grocery and foodstuff shipments in 1885, had 99.9 tons in 1890 and 150 tons in 1900.[15]

The shops were selling crockery—first only for holidays and Sundays, then for everyday use—and tableware, so that by 1900 in many Mazières houses people began to use table knives and even to change plates for separate courses. The shops also sold wine, at first an exceptional luxury, like coffee, sugar, chocolate, and macaroni. They sold umbrellas, once evidence of solid comfort, which were now the right of all and were even a feature of some public demonstrations.* They sold tobacco—for a long time in the form of snuff, a luxury incorporated into the "matrimonial rites of our countryside," where brides-to-be came to expect the gift of a silver snuffbox. This suggests that, like all market goods, tobacco was rare. As late as 1893 it was still a "recent custom" in Côtes-du-Nord to sacrifice a few packages of tobacco in laying the foundation stone of a farmhouse. Joseph Cressot remembered very little smoking in his village of Haute-Marne in the 1880's. "Who would be so crazy as to turn *sous* into smoke?" The Upper Breton peasants called a free pinch of snuff *tabac de diot*—fool's tobacco. It was the soldiers who, after seven or five or three years of service, returned to their villages won over to the rolled cigarette. Cressot's father, a twenty-year-old recruit in 1870, lit his first cigarette as a counter to typhus and went on smoking for the remainder of his life. The war of 1870, which brought a far greater number of men into the ranks than ever stood regular duty before or after until 1889, must have been important in spreading the smoking habit.[16] And indeed Caporal, sold in army canteens, soon became a synonym for tobacco itself.†

Above all, perhaps, the shop sold clothes, and more and more people bought them. Jules Michelet has celebrated the calico revolution, when cheap cotton prints permitted working-class women to shift from drab, dark garments worn for ten years or more to "a dress of flowers." This sort of thing took time to percolate down to the rural level, where poverty, local materials, and local craftsmen favored old modes of dress. In 1845, as Michelet was writing of *The People*, meaning almost entirely the city people he saw around him, peasants were still wearing knee-breeches and cocked hats inherited from the upper-class fashions of the seventeenth and eighteenth centuries.‡

The very notion of dressing up was alien to everyday experience, the term

* Roger Thabault, *Mon village*, p. 173. In Allier, where Socialist propaganda had made headway in the 1890's, the conscripts of Commentry, Marcillat, Montmarault, and thereabouts carried red ribbons and red banners. When these were banned by the prefect in 1895, large red umbrellas were used instead (Georges Rougeron, *Le Département de l'Allier*, p. 84).

† Caporal got its name because it was supposed to be superior to the ordinary issue that army privates could buy "à deux sous la brouette." This alleged superiority did not prevent the term from becoming a synonym for bad, cheap tobacco (Paul Sébillot, *Le Tabac*, Paris, 1893, pp. 3, 4).

‡ *Le Peuple*, p. 73. And even then, for all his sympathy for the common man, Michelet found contact with the man on the street difficult: "Je suis né peuple, j'avais le peuple dans le coeur … mais sa langue, sa langue, elle m'était inaccessible. Je n'ai pu le faire parler."

(in Franche-Comté) also used to mean a disguise—to put on Sunday clothes, something out of the ordinary and, somehow, ornate. Linen and clothes that were not homemade, or handed down, or bought secondhand, and not worn and patched and worn until they fell to pieces, were strange and wonderful things.[17] The crowds that filled the Boulevard du Temple—dubbed the Boulevard du Crime, not because of its whores and pickpockets, but because of the kind of shows its theaters put on—seem to have been fascinated by costumes, and the actors' dress received special mention in the barkers' puffs. "Mr. Pompey will play tonight with all his wardrobe.... See the apparel of the first act.... Come in, come in, hurry to get your tickets, Mr. Pompey will change costume 12 times. He will carry off the Commander's daughter dressed in a frogged jacket, and will be struck down in a spangled suit." If the public admired gaudy costumes, it was because they were so rare.

Everyone who could manage it owned a dress or a suit for the great occasions, or to be buried in. A friend of Charles Péguy remarked that the fine clothes of the women of the people were always mourning clothes.[18] He might better have added, or their wedding dresses. (Men were nearly always buried in their wedding suits.) Urban influence is most clearly seen in the evolution of women's wedding dress. For a long time, girls got married in bright-colored dresses, the color sometimes being set by local custom: green, color of hope, trimmed with silver, in Bresse and Languedoc; blue adorned with stars, color of the Virgin; or, as in the Morvan, any vivid color. In more economically minded regions the bride wore a black dress with a multicolored scarf draped over her shoulders and (in Ariège) a coronet of flowers and gilded leaves or (in Châtillonais, Côte-d'Or) a marriage shawl, reflecting her family's riches, which would be used as a table carpet or bedspread until it fell apart.[19]

White dresses and white veils came in from the cities. The veils arrived first (for example, in the mountains of Ariège about 1890), since they were relatively cheap and could be worn conveniently with any dress. White wedding gowns, impossible to make out of local stuffs and more ostensible marks of conspicuous consumption than other ceremonial garb, took their time—as a thorough survey carried out in the northwest corner of Loire, in the area around Roanne, shows. White dresses are mentioned first in 1890, at Saint-Germain-l'Espinasse, an important crossroad on the main road from Roanne to Moulins. But at Saint-Forgeux-l'Espinasse, a little way off, the first white dress did not appear until five years later, and the fashion was only generalized there after the First World War. At Villerest, beside the Loire, not far from Roanne, many girls had worn white since 1900. But at Sail-les-Bains, an isolated village in the far northwest, white was "very rare in 1899." The same is true at Saint-Haon and at Saint-Alban, on the edge of the Allier forests, where white was said to have appeared "mostly since the war," and to have been little known before the war, when "Bismarck brown" had been very popular. Dark, serviceable colors—blue or black—as at Mably, quite near Roanne but rather isolated, where families sometimes splurged on a white veil for their daughters, but never on a dress until after 1914, and notably after 1922, when white gowns, which could now be bought ready-made, became the norm; or at Villerest, where until 1890–1900 the dresses were of black cashmere or satin and could later be worn on all appropriate occasions—marriages, communions, processions, and into one's own grave.[20]

Presumably the first step in the change was ready money, the second readymades. Yet even in distant Aveyron, by one account, the countryside had been invaded by ready-made clothing in the 1880's (a suitable delay, though a short one after Mazières); and we hear that by 1909 a milliner could do quite well in a modest village, and that, at least on Sundays, the young country girl dressed like her working sisters of the cities: feathered hat, corset, brightcolored dress, frilly underpants, black hose, yellow boots, and parasol. Peasants were beginning to look like everybody else.[21]

We know that for a long time they had looked different—even from each other. They had worn their coarse, rough-cut outfits with a difference, dyed in traditional dyes that varied from one district to another, cut in traditional cuts that reflected some local tailor's petrified fantasy, the image of a variegated society illustrated in garb and headgear, stressing the peasant's perception of geographical differences.[22] Pays had their uniforms—in different dress for great occasions, and different hats and bonnets. So had the crafts, with millers dressed all in white, even to the hat. Even road and construction workers could be identified by their corduroy or moleskin trousers, colored flannel belts, surcoats, and felt hats. Then, around the 1850's and 1860's, came one of the first articles of wear that men bought in the market, the *blouse*, worn at first only on days of rest. And with it came the first murmurings about the growing uniformity of dress. But under the smock the homemade cloth, scratchy and stiff as cardboard, soldiered on.[23]

In the late 1880's, when Dieudonné Dergny published his *Book of Curious Things*, he opened the work with the remark that modern fashions, which had been penetrating the countryside since mid-century, had crushed local costume and headgear out of existence. But Dergny lived in Eure, and the lower Seine valley was more easily penetrated by city fashions than other parts of France. In Lauragais, Mâconnais, and Bourbonnais the old local costume persisted through the Second Empire, traditional headgear until the 1880's.* In Auvergne clothing was locally made until the end of the century, a suit lasting for 20 or 30 years. The father often carved the family's sabots, the women knit hempen stockings that never wore out but did not keep one warm. Only the *blouse* was bought in town. The situation remained essentially unchanged until the war, when ready-made shoes and clothes completely displaced home products. Yet an 1886 guidebook boasted that current fashions

---

* Dieudonné Dergny, *Images,* 1: i; M. F. Pariset, *Economie rurale . . . Lauragais,* p. 104; Emile Violet, *Clessé,* p. 112; Francis Pérot, *Folklore bourbonnais,* pp. 49–50. Pariset noted in passing that the tailor and shoemaker used to come to the farm and work by the day so as to get their meals there; but now (1867), "se procurant facilement leur vivre," they did their work at home.

were to be found everywhere, and that the ways and manners of Auvergne were "now those of all our beautiful France." Whatever some might say, the Auvergnats "are got up, speak and act like the generality of French people." There was evidently some need to reassure or warn a potential visitor.[24]

We must not cry too much over the passing of these bucolic ways. Martin Nadaud remembered his homemade clothes with little love, the coarse, stiff cloth that made the wearer "awkward and heavy, stirring clumsily, turning with difficulty." The best testimony to the exactness of his memory is that those clothes were abandoned at the first opportunity. Both the Félibre Frédéric Mistral and the Breton poet Théodore Botrel insisted that their wives wear local costume. As soon as the men died, in 1914 and 1925, respectively, the widows abandoned what they seem to have regarded as an imposition.[25] By then, local costume had become costume *tout court*. But if this happened, it was because everywhere the young had turned to modern city clothes.

In every place where local clothes persisted toward the end of the century—the Limousin, Auvergne, Velay, Brittany—the young were trying to escape from them. Lads wore the smock at least, or broadcloth jackets, or suits of tweed or twill; the girls wore store-bought dresses and carried "flashy sunshades that make them look a perfect fright."[26] Even hats with flowers and feathers were making headway. And so—great novelty—was the jewelry of the city. Traditionally, women had carried their wealth upon them, in chains, trinkets, earrings; the more backward the region (for example, Velay), the longer this practice would last.* After 1885 or 1890, after 1900 and 1914, heavy gold chains went out. On the other hand, engagement rings came in, like those of the middle classes, especially after the war, when one could get to town more easily by car or bus to buy one. As an informant in Poncins (Loire) said, in 1936: "In the past, one had a watch and a chain [to mark an engagement]. Today people do what they do in town, they buy an engagement ring."[27]

To do things the way they were done in town, to dress the same way especially, was clearly to move up in the world. Peasant costume was often despised as the mark of an inferior condition, not least because so many bourgeois forced their servants to wear it. Looking like Bécassine was not conducive to self-respect. But traditional costume was also ill-adapted to modern life: high coiffes, long, heavy, voluminous skirts, rough materials less interesting than what could be bought and finally too long wearing, when even cheap ready-mades now began to go out of style relatively quickly. In any case,

* One imagines this was connected with the equation of beauty, wealth, and luxury. Peasant speech reflected the identification when it called a woman beautiful to say that she was wearing her best attire (see Charles Péguy, *Victor-Marie, Comte Hugo*, in *Oeuvres en Prose, 1909–1914*, Paris, 1968, p. 694). In the same way, quantity could stand for quality. Robert Jalby explains that Languedoc peasants normally wore few clothes except on feastdays when, however warm the weather, they donned their winter finery over their summer best, provided both could be seen, "for on such occasions luxury consists in wearing a great deal" (*Folklore*, p. 194).

peasant costume like the clothes of city folk had always evolved and continued to do so through much of the nineteenth century. As local industries declined and national fashions penetrated the last bastions of isolation and of poverty, costume lost contact with people's lives. It did not make sense any more. And the competition was too strong. In a paper delivered to a Provençal congress in 1906, the writer pointed out that Arlesian costume dated back less than a century, and that its current form was only 10 or 15 years old. True costume for ceremonies and dances, it settled ever more within narrow rules, stiff, heavily ornamented, and clumsy. The unfortunate upshot was that "French dress," so convenient by contrast, so easily slipped on, was gaining ground. "In some villages, even on Sundays, they wear this [French] rig to a dance or promenade. The bodice is so convenient to put on! Only the hat is missing to make the costume that of a lady: the step is easy to take." It was all connected, as the speaker said, to "a more active way of life, more casual relations, all the protocol of the old life of Arles that disappears."[28]

Coiffes and costumes disappeared, finally, because they were too costly. The local bonnet- and lace-making industries serving them decayed; tailors closed shop one after the other; so did the embroiderers; local touches on *blouses* disappeared as a unique Paris pattern came to provide the model for all provincial buyers; sabots, especially the luxury sort, went out, as did the locally made leather shoes that came in their wake, unwanted now that manufactured Paris wear could be obtained. A fair-minded observer remarked that the changes made dress "more banal no doubt, but also pleasanter, lighter, often stylish." This is worth remembering when expressing regret at the disappearance of traditional costumes.[29]

Innovations, an accumulation of disparate novelties, a gradual process, more or less perceived: the ready-made replacing the homemade; rolled cigarettes replacing snuff, with the change of gestures and of terminology all this involved; rings replacing chains; and a wardrobe and mirror that had to be bought in a store replacing the wooden wardrobe that a local man could make. All this strained the cat's cradle of communal relationships and constraints, strained and modified it. For the old structure did not in fact break; it stretched, it twisted new turns into the old shapes, incorporating the newfangled and the up-to-date into familiar patterns. So it was with bicycles, which permitted farm laborers who had generally eaten in the fields to cycle back home for meals, and thus increased the similarity between life on the farm and life in the city—though mostly after the First World War. And so it was with photography, which was enlisted very soon to accompany the great ceremonies and feasts of life, to fix them for eternity, and to add to the solemnity of the occasion.[30] First for marriage, the major family feast, eventually (though a good deal later) for christening and first communion, the photograph, formal and stately, entered the circuit of ritual gifts and gestures: a new rite, like a new costume or locution, adjoined to the old ones or replacing them.

Chapter Fourteen

RUS IN URBE

I shall say nothing just now of the peasantry because they live in a world of their own, with its own uses and traditions, which must be studied separately.

—P. G. HAMERTON

"IT WASN'T THE countryside, there were houses; it wasn't a city, the streets had ruts like turnpikes and the grass grew upon them; it wasn't a village, the houses were too high." Victor Hugo's description of the Faubourg Saint-Marcel, valid for the July Monarchy, could easily apply to many a country town one generation later—and even two! Country and town interpenetrated in small, sleepy centers like Cérilly (Allier), Millau (Aveyron), Brioude and Yssingeaux (Haute-Loire), Florac and Marvejols (Lozère), Saint-Flour (Cantal). Such towns, which acted as "tiny capitals" for perhaps half a dozen communes, were sleeping not-quite-beauties periodically awakened when the brief bustle of the weekly market or seasonal fair broke their quiet. Yet it was through these towns that the national culture and the changes it suggested were transmitted to the surrounding countryside. "Laboratories," Adolphe Blanqui called them, "where the enterprising spirit of the bourgeoisie prepares the experiments from which the country people benefit."[1]

When Blanqui wrote and for a long time after, these little country centers were really closer to rural than to city standards. Large bourgs or villages in most respects, they struck city folk as primitive, dreary places, "gloomy and isolated" like Parthenay (Deux-Sèvres) in 1882, from which "all intellectual life was banished," or like Vic-le-Comte (Puy-de-Dôme), dragging along in anachronistic unpicturesqueness in 1903. In 1904 Mende (Lozère), capital of wild Gévaudan, was a "gloomy and sinister" place of exile for the teachers, officers, and civil servants who were forced to live there. The numbers of such rusticated exiles were sometimes remarkably large—in Mende proper, for example, they and their families accounted for 1,234 of the 5,261 residents—and where this was so, the trade and life of the town turned around their activities. There were a great many towns like Tournon (Ardèche), population 5,000, which "lives only by its sub-prefecture, its tribunal, and the strangers that the two attract. Take them away and you reduce half the population to misery."[2]

The presence of a community of strangers in little towns like these, unrelated to their normal life, created something very much like a colonial situation. Taine had sensed this when, in 1864, he had described the provinces as being under the trusteeship of Paris, which civilized them from afar by sending them its commercial travelers, its civil servants, and its garrisons.* The situation had changed little two score years later. Ardouin-Dumazet, the professional traveler, noted that the town of Bellac (Haute-Vienne), without its garrison and functionaries, would not be very much. It had little industry, merely a bellows factory and a tannery, but at the marketplace "the peasant women stand in two rows by their meager wares: a cheese, a few cherries, strawberries, a rabbit or a chicken. Between them come and go the ladies, civil servants' wives followed by a maid, officers' wives accompanied by the orderly."[3] Here is the typical colonial marketplace with its pitifully small heaps of produce, its endlessly patient sellers, making tiny but significant profits from catering to creoles or to colonists.

Where towns were not islands for marooned representatives of the central power, they were (as M. F. Pariset said of the Languedoc) dependent extensions of the countryside. By and large living conditions in such towns were remarkably similar to those on the farm; the more so since a good proportion of their inhabitants were often actively engaged in agricultural occupations. Many doctors and travelers spoke feelingly about the lack of sewers in these farming towns, the utterly filthy streets, alleys, and courts, all used as public sumps, which made walking dangerous at all times, heroic after dark. There was the "primitive habit" of relieving oneself in the street, the only resort when most homes lacked any kind of cesspool. And there were the ubiquitous domestic animals—horses, oxen, chickens, ducks, geese, and man's best friend, the pig—worsening the muck and smells. In 1851 there were 185 pigs in the town of Florac (Lozère), about one for every ten inhabitants, and almost as many pigsties, attached of course to the homes. As Doctor Allaux noted at Pamiers (Ariège) in 1866, the general mess was much increased by the blood and offal of pigs slaughtered at home. But despite a good few complaints from sanitary councils, the "stubborn inertia" of the pigs' owners probably held out there through the 1890's, as it did at Privas and Tulle. It was difficult, as the doctor himself remarked, to ask that people cease to raise "pigs, geese, ducks, etc." in their homes; too many families lived off them.[4]

There was another consideration: in areas like Provence, poor soil, relatively

---

* Hippolyte Taine, *Carnets de voyage*, p. 321: "La province est une autre France en tutelle de Paris, qui la civilise et l'émancipe de loin par ses commis voyageurs, ses garnisons mobiles, sa colonie de fonctionnaires, ses journaux, et un peu par ses livres." What other country, one wonders, would consider itself the province of its capital?

few animal droppings, and lack of means to buy artificial fertilizer made manure precious. Town and village streets were strewn with branches and leaves of aromatic plants (box, lavender, rosemary, sage) carried down from the mountains and left to rot in the streets and alleys, mixed with whatever contributions men or animals made. So there were permanent dung heaps in every street and alley, along with the rats that thrived in such singularly favorable conditions. A century-long battle of municipal and sanitary authorities to change this state of things had tough going against the opposition of the little man with no other source of manure for his patch of land, not even a privy. It was a long time before the sewage legislation of 1894 made an impact. But the removal of the family dung heap, together with the disappearance of the family hog, would radically alter the landscape of rural towns.[5]

Meanwhile, other important steps had been taken to alter the face of small and middling towns, where the pulling down of picturesque houses and streets that we regret today came as emancipation. Age withered, years condemned. Old towns were ugly and grimy. Exceptions to this rule called for special comment. "Pézenas (Hérault) is quite handsome, despite its age," marveled one officer. "Despite its antiquity, Dax is a pretty town," reflected another. And Privas would have been quite pretty but for the irregularities and the barbarian architecture of squares and houses that recalled feudal times too much for the modern eye.[6]

By 1876 an architect pronounced Privas liveable enough, provided one stayed beyond the new boulevards built outside the old center. Some towns, like Orléans, cleared new streets in the center itself, as Paris was doing; in most the surrounding walls were torn down and replaced by broad boulevards to "give the city air" and free it from the constrictions of a hemmed-in past, conservatism, and narrowness of spirit as well as physical space. There was no voice of consequence that did not welcome the destruction of dark twisting lanes to let in air and light; the razing of ramparts to make way for "magnificent promenades"; the leveling of damp, ramshackle, unhealthy buildings to permit the building of "elegant new ones," better for health and comfort. The "strangled" towns, once stifled by their parapets, advanced to freedom, progress, and civic beauty. A newspaper in Var voiced the general pride and sense that new streets and buildings were not only superior to the old ones, but more beautiful, besides. "If our fathers, so proud of their strangled, tortuous streets, their tiny squares, with their banal fountains...their heavy cloaks of stone,...came back to life," imagine their amazement to see "spacious avenues, princely residences, charming homes...open to sun and light,...squares and walks shaded like lordly parks,...pleasing gardens that would do the most opulent squire proud."[7]

By the end of the century there was even artificial light. And if a city employee went around to put out the flickering gaslights at 11 P.M. or so, when honest people had long been in bed; and if as in Laval in 1902 only one street lamp in four was lit on nights when the almanac predicted moonlight (even if there were clouds);[8] at least these marvels of modernity softened the hold of darkness, moderated the grip of interminable winter evenings, and burned like promises of a new world in store.

Cynosure of surrounding villages, the little town tended to be deadly dull. Boredom, ennui seems to have been the chief pastime of the small-town bourgeoisie. Many people in traditional societies may well have spent most of their leisure time being bored. But like all those who worked for a living, they had few leisure hours to fill. Those who did not work were largely concentrated in small towns, and there we find ennui practically a way of life.* Parisians banished to the provinces bear eloquent testimony to this. We hear the same bitter complaint from workers, from teachers, from noblemen forced to take up residence to tend to business, and from officials who despaired of finding anything to say in their reports. "In a district like this," apologized the subprefect of Céret (Pyrénées-Orientales), "there is very rarely an incident of any importance ... and I ask myself with real uneasiness what I might possibly find of interest to report next week."[9]

There were cards and pipes. There were ritual promenades. There was (where there was a courthouse) the occasional titillating trial, a sure draw to which the public could flock in such numbers as to make the floor collapse, as in Vic-Fézensac (Gers) in 1874. There was (eventually) the railway station, where idle strollers met to stand and watch the trains pass by. Ardouin-Dumazet arrives at Sainte-Foy-la-Grande, on the Dordogne, one Sunday afternoon. The year is 1901 or 1902. Around the station a great crowd. They have come, he explains, "voir passer les trains [should it have been *le train*?], occupation régulière et dominicale de tant d'habitants de petite ville."[10]

There was the occasional burial; *un bel enterrement* was never scorned. And sometimes a hall where traveling actors could put on a show. The censors kept a vigilant eye on such troupes through the July Monarchy and the Second Empire, but small towns saw less and less of them after mid-century. Then, in the 1860's one begins to hear of cafés-concerts, cafés-chantants, alcazars, casinos, ever more numerous, patronized not only by the habitually idle, but by working-class families (lots of children), attracted by the moderate price of a *consommation* for which one got to hear an orchestra, singers, perhaps be treated to a pantomime. By the 1870's, "the least little town has one," reported a traveler through the Midi.[11]

There was, of course, gossip. And what gossip: "mesquinerie ... taquinerie ... bassesse," reported one Vogüé to another in 1881. "C'est l'envahissement de

---

* A song of 1848 entitled "Tuer l'ennui" throws a suggestive light on this problem of boredom (which Musset's *Fantasio* had also encountered): "Je ne sais rien en politique / Mais j'ai besoin de mouvement! / La rue éclate en fusillades, / Le peuple va droit devant lui; / Allons faire des barricades! / Que voulez-vous! Il faut tuer l'ennui!" (Eugene Pottier, *Chants révolutionnaires*, pp. 27–28.)

la médiocrité ignorante et paresseuse ... s'agitant sur le théâtre rétréci du canton ou du département ... triste spectacle."[12] Above all, there was the club and café.

Somnolence, lethargy, idleness, reported the police superintendent of a small town in Ardèche in 1863; a backward civilization, an apathetic spirit, a population that never looked beyond the parish pump. "Three-quarters of our fellow citizens" (of the men, that is) spent their life in the café. Cafés were less for drinking than for sitting in, and for looking out of. There were cafés for different cliques and political groups, but there was always one main café where public opinion was made and whence it spread abroad, where the local paper might be written, where one could exchange all of the gossip and news of a small realm ruled by the idle, bored, and curious habitual customers. Interestingly, at Draguignan in Var the supremacy of the chief café (and of its twin, the circle) began to wane with the Second Empire and the 1870's, their eminence killed by the spread of an affluence until that time restricted to a few. "Now," the historian Frédéric Mireur wrote in the 1890's, "the idle are everywhere and nowhere." The former idlers were impoverished, idleness itself too diffused to prove one's eminence, and "the bourgeoisie has given place to merchants," with their altogether different tone.[13]

So by the 1890's the bourgeois class, if we may use the term, was seen as differentiated: the merchants and wholesalers who sat in the cafés of Draguignan were not the bourgeois, the old urban aristocracy, but the jumped-up something else. They were not the bourgeois, for one thing, because they were not idle, and idleness was one important element of the old definition of the bourgeoisie. Yet they were bourgeois because they lived in cities, and their growing prominence indicated that society and social classifications had become broader and more complicated over the past decades. Blanqui, in 1851, had found no reason to distinguish among the bourgeois inhabitants of small towns. For him the bourgeois were still defined simply as those who did not work the land, rather than as one segment of the urban population as opposed to another, let alone as today to an industrial working-class.

The traditional bourgeois was the man whose primary attachment was to the bourg, the agglomeration that had an urban style and vocation amid the dispersed farms and villages of the countryside. But we have already seen that this was a very wide category. It could include quite humble artisans whose base was in the bourgs at one end and nobles at the other. In part because nobles also lived in town, and their urban ties seemed so significant in peasant eyes, in part because the landed aristocrats lagged in numbers, riches, and power behind the rising business classes, noblemen were easily classified as bourgeois. Popular speech incorporated the traditional sense of dependency: the peasant's master was, by definition, a bourgeois. As H.-F. Buffet has said of the landowners of Upper Brittany: "Though they were often nobles, their tenants called them 'not'bourgeois.' They also said 'not'maître'—our master."

In Emmanuel Labat's Gascony, too, there were only peasants and bourgeois, the latter including nobles, who lived and drew their revenues in much the same manner as their untitled peers, so that "one makes no distinction between the two."[14]

Perhaps it was a matter of perception: "At Montluçon," explained a sub-prefect writing from Allier, "every person who doesn't get his living from his work or from revenues acquired by his work is called a bourgeois. The bourgeois is the man who does nothing and who has never done anything." Though by any definition the bourgeois constituted a small proportion of the population, something like 10 percent, many men clearly qualified under this description, and more appeared to do so. Madame Lafarge, star of a famous murder under Louis Philippe, remembered the men of Tulle (that is, the men of the only social group that counted) passing their lives in the cafés or around the law courts: "They're almost all lawyers, solicitors, doctors, and Republicans."[15] A large share of the income of professionals came from private revenues, inherited or through marriage, and they cannot have worked hard or long. Many positions, like that of Maurice Barrès's father at Charmes, were in any case nominal, providing a function or title in keeping with a man's social position, while making few demands on his energy or time.

But there were also those who lived on rentes alone, whether from stocks, bonds, loans, or the renting of land, more than 6 percent of the population. Such rentiers were especially numerous in smaller country towns. According to the 1872 census, some 10 percent of the males in Cahors lived exclusively from private revenues. So did more than 8 percent of the men in and around Rennes, in 1874, and another 20 percent had some such income, which was supplemented by "professional activities." But in a really small town, like Florac in Lozère, where in 1851 almost exactly 10 percent of the inhabitants belonged to the bourgeoisie, 17 of the 100 heads of bourgeois families gave their profession as rentier or as living from the revenue of their property. Together with the town's five pensioners, we thus find an important proportion of men with time on their hands. The influence of such men while they lasted and the effects of their disappearance as a significant force in the small towns have never received adequate notice. And this in spite of Henri Febvre's perceptive remark that between 1880 and 1940 he had seen, as all men of his age could see with their own eyes, "the downfall of the man who does nothing, the man who does not work."[16]

As long as they lasted and as long as the way of life that they represented lasted, people like these must have been at the very center of small-town life. Their means were limited, but their time was not: they could afford a good deal of it for desultory talk. If they were not all Republicans, as Madame Lafarge would have it, they were at any rate politicized, for politics—local and national—furnished matters for concern and debate where there were relatively few other matters to consider. In any case, they were brought up to it.

A bourgeois's son was raised on classical studies. The ideals these taught him, however vague they were, accorded with the pursuits available to him and intensified their effect: to oversee the administration of an estate (albeit from a distance), to fill some public charge that would not prove too time-consuming, to make an occasional appearance "on the forum," and to reserve plenty of hours for the "pleasures of the spirit and of friendship" were worthy of the teachings of the Roman texts.[17]

Roman or not this bourgeoisie was rural. Often it lived on an estate or within visiting range of it. Landed property meant first electoral rights, then economic prestige right through 1870. The bourgeois "measured his influence by the size of his lands." Even when an office, a profession, or a trade required him to settle in town, the land remained close and he stayed close to it because that was the true source of his fortunes, hence of his influence and status.[18]

Needless to say, not all bourgeois did nothing. And clearly bourgeois was (and is) a confusing term that conceals even more differences than it reveals. According to Emile Guillaumin, in the first 20 years of the Republic, the population of Cérilly fell into four major groups: great landed families, aloof from all the other groups and anchored firmly in their caste; a more accessible lot including doctors, pharmacists, notaries, the richest merchants, and a few civil servants; a third group composed of businessmen (traders, cattle dealers, and storekeepers), stewards and other estate agents, and the prosperous farmers who ensured the liaison with the fourth group, the "little people," small shopkeepers and artisans. It was chiefly the last group who emphasized the town-country opposition, wearing suit jackets and putting on the dog to mark themselves off from the "peasants in blue smocks, whose speech [was] harsh, uncouth, and *patoisant*."* Yet it must have been the same men, closest to the peasants whom they despised and who resented and envied them in turn, who were the great carriers of the ways and manners that they themselves tried so hard to ape.

This is where the term bourgeois can easily betray us. Where the bourgeoisie ended and the "people" or "little people" began depends entirely on the point of view. For most officials, after Guillaumin's second group. For the lower orders, somewhere in the fourth. Where the line is drawn does not really matter much, as long as we remember how flexible the term bourgeois was—and that the label *did* matter to people at the time, who made fairly refined distinctions (though these vary rather confusingly). Peasants were very much aware of what the Dauphinois Barnave had once denounced as *importance*, and this at all levels. Thus, the Beaujolais description of social mobility: "The

---

* *Charles-Louis Philippe, mon ami*, pp. 10–11. Guillaumin has further distinguished subcategories within each group, noting, for example, a "sharp boundary between *sérieux* and *chopinards*" among artisans and small shopkeepers. See also in André Armengaud, *Les Populations de l'est-Aquitain*, p. 254, the 1871 report of a Toulouse magistrate named Carol (Archives Nationales, C 2854), which reveals the rise of an intermediate class between ouvriers and bourgeoisie, a stream feeding Gambetta's *nouvelles couches sociales*.

father had straw in his sabots, the son puts hay in his boots." Mistral, who belonged to the boot-shod sort, tells us that in his family of very prosperous farmers (a sort of "transition between peasants and bourgeoisie") the parents became obsequious before messieurs who did not speak like them, and that his father, who normally called his wife "the mistress," called her *ma mouié* (woman or wife) in front of his social superiors.[19]

What mattered even more was that one could quite easily move from one class to the other, then rise from shabby to less shabby bourgeoisie. And that the social hierarchy of the little towns was so structured that those who moved up a step remained close to each other and to those behind.[20] This was yet another aspect of the bourgeoisie: on the one hand, idleness and the time to talk to others; on the other, activity and the opportunity to influence others, not only by argument but by example, too. It is a point that the sub-prefect of Aubusson in Creuse expressed well in 1853, when he explained that the bourgeoisie of his area was new, its popular roots still very much in evidence. "It is still the people, but richer and better schooled. Its intelligence and activity are remarkable, its pride and ambition immeasurable.... A bourgeoisie [like this] holds the people in its hand as I do my pen at this moment. It does their business, lends them money, flatters them by innumerable family connections."* Here was the aspiring bourgeois, pushing out the old.

Costs and wages were rising, crop prices were not, because railroads prevented shortages by carrying grain all over the country. Yet land hunger kept land prices up. By the end of the Second Empire land fetched such high prices that even with the best management it paid no more than 2 or 3 percent, whereas safe bonds or stocks could bring returns of 5 percent or more.† By the turn of the century, the landed estate had become a burden; the shortage of hands had cut its income further and the prestige of the rural bourgeois, whose sphere of action shrank with their revenues, was singularly diminished. Increasingly isolated, the old bourgeoisie was being overtaken by new men who imposed themselves by wealth and services that brought them into broad contact with the peasants, with whom they dealt professionally, in office, shop, or

---

* "In all," he continued, "the bourgeoisie and the people live in a close relationship where the decisive influence necessarily belongs to the more intelligent." But for all that he felt the bourgeoisie's origins and "passion for equality [made] it essentially democratic" (Archives Nationales, F¹ᶜIII Creuse 8, Aubusson, June 26, 1853). One might also cite in this connection Henri Béraud's *Maître Anselme*, the *patron* of a small ironworks, "dont les gens s'étonnent qu'il préchât le désordre et qui répond: 'On est patron, c'est vrai, mais on est du peuple, et ça se verra s'il le faut' " (*Les Lurons de Sabolas*, Paris, 1932, p. 92).

† In a lecture delivered in 1877 a Champagne veterinarian explained that investment in a farm brought an average return of 2.5 percent. So the man who bought one did so not as a money-making proposition, but as an "affaire de luxe, de convenance," since he could get better returns elsewhere (*Conférence agricole faite par M. Boulland, vétérinaire, Joinville, Haute-Marne, 1877*, p. 15). Same song from M. F. Pariset, writing about Aude and Tarn in 1882: "C'est un très grand luxe, aujourd'hui, que de posséder de la terre; un grand luxe quand toutes les choses de la vie ont singulièrement renchéri, de ne retirer de sa fortune qu'un intérêt de 2 et 2.5 à 3 pour cent" (*Economie rurale ... Montagne Noire*, p. 65).

market, or into whose homes or stables or dram-shops they entered in a routine way to tend or heal. Meanwhile, as the large landholding became increasingly unprofitable, peasants made better money out of the acres that they could work themselves with the help of their family and at most a few closely supervised hired hands.[21]

To live in a bourgeois way cost more. Comfort, food, social life all became more expensive. Small revenues from landed property would not keep pace. The men whose social and economic status depended on them reacted in three ways: by saving and drawing in their horns, by selling off, and by family planning or voluntary celibacy. The first method limited their everyday impact on society; the second removed the base of their influence and prestige; the third, which many times left a family without a direct heir, affected continuities that had been an integral part of the propertied class's regional influence. The alien heir of a local family that died out did not command the prestige or the interest his forerunners had enjoyed. In any case, he often sold out.

Nowhere were all these developments clearer than in the southwest, where after the 1860's large estates began giving way to smaller holdings,* land passing to peasant farmers who could save more because they used the family labor force, hence did not have to worry much about high salaries; who worked the land harder than the hired hands of the large domains had ever done; and who diversified their farming and so were less affected by the fluctuations of grain prices. In any case greater demand sparked by rising living standards, coupled with improved transportation, meant that more crops could now be bought and sold in the market, and at better prices, at least from the point of view of the small producer, who ended up with more cash even if the market price was not so very high. More money meant more land, but also bigger, better-built houses, better diet, better dress, and better tools to turn out more produce. It also meant better education—for the peasant through broader social contacts, for his children through the school. Better able to learn the lessons that the rural bourgeoisie had to teach, the peasant tended in due course to take over their functions. By the eve of the First World War, Labat found the prosperous peasant of Gers replacing his erstwhile betters—not only in the country house or small chateau he bought from their heirs, but in their seats in the municipal council and mairie, as deputy to the justice of peace, on juries and schoolboards, as part of the prefectural administration. The peasants had become the "masters of village and of the countryside."[22]

---

* A process that Pariset identified early on, in 1867: "L'ambition de posséder, l'inquiétude, l'agitation, descendent des classes aisées dans les classes rurales et pénètrent celle des métayers" (*Economie rurale ... Lauragais*, p. 128).

Chapter Fifteen

PEASANTS AND POLITICS

*Ce qui est grave pour ce régime et pour sa gloire, c'est qu'il risque
fort de n'être raconté que d'après les publications du Journal Officiel.*
—LOUIS CHEVALIER

THE POLITICIZATION of the French peasantry has been variously assigned to
the French Revolution and its aftermath or to the feverish days of 1848 and the
bustling propaganda of the years that culminated in the rising of December
1851. Maurice Agulhon has written a seminal work showing how the rural
and small-town population of up-country Var awoke to national politics, how
the politics of the bourgeoisie became the politics of the peasants; and Philippe
Vigier has traced similar developments a little to the north, in the Alpine
regions. Despite Agulhon's warning that the prehistory of modern democracy
in France runs well into the 1860's,[1] it is still commonly assumed that, somehow, political tendencies that were suspended during the imperial interlude
revived and expressed themselves when they were freed at last after 1871 and
1877. Stabilities in political orientation, which François Goguel and his fol-
lowers have carefully plotted on maps, as well as evolutions explained by André
Siegfried and others, appear to confirm such views.

My purpose here, as throughout this book, is to suggest that over great parts
of France the process of politicization was slower than we think; that, though
many regions did indeed move at the pace historians indicate, others took
more time. To be sure, some building blocks of political attitudes were laid
out to some extent in these regions by the Revolution, the Terror, 1848, and
Louis Napoleon's coup of December 2, but these fitted into earlier structures
founded on other memories, like the Reformation, and served other interests,
above all, local ones. Politics in those parts of rural France that I have looked
at remained in an archaic stage—local and personal—into at least the 1880's.
In these areas evolution toward modernity, that is, to an awareness of and concern with issues on a national or international plane, *seems* to begin after the
1870's. It came as part of the integration of these areas into France—as part
of the same slow, complex process that we have watched so far, of city ways
and values flowing into countryside, of the country's colonization by the town.

The question is not whether politics existed in the countryside. Every community was, in some sense, a polis. The question is whether the local, sui generis interests there thrashed out can be interpreted in the familiar terms of national politics. It is not a question that would have troubled many Frenchmen of the time. Jules Vallès, who knew something of underdeveloped France for having been born at Le Puy, in Velay, reflected the dominant view—one that was at best the view from the country town. In the summer of 1880 he published an account that we might call historical fiction of a grain riot that shook the important market town of Buzançais in Indre in 1847, the starvation year.[2] In this story Vallès complicates what amounted to a small-scale jacquerie by introducing the paraphernalia of contemporary politics: revolutionary ideas, secret societies, policemen, all the stage properties of the urban political scene, the backdrop against which the countryside was inevitably viewed, even by sympathetic observers.

But peasant politics were not like the politics of Le Puy or Nantes or Caen that Vallès knew, let alone like those of Clemenceau's *La Justice* in which Vallès's story appeared. And if it is difficult to say just what peasant politics were, it is not so difficult to show what they were not. This I shall try to do.

The transition from traditional local politics to modern national politics took place when individuals and groups shifted from indifference to participation because they perceived that they were involved in the nation. This did not mean only intellectual evolution—learning that one was part of a wider entity. It meant that men and women, as private persons and as members of particular groups, had to be convinced that what went on in that wider entity mattered to them and had to be taken into consideration. In other words, national politics became relevant when national affairs were seen to affect the persons and localities involved. Before this could be seen, it had in effect to happen. Until it happened, that is, until roads, markets, goods, and jobs became part of the national whole and dependent on national developments, archaic politics, as we might well call them, made perfectly good sense. And we shall see that such politics did effectively survive as long as the conditions they reflected and served survived; and that, when they broke down, they left their mark on modern politics as we know them.

We have already said that government and state in the first half of the nineteenth century were dimly seen as agencies for the exaction of taxes, occasionally interfering to impose public order (not necessarily identical with local custom) and to mete out justice (not necessarily identical with equity). Like the Alpine peasants Adolphe Blanqui described in 1848, like the Bretons Emile Souvestre wrote about in 1843, the country people of these times knew only "la douane et le fisc." Government, its form, its name, the names of its leaders and its institutions, remained unknown or almost so. And such parties as existed were political only because they represented something else, like religion. The author of a guide to Aulus in the Pyrenees put it well. For the local peasant, he wrote in 1873, government was a being "given to mischief-making, hard on little people, that demands taxes, prevents contraband, and dwells in Paris." It was no part of the peasant's life, he had no share in it; that it might represent him would seem nonsense.[3]

The thousands of officials—policemen and gendarmes, judges and public prosecutors, prefects and sub-prefects—who kept close check on the "public spirit" of the countryside lived in the towns. Their reports reflected opinion there. It is important to remember this, because even the lower orders in the country towns participated to some degree in a national politics that their fellows in the countryside were oblivious of. The officials knew there was a difference, and they said so—when they could be bothered to make the point.

Politics were for nobles and for bourgeois, explained the Republican mayor of Saint-Aignan (Loir-et-Cher) in 1848. As for the poor farmers, they were divided into two categories: "the misguided and the stupefied." You had to distinguish between rural populations and townspeople, wrote the imperial prosecutor at Bordeaux in 1864. The country folk were indifferent to political debate and to issues that did not affect them directly, whereas "in the enlightened classes and among the working populations of the cities," political life, the "spirit of criticism and discussion," took a new dimension.[4] Platitudes, of course, hence so familiar that we tend to overlook them, here are two themes that would be repeated until the end of the century. The first, that political activity or at least discussion was confined to towns, and that the country, indifferent to politics, was interested only in its labors. The second, that beyond this, there were certain "enlightened classes," their numbers clearly limited, thus paring down still further the politically significant minority.

"Only the most enlightened part of society" (Issoire, Puy-de-Dôme, 1841). "The newspaper-reading classes" (Ariège, 1866). "The upper and enlightened class that forms the opinion of the masses" (Lombez, Gers, 1867). "The literate class" and "the restricted circle of people who take an interest in politics" (Murat, Cantal, 1867), those few who are "a little more literate than the mass of the population" (Mauriac, Cantal, 1866). "The lettered part of the population," and "the other part... which takes no interest in politics" (Epinal, Vosges, 1869). Townsmen alone are interested in political questions (Angers, 1866). "Only those in comfortable circumstances" (Limoges, 1867). Meanwhile, "country people,... the immense majority, are exclusively preoccupied with their agricultural labors and indifferent to the events that stir opinion in the larger centers" (Angers, 1866). "The unenlightened working population isn't interested in questions of principle" (Limoges, 1867). "The countryman proper is absorbed by his tasks" (Mauriac, 1866). *Les populations* "take no interest in political questions. In the towns, where newspapers are read and discussed, the Chamber debates are followed with great interest" (Mauriac, 1867).[5]

The peasants lent an ear when things plainly affected their own lives, such as the projected army reorganization and the cost of exemptions from military service. Let their "private interests [be] touched, which alone dominate their aspirations" (Cantal, 1866), and officials noted with some surprise, "even" country people began to stir. Most of the time, though, indifference reigned; and the Third Republic does not seem to have wrought any great change at first. "Only the few better-off literate persons" paid any attention to politics, wrote a policeman from Plaisance (Gers) in 1875. The constitutional laws, reported the commander of gendarmes at Bordeaux in 1875, "fascinate the towns, but pass almost unnoticed in the countryside preoccupied only with the way wine is selling." Even the political crises of 1876-77 had no effect on people interested in the Phylloxera, not politics. And May 16, 1877, found the once ardently revolutionary Gers with scarcely a reaction outside the bigger centers like Lectoure.[6]

I shall presently show how all this changed. But, at least in the Pyrenees, the official reports suggest that the process was painfully slow. Public opinion "remains that of the towns and of the bourgeoisie." *The public* seems to be identified as those few voters who read the newspapers, *the population* as that tiny portion of people who were "intelligent and literate." Finally, in 1898, a police superintendent at Perthus hit on the right descriptive phrase, singling out a "political population" as opposed to a "general population" that was indifferent to politics. The political population remained small—perhaps the four or five in every village who the sub-prefect of Pamiers, writing in 1905, thought would pay attention to national or international news.[7] Even so burning an issue as the Dreyfus Affair, whose ins-and-outs "fascinated public opinion" at Limoges, left country people quite indifferent and kindled little interest outside of the provincial capitals with a political class.*

But political awareness can exist outside those persons, a limited group in any age, who sustain an interest in political news and political debate. If it is misleading to suggest that the views of a few men constituted public opinion, surely it is just as misleading to suggest that the majority had no opinion. Yet that opinion was doubtfully as coherent as some would have it. Marxist historians in particular have sought to show that political tensions of quite a modern sort affected the peasantry, and that their struggles against landowners

---

* Jacques Duclos first heard the name of Dreyfus four years after the Rennes trial, in a discussion during the feast of Saint Anne at Tarbes. The younger men (from Bordeaux and other centers) were for Dreyfus, the older men against him. In his own village, Louey, Socialism was unknown, and the separation of Church and State, though an issue of some interest, caused no trouble. The disturbances that shook Hérault in 1907, by contrast, stirred much talk. (*Mémoires,* 1: 49.) Maurice Halbwachs points out that the downtrend in suicide rates during the Dreyfus Affair was of much briefer duration in the French countryside than in the towns, lasting only from 1899 to 1902, and that over the larger period 1898–1905 the reversal was much less marked there, with the rate in the country falling less than half as much as in the towns, an indication of a very incomplete participation in national affairs. (*Les Causes du suicide,* pp. 344–45.) On the impact of the Affair in the countryside, see Archives Départementales, Haute-Vienne 1M 191 (commissaire spécial Limoges, Nov. 1898; préfet, Sept. 1899), and Pyrs.-Ors. 3M1 167 (telegram of Jan. 31, 1898, and *passim*).

and officials involved a political vision and a kind of protest that fit a recognizable pattern of class struggle. Marx knew better than that. For Marx, French peasants were not a class because "identity of interests" had engendered in them "no community, no national bond, and no political organization." Having come to this conclusion in 1850 in *The Eighteenth Brumaire of Louis Bonaparte*, Marx saw no reason to change or qualify the statement with a footnote for the second edition of 1869, no more than Engels did for the third edition of 1885. Both saw quite correctly that isolation, mode of production, and poverty, "increased by France's bad means of communication," made for a life that had little to do with society—meaning the political society with a recognizable class structure that interested them. Both concluded from this that the peasantry, unable to see itself or to function as a class, was an inchoate "addition of homologous magnitudes, much as potatoes in a sack form a sack of potatoes." The famous phrase bears witness to the incapacity of even the most perceptive to see the structure of the peasant world: "a small holding, a peasant and his family; alongside them another small holding, another peasant and another family. A few score of these make up a village."[8] Nothing but potatoes, because the forms of organization, the solidarities, and the values of the peasant world were not reducible to urban terms—not yet.

In my own view, it seems rather that peasants saw (and see) themselves as participating less in a class than in a condition, a way of life with its own hierarchies of the old-fashioned sort (rich and poor, more or less valiant, and so forth), which for a long time served them very well. Social divisions were marked: between those who had and those who had not, between those who owned land and those who rented it (but among these last, the large-scale tenant could well be a monsieur or a bourgeois), between journeymen-smallholders and landless farmhands. Groups of this sort did not intermarry—any more than woodcutters and farmers' daughters intermarried.* They kept to themselves, stayed separate at dances and festivities. In Lauragais, for instance, in the 1860's sharecroppers and domestics danced to the bagpipe and stuck to old standbys like the rigadoon, while smallholders enjoyed a three-piece band of trumpet, clarinet, and drum, and swung around in waltzes, polkas, and quadrilles "as in the towns."[9]

Wealth was a crucial factor, of course; the more so since the rich and poor were usually related. Village society distinguished between "Brélet, the rich" and "Brélet, the poor"; between a domain that raised cattle and a holding that had only cows; between an ordinary cottage and a chateau with an upper story and a weathervane on the roof; between the Miyette whose forename sufficed, La Coulaude who carried her husband's name, the bourgeoise who

---

* Or at least if they did, it offended everybody's sense of propriety. See Pierre Gilland's story "La Fille du braconnier" for an illustration of the deep gulf between the rich farmer (considered a bourgeois) and the landless peasant. When a lowly woodcutter marries the farmer's daughter, no one approves of the incredible mésalliance. But note also that the story treats the gentry of the chateau with sympathy and the "bourgeois" with dislike. This, of course, in the 1840's.

had shed peasant garb, and Madame Lepaud who sold groceries. The social hierarchy asserted itself in the relations between the sexes. At a dance the youngest son of a middling farmer could not dance much with the daughter of a rich farmer without exciting comment. There was a gulf between "the big house" and the rest, the former easily recognizable by a second story, a monumental gateway, or some other expensive embellishment. To this day, says Pierre Bourdieu of his Bigorre, the girls look at the gateway more than at the man.[10]

Inevitably, wealth affected political alignments. "The peasant of Nord is a bourgeois," declared a Democratic-Socialist ("red") Tulle newspaper in May 1849; "next to him the peasant of Corrèze is almost a beggar." The conclusion to be drawn was clear. In 1849 around Tulle the peasants dubbed the conservative electoral list *la liste des riches*. The conservatives lost heavily. All over the Limousin, the public prosecutor of Limoges reported, the peasants voted for the "reds" expecting "le partage des biens des bourgeois."[11] Radical ideas penetrated the countryside clad in old rancors and even older hopes. It was not surprising. But it should be borne in mind when interpreting their success.

Yet wealth was far from the only consideration. Olivier Perrin's excellent portrayal of the Quimperois emphasizes the diversity of classes and of rankings (not used in a Marxist sense) to be found in Breton villages, especially the distinctions between those who owned, who rented, and who sharecropped the land they worked, and within each group the further ranking based on antiquity. "Vanity," wrote Perrin, "presides over marriages as much as arithmetic," and rustic aristocrats would have thought it a derogation to marry outside their "caste." The more plebeian remainder was just as careful about whom it wed and whom it consorted with in general. People looked down, not up. In 1909 leaders of peasant unions in Allier denounced the peasant hierarchies, above all the sharecroppers, who exploited and despised their putative "inferiors," showing "contempt," "pride," and "arrogance" to the servants and hired hands whose life-style they often shared. Scorn seems the leitmotif of class relationships, from one group to another, every society a small cascade of scorn explained or rationalized on a variety of grounds. But it is hard to fix such archaic attitudes into a modern model. The comparatively high rate of endogamous marriages in Vraiville (Eure) operated most visibly on an occupational basis, with farmers and weavers keeping largely apart, and marriages reflecting more family traditions than purely economic considerations. At Chablis (Yonne) the two "classes" were smallholders and winegrowers, as divided in politics as in interest. In the Limousin farmers despised mere wool carders. In the Alpine regions, Philippe Vigier could discern no clear-cut social classes, only different groups, distinguished by profession, fortune, and local influence.[12] Social interaction of this sort is better depicted if we replace the familiar image divided by horizontal lines with one in which several circles overlap and intersect.* That would account for instances of "vertical" solidarity, peculiarly numerous in 1848 (and before that), where local authorities (mayors, priests, or rich men) sided with the peasants against the national authorities and their representatives and against members of "the wicked rich" like usurers and absentee landowners.[13]

But the very use of the word class tends to be misleading, because it suggests real social oppositions and solidarities that go beyond specific instances. The fact is, as Roger Brunet has shown of Comminges in the mid-1880's, tensions arose mostly between groups engaged in different activities, or between rival villages, or between rival sections of one village. As long as the social horizon remained limited, political categories remained limited too. It would take some time before the didactic affirmation and the experience that make a class would cut across the community of site; before accessible, visible, local hierarchies and tensions gave way to more abstract national ones; and before the transition was made "from a system of social orders based on localities to a national system of social classes."[14]

It is within this context that we must take a quick look at the main argument for peasant politicization before the Third Republic, above all, the events of 1848–51. It would be unfair, though it is tempting, to quote Richard Cobb on the Great Revolution "as a magnificent irrelevance"—unfair, because out of context, since Cobb writes of marginal groups, however numerous these may have been.[15] Yet in important ways Cobb's words apply more broadly: for the Revolution did little to modify the conditions of labor or pay, or to change the customs and traditions that bound villagers to each other, and sharecroppers or domestics to their masters. As Emmanuel Labat noted of Gascony, the Revolution "passed above the villages, hamlets, farms, without affecting social and economic life, the everyday routine of life." New leases simply repeated the old with new taxes added. Thus a Republican master, who had changed his name from Pierre to Scaevola and vowed to follow "the sacred principles of the Mountain," entered in his journal a new lease for his sharecropper (not dignified as a citizen in the description) incorporating traditional terms and obligations—chickens to be offered at Saint John's feast, capons at All Souls, hens at Christmas. Under the July Monarchy, the taxes the sharecroppers of Haute-Vienne paid were still called a poll tax; and in Gers and the Landes some sharecroppers' contracts included tithes up to the First World War.[16]

Official or semiofficial commentators of the day insisted that the lower classes had been politicized. But even they admitted that this went no further than concern for material interests. In any case, who were these lower classes? The evidence suggests that they were urban. In the Limousin, for example, Alain

---

* Not too far off from Soboul's remark that there was no one French peasantry in 1848, but rather various "peasant classes, often antagonistic," with many nuances in their social attitudes and political stance ("La Question paysanne en 1848," p. 55).

Corbin has found that urban populations at all levels were open to political ideas, while in the countryside mass reactions reflected an older, deeper peasant revolutionary tradition. When rural disturbances were not caused by food shortages, they arose in traditional animosities, as at Saurat (Ariège), where in 1834 "hundreds" of village children, armed with wooden weapons, clashed on the commons; or in anxiety and anger over infringement of traditional forest rights, best documented in Provence and the Pyrenees; or occasionally under the influence of a nearby town. Yet in the end, as a report on the food riots that broke out near Bellac in the winter of 1847 put it, "It was the war of those who have nothing against those who own."[17] Not politics, but want made for trouble. And when there was trouble communities "acted as one," as they had always done, as they would go on doing, voting en bloc whether for government or for opposition, traditional solidarities expressing themselves even in electoral terms.*

Traditional ideas, too. The peasant's ideological arsenal, like his vocabulary, remained anachronistic. In 1848 the idea of a Republic seemed difficult to accept not just in Brittany, but in the Limousin and the southwest. "If there's no King, there's no government," the peasants told a tax collector at Ajain in Creuse. When would a new King be appointed, they wondered in Gironde. "Le Duc Rollin (Ledru-Rollin) who governed was no King." As for Lamartine, who was this woman Martine? (*Qu'ès aquette Martine?*) Changes of government meant little at that level, and a different system of government seemed little different in a peasant's eye. Duchatellier found that, for Breton peasants in 1863, Emperor and King were much the same; and the brief Second Republic was connected with vague memories of 1793 but was personified, leading many to remark that "by today the lady must be pretty old."[18]

Are these only tall tales? One is inclined to doubt it, the more so since there was little reason for successive regimes, successive governments, to have meant very much. But memories did mean something, and the association of ideas. Fears that the Ancien Régime might be reestablished persisted for a long, long time. Many times these were kept alive by local or family traditions: during the Revolution one had thrived or suffered, sometimes by sheer chance. But there were also more general folk memories. For a decade after 1848 the propaganda of the "red" party, the Mountain, denounced its enemies as whites. In 1858 the prefect of the Drôme explained that the reds still found popular support when they referred to "the party of order" as "nobles, royalists, representatives of the reaction of 1815," which had left bad memories behind.[19]

* In the elections of 1849 the Democratic Socialist "reds" did particularly well in poor and remote rural areas, where their majorities were often higher than in working-class areas. In Corrèze and Haute-Vienne, 39 of 56 rural cantons gave them an absolute majority, and in 17 of these they won 70–80 percent of the vote (Jacques Bouillon, "Les Démocrates socialistes," p. 88). Such unanimity can be explained only in terms of an archaic approach to political action. See also Alain Corbin, "Limousins migrants," p. 1269, on the elections of 1857.

Many villages remembered small local tyrannies, often magnified and embroidered: the game laws prohibiting free hunting and fishing; the injunctions against organizing a dance without the lord's permission; the squire's monopoly of selling wine or keeping dovecotes.[20] They had gained the right to hunt at the Revolution, and they held it dear—first as a resource, but also for the simple pleasure of killing game, a right the nobler for its having been so long reserved for the squire. The institution of a hunting permit in 1844 was unpopular not only because it struck a blow for gents against the peasant, but because it suggested that freedoms or privileges achieved within living memory might easily be lost again.* This applied particularly to tithes and corvée service, which must have been uppermost in peasants' memories. In 1848 some rash legitimists (in Lot-et-Garonne) declared that before long tithes and feudal rents would be reestablished. In May 1849 the peasants of Dordogne voted en masse for "Republican Socialists" because (explained the general prosecutor in Bordeaux) they feared that the "old nobles and bourgeois would reestablish tithes and the corvée."†

In Périgord, Mâconnais, the Morvan, and elsewhere the nobles had left bad memories behind. Popular tales recalled them as brutal, bloody, and greedy: ready to shoot a mason off the roof for fun or torture a tenant who refused his daughter; hypocritically claiming they treated their subjects well and struck down for perjury by the wrath of God; turned into the beasts of prey that resembled them, wolves, wild dogs, or other nocturnal wanderers. Peasant language, too, kept alive the image of the *méchants châtiâs* and their *zeu-z-oubyettes* (the evil castles and their dungeons), not forgetting the *batteurs des queurneuilles*, kept up all night to beat the moats and ponds to keep the frogs from croaking. And where the local ferruginous sands were red-tinted, peasants insisted to the twentieth century that castles (and churches) were built with *mortier de sang*, a mortar mixed with the blood of sacrificed victims. In Périgord especially, the bitterness lingered: the old songs of 1793 voicing the peasants' resentment of rich farmers and messieurs were revived in 1848 and still sung in 1909; in 1830 castles were pillaged; in 1848 the local gentry made preparations to defend their halls; and in 1849 the rumor spread that the moderate candidate in that spring's elections had stocked 100 yokes or more

---

* See Eugène Le Roy, *Moulin du Frau* (Paris, 1905 ed.), especially p. 58. It may even have provided an opening for urban social propaganda in the countryside. The revolutionary Paris chansonnier Charles Gille wrote a song against the hunting law—"Bons paysans du Beauvoisis / Cachons, cachons bien nos fusils"—which he could well have sung in Vexin and Braye while spending time on a friend's farm in the area (Pierre Brochon, *La Chanson française*, 2: 127–28).

† Albert Soboul, "La Question paysanne," p. 32; Eugène Bonnemère, *Histoire des paysans*, 2: 418. In places, of course, the old practices survived with only little change. At Saint-Lary, in southwestern Haute-Garonne, where in the late 1840's the old men still wore pigtails and knee breeches, "les usages gardaient encore une sorte de couleur féodale." The tithe survived in the shape of gifts, the corvée as more-or-less voluntary services. "Quand mon père avait besoin d'un gros charroi, de pierres par exemple, il le faisait crier au sortir de la messe et c'était à qui se présenterait; on leur donnait à souper." (Comte de Comminges, *Souvenirs d'enfance*, pp. 28, 29.)

in his castle to use on his ex-vassals if he won.[21] How long such hatred and suspicion lasted is mirrored in the success of Eugène Le Roy's *Jacquou le Croquant*, published in the last year of the century. Jacquou is the heir of an old revolutionary tradition. When, on the eve of the revolution of 1830, he wreaks revenge against his wicked local baron, he avenges not only his own wrongs but those heaped on his father and his kind. Under his leadership, his fellow peasants set the oppressor's castle on fire and, more important, assert their own right to the land; the same land that was sung by the Gascon poet Jasmin, "from which alone could issue forth the balm that would put an end to the plague of misery." Four acres and a cow, if one may say so, were scarcely the inspiration for modern politics.

And that is just the point. For all the way into the 1870's fear of a restoration of the Ancien Régime and its servitudes hung in the back of many peasants' minds. In 1871 a Republican newspaper in Gers campaigned against the Monarchists by arguing that they would reestablish tithes. In 1873 the commanding general at Bordeaux reported relief in the countryside when the Count of Chambord eliminated the possibility of a royal restoration, because "right or wrong they believed tithes and forced labor were about to be reestablished." That same year a sub-prefect in Lot remarked that the peasants would accept the monarchy if only they were persuaded that they need not fear tithes or feudal dues.[22]

These were the sentiments that lay behind the curious jacquerie that ran through Dordogne and the Charentes in the late spring of 1868, and that appears to have begun when the de Lestranges, an aristocratic family of Chevanceaux (Charente-Inférieure), put their coat of arms in a stained-glass window of the local church. This persuaded villagers that noble privileges were on the point of being reestablished. It was not long before alarming rumors began to circulate throughout the entire area to the effect that very soon the priests would be demanding every thirteenth ear of corn and noblemen would be back sucking the peasants' blood. Official reports noted great disquiet in the region, made worse by the fact that the local population was "ignorant, irreligious, [and] exclusively attached to its material interests." Ribérac (Dordogne) was full of "absurd stories." At Saint-Paul-de-Lissonne an old woman asked the mayor if it was true that the Empress Eugénie had wed the Pope. Troubles broke out at Cercoux (Charente-Inférieure) and spread to Saint-Pierre-du-Palais nearby. Most of the troubles had to do with churches. At Saint-Michel-Lepauou (*sic*), near Barbezieux (Charente), some 20 peasants armed with sticks sought to remove clusters of flowers and grain (apparently including lilies) from the church altar because, they said, these signified the coming reestablishment of tithes. Another church, near Cognac, was invaded by several hundred persons bent on removing a (nonexistent) painting of Saint Joseph carrying a bunch of lilies and an ax, the which announced the return of feudalism. Priests were beaten up (as at Gigogne,

Charente), insulted, threatened; all were accused of planning to reestablish feudal dues.[23]

Only two years later these and similar hatreds found an outlet in the terrible murder of a local nobleman in the marketplace of Hautefaye (Dordogne). Seized by the peasants, accused of Prussian sympathies, the lord of the manor was brutally beaten, dragged around, tortured, and finally, still breathing, thrown on a pyre to be burned alive. André Armengaud has suggested that hatred for inaccessible foreign enemies was transferred to more accessible ones (such as the nobility, the rich, the clergy, or Protestants), who were regarded as traitors or the next thing to it.[24] That may be so. But would it not be simpler to recognize instead an old existing hatred to which moments of high tension offered an outlet and official hostilities a convenient label? This was why during the war of 1870–71, as Philip Hamerton tells us, the Burgundian peasantry so readily believed that all priests were Prussian agents, and that all the monies they collected went to the German cause.* Before bad motives are ascribed to a particular group, there must be a presupposition of their potential for evil. Where that potential was attributed to nobles or to priests, it was easy to hold them responsible for every sort of misdeed. The "faint underhand rumors" and "slanderous imputations" reported by the imperial prosecutor at Toulouse merely reflected what the peasants thought of those they blamed, and what they feared from them.[25] Historical memory and plain interest combined to make the peasants hate these groups more than foreign enemies. Nothing had happened yet to suggest that such priorities might be improper.

A simpler, inner-looking world reacted to political events that came from the outside in terms that it understood, and that urban observers scorned as ignorant and petty: would it lose liberties held uncertainly, regain liberties lost in forest rights or hunting, be made to pay more taxes, or be freed to pay none? At Draguignan the initial reaction of the procession that celebrated the news of the Second Republic in 1848 was to sack first the toll offices, letting the mistral blow their papers off, and then the chief tax agency, where the records were burned. At Avignon the committee that proclaimed the advent of the Republic simultaneously abolished the tolls and the tax on wine. Elsewhere, peasants seized former commons and forests that had been lost, or ravaged new plantations that had encroached on their pasturelands. In Yonne and elsewhere enthusiasm in February turned to disgust in March, when liberty turned out to mean additional taxes. In Lot, a police official maintained the

---

* *Round My House*, p. 213. Again in the First World War the charge was made that nobles and priests had subsidized Germany's attack on France. In the hilly, wooded country around Nontron in northern Dordogne many believed that the Kaiser was hiding in a local chateau, where the marks left by his nightly walks could be plainly seen on the sandy paths (Georges Rocal, *Croquants du Périgord*, pp. 131–33).

troubles that broke out in June 1848 had only the vaguest relation to the Paris rising; it was just that people were determined to seize the first opportunity to rid themselves of the tax collectors. If government was above all the collection of taxes, there was little reason for liking the Republic. Peasants and artisans acted logically in suspecting it, the more so since "the principle of equality crudely understood had spread through the ignorant and credulous masses."[26] Memories of an earlier tradition tended to leveling, and there was little need of political propaganda to stir the embers of such tendencies. But they expressed themselves in the attempt to eat and drink at the expense of the rich (if need be at their table) and the pulling down of that most conspicuous sign of their wealth, the weathervane perched on their roof.*

Amid hunger, want, and political confusion, coupled with disunity at the top, traditional hostilities created fears, myths, hopes, and mobilizing images enough. Everyone recollected the lessons of the past. Nobles and townships feared their peasant foes.† The peasants hated the "bourgeois" and thought to march on them. One hears a great deal about secret societies and the effect of their propaganda in small towns and in the countryside between 1849 and 1851. Certainly their organizations seem to have been effective enough to produce local insurrections in numerous areas after the December 2 coup. But it is very doubtful that any countryman stirred to defend the Republic or the constitution, or to oppose Louis Napoleon's coup. One is struck by the political ignorance of the peasants enrolled in such societies. "They put me in a club; I always thought it was a benevolent society," said one, and though he may have been lying, like the good soldier Schweik, the evidence suggests this was frequently the case. There was certainly confusion on what both clubs and insurrections were about. In Ardèche several rebels testified that they had been told the prefect awaited them in Privas to collect their votes. Even the prosecutor admitted that many insurgents did not know what they were doing: some thought they fought to abolish taxes or to obtain work; some believed they were answering the President's appeal for help or his call on the people to march on country towns; many were simply pressured into going along with the crowd. This last often counted heavily, as for the peasant in Zola's *Fortune des Rougon* who, brought to trial for taking part in the in-

---

* For examples of such incidents, see Alain Corbin, "Limousins migrants," pp. 665–66. Thus at Mazeau, near Ambazac, "the gang [of insurgent peasants], having gotten a written promise from the steward to pull down the weathervanes within two or three days, dispersed slowly and returned to their respective villages singing" (Archives Départementales, Haute-Vienne M 741).

† In Cognac and other urban communities of the Charentes, Raymond Doussinet tells us that the townsmen were singing: "Pan! Pan! Rantanplan! sus la goule! sus la goule! / Pan! Pan! Rantanplan! sus la goule aux pésants!" (*Les Travaux et les jeux*, p. 355.) No wonder that local loyalties, especially urban versus rural ones, overrode economic or class resentments. Gilbert Garrier has noted the division in the Lyonnais: "cloisonnement entre Lyon et son département rural; les idées ne circulent pas plus que les hommes." The same at Givors, where Red *voraces* held the town until June of 1848 but never managed to affect the neighboring countryside. (*Paysans du Beaujolais*, 1: 317–18.)

surrection, could only stammer, "I'm from Poujols." For him this was enough; and village solidarities (whether red or white, the men marched to the church bells) or the prestige of a local notable (like the notary who led 100 men out of his village to march on Mirande, Gers) or hatred of towns, of usurers, of the rich, sufficed to account for most of what took place.[27]

The authorities accused the rebels of social revolution. That it was—but in limited ways: "We wanted to maintain the rights of the people," explained one prisoner from Bourg-Saint-Andéol. "What do you mean by people's rights?" "I do not know." We hear of calls for "five hours of pillage," and if an incentive was needed, "aren't you tired of being poor?" Antoine Souliès of Saint-Privat (Dordogne) was taken in custody for declaring that he had sharpened his scythe to weed the houses of Saint-Aulaye. The urban agitators tried to appeal to peasants by playing on their hatred of the towns: they promised that they would be razed or set on fire, or better still, that they were already in flames (Limoges) or had been burned down. And the revolutionary language harked back to sources of the traditional sort. In Ardèche they sang a couplet about the unclean blood soaking through their furrows, raising the chant: "Let us march on Privas and set the mortgage registry and the tax office on fire." At Thiers the password was "Marat and Revolution," the war cry "Death to the rich!" The 2,000 countrymen marching on Agen roared "Vive la guillotine!" And at Narbonne a ditty was selling well: "Song of the Guillotine." At Carcassonne Léon Wralier of Moux was heard to shout: "We must play bowls with rich men's heads." At Seyches (Lot-et-Garonne) one leader of the crowd assured his listeners that the poor would not be happy until every monsieur and every priest had been cut in two.

The imagery was unmistakably that of the Revolution: I want to drink a pint of blood and carry off a head on my staff....I want a belt made out of their guts....I'll throw their liver to the dogs....Let blood run in the streets like water on a stormy day. But the mood was festive, for rebellion was a break in the everyday routine, a letting-off of steam much like Carnival. "Tomorrow," shouted an agitator to a Limousin village crowd, "tomorrow we'll be 50,000 at Limoges. It will be the finest festival we have ever had in our life." The woodcutters hesitate to join; they are promised chicken, turkey, champagne, and Bordeaux wine. "It's not today, but tomorrow surely we'll celebrate *le grand carnaval*. The peasants' Republic is here; tomorrow we'll have the harvest feast." Even in failure, when a courier arrived to warn that the cause was lost and the insurgents should disperse, the language remained consistent with the mood: It is too late to disperse now, came the response, for "the wine is tapped; it must be drunk!"[28]

A revealing scene unfolded at Béziers, where the surrounding villages rose en masse and filled the town with armed and angry men by daybreak on December 4. A band of these, hunting for enemies, encountered a local lawyer and his father-in-law, both Republicans. The gentlemen cried out, in

French, that they were Republicans and friends. The peasants cried out, in patois, "Let's get them!" They killed one and severely wounded the other. For these rebels "of the poorest and most ignorant portion of the *peuple* of Béziers," the foe was simply the bourgeois, and a French-speaking bourgeois at that!

When we are told that in 1849 Republican politics penetrated areas and levels of society that had been unpoliticized up to that time, we have to ask just how new this could have been. Alternatives to traditional resignation were greeted with delight, but the forms of expressing rebellion were traditional—farandoles, songs, threats—and the objects against which such rebelliousness was aimed were traditional too. As Philippe Vigier points out in masterly detail, the themes of the time were old themes warmed over, and the tensions that exploded after December 2 were familiar tensions: town against country, poor against rich and against usurers, people against notables, not workers against employers. "The Socialist infection" that was spreading so deplorably fast among poor peasants in the Alps, and elsewhere no doubt, caught on because it had a familiar ring. "It's frightening how they let themselves be caught with the snare of riches coming to them in their sleep," commented a Bonapartist agent. Why not, when this was a traditional theme of peasant tales and, anyway, only a miracle could bring the peasant riches? "Surprising continuity of peasant reactions," comments Albert Soboul. Why should it be surprising, when so little had changed?[29]

Seen in this perspective, the Second Empire was not an interlude of repression for a newly politicized peasant "class," but a period of relative well-being, during which, with order and economic activity restored, the possibilities of urban or urban-led economic growth percolated into the countryside to give men satisfactions on their own terms. The people of his town, announced the mayor of Courgis (Yonne), were pretty satisfied with the new constitution of 1852, the more so since their wines were selling reasonably well.[30] Peasants often identified opponents of the Empire with reactionary forces set on restoring old oppressions, rather than with those forces concerned to preserve or recapture some vague new liberties.* And concrete evidence that things were going well *for them* made peasants identify the Empire with prosperity. "The peasants vote for the Emperor not because they are unfree men," wrote Eugène Ténot in 1865, "but because they are satisfied, and because they have

---

* The argument has been made that the Second Empire helped introduce the peasants to political life and that rural Bonapartism was the beginning of the *fin des notables*. A vote for the official candidate was a vote against the local notable or priest: "a revolt of small rural democracies against the oligarchy of departmental notables," as Jacques Rougerie puts it in Georges Duby, *Histoire de la France* (Paris, 1972), 3: 117. Conversely (and bearing him out), Patrice Higonnet tells us that in one Lozère village, at least, before 1870 "a vote for the Left was a vote for Napoléon III" (*Pont-de-Montvert*, pp. 121, 124). It is worth noting in this connection an observation of Alain Corbin's: "Tout se passe comme si l'histoire de l'opinion politique se situait à deux niveaux, dans le cadre de deux systèmes de psychologie sociale différents" ("Limousins migrants," p. 1375).

their way of looking at things which is different from that of townspeople."
There was no one like Napoleon III, the peasants said, for keeping up hog
prices.[31] And the sub-prefect of Brive reported the success of the big fair of
1853: "The peasants return home with fervent cries of 'Long live the Emperor!'"*

Martin Nadaud grown old, appointed prefect of his native Creuse in 1870
by Gambetta, found that men no longer talked as they had in 1849, about
bravery, selflessness, self-sacrifice. Their sights had shifted from abstract formulas they barely understood to concrete objects brought within their reach.
Politics was about the way life was lived, and on the whole life was better
lived; so talk was about how to produce more crops (now that communications and trade made increased productivity possible and relevant), and about
the price of cattle.[32]

Such attitudes have generally drawn pejorative comments even from sensitive and sympathetic observers. Paul Bois, discussing the elections of 1790
and 1791 in Sarthe, shows how the 1790 elections, involving departmental posts,
drew a very high participation from the same peasants who the next year
turned out in incredibly low numbers to vote for representatives to the Legislative Assembly. In 1790 local government and local interests were at stake;
in 1791 the government of France was being decided. For the countrymen,
"ignorant and selfish, political deliberation was pretty much devoid of sense";
national issues did not move them, only "the sentiment of their interests."
Indifferent to news of the King's flight to Varennes and his capture, fall, and
execution, the peasants showed concern about grain shortages, the plundering
or requisitioning of grain, rising bread prices, and the falling value of the
assignat, and about troubles that involved local priests and churches.[33] Was
this so strange, regrettable, wrongheaded? Questions of national interest must
remain of little concern to those who do not see what they can mean to them.
A lively interest in matters that do concern them, that can be seen to matter
because they are close to home and that one can hope to do something about,
seems eminently sensible. But setting such value judgments aside, if that can
be done, it is true that indifference to questions of more than local interest
reflects mental and practical isolation: conditions that make the outer world
unimportant also make one feel powerless to affect it. By the end of the
Second Empire, greater material involvement would be translated into broader
political scope. But only barely.

The peasants were moving into the modern world, but the shift was ambivalent and inevitably uneasy. Politics continued to be personalized, and so

---

* Archives Nationales, F[1c]III Corrèze 3 (sous-préfet Brive, Jan. 1853). Conversely, consider the
case of a village carpenter near Orléans who got ten days in prison in 1859 for shouting that
the Emperor was a pig for having raised tobacco prices (see correspondence in AN, F[1c]III Loiret
12); and, significantly, Hamerton's remark that President MacMahon had a bad press with the
peasants because the removal of Thiers had coincided with a fall in the price of cattle (*Round My
House*, p. 270).

were programs and policies. We are ill-placed in the twentieth century to denounce the personalization of political issues as evidence of a primitive mentality. It may simply reflect a realistic understanding of how politics work. Yet the predominance of personalities over issues remains an indicator (however faint) of an earlier stage of politics and of a time when the role of intercessors, leaders, and interpreters was more readily admitted than in the popular politics of today. This is in part because that role was objectively greater, and in part because mentalities had not adjusted to abstraction, which is the supreme characteristic of the modern world and mind.

Personalized politics are the introductory stage of modern politics, and the elections of February 1871 very quickly turned into symbolic plebiscites: a battle between Thiers and Gambetta, heading their respective lists in many departments, embodying the major issue of peace versus continued war but also providing a personalization of the conflict. No wonder, in these terms, that Bonapartism endured as myth, as model, or as the mainspring of local supremacies. Policies, issues, governments were abstractions. Most people "vote for a man," reported a police official in Gers in 1876, "not necessarily against the government." No wonder that a Republican paper wrote bitterly in 1878 that peasants still thought Napoleon III responsible for the fine harvests of the Imperial years, still felt they had to have as a leader a man "who must be to some extent *thaumaturge*"—healer and sorcerer—in times of need.[34] When peasants in Charente said, "we need a man," and voted for Boulanger, they may have meant a strong man, but they also meant quite simply a recognizable and recognizably symbolic figure—the "man on horseback," not necessarily an image of reaction, but something concrete.*

The personalization of politics was particularly evident at the local level, where those national issues that did arise became rallying points for local factions, feuds, and interests. The rivalry of clans and partisans joined national politics to unrelated local issues and provided labels that can easily mislead. In eastern Périgord, scene of fierce rivalry between the two great river-trading houses of Barbe from Auriac and Chamfeuil from Espontours, none could avoid taking sides with one or the other. "You have to be for Barbe or for Chamfer" went the popular saying, and national politics had little to do with it.†

* *Le Figaro*, March 9, 1888; Emile Faguet in the introduction to Arthur Meyer, *Ce que mes yeux ont vu* (Paris, 1911), p. vi. In chapter 11 of *L'Appel au soldat*, Maurice Barrès remarks in passing that, after Gambetta, the peasants of the Moselle valley did not know a Minister's name until Boulanger came along. To what extent did the "American" methods that Comte Dillon used to spread the General's fame serve as a politicizing agent, as the enthusiasms and tensions of 1848–51 had done?
† Eusèbe Bombal, "La Haute Dordogne," pp. 391–92. Such divisions often ran deep, as in the small town of Sarlat, whose two religious fraternities (into which one was born) were at daggers drawn—"Capulets et Montagus dont les querelles ont défrayé les chroniques de Sarlat" (Alfred de Tarde, *L'Esprit périgourdin*, p. 10). Or in the Picard village of Bienvilliers, where well into the nineteenth century there was a bitter feud between families faithful to the sanctuary of Saint Etton,

It is not that national politics were totally irrelevant, but that, enlisted in the service of a local cause, they became part of local politics. Memories of 1793 or 1815 affected the orientation of a local clan, and sociopolitical interests expressed themselves by gravitating around a man or family. According to one analysis of the elections of 1869, the votes of different areas in Vendée tended not to divide along economic lines but rather to reflect local historical experiences. A conservative traveler writing about the Monarchists of Carpentras in 1873 remarked that they hated not so much the Republic as the Republicans. In upper Maurienne "one belongs hereditarily to reds or whites, and many would find it difficult to explain their political beliefs." In Vivarais, too, "one is red or white." The Revolution redefined the struggles between Protestants and Catholics; Right and Left would carry on their feuds. Interests, sympathy, experience involved one in the traditional factions but scarcely altered the factions themselves. One became white or red because one was a carter or because a relative had been ill-treated by the government; and perhaps also because of "individual and family temperament."[35] National themes, adopted for local consumption, enabled one power group to oppose another that was often very similar in wealth and social standing. "It is not that one doesn't seize every occasion to hide questions of personal interest behind the mask of politics." But everybody knew that this was what was being done.[36] Thus, 1848 found the little community of Martel (Lot) "divided from time immemorial into two camps," both led by "honorable families," one camp standing for "progress," the other necessarily for "resistance" to it. But as a judge commented when troubles broke out at Le Vigan, nearby, though the leaders of the two parties may have been involved in politics, "in the ranks it's a choice of persons." And in 1853 the sub-prefect of Avallon spoke for more than his district when he wryly described "all these internal struggles quite devoid of political coloring, turning within a narrow circle of personalities."[37]

The rich mass of official reports harvested by the Second Empire and the Third Republic shows that politics continued to be local, and local politics continued to be personal. "There are no political parties properly speaking," reported the sub-prefect of Mirecourt (Vosges) in 1869; "there are only local parties." Like the Sarthe peasantry described by Paul Bois, the peasants in every region I surveyed, from Vosges to Brittany, remained indifferent to national politics, concerned with local issues and local personalities. The prefect of Vosges found reason for satisfaction in 1870: "The temper of the countryside is excellent: political opinions are almost totally unknown." And from Agen: "General politics leave the masses indifferent." Local notables exercised political influence not only because they wielded power, but because political issues mattered to them more than to the peasant; by his simple sup-

---

destroyed in 1720, and those who accepted the new parish church dedicated to Saint Jacques, each party refusing to celebrate the other's saint, each frequenting its own cabarets and avoiding marriage with members of the other group (Marcelle Bouteiller, *Médecine populaire*, p. 99).

port, the peasant could thus at no pain oblige associates or superiors who seemed to care about such useless things.[38]

Physical and economic isolation, where they obtained, limited the alternatives or the access to them, and imposed a hierarchy of priorities. Strangers hawked strange ideas in strange language, often quite literally incomprehensible.[39] Work, crops, and land were what mattered; access to them, to cash, to help in need; and all these were tied to personal relations. So was the general welfare of the community, whose fate rested in the hands of a strictly limited few: a family or two. Personal pride and minimal means might assert independence, but this would be personal, too, with the general cause, vaguely articulated and vaguely understood, adopted to stress a personal stance, not an ideological commitment. Judicious regard for private and community interest made conformity with the concerns of notables hardly a sacrifice, and possibly quite profitable. Being courted by one's social superiors was a rare occasion that increased one's self-respect. But in any case selling one's vote or giving it to one's master was seen as the trade of an empty right for concrete advantage. All sides recognized this in contested elections, with the Republicans fully as eager to provide free drinks as their opponents, and drumming peasants' votes on their estates and those of their relatives.*

Interpretations must perforce remain tentative, but I am struck by the lack of comprehension in a remark like the one made by the commissaire of Plaisance (Gers), who noted that the people "don't try to understand the consequences of their votes: they vote for these gentlemen and that is all."[40] Of course, they voted for the gentlemen. Who else would they vote for, and why shouldn't they, in light of what has been said above? But within these limits they also voted hoping, as voters do today, that they might achieve a tax cut; and though, like more modern voters, they were only too often disappointed, this was a reasonable basis for choosing where to cast a vote. So was the interest in personal protection, which could transcend ideological differences. So was the concern that representatives, whatever their opinions, should stand in well with the national administration, once this had been recognized as a potent source of largesse. This was what made the second district of Riom reject Alexandre Varenne for the General Council in 1907, as the prefect explained, for while appreciating his "advanced opinions," the electorate, "essentially pro-government," did not want their representatives on bad terms with Authority.[41] They knew what this could cost them, and though they did

---

* Jacques Lovie quotes the corporal of gendarmes at La Roche in Faucigny, where the Republican Jules Favre ran against the government candidate in the elections of 1869: "Il serait nécessaire et même très urgent de payer à boire.... Déjà ... nous avons eu lieu de remarquer l'effet produit ... par quelques bouteilles de vin et de bière. Ainsi, par ce procédé, les partisans de Jules Favre ont réussi 150 suffrages en deux jours seulement, chiffre énorme sur quatre communes rurales." (*La Savoie*, p. 468; see also Archives Nationales, BB 18 1785, quoted by Guy Palmade in Louis Girard, *Les Elections de 1869*, p. 210.)

not mind electing a Socialist, they wanted him to stay on friendly terms with the men in power.

Apart from (or around) such considerations, national politics at the local level remained a travesty of local politics, just as before. Local rivalries and family quarrels divided the inhabitants (Aubenas, Ardèche, 1874). Political parties were essentially nonexistent, the vast majority paid no heed to them; only local issues mattered, not political ones (Bourg-Madame, Pyrénées-Orientales, 1876, 1882). The peasants were too busy with the potato harvest and with winnowing to notice the manifesto of the Comte de Paris—widely circulated by the Monarchists (Rambervillers, Vosges, 1887). Politics consisted of one man against another; there was no political spirit in these parts (Saint-Flour, Cantal, 1889). Parties concerned themselves with politics only at election time (Billom, Puy-de-Dôme, 1890). Utter indifference to political matters (Riom, Puy-de-Dôme, 1892). Local affairs and local hatreds (prefect of Pyrénées-Orientales, 1892). In this district there were no political differences, just personal ones (Thiers, Puy-de-Dôme, 1896). Political ideas played only a small part, but everywhere there were many personal quarrels and animosities (Issoire, Puy-de-Dôme, 1897). Elections were built on the name of a man, not on the principles and ideas the man represented (Gourdon, Lot, 1897). There were no true parties, concluded Raymond Belbèze in 1911: "The [typical] peasant chooses his candidate according to family tradition or what he believes his immediate interest to be."[42]

I do not want to suggest by all this that such motives do not enter into politics today. Far from it. It is only that now they are weighed against other considerations, whereas at the time they were dominant. Personal bonds are fitting and necessary in aristocratic or oligarchic societies, where they provide working substitutes for the more complex institutions of societies built on a larger scale. The waning of personal allegiances in the politics of the French countryside was an effect of scale, of a growing number of participants, along with improved techniques of communication, of what we call modern politics. Yet there are certainly places where personal and local ties continue to be an important and even the most important political factor. Writing about a rural canton in Santerre between the wars, Jacques Bugnicourt has shown how personal and clan rivalries still ruled local politics there. "On employe pour mieux s'insulter, un certain vocabulaire, on établit un lien entre les tendances locales et ce qu'on croit comprendre des tendances nationales." In the end, though, "the election is only one episode of the rivalry of the clans ... a convenient means of stressing old animosities."*

* Bugnicourt in Jacques Fauvet and Henri Mendras, *Les Paysans et la politique*, pp. 463–75. This is borne out in a remarkable article by Claude Karnoouh on kinship and politics in a Lorraine village. In that village, she writes, "les notions de droite et de gauche s'estompent au profit des catégories parentales et familiales. L'intérêt public se confond avec des querelles dont

Maurice Agulhon has suggested that this adaptation of alien themes was important in the transition period, when rural populations little affected by the outside world could be swayed with ideological slogans that corresponded with local hatreds or aspirations, and that the interaction of these themes with local folklore was part of the acculturation process.[43] Quite so. But it is well to remember that what Agulhon says about village society before 1848 holds good half a century later in many parts of France, where the acculturation was still very incomplete; and that the ploy was used for at least 100 years.

By then, the village in Picardy that Bugnicourt has studied was fully integrated into the modern economy, so that the persistence of personal politics must mean something more. For old animosities to survive, they have to be remembered; for clans to endure, there has to be continuity. The less mobile the society, the greater the stability of its themes and of its categorizations. Though no rural society was ever fixed in its composition, the proportion of newcomers was always small enough to allow for assimilation and indoctrination in the local lore. Themes could persist and so could families in a way that urban politics, at least since the nineteenth century, did not need consider. The degree to which this affected political activity and language in the countryside can serve as one index of modernization.

Another explanation of the persistence of personal politics comes from Henri Mendras, who sees rural society as founded on a confusion of roles. That is to say, every participant has less a functional than a total perception of every other: the postman is also a neighbor, a cousin, a creditor; the shopkeeper sells, but he also buys things himself, drinks with you, is a political ally; and so forth.[44] Functions and institutions are incarnated in men (as they are in the Welsh usage "Jones the chapel"), so that the church is the priest, the school is the teacher, the townhall is the mayor or his substitute. Social life is conceived as the interaction of individuals, and all events are attributed to some person's will. It follows that the operations of institutions, of abstract functions, trends, or forces, are not realities in the experience of villagers who have difficulty in understanding the workings of politics and economics beyond their immediate ken. This difficulty may diminish as acquaintance with the operation of unfamiliar institutions grows. But it will never disappear altogether. It has not done so in the urban mind. Once again, the difference is one of degree; but a watershed comes at the point where a peasant of the Mendras model admits, however grudgingly, that politics is an indirect way of dealing with matters of direct concern.

---

la génèse s'est parfois estompée dans la mémoire des acteurs. Ici les concepts de bourgeois, de prolétaire ... se révèlent sans pouvoir sur les faits." ("La démocratie impossible," *Etudes rurales,* 1973, p. 34.) We find a curious comment on all this in an article by Margaret Peil, reviewing two books on Nigerian politics: "Factions arising out of personality conflict between individual leaders often continue long after these leaders have passed from the scene, because politics is based far more on personal relations and the struggle for personal advantage than on ideology" (*Times Literary Supplement,* Oct. 17, 1975, p. 1241).

One other tendency, still surviving though enfeebled, reflected the enduring archaism of politics. The prefect of Pyrénées-Orientales put it very well when he explained the electoral situation in 1889. Not party labels, but regionalism determined the vote: "Local rivalries... will reawake as strong as in the past; it suffices to have one parish vote for Mr. B, for the rival parish to give its votes to A."[45] Again and again, since labels were masks for local politics and local sentiments, the roots of a candidate counted more than his political label. So that in several instances Left-wing parishes were led to vote for a candidate of the Right because he was "their man," and Right-wing areas to vote Left because the candidate happened to be a local doctor, or just to spite the hated rival from up or down the hill.

Here too the permanencies are suggestive. Age-old oppositions were simply redefined when the plains went Left and the mountains remained obstinately Right and Catholic. A pastoral economy surviving on the upper slopes would be reflected in the clinging to old ways that were rapidly disintegrating below. The process would be hastened when, as in Maurienne, industrial development turned the peasants into proletarians and brought in immigrant workers from outside.[46] All this created hierarchies to rival old familiar ones, class divisions of a modern kind, and estrangement from traditional practices and loyalties: tensions that opened the door to modern politics. But there was no consistent pattern.* All one can say with certainty is that isolation and self-sufficiency made for political (or rather apolitical) stability, or put another way, the refusal to entertain new ideas; and that they coincided with a political orientation toward personalities, rather than toward either Right or Left.†

Proximity to towns and their markets, on the other hand, with all the traipsing back-and-forth this implied, accelerated the tendency to movement and evolution. However small it was, the town had a few civil servants, shopkeepers, doctors, veterinarians, men of law; clubs or societies, perhaps a Masonic lodge; and a "press" put together in the café and published once or twice a week—all likely carriers of outside ideas. The tension between the little town—sub-prefecture or district center—and the surrounding countryside was increased and complicated by urban novelties. In turn, the small town

---

* The mountaineers of Ariège, smarting under the injustices of the wood-greedy iron forges and their usurious owners, voted heavily for Republicans and "reds" in 1848 and 1849. But during the Second Empire, the Ariège forges declined, the population thinned out, wood was more readily available, popular dissatisfaction waned, and the political coloring altered.

† Thus the people of the Thônes valley in Savoy were known as the Bretons of Savoy, and their valley as a Vendée savoyarde; yet nearby Nancy-sur-Cluses, wealthier and closer to the more politically sophisticated Cluse d'Arve, "se paie le luxe de voter quelquefois à gauche par pure fantaisie" (Paul Guichonnet, "Le Géographie et le tempérament politique," pp. 70–71). On the coincidence of isolation and personal politics in Isère, see the map in Pierre Barral, *Département de l'Isère*, p. 450. Of the poor, undeveloped *terres froides* in the department's northwest, the subprefect of Vienne remarked in 1905: "Les courants politiques sont moins accusés, les questions de personnes et les petites querelles de clocher tiennent plus de place" (Archives Départementales, Isère 8M 37).

often introduced new political tensions into the countryside. Thus, in Allier the political emancipation of the rural areas from the domination of great landowners seems clearly due to the vitality of certain bourgs, "kernels of opposition," which gave the countryside around them an alternative political lead. Whether a village or township gave such a lead or not may have depended on the degree to which the town itself was part of the wider world. In Ardèche, for example, Le Cheylard, which remained outside economic currents until the 1880's, was politically quiescent, and so was the region around it. But to the south, Largentière, an important center for trade between complementary areas, and its environs were politically alive.[47]

Other tensions with political possibilities developed on the land itself. Cracks had appeared and were deepening in the foundations of rural society—in that "submission and respect to the laws and regulations and respectful deference toward the agents of authority" reported by the gratified police superintendent of Céret.[48] But this was in 1876, and Céret lies in a Pyrenean valley. Elsewhere the seeds of change had sprouted long before. They had come with alternatives: the possibility of choice, and of escape from authority. Baudrillart, traveling in the south, noted that local speech had no term for respect and hence used "fear." In fact, respect (*respe*) appears at least in dictionaries. But so does *crainto*, which covers both respect and fear. Awe and reverence are not far apart. A child was taught that he should fear his father, an underling his superior. External manifestations of deference symbolized submission: kissing the father's hand, kneeling before one's master, as peasants in Brittany still did in the 1840's. Deference based on fear, dependence, and submission did not avert spite, but rather helped to breed it. Popular proverbs reflected the malice of underlings who rejoiced at the discomfiture of superiors: "When the master's foiled, the menial laughs."[49] And in Lauragais, where the big domains grew wheat and the smallholders corn, the poor greeted summer rains that threatened the one and helped the other with "It's raining insolence." If the squire's harvest was ruined and the little man had plenty of corn, he could afford to set fear aside and to be as "insolent" as he pleased.*

The opportunity for insolence was slow to come, though sources beginning in the 1830's deplored the waning of respect toward authority of every sort, especially toward masters. The Agricultural Survey of 1867 lamented that though conditions of rural labor had improved, relations between workers and employers had deteriorated. The two things were of course related; the possibility of leaving the land, the thinning out of rural populations, however

---

* M.-F. Pariset, who quotes this saying, provides another of similar sentiments: "When it's wet, the servant laughs, and the master's pretty mad" (*Economie rurale . . . Lauragais*, pp. 59, 135). A proverb of the Lower Vivarais reveals another aspect of the same yearning: "Windy March, rainy April, make the peasant arrogant" (Pierre Charrié, *Folklore du Bas-Vivarais*, p. 165). April rain promises a fine harvest, but the peasant looks forward just as much to the prospect of holding his head high.

limited at that time, had nevertheless raised wages. A decade later, in the 1870's, a doctor in Tarn wondered at the disappearance of the sharecropper of yore, "full of deference for his master." Sharecroppers now were "less slaves of routine, more competent, more hard-working, but very independent, treating the master as an equal, very selfish ... less obliging than they used to be and inclined to sacrifice all for their own interest."[50] There it all was: the change, and the observer nonplussed at inferior groups beginning to set their own interests before their masters', indeed discerning a difference of interest at all.

The mere existence of alternatives had encouraged higher expectations, and had to some extent brought gains. But the gulf between actual gains and expectations that grew at an unprecedented rate (however modest they may seem today) intensified the existing frictions and evoked remarks about the malevolence and hostility of the inferior classes toward the higher ones. In conjunction with this came another development, rued by Théron de Montaugé in 1869: "The bond of patronage, so powerful in the past, ... has no force today." Hence, the superior classes "no longer constitute a mainstay for the state."[51] There was the rub. The superior classes had diversified to such an extent that they provided a whole series of alternative authorities. Deference did not need to die out in order to wane, but simply to be transferred from one object to another. Yet the multiplication of authorities, and their rivalries, sapped the notion of authority itself.

From the very beginning of the nineteenth century, rural society and its hierarchies had become increasingly complex. The acquisition of national property by bourgeois, the greater number of nobles living on their lands, especially after 1830, and the increasing number of professionals and officials in small country towns had raveled what had once been a fairly simple social fabric. This happened at a time when prosperous farmers, enriched by the suppression of feudal survivals and by opportunities to purchase property, began to assert their new social position. Still close to their fellow peasants, they nevertheless sought to mark their distance from them by imitating higher social groups.* Inevitably, their relations with their workers changed in the process. A life of common hardship had long established a rough equality between a farmer and his neighbors, even more strikingly between a farmer and his help, who shared his board and, if they slept in the cowshed, felt not much worse off than he. Whom poverty had united, prosperity set apart. The *domestique* (part of the household) became an *ouvrier*. In some families two sorts of bread began to be prepared, the better quality for the masters, who learned to eat from crockery and to drink wine, the customary black bread for the hired hands, who washed it down with water or thinned wine. The division was sharper still if a wealthy farmer turned from land to horse- or cattle-

---

* As can be seen, for instance, in George Sand's *Valentine* and *Le Meunier d'Angibault*. But all these developments were slow-moving until after mid-century.

breeding, for then labor in common ceased. The workers and their employers no longer shared the same timetable. The farmer went to the market, where he drank and gossiped. The worker who stayed behind resented this, especially because it flouted traditional modes. Here was privilege. Leisure came to be enjoyed separately, just as work was now done apart. The workers left the common table and ate separately in the stable or, on a holiday, at the cabaret. Everyday relations reflected the new tensions, the new frictions, so that by 1884 the village landowners who used to be cordially greeted by their fellows were now looked on askance.[52]

This trend, suggestive of new divisions through the whole of peasant society, in due course propelled successful farmers into the list of local notables. Farmers too could become bourgeois, especially when they began buying up the properties of urban absentee landowners. They joined the struggle for political places (henceforth symbols of status and proofs of influence), and they vied among themselves and against others in municipal politics and in the struggle for honors.[53]

All this competition in an increasingly open political market created perplexities and some confusion, but also provided lesser men with opportunities for maneuver or, at least, with a sense of discretion and the possibility of choice. It also helped improve their self-respect. Writing about Berry in 1913, Hugues Lapaire noted that the peasant had left servility behind. He no longer bowed to any city slicker, to any gent. True, he still used polite formulas when he talked to you, but when you turned your back he called his pigs "gentlemen" or "nobles." He may have done that before, out of the master's hearing (though it is doubtful that he would have dared). The novelty lay in the self-assured tone, in the shedding of "servility," in the refusal to regard the city slicker as automatically superior.[54]

The peasant was simply doing better, and he was seeing more of city people, too. But the opportunity to choose among his betters must have helped build up his self-respect. It was not that dependency did not continue; the little man was still under pressure from his creditors, from men who employed him or lent him their team of horses to plow his land, above all from the local landowner, noble, or bourgeois—"masters of the land, of life, of souls." As late as the turn of the century the squire at Chanzeaux in Vendée still required his tenants to gather at his chateau before Sunday mass, march to church behind his carriage, and then return to the chateau for a quiz on the day's sermon.[55] The interesting thing is that such types maintained their hold less by straightforward economic bonds than by sustained relationships and attention, once the rural voter had a chance to choose.* Where the lord of the manor was a

* A study of the account book of Albert-Auguste Flahaut, a country notable, owner of some 250 acres of good land and mayor of his village in the Pas-de-Calais, shows the devices he used to maintain his authority over the workers on his estates near Béthune: he lent money to those who preferred to borrow from him rather than the notary; he kept surpluses he might have sold elsewhere to sell to those of his workers who had to feed themselves; he provided essential services

tangible presence, as in the case of the Baron of Rochetaillée, who opened an account with the butcher and the baker for all the poor of his village close to Saint-Etienne, traditional loyalties were bolstered by gratitude. Where a great family had the wealth and influence to wangle for a community a church, roads, a bridge, schools, a town clock, and a telegraph office, as the Dampierres did at Cazères on the Adour, "this is known, judged, valued by all families, even by those undisposed to gratitude." But in most cases, the great landowners did not live on their land. They visited the estate intermittently, transmitted their instructions through their stewards, and lost touch with an electorate that was increasingly choosy and susceptible to suasion. Local families, notaries, solicitors, veterinarians, and especially doctors—some of whom had served the region for several generations—provided an alternative elite, and one that cultivated the voters more assiduously.[56]

When, in 1871, Léonce de Vogüé, though elected to the National Assembly just behind Thiers on the conservative ballot, lost his seat in the General Council of Cher to a country doctor, he attributed this to the opportunities that had "excited all the ambitious mediocrities (notaries, doctors, justices of the peace)." People like these, he contended, "live closer to universal suffrage and avail themselves of this to canvass votes." In Vogüé's eyes, as in his terms, this was somehow demeaning. Nor did he mention, as his grandson would, that the doctor in question, though an indifferent practitioner of his art, was honored in his canton for the many services that he had rendered his fellow citizens.

A generation later we find Melchior de Vogüé carrying elections for the Cher council, through the 1880's and 1890's over "a little village doctor," who finally succeeded in defeating him in 1904. A friend wrote to console Vogüé on his failure, assuring him that there could be no fair contest "between the charlatans who promise that the state will change the lot of workers ... *and who repeat this 365 days a year in the local pub*, and a private individual, who *once every four years* speaks to them of efforts they may have to make."[57] The point was not the content of the propaganda, but its intensity and its continuity. One man was a permanent presence, talking and to be talked to, the other was available only periodically. The presence created bonds of reciprocity; social encounters strengthened these bonds; small attentions and interested concern flattered the self-respect of men who by custom, manners, dress, education, and sometimes even language were in a class apart. French was the language of ceremony, but it was important to be able to address the lower classes in their speech. They were hungry for personal recognition from

---

to those employees who owned some land of their own; and he took the earnings of employees on deposit, "managing" the money and requiring the depositors to state how they were going to use their money when withdrawing any. But all this was subject to change at the peasant's initiative. (R.-H. Hubscher, "Le Livre de compte," pp. 380, 400.) On the ambiguity, see Georges Rougeron, *Le Conseil général*, pp. 171–72; Jean Bécarud, "Noblesse et représentation parlementaire," *Revue française de science politique*, 1973, pp. 986–87; and Archives Départementales, Puy-de-Dôme M 0162 (Thiers, May 1892).

their superiors, and grateful to those who offered it. "One thing torments them more than questions of salary," wrote Audiganne about the workers of Rouen. "It is the need for some consideration." Attention of this sort "elevates them in their own eyes and narrows social distances, without hurting the hierarchy." The moment would come (and Melchior de Vogüé predicted it in 1886) when "the inferior ranks" would choose their representatives among themselves ("What will become of our beautiful France then!"). But that was far away, and for the moment, those who succeeded in combining the traditional virtues of generosity and some kind of public munificence with a new "familiarity" pleased the crowd.[58] Social distances were still so great that to be "not proud" was the supreme praise peasants and artisans could heap on a bourgeois.*

More sensitive to the symbols of status than to supposed class antagonisms, flattered by fair words that heightened their sense of dignity, the lower orders responded with particular readiness when notables showed signs of wooing them.[59] Politicization was one aspect of acculturation, of listening to the language of one's betters and imitating it, as one imitated dress when one could afford to. Political manners were part of urban mannerisms slowly and awkwardly being assimilated by another world, but one increasingly predisposed to learn.

How was the new language of politics assimilated? To put it differently, how did the unpoliticized many begin to act as if politics was not the interest and the preserve of a very few?

We may safely say they did not learn it through reading. "The peasants don't read electoral literature," reported the sub-prefect of Rochechouart (Haute-Vienne) in 1857. They did not read very much of anything else, either. Opinion in traditional communities was consensual, not a privately developed view of things. Founded on personal relations, opinion was affected by the spoken word, not the written word. Whether in the 1850's, when publications were being distributed free through the countryside, or in the 40 years before 1914, political propaganda remained chiefly verbal.[60] Indeed, speech was an act that transcended words.† Words, in any case, tended to generalities that left men who were concerned with immediate problems quite unmoved, or moved them in unexpected ways. Ideals could easily appear as threats to peasants for whom patriotism meant war and military service, order meant the rule of the chateau, and progress meant disturbing novelties, incomprehensible laws, and more gendarmes. Only when interpreted and translated into familiar terms could the political language of the cities carry positive attractions.[61]

---

* Frédéric Mireur, Les Rues de Draguignan, 3: 156–58. When Martin Nadaud was addressed by a medical student in a reading room, "c'était la première fois qu'un bourgeois me donnait la main, et j'avoue que j'en fus très flatté."

† Speaking of the Vivarais peasants, Gaston Rioux wrote in Foi et vie in 1912: "Ils ne s'interessent qu'à la parole, qui est un acte" (June 1, 1912, p. 332). But, then, consider these two Basque proverbs: "Words are female, acts are male"; "Words and feathers fly in the wind" (Sylvain Trébucq, La Chanson populaire et la vie rurale, 1: 248).

The role of the interpreters, therefore, was crucial; and just as crucial were their numbers, their variety, and their penetration into the depths of rural society.[62]

At the grass roots, we find a political "class" containing a few men whose functions brought them into some sustained contact with the outside world: innkeeper or publican, shopkeeper if there was one, mayor, teacher, priest, road surveyors, inspectors of highways, the odd customs or excise agent, the corporal of forest guards or commander of the gendarmerie. To these one can add their underlings: the postman, the rural constable, cantonniers or road gangs and their overseers, perhaps also the sexton. All but the first two were invested with official functions. They were servants not of the public, but of the state that paid them and that they represented. They were the personification of government, and more specifically of a given regime. It was an important fact of rural political life that these offices changed hands as the regime changed.[63] Precisely because politics were not abstract, regimes and governments were identified with the functionaries who represented them; a multitude of rural reports emphasize this, and the dismissal, appointment, or exile of judges, justices of the peace, tax collectors, tax receivers, tobacco agents, teachers, postmen, and constables shows that the reports were taken seriously.

But the authority of such minor public servants stemmed from more than their official position. In an illiterate culture, these men could read and write, however clumsily; in a particularist culture, they were conversant with the official language—French. The postman could read out letters and vaguely explain official documents. The constable could draft notes, a report, a police citation. They were the first to hear news from the outside, from notables like the mayor, who actually read the paper, and to transmit it in relatively garbled form to fellow villagers and outlying hamlets. News of the outside world probably traveled much as in those children's games in which a word whispered from ear to ear reaches the end of a human chain transformed beyond recognition. It was news nevertheless, a link with civilization. And such links were more numerous as easier travel brought city vacationers into the countryside. A Paris pharmacist begins to pass each summer at Cuers, up in the hills behind Toulon, brings with him new ideas, and keeps up a correspondence the rest of the year that lets people know what goes on in the capital.[64] The influence of the carriers and interpreters of civilization, the humblest among them most likely also the most effective, should not be ignored.

With the years the number of such carriers grew. So did the amount of news they carried. There were more letters, more postmen, simply more information. Wars awoke the countryside to the existence of a distant world. What the campaigns of 1792–1814 began, those of the Second Empire settled. A steady flow of reports, rumors, hearsay, and tall tales about the Orient, the Crimea, Italy, China, Africa, and Mexico irrigated France with curious anecdotes and intelligence. Events more or less current penetrated the news-tight world of the countryside, because factions and governments became interested in en-

listing voter interest in their enterprises. They were welcome because they offered something new and colorful to talk about: victories were fun. No wonder
the villagers were "avid for news of Italian feats and glories," and enjoyed hearing about Garibaldi's successful boldness, which must have fitted into familiar
tales of derring-do. But foreign news was also increasingly recognized as
relevant. Relations with strange lands were recognized to affect local prosperity, even in unlikely places like Ardèche, which got its silkworm eggs from
Italy. Conscription affected peasants sharply, if only in the rising cost of replacements for the draft. Taxes to pay for war hit even closer home, especially
when, as in 1862, they threatened a rise in the price of salt.[65]

The Third Republic was as eager as the Second Empire to increase its
prestige with international success. Republican politicians, determined to persuade the general public how well they managed the interests of France,
taught the peasants even more about the wider world. These lessons were always recited in a particular context—the Prussian menace, frictions with
Italy, or Russian friendship—but once again they introduced new areas to
popular consciousness. The war of 1914–18 capped the process. The impact
of all this should not be exaggerated; knowledge of the wider world remained
vague, interest in its details slight and at best anecdotal.[66] But the growing
awareness that international affairs were capable of affecting one's life and
the life of the locality carried with it a growing awareness of the nation. Willy-
nilly, the inward-looking rural islands, self-sufficient at least in their own view,
were being forced to attend to wider complications.

Taverns, the liveliest centers of the rural man's social activities, were forums
for political talk as for every other kind. A deliberate resort for mutual aid
or a social center for regular customers, the tavern gave workingmen the
chance to mix with tradesmen and artisans, and gave the young who idled
around the bar the chance to indulge in opposition for the sheer pleasure of
it.[67] In or near the tavern, inn, or café, there grew clubs, circles, or associations
in great variety. Originally designed to provide distinction, privacy, special
comfort, easy access to newspapers, mutual aid, common entertainment, or
simply cheaper drinks, these could easily become political circles. They certainly offered opportunities for talking politics. But clubs and circles tended
to be urban and to recruit their membership rather in terms of social status
than of political sentiment.* For obvious reasons, those associations that needed
to draw on a relatively numerous recruiting base were also urban organizations: fire companies, singing societies, bands, religious fraternities, mutual-
aid associations. We would not expect to find them any lower than the *chef-*

---

* On the other hand, at the end of the nineteenth century we find a countrymen's club, Le
Cercle des Bastidans, with about 100 members, in the little town of La Garde-Freinet (Var). In
its quarters in a building in the center of town country people could gather on Sundays (only
Sundays!) to talk, drink wine, and play cards. The Bastidans remained neutral in the political
conflicts that divided the town. (Léon Sénéquier, *Connaissance de la Garde-Freinet*, pp. 134–36.)

lieu-de-canton (Cazals, Lot), and most would have been at the level of the sub-prefecture (Bonneville, Haute-Savoie) or above. By 1870 many of these social groups did in fact become politicized, at least in those regions where politics were already a part of run-of-the-mill social life; so that in Provence "innumerable" Republican circles flourished, and Monarchists tried to oppose them with circles of their own.[68]

Here is a description of one of the latter, the Cercle de la Concorde, quartered in a side street of Carpentras: "Around a table sit a dozen peasants, their staffs beside them, drinking their coffee. A handsome young man, who seems to be from the town, reads aloud an article from [the Monarchist paper]. He stops at almost every sentence to explain it in Provençal. This is greeted with cries of approval."[69] Here is the urban club at work: the visiting peasants, the paper they never saw and would not have known how to read anyway, because it was written in French, the young man from town acting as interpreter, presumably preaching reactionary ideas, yet helping to detach these men from the old world, and easing their passage to a new French one. There is no way of telling the incidence of clubs even at the urban level. The authorities seem to have regarded most taverns as potential havens of political propaganda and to have kept a sharp eye on all of them; but the popularity of the club as such appears to have varied a great deal. The north, south, and southwest, for instance, seem clearly to have been more prone to organized sociability than the center regions and possibly the west as well. This was in part a function of available means, in part perhaps of tendencies bred by living in dispersed parishes or concentrated ones (though Lorraine, where villages were fairly large, had far fewer clubs than Provence).

We know that throughout Languedoc, Gascony, and Provence, an old urban orientation in the countryside made clubs popular. But in the Limousin Corbin finds none of the imitative tendency of Agulhon's Provence; and in the Vosges in 1901 we find only 287 clubs in 138 localities, in a department with 531 communes and a population of 421,412.[70] In Pyrénées-Orientales, too, a dip into the files on associations shows that these were scarce outside the region of Perpignan. The six cantons (113 communes) of the electoral district of Prades seem to have had fewer than 40 associations by the end of the century. The official file is not exhaustive, but it does suggest that where a group was not a social club for the upper classes, joined by the judge, the retired army officer, and the mayor (Cercle de France, Vinça); or a society of artisans and shopkeepers, "formed to put each other in the way of work" (Cercle des Ouvriers, Ille-sur-Têt); or "a device for the café-owner to keep his establishment open after hours" (Mosset), associations were politically based. The politics were very probably local politics, as when, following the municipal elections of 1896, the little township of Corbère saw the founding of a circle in opposition to the existing one. Nevertheless, by that time, and considerably earlier in some places, local and national politics had become inextricably mixed.[71] Once that happened, party allegiance would thereafter be reflected in clubs, dances, various festivities, and other "public amusements" connected with the political orientation of their participants.*

One step below the relatively formal clubs came more ad hoc affairs—*chambrées, chambrettes*—of the sort studied by Maurice Agulhon and Lucienne Roubin. They could be offshoots of local gatherings, such as we find before 1870 in the Seine valley between Vernon and Mantes; there after dinner, while the women gathered in veillées, the men went to smoke and talk around the stove of some late-working tailor, weaver, or sabotier, producing several so-called clubs of ten or fifteen per village. They could result from the initiative of an individual or a group of friends seeking the privacy their bourgeois betters enjoyed. They could also be answers to the need for mutual assistance and support, didactic institutions established for the informal transmission of information, the facilitation of rites of passage, and the performance of certain local chores (for example, a special role at Carnival).[72]

A rented room, preferably near a tavern whence one would fetch the wine, some chairs, and a table, and a quasi-club was born. It offered a respite from the overcrowded quarters that drove men into taverns, a chance for physical escape from the home. There one could drink more cheaply, play cards ("gambling" was frowned on by the authorities), and chat. In bigger villages, which could have a score of such "roomlets," membership would be based on neighborhood and affinity. The group, already sharing the minimal rent and cost of buying drink, might also assess itself to subscribe to a regular newspaper. Even limited social purposes could bring involvement in economic, hence political problems, as when the authorities tried to tax the group's drinks. In any case, the solidarity that brought members together was reinforced by regular association. We hear that group members got the same voting bulletins and went together to the polling booth. By 1905 Thorame-Haute, a little village in the Verdon valley, had four such associations, made up of heads of family, youth, radical Republicans, and residents of Riou, a hamlet on the slope above the village.[73] We see here the traditional division into age groups, each with a role to play in the life of the community; an equally traditional neighborhood division; and the incorporation of politics in traditional structures—just as these were now recognized by national law.†

* La Garde-Freinet was one of the places where the politicization of clubs came relatively early. The Union Philharmonique split into two factions in 1879, the Bravade broke up and eventually died in the 1880's, hunt clubs divided, and so forth. In the end the local youth began to react against this trend and took to frequenting cafés and dances and courting girls irrespective of political camp. Unfortunately, just when this reaction set in is left vague. (Sénéquier, *Connaissance*, pp. 104ff, 125, 172.)

† Emilien Constant, who has also studied the much-plumbed *chambrées*, feels that these helped to introduce their members to the practices of modern political life: the nomination of officials, discussion of issues and doctrine, diffusion of slogans and programs. Constant cites a letter replying to Prime Minister Emile Ollivier's circular of 1870 that was published in the "democratic press" of Var and signed by "the delegates of all the peasant chambrées of Draguignan." But it is

But the most effective politicizing agent was politics itself, that is to say, electoral practice. Abstention from voting is more common and more routine, remarks Alain Lancelot, to the extent that voters belong to categories or communities ill-integrated in "global society." Put in our own context, isolation tended to result in nonparticipation and abstentionism. But we are not talking about mere physical isolation; voters living away from it all may in fact relish the chance to take a little trip to town to do their civic duty. There is a sort of isolation that makes "global" affairs irrelevant, and makes the effort of voting meaningless.[74] Precisely the sort of economic and cultural isolation we have documented right along. After all, going to vote meant taking time from work, plus perhaps the costs of an unusual trip.* The problem of getting to the polling place remained a real one, especially before 1871 when voting took place in the chief town of the canton. We know that country roads were bad and few. Easier movement as communications improved in the latter part of the century, together with the expansion of polling places, now no farther away than the parish bourg, encouraged participation.[75] But intellectual conditions also mattered. There is a direct relationship between literacy and electoral participation, just as there is between poverty, isolation, and literacy—or rather illiteracy. Georges Dupeux has shown this relationship in Loir-et-Cher, and Serge Bonnet has found a similar correlation in Lorraine, where, in the early years of the Third Republic, the villages with the poorest voter turnout also showed poor attendance at school and church.[76]

Ignorance made it easier for politicians and local leaders to manipulate and confuse their constituents: to argue that repeal of the Falloux Law on education was tantamount to the abolition of taxes; to put it about that Republican voters would be deported to Cayenne, as was done in Allier in 1873; to intimidate villagers into abstention, so that in one Finistère village in 1889 only 11 of 396 voters dared cast a ballot; or as in Isère in 1887, to put Republican ballots on a chair at the door of the polling place because "the major part of the population being illiterate, voters take what they find to hand." The secrecy of the ballot was not particularly well preserved until 1914, when voting booths and envelopes to put the ballots in were instituted. And even then, the suspicion of discovery made deviation difficult in small communities.[77]

Still, each election, with the campaign preceding it and the talk this caused, introduced indifferent populations to new practices and issues. Political wastes

---

well to note that this letter was presented by a well-known militant of Var, Dr. Félix Brémond; and while admitting the following he had among peasants, one may wonder how far such a document really reflected their thinking. (*L'Esprit républicain: Colloque d'Orléans 1970*, Paris, 1972, p. 287.)

* Hence perhaps the elections of April 23, 1848, held on Easter Sunday when whole villages were bound to assemble for high mass (Anacharsis and Hippolyte Combes, *Les Paysans*, p. 81). Similarly, after May 16, 1877, the date of the elections was set at the uttermost legal limit (October 14), not only because this would give the government time to "prepare" public opinion, but also, as a provincial newspaper in Loire pointed out, because the grain and grape harvest would be over by then, and the rural voters free to go to the polls (*Journal de Montbrison*, July 22, 1877).

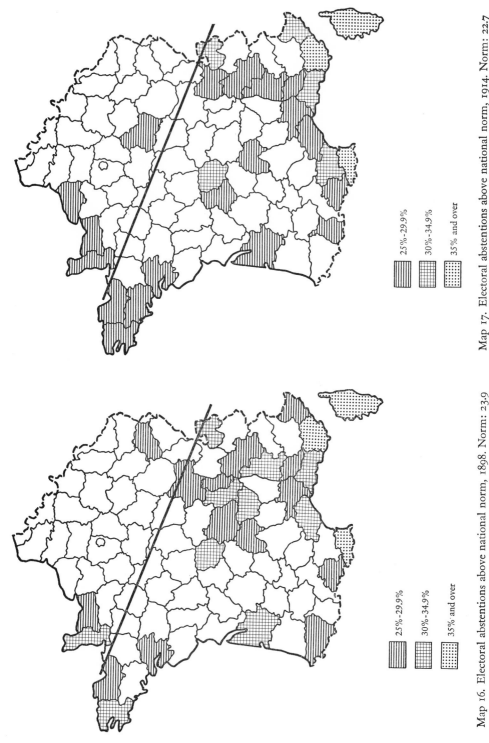

Map 16. Electoral abstentions above national norm, 1898. Norm: 23.9 percent. SOURCE: Alain Lancelot, *L'Abstentionnisme électoral en France* (Paris, 1968), p. 58.

25%-29.9%

30%-34.9%

35% and over

Map 17. Electoral abstentions above national norm, 1914. Norm: 22.7 percent. SOURCE: Same as Map 16, p. 59.

25%-29.9%

30%-34.9%

35% and over

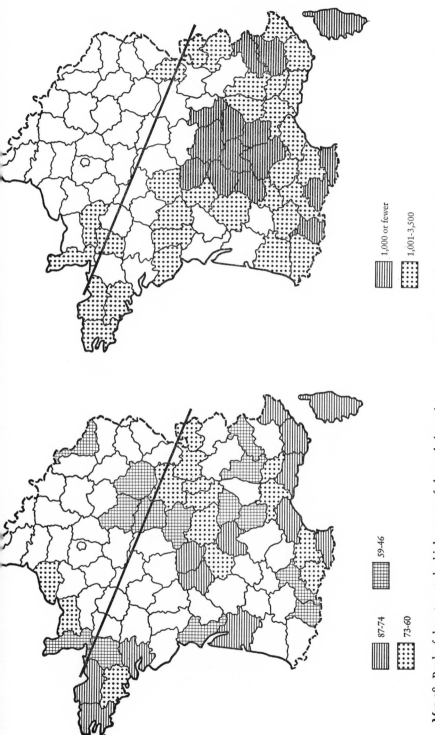

Map 18. Rank of departments by highest rate of electoral abstentions, 1876–1914. SOURCE: Same as Map 16, p. 72.

87-74

73-60

59-46

Map 19. Number of velocipedes (both 2- and 3-wheeled cycles), 1899. SOURCE: 1899 tax rolls, *Annuaire statistique de la France* (Paris, 1900). NOTE: By comparison, 16 of the departments north of the line had more than 5,000 vehicles, and in 6 of these the number surpassed 10,000.

1,000 or fewer

1,001-3,500

were being cleared and plowed: as the term has it, cultivated. In 1860 a Savoy peasant was quite certain that his local squire would win in the elections; for after all, "the mayor thinks so, the priest thinks so, everyone thinks so." Personal relations and local orientation were still dominant. But the peasant added in passing, "I've heard say in the market," and what he heard there would in due course reveal unsuspected alternatives.* By 1869 the sub-prefect of Saint-Dié was claiming that political issues had brought politicization and a new spirit of criticism to an area where political ignorance and indifference had once reigned. Political agents soon ranged the countryside. Their rival arguments and their political meetings (well attended as long as there were few other sources of entertainment) imparted a new terminology and new interests. Officials mocked the "banal, vulgar language" and the "democratic optimism" addressed to the *gens du peuple*. But it was not in sophisticated terms that one would wake them up.[78]

Pierre Barral has remarked that the Republic won peasant support in the 1870's on a purely political level, with no reference to socioeconomic measures or state aid, concerns that developed only in the (later) 1880's. This makes good sense, especially in those parts where the relationship between politics and the market was late to be appreciated, so that political awareness developed first. The precipitation of political activity and the frequent change that marked the 1870's made political subjects more intriguing and more disquieting too. At fairs and markets now, in electoral periods, there was more talk of politics than of business. And politics, since 1877 at least, had made their official appearance in the village, where, thenceforth, the mayor was no longer appointed from above but elected by the municipal council, themselves elected by all males over twenty-one. For Daniel Halévy, this *révolution des mairies*, affecting the very fabric of society, was a far more important event than the Revolutions of 1830 and 1848, which affected only the state. For contemporary observers, too, the result was not in doubt, especially when this measure was coupled with the decision that senators would be elected in an assembly where delegates of rural communes were overwhelmingly preponderant. "C'est introduire la politique au village," exulted Gambetta. And indeed, as Doctor Francus wrote in 1879: "Politics has been everywhere for the last few years."[79] By the 1880's the polarization of political issues was training "apprentice citizens" to new awareness and independence.[80]

Even in remote places modern competitive politics replaced the tensions and alignments of the traditional world. Few people were indifferent today, reported a police superintendent in Gers in 1888. "All pay attention to politics,

---

* *Courrier des Alpes*, December 7, 1860, quoted in Jacques Lovie, *La Savoie*, p. 370. This is the significance of the electoral "consultations" that Daniel Halévy has dismissed as irrelevant (*Décadence de la liberté*, Paris, 1931, p. 21). Perhaps—but each was one more experience, familiarizing people with things that had indeed been irrelevant to them for a long time.

more or less, talk about current events, analyze, discuss them." The Puy-de-Dôme reports reflect this aroused interest by the 1890's. Peasants realized that laws and national politics affected them; they talked about and called for laws on taxes, credit, protection, and health insurance, and the authorities noted the novelty. In remote Ariège the tone of the official reports changed as local politics gave way to the politics of national parties. The character of the issues discussed had become "modern" and the department "civilized."[81]

A work devoted to Aulus-les-Bains, close to the Spanish border, reflects in its second and third editions the change that took place there between 1873 and 1884. The second edition described the local people as caring only for local issues and utterly indifferent to national politics. The right to vote was seen as drudgery with no meaning or profit. Official lists of the votes cast were regularly filled in with imaginary figures that bothered nobody. This, said the writer, Adolphe d'Assier, was the routine practice in all the parishes of the upper valleys, and in a great many others besides. By 1884 d'Assier had to correct himself: voting was taken as seriously at Aulus as it was everywhere else. Left to themselves, the men of the older generation would be as skeptical and as indifferent as they had been in the past. But the young men and the village artisans were keen and full of zeal on election day. This made the elders think, and prompted them to vote as well.[82]

By the turn of the century, the force of inertia that had made for indifference earlier now made for familiarity, however vague. Most Frenchmen had grown to manhood under the new system and were little inclined to question it in a fundamental way. They had learned to combine modern politics and local tradition, political campaigns and traditional farandoles.* They stepped into a world whose social mechanisms were alien to them, whose political and economic workings they understood only imperfectly or not at all. They were not clear on how economics, politics, law, and science worked, but they knew they were affected by them. Their ever-increasing, ever-more-significant numbers created a public for the miracle-working panaceas of isms that traded on ignorance and anxiety—Boulangism, anti-Semitism, nationalism, Socialism, too—before further integration and adjustment could take place. Even aggressions shifted from the village society where they had been worked out to a wider context. We know by now that political claims that seem to chal-

---

* Thus, around 1880 in the Bonapartist Charentes the ogres invoked to scare children turned into Gambetta, pronounced Grand-Beitâ, while Republicans spoke of their opponents as Bounat-trapistes—partisans of *Poléyon Boune-Attrape, neveur à son onc'*. (Raymond Doussinet, *Le Paysan santongeais*, p. 130, and *Les Travaux et les jeux*, p. 421.) In the same period, the traditional Provençal ritual known as "giving the feet" (*douna di cambo*), when an infant was allowed to take his first steps in church, preferably at the moment of the elevation of the host, was shifted to a Republican context. At Arles, around 1885, toddlers would take their first steps in the vestibule of the city hall, under the benign gaze of a bust of Marianne. Similar substitutes seem to appear about the same time in the surrounding countryside. (Fernand Benoît, *La Provence*, p. 139.)

lenge a society actually help integrate the claimants into the society they purport to fight.* The near-insurgency that stirred the Midi in 1907 showed an immense advance of political sophistication from the days of the Second of December, when the peasant prisoner could only mutter in his defense, "I'm from Poujols."

The southern vintners did not rebel blindly, but in support of a well-understood interest. Their leader was a local man and not a burgher, but he was also a product of the country schools. The rebels conducted a remarkably efficient and sophisticated campaign, which included moving large numbers of demonstrators about by special trains that the railway companies put on at their behest, enlisting the cooperation of municipal authorities over a wide area, and organizing a tax strike directed against the national government.[83] Particularism and historical references (these last facilitated more by history taught in school than by folk memory) were incidental to the modern project of bringing political and economic pressure to bear on the government of the day. It does not matter that the project failed. What matters is that those who undertook it saw a direct relationship between their problems and the total society, and sought to act in terms of this new perception. They made political choices, determined their particular ends and how to employ their resources, and mobilized to achieve their goals. They had passed from the realm of local consensus to that of national contention and debate. Their collectivity no longer ended at the borders of a small pays: it was recognized as part of the larger one.

Political dispute, even rebellion, on the national level played its part in diminishing the significance of local solidarities, suggesting new rival ones, like the new-fangled idea of class. At mid-century, local solidarity had reigned supreme. By the end of the century it had lost its exclusive relevance. The autarkies characterizing most of the nineteenth century were breaking down. Great local questions no longer found their origin or solution in the village, but had to be resolved outside and far from it. The peasantry gradually awakened to urban (that is, general) ideas, abstract (that is, not local) concerns.[84]

Consciousness of "social" or "economic" conflicts helped to advance national unity, partly because it reflected the disintegration of traditional homogeneity and consensus, and the permeation of ideologies imported from outside; partly because it spurred the process of disintegration and looked for its resolution on a much broader stage. The doctrines of rebelliousness and of social war that play such a great role in modern politics could not have gained a hold where and while the social structure continued to be considered absolute

---

* On this point, see Remy Leveau, "Le Syndicat de Chartres (1885–1914)," *Mouvement social*, 1969, p. 63. This peasant union set forth as its aim: "changer l'âme villageoise et débarasser les paysans traditionnels de tous les éléments irrationnels de leur comportement pour mieux les adapter à leur travail et à leur rôle dans la société française."

and immutable. In a society where no break exists between the group and the individual, the existing social order is the only conceivable order. The individual cannot oppose it; he can only transgress. Of course, there had been insurgency and there had been rebellion in the past: sporadic, spontaneous, and explosive, aiming to shake a fist at fate, not change it. This was no basis for politics, which calls for analysis and debate about choice. Only when and as this seemingly monolithic traditional society began to disintegrate could individuals begin to see themselves as separate or separable from the group.

Public sensitivity grew as the standard of living climbed. In a world where riches and poverty had seemed prescribed by a predetermined and unalterable order, the chief question for most had been to survive, and economic injustice in the modern sense did not affect the collective consciousness. Once elementary needs began to be satisfied, there was time to lay claim to more: better conditions of work, better conditions in general. Time, above all, to consider possibilities hitherto unsuspected, which towns, schooling, and, yes, political parties were beginning to suggest. Ideas that had invaded the towns long before now implanted new claims among the rural masses. And politics were there to spur them and to provide them an ideological garb. Doctrines found currency that taught that destiny is only a concept and society another, both of them open to question, challenge, and eventual change. And with this lesson learned, the questioning, challenging, and changing that seem so much a part of modern politics began their work in a countryside hitherto immune.

Chapter Sixteen

MIGRATION: AN INDUSTRY OF THE POOR

Partir c'est mourir un peu.—EDMOND HARAUCOURT

IT WAS AN obscure French writer of the late nineteenth century who said that to go away is to die a little. For many in France, staying put would have been more likely to threaten their lives: leaving home was the price paid for survival. In those parts difficult of access, where roads were scarce and railroads late in coming, the only easy export was men. The poor sought out the richer regions, the mountaineers went down into the plains.* Their earnings supplemented scarce resources, their absence eased the pressure of a population too numerous for the land to feed. Where the pattern of temporary and seasonal migration in the 100 years or so from the late seventeenth century on has been studied, for instance, in Auvergne, we find an expectably close relationship between misery and the search for resources, between the high price of bread and the number of passports delivered in a given year. Similarly, in the Morvan it was the pressure of need, the endless search for a bit of cash to make ends meet, to pay an outstanding debt, to buy a tempting field, to re-roof a house or build one, that drove peasants out as carters, herdsmen, harvesters, thatchers, and domestics, going away from home because that was the only way to keep the home going.[1]

In the high Alps winter blockaded families for six months a year. To the end of the nineteenth century, most men, women, children, and beasts had had to live that half year out crowded together in the stable: table, benches, coal stove, perhaps three or four beds with two or three persons sharing each; between the beds goats and sheep; calves in the middle; and at the back the horses, cows, and oxen. Pigs were relegated to the corner closest to the door and farthest from the beds. As winter drew on, the air grew more noisome and garbage turned to manure underfoot. If the family also went in for trading,

* But there were exceptions. Unlike the Alps, for example, the Jura had almost no history of temporary migration, because the Jurassiens had small family and artisanal industries—a more difficult solution, perhaps, than going away, but one that forestalled the need to leave home.

selling wine or some groceries, the clients coming in and staying to exchange a few words added to the overcrowding, and also used up the scarce air. In such conditions, one person less to breathe the air, take up bed space, or consume scarce food made a contribution to the family's wellbeing even if the migrant brought back no cash at all.[2]

In earlier centuries, population had been limited by plague and famine. To the extent that these were mastered, idle hands survived to find employment only at times when the demand for labor called on every member of the community—sowing, haying, harvest. To make a living, they had to go away, even more than in the past. They had done so from time immemorial. Gangs of harvesters had regularly left areas where crops ripened late to gather other people's, before returning home to work on their own fields. Vintners and vineyard workers had sought employment away from home in the middle of summer and sometimes in winter, to raise some cash with which to pay their taxes and their debts. Cities like Arles sent out annual couriers to recruit the labor for the coming crop. The numbers involved were large. The Agricultural Survey of 1852 found nearly 900,000 seasonal workers mobilized for harvesting alone.[3]

Such migrations often followed traditional routes based on mutual need. The southern Limousin long saw a "natural" migration from Corrèze to the moors of Millevaches, from the Ségala of Rouergue to the Margeride, and from the Causse valleys to the Causse plateaus, as men in need of work trekked to areas that lacked the hands to harvest the rye crop with a sickle. These movements died out in the last third of the nineteenth century as the poverty (of men and of labor) that had triggered them was reduced. Similar migrations continued further to the north in the Upper Limousin, which was still poorer, to the eve of the First World War. On the other hand, haymaking gangs went on serving Upper Cantal and the Mézenc area, because farms there were prosperous and able to pay higher salaries.[4]

Other periodic migrations put to use locally developed specialties or skills. In Franche-Comté, where sawyers and woodcutters came from Cantal and Puy-de-Dôme, the long saw was "the banner of Auvergne."[5] The poor Cantal (which supplied important numbers of workers for the hardest and worst-paid urban jobs) had a century-long tradition of sending the men of many villages into Castile as bakers, clothiers, and ironsmiths.* And all over France,

* One effect of these border crossings was to establish remarkably close relations between southern Auvergne and Spain. Educational surveys show that the people of Cantal overwhelmingly favored having Spanish taught as the required foreign language in the schools, and many Spanish children were sent to the Cantal schools to learn French. By the middle of the nineteenth century there was not one commune in the arrondissement of Aurillac that did not have a family in Spain. Indeed, in 1845 the Aurillac municipal council went so far as to set up a chair of Spanish. Similarly, reports from Mauriac show that hundreds of residents spent a great part of the year in Spain or had to travel there on business several times a year. (See Archives Départementales, Cantal, IT 442 [1893; educational surveys], 99 M1 [Aurillac, Mauriac, Murat, St.-Flour, *passim*, 1808–

the little gangs of chimney sweeps and beggar-children were known to be coming from Savoy. In 1628, when Cardinal Richelieu built the great dike blockading La Rochelle, he called on good Catholics to help him. Among those who responded were men of the Marche—now roughly the department of Creuse. They found that they made some money at it, starting a tradition of periodic migration by men of the region to sell their skill in towns as construction workers.[6]

Peddling and trading had long been important occupations in some poor areas, but these activities sprouted in many parts with the new availability of certain goods and of roads between manufacturing towns and isolated hamlets. Some peddlers, like those who came out of the bocage of Normandy—the end of the world as many called this roughest, poorest, rainiest area in southern Manche and western Calvados—sold goods produced by their own rural industries: ironworking, cooperage, fabrics, paper. Others jobbed horses, especially at Breton fairs, specializing in buying and selling sick, worn, sorry nags good only for the glue factory. But most of the men who hit the roads were simply hawkers, selling trinkets and tawdry, spectacles, pins and needles, thread, vanilla, devotional objects, scythes and grindstones; whatever the market and their backs would bear.*

All migrants timed their departures with the seasons. Most left during the winter when work was slow at home. Some went out in the spring and summer because the going was better on difficult country roads or because, as in the case of construction workers, the job prospects were brighter. But migration was not haphazard. The process was dominated less by private enterprise than by the family's common interest in finding additional resources. In the Alps girls migrated from those areas where some winter labor was possible for men, and men from those areas where long, rigorous winters prevented any work except the indoor jobs that could be done by women.[7]

Local economic changes forced certain populations with no habit of migration to begin the practice. When, in the 1840's, the local industries of Ariège (mines, ironworks, charcoal burning) suffered in the general economic crisis, the peasants had no option but to fan out. Most of them begged; some worked,

---

46; "Notice sur les émigrations . . . du département du Cantal," n.d., 1812?]; and Mazières, 1: 127. See also AD, Cantal IT 754 [156] of Aug. 1870, and IT 772; and M. Trillat, "L'Emigration de la Haute-Auvergne en Espagne, du XVIIIe au XXe siècle," *Revue de la Haute-Auvergne*, 1955, pp. 257–94.)

*Placide Rambaud, *Economie et sociologie de la montagne*, p. 196, gives the contents of a peddler's pack in 1841: 507 dozen spools of thread; 24 lengths of cotton; 3 dozen combs; 3,000 needles; 9,800 pins; 4 dozen pencils; 27 gross (3,888) buttons; 18 snuffboxes; 3 dozen thimbles; 3 boxes "Limoges"; 4 dozen pens; 200 quills; 2 dozen scissors; ½ dozen each cakes of soap, knives, notebooks, suspenders, and hooks and eyes. There could have been little profit after paying for the stock, invoiced at 294.42 francs. But there was the pride of handling cash and being left with some, the benefit of conserving home resources, and the new ideas, objects, techniques, and above all tales brought back from faraway places. For details on peddling in general, see Marcel Gautier, *Chemins et véhicules*, pp. 47–50; R. Musset, "Les Genres de vie anciens," pp. 5–7; and the articles of Abel Chatelain.

some traded. In any case, the seasonal exodus became part of the annual rhythm. Later, in the 1860's, when new roads permitted the use of carts, wagons, and eventually coaches, opening the mountains to travelers, the people of the lower valleys took to hawking, both to their neighbors and farther afield. The interesting thing is that as the area emptied and such enterprises (as well as permanent emigration) drew off the surplus population, temporary migration fell off, to disappear entirely in most places between the 1880's and 1914. Too many hands had driven potential labor away. Too few hands had raised agricultural wages for those who remained. The process of demographic decompression helped those who stayed behind; but so did modernization. The roads that made the hawker's enterprise possible also removed the need for it. On the Oisans plateau, in Dauphiné, where poverty and isolation drove one family head in three to go peddling around 1880, roads and prosperity had by 1911 cut the figure down to one in 18. By 1921 only one in 37 still hoisted the seasonal pack.[8]

It is important to note that traditional seasonal migration made little contribution to cultural change. Moving, as a rule, along traditional routes, often involving gangs or groups from the same village, these migrations did not break up the solidarity of the village but on the contrary reinforced it, staving off a deterioration that might otherwise have come sooner. Such passages from stability to movement then back to a new stability suggest that the crux of traditional society is not immobility but mobility of an impenetrable sort. However far the masons of Creuse, the harvesters of Tarn, the lumbermen of the Livradois, or the peddlers of Savoy and the Pyrenees traveled, mentally they scarcely left home.

Much rural migration was to rural regions: a circuit of backward men and women visiting backward regions in which each side preserved its integrity. The more so since most migrant labor gangs camped together, with women sometimes brought along to do the cooking, and with a minimal desire or need to share the ways or learn the speech of a different *pays*.[9] The cultural wall would be breached to some extent where seasonal migrants were exposed to a higher degree of "civilization": not just to the societies of regions similar to theirs, but to the temptations of an urban world, alien and superior. Yet, even then, migrating gangs kept up a reasonably efficient insulation. Part-time farmers with wife, mother, and family at home, their ambitions differed from those of city workers: their chief aim was to preserve or increase the family holding and to be treated with the respect and deference to which their role as the family breadwinner entitled them.[10] Cultural integration on such divergent terms was hardly possible.

All sources show the masons, stonecutters, and tilesetters from Marche or Creuse keeping to themselves in Paris, lodged in dormitories or living in bare, furnished rooms rented by one of them or provided by the contractor. The contractor or a wife of a member of the gang looked after food and laundry.

The very numbers involved encouraged the maintenance of traditional solidarities. In many communes almost all able-bodied males went off for the working season, and carried most of the group's normal constraints with them.[11] Reading the memoirs of Martin Nadaud, one wonders what impact Paris could have on such men. They marched down in their seasonal thousands, camped in quarters of their own, passed from there to the work site and back twice a day in their great bands, talking in their own speech, strangers in a strange land.

A mid-century book describing Paris workers marvels how migrant masons (about half of the capital's building workers) remained completely unaffected by the environment. Indifferent to what went on around them, they persisted in taking nothing, learning nothing that Paris offered them: "impossible to break down [their] apathy."[12] Alain Corbin has found things little changed 20 years later, at the fall of the Empire. In his view, the Limousin migrants' poor integration into the urban milieu accounted for their failure to share in the popular hostility to the regime rising among urban groups in 1868 and 1869. As late as the eve of the First World War, this same particularism was still exhibited by such migrant workers as the glaziers from the Val Soana in Savoy, who lived all together in "tight and homogeneous" communities, speaking a special jargon that not even Savoyards could understand. Such "tight homogeneous" communities resulted in Parisian ghettos of immigrants from certain regions: Auvergnats clustered around the Rue de la Roquette in the eleventh arrondissement, Bretons around the west-country railway terminal at Montparnasse in the fourteenth and fifteenth arrondissements, Alsatians around La Villette to the northeast, in the nineteenth arrondissement. Even in isolated outposts like Jean Ajalbert's father's farm in Levallois-Perret at the gates of Paris, one heard mostly the patois of Cantal, "for my parents had come straight from the mountains with cowhands and servants from the same villages."[13]

Though people such as these came to the city for months or even years, their eyes remained fixed on home society. Their work did not insert them into the urban realm that permitted them to realize their aims, but screwed them more firmly into the limited world of the parish, family, and culture of their birth.[14] We shall shortly see that their imperviousness was relative, and that even though their eyes were focused on home, such migrants could not help acting as carriers of modernization. Temporary migrations do, as we have said, maintain traditional societies by furnishing resources that enable them to resist the crises of rural life; they also pave the way for a later exodus and later changes. The road was not just a facility for going and returning; it was also an opportunity to compare conditions and modes of life. It affected the peasants who set out on it, getting them used to strange places, showing them the way, permitting alien notions and a sense of different prospects to germinate in them or in those listening to the tales they told.

This kind of effect can most easily be noted in looking at a type of migrant who lacked the support of a surrounding group: the wet nurses of Yonne and Nièvre. Wet nurses had been going from the Morvan to Paris at least since the late eighteenth century: milch cows as they were called in Nivernais. One of them nursed Napoleon's heir, the *roi de Rome*; others, the sons and grand-sons of Louis Philippe. But comparatively few undertook the difficult trip until the railway, which at the same time ruined the region's traditional log-floating industry, brought easy access to Paris. As lumbering, which had been the Morvan's chief source of revenue, declined in the 1840's and men began to seek work on Paris wharves or building projects every spring, nursing be-came a large-scale local industry. What had been the exceptional indulgence of rich or ailing city folk began to be commonplace in bourgeois families, and to be used sometimes even by working-class couples when the woman had to provide a second income; and the demand was rising. On the eve of 1848 the third verse of Pierre Dupont's popular "Chant des ouvriers" was devoted to the women who hired out their breasts to strangers' offspring. By 1853 the sub-prefect of Avallon reported that the revenues from wet-nursing were spreading a certain comfort in areas where poverty had always been the norm; after three *nourritures* a woman had the wherewithal to build a house. In cer-tain districts two of every three nursing mothers left for Paris; most of the others took city babies into their homes.[15]

Many Morvandaises became wet nurses simply to conform, or under the pressure of husbands or family. One young woman actually committed sui-cide when her milk dried up and she was unable to contribute her share to the family's revenue. By the middle 1860's a doctor denounced this most important of Morvan industries for the deadliness of its effects on babies. Some saw other no less troubling effects. The women, complained a government official, re-turned from Paris with disturbing ideas of unwonted luxury. They had got used to comfort: no more buckwheat porridge, no more boiled potatoes, no more thatched roofs.[16] New buildings blossomed in remote areas, with win-dows, several rooms, and the furniture to fill them—*maisons de lait*. Fresher bread was eaten; pork became a daily staple; "meat," i.e., beef, once quite un-known, entered the diet, and so did little drinks of great sophistication, such as one had tasted in the wine shops of Paris.[17] In Brittany, too, in the 1890's we hear that half the women in some parishes left for one, two, or three years, returned with new tastes, denounced their traditional condition as bondage and were bent only on bearing a child so they could leave again. Worse still, their stories sparked such dissatisfaction among the local young that they too thought only of getting away.*

* Abbé Elie Gautier, *L'Emigration bretonne*, p. 58; Georges Rocal, *Croquants du Périgord*, pp. 208, 303. Périgourdine wet nurses could make good money in town: 20 francs a month in 1884, 25 in 1888, plus a weaning gift. Indeed, we are told that around 1900 a father rejoiced if his unwed daughter bore a child: "Me val autan que ma vaco!"

If dissatisfaction rose rather than abated, it was because exposure to a different life created expectations that could not be fulfilled outside the towns; but also because there was now an avenue of escape that had not existed before. The nursing industry would never have developed without the railways. And railways stood at the core of the increase in migration, just as they did in so much else.

When the fourteen-year-old Martin Nadaud, wearing his homespun suit, went off to Paris in March 1830, the wailing of his womenfolk could not have been more piteous if they had buried him. This was not surprising. Three other youths who left the village at the same time as he were soon to die. The something over 200 miles from Creuse to Paris took four days, three of them on foot, the fourth in a bad, expensive coach from Orléans. Nadaud speaks of a golden age beginning in 1856, when a railway station at La Souterraine allowed his countrymen to make the trip in comfort. In the new conditions, more men could go to work and more survive. The enterprise seemed less fearful.[18] The distant trip that had put off so many became a temptation difficult to resist. The postal service made communications easier. The letters the postmen carried suggested the possibility of leaving to those who had not yet taken the plunge. The railroad line, complained a politician, became a magnet attracting the filings of humanity.[19]

New rail facilities greatly increased the seasonal migrations from certain poor areas like the Oisans and Côtes-du-Nord, which seem to have reached their peak in the 1880's and 1890's.[20] With the coming of a rail line to Rodez in 1860, increasing numbers of migrants streamed out of the once-isolated parts of Rouergue that had seen their first migrants depart only in the 1840's. War and the Commune stemmed the flow, but only temporarily. Thus in the 20 years after 1890 about two-thirds of the young men of Saint-Chély (Aveyron) were consistently to be found in Paris; and in 1908 half of the conscripts of the district of Espalion reported to the draft board in Paris. Railways eased and encouraged the great migrations of the 1880's out of the southwest and west hard-hit by the Phylloxera, then in due course the immigration into these same regions (Poitou, Saintonge, later the middle Garonne valley) of westerners from poor, overpopulated Brittany and Vendée, who turned the abandoned vineyards into farm and pasture.[21]

Rails also began to change the nature of migration in a deeper way. They struck hard at such subsidiary occupations as peddling, but even more so at the local manufacturing of the things peddlers peddled. Once nails no longer came specifically from Forez or from the Pyrenees, once spectacles could be obtained easily outside the Jura, a trader's local base became irrelevant. The sabotiers in Brittany and elsewhere no longer needed to migrate from one copse to another for raw material that the railroads now brought to them, or to wander about selling products that distributors now collected from them. The spread of shops in market towns and bourgs meant less trade for hawkers, who gradually gave up their accustomed ways and settled down, either returning to the land as full-time farmers or setting up a new home with a store and perhaps a carriage to make country rounds within a small area. Meanwhile, many of the men who had once migrated seasonally began to settle in the cities where they worked, especially in the building trades. The introduction of new equipment under the Second Empire—lights that permitted working after dark, steam engines that pumped out flooded ground more quickly, waterproof canvas that sheltered workers and scaffolding—made building feasible through most of the winter, shortened the period of unemployment when weather had sent men home from work, and broke the rhythm of seasonal migrations. Workers now stayed longer on the job and might not return home for years at a time.[22]

By 1885 women were accompanying their husbands to the city. By the turn of the century half the married couples in the godforsaken northeastern parts of Aveyron were leaving for Paris; by 1911 four of every five newly married couples were fleeing Saint-Chély. As a case in point, Emile Guillaumin traces the fate of five peasants found hoeing a field of beets on a hot summer day of 1902, not far from Moulins. By 1910 one had become a janitor, one worked for a concession company at Vichy, another had a job in a furniture factory, and a fourth had become a footman; only the fifth was left to work the land. At Saint-Alban, in Loire, an old woman later remembered that "around 1900 all the young people went off, they went off to town." Migration had gradually been turning into emigration. Where once migration had been undertaken to perpetuate the peasant community, it was now becoming an end in itself: an opportunity to break with the community, its ways, its heavy pressures, to free oneself from the charges and restrictions of the family, and also from the slavery of agricultural labor.[23]

Migration, seasonal or otherwise, had always incorporated an element of adventure. To leave home was an anxious act, but also an eventful enterprise and a release. A search for work, for supplementary income, for profitable activity when home offered none, provided socially acceptable explanations for motives more difficult to express. Of course, there was higher pay to be earned in town. One could make money fast, so it was said. But there was also escape from the conditions of life in the country. Life in the towns was easier and more pleasant; work was not so hard and working hours lighter; medical aid, charity, organized help in need were easier to obtain. Above all, towns were fun. In the village "amusements were few and church services numerous"; in town there were "coarse, dissolute delights," and furthermore "in the crowd, no one knows you." One did not need to seek debauchery in order to appreciate a certain anonymity, an easier access to entertainment, the readier availability of company. For Breton peasants Paris was like the enchanted fairy-tale city of Ys. "Since Ys sank down beneath the sea, there is no town to match Paris" went the common saying.[24]

With the continuous bustle of its thoroughfares, its streetlights, shops, cheap shows, and easy women, the town was an unending fair or feast. "Attracted by city splendors like the moth by light," wrote Jules Méline in an apt simile (for light was important, even crucial, in somber villages condemned to long dark nights), the peasants dream of "magnificent theaters, sparkling cafés, brilliant festivals, luxury, pleasures," and reject their drab cottages. Life was indeed drab in the cottages, as we have seen. For all the horrors of life in the industrial cities, the peasants voted for the city with their feet. It offered more (and more constant) diversions than home ever did, and better means to take advantage of them. A school inspector, attempting to refute accusations that education taught children to flee the country for the town (of course it did!), advanced his own list of determining factors: a person got regular pay, higher of course but above all without unemployment; dressed like ladies and gentlemen; could see far more people and more interesting things; exerted less effort or at least was better rewarded; and did not have to bear with the rain, wind, sun, and cold. And all this only a few hours away![25]

We must not lose sight of the fact that urban unemployment, especially in the latter part of the century, seemed far less drastic than the seasonal unemployment of country life. Moreover, the urban worker worked shorter hours and received regular pay regardless of the weather. Above all, if he could secure the sort of permanent job that carried a pension at the end, the constant nightmare of insecurity would be laid to rest.

It was very tempting. The young and the women felt the temptation most. Jules Vallès mentioned that peasant lads objected less to military service than the city boys because the barracks were in the towns. And military service, as we shall shortly see, was a big recruiter for the urban life. As for the women, all witnesses emphasized their role in persuading men to abandon land and village, a life that so far as they were concerned added up to fear, insecurity boredom, and overwork. If the young men could not be persuaded, the girls went alone. In one Eure village in 1900, 42 of 100 sons of agricultural workers stayed on the land, against only 15 of 100 girls.[26]

Finally, to dwell in a town was to rise in the world. The peasant felt inferior because he was a peasant, bound to a condition he despised. In scorning his own station, he shared the scorn of the burghers, whom he both resented and envied for having made good their escape from the land. And as more and more people left, the self-esteem of those who stayed behind dropped still further. Many would have agreed with the Socialist leader who told the Party Congress of 1909 that "those who stay on the farm are poor clods incapable of any intellectual experience, soaked in ignorance and alcohol, condemned to shuttle from church to tavern, and from tavern to church." Parents were proud to see their children "well-dressed, moving in town society, *fashionable*," and seized on opportunities that would permit promotion of this sort. In 1900 a student of the "rural exodus" placed "the parents' vanity" first among the

factors that encouraged this exodus. The others, in order, were the school certificate, which facilitated escape; military service, which cut youths loose from
their home surroundings and exposed them to the facilities of the urban life;
the scorn of farming, as both an unprestigious and an unrewarding occupation; the fear of boredom; the attraction of unknown pleasures; the hope of
an easy life and of ready fortune; and, finally, the contagious example of
others, the more powerful since transport permitted their return to show off
their new clothes, wealth, and status, and leave the impression that city people
seldom if ever did a stroke of work.[27]

However false such images might have been, the envy felt by stay-at-homes
and the "vanity" of parents who encouraged their children to leave the land
were nevertheless objective estimates of the situation. And the very image that
country people formed of the city now—a place of greater job and personal
security, of comfort, leisure, and entertainment, of schooling and welfare—
reflected a revised scale of values and a new sense of alternatives.

Yet if the motives for emigration were increasingly admitted to be personal,
its effects were and continued to be social. One of the first effects to be noted
was the impact of migration on rates of pay. As workers gradually left regions
where pay was low, depleting the labor supply, the competition for hands
pushed wages up. Officials and employers showed great concern at the "ex-
orbitant pretensions" of the stay-at-homes as once densely populated areas began to thin out. The Agricultural Survey of 1866 produced a rich crop of grumbles about hands who cost more to hire, did less work, and were more demanding than in earlier times. But the most marked improvements took
place in the 1890's and after, when a shortage of labor and greater productivity,
coupled with the spread of acquired tastes, made for better pay, quarters, food,
and savings opportunities almost everywhere, especially in the regions that
had been and still were the most backward. Farmhands who had been accustomed to sleeping with the cattle began to get small rooms of their own.
Sharecroppers who had lived in hovels got larger, lighter, "modern" dwellings.[28] Domestics who had been forced to work in the fields on Sunday morn-
ings and get their church finery wet with dew, stipulated as a term of hire
that they would be free all day Sunday "to ramble, laugh, and drink" to their
heart's content.*

Emigration contributed to these advances in two ways: the first was the
decompression that it brought to the labor market, the second, which may have
counted more, was the ideas it put about. A landowner from Puy-de-Dôme

---

* Francis Le Bourhis, *Etude sur la culture*, p. 77. Still, one must be cautious about talk of improved conditions in official sources. In 1894, for example, the police superintendent of Brassac
forwarded a report to the prefect of Puy-de-Dôme describing the harvesters' diet: six meals a day,
plus two liters of wine or *piquette*, "which is not very good." A few days later the prefect put
this information into a report of his own designed to show how well agricultural workers were
doing, leaving out the last comment and not explaining that this was the special case of harvest
fare. (Archives Départementales, Puy-de-Dôme, M 04469, fall 1894.)

complained in 1866 that workers insisted on shorter hours (they now began at 5 A.M. instead of 4 and took a whole hour for lunch instead of half), demands he felt sure were inspired by the subversive principles that emigrants had brought back. As soon as a construction worker returned home, he "spread demoralization through the countryside." The emigrants were used to higher pay and different conditions. "Their presence manifests itself by immediately disturbing the local workingmen." A witness from Creuse agreed: "The insubordination of the workers grows on contact with the emigrants."[29] It was not that there had been no reasons for dissatisfaction, but that there had been no reasons to hope for a change. The laborer who came home in effect taught his fellows that things were different elsewhere, and that changes were not completely impossible.

Despite the emigrants' remarkable isolation from the urban environment that employed them, they nevertheless spread its germs among their fellows at home. An Auvergnat, writing on the eve of the Great War, noted how quickly migrants returned to local usages as soon as they were back home. Yet, though almost impervious to strange ideas, they brought different manners with them, "they became easier and more polite."[30] They sent back letters, tracts, and newspapers; they suggested new practices and tastes; they sent home parcels containing all sorts of curious sweets, spices, and fabrics; they came home for holidays and they retired there, bringing with them the notions and the fashions of the town. They were first to use dishes at the table, to show off a bicycle, to paint their houses or install lighting.* First also in many places to speak French, as part of their "city dress." We hear of them returning to the village, showing off their fashionable garb and describing the marvels of the city "with French words that they do not know too well."[31]

If they did not know them, at least their children would. Migration advanced literacy on two fronts: migrants found that reading, writing, and arithmetic were useful in their work and in keeping up links with the family by mail; and they wanted their children to learn what they themselves in many cases had only a shaky hold on. In 1881 it was noted that the Ambert district of Puy-de-Dôme, though ill-equipped with schools, turned out a singularly small number of illiterate conscripts because—said the school inspector—men who migrated appreciated the use of writing for their correspondence, and wanted their children to read and write better than they. But this was a detail. Instruction was a ticket of leave from the straitened village life and a pass to urban opportunities. As a school inspector from Murat (Cantal) explained: "Not only do the parents...want schooling for their children, but the children themselves seem to appreciate the practical advantages that may follow from what they learn at school." The fat basin of Brive apart, literacy rates in Cor-

---

* Yet did emigrants always bring new ideas, or only different ones? We are told that in Savoy men returned with books of magic like the *Petit* or *Grand Albert*, "which confused those with little learning" (Antoine Balleydier, *A propos d'un mal mystérieux à Morzine sous le Second Empire*, Chambéry, 1949, p. 9).

rèze were consistently highest where migrants were thickest on the rolls. And though in Haute-Vienne as a whole only one child in three was enrolled in school in 1872, "almost all the boys" attended in the district of Bellac, where immigration was a notable and continuing phenomenon.[32]

We can observe the impact of these attitudes on farming communities, in which farmers as a group had always been less literate than other rural categories (artisans, masons, tradesmen). In those regions of Haute-Vienne that had the highest rates of migration, there was the least difference in literacy between farmers and the other groups, because by the third quarter of the nineteenth century, the farmers too had cottoned on to the advantages of schooling. In other words, migrants spread literacy in concentric circles, first in their own families, then among their neighbors.[33]

Inevitably, literacy would in due course mean greater political awareness. I doubt that the migrant workers of the Limousin, Marche, and Savoy were very soon "proletarianized," as Abel Chatelain and other students of the subject have suggested. My argument is that the overwhelming majority of those who migrated remained peasants with peasants' values for most of the century, and that until the great explosion of change after 1880 what they introduced from town was little and easily assimilated. Nevertheless, as the authorities complained, they were carriers of urban ideas and urban notions of emancipation.[34]

Certainly the migrants were more politicized. When, in the elections of 1857, a Norman was put up as the government candidate at Guéret, Norman workers in Paris taunted their mates from Creuse because they could not find a candidate of their own. What Norman peasant still in Normandy would have even known about it? In 1870 remote villages in Cantal heard about Henri Rochefort, "defender of the people": "It is the emigrants coming home who report what they have heard said in the cities where they work." In Puy-de-Dôme in 1871 the new "Lyonnais" came back to teach their fellow villagers the politics that they had picked up in that rebellious town. Villages like Sornac (Creuse) and Saint-Sétiers (Corrèze) sent hansom cabdrivers to Paris, who returned "dressed like gents," dazzling their compatriots with their gift of gab, and preaching radical and socialist doctrines. In 1908 the Diocesan Congress of Aurillac charged that migrants who had lost their religious principles (and accounted for "almost all the civil burials in our parishes") were contaminating their fellows.[35]

The kind of employment matters here. Chimney sweeps had few opportunities to establish the sort of relationships that would alter their mentality. The porters and stevedores who worked in the markets, dockyards, or railway stations of Paris, the laborers who went to work in the southern vineyards, above all the petty civil servants, who however low their station were endowed with much prestige, were likely to return home with the radical and anticlerical ideas they had picked up in town, and to infect their village. We hear of libraries being set up in isolated villages of the Limousin or Savoy out of the books the emigrants sent back, playing their part in the advance of radicalism. The political complexion of a village could be changed by the votes and the influence of emigrants who returned to retire.[36] But there are more subtle subversions than those of politics. Changes in dress, manners, diet, the gradual rise in expectations (especially among women), the very breakdown of isolation, may well have counted more than radical politics. Nor, possibly, would politics have been much radicalized without them.

The increasing ease and practice of migration (and emigration) meant that strangers entered once insulated communities in such numbers as to affect their cohesion and their way of life. In the formerly homogeneous department of Hérault, for example, where in 1851 outsiders accounted for a mere half of 1 percent of the population, the percentage of foreigners rose to 2.46 by 1896, 3.5 by 1901, and 10.7 by 1921. In France as a whole, the percentage of the population born in one department and living in another, 11.3 in 1861 and 15 in 1881, climbed to 19.6 in 1901. By the end of the First World War one-quarter of the French people lived outside the department where they were born.[37] It would be interesting to focus more narrowly, and see how particular regions were affected by this. I have been forced to limit myself to a more general view. One thing is clear, however. The massive influx of "foreigners" into the cities shattered the hold of local speech and lore in the urban centers. Arnold Van Gennep has noted the disappearance of the local folklore of Passy, Montrouge, Montmartre, and other Parisian neighborhoods as alien "colonists" submerged the local populations.* Similar developments took place at Lille and in the industrial centers of the north. So, large-scale immigration into the cities and especially into Paris not only increased their sphere of influence throughout France; it also had a homogenizing effect on them.

The countryside held out longer than the cities. The impact of alien influences was less massive, the pace of change slower.† But there too "civilization," "luxury," and drink were making inroads—the deeper where migration and emigration contributed to the process, notably in the Massif Central, Côtes-du-Nord, Ariège, and parts of the southeast.[38] Familiarity with the urban economy eased the move away from local traditions of self-sufficiency and

---

* *Manuel de folklore français*, 1: 55. In 1864 school officials noted that La Villette was heavily populated by German workers from Alsace and other areas close to the Rhine who knew only a few words of French and whose children found it hard to get into school because they knew even fewer (*Instruction primaire*, 2: 220). One has to ask to what extent these workers and their children provided an inspiration and a recruiting ground for the Parisian anti-Semites of the 1880's and 1890's, for *les bouchers de La Villette* would be the storm troops of anti-Semitic violence into the twentieth century.

† Even slower, perhaps, than I wish to suggest. Consider this comment of Henri Bachelin's in 1919: "Il y a les gars qui reviennent du régiment avec des habitudes d'élégance et des besoins de comfort, mais cela leur passe vite. Il y a les filles qui, pour huit jours, rapportent de Paris, où elles sont femmes de chambre, du linge, des provisions et des nouvelles. Mais, dès qu'elles sont parties, on range le linge dans l'armoire . . . et l'on ne pense plus aux nouvelles." (*Le Village*, p. 4.)

barter. Lessened concern with sheer subsistence as job opportunities increased helped in the "dissolution of social bonds," encouraging "insubordination" to all authority, including that of the family elders. An increasing unwillingness to bow to natural contingencies expressed itself, among other things, in the earlier practice of birth control. A growing belief in the possibility of social advancement spurred the development of personal ambition and a sort of individual enterprise subversive of old family and communal bonds. Literacy, together with access to books, newspapers, and other sources of information, forged a new attitude to politics, and this in turn cast up new leaders, different from and competing with those molded by the local hierarchy. None of this was entirely new, not even in isolated areas at mid-century. But only improved communications turned a tiny trickle into a mainstream. As Agulhon has put it in another context, the fundamental point is not the appearance of new ideas, but the appearance of conditions that made such ideas relevant.[39]

Chapter Seventeen

MIGRATION OF ANOTHER SORT: MILITARY SERVICE

Honneur! Honneur aux conscrios!
Honneur à notro patrio,
Accourons à sa voix chério
Servir notro payo!

———

Catineto ploures pos,
Toun galant partira pos.

—CONSCRIPT SONGS OF ARIÈGE

SYSTEMATIC CONSCRIPTION in France dates back to 1798. Its general lines for the first four score years were set under the Empire, when Napoleon introduced the draft lottery (*tirage au sort*) and defined the basis of exemption from service. Every canton of France was responsible for a certain number of recruits. The lots were drawn annually, and the youths with numbers higher than the required contingent were exempt. So were married men, priests, and those who could afford to pay for a substitute to serve in their stead. Once the law was set in motion, there ensued a great many religious vocations, and the rate of marriages among eighteen-year-olds increased considerably. A new job opportunity also appeared: hiring oneself out as substitute for those who could afford to pay the fluctuating price that would save them from hard and dangerous service.

In 1818 the recruiting policies of the nineteenth century were set by a new law, which bore the name of Louis XVIII's War Minister, Laurent Gouvion-Saint-Cyr.[1] In its essentials the new law did not differ from the earlier system, though it did free those who drew "a good number" or paid for a substitute of all liability from further calls to service, something that Napoleon had done when he ran short of men. The long term of duty (six years after 1818, eight years after 1824, seven years between 1855 and 1868, five years until 1889) meant that comparatively few men were inducted yearly: 10 percent or less of the age group subject to the draft. Of these, until the late 1850's, at least a quarter or more were substitutes—poor lads seeking a way to raise some money, or veterans who meant to re-enlist in any case and who, this way, made a profit on their decision.*

---

* In 1868 the draft (in imitation of some aspects of the Prussian system) was divided into two "lanes," one involving five years' active service followed by four in the reserve, the other involving service in the Garde Nationale Mobile, which made its brief historical bow in 1870–71. From 1872 to 1889 the military contingent was still divided in two: those who drew "un bon numéro" served for one year (in practice, six months); the rest served five years.

The finding of substitutes was a haphazard process until around 1820, when the agents of newly founded insurance companies made their appearance in the countryside. Then, in the 1830's, Louis Philippe's government encouraged the organization of "mutual" and "family" associations that would offer more solid guarantees against induction than the dubious promises of ad hoc merchants of men, whose enterprise was often rather fly-by-night. For something between 1,500 and 1,800 francs a "casualty" or "victim" of the draft (as company language had it) could buy his way out of service, and about 20,000 men a year seem to have done so, thereby setting a great deal of money into circulation.*

The investment made sense. Through most of the nineteenth century still, the peasant's basic capital and the major factor in his productivity was his working capacity and the number of hands at his disposal. A loss of hands could have serious repercussions on the fortunes of a family or parish, as can be seen at Plozévet (Finistère), where in 1860 the village mayor begged remission for a peasant's son, "for if he has to return to service ... his father will be forced to abandon his farm"; and where statistics of 1873 translate the loss of manpower during the war of 1870–71 into a shrinkage of the lands under cultivation. "The peasants accept the heaviest sacrifices to keep their sons," wrote the imperial prosecutor from Angers in 1866, "not out of affection for them, but because labor is scarce and expensive." It was to the farmer's benefit to buy off his son, but he grumbled and thought of the time when it had cost him only 1,000 francs, half as much as he had to pay now. In Vendée even hired hands preferred to go into debt rather than leave for seven years' military service, though it meant that their entire salary was given over to paying off the money raised to hire a substitute.[2]

Substitution was abolished on January 1, 1873, in the first military reform of the Third Republic, which also confirmed the five-year term of service. At the same time the government introduced a wealth of dispensations, mostly for the educated classes, ranging from outright exemptions to a "voluntary" tour of duty for one year on payment of a fee of 1,500 francs. By then, sections of public opinion favored universal service, partly because military discipline could be expected to reestablish respect for authority, partly because they saw in military service a means of making instruction general. Suggestive motives;

* According to Louis Peygnaud, the total yearly expense of securing substitutes came to over 70 million gold francs (*Le Bal des conscrits*, p. 149). The commutation rate varied widely from region to region. During the 1860's over 40 percent of the draftees in Eure, Lot-et-Garonne, and Hérault took this way out, against 8 percent in Alsace and Brittany and a mere 2 percent in Corsica (N. Sales, "Remplaçants, remplacés, marchands d'hommes et assurances pour le service militaire," unpublished manuscript, 2 vols., Paris, 1964, 1: 72–74; Sales, *Comparative Studies*, 1968, p. 263). But everywhere saving the young from the rigors of service was recognized as a meritorious act. Thus, a collection of edifying stories for the young, published during the July Monarchy, includes one in which a whole class contributes the money to buy a substitute for the man-servant employed at the school (cited by Marie-Thérèse Latzarus, *La Littérature enfantine en France dans la seconde moitié du XIXe siècle*, Paris, 1924, p. 70).

but they had to wait. Shorter and more general service, initially advocated by the Minister of War, General Boulanger, and by the radicals, was in the end voted as an anti-Boulangist measure, passed in the hope that it might cut some ground from under the dangerous General's feet. In 1889, at last, the term of service was reduced to three years, the 1,500-franc dispensation was abolished, and all who had been exempt before (notably, students, teachers, priests, seminarians, and the oldest sons of widows or of large families) were required to serve one year under the colors. The measure was popular.[3] This was the crucial point at which all Frenchmen who were physically fit began to see service under the national colors. In 1905 the term of service was made two years for all; in 1913 it went back to three again. But the institutionalized migration and kneading together embodied in universal military service had gone to work in the 1890's.

It is important to note that in its limited form conscription had little effect on the country mind.[4] Yet it had sufficient impact to color the peasants' reactions to national policy and international politics. The Crimean War in 1854, for instance, remained popular as long as it involved "no actual and direct sacrifice." The Italian War of 1859 was greeted with a plain lack of enthusiasm and an awareness that it might raise the cost of substitutes. The middle 1860's brought a "lively demand for peace and economy," especially since a cut in the village levies would lower the price of a discharge; whereas in 1867 news of a reduction in the official cost of a discharge (whose high price had been taken as a sign of preparation for war) brought calm to a countryside anxious about its pockets and its sons. A new army law began to be discussed in 1867. In the southwest, where "military spirit is so little developed," people did not like the uncertainty that would be introduced by the proposed changes (notably, a reserve period subject to recall). The standard term of service might be shorter, but people would not know when they might be called to serve for a longer time and, anyway, reported the imperial prosecutor in Rennes, "there won't be any more good numbers"—things would be the same for everyone.[5]

Nor did the upper classes like the idea "of seeing their sons called to serve side by side with peasants' sons." In the event, the two groups did not have to mingle. But we hear, and it is illuminating, that "of the different measures brought before the legislature, the military reform is the only one to have gone to the heart of the country; the masses pay little attention to the question of public liberties."[6] Perhaps rightly so; public liberties were scarcely likely to affect them. Nor as a matter of fact was conscription. At least, in their way of life. In any given year in the period between the wars of the late First Empire and 1870, one, two, three, or none of a commune's young would actually be conscripted. We shall soon see that few of those who went returned after their long term of service. And this was just as well, since conscription was seen not as a duty owed to some larger community or nation, but as a heavy tribute exacted by an oppressive and alien state.*

The most visible reactions to conscription lie in the continuing tale of draft evasion or desertion wherever and however it could be contrived. The record that Richard Cobb paints for the 1790's and that Ladurie's study confirms as true a generation later persisted under the Second Empire and the early Third Republic. The elementary schools of the 1830's, whose pupils still drilled to the drum as they had done a quarter century before, were suspect as recruiting grounds and avoided for that reason. Everywhere one turns, the evidence of a lack of appetite for soldiering is abundant. "Little inclination for military service" (Hérault, 1825). "Pronounced antipathy for military service" (Cantal, 1832). "Very reluctant to join the army; all farmers with any means buy a man to replace their sons" (Loiret, 1839). Basques tend to desert to Spain to escape military service, which they dislike, just as they deserted the imperial armies (Pyrenees, 1840). Great tendency to avoid service by self-mutilation, decamping, or attempted bribes (Ariège, 1856 and 1857). Little taste for military service and continued practice of self-mutilation to avoid it (Loir-et-Cher, 1859); same note a year later, insisting on the numerous self-mutilations at conscription time. Only those who are forced to will be soldiers—a trade held in very low regard (Eure-et-Loir, 1860). Military service is looked on as a tax exacted by the state, a sort of theft; it follows that the army would meet a poor reception, because it reminds them of conscription (Ille-et-Vilaine, 1860). Profound horror for military service (Seine-Inférieure, 1860). In Vendée "they were hard to budge before 1850, they hid or ran away. After 1850 they redeemed themselves."[7]

Stendhal had noted the anxiety and horrendous tales surrounding military service. Rumors said that no conscript survived more than four years. The regimental barracks took on the aspects of a Bluebeard's castle. Nearly two score years later, in 1869, Bruno's *Francinet* (one and a half million copies of which would be sold) held the avoidance of military service to be a natural desire, escape from service the reward of virtue.

Auvergne and the Pyrenees specialized in desertion. In 1844 an officer was shocked to hear "one of the richest and more civilized farmers" of Gévaudan boast that in 1813 he had deserted together with five other men: "What did the wrangles of the Emperor and the other rulers mean to us!" Such wild people, commented the officer, were so devoid of all honorable feeling that they "would not distinguish between compatriots and foreigners, and treated all of them as enemies." The judicial archives of the Pyrenees are full of proceed-

* In Emile Guillaumin's description of nineteenth-century Bourbonnais, the mother wails that she would rather see her sons dead than have them go off to be soldiers. "Anyway," comments the author, "in our countryside one did not have the least idea of the outside world; beyond the limits of the canton . . . there lay mysterious lands . . . full of dangers and peopled by barbarians" (*La Vie d'un simple*, p. 57).

ings and lawsuits against deserters, draft evaders, insubordinate recruits, crooks selling fake draft insurance, men known to have maimed themselves to avoid service, and frauds who tried to slip through by offering substitutes already found unfit for military service. In Savoy migration was a favorite way of seeking to escape the army. At the end of 1872, after the new five-year service law had passed, a third of the 50 young men who applied for passports belonged to the age group being called up. Among the youths of fifteen to twenty years, 95 future recruits had left officially, and many others had slipped away without any papers. In 1875 the village of Méry could present only one conscript out of the 18 on its list.[8]

In other words, the war of 1870 had changed very little. Traditionally, in one small Bourbonnais village near Lavoine, in Allier, "almost all boys at birth were declared as girls," and this subtle avoidance of conscription was still practiced in the 1870's.[9] Five years of service removed indispensable labor from farm and fields, raised local wages, delayed marriages, prevented the young from settling down. Military reports continued to reflect the countryside's antipathy. Detestation (Basque country, 1873) or at best indifference (Landes, 1874, Ille-et-Vilaine, 1876). No sense of the general weal (Haute-Garonne and Gers, 1876). Underdeveloped military spirit and frequent emigration to escape service (Haute-Garonne, 1877). Anxiety and effort to avoid military service (Sarthe, 1878). Official relief to see recruits go off without problems in a department where "recruiting has always been a little difficult" (Pyrénées-Orientales, 1879). There was no end to all the practices that had been used to escape conscription, Francis Pérot noted in his study of the folklore of Bourbonnais. For one, there was the renting of wedding rings of widows of irreproachable virtue, which were reputedly potent in securing a good draft number and which fetched rates that suggested both rarity and demand. In Brittany, too, conscription continued to be surrounded by rituals and sorcery designed to elicit a good number and to ensure escape from dreaded service.[10]

Popular lore absorbed conscription and incorporated it in its ways to such an extent that the cockades traditionally worn by conscripts, originally adopted to sport more visibly the number they had drawn, remained part of their paraphernalia even after the lottery had been abolished in 1889. Witches, saints, even miracle-working fountains were enlisted to protect the recruit. Masses were said; bones, rings, coins were sewn in his hat or uniform.* As late as 1913, when the two years of service were raised to three, the authorities feared that the response would be mass desertion. Nothing of the sort happened, but the anxiety and subsequent relief testified more to reflexes that several genera-

---

* Francis Pérot, *Folklore Bourbonnais*, p. 10; Jean Vartier, *Sabbat, juges et sorciers*, pp. 209–10. But note the shame of being rejected as physically unfit in a society where health and strength were essential. In Brittany the consequences were insults and difficulty in finding a wife. In Bourbonnais girls would not dance with a réformé or accept his attentions. (Paul Sébillot, *Coutumes populaires*, pp. 82–83; Joseph Voisin, "Entre Loire et Allier," p. 24.)

tions had conditioned than to the anti-military propaganda of the twentieth century.[11]

Anti-militarism is generally regarded as a creation of red propaganda after the turn of the century. It makes more sense to see that propaganda as a play on prejudices still very much alive in many minds.

Until 1889 the army was one of the countryman's bogeys, and soldiers were feared and suspected even in their own communities. Men who returned home had picked up alien ways and probably bad habits. "He went to the army a horse and came back a mule," they said. The nicknames by which the village knew its veterans revealed their oddity and identified them as different in kind: Carabineer, Swashbuckler, Swordsman, Military, Dragon, Moustache. To go asoldiering was humiliating, remembered an old man in Périgord. "Only the poor, the landless, and the roofless would do it."[12] And since so few went from any parish, their effects on the overpopulated communities of the nineteenth century were slight. The handful who chose to return were forced by community pressure to conform. Many had scarcely learned to speak the national language. Writers right through the 1870's remarked on the presence in Brittany of old soldiers—veterans of the revolutionary and imperial armies— who had never learned to speak French, or who unlearned it "out of respect for the prejudices that prevent its use."*

There was, in short, little sense of national identity to mitigate the hostility and fear most country people felt for troops. The record suggests that soldiers (except in garrison towns, where the middle classes appreciated their presence highly as a source of revenues) were treated like an army of occupation, with little or no sense that they represented any kind of common weal. "The troops have to be careful to avoid quarrels and trouble," warns an early report from Hérault: "*Even in cities* [my italics] garrisons are sometimes exposed to the provocations of inhabitants of all classes who show a decided malevolence for the military. Soldier and officer are more ill-regarded ... than in enemy country." Throughout the Landes, we hear in 1843, the natives viewed soldiers as "strangers whom they are forced to receive in their midst." Difficult relations (Rhône, 1859). We might meet some resistance (Allier, 1860). We expect help only if they gain from it (Côtes-du-Nord, 1860). Strong disillusion (Deux-

---

* A. M. Duchatellier, *De la condition du fermier*, pp. 6, 221; Archives de la Guerre, MR 1236 (1826); Louis Ogès and F. M. Déguignet, "Contes et légendes," p. 114. Stendhal, writing about the men around Vannes and Auray in 1838, remarked: "A peine les soldats qui ont servi 5 ans sont-ils de retour au pays, qu'ils oublient bien vite tout ce qu'ils ont appris au régiment et les cent ou deux cents mots de français qu'on leur avait mis dans la tête." Three-quarters of a century later, René Bazin voiced the same sentiments about the three-year men: "Eh bien! ramenez-les chez eux, les soldats d'hier: au bout d'un an, la terre les aura repris. Ils ne différeront pas, sauf peut-être au fond de leur cœur par la réminiscence malsaine des mauvais lieux et des propos de caserne, des anciens qui n'ont jamais quitté la commune.... Oublié le passé.... Les trois ans n'ont été qu'un épisode.... Rien ne subsiste ... pas même une curiosité." (*En Province*, p. 237.) I would argue that these lines, written before the Great War, ignored fundamental differences in the impact of the military experience.

Sèvres, 1862).[13] Dislike and scorn were mutual; soldiers and civilians regarded each other with an equal lack of sympathy and trust. The military archives of the Second Empire show numerous cases of soldiers attacked or stoned, of rocks thrown at detachments on the march, and of fights between soldiers and workingmen, even in very small urban centers.[14] Of course, violence was endemic, friction between local people and strangers natural, drunken squabbles fairly commonplace. Yet it is fair to assume that an unrepresentative army, almost a professional army in terms of the period of service, was conceived by ordinary people as the creature of others—the "thems"—and hence the more readily rejected.

In 1889 an English writer observed that the army had come to be recognized as national after 1870, and that soldiers and military service were now accepted, which was not the case before that date.[15] We have just seen that resistance to military service survived at least to the time when this remark was made. But it is likely that the war with Prussia, which mobilized unusually great numbers while focusing attention on their fate, a war also in which the connection between local and national interests became more evident to large numbers of people, marked the beginning of change. The old prejudices took their time to die, and the 1870's offer scattered instances of enduring antipathy.* But the role played by war in promoting national awareness was reinforced by educational propaganda, by developing trade and commercial ties, and finally by something approaching universal service. By the 1890's there is persuasive evidence that the army was no longer "theirs" but "ours."[16] Ill-feelings between troops and civilians were countered by the sense of nationality being learned in the school, and in the barracks too. At least for a while, the army could become what its enthusiasts hoped for: the school of the fatherland.

A school in several ways. For one thing, quite literally: the law of 1818 linked promotion within and from the ranks to literacy, and led to the creation of regimental schools where soldiers could learn how to read, write, and count—and what it meant to be a French citizen. Regimental festivals celebrating the unit's feats of arms began in the 1870's; regimental colors became the centerpiece of special ceremonies; every barracks had a special room that served as a regimental tabernacle; the presentation of the flag to the recruits and the oath to the flag became quasi-religious ceremonies. For two score years the result of such observances may merely have been that local patriotism was replaced by regimental allegiance, that attachment was shifted from the parish pump to the regimental flag. But they prepared the way for national allegiance, too.[17]

* As a case in point, on June 18, 1876, a detachment of the 88th Regiment met a hostile reception at Montestruc, specifically from the innkeepers and shopkeepers, who refused to have anything to do with the "voleurs" and "pillards." Moreover, the commanding general reported that this was not the first time his troops had been treated this way. (Archives Départementales, Gers M 2278.) Note the difference, though, between garrison towns, in which the army meant good business, and mere way-stops such as this.

As a school for the French language, the army often had to deal with obstinate recruits, and again the advances seem to have come slowly. We hear of Breton conscripts in 1849 refusing to understand orders in French; and half a century later they still used their own speech. Recruitment was regional. Men served in local units. Successive regimes expressed concern over the excessive regionalism and isolation that kept the army from becoming "truly French," but the very reiteration of measures designed to remedy this condition suggests that it endured.[18]

As late as 1907, when the southeastern departments seemed ready to erupt around Agde, Narbonne, and Béziers, the locally recruited army units showed where their loyalties lay. The 100th Infantry Regiment mutinied in sympathy with the crowd. The 17th Regiment of Infantry mutinied, too, its disaffection set off by rumors that it was to be posted far from home—to the Vosges, the Alps, or at least Rodez. The 139th, a Cantal unit brought down from Aurillac, was initially friendly but lost its sympathy under the hail of stones and other missiles that greeted it. The proceedings of the board of inquiry into the events of those days bring out precisely this: the initial friendliness between the crowds and the infantry troops who were either local or spoke a recognizable dialect; the hostility to units brought in from other regions, and to regimental officers, also "foreigners" to a man.[19]

This last suggests that the army must have been the last official institution to keep up the Ancien Régime's practice of bilingualism, with officers addressing the ranks in French and the noncommissioned officers interpreting when necessary. Nevertheless, in this very process even the most reluctant troopers could not help picking up a smidgen of French, learning at least to understand it and in all probability more than that. Military service rendered "inestimable services," reckoned a report from Rennes in 1880. "The young Bretons who don't know how to read, write, or speak French when they get to their units are promptly civilized [*dégrossis*], ... lose the prejudices of their *pays*, abandon native suspicions and backward opinions; and when they return to the village, they are sufficiently Frenchified to Frenchify their friends by their influence."[20]

Once home conditions became appropriate, that is, when the command of French was recognized as an advantage and was accepted socially, the very forces that had formerly prompted people to resist acquiring it made them eager to take it up. By the last quarter of the century we hear that returning veterans in Bourbonnais were showing off their new knowledge in ridiculous but significant ways. By 1893 Cantal dialect, barely breached until late in the century, was dying out perceptibly because "now everybody goes off" to the army. Such scattered evidence is suggestive and not much more. On the one hand, local speech persisted well into the twentieth century; on the other hand, it was crumbling before 1889.[21] But if it crumbled as fast as it did and if a garbled French replaced it, the army's role in this cannot be ignored.

The army was a school in still another way, and perhaps its teaching there acted more rapidly on more willing pupils.* In 1827 a military officer found it puzzling to have such difficulty wringing the annual contingent out of Puy-de-Dôme when the recruit would be "infinitely better off than he is in his vile shanty." Twenty years later in Haute-Vienne, young men who had returned from military service stood out as less habitually dirty than their peers, and had picked up a little French, otherwise quite unknown in the countryside ("as well as the more virile bearing of the north"). Could the "virile bearing" have been the result of better nourishment? Certainly army fare, however spartan, set standards far above those of many a home. "The army is good, it cannot be better. And the soup is good, it cannot be better," goes the Flemish conscript song:[22]

> Everyday, meat and soup,
> Without working, without working.
> Everyday, meat and soup,
> Without working in the army.

In diet, lodging, bedding, hygiene, dress, the soldier's wellbeing was well above the standards of the rural working class. Indeed, during the 1860's the soldier's average daily ration of 1.4 kilograms of food exceeded the national average of 1.2 kilograms, a figure that included the vast quantities ingested by the rich. The mortality rate for young men between the ages of twenty and twenty-seven was 11 per 1,000 among civilians, 10 per 1,000 among soldiers; the rate of sickness was 43 per 1,000 among civilians against 41 per 1,000 among soldiers. In noting these disparities, we should bear in mind that the vast majority of soldiers came from the poor classes, whose food consumption was a good deal lower and whose rates of sickness and mortality were a good deal higher than the national average.[23]

Equally revealing are commissary reports showing that in the 1870's soldiers ate well over half a pound of meat a day, plus about half a pound of bread and some two pounds of vegetables, including potatoes. The bread they got was often white (because the men rejected the regulation fare); and, in exceptional circumstances, they were issued coffee, wine, and sugar. The work schedule in barracks was comparatively easy next to the farm routine. Thus at Le Mans in 1872, we see the troops shifting earth from 6 to 9 A.M., eating at 9, resting at 11:30, working till 4:30, and then returning to barracks for the evening meal. "It was the best time of my life," remembered a cowherd from

---

* They may not all have been willing, but most learned something. Around 1890 Edward Harrison Barker, *Wandering by Southern Waters*, met a man with a donkey gathering wood. "The army, he told me, was the best school for learning to treat a beast with proper consideration.... When a soldier is caught beating a horse, he gets eight days of *salle de police*" (p. 54). In 1906 Marcel Baudoin noted that Vendeans learned "more respect for modern laws" in the service. *Le Maraichinage: Coutumes du pays du Mont (Vendée)*, Paris, 1906, p. 187.

Cheylade (Cantal). "We would go out every evening at half past 5, we were well fed, we had meat twice a day, fresh meat you understand, and what a broth! It had globs of fat in it; one would have said it was oil! White bread at every meal and coffee in the morning!"[24]

Even so, when Hubert Lyautey, then a major, took command of a cavalry squadron at Saint-Germain in 1887, about the time the cowherd spoke of, his unit had no mess hall, let alone any canteen or common room. Lyautey's recollection of the situation indicates the gulf between the expectations of the common people and those of the better off. There was always the same soup, a bit of meat swimming in greasy liquid; vegetables and bread were served in a mess-tin twice a day, and wolfed down while sitting on the bunk, or beside a trestle table in the barrack room. "No one thought to complain," not only because conditions in the squadron had always been thus, but also because the conditions back home made the present seem pretty good. Lyautey, shocked by such primitive style, introduced a mess hall where men sat on benches at proper tables, ate from plates and drank from glasses, were served roast meat, fish, and properly cooked potatoes, as well as a games room where they could play billiards and otherwise relax in comfort unheard of outside real cafés.[25]

Lyautey was an exceptional man, and his reforms took time to spread. But by the turn of the century they had made great progress, as had his ideas on the social role of the officer, who was strategically positioned, as he said, in the only place "where one has all the nation in one's hands." The mere experience of a radically different way of life made a tremendous impact.* A student of Breton emigration has attributed that phenomenon to the three-year service law, writing that the Breton conscript "notes that ... one eats white bread and meat every day, which is better than rye bread and porridge. He notes that fatigue duty is less hard than threshing."[26] It was an exodus that would be hastened and expanded by habits formed during four long years of war, when masses of men ate and drank better than they ever had before.

No wonder that in these circumstances, knowing what conditions were like at home, a good proportion of peasant soldiers chose not to return to their villages. The livelier spirits would serve as orderlies and go on from there to get a job as footman, coachman, or domestic servant in a bourgeois house. Most of those who had earned some stripes either reenlisted or sought a job suitable to their rank in another branch of the government, such as the gendarmerie, the water-and-forest service, the railroads, the public works department, or the post office. The army, we hear from mid-century onward, untaught work and taught idleness, became a breeding-place of petty public servants, a recruiting ground for urban jobs. Regiments set up their own job agencies, which

* One result of the troubles of 1907 was an official move to get the army to buy larger quantities of wine, a decision that helped spread the habit to a number of units (Pierre Barral, *Les Agrariens français*, p. 101).

further encouraged this tendency by offering men who had been farmers posts as servants, bus conductors, delivery boys, or maintenance men.[27] The result was striking: over the ten-year period ending in 1896, reported a correspondent from one rural parish, one in three conscripts failed to return when his service was done. The record of a Doubs village shows that only a little better than one in two opted to go back:[28]

Year	No. of recruits	Returned on discharge	Year	No. of recruits	Returned on discharge
1887	6	3	1893	6	3
1888	5	2	1894	8	4
1889	4	2	1895	4	2
1890	5	4	1896	4	4
1891	4	1			
1892	5	2	TOTAL	51	27

In sum, the army turned out to be an agency for emigration, acculturation, and in the final analysis, civilization, an agency as potent in its way as the schools, about which we tend to talk a great deal more. Its contribution in all these realms matters less in and of itself than as one factor among many. It was the conjunction of a multiplicity of factors, like the bound rods in the lictors' bundle, that made their force; it was their coincidence in time that made their effectiveness and their mutual significance.

Chapter Eighteen

CIVILIZING IN EARNEST:
SCHOOLS AND SCHOOLING

La République a fondé des écoles,
Aussi maint'nant le peuple sait compter,
L'peupl' ne veut plus qu'on lui donn'un obole,
Il veut son compt' et non la charité.
—MONTÉHUS

THE SCHOOL, notably the village school, compulsory and free, has been credited with the ultimate acculturation process that made the French people French—finally civilized them, as many nineteenth-century educators liked to say. The schoolteachers, in their worn, dark suits, appear as the militia of the new age, harbingers of enlightenment and of the Republican message that reconciled the benighted masses with a new world, superior in wellbeing and democracy. Observers have pointed out that there were schools before the 1880's, and have quarreled with implicit assumptions or explicit statements that there was no popular education under the Ancien Régime. But we shall see that the now-classic image of a profound change of pace, tone, and impact under the Third Republic is roughly correct if it is placed in the proper context.

The context matters because schools did in fact exist before Jules Ferry, indeed were numerous; and so, to a large extent, did free education. What made the Republic's laws so effective was not just that they required all children to attend school and granted them the right to do so free. It was the attendant circumstances that made adequate facilities and teachers more accessible; that provided roads on which children could get to school; that, above all, made school meaningful and profitable, once what the school offered made sense in terms of altered values and perceptions.

It is my purpose in this chapter to sketch the development of schooling in this particular context, to suggest how it fits the changes indicated above, and to show that its success was an integral part of a total process. It was only when what the schools taught made sense that they became important to those they had to teach. It was only when what the schools said became relevant to recently created needs and demands that people listened to them; and listening, also heeded the rest of their offerings. People went to school not because school was offered or imposed, but because it was useful. The world had to change before this came about.

The schools that priests or laymen ran for the poorer classes before the last quarter of the nineteenth century tended, in the nature of things, to put first things first. First things were those the masters thought important: the ability to gabble the catechism or a part of the Latin service. The teaching of even elementary reading, writing, and arithmetic was rare before the Revolution, reflected the prefect of Yonne in 1810, and teachers were little interested in "broad public education, I mean the sort concerning the greatest number of people."[1] In any case, a great many teachers taught whatever they taught with limited competence. Until 1816, no title or proof of competence was required from a teacher. And though in the cities and larger towns this could be remedied, popular schooling suffered. It went on suffering on this score for quite some time, under the rod of men like the dominie of the secondary school of Noyers (Yonne), whose schoolroom was so ill-swept and so full of spiders "that one could hardly make out Citizen Colibeau through the spiderwebs, especially when he gave his lesson as he habitually did in nightcap, dressing gown, and sabots."[2]

The schoolroom or schoolhouse tended to be ramshackle. At Moulle (Pas-de-Calais) a whole wall collapsed in 1828 during a friendly scuffle between teacher and pupils. In 1850 the school at Sauvat (Cantal) was an abandoned bakehouse whose roof was separated from the walls, so that the snow got in. Throughout the 1870's we hear of ceilings crumbling, floors collapsing, paneless windows—sometimes no windows at all, the chimney providing the only ventilation. Living and teaching quarters were hard to tell apart; in Eure-et-Loir teachers or their wives did their household chores, prepared meals, and baked bread during class, and some also slept in the classroom on a folding bed. Perhaps just as well, since otherwise the schoolroom might have been even more poorly equipped: quite a few lacked tables; some until the 1880's had neither seats nor stove. Body heat helped, and we find one mayor (in 1837) asserting that the children's breath ensured a reasonable temperature. Dark, humid, crowded, unventilated, unfurnished, unlit, unheated or smelly and smoky when a fire or stove was lit, drafty, unwelcoming, and ugly, such was the great majority of schools right through the end of the 1870's. Most had no yard, let alone a latrine. In 1864 a school inspector, reporting on the lack of cesspools or other sanitary facilities, noted that some schools did provide a fenced-in area in a corner of the backyard. The manure amassed there was removed from time to time and used as fertilizer—"the beginning of progress, ... unknown a dozen years ago."[3]

At Nouvion-en-Thiérache (Aisne) there were "no maps, no blackboards, no tables or desks" in the 1850's. Each pupil had a wooden plank that he placed on his knees for writing; the master sharpened the students' quills, and when he was called away to sing in the church, his sister kept the class in order while she cleaned her salad.[4] This was not unusual, and informality of this sort must have interrupted many a dreary lesson. If the schoolroom was in the village hall, the community's records were likely to be kept in a corner cupboard, with adults filing in at any time to verify a document or to seek the teacher out for other functions; and it was not unknown for a wedding celebration to be held there, even sometimes during class.[5]

The teacher himself was another problem. In the first half of the nineteenth century, he could well have been a retired soldier, a rural constable, the local barber, innkeeper, or grocer, or simply a half-educated peasant's son. Seven of the 15 teachers in Rennes in 1815 were ex-convicts. Balzac's figure of the village teacher, Fourchon, who ended as a poacher, part-cordwainer, part-beggar, and fulltime drunk, was evidently an acceptable stereotype under the July Monarchy. In any case, most teachers worked at another job, ranging from farming their own land or someone else's, weaving (in Eure-et-Loir one kept his loom in the schoolroom), mending shoes, and digging graves to serving as the village choirmaster or village registrar. Even in 1872, when teachers had moved up in the world from their low condition of the 1830's, we find what must have been most if not all of the 395 public teachers of Eure-et-Loir doing something else on the side: 359 acted as registrars, 273 as choirmasters or church organists, and 14 as sextons, beadles, or bellringers; two were janitors and sweepers, one a gravedigger, and ten tobacconists; two ran the local telegraph office, and 36 sold insurance.[6]

Teaching was a trade like any other, and a man or lad would hire himself out—sometimes at the fair, like the "mercenaries" who "taught what they didn't know" from Hautes-Alpes to Ardèche into the 1850's. They wore one quill stuck in their hats if they taught how to read, two if they also taught arithmetic, three if their mental equipment included Latin.* The peasants would put their heads together at the autumn fair to hire such a teacher, himself but a more learned peasant, for the winter. If they did not know him already, they gave him an informal examination at the inn, and during his stay they took turns in providing his bed and board, a place in the stable for classes, and light and ink for the children he taught. In the spring the teacher returned to his farm with a bright golden *louis*, 20 francs the richer.[7]

The moral worth of such teachers was often as shaky as their enlightenment. Physical and intellectual isolation permitted them to play strange tricks with their slender powers. In Yonne we hear of a village teacher being fired in 1853 because he used cabalistic formulas to heal the sick, touted toads as a cure for cancer, sold cheap brandy, and "excited his pupils to drink." Such schoolbooks as could be found were ancient. Authorities denounced them as Gothic, anachronistic, and absurd. They seem to have been all of these things. We hear of an alphabet book in Latin, of a work called *Christian Civility* printed in Gothic characters; of a life of Christ dating back to the fifteenth

---

* *Annuaire départemental pour les Hautes-Alpes*, 1844, quoted in Elie Reynier and Louise Abrial, *Les Ecoles normales primaires*, p. 72. In Ardèche they were known as Briançonnais or Matinaux because they came from the Dauphiné mountains, to the east. They are also mentioned in Victor Hugo's *Les Misérables*.

century "full of miracles, superstitions, and fear of devils"; of a text telling how the Virgin Mary spent her youth in the temple learning the psalter and the prayer book, as a good saint should. Once the basic essentials were learned, children practiced reading in old family papers, legal documents, marriage contracts. They learned to read old scripts, to know and remember the ways of the past, not very different from the world they lived in under Louis Philippe.[8] This "vicious usage" began to disappear in the 1840's as more and more schools were equipped with standard texts.* But most of these texts were, in their own fashion, equally useless; and teaching standards continued to be sadly low.

One hears of village schools that imparted a good fund of knowledge, and of countrymen who knew how to read and actually did read. But these were the exceptions. Most country schools must have been more like the one at Selins (Cantal) in the 1840's, which was conducted by Sister Gandilhon, who could teach only prayers, the catechism, and the first two rules of arithmetic ("she had heard of a third, but never learned it"). In consequence, if poor men read, it was because they had taught themselves. And that came hard. When Martin Nadaud was elected to Parliament in 1849, he could not write a letter, though he had worked at educating himself for over a decade. Where French was not native to the region, some teachers were as ignorant of it as their charges; and others bent it to their needs in a special pidgin, as in Cerdagne, where the school idiom was a strange mixture of Latin, Catalan, and French. At Olette (Pyrénées-Orientales) in the 1840's, where the teacher did not know French but had Lhomond's Latin grammar by heart, those children who progressed beyond simple spelling read *The Imitation of Jesus Christ* and *Telemachus*. But, recalled a survivor, they read only in a manner of speaking: no one could read a book that was written in French for the simple reason that the teacher could not read it either.[9]

It takes real effort today to conceive such an educational system, one in which both teacher and taught were ignorant of the material they were dealing with, and in which the capacity to draw letters or pronounce them completely outweighed any capacity to comprehend. Letters, words, and sentences were formulas and spells. "No child understands what he reads," reported a school inspector from Var in 1864. And in Brittany the inspectors noted that, though the children read along with fair fluency, "no child can give account of what he has read or translate it into Breton; hence there is no proof that anything is understood." In such circumstances, Latin was no more difficult, no more incomprehensible than French, and many a bright village child "learned" Latin in this fashion and left school full of bits of scripture, canticles, and the catechism, "rattling along in Latin like a phonograph, without understanding a word of it," and capable of writing in four different hands, accomplishments most impressive to his illiterate parents.[10]

---

* Yet as late as 1879 a school inspector in Charollais found children using the Royaumont Bible as their only text (cited in Pierre Zind, *L'Enseignement religieux*, p. 134).

Most simply learned by rote. At Soignes (Vaucluse), school authorities reported in 1864 that up to 40 girls were admitted to school every year for a few months, just long enough to learn the catechism by hearing it repeated, so they could make their first communion. Thirteen years later at Privas (Ardèche), nearly half the children were enrolled for this purpose alone. From Louis XVI to Louis Napoleon, the words of one of Grégoire's correspondents continued to apply, though less and less: "Education in the countryside comes down to enabling pupils to help their pastors on Sundays and holidays to sing the praise of God in a language they don't understand."[11]

No wonder in such circumstances that outside reading continued rare. In 1864 a survey tells us: "very little" (Vaucluse); "the local paper, a letter, the prayerbook" (Doubs); "no one thinks to read in the countryside" (Landes); "the taste for reading doesn't exist" (Lot-et-Garonne); the same in Basses-Pyrénées. As for writing, it was rarer still. "To write several pages, one needs a practiced hand," a Dordogne priest had written to Grégoire in 1791.[12] Two generations later few could trace even a few words. Children left school able to make their way painfully through thickets of letters, but only a handful had been taught to write. Writing was a stage of learning to which few aspired, the fewer since it called for higher fees.[13]

I have quoted the reports of school inspectors. They came into existence in 1833 as part of a law introduced by François Guizot, then Minister of Public Instruction. That law set the foundations of the people's schooling. It required every commune or group of neighboring communes to set up and maintain at least one elementary school; it reaffirmed the standards of competence for teaching that had been set by royal ordinance in 1816, and prohibited the operation of a school without an official certificate that such standards had been met; it decreed that each department should set up, alone or jointly with its neighbors, a normal school to train primary school teachers; and it produced quick results. In 1833 France had 31,420 schools attended by 1.2 million children; by 1847 the number of schools had doubled, and the number of pupils had increased almost threefold. In the same period the number of normal schools increased from 38 to 47. This last had its importance. We must realize that the mass of the teachers in the public elementary schools in the mid-1880's probably came out of these normal schools of the July Monarchy; and that, however slowly, their training and quality improved as a result.

We can see that Guizot's was an important measure. We must be careful not to overrate its effectiveness. The normal schools continued to provide only rudimentary training. The "schools," as we have seen, varied in grandeur and facilities—but varied mostly downward. They were (I speak of the countryside) still supplemented by the ad hoc establishments of religious teaching orders, like the *béates* of Haute-Loire and Ardèche, who could not teach their charges how to read, but were very effective babysitters and cordial hostesses for feminine gatherings where one embroidered, gossiped, and prayed. Beyond this, there were unofficial, or "clandestine," establishments, numerous into the

1850's, where some local man or woman gathered a group of paying students during the winter nights. In 1880 the school inspector of Vannes (Morbihan) reported on the clandestine school he had discovered, with more than 40 girls from three to thirteen crowded in a tiny room already filled by a wardrobe, bed, and chest. The woman who kept the school taught them "neither reading nor writing, and no word of French. Only the catechism and prayers in Breton, and songs in a Latin book for the bigger girls." In 1881 the béates still flourished in Velay and Vivarais, to the great indignation of the local authorities. Though they were officially suppressed in 1882, Ardouin-Dumazet found them still operating at the turn of the century and avowed that without the shelter they offered the women for their work and the children for their catechism, long winters would have been unbearably dreary.[14]

As for the public schools, official attendance figures are scarcely credible. For one thing, the claims made for the 1840's equal the more reliable figures that appeared in the 1860's. And for another, in drawing up statistics, no one gave any thought to girls. When not taught at home—scarcely a frequent case among the masses—girls were left to local hazard, which often meant no school. In 1867 a law was passed requiring every commune of 500 souls and over to have a girls school, but it provided certain outs, with the result that at the end of the 1870's half of the communes in France still lacked such facilities.[15]

Despite all these shortcomings, from 1833 onward the government, supported by a steadily growing vested interest, bent itself to advance and develop public education. Nationally, the conscripts affected by the law of 1833 showed a much smaller measure of illiteracy than their forebears. And in an illiterate department like Corrèze, the change was equally evident. The proportion of conscripts who knew the elements of reading rose from 14.3 percent in 1829 to 31.9 percent in 1855, 34.8 percent in 1860, 41 percent in 1865, 50 percent in 1868, and 62 percent in 1875.[16] By 1863 only about one-fifth of the children between seven and thirteen received no instruction whatever. What we want to know is the kind of instruction that was given and who got it. The evidence suggests, and so does common sense, that urban areas had more schools than rural areas, that these schools were more regularly attended by more of the local children, and that the quality of the teaching in them was better. By 1876 nearly 800,000 of 4.5 million school-age children were still not registered in any school. Most of these belonged to rural communes; and many who were registered hardly ever attended class.[17] This was the enduring problem.

The next great change came in the 1880's. It would have come earlier had the Minister of Education Victor Duruy had the chance to develop the plans he elaborated in 1867. But he did not, and most of his initiatives remained in the project stage.[18] Hence the importance of the reforms introduced by Jules Ferry. In 1881 all fees and tuition charges in public elementary schools were abolished. In 1882 enrollment in a public or private school was made compulsory. In 1883 every village or hamlet with more than 20 school-age children was required to maintain a public elementary school. In 1885 subsidies were allotted for the building and maintenance of schools and for the pay of teachers. In 1886 an elementary teaching program was instituted, along with elaborate provisions for inspection and control.

We may observe that the adoption of these policies coincided with the vast expenditures of the Freycinet Plan. The millions that were spent on building roads were matched by vast sums for schools: 17,320 schools had to be built, 5,428 enlarged, 8,381 repaired. A school fund set up in 1878 dispensed 311 million francs in subsidies, 231 million more in loans in the space of seven years. Meanwhile, the budget for public instruction rose from 53,640,714 francs in 1878 to 133,671,671 in 1885, enough to set money flowing through the country and to convince the undecided of the virtues of the new policies.[19]

In certain parts of France the educators had their work cut out for them. South of the line that marked off the best and worst areas in primary education, a diagonal running from Saint-Malo to Geneva, 16 departments, representing a population of 6.5 million souls, showed a higher than 20 percent rate of illiteracy among conscripts in 1881; nine of these ranged between 26.1 percent (Corrèze) and 41.3 percent (Morbihan).[20] Even these figures underrated the degree of illiteracy by several percentage points. They did not include males who were not conscripts. They did not include women, who had a much higher rate of illiteracy than men. And they did not discriminate between urban and rural areas to show that even in the most backward regions—Lower Brittany, the center from Cher to Dordogne and Ardèche, the Pyrenees—rural areas were consistently worse off. In this same year, 1881, teachers in Lot reported that in their communes seven persons in ten were illiterate, and that only one of the three who could read could also write, and then "very badly." By the turn of the century conscript literacy in Finistère was not far below the national average. But when the 1901 draft board examined a group at Châteaulin, it found about one in three of the men from Pleyben, Châteauneuf, Huelgoat, and Carhaix to be illiterate.[21]

In a society recently come to mass education, the rate of literacy among the conscripts would necessarily have been higher than the rate among adults. This means that in the 1880's the illiteracy rate among men in their fifties (the figures for women being even worse) would have corresponded to the rate found among conscripts in the later 1840's, and the illiteracy rate among older people to the rate noted in the conscripts of the early 1830's, which ran between 60 percent and 80 percent throughout the 54 departments of the center and south of France.

It is because figures and statistics tend to be misleading that an impressionist account may come closer to the truth. School inspectors of the 1870's plainly appreciated the point in expressing a certain skepticism about the lists of literate and illiterate children that they themselves passed on. "Reality has nothing to do with administrative figures or statistics," complained Félix Pécaut in 1879.[22] The number of those who could not read or write belied the official claims. Passing remarks give us some useful clues. Jean-Paul Giret in his study on popular education in Eure-et-Loir observes that to say people knew how to read or write does not mean that they could in fact do it, but says only that they had been taught to do it. A teacher in Vosges remarked on the enormous difference between being able to sign one's name and being able to read, let alone write (1889). In 1871 the General Council of Haute-Loire found occasion to point out that most of the people statistically listed as able to read and write were completely illiterate. A year later, a local official confirmed that school attendance often resulted only in the ability to scrawl a questionable signature and to spell out the shop signs (1872). And the reports to that effect are endless. Many conscripts have attended school but have retained nothing from it (Allier, 1864). They learn how to sign their names and think they know everything (Charente-Inférieure, 1861). In any case, the lads who had left school at twelve would return for a winter's cramming before they faced the draft board, to give them a minimum appearance of literacy (Cantal, 1880). Conversely, other men claimed illiteracy in order to escape service, and lists of illiterates in Ariège in 1865 included a fair measure of seminarians, students, and teachers.[23] The statistics clearly must be taken with more than a few grains of salt.

One reason for the slow progress in eliminating illiteracy, strangely ignored by even the best accounts of education in France, was the fact that so many adults—and consequently children—did not speak French. As we have seen, in 1863 by official tally (as reproduced in the Appendix, pp. 498–501, below) some 7.5 million people, a fifth of the population, did not know the language.[24] And as we have also seen, even that figure is questionable. The actual number was probably much larger, particularly if one includes those whose notions of the language were extremely vague.

The greatest problem faced by the public schools in the 8,381 non-French-speaking communes, and in a good few of the other 29,129 where French was said to be in general use, was how to teach the language to children who never or hardly ever heard it. The oft-repeated claim that they were learning their mother tongue could hardly have rung true to those whose mothers did not understand a word of it. "The children [of Lauragais] don't have to learn simply how to read and write," commented M. F. Pariset in 1867. "They have to learn how to do so in French, that is, in another language than the one they know." The result was that, for a lot of them, the instruction received in school "leaves no more trace than Latin leaves on most of those who graduate from secondary school. The child . . . returns to patois when he gets home. French is for him an erudite language, which he forgets quickly, never speaking it."[25] Officially, the problem was faced by denying its existence and forcing even those who could scarcely master a few words to proclaim, as in a catechism, that what *should* be true was true and what they *knew* to be true was not: "(1) We call mother tongue the tongue that is spoken by our parents, and in particular by our mothers; spoken also by our fellow citizens and by the persons who inhabit the same *pays* as us. (2) Our mother tongue is French." So read an army examination manual in 1875. Unofficially, the schools continued to struggle to make the slogan true. Teaching French, "our beautiful and noble mother tongue," asserted Ferdinand Buisson, the leading light of Republican education in the 1880's, "is the chief work of the elementary school—a labor of patriotic character." The labor proved long and hard.[26]

The printed forms school inspectors used in the 1870's in making their rounds included a section headed "Need to teach exclusively in French. Regulations to be reviewed in *pays* where Basque, Breton, Flemish, German patois, etc., are spoken." The section was put to use, and one may assume that the rules were reviewed with some frequency at least for some decades. Yet the results were patchy. "We have been teaching French regularly for 30 years in nearly every commune of the Empire," exclaimed a schoolteacher of Châteauneuf-du-Rhône, a village near Montélimar, in 1861. Yet what were the results? "Look at the difficulty with which young peasants manage to mumble a few words of French!" The situation in Vaucluse was no different: "They leave rural schools with scarcely a notion of French." And how could one ask more of them, especially when "only high society habitually speaks French"? In Dordogne reports of 1875 tell us that French was studied "without much result," and young people read without understanding. In Basses-Pyrénées the French language was known by only a few, and children could hardly cope with a language they never heard. When the two young heroes of Bruno's *Tour de France* (1877) stop at a rural hostelry south of Valence, they cannot communicate with the nice old landlady or any of the other patrons, who speak only patois—that is, the Franco-Provençal dialect of the Drôme. Little Julien asks his older brother, "Why is it all the people of this *pays* do not speak French?" "It is because they have not all been to school," André answers. "But in a number of years it will be different, and everywhere in France people will know how to speak the language of the fatherland." Symbolically, at this point the landlady's children come home from school. *They* can speak French: Julien and André are no longer isolated.[27]

Here was the promise of great change to come. And Bruno's scene is confirmed from all quarters. By 1875 in the schools of Hérault French "tends to replace the patois idiom." By 1878 in the Cévennes "all the youths today know how to speak French." And by 1873 in Tarn-et-Garonne "even the country people want their children to know how to read, write, and do sums."[28] Unfortunately, what they wanted was not that easily accomplished. The fact that classes were taught in a foreign language played its part in maintaining a high rate of illiteracy, making it that much harder to assimilate courses that were strange twice over. It helps explain complaints about how, for all the number of schools, there were so few graduates who could read and write. It also explains why priests continued to preach and teach the catechism in the only language most of their parishioners really understood.[29] Even where acquaintance with French was spreading, the children affected remained a minority for many years. Only in the 1880's at the earliest, more likely by the turn of the century, could one expect the efforts of the 1860's and 1870's to have produced a majority of adults familiar with the national tongue.

"In the villages, anyone who tried to speak French wouldn't escape the jeers of his neighbors," explained an educator in Loire in 1864. "He would be turned to ridicule."[30] This and other kinds of pressure have to be taken into consideration. Regard for the majority or simply for one's elders, the presence of non-French-speaking relatives in a family or a congregation, kept local speech in use. Jacques Duclos was born in 1896. His parents knew French (the date is right for that), but did not use it at home, perhaps because his grandmother did not understand it. The little boy only learned French at school.

So the transition was bound to be slow. Until a large enough segment of the population had been reached to shift the balance in favor of French, the pressures of environment, that is, of general practice, worked to protect and enforce the use of local speech, and schoolmasters felt that they were fighting lonely battles. Even when parents began to want their children schooled, the war was not won: the "teaching of French makes no progress,... everyone speaks Gascon" (Tarn-et-Garonne, 1873); "teaching is everywhere in French but everywhere outside school one speaks patois" (Tarn-et-Garonne, 1877); "pupils express themselves badly in writing.... It's difficult in a *pays* where patois is spoken constantly" (Puy-de-Dôme, 1877); "it is necessary to teach French to students" (Vaucluse, 1883). The best one could say of Corrèze in 1893 was that "everyone speaks and understands French well enough, but the usual language is still patois." Yet here, by the end of the century, the balance had swung to the side of French; witness the local priest who discontinued giving the sermon and the catechism in Limousin.[31]

But the effort that produced this result had to be made in the 1870's. Article 24 of the official regulations for public schools in the Basses-Pyrénées, published in 1874, "expressly" prohibited the use of patois in Béarnais schools where French had made progress and recommended "translation exercises and other methods" to make Basque children "acquire the usage of French."* As late as 1876, a report emphasized that teachers in Basque schools who did not speak Basque had great difficulties, since none of the children could speak

---

* Vicomte Sérurier, "De l'instruction primaire ... en Béarn," *Bulletin de la Société des Sciences ...de Pau*, 1873–74, p. 230. Similarly, late in the century we hear the suggestion in Ariège that a good way to make sure children understood what they were taught was to "make them translate the French text into their local tongue" (Archives Nationales, F[17]10757, Ariège). Just as in secondary schools pupils translate Latin or Greek texts into French.

a word of French. By 1881, though both Basque and Béarnais children never spoke French except at school, the latter were at least beginning to "join in the general movement," whereas the Basques persisted in avoiding "the emancipating action of French genius." Many Pyreneans seem to have stubbornly resisted this "emancipation" from their local speech. From one end of the mountain chain to another, Basque, Béarnais, Catalan, Gascon, or other Oc dialects predominated, and teachers in the late 1880's found French the most difficult thing that they had to teach. In 1897 Paul Beulaygue, a schoolmaster in Ariège, pointed out that pedagogic works assumed children spoke French when the "truth is quite different. In the great majority of our rural schools, children come ... knowing only a little French and hearing only patois spoken at home. This is and will long remain a general rule."[32]

Perhaps Beulaygue generalized too much from his Ariège experience; but surely not too much where Brittany was concerned. Inspection reports of the 1870's bear witness to the slight effect schools had on regions where thirteen- and fourteen-year-old boys at school could hardly understand the things they read or learned in French—"and the number of those who attend school as long as that is very limited," added one inspector. Rector Baudoin of Rennes, in his great report of 1880, spoke of the need to "Frenchify" the peninsula— especially the three departments of Lower Brittany—by the spread of schools, which alone could "truly unify the peninsula with the rest of France and complete the historical annexation always ready to dissolve." Ends set so high justified all means. Breton was hunted out of the schools. Children caught using it were systematically punished—put on dry bread and water or sent to clean out the school latrine. Rector Baudoin had cited as an example worth following the methods used to Germanize Alsace-Lorraine; in 1895 a Breton patriot from Saint-Brieuc compared the school policies of France unfavorably to those of the Germans.[33]

A favorite punishment, inherited from the Jesuits (who had ironically used it to enforce Latin on their French-speaking charges), was the token of shame to be displayed by the child caught using his native tongue. The token varied. It could be a cardboard ticket (Dorres, Pyrénées-Orientales), a wooden plank (Err and Palau, Pyrénées-Orientales), a bar or a stick (Angoustrine, Pyrénées-Orientales), a peg (Cantal), a paper ribbon or metal object (Flanders), or a brick to be held out at arm's length (Corrèze). A child saddled with such a "symbol" kept it until he caught another child not speaking French, denounced him, and passed it on. The pupil left with the token at the end of the day received a punishment. In the country schools of Brittany the symbol of shame was a sabot. Morvan Lebesque, who attended those schools in the years after the First World War, remembered the punishment with bitterness, which suggests that Breton did not die lightly. Yet by 1895 our anonymous Breton patriot could decry "the systematic exclusion of the Breton language," which helped discredit it in the eyes of those speaking it, who saw it as a badge of ignorance and shame.[34]

Our friend from Saint-Brieuc was both right and wrong. French was gaining ground. But not so much through persecution as through the peasants' growing appreciation of the usefulness of a less parochial language and of the skills learned in the schools. Universal military service both spread the use of French and made at least a smattering of it important to more people. The introduction and spread of kindergartens—*salles d'asile*—to relieve teachers of the care of three- and four-year-olds given into their charge familiarized very young children with authority figures who spoke French rather than the mother's language.[35]

Most important of all, perhaps, more girls were being schooled, more girls and women learned French, more mothers could speak French to their children if they chose to do so. Women had willy-nilly perpetuated local speech. Girls had been left untaught at the village level much longer than in bourgs and towns, a fact that the available statistics hardly mirror at all. Only in 1867 were communes over 500 souls required to provide a girls school (they had been required to provide schools for boys in 1833), and it took some time before the results of this law were felt. In any case, girls schools were generally run by members of religious orders, and their standards remained quite low until the 1880's. Nor did the girls have the benefit of military service as a refresher course in French and "civilization." It follows that the school laws of the 1880's had the broadest impact on the literacy and schooling of girls, both of which had lagged far behind.[36] And that when the results came to be felt in the 1890's, the women's cultural role in the family would suddenly change and, with it, attitudes to schooling and to the use of French.

There was another great problem that had to be mastered before French could truly be made the national language: the teacher's own poor knowledge of the language that he had to teach. "Most teachers don't know French," complained a report of 1803 in Ardèche. Half a century later things had hardly improved. A special summer refresher course for teachers held in 1839 at Privas reported great success: when it ended those who began with 60 to 80 mistakes in a page of dictation made only 25 to 40 errors when the exercise was repeated.[37] Through the 1840's and 1850's many teachers still found it difficult to spell or to form a proper sentence.*

During the first two-thirds of the century, normal schools south of the Saint-Malo–Geneva line reported grave difficulties in teaching apprentice teachers French. At Salers (Cantal) "every kind of trouble getting the students...to speak French out of class." Even some of the normal school's teaching staff found the national language awkward, and students made fun

---

* Consider this note penned by the teacher at Saint-Brancher (Yonne): "Je vous observeré que je sui infirme de la main goche, qui motte totallement la fagulté de men servire. Je sui attaqué de leul goche par une galle qui le couvre, qui motte la fagulté de voier. Dotre cotté je sui apsent desprit enpartie par mon grand âge qui me donne une timidité insuportable, surtout lorce que japersoit des gendarmes." (Quoted in H. Forestier, "Perrette décoiffée," *Annales de Bourgogne,* 1955, p. 182.)

of the way they spoke. This was in 1836. By 1875, some 40 years later, the normal school had moved from Salers to Aurillac, but "the study of French [was] still the greatest problem because of the patois." Two years later the director took further stock, to find that "for most of our students French is almost a foreign language." In Gard the inspector reported from Nîmes in 1872: "The use of patois, the students' backgrounds, and the relatively brief time they spend at [normal] school make teaching in the French style pretty difficult." At the normal school in Mende (Lozère) in 1872 the student teachers were weak in French, "primarily because of insufficient knowledge on admission." A decade later every student in school still spoke the Lozère patois at home. French "comes down to purely grammatical exercises."[38]

Neither students nor teachers read enough to be familiar with, let alone teach, French literature. In Basses-Pyrénées we hear that cultivated people knew French (1874). But what kind of French? A year later the normal school at Lescar reported having problems with the language because "even the cultivated who speak it don't speak it very well, and that's all the students have heard when they have heard it." In Dordogne in the same year, 1875, examiners for the teaching diploma were warned to make sure that every teacher "*knows at least how to write his language correctly*." (To be certain the point got across, the warning was underlined.) In the Landes in 1876 student teachers and their mentors had mastered the language only shakily. "Many masters read no better than their students," and in explaining a reading both sides offered plain absurdities. At the Avignon normal school, also in 1876, "the master himself knows French badly." At Perpignan in 1878 student teachers read and understood French badly; they were used to Catalan and only great efforts could "familiarize them with French." Much the same thing in Puy-de-Dôme in 1877: "Detestable local accent," and patois hindering everyone. The reports of 1881 carry similar criticisms. The teachers don't do very well in French because they have been insufficiently prepared to handle it (Lot-et-Garonne). The teachers are insecure in their use of French; they lack solid training in using it on their own account (Basses-Pyrénées). Even many of the normal school teachers are local men who have never left the department; they retain the local accent and habits, and pass them on to their students (Aveyron).[39]

In short, with few exceptions teachers were merely peasant lads who hoped to improve their condition or wanted to escape military service. Only in extraordinary circumstances would a man who expected to inherit property have wasted his time on something that until the 1880's brought little profit or prestige. The reports amassed in the government's survey of the state of primary instruction in 1864 show that student teachers came from the "working class" and from families of small farmers chiefly interested in getting an exemption from military service for their sons (Dordogne, Eure, Savoy); that they were recruited from the poor families of the countryside (Lot-et-Garonne); that they had the defective pronunciation and habits of the peasants (Calvados). A motion of the governing board of the normal school of Montpellier encapsulates the problem in blunt terms: "Whereas the department's ... wealth offers young men of intelligence and a little money careers much more profitable than that of elementary teaching and which they in fact prefer; whereas the students of the normal school are recruited only among the poor inhabitants of the mountain areas in the department's north and west ..." Even as late as 1881 we hear that recruitment came easily in the poorer regions; but that in wealthy ones, where families had few children, only those who were useless in the fields were sent to normal schools. Many must have gone off with the greatest reluctance to what we could generously describe as miserable holes, far worse than barracks. "A sorry, mean, and shabby dump materially and morally" was how one report described the normal school at Parthenay (Deux-Sèvres) in 1882. "Intellectually nonexistent, depressing on all counts, it forms or deforms poor young peasants to become poor old teachers."[40]

Also, we may add, acolytes of the priest. "Elementary education properly understood ... is the fraternal union of presbytery and school," pronounced Rector Denain at an awards ceremony in 1862. Just how fraternal, the readers of Flaubert's *Bouvard and Pécuchet* could learn. "The teacher is no more than a mnemotechnical auxiliary of the priest," complained Félix Pécaut, less mellifluously than the rector. Yet by then things had improved since the day when the teacher's first duty was to assist the priest, sing all the offices, sweep the church once a week, dust and polish the ornaments, see that the bells were rung and the clock was wound, and finally keep school and instruct the children according to the true faith. But inspectors in the day of Marshal Mac-Mahon still checked to make sure that "teachers show themselves useful auxiliaries of the priests." The peasants greatly appreciated teachers when it came to practical matters such as surveying land and measuring properties, remembered a beginner of those days; but their subjection to the priests was horrid. One need not wonder at the consistent devotion of teachers after the 16th of May to a Republic that emancipated them from their humiliating bondage.[41] One need not wonder either that it should take something of a revolution—in training and consequently in outlook—for the village schoolteacher to blossom into the dynamic missionary illustrated in our books.*

But before teachers could take on the role of missionaries, they had to learn to live the part. Too many teachers "dress like peasants, think like peasants. They are peasants who have a slightly different trade." They mixed with the villagers, went off to fairs with them; there was no distance here and certainly no respect. "One has a lot of trouble to make them give up such habits." The 1880's saw a campaign to turn these browbeaten peasants into models of the

---

* André Burguière describes a revealing scene that took place at Plozévet (Finistère) in 1910. The local priest attempted to speak at a political meeting, was interrupted, and called on the teacher to clear the room. "Monsieur le curé," answered the teacher, "I am neither your servant nor a policeman!" (*Bretons de Plozévet*, p. 285.) Not long before he had been a bit of both.

new enlightened style. Above all, they were not to go around "dressed in smocks, caps, and sabots, keeping their heads covered in class like their students...as uncivilized as the populations in whose midst they live."[42] In their persons and in their actions teachers were expected to maintain standards that would reflect their elevated functions and their representative role.

Though pay improved somewhat, such standards were difficult to maintain. Beginning teachers earned 700 francs a year in 1881, 800 ten years later, and 900 between 1897 and 1905, when the starting salary was raised to 1,100 francs. The highest pay doubled in the same period. By the turn of the century, after withholdings for pensions and other things, country teachers at last earned as much as a miner and more than a Paris laundress or a textile worker.[43] But they had to "dress suitably," and to keep up at least outwardly a style of living that went with their position as *fonctionnaires d'Etat* (1889) and aspiring notables. That they were willing and able to make the attempt was due to the training inculcated by the reformed normal schools.

A monograph on the normal school of Puy-de-Dôme shows how impoverished the curriculum of such schools was until late in the century. Only a handful of subjects was offered: religious instruction; grammar, a cat's cradle of formal rules far removed from everyday speech; writing, that is, calligraphy; drawing; music, a course in which the future teacher learned plainchant for the masses he would have to help serve, then got some instrumental training because most teachers sang badly; horticulture, a subject offered primarily in aid of the teacher's own garden; and arithmetic and land-surveying, the only practical skills most teachers truly mastered, recognizing, as did villagers and schoolchildren, that they related to practical needs. Only the 1880's saw innovations—an enrichment of the teaching of French, the introduction of history and geography, an attempt to relate dusty formalities to living experience. The whole character of the normal school changed. Students formed clubs, went in for hiking and mountain climbing. "The school is no longer the sinister establishment that it used to be; ...it lives, it acts."[44] Doubtless we would think it stiff and stilted. But the tone had clearly changed, and the new teachers trained at Clermont or Mende—as in Péguy's Orléans— would indeed be the conquering army that Charles Péguy has sung.

They already enjoyed a basis for prestige in their literacy and command of French, a knowledge that they shared with very few others.* This put them if not quite in the class of notables—not while their subjection to the priest

---

* And for concrete advantages and rewards that went with this, which the mother of an apprentice teacher voices in Simin Palay's play, "La Reyente mancade" (quoted in Gaston Guillaume, *Le Théâtre Gascon*, Paris, 1941, pp. 124–28). "Ue reyente!," says the mother:

"Mes, sàbes pas quin ey beroy, per u paysa,
D'abé ue reyente à case! Ue reyente! . . .
Ue hilhe qui sap de tout, e qui n'a pas
Besougn, ta bibe, de trima coume nous autes,
Pous camps, per la parquie, au darrè dou bestia,
Ha lou hariat dous porcs, afena, hemeya."

endured—at least in a position of influence. The teachers were recorders and scribes, very often secretaries to the mayor and municipal council. In many places the village councilmen conducted their business in the local tongue, leaving it to the teacher to keep the minutes in French. As *secrétaire de mairie*, the teacher prepared the documents required of the mayor, and often wrote all his letters as well. Many mayors, many municipal councilmen, were illiterate or as good as. Throughout the July Monarchy and the Second Empire the odd remark surfaces in some documents to say that most mayors "hardly know how to write," that lacking schooling they did not understand the forms they were to sign, that municipal councils and mayors were "practically illiterate." In a department where a third of the mayors were completely ignorant of the French language and five-sixths of the fonctionnaires could not write it, reasoned the prefect of Bas-Rhin in 1853, the teacher was indispensable. Such conditions still prevailed much later in isolated areas, so that in the Pyrenees in 1896 "most of our mayors can hardly read or write" (quite natural for men who had grown up unschooled around mid-century). They could not read, did not know what the official regulations were, and left everything to their secretaries.[45]

As early as 1865 the teachers' growing influence rated an official warning. Teachers were running the affairs of negligent, often illiterate mayors. They had become legal advisers to the villagers; lent farmers money, wrote their letters, and surveyed their fields; had "become occult powers." Their prestige was great, their status in the community almost "sacerdotal." Most alarming of all, warned the sub-prefect of Joigny (Yonne), teachers were even beginning to go into politics.[46] Hardly the browbeaten figure that Flaubert etched.

Such forebodings became serious fact when village teachers, trained to greater competence and new self-respect, became the licensed representatives of the Republic. By the 1890's they not only ran the administration in almost all the communes, but also in some instances worked as correspondents for the local newspapers, earning a useful increment in salary and prestige. A theme that recurs frequently in political accounts is the observation that the local schoolteacher "had turned the commune round politically by his influence on the young." The teacher was the municipal lamppost, the *bec de gaz municipal*, a half-friendly but suggestive nickname.[47] The political influence attributed to him was probably a reflection of shifts that we have seen to have had more complex roots. But even if exaggerated, such reports attest to the growing role of the man whose light, however dim, glowed strongly on his parish.

This could not have happened as long as schools remained irrelevant to a great many people; and this they did into the last quarter of the century. Most peasants wanted their children to work and contribute to the family budget. If they sent them to school at all, it was usually for the sole purpose of getting them past their first communion, a crucial rite of passage. Once that was accomplished, the child was withdrawn. Parents send their children to school for a few winter months before their communion, grumbled a Breton teacher in 1861, and that short time was almost exclusively devoted to learning the catechism, an awkward business since the children could not read. For this reason communions were made as early as possible, between the ages of ten and twelve. As a result school enrollments of children past that age diminished sharply, and children soon forgot the little they had learned, mostly by rote, lapsing once again into a "state of complete ignorance."[48]

In any case the country school provided little stimulus to learning for its pupils, not even the challenge of exposure to more motivated students. Parents in comfortable circumstances who were willing and able to keep their children in school for a time preferred to send them to the bourg or to a boarding school. More important, the offspring of wealthier parents, aware that schooling would play a part in their later activities, assimilated more and retained more of what they learned. The parents took more interest in their work.[49] Thus the children of the poor had access to poorer schools, less time to attend them, and far less reason to make the most of such opportunity than their better-off mates.*

Some poorer families kept their children out of school under the pressure of local landowners who did not want their future work force to be subverted or diminished by even a modicum of book-learning. More were discouraged by the distance the children had to cover to get to school and by the state of the roads. Where the peasants lived in small, dispersed settlements or in isolated houses the problem was twice as difficult. One village in Finistère refused to build a school because "the distance from the hamlets to the center does not permit farmers to send their children there. In summer they need them to watch the cattle; in winter they could not get to school because of the bad state of the roads." Another, in Ille-et-Vilaine, pointed out that though the present school seemed to have cramped quarters, the space was adequate because no child could make his way to school before the age of eight or nine, which cut the potential attendance by half. In Sarthe the rural roads were too bad for children to negotiate in the winter months; in Maurienne, Tarentaise, and Savoy generally, only the twelve- or thirteen-year-old child had the stamina to get to school regularly. At that point they left! Not especially surprising,

---

* But little attention has been paid to the institution of *caméristat*, in which a teacher or a poor family of the bourg took in boarders from outlying farms and hamlets. Around 1880 Pierre Besson's mother placed him *chez la Tinoune*, who lodged him (his mother supplied the bed), provided soup, and cooked whatever he brought to eat. For these accommodations Tinoune received 1.5 francs a month, plus a pound of butter and a cartful of firewood a year. There were 20 caméristes of both sexes at Tinoune's. (*Un Pâtre du Cantal*, p. 6.) See also Archives Départementales, Cantal 931 (299), 1903; and IT 533, 1895.

considering that they might have had to cover three to five miles on foot each way or use a boat to get there. In the Lannion district of Côtes-du-Nord where, in 1877, one child in three was not enrolled in a school though nearly every parish had one, the figures show that distance from isolated farms and hamlets made a significant difference, with the loneliest cantons averaging only half the enrollment of the others.[50]

Nor was the problem by any means a rare one. In many mountain communes less than a tenth of the population lived in the parish center. In Vendée, too, where in 1881 one-third of the twenty-year-olds could not spell out a word, the population was widely scattered. Only 224 of the inhabitants of a commune like Saint-Hilaire-de-Talmont lived in the bourg; the remaining 2,515 were spread over 83 km. La Garnache, with a population of 3,617, had three large villages (as well as many farms and hamlets), each 8 km from the bourg, where fewer than 500 people lived. Reports from Brittany ring with desperation. No one could understand who had not been there to see the conditions and terrain, an official reported in 1880. He selected as an example the commune of Lanouée, which was spread over 22,500 acres divided by a great forest. The bourg had 250 inhabitants; more than 3,200 other people were dotted about in solitary farms.[51] Here, as elsewhere, schools set up in the bourgs served a tiny minority, leaving the vast dispersed majority illiterate and untouched. The roads were impossible from November to March, which was just the season when most children would be free to attend them.

This problem would cause much ado into the 1880's, when better local roads began to help the situation, and the school-building program provided even hamlets with schools of their own. Yet the pressures exerted by landowners and difficult communications were minor obstacles compared to those raised by indifference and poverty. Poor, isolated departments maintained expectably low attendance rates. In 1867, when the national average was 69.1 percent, Corrèze had a rate of 40.7 percent, and Haute-Vienne's was 39.2 percent. In 1876, against a national average of 73.6 percent, the Limousin departments sent 60.3 percent and 55 percent of the school-age children to their schools. In Perche attendance in 1888 was lower than in the rest of Eure-et-Loir. The Breton departments made a still worse showing. A general report of 1880 shows that more than a third of the children in the 6–13 age group did not go to school:

Department	No. attending	No. not attending
Morbihan	40,842	31,434
Ille-et-Vilaine	59,309	30,810
Loire Inférieure	58,016	27,044
Côtes-du-Nord	60,421	30,000
Finistère	44,084	49,234

The proportion attending must have been far lower than two-thirds in rural areas—even if one provides for some undue optimism in the figures.[52] "The parish school we have suffices for the poor," reported a Cantal mayor in 1839, because, as he explained, their children left it at the earliest possible age to work. Once they had gone to work, learning was out of the question: they were at their tasks "by candlelight in winter, and in summer from one twilight to the other." There was no time or energy for anything else. In the Nive valley of the Pyrenees an officer found little trace of school enrollment in 1844. "The land is so poor that its people cannot make any sacrifice. The children guard the cattle in the mountains, while the parents work without a stop." These statements might as easily have been made a quarter century later, when many a country child still attended school—as they say in Franche-Comté—behind a cow's arse.[53]

Where there were mills, as in Ardèche or Franche-Comté, for instance, children could find work at the tender age of eight or nine. By 1867 only a "very few" children under eight were still working 15-17 hours a day in the mills of Privas or Annonay, but there were plenty of children aged eight to twelve who continued to do so.* The ones who interest us, however, mostly stayed close to home where they were needed to guard birds and cattle. Age was no object, provided they could trot. In Rouergue and Lauragais all children were clearly put to work at the age of six or seven throughout the 1860's, and boys as soon as they were strong enough were put to plowing or leading the plowing team—heavy work that stunted their growth, as draft boards commented. In 1875 we have a police report from Seissane (Gers) concerning a seven-year-old girl who set a rick on fire while guarding turkeys. As late as 1899 at Billy (Meuse) children were still being put to work at around the age of eight. Unfortunately, said the teacher, those who should have enforced attendance were the very persons interested in hiring them. Another teacher, at Sainte-Alauzie (Lot), put the blame more squarely on parents, complaining about how easily they sacrificed their children's schooling to the gains they could make from their work. The simple fact is that the sacrifice was easy because it was scarcely a sacrifice. The gains were important because the children's contribution, however skimpy, was crucial to the budget of households on the brink of misery. Small wonder that the Socialist *Egalité* should oppose compulsory schooling, which threatened to "force the poor man's child into school" and to "wrest from the working family a resource it cannot spare." Sauce for the rural as for the urban poor. More so, indeed, for country parents who depended on their children's services to meet the family's immediate needs.[54]

Where and when children were registered in school, what matters, after

* Elie Reynier, *Histoire de Privas*, 3: 172–73. The situation was no different in Meurthe-et-Moselle in 1888. At Croismare, where a local glassworks hired ten-year-olds, that was the age when boys left school. At Baslieux the possibility of working meant that some children never set foot in school, and others left it as soon as they had made their first communion. At Moutiers in the many families where both parents worked in the local textile mills, the children stayed home "to take care of the house." (Serge Bonnet et al., "La Vie ouvrière vue par les instituteurs...," *Mouvement social*, 1965, pp. 88–89.)

all, is not their enrollment as such, but their attendance.* This varied with the region and its ways, but tended generally to be restricted to the winter months. As actual or potential workers, children were free for school only when there was no work. In the Limousin they did not say that a child had been in school for three years but that he had three winters in school. He entered it in December, after the chestnuts had been gathered and the migrants he had helped replace had returned home, and left in late March or early April when the migrants set off again. Similarly, in Côte-d'Or and the Jura, which had more elementary schools for their outlying villages and hamlets than most departments, children usually had to work much of the year, and attended class for only a few months in the winter, forgetting in the interval whatever they had learned. The only ones who benefited from schooling were the sons of those with sufficient means to do without their help. In the Doubs, on the other hand, winter is hard and long. This kept the children in school longer, and they picked up more. Yet even children who did not help their parents left school in March or April. In Lozère children attended school four months a year at most. After Easter, only infants were left; schools were either closed down or turned into day nurseries (1877). In Manche parents were happy to leave children in school during the years when they would only get underfoot around the house, but wanted to withdraw them as soon as they were able-bodied, precisely when they would be at their most teachable (1892). Alain Corbin concludes that child labor disappeared only slowly, between the 1870's and the late 1880's. By the end of the century, at any rate, inspectors could note a greater regularity in school attendance in the winter. Continued complaints of irregularity now referred to the rest of the year. Grumbles were bitter, but standards had been raised.[55]

It is important to realize how regional conditions affected these gains. In the Doubs, about which we have heard already, some of the explanation for the department's slightly greater literacy may well be found in the Protestant influence radiating from Montbéliard. A more important factor may have been the predominance of the cattle industry in the mountain country around Pontarlier. With little cultivation, there was less call for children to work in the fields or be otherwise employed, so they were sent to school more often during the winter than elsewhere—"if only to get them out of the way." At Bansat (Puy-de-Dôme), on the other hand, attendance problems were made worse by the seasonal migrations that required the additional use of children to fill in for their absent fathers or elder brothers. In Sarthe, despite roads best described as excruciating, the "children of indigents attend more regularly [than others], since their parents have no lands on which their work is needed." In Cher and Indre, where cattle were kept and fed in the

---

* As usual, one must be wary of figures provided by the Ministry of Public Instruction. Checking these against the *Annuaire du Bureau des Longitudes*, Sanford Kanter concludes that in 1864, of 4,277,724 children between seven and thirteen years of age, 1,666,440 did not attend school ("Defeat 1871," p. 122).

fields, and sheep were tended in separate flocks based on sex and age, there were greater demands on the services of children than in neighboring Nièvre, where such practices were not followed. As a result, the absentee rate among school-age children in Nièvre was about 22 percent, compared with a rate of 30 percent in Cher and 45 percent in Indre.[56]

In Vendée, where agriculture had made great strides, children were in great demand to pull out weeds, which the humid climate treated with special favor. In Loire job opportunities had a marked effect on the school attendance of the two sexes. Thousands of boys went into the factories and mills of Loire as soon as they had made their first communion, but girls had no hope of finding work before they were fourteen or so. As a result, in 1878 only six in ten school-age boys attended school, against almost eight in nine girls. Within a single department like Saône-et-Loire there were significant differences between the Mâcon region, whose vineyards called for no child labor and whose dense population had put schools within relatively easy reach; the Autun region, mountainous, harsh, less densely populated, where peasants could not afford to hire workers and used their own children instead; Charolles, a thinly populated pastureland, where children grazed the fat, white cattle in summer and found the roads to school too long in lonely winter; and the low-lying plains of Louhans, easily inundated, full of meres and ponds, where the high rate of fever cut further into school attendance.[57]

Such regional differences may explain how Ardouin-Dumazet, crossing the Millevaches plateau at the turn of the century, could still find the cattle being tended from April to November by boys of ten to twelve, "fairly wild in manner," despite the school laws that had been in operation for nearly 20 years. Was the need of the parents still greater than the promises that the schools held out? Had their perceptions not yet awakened to new possibilities? Or were they merely waiting for pastures to be enclosed by wire or wood, so they could hand the small shepherds over to the mercies of the schools?[58]

After the 1880's the striking regional inequalities mirrored in school attendance tended to recede. Laws played their part in this. So did improvements that facilitated access to school or made the economic and physical effort of attendance seem worthwhile. In Sarthe, where inequalities between the schools of the eastern and western parts of the department had been very great, Paul Bois has found that "after 1885–1890 these regional inequalities in popular instruction practically disappear."[59] Another step in cultural homogenization was being taken.

It had been helped along by the law of 1881, which made schooling free. Free schooling for the poor, or some of the poor, had long been a fact. Church schools, at least in theory, had always opened their doors to those who could not pay. The First Republic had set a quota by which a quarter of the children could be admitted free; the Guizot law, like the ordinance of 1816, had reaffirmed that practice. By 1837 one pupil in three attended public elementary schools free of charge. Victor Duruy, the great reformer, supported the principle of free schooling for all. His education law of 1867 gave municipal councils the option of eliminating all tuition fees by the use of local taxes. Results on the national plane were striking: the proportion of free students in the school population, 38 percent in 1861, rose to 54 percent in 1872, and to 57 percent in 1877. Seen from this angle, the law of 1881 was the logical conclusion of a long process.[60]

However, the process of free schooling did not move forward as smoothly as these developments may suggest. National figures once again provide only a general view. In Eure-et-Loir the proportion of free students in 1862 was 26 percent, in 1878, 36 percent, well below the national average of 38 percent and 57 percent at those dates. In Gers the percentage of free students almost doubled in ten years, rising from 26 percent in 1861 to 46 percent in 1872, but still remained below the national average. On the other hand, by 1872 68 percent of the schoolchildren in Hérault and a full 86 percent in Lozère were free students.[61] Clearly the course municipal councils chose to follow varied greatly. As we have seen, the people of some means generally chose to send their sons to school in town. At Oulins (Eure-et-Loir) "indifference or misery of most," reported the teacher in 1873, who was left with such students because it was "easy for the better-off to send their children to good neighboring schools"—presumably at Anet, or even Dreux or Mantes not too far away. Similarly, in Finistère, those who could afford to do so preferred to send their children to Quimper, Morlaix, Quimperlé, or Pont-Croix. It is not so surprising, after all, to find notables reluctant to subsidize schools that their children did not need, and that might produce French-speaking competitors for their offspring among the lower orders.[62]

The authority to exempt students from school fees rested with municipal officials, and this gave rise to abuse. In Cantal, where school inspection reports reflect the rising numbers of free pupils, a mayor in 1852 certified three-quarters of the school's students as needy. Many local mayors played favorites in deciding who was to be certified as indigent. In 1853 one man was found to have listed his own grandson and the son of his deputy, boys who came from the two richest families in the commune. In 1859, and again in 1862, official circulars invited prefects to hold local magistrates to the letter of the law.[63]

Some schools themselves—especially those that were run by nuns—violated at least the spirit of the law by making a distinction between paying pupils and indigents admitted as free students; and not only in their treatment but in the quality of their education. In Loire-Inférieure many church schools in 1875 had separate classes for poor children and neglected them. There and elsewhere the indigent schoolchild was made to feel his inferiority. There were quite a few such children in the school at Dammartin-en-Serve in 1875, but it was painful to be admitted on that basis. "It was then practically a disgrace," remembered a teacher who had had to endure the pain himself. The poor did not want to send their children to school, explained the parish doctor of Pouldergat (Finistère) in 1852, because they were badly clothed. In any case they had to find bread and firewood. This last suggests that gratuity was only a partial answer when need was very great.[64]

We hear of a large Périgord village, with a quota of 20 scholarships, whose school in mid-century was attended by only three paying and three non-paying pupils. It was not enough to admit the needy free. In 1884 Georges Clemenceau met a peasant in a field with his son, and asked him why the child was not in school. "Will you give him a private income?," the peasant answered. The child who went to school had to bring a log for the fire, or a few sous instead. He had to provide his own ink, pen, and paper for writing—and though a slate could be used, the results were less than satisfactory. "A great number of children admitted to schools free get no benefit because they cannot acquire the indispensable books and class materials," read a report of 1875. "The well-off send their children away to school," reported a teacher from Tarn in the 1860's. "The poor don't send them to the elementary schools, because it costs 18–24 francs a year plus books, paper, etc., which can raise the cost to 30 francs." So, even if tuition was free, the child attending school, a useless mouth around the household board, was an expense. The "inexplicable inertia," the "indifference" that perplexed and annoyed apostles of the school, was in good part due to poverty—a lack of cash so great that, as a pastor in the Pyrenees explained in 1861, "even if the school fees were only 50 cents, they would still be a painful subject of anxiety and concern for the farmer." We must conclude, with a correspondent from Gironde, that "it is not enough for schooling to be free; the child's work must bring in some revenue to cover his keep or simply because the family needs it."[65]

But the same report held out the hope of change: "The remedy to this state of things lies in public opinion. Even the most ignorant portion of the masses begins to understand that instruction is useful to all [and not just to their betters]. Country people know now that reading, writing, and arithmetic are means of rising in the world."[66] Let us say at least that they began to know it. Free education had been gratuitous, that is, seemingly useless, to the children of the poor because it did not serve any needs that their parents could discern.* The remitting of fees did not prove a critical factor in rural school attendance. There is no good evidence that the poor children who were admitted as free students attended school more diligently as a result; indeed, often they attended less regularly than the paying students. The crux of school attendance lay in the social practice: when going to school was the thing to

---

* In the patois of Picardy *bibloteux* (bookish) describes a person engaged in a useless task (A. Morel, "Le Pouvoir au village: en Picardie," *Annales: Economies, sociétés, civilisations*, 1975, p. 166).

do, all would do it. It also lay in the dawning comprehension, related to changing circumstances, that instruction was useful. With this realization, even lack of means would not deter many from sending their children to school.[67]

We have arrived at the fundamental cause of that "indifference" to book learning that Philippe Ariès, like Destutt de Tracy before him, finds indigenous to the countryside. The urban poor had occasion to use the skills picked up in parish schools and to observe the opportunities of improving their position with that learning. In the countryside, such skills brought little profit, their absence small disadvantage, and there were fewer chinks in the armor of misery through which curiosity or enterprise could find escape. The *Statistique* of Vendée, regretting in 1844 that the department's inhabitants "showed little inclination for the study of sciences and polite literature, or for the culture of fine arts," sounds ridiculous until it shows that it understands why this was not surprising: "Far from the sources of inspiration and taste, they were rarely in a position to know their value or [to find] any object of emulation."[68] Objects of emulation were scarce in the countryside, sources of inspiration even scarcer.

School was perceived as useless and what it taught had little relation to local life and needs. The teacher taught the metric system when *toises, cordes,* and *pouces* were in current use; counted money in francs when prices were in *louis* and *écus.* French was of little use when everyone spoke patois and official announcements were made by a public crier in the local speech. Anyway, the school did not teach *French,* but arid rules of grammar. In short, school had no practical application. It was a luxury at best, a form of more or less conspicuous consumption. Corbin has pointed out the significant role that all this played in the lack of interest displayed by parents and children.[69] When Martin Nadaud's father wanted to send him to school, neighbors and relatives argued that for a country child school learning was useless, enabling him merely to make a few letters and carry books at mass. Teachers and school inspectors failed to persuade the peasants that reading and writing had any value in themselves. And parents found their reticence justified by the slight difference in the situation of those who attended school and of those who did not. When Ferdinand Buisson linked poor school attendance to a lack of concern for the moral benefits that children could derive, he was in the great (abstract) tradition. Yet show people a practical benefit that they could understand, and the problem would shrink to manageable proportions. Rural inhabitants, explained a village mayor, were "only very vaguely conscious of an intellectual or moral culture that has no immediate or tangible relation to pecuniary profit." That seemed to make sense. Before a man could want his child to go to school, he would have to abandon "the gross material interests" that were all he understood. Not so. It was when the school mobilized those interests that men began to care.[70]

In darkest Finistère, while the other local councils squirmed uncomfortably before the requirements imposed by Guizot's education law of 1833, the council of Audierne alone voiced a positive response. Since most children in the little port "belong to families of sailors and soldiers, and are destined, like their fathers, to defend the fatherland [on] sea or land, where they can expect no advancement if they lack basic instruction and cannot read, write, or reckon sums," the council decided that "a school appears necessary."[71] Not all municipalities enjoyed such enlightened majorities and many, we have seen, placed the personal interests of men who could fend for their children's schooling above the training of potential competitors or social rebels. But the connection between practical interest and school, when it became apparent, was a potent force.*

A number of individuals had overcome the disadvantage of illiteracy by self-education. Others, faced with the need to keep accounts, devised private systems of notation. By their nature, such records were not likely to survive; but we do know about a Loire mariner who, around 1830, kept track of his expenses by drawing the objects of his outlays or figures of little men accompanied by ciphers to show francs and sous. Clearly, mariners were involved in trade and in commercial transactions long before the peasants of the isolated countryside had reason to engage in such activities. Yet by the 1870's even sharecroppers in Brittany were being pressed to keep accounts. Manuscripts of the accounts maintained by two illiterate sharecroppers in Finistère have survived to show the new need for records. Each man separately seems to have devised a system of figurative notation to identify purchases (rope, horseshoe, horse collar), hired help (a man with a spade to dig up a field or an expensive sawyer), the number of horses or cattle sold, and coins (*sol, réal, écu*). These rough records, with their crude, ingenious shapes reminiscent of children's drawings, were preserved by offspring who went to school. The very treasuring of them as artifacts suggests the reasoning that led to that decision.[72]

My point is that it needed personal experience to persuade people of the usefulness of education. Certain migrants had learned this, and we have seen how they and their children recognized at an early date "the value of instruction and the profit one can derive from it in the great centers." Through the second half of the century, school attendance in migrant Creuse was far better than in neighboring Haute-Vienne and Corrèze—higher by 7 percent and 12 percent, respectively, in 1876.[73] Another spur to schooling came from the military law of 1872, not only because it abolished the purchase of substitutes, but also because it provided advantages for men who could read and write and threatened illiterate conscripts with an additional year of service. The

---

* According to Armand Audiganne, of all the workers at Saint-Etienne the lace-and-braid workers were the best educated for the simple reason that they had to keep tabs on their daily output and transactions. As a result, they well appreciated the usefulness of writing and did not forget the skill as soon as they left school (*Les Populations ouvrières*, 2: 103).

school authorities made haste to refer to these facets of the law to persuade parents to send their children to school. In Isère a poster was even displayed in every schoolroom, and teachers were required to read and discuss it at least every two weeks, presumably arguing that the fulfillment of one patriotic duty could help lighten the burden of another.[74]

But another army was growing, as important as the regular one—the body of public and private employees, access to which was opened by the school certificate, the certificate of elementary studies. The little school of Roger Thabault's Mazières put its graduates into the numerous jobs that opened up there (and elsewhere), with economic, social, and political development: the town's 15 civil servants in 1876 had become 25 in 1886, and there were seven railway employees as well. Ambition was encouraged by propaganda. "A good primary education allows one to secure a post in several state services," the student was told in a first-year civics text published in 1880. "The government servant has a secure position. That is why government posts are in great demand." They were. Given the chance, many peasants wanted to stop being peasants, to change to something else. In 1899, 40 former natives of the little village of Soye in Doubs, population 444, worked as functionaries elsewhere, and 14 inhabitants worked as domestics in town. The prefecture of Seine received 50,000 applications for 400 openings in its departments.[75]

Other times had seen the growth of a state bureaucracy that triggered the expansion of education to fill the available posts. Such educational booms, however, had been restricted to relatively high social groups. Under the Third Republic the means for those too humble to have gotten their share of the educational pie were made available just when the ends (i.e., the jobs) emerged to reinforce and justify their use. Around the 1880's even rural laborers began to lend attention to the schools. As the number of jobs expanded and getting one became more than an idle dream, the education that would help secure such prestigious jobs became important. Even more so the certificate to which it led. Scattered encomiums to its practical uses appear in the late 1870's. By 1880 Pécaut could report that the school certificate "is slowly being accepted. Families realize that this small diploma can be of use for several kinds of jobs; hence they consent ever more frequently to leave their children in school for a longer time." Schools were still badly housed, still far from home, but children now were made to attend even when they lived six km away, because "the idea of the utility and the necessity of elementary schooling" had caught on so well.[76]

The recognition of new possibilities and of the school as a key to their exploitation was in full evidence by the 1890's. By 1894 practically every child in a village of Lower Provence that had been almost totally illiterate a generation earlier was attending school, even those who lived one and a half hours' walk away. In the southwest the image of little boys doing their homework of an evening by the light of the dying embers became a reality. Municipal councils voted rewards for teachers whose pupils won the coveted certificate. Families became avid for it; they celebrated when a child got one; too many failures could become issues raised at council meetings.[77] In a natural evolution, the school certificate, significant because of the material advantages it could help secure, became an end in itself.* "It is an honor to get it," wrote a little girl (and wrote it very badly: "être ademise s'est un honneur davoir son certificat d'étude"), about what popular parlance dubbed the "Santificat."[78] The passing of the examination became an eminent occasion, competing in importance with the first communion. Men who had taken it in the 1880's remembered the questions that they had to answer, had every detail of their examination day graven in their memories. To take one example among many, here is Charles Moureu, member of the Academy of Medicine and professor at the Collège de France, speaking at the graduation ceremony of his native village in the Pyrenees in 1911: "I could if I wanted to recite by heart the exact details of the problem that turned on the things Peter and Nicholas bought and sold."[79]

There were of course more immediate gains: there would be no more need to go to the nearest town to consult a solicitor or a notary when one wanted to draw up a simple bill or promissory note, make out a receipt, settle an account in arrears, or merely write a letter, explained a thirteen-year-old schoolboy in the Aube. The literate man did not have to reveal his friendships, his secrets, his affairs to some third party. *And* he could better himself—in local politics, or teaching, or the army (whence he returned with a pension and decorations, achieving a position "that places him above the vulgar crowd").[80]

The vulgar crowd was full of the sort of peasants whose stereotyped image filled current literature: they spoke ungrammatically, used characteristic locutions, mishandled the small vocabulary at their command, and "do not look more intelligent than other peasant farmers around them." The only escape from this was education, which taught order, cleanliness, efficiency, success, and *civilization*. Official reports coupled poor education with rude, brutal ways. Where schooling did not take hold, "ways are coarse, characters are violent, excitable, and hotheaded, troubles and brawls are frequent." The school was supposed to improve manners and customs, and soothe the savage breast. The polite forms it inculcated "softened the savagery and harshness natural to peasants." Improved behavior and morality would be attributed

---

* Honor and profit lay in scholarly accomplishment. This may be why horticulture courses seldom caught on: "Occupation manuelle nuisible au travail intellectuel," it made no contribution to passing exams. See C. Desprez, *Congrès pédagogique de 1880: Doléances et voeux des instituteurs* (Chartres, 1880), p. 48. Louis Chevalier remarks that the teaching of agriculture was also generally considered reactionary. Around 1900 and after, he claims, such courses were left largely to church schools; the secular schools made vague gestures toward competing with them but abandoned the field when the church schools closed (*Les Paysans*, p. 209). I am not certain this was so, but for all the attempts to teach "useful" topics, the school in fact concentrated on and glorified intellectual attainments, which were increasingly perceived as even more useful.

to the effects of schooling. Schools set out "to modify the habits of bodily hygiene and cleanliness, social and domestic manners, and the way of looking at things and judging them." Savage children were taught new manners: how to greet strangers, how to knock on doors, how to behave in decent company. "A bourgeois farts when his belly is empty; a Breton [peasant] burps when his belly is full," declared a proverb that seems to confuse urban and rural differences with race. Children were taught that propriety prohibited either manifestation; and also that cleanliness was an essential part of wisdom.[81]

The schools played a crucial role in forcing children to keep clean(er), but the teachers had to struggle mightily to that end.* Hair, nails, and ears were subject to regular review; the waterpump was pressed into frequent use; the state of clothes, like the standards of the child's behavior out of school, received critical attention and constant reproof. Study, ran the text of one exercise, "fills the mind, corrects false prejudices, helps us order speech and writing, teaches love of work and improves capacity for business and for jobs." What does study tell us? Among other things: cold baths are dangerous; the observance of festivals is a religious duty; labor abuses the body less than pleasure; justice protects the good and punishes the wicked; tobacco is a poison, a useless expenditure that destroys one's memory, and those who use it to excess live in a sort of dream, their eye dead, incapable of paying attention to anything, indifferent and selfish. And then there was the lesson of Jules and Julie, who are rich and therefore do not work at school; and who, having learned nothing, are embarrassed later by their ignorance, blushing with shame when people laugh at them for the mistakes they make when speaking. Only the schools could "change primitive conditions," declared Ardouin-Dumazet.[82] The primitive conditions themselves were changing, and schools helped their charges to adapt to this.

Of course they did more—or they did it more broadly. If we are prepared to set up categories with well-drawn limits, society educates and school instructs. The school imparts particular kinds of learned knowledge, society inculcates the conclusions of experience assimilated over a span of time. But such a view, applicable to specific skills and subjects, has to be altered when the instruction offered by the school directs itself to realms that are at variance with social education (as in the case of language or measures), or that social education ignores (as in the case of patriotism). In other words, the schools provide a complementary, even a counter-education, because the education of the local society does not coincide with that needed to create a national one. This is where schooling becomes a major agent of acculturation:

* Mightily, and long! At Plozévet (Finistère), school inspectors never cease criticizing the grubbiness, long hair, and bad manners of students. In 1893 "les élèves sont malpropres. . . . Une grande partie viennent en classe pieds nus et sans chaussures, les vêtements en désordre, la figure et les mains noires de crasse." In 1897 "l'éducation des élèves est complètement à faire *quand ils arrivent en classe*" (my italics). André Burguière, *Bretons de Plozévet*, p. 294.

shaping individuals to fit into societies and cultures broader than their own, and persuading them that these broader realms are their own, as much as the pays they really know and more so.

The great problem of modern societies, or so François Guizot considered in his *Memoirs*, is the governance of minds. Guizot had done his best to make elementary education "a guarantee of order and social stability." In its first article, his law of 1833 defined the instruction it was intended to provide: the teaching of reading, writing, and arithmetic would furnish essential skills; the teaching of French and of the metric system would implant or increase the sense of unity under French nationhood; moral and religious instruction would serve social and spiritual needs.[83]

What these social needs were is laid out clearly in various writings, both official and unofficial. "Instructing the people," explained an anonymous writer of 1861, "is to condition them to understand and appreciate the beneficence of the government." Eight years later, the inspecteur d'Académie of Montauban concurred: "The people must learn from education all the reasons they have for appreciating their condition." A first-year civics textbook set out to perform this task:

Society (summary): (1) French society is ruled by just laws, because it is a democratic society. (2) All the French are equal in their rights; but there are inequalities between us that stem from nature or from wealth. (3) These inequalities cannot disappear. (4) Man works to become rich; if he lacked this hope, work would cease and France would decline. It is therefore necessary that each of us should be able to keep the money he has earned.[84]

The ideals of the educators were to be fulfilled at least in part.

Schools taught potent lessons of morality focused on duty, effort, and seriousness of purpose. Hard work and rectitude were bound to bring improvements, internal and external. You must be just and honest. The Roman Camillus refuses to take a town by treachery: the people of the town become the allies of Rome. Never forget that no end, however useful, can justify injustice. Progress is good, routine is bad. "Routine consists in refusing to make any improvement and in following the methods of our ancestors." Progress was new schools, fire companies, municipal bands. It was Monsieur Tardieu, mayor of Brive, who built a bridge that permitted people to sell their goods in the market on the other side of the river, and thus increased the prosperity of his town: "The Brivois perceived the possibilities of gain, and the more they worked, the richer they got." A Vosges village teacher's report of 1889 echoes what he taught and what his students learned: "The farmers are better educated and understand that they have to break with their routine, if they want to earn more. In 1870 they only did what they had seen their forebears doing."[85]

"Believe in progress with a sincere and ardent faith.... Never forget that the history of all civilization is a perpetual glorification of work." Perhaps it is true that men are seldom so harmlessly employed as when their energies are bent on making money. "Work draws men together and prepares the reign of peace." "Work is the instrument of all progress." Francinet and his little friends are told the story of the sago tree, which feeds a man during a whole year in return for only a few hours' work, but in so doing, destroys his moral values. Conclusion: "Work is moralizing and instructive par excellence. But man only resigns himself to constant and regular labor under the pressure of need." One rises in the world by work, order, thrift: "Not all at once, of course. My father had nothing, I have something; my children, if they do like me, will double, triple what I leave behind. My grandchildren will be gentlemen. This is how one rises in the world." The speaker is the shoemaker Grégoire, hero of several little moral tales in a collection published by Ernest Lavisse in 1887. They warn against idleness, indolence, and thriftlessness, and make their point with lots of solid detail ("his charming wife brought a dowry of 5,000 francs; he had 3,000 ..."), with useful explanations of things like bankruptcy law and fraud, and not least, with a profoundly realistic sense of values.[86]

Such is the tale of Pierre, who, called to serve in the 1870 war, escapes death when a German bullet is deflected by two five-franc pieces sent him by his father and his brother as tokens of their affection. Decorated with the military medal, which the proud father frames and garnishes with flowers, Pierre "will go every year to draw the 100 francs to which his medal entitles him until his death, and place the money in the savings bank." Both family affection and heroism are expressed and rewarded not only in elevated feelings but in concrete terms: a thoroughly sensible view. No wonder that patriotism was advocated in similar terms. The fatherland was a source of funds for road repairs, subsidies, school scholarships, and police protection against thieves—"one great family of which we are all a part, and which we must defend always."[87]

We come here to the greatest function of the modern school: to teach not so much useful skills as a new patriotism beyond the limits naturally acknowledged by its charges. The revolutionaries of 1789 had replaced old terms like schoolmaster, regent, and rector, with *instituteur*, because the teacher was intended to *institute* the nation. But the desired effect, that elusive unity of spirit, was recognized as lacking in the 1860's and 1870's as it had been four score years before.[88]

School was a great socializing agent, wrote a village teacher from Gard in 1861. It had to teach children national and patriotic sentiments, explain what the state did for them and why it exacted taxes and military service, and show them their true interest in the fatherland. It seems that there was a great deal to do. The theme remained a constant preoccupation of eminent educators. Twenty years after this, student teachers "must above all be told ... that their first duty is to make [their charges] love and understand the fatherland." Another ten years, and the high aim is again repeated, that a "national pedagogy" might yet become the soul of popular education. The school is "an instrument of unity," an "answer to dangerous centrifugal tendencies," and of course the "keystone of national defense."[89]

First, the national pedagogy. "The fatherland is not your village, your province, it is all of France. The fatherland is like a great family." This was not learned without some telescoping. "Your fatherland is you," wrote a thirteen-year-old schoolboy dutifully in 1878. "It is your family, it is your people [*les tiens*], in a word it is France, your country." "The fatherland is the *pays* where we are born," wrote another, "where our parents are born and our dearest thoughts lie; it is not only the *pays* we live in, but the region [*contrée*] we inhabit; our fatherland is France." The exercise was a sort of catechism designed to teach the child that it was his duty to defend the fatherland, to shed his blood or die for the commonweal ("When France is threatened, your duty is to take up arms and fly to her rescue"), to obey the government, to perform military service, to work, learn, pay taxes, and so on.[90]

At the very start of school, children were taught that their first duty was to defend their country as soldiers. The army—and this was important, considering the past and enduring hostility to soldiers and soldiering—"is composed of our brothers or parents" or relatives. Commencement speeches recalled this sacred duty in ritual terms—our boys will defend the soil of the fatherland. The whole school program turned on expanding the theme. Gymnastics were meant "to develop in the child the idea of discipline, and prepare him ... to be a good soldier and a good Frenchman." Children sang stirring songs like the "Flag of France," the "Lost Sentry," and "La Marseillaise." Compositions on the theme were ordered up, with title and content provided: "Letter of a Young Soldier to His Parents. He tells them that he has fought against the enemies of the fatherland, has been wounded ... and is proud (as they must be too) that he has shed his blood for the fatherland." And teachers reported with satisfaction how they implanted the love of the fatherland by evoking "those memories that attach our hearts to the fatherland" from history, and then "develop[ed] this sentiment by showing France strong and powerful *when united*."[91]

There were no better instruments of indoctrination and patriotic conditioning than French history and geography, especially history, which "when properly taught [is] the only means of maintaining patriotism in the generations we are bringing up."* Could it be that other social forces were doing little to stir or inculcate it? Unfortunately, most teachers knew history badly,

---

* Archives Nationales, F^{17}9276 (Tarn-et-Garonne, 1877). The point was well taken. When in 1897 candidates for the *baccalauréat moderne* were asked to discuss the uses and purpose of history in education, 80 percent replied essentially that it was to exalt patriotism (Ch.-V. Langlois and Ch. Seignobos, *Introduction aux études historiques*, Paris, 1898, pp. 288–89).

geography still worse. When, around the 1870's, they taught French history—or began to teach it—they tended to string out reigns and dates, and seldom seem to have got further than the Middle Ages. History was ignored, and civics absent from the teaching program, complained Félix Pécaut in 1871. It was quite possible "to use French history to form French citizens, make the free fatherland be known and loved; but no elementary attempt of this sort has yet been made." This was not surprising. "Teachers certificated in 1850–1868," more than half those teaching in 1879, "have never studied French history and do not know it," grumbled a school inspector in Vendée. And "teachers begin, it is still new and rare, to present the chief events of French history," reported another in Haute-Saône.[92] The job would be undertaken in textbooks like Lavisse's *First Year of French History*, a book thoroughly bent to show and to justify the rise of French patriotism and unity—refocused from the *petite patrie* to the larger one. Reading it, children were told, "you will learn what you owe your fathers and why your first duty is to love above all else your fatherland—that is, the land of your fathers."[93]

Just as the mother tongue was not the tongue of their mothers, so the fatherland was somewhere more (indeed, something else) than where their fathers rather obviously lived. A vast program of indoctrination was plainly called for to persuade people that the fatherland extended beyond its evident limits to something vast and intangible called France. Adults were too deeply rooted in their backwardness. But it was hard work to persuade even children, for all their malleability, without the panoply of material that became available only in the 1870's. Under the Second Empire, "children know no geography, see no maps, know nothing concerning their department or their fatherland" (Lot-et-Garonne). Children "were completely unaware of the existence of their department or of France" (Dordogne). "Notions of geography have become a general need" (Doubs).[94]

Maps of France began to be supplied soon after the Franco-Prussian War, distributed by the state. First urban schools, then rural ones, were endowed with wall maps. By 1881 few classrooms, however small, appear to have lacked a map. Some, of course, served "only as ornaments."[95] But they inculcated all with the image of the national hexagon, and served as a reminder that the eastern border should lie not on the Vosges but on the Rhine. They were also powerful symbols, not only of the asserted fatherland, but of the abstractions young minds had to get used to. How difficult this latter exercise remained is suggested by a circular of 1899 announcing the distribution of engravings of "views of different French regions that will lend concreteness to the idea of the fatherland."[96]

By the 1880's the determined assault against provincialism began to show results. "France ceased being a Kingdom and became a fatherland." Little boys in country schools were fascinated by tales of past French glories. Preparing for the school certificate examination in his lost Cantal valley, Pierre

Besson bought the fat history text of the advanced course and spent the class breaks learning Napoleon's campaigns by heart. Going home in the evening the boys would shout snatches of Hugo or Déroulède to each other, and the valley would resound to the echoes of Waterloo.[97] The young Auvergnats were joining the rest of France, now that the once abstract notion was taking on concrete and epic forms.*

The stirring deeds of derring-do were themselves part of a transcendent theme. By 1884 Bruno's *Tour de France*, published in 1877, had gone through 108 printings, and by 1900 or so, sales exceeded eight million copies. Every child knew, read, and reread the story of the two Alsatian boys who left their home after their father's death to fulfill his wish that they should live as Frenchmen. With great simplicity the book managed to introduce its readers to almost all the regions of France, their ways, scenes, history, and people. It can still be read today with pleasure, and it still leaves the feeling of a charming world—not easy, but helpful and decent, where the right sentiments would get you by. A reading makes one wish to repeat Julien's and André's circuit, and forges strong links of sympathy for France and the people in it. The millions who pored over the book and its illustrations learned that French patriotism was a natural complement to their own: "France is a garden, the provinces are the flowers in it." And while everyone the children meet along the ways sings the praise of his particular home, all agree that France includes them all: Vive la patrie française! Love of France is a leitmotif, becoming more insistent as the book draws on, and what this implies is made evident. Bayard "dies for his country"; Du Guesclin is represented as a French patriot fighting the English (when he fought mostly Bretons). When the two children tire, they remind each other that they want "to remain French at any cost." And the last words of the book are "Duty and Fatherland!"[98]

Though written in the wake of the war with Prussia, the *Tour de France* did not preach revenge. The children encounter no soldiers on their circuit, and there is no war talk among those they meet, only talk of escaping from war and rebuilding life. Alsace and Lorraine are mourned, but the grief of their loss is to be effaced by work, not fighting. Ernest Lavisse, who was younger than Bruno and still in his twenties in 1870, struck more pugnacious notes in his edifying tales and histories: it was the duty of sons to avenge their fathers; it was the duty of children to wreak revenge for past defeats. His books and others like them were also widely read. But it is my impression that the patriotism they advocated placed national integration first, re-

---

* Of course, there had been teachers in an earlier day who had infused their students with their own patriotic enthusiasm, but one suspects they may have been found more frequently in urban schools. At any rate, we know from Arsène Vermenouze that he was so flushed with patriotism as a schoolboy at the Ecole Supérieure des Frères des Ecoles Chrétiennes at Aurillac in the mid-1860's that he learned to play the trumpet simply so he could play "La Marseillaise" (*Croix du Cantal*, Aug. 11, 1895; July 30, 1903).

venge only second. It is difficult to discriminate; the themes are often mingled. But simply making military service acceptable was itself an immense task. The theme of a good citizen's duty to serve his country and to defend the fatherland, constantly recurring, can easily be taken for militarism, unless we remember that it sought to inculcate sentiments whose total absence endangered a modern state.[99]

The problem of national integration went far beyond the army. Whole generations had to receive a basic training, quite simply to become amenable to being trained in radically new ways. All the efforts of the schools were none too great to civilize a citizenry—or even half of it: "well-taught children will make wise citizens. They will also make good soldiers." Note the order. The four *essential* obligations of the citizen were to get an education when young, and later to make sure that his children got one; to carry out his military duty zealously and always be ready to defend the fatherland; to pay taxes regularly; and to vote and elect the most honest and capable candidates.[100] We have seen how much there was to do on every score, and it is well to view teachers and textbooks in that context.

Teachers taught or were expected to teach "not just for the love of art or science ... but for the love of France"—a France whose creed had to be inculcated in all unbelievers. A Catholic God, particularist and only identified with the fatherland by revisionists after the turn of the century, was replaced by a secular God: the fatherland and its living symbols, the army and the flag. Catechism was replaced by civics lessons. Biblical history, proscribed in secular schools, was replaced by the sainted history of France. French became more than a possession of the educated: it became a patrimony in which all could share, with significant results for national cohesion, as the 1914 war would show.[101]

But the effects of school went further. In the first place, the literary or written language children learned in schools was as alien to the spoken tongue as spoken French itself was to their native dialect. In other words, schools began their work by propagating an artificial language, and this was true even for French-speakers.[102] They did this largely through the discipline of dictations, "the instrument of a learned and universal language" beyond the local ken. As a result, many students learned to express themselves freely and easily in speech, but had difficulty when it came to writing or to expressing thought in an idiom close to that of the written word. We can glimpse this best in the surviving files of gendarmerie reports, which are often drawn up in a stilted administrative style and relate even simple events in an awkward and convoluted manner.

A striking result of this (much worse in areas estranged by dialect) was that "for months or years [the children] give no sign of intelligence, merely imitate what they see done." Just as legislation can create crime by fiat, so education created stupidity by setting up standards of communication that many found difficult to attain. "Our children cannot find, and indeed have no way to find, enough French words to express their thoughts," reported a Cantal teacher. The result was a divorce between school learning, often acquired by rote, and assimilation, which helped slow down the progress of the schools. Memorization saved the trouble of "having to translate one's thoughts into correct French." It also divorced word from reality. Many children "can spell, but syllables have no meaning for them; can read, but fail to understand what they read, or to recognize in writing some words they know but whose orthography is alien," or to identify words learned in French with the objects around them. "You will learn it, this language of well-bred people, and you will speak it some day," promised a prize-giver in Dordogne in 1897. The future tense used in such improbable circumstances suggests a possible reason why, by 1907, the number of illiterate conscripts seems to have been slightly higher than in the immediate past. The absolute banning of the native tongue, which had been helpful in teaching French as a second language, inhibited the learning of idiomatic French and impeded its full assimilation.[103]

This is not to say that French did not make great strides forward. It did. But writing remained a socially privileged form of expression, and the French of the schools and of the dictations was an alienating as well as an integrative force. Perhaps that was what a school inspector meant when, looking back from 1897, he declared: "Ignorance used to precede school; today on the contrary it follows schooling."[104]

Of course there were (from the school's point of view) positive results; and these too went beyond the immediately obvious. The symbolism of images learned at school created a whole new language and provided common points of reference that straddled regional boundaries exactly as national patriotism was meant to do.* Where local dialect and locutions insulated and preserved, the lessons of the school, standardized throughout France, taught a unifying idiom. In Ain, the Ardennes, Vendée, all children became familiar with references or identities that could thereafter be used by the authorities, the press, and the politicians to appeal to them as a single body. Lessons emphasizing certain associations bound generations together. The Kings of France were the older sons of the Church, time was the river that carried all in its waters, a poet was a favorite of the muses, Touraine was the garden of France, and Joan of Arc the shepherdess of Lorraine. Local saws and proverbs were replaced by nationally valid ones, regional locutions by others learned in books:

---

* In a lesson given in the second year (four- to seven-year-olds), for example, children learned to interpret road signs. They began with the one all knew as a cross, then were taught to recognize it as a sign helping a person to find his way, and further, as an indication of how much better roads were in their own day ("Il n'y avait pas de routes dans le temps..."). *Devoirs d'écoliers français*, pp. 356–60. This cross-as-signpost image, as Renée Balibar has shown (*Les Français fictifs*, Paris, 1974, p. 194), played an important role in the writing of Charles Péguy, who had undoubtedly been taught the lesson.

castles in Spain rose above local ruins, and golden calves bleated more loudly than the stabled ones. The very mythology of ambition was now illustrated by landscapes that education had suggested, more stirring than the humbler ones at hand and by this time no less familiar.[105] These are only aspects of the wide-ranging process of standardization that helped create and reinforce French unity, while contributing to the disintegration of rival allegiances.

The cultural underpinnings of rural society, already battered by material changes, were further weakened by shifting values. First of all, manual labor was devalued—or better still, the natural aversion to its drudgery was reinforced. The elementary schools, designed to form citizens, neglected producers. The school glorified labor as a moral value, but ignored work as an everyday form of culture. The well-established contrast between the plucky, mettlesome spirit of the *courageux* and the idle *fainéant*—the one hardworking, especially or only with his hands, the other avoiding manual labor—was translated into scholastic terms. Soon, the idle boy was the one likely to be the most pressed into hard physical labor, the plucky boy the one most enterprising with his books. It made good sense, for the rewards of work now came to those not doing what had once been recognized as work. But it opened a crack—one more—in age-old solidarities.

In a great many homes, illiterate adults depended on small children to carry out what were becoming essential tasks—accounting, correspondence, taking notes, reading aloud pertinent documents or newspaper items. And new literacies at whatever level made new ideas accessible, especially to the young, to whom certain profound changes in the political climate of country districts were now attributed. In any case, the relationship between school and social claims was not ignored in their own time: "The Republic has founded schools," sang Montéhus, the revolutionary chansonnier, "so that now the people have learned how to count. The people have had enough of the pauper's mite; they want an accounting, and not charity!" More important, where, as in Brittany, a determined campaign taught new generations French, "children and parents form two worlds apart, so separated in spirit, so estranged by speech, that there is no more community of ideas and feelings, hence no intimacy. Often, as a matter of fact, any kind of relationship becomes impossible."[106] This is both exaggerated and suggestive of a generation gap more easily discerned in modern societies than in traditional ones. But even granting the exaggeration, the corrosive effects of one sort of education on a society based on another kind are undeniable.

Like migration, politics, and economic development, schools brought suggestions of alternative values and hierarchies; and of commitments to other bodies than the local group. They eased individuals out of the latter's grip and shattered the hold of unchallenged cultural and political creeds—but only to train their votaries for another faith.

Chapter Nineteen

DIEU EST-IL FRANÇAIS?

There's good and evil, God and the devil. God is good, we pray to
him in church, we give him his due, that is religion. But religion
does not allow us to ask God for earthly goods—at most, one
can pray for *everybody*. Now, what's good for one isn't good for
the others; for if my neighbor's land is struck by hail that's so
much less [grain] on his land and my wheat, if I save it, will
be worth double. Thus religion is about saving our souls from
the eternal fire by observing the prayers and the services of Sundays and feastdays. But religion has nothing to do with our private
interests. In the same way, the priest preaches that our happiness
is not of this world and that we have been put here to suffer.
That's well said, but too much is too much!

—GEORGE SAND

IN THE MID-1870's 35,387,703 of the 36,000,000 people in France were listed
in the official census as Catholics. The rest declared themselves Protestants
(something under 600,000), Jews (50,000), or freethinkers (80,000). The secular clergy of the Catholic church alone included 55,369 priests, one for every
639 inhabitants. Roman Catholicism remained, as it had been in 1801, "the
religion of the majority of Frenchmen."[1]

Whatever else this meant, it meant that the Church was an integral part of
life. It presided over all the major occasions in a person's life—birth, marriage,
death—and over the welfare of the community and the conduct of its members. It helped the crops increase and the cattle prosper. It healed, taught, and
preserved from harm. Its pervasive power was apparent in the appropriation
of godly terminology for more vulgar use: *kyrielle* (litany) for a long string
of words or a tedious story; *gloria* for a confused noise of voices; *glose* for
carping; *peromnia* or *faire des dominus* for hollow chatter; *brimborion* (from
the breviary) for empty baubles or knickknacks. Most of the terms refer to
uselessness or confusion, like *rapronobis* or *orapronobis,* used to describe something incongruous or stupid, or at any rate complicated, expressed in incomprehensible words taken from the most obvious place where the people would
hear them—the language of the Church.[2]

Dialect imitations of vespers, hymns, or canticles were abundant. Even more
so, jocular graces thanking God for the soup being poured and praying heaven
that no more mouths should appear to consume what was not enough already.
Such playful familiarities do not tell us much about people's feelings, only
that religious practices were part of everyday experience. They offered formulas that were repeated as charms and benedictions, even though their meaning was inevitably obscure. Witness this "Latin" grace pronounced after supper with no intention of levity:[3]

Rogimur tibi garcias,	Agimus tibi gracias,
jarnipotens Deus, pru-	omnipotens Deus, pro
nas d'hiver, per un inficit,	universis beneficiis tuis:
qui a vit lou renard, per	qui vivis et regnas, per
caromnia cercla cercloron.	omnia secula seculorum.
Amen!	Amen!

Religion provided spells and incantations, often written down and passed on preciously like amulets. These, like its ceremonies, were efficacious and protective. The peasant, noted Father Gorse in 1895, was proud to recite his prayers. "He has prayers for thunder, for sickness, for going to bed at night. They are good, very good, these prayers, says he, though he doesn't understand them very well, since they are in French," or in Latin. The ritual lent solemnity to private and public occasions, as the term solemnization applied to ceremonies like marriage attests. This was particularly important in rites of passage. The first communion, the first time one received the Eucharist, was crucial—a "great matter for country children; many cannot find a job before they have done it." Marking admission into the world of workers and of earners—almost an adult world—the first communion and the preparation for it, the catechism, provided the basic initiation into the moral mysteries of life. "The children did not know how to read, so the priest was teaching them the catechism by heart [which was] full of extraordinary words and which they laughed at," recorded Charles Péguy.[4] They must have had a sense that obscure powers were properly invoked with obscure incantations. Only, when one spoke more clearly, the borrowed terms expressed sentiments on which the Christian message seems to have had little impact.

Was Christ's personal message communicated in many a village church? We cannot tell. Those sermons that one finds concern themselves with the proprieties and transgressions of everyday behavior. Policemen were less concerned with immanent justice than with infringements of petty human laws; and village priests seem to have taken a similar view. This was their civilizing function. Along with this, it was their duty to see that their flock observed all of the formal and routine religious rites. It is by the practice of such rites that adherence to religion is generally measured. When there is little participation, even on high holidays, or when it declines, religion is said to decay. Yet what did church attendance mean to churchgoers?

"Sunday, the peasants go to church," wrote Madame Romieu at the end of the Second Empire, "some moved by religious feeling, most by habit or by fear of what people say." One went to church because it was the thing to do on Sunday, because it was one of the few social occasions of the week, because it was an opportunity for talking business or meeting friends, acquaintances, relatives. It was—especially for the women, once men had grasped at the opportunities that fairs held out—the sole occasion to escape the isolation in which many lived, the major recreation or diversion in a restricted life. Observance, business, and pleasure were combined. One went to mass wearing one's Sunday best, and given the muddy cart tracks, this often meant special paths—mass roads, *chemins de messe*. Public announcements were made by the village crier as the congregation left the service, public sales were often timed to fall after it, one could slip off later to call on the notary or the doctor, or drop in to the tavern, circle, or café. Even if a majority did not attend the service but went about their work as on any other day, "a multitude of peasants gathered in front of the church, discussed politics, made deals, filled the taverns."[5]

In a world where entertainment was scarce, church provided a certain festive diversion. Those attending might well "love the high mass, the rich ornaments, seeing a great many statues of saints in their churches." Writing about his grandmother, Charles Péguy presented church attendance as a treat for the lonely child raised in a woodcutter's hut in Bourbonnais in the early 1800's: "When she was good, she was allowed to go on Sunday to mass in the village—she wore her sabots because one doesn't go to church barefoot, and she was happy because that's where everybody met, where they exchanged news, where one heard about deaths, marriages, births, where gossip flowed about what was going on, where servants were hired."[6]

Observance clearly varied according to local tendencies. In a classic study, André Siegfried has pointed out the relationship between granitic terrain and the isolation, conservatism, and priestly vocations the rocky soil engenders. More recently, Serge Bonnet has sketched out a hierarchy of observance that runs from grainland down through vine to forest, where it is least prevalent.[7] But the belief and behavior of the peasants never ceased to oscillate between observance and transgression. Until the Revolution church attendance was compulsory, and religious sanctions that could cause serious social embarrassment menaced those who skipped their Easter duties. The elimination of constraints broke this decreed unanimity. Those who had been quietly uncommitted (as in Aunis-Saintonge, where the forced conversion of Protestants had made lukewarm Catholics) were free to fall away.[8] Political divisions and internal schism during the 1790's confused many more, and deprived parishes of pastors or cut sections of a community off from the only priest. For a decade or more, at least until the Concordat of 1801, a good number of young people grew up without catechism, whole communities did not attend church, and others ceased to celebrate traditional festivals. The Décadi created the habit of working on Sunday.* The absence of priests left marriages to civil

---

* With Napoleon on Elba, the mayors of several communes in Yonne complained that the priests were trying to restore holidays abolished by the new calendar, and that they were abetted by *cabarétiers*, who encouraged "this false piety" so that "domestics on those days won't do anything." One mayor remarked: "Les habitants des campagnes qui avaient regretté autrefois la suppression de certaines fêtes, les verraient rétablir aujourd'hui avec répugnance, parce qu'ils savent qu'un trop grand nombre de fêtes fait perdre aux cultivateurs et aux ouvriers du temps et de l'argent, et leur donne des occasions de dépense." And another wrote: "Le peuple n'est cependant pas si dévot pour lui donner tant de fêtes; elles ne servent qu'à lui faire perdre du temps et dépenser de l'argent." (Archives Départementales, Yonne III M¹47, Dec. 1814; Jan. 1815.)

authorities and led to prolonged delays before baptism, if the ceremony was performed at all.

Some communities came to rely on the services of laymen, who took over the functions of absent priests, performing baptisms, marriages, and burials. Archives contain numerous complaints on this score, especially against village teachers, whom peasants generally chose to take the place of the absent priest. Ad hoc arrangements of this sort could prove enduring. As late as 1837 we hear that Rouvres in Loiret refused to accept a priest and, worse still, prospered in its iniquity: "Baptisms and burials are performed right and left after a fashion; there is no mass or confession; the churchwarden tolls the Angelus, the schoolmaster recites the prayers for the sick, and all goes well."[9]

Canon Fernand Boulard doubts that the Revolution really affected rural religious practice very profoundly, or that much changed in this realm until the last decade or two of the nineteenth century. He may be right. But there were discordances where there had once been at least outward unity. Men who had acquired Church property and would not submit, men who had married in a civil marriage and would not seek absolution for their sin, became centers of local opposition. Not many cases of this kind of sturdy opposition developed in communities that remained cohesive, but it flourished in areas where, as in Burgundy, the memory of clerical harshness and exploitation survived, along with the fear of a reconstitution of their great domains. In Mâconnais, where it was said that it was better to meet a black wolf in a forest than run into a white (Cistercian) monk—crafty, vindictive, and rapacious— the devil appears as the hero in some local legends and triumphs over Christ, disgraced by the men who served him. The peasants had burned churches there in the Middle Ages and did so again in 1789, or stayed away thereafter. But even where the road had not been so prepared, hard times frayed clerical authority. Priests were forced to ask for help from their parishioners. Rival clergymen accused each other of the worst transgressions, diminishing still further the influence of the cloth. "People begin to separate religion from its ministers," asserted the *Statistique* of Lot in 1831.[10] But religion *was* its ministers, just as the state was bailiffs and gendarmes. And when, after 1830, liberal local mayors opposed the influence of priests loyal to the old order, they sought to sap their authority by encouraging the drift of men away from the sacraments.*

---

* Note that when, after the Restoration, the Church refused the last rites, especially burial, to Catholics accused of flouting its authority, rival authorities encouraged by recent experience were ready to replace the priest in his functions. Thus we hear in 1834 that at Gaillefontaine, not far from Rouen, the mayor "has forced entry into the church to bring in the coffin, has had the bell rung, has himself with a few supporters sung the Office for the dead, and ... has completed the burial in the absence of the priest" (Nadine-Josette Chaline, "Une Image du diocèse de Rouen sous l'épiscopat de Mgr. de Croy," *Revue de l'histoire de l'église de France*, 1972, p. 59). The next logical step would come, as it did in Provence, when local populations "unexpectedly and spontaneously" replaced the customary religious ceremonial with solemn civil burials. Maurice Agulhon finds in this "the first public symptoms of a still-unselfconscious dechristianization"

We see that in the churches, as in the schools, non-attendance is a way of measuring ineffectiveness. The growing numbers of migrant workers going to the cities added to this trend. Urban workers worked Sundays and holidays, or did so very often. The more earnest the man, the more he worked. The less responsible were the more likely to get drunk during their free time. The Church did not see them either way. Like the Revolution, acquaintance with the city did not destroy religious sentiment. It simply made nonconformity possible or created another kind of conformity. Men who attended church at home because their peers did ceased to attend church where such attendance was exceptional. The city merely provided an opportunity for the collapse of practices "shallowly rooted in the personality." Returning migrants may well have lost whatever impulse to religious conformity they had left with. They did not necessarily bandy this about so long as the priest retained his influence in the community. But they were ready to welcome emancipation when it came.[11]

At any rate, all observers seem to have sensed the shallowness of faith behind the slackness of observance. In Beauce respectable farmers, "preoccupied by the care to augment their fortune, work to this end even on Sunday during the services, so that the churches are deserted." Not that they lacked respect for religion, "but they consider that the time they would spend in church would be lost for their work and their fortune."[12] Not challenge, but indifference and hardheadedness. One farmer declared that he would rather go to hell, since heaven was too high and far away. He was not interested in salvation ("it's not in my way of thinking; . . . it's not done"). The paradise he sought was here on earth. "The absence of religious sentiment [in the countryside, especially] is such that there are communes where scarcely one marriage in six is blessed in church" (Yonne, 1862).[13]

In 1874 the bishop of Limoges bewailed "this grievous inertia of the masses." Alain Corbin, who has found no evidence of a great increase in religious indifference in the Limousin before 1870, notes a "brutal fall of religious practice" just about that time—not yet the godlessness the bishop of Limoges described in 1875, "but indifference, an incurable apathy, the total abandonment of religious duties, [and] universal disaffection." In the Limousin the Church's identification with the Moral Order brought anticlericalism. But even there, as almost everywhere, the most detached or hostile maintained their loyalty to rites of passage and local festivals. More generally, as in Puy-de-Dôme, "the religious question leaves our countrymen indifferent." though they "continue to go to church on Sunday out of habit." And on the other side of the Massif Central, "unfortunately" rural inhabitants "are often as yet unconverted to Christianity."[14]

(see Edouard Baratier, ed., *Histoire de la Provence*, p. 448). For my own part, I find it evidence that ritual itself is more important than who performs it. The Church is fine, but one can do without it.

Whether unconverted or disaffected, people lost their respect for Church rules and Church prohibitions. The proportion of civil marriages grew, the delays between birth and baptism became longer. Once set at 24 hours of birth, the outside limit for baptism was extended to three days in 1830, to eight days in 1887, to "the soonest possible time" in the twentieth century. In one Sologne parish the average delay between birth and baptism, which was 2.73 days in 1854, had stretched to 15.12 days by 1901; in 1950 it ran well over three months. Less fear for the newborn's life, fewer epidemics, greater closeness between husband and wife, who was increasingly expected to play a part in the ceremony, but also indifference to what the sacrament of baptism meant and to the authority of the priest. Until 1902 in the Eure villages Martine Ségalen has studied marriages were extremely rare during Lent and Advent. This also changed.[15] One could do without the priest if one wanted to get married when he could not, or would not, perform the ceremony.

From the Church's point of view, every innovation only made things worse. The bicycle was blamed for enabling young people to avoid mass. Tourists, visitors, and returning emigrants felt increasingly free to speak of their indifference to religious practice or even their scorn of it. Military service side by side with "pagan" urban workers made some peasants ashamed of a show of piety as a mark of their bumpkin backwardness. Finally, with war in 1914 there came a culmination of the pressures toward detachment. Yet, how far and fast would all these factors have worked if religion had been solidly anchored in personality?[16]

Religion was an urban import, like education, and, just like education, it reflected the scholarship of the Counter-Reformation and the Enlightenment—the two at one, at least, in being alien to the countryside. Tridentine and post-Tridentine missionaries, where they could, replaced familiar native rites and practices with new ones that were strange. These had no time to settle into tradition before the Revolution and the cascade of changes following it. Religious custom remained superficial, even though convention and the need for ritual kept it in being. In this respect, reputedly devout areas appear little better than incredulous ones. For the outwardly pious Solognot, religion was "an artificial system that he bore without understanding, lacking in efficacy and well above his preoccupations." A student of Normandy sounds the same note when writing of the Caux region, where Easter services were well attended compared with the Bray region, nearby. Here, around Doudeville-en-Caux, we are in the *pays églisier*. But even in this churchly area, "the people are no more knowledgeable about religious matters; ... they just practice more."[17]

Such comments may explain the frequent conjunction between indifference and some form of practice, as in Bourbonnais where peasants "have recourse to religion in all great circumstances, but following ancestral traditions rather than any real faith." Religion had didactic uses: "It fills the young with fear," and that was good and necessary, "but when we're dead we're dead," and that was common sense. Even those peasants who eschewed religious practice wanted a resident priest, for one thing, because he would teach the children to respect their parents and authority, but above all "for rites needed in social life and to ensure good crops, for festivals often connected with a healing saint."* In short, the ritual and the ceremonies that were the very core of popular religion were fundamentally utilitarian. Accordingly, we might expect such pragmatic formalism to decline when its utility no longer seemed apparent, or when rival authorities and formalities beckoned.

This of course is advanced as merest supposition. I know no way of telling the spiritual hold that the Church had on people.† At the visible level, however, its influence was based on practical services and subject to its ability to keep these up: consecration (in an officially acceptable sense), healing, protection, making wishes come true, and not least providing a center for traditional practices. In all these things, official religion drew generously on the popular cult of saints, of healing agencies and other useful "superstitions." Superstitions have sometimes been described as religions that did not succeed. Perhaps, in our case at least, it is they that should be called successful, since so much official religion depended on them and survived largely by indulging practices endorsed by popular belief. The people of Balesta in Comminges, noted the village teacher in 1886, "are the more religious, the more superstitious they are."[18] A teacher is apt to be a prejudiced, hostile witness. But it would be wrong to doubt that the connection loomed large in the public mind.

We know about the widespread usage of the cross—about how the plowman signed himself before he drew the first furrow, and again before he sowed the first handful of grain; about how he would not cut a slice out of a loaf without first tracing a cross on it. But how far did this, or prayers, or kneeling in the fields when the Angelus tolled, go beyond the propitiation of powers that were feared but little understood? Religious practice had not been affected by the Revolution, reported a correspondent of the Abbé Grégoire in 1790, and as for the principles of religion, they had never been comprehended: "people believe more in hell than in God; they fear the priest more than they do the devil."‡ If this was true under the Ancien Régime, it continued in its

---

* M. Bardoux, "Des caractères ... des paysans au Bourbonnais," p. 236; Yves-Marie Hilaire, "La Pratique religieuse," pp. 61–62. In the 1870's Philip G. Hamerton described Burgundian religiosity as a mixture of faith and skepticism. But the faith rested in old wives' tales and traditional cults, whereas the skepticism focused on the Church, its claims, and even its miracles! (*Round My House*, pp. 262–63.)

† Jules Marouzeau suggests that the Limousin term for religion in fact referred to *ceremonies*, not sentiment (which could well have been there, but remained unexpressed). See his *Une Enfance*, p. 36. On the rare occasions when sentiments are expressed, however, they appear skeptical indeed, as in the Auvergnat saying, "If only the Good Lord was a decent man!" (M.-A. Méraville, *Contes populaires*, p. 336.) No wonder that a Limousin description of a task carelessly carried out was that "it's done for the love of God" (Léon Dhéralde, *Dictionnaire de la langue limousine*, Limoges, 1969, 2: 278). The love of God did not go very far.

‡ *Papiers de Grégoire*, p. 10 (St.-Calais, Sarthe). The same letter attributes the persistence of belief in ghosts to the curés, who encouraged it so that the haunted would pay for masses to

essence in the new one. One Allier farmer, talking to Daniel Halévy about his youth in the 1860's and 1870's, thought priests merely sorcerers who always prescribed masses along with their other spells—one sort of magic bolstering another. At Larcau (Haute-Garonne) the priest was described as "the foremost village witch."[19]

Much that was expected of the priest indeed fell in the category of magic—white, of course, as when the priest said masses to cure animals that were under a spell, or when, during the traditional processions that wound their way through communal territory on Rogation Sunday, he threw stones plastered with a small wax cross (priest's dung in Franche-Comté) into the fields to keep the storms and hail away. We have already seen the power over natural phenomena attributed to priests, and the logical belief that some men of the cloth wielded more powers than others. A country priest deplored the way in which the Morvandiaux blamed crop failures, rust, or distemper on their divines. It seems quite natural that when, in the early 1890's, the bishop of Mende visited the village of Saint-Enimie (Lozère), his flock should find that his blessing of their valley made the almond harvest more abundant. In Bourbonnais "everything was blessed: the seed, the fields, the herds." In Meuse several priests were held to sit on clouds, thus helping to disperse them; and the Abbé Chévin, of Bar-le-Duc, who died in 1900, was accused of having made a violent storm break over his own parish.[20]

For those who connected Catholicism and sorcery, plainly, priests could be sinister figures, holding the powers of black magic as well. As a result of natural associations, the Limousins of the twentieth century still dreaded that "priests would usher death" into the homes they visited.[21] The fear that stalked all the inhabitants of the countryside found in the church service not only appeasement but fuel. When sermons did not deal with public discipline, they frequently stoked the fires of brimstone and hell. That was the only way "to move such an almost savage populace," remarked a Breton. "A voice like thunder, dire threats, fists belaboring the pulpit, sweat running down his cheeks, the eloquent pastor fills his hearers with delicious terror."[22]

Benoît Malon (another hostile witness) has denounced the obsessive effects this sort of thing could have on people, especially children, haunted throughout life by the dread of hell-fire, torments, retribution, and circumambient fiends. But priestly menaces were bound to be intimidating to the most sober when menace was the staff of everyday life. Living was marginal, disaster inexplicable and uncontrollable. This added to the countryman's Winnie-the-Pooh syndrome of seeing the trace of fantastic monsters in tracks that he had made himself.[23] Where harm and ill-fortune were swiftly come by, nothing was easier than to claim that they were punishments of heaven. Long

---

lay the errant souls. But if priests were suspected of feeding superstitions, superstitions also fed the priests; witness the Béarnais saying that witches and werewolves make priests eat fat capons (cited in Claude Seignolle, *Les Evangiles du diable*, Paris, 1967, p. 134).

centuries of trying to mollify and coax the powerful conjured up a religion where fear almost excluded love, a faith bent to flatter and do honor to the heavenly lords in order to obtain their protection or avoid their ire. Power and irascibility were what impressed. The peasants would not work their cattle on the feasts of the nastiest saints, the ones most likely to resent and revenge any irreverence; they sought to discover what "thrashing saint" lay behind their illness. Kindly saints could be invoked when they were needed; in grimmer mood, they evoked well-conditioned submission.[24]

God was far away. The saints were near. Both were anthropomorphic. Saints were intercessors. One did not address God directly, but prayed to saints to request his favors, rewarded them if the crop was good or the weather fair, even chastised them, as at Haudimont (Meuse), where Saint Urban, accused of permitting the vines to freeze on May 25, his own feastday, was dragged in effigy through the nettles around his church.* The greatest saint of all, of course, was the Virgin, an unparalleled source of delivery from harm. The *gwerz* (ballad) made up when a new pilgrimage to her was launched in 1894 at Plounéour-Menez recited only recent and concrete miracles: saving men from falling, drowning, prison, and so on. These were the functions of a saint.[25]

But the chief function of saints on earth was healing, and every malady was the province of a particular saint. The attribution could vary from region to region, with some local patron saint taking over duties another saint performed elsewhere; but it was a creation of popular design. The conjunction between saint and illness was determined by associations, some naively evident, others lost in the mists of time. Thus Saint Eutropius healed dropsy (*Eutrope = eau en trop*); Saint Cloud healed boils (*furoncles* are also known as *clous*); Saint Diétrine dealt with herpes and scurf (*dartres = diètres* in Morvan); Saint Aignan coped with ringworm and scurvy (*teigne*). Saint Clare (Claire) helped eyes see more clearly, and Saint Loup, by fine contradistinction, healed fright. Berry had its own array of saints destined by alliteration or obscure fiat to heal. For the deaf there was Saint Ouen; for the gouty, Saint Genou; for crabbed and peevish women, Saint Acaire (in reference to *femmes acari-âtres*). In Finistère Our Lady of Benodet healed aches, depressions, madness, or simplemindedness—disorders associated with the head. Benodet literally means head of Odet, that is, the mouth of the Odet River.[26] In Veurdre

---

* Some rituals involved playful threats should the saint not do his duty. Thus, in Aude girls went to pray for a husband at a sanctuary of Saint Salvaire. They entered the saint's grotto and threw a stone, as hard as they could, at a rock at the far end of the cave while reciting the verse "San Salvaire, / Douno-me un fringaire / Ou te fiqui un pic /Sul nic." (Vouchsafe me a lover / Or I shall strike you a blow / On the nose.) Robert Jalby, *Le Folklore de Languedoc*, p. 78. The point of view was not limited to peasants. A traveler in Provence tells how, in 1887, in the parlor of a convent he found a statue of Saint Joseph turned with the face to the wall, in penitence for not answering the nuns' prayers for a legacy they coveted. Claude Seignolle, who cites this, claims that the practice was followed in other houses of the same order (*Evangiles du diable*, pp. 130–31).

(Allier), not far from Bourbon-l'Archambault, Saint Faustin, whose statue stood in the church, became in popular parlance Saint Foutin, the resort of barren women.*

Probably the most notorious saint born of popular whimsy and need was Saint Grelichon or Greluchon (from *grelicher*, which means to scratch or tickle). Saint Greluchon had started life as the funeral statue of a local lord of Bourbon-l'Archambault, Guillaume de Naillac, but we rediscover the figure in a recessed nook of that city's streets. Childless women came from afar to scratch a little dust from the statue's genital area and drink it in a glass of white wine. By 1880, when Sir Guillaume's lower parts had been scratched down to nullity, the dust was obtained from under the statue's chin. Finally, the statue—which had become a bust—was transferred to the museum for safekeeping.†

I do not know what popular rumor the decision to remove Saint Greluchon aroused in Bourbonnais. Perhaps no one cared as the century ended and prolific motherhood began to be regarded with a cooler eye. But miracle-working agents enlisted strong popular loyalties. So did the traditions that called for rites to be performed in scrupulous detail, or otherwise fail in their intent. At Maizey (Meuse) the relics of Saint Nicholas were carried in procession through the streets in May, and the following Sunday's services then had to be celebrated in a country chapel about a mile away. In 1889 the priest tried to avoid the chore and to say mass in his own church. This disturbed his flock, and most of the men in his congregation, dressed in their holiday clothes, marched to the designated chapel so that the rite would be

---

* Camille Gagnon, *Le Folklore bourbonnais*, 2: 77. Many of these local saints were pure figments of the popular imagination, with no tradition or standing in the Church. Thus, in Saintonge, Saint Bavard healed mutes, Saint Braillard healed convulsions, Saint Pissoux healed urinary incontinence, Saint Lacolique healed stomachaches. In one Saintonge village, Raymond Doussinet tells us, when a child was very ill two candles were lit: one to Saint Rémy, the other to an imaginary Saint Finit (St. Remis = healed; St. Finit = lost). If the first candle outlasted the second, the child was saved (*Les Travaux*, p. 436). One might add two other cases among many, where association or alliteration suggested a connection. Saint Fiacre was the patron of gardeners and was usually pictured holding a spade. But, as it happened, the first cab firm in Paris operated from the Hotel Saint-Fiacre, which bore a sign showing the saint, and he soon became the adopted patron of both cabs (*fiacres*) and their drivers. More important so far as the countryside is concerned is Saint Donat, the legendary martyr of the Roman legion Fulminans, who protected against thunder, lightning, and hail, and whose name can be found engraved on many a rural church bell.

† *Ibid.*, pp. 76–77. Popular canonization created many other healing or helpful saints of persons of local renown. Thus the Rhône rivermen of Arles had adopted as a saint one Isabelet, the daughter of a ship captain who had always watched and blessed all sailings from the city's Quai de la Roquette. After her death in 1826 her remains were said to work miracles (Fernand Benoît, *La Provence*, p. 189). There were also converted rogues like Saint Lénard of Andouillé-Neuville (Ille-et-Vilaine), who mended his ways only to be mortally wounded by a carter he tried to help; pious folk like the oysterman Jo Camu of Cancale, who in 1860 offered his life for the welfare of his parish from which the oysters had disappeared (he died soon after his vow, and the oysters returned); and martyrs of the Revolution like Saint Poufra of the Republican light infantry, who cured fevers at Missiriac (Morbihan). See Henri-François Buffet, *En Haute-Bretagne*, pp. 340–42.

carried out properly. On the other hand, it appears that the change of a patron saint was often treated with equanimity, as was a substitution of the supposedly sacred image itself. At Villeneuve-de-Berg (Ardèche) the blacksmiths had no statue of their patron, Saint Eloi, to parade on his feastday. They solved the problem routinely by borrowing Saint Vincent from the vintners' corporation, removing the statue's pruning knife, and replacing it with a little hammer. Similarly, in the Alps, at the feast of Saint Besse the saint's devotees bought medals "of him" bearing the legend "St.-Pancrace." When the discrepancy was pointed out to them, it bothered them not at all. The fact was, they said, the likeness was close, and the effects were the same. To the traditional mind the patron saint was secondary to the rite, and to the site as well.[27]

We can see this in the cult of "good" [i.e. healing] fountains, a cult that was generally abetted by the clergy on the theory that the saints who protected the fountains would be given a share of the credit for their restorative powers. Yet popular customs connected with healing fountains were, as a student says, "often purely secular," and certain spas kept their appeal with or without the Church's blessing. Near Areich (Gers) a long-established pilgrimage to the sanctuary and spring of Our Lady of Pibèque lapsed from the Revolution until 1880. But the source kept its prestige and its magic powers through the whole period. On Batz island, off the Breton coast, the old chapel dedicated to Saint Pol (de Léon) was shifted to the patronage of Saint Anne when, at the end of the nineteenth century, she was officially declared the patron saint of the peninsula. The pilgrimage continued as before. It was the place that mattered![28]

Familiar venues and familiar rites and actions could not be tampered with with impunity. When obstacles were raised to established ways, rebelliousness ensued. Thus, at Nourard-le-Franc, near Saint-Just-en-Chaussée in Oise, the cemetery chapel had statues of Saint Vaast and his bear. The bear was made of wood and stood on rollers. The chapel was a popular place of pilgrimage for mothers, who took their young children with them hoping that Saint Vaast would help them learn to walk. Ritual required that they tip the sexton to place the children on the bear's broad back and pull them for three turns around the chapel's crypt. At the end of the nineteenth century the incumbent priest, hoping to discourage this superstitious practice, had the bear burned. This caused an uprising in the parish, and delegations pleading with the bishop of Beauvais obtained a new bear, which apparently served Bray, Vexin, and Picardy until the war put an end to the pilgrimages.[29]

Alphonse Dupront has written that all pilgrimages are made to a source of healing. But we should add that the pilgrims as often seek protection and favors, too. In Bresse one went to pray to Saint Anthony that one's pigs should "gain" during the year. In Bourbonnais shepherdesses attended the annual pilgrimage to Saint Agatha's shrine at Saint-Désiré "in the first place to divert themselves and to secure a blessed hazel switch" with which to control their herds and be free of the fear of wolves.[30]

Conditions obviously varied depending on the stand of the local priest; but priestly decisions were interpreted without illusions. At Carnac (Morbihan) the pilgrimage to the shrine of Saint Cornelius (Cornély), patron of horned beasts, was very profitable. Oxen and calves were offered to him; they were made to kneel in adoration of his statue, which stood above the portal of the church, then blessed by the priest and auctioned off under the saint's banner. Then, in 1906, the priests refused to bless the gathered beasts. "They haven't been paid enough," explained a hawker selling his toys at the local fair. "You don't find the church giving its blessing for nothing—at least not these days. But there, I daresay they will get on just as well without it."[31] The year 1906 was a year of turmoil. But priests too galled or too rigorous to keep up traditional devotions were in a minority. As a general rule, they accepted current beliefs in healing fountains, stones, and megaliths. For one thing, as all observers hastened to point out, the gifts offered to their patron saints contributed to clerical revenues. Saint Anthony was offered pigs' feet, Saint Eloi horses' tails, and Saint Herbot cows' tails. More important, many saints were offered the beasts themselves, calves, lambs, chicken, and other gifts in kind. These would be sold by the verger after the ceremony, and the revenue could rise to as much as 1,500 or 2,000 francs—riches for men whose yearly income was only half as much.*

For some priests the launching of a new pilgrimage spot meant big business, like the shrine in Picardy, complete with publicity, signposts, hostels, and eateries, which had to be suppressed in 1882 by the bishop of Beauvais. Others were satisfied with a modest but regular income gained from the sale of some small item, like the *saint vinage* at Miremont in Combrailles, a mixture of 10 liters of water and one liter of wine that was blessed by the priest and sold by the sexton at very moderate prices, and that was said to cure all cattle ills. Still other priests intervened to keep a pilgrimage site alive when people no longer had good reason to visit it. In Morbihan the church at Forges-de-Lanouée was dedicated to Saint Eloi as a patron of metalworkers. When the local forges closed down in 1886, the pilgrimages declined, and so did the church's revenues, until in 1908 the local rector instituted a blessing of horses (Saint Eloi was the patron of blacksmiths and, hence, of livestock in general), which soon revived his trade.[32]

---

* Archives Nationales, F^{17}9261 (Finistère). Stendhal, admittedly on the lookout for such matters, contributed two stories in this vein. Around Lorient one village priest made (it was said) 1,500 francs a year out of the handfuls of horsehair that he got for blessing horses or oxen. ("Blessing does not heal ailments, which would be difficult to prove; it protects one from them.") At Uzerches (Corrèze) rheumatics brought big balls of wool to throw at the statue of the patron saint, which stood about 20 feet away behind a railing. To be effective, the wool had to hit the statue on the exact part of the body to be healed, and petitioners had to keep throwing the wool until the right spot had been hit. (*Mémoires d'un touriste*, 2: 50.)

That priests and their parishes profited from such religious undertakings does not make the undertakings any the less valid or the participants any the less sincere. Utility underlies most human enterprise, and in no way demeans it. The mother who trudged off carrying her child that it might be strengthened or healed was an admirable figure. The priest who sought funds to glorify the source from which such healing sprang—and perhaps its guardian as well—was human and perhaps even saintly.

But to return to pilgrimages: these were perhaps important above all as a form of access to the extraordinary that was so rare in the cycle-bound life we have been talking about. The pilgrimage offered an excuse to leave the village, and with it, for a time at least, an inescapable fate.* Pilgrimages were festive occasions involving food and drink, shopping and dancing. The most ancient pilgrimages coincided with great fairs; markets and sanctuaries went together; the connection between trade and devotion seems to go back as far as Herodotus. Bakers and butchers, clothiers and peddlers, set up their stalls; people treated themselves to sweetmeats, wine, or lemonade, and purchased images, traditional cakes, and other ritual ex-votos to deposit in the sanctuary or tie to the branch of a nearby tree. The healing statue of Saint Stephen at Lussac-les-Eglises (Haute-Vienne) was invoked, like a good many others, by binding a ribbon on the statue's arm. The ribbons were bought from cloth merchants or from the stalls local women set up in the village streets. So were the wax limbs carried in the procession of Saint Amateur at Lamballe (Côtes-du-Nord); the "saffron-flavored cakes shaped like hens," sold to the devotees of Saint Symphorien at Vernègues (Bouches-du-Rhône); the yellow wax breasts offered by women to Saint Anthony's fountain near Brive (Corrèze); and the amulets or priapic figures, in cake or wax, sold from Normandy to Var at least since the seventeenth century. No wonder the peasants felt that priests were necessary because they made business go![33] And it is easy to dwell on the commercial aspects of religion. The point is that there was commerce because there were people, and people congregated because this was the only sort of festivity they knew.

"It's more a pleasure trip than a pious action," caviled an eastern teacher in 1888. What was wrong with its being both? At this unexalted level, the pilgrimage and traveling were one and the same thing. Indeed, in the Dombes *vyazhou* (voyage) was a synonym for pilgrimage. Relations and friends met at pilgrimage places regularly every year, and such predictable gatherings were convenient in times when communications were rare and difficult. They also afforded welcome breaks, especially to women. The pilgrimage was chiefly a feminine activity—perhaps because it was the woman's only socially

---

* And for some, indeed, a way of escaping that fate. As Augustin Collot points out, there were professional pilgrims, of both sexes, who undertook to fulfill the vows of those who could not carry them out themselves. In Mâconnais and Côte-d'Or this practice seems to have waned around 1860 (railways or faith?). In Brittany it lasted longer. (*De quelques anciennes traditions*, pp. 11–12.)

sanctioned means of escape from home and its daily routine. Men had opportunities to visit fairs or to travel to farther places. Their lives were far more
varied than those of womenfolk. These found their opportunity in pilgrimages, which they often undertook alone over great distances. A middle-aged
woman around mid-century made her way on foot from Pommard (Côte-
d'Or) to the shrine of Sainte Reine in Haute-Saône, a hefty march for anyone. The same peasant woman went to see the holy curé of Ars, a good way
south in Ain. There was no healing involved and no particular vow.[34] Dare
we attribute her enterprise to the quest for personal satisfaction and to curiosity? Here was an eager public that the Assumptionists tapped when, in the
mid-1870's, they enlisted the aid of railway companies in transporting the
mass pilgrimages they organized, which were patronized largely by humble
men's wives.

But let us hazard further. Even quite humble trips, for secular or devotional ends, took a person out of his element and opened up unfamiliar
spheres. The extraordinary began much closer to home then than it would
do today, and a trip of any kind was an understandable aspiration for those
whose ordinary lives offered so little change.

What could be more extraordinary than the miraculous? Perhaps this was
what humble people welcomed in the news of the great miracles of the time.
Miracles promise deliverance from the routine unfolding of predictable destinies; and they create a sense of expectancy and excitement the more potent
for being the more vague. Millenarianism, which embodies all this in its
most extreme form, is commonly attributed to bafflement—a sense of privation and restraint with no conceivable relief in sight. The promise carried by
evidence of supernatural forces heals bafflement and frustration, and rein-
forces hope. It also holds out an opportunity to escape from the commonplace into the realm of the prodigious, to wonder over marvels and possibilities beyond familiar ken. Like the sensationalist *canards* the villagers were
so fond of, rumors of a new miracle provided a semblance of diversion.

Whatever the explanation, the rural world was eager for miracles. It exploited the regular sources of awe and thaumaturgy, and flocked when new
ones were announced. Most of the time rumors of local miracles did not go
beyond a limited radius. In 1840 the Holy Virgin seems to have manifested
herself in several places in Vendée. But this was treated as local superstition.
In the early 1860's the Ursuline nuns of Charroux in Poitou discovered what
they claimed to be the Sacred Prepuce, removed from the Infant Jesus at the
circumcision and, in the words of Monsignor Pie, bishop of Poitiers, "the only
part of Christ's body left behind when he ascended into heaven." The name
Charroux was associated with *chair rouge* (the red meat of the cut-off prepuce!), and an elaborate festival in 1862 brought the fortunate convent into
the public eye. But the miraculous discovery was unfortunately connected

with Legitimist politics, and its later fortunes are lost in mists of contentious ribaldry.[35]

At about the same time, in the fall of 1862, the sixteen-year-old daughter of a rural postman of Saint-Marcel-d'Ardèche began to preach, predict the future, and promise miracles. The people came en masse from all surrounding communes until, in a few days, the furor died down.[36]

In other cases the feverish excitement did not pass so quickly. When, in September 1846, two shepherd children guarding their herds on the deserted mountainside of La Salette saw an unnatural light and a tearful lady announcing the wrath of Christ in their own patois, curious pilgrims hastened there at once. The veracity of the children was contested, especially by the Church authorities, but the enthusiasm was too great to stifle. The evidence makes clear that miracles were validated and imposed by popular opinion, which the authorities—civil and clerical—accepted only unwillingly and under pressure. In a notorious trial of 1857, concerned with the reality of the miracle of La Salette, the lawyers continually referred to the supernatural needs of the lower classes (explained presumably by their ignorance). It was wholly understandable, they said, that the common people should believe in such things, but they expressed some surprise at finding members of the upper classes sharing these views.[37]

This same division and the same pressure of popular need appear in the earliest stages of the first and perhaps the greatest modern pilgrimage site—Lourdes. In February 1858, eleven-year-old Bernadette Soubirous encountered a "Beautiful Lady" beside a stream. The local nuns, priests, and civil authorities, afraid of complications, refused to believe Bernadette's story. The local gendarme sought to tell "the people ... that it is not in the nineteenth century that one lets oneself be carried away by such a belief." Yet belief was stronger than skepticism. It spread like wildfire. Within a few days large crowds, mostly women and children, began to gather at the grotto of Masabielle. By the beginning of March they numbered 20,000 (the population of Lourdes was less than a quarter of that). "Disorder caused in the name of God is none the less intolerable disorder," warned the gendarme. All his superiors clearly thought the same. The records are full of it: "disorder," "regrettable agitation," "preserve order," "undeceive the population," "regrettable facts." But the population did not want to be undeceived. For it, disorder was hope and holiday. "The population ... wants to believe. When there are no miracles, it invents them; it insists on baring heads, kneeling, etc."[38]

There were few priests, sometimes no priests, in the assembled crowds. The clergy, as the imperial prosecutor reported, "maintained an excessive reserve." But the ritual pilgrimages developed without their intervention and despite that of the civil authorities. It was several years before the bishop of Tarbes confirmed the miracles in 1862, proclaiming the authenticity of the Virgin's appearance and the healing virtues of the grotto's spring. But clearly the voice of the people preceded the voice of God. In 1867 a railway line became available. By 1871 the pilgrimage had become international, and in 1876 the great basilica was consecrated before 100,000 pilgrims—a new tide in the affairs of men, flowing in the wake of the railroads.[39]

The people wanted to believe—when there were no miracles, they invented them. They also invented appropriate ends for some of the official actors of the early drama, damned in their eyes for their skepticism. When the police superintendent of 1858 died in 1873, full of professional honors and properly buried with the last rites of the Church, popular lore invented tales of heavenly retribution. He had gone blind, it was said; he had first massacred his wife with a meat axe, then ended his own days; the horses had refused to pull the hearse bearing his remains. Similar tales were told about the local prefect, alleged to have been stricken cup in hand in the midst of a banquet while blaspheming Lourdes. The retributive fantasy went on to kill his wife, who broke her neck in a fall, and his daughter, who choked to death while eating a cold chicken. The people loved their miracles so much that they pursued those who would deprive them of their prodigies with implacable hatred. As a great prelate said in 1874: "On every side today ... all that one hears is miracles and prophecies."[40]

What does all this tell us about religion? Conclusions do not come easily. That it was local and specific. That a peasant who did not believe in the Church, its foolishness or its saints, to quote a country priest, could share in local reverence and worship Saint Eutropius. That men who would not go to mass would undertake long pilgrimages to be healed or to have their beasts healed. And that, in one way or another, religious practices were interwoven with every part of life, but hardly in a manner that one would call specifically Christian.[41] Leaving aside the entertainment that these practices offered, divinity was associated with vast unknown areas. God and saints—like fairies—possessed knowledge that was forbidden to men. They had to be propitiated and persuaded to perform tasks that men accomplish only imperfectly (like healing) or not at all (like controlling the weather). The more men came to master such tasks, plumb the unknown, shake the tree of knowledge, the less they needed intercessors.

The sales of the *saint vinage* at Miremont declined, to the despair of the sexton. In Sologne good Saint Viâtre, who had done so much to heal the local fevers (malaria), was badly hurt by the spreading use of quinine and by the drainage and sanitation projects beginning to show results in the 1880's. At Hévillers (Meuse) the priest read the Lord's Passion every day from May to September "to bring heaven's blessing on the goods of the earth"; then, before Christmas, the church treasurer went from door to door to collect grain in payment for this service. In the 1850's the treasurer got 800 lbs and more. By 1888, for all that things were better, he garnered only 330. Things were worse still in Périgord, where the popularity of Saint John the Baptist, whose accompanying lamb had made him the patron of the local sheepruns, declined with the century. At La Coquille, in northeastern Dordogne, where the *ballade* of June 24 brought some 5,000 pilgrims every year, the priest would get 40 or 50 lambs for his pains. By 1900 he got only three. By 1920, what with the rising price of wool, he scarcely got a pound of wool.[42]

In 1886 at Ligarde (Gers) a youth group voted to shift the local festival from January 14, the feast of the patron saint, to the last Sunday in September, which was more convenient from the point of view of work and weather. The observance of Rogation week declined—even in Brittany. The turn of the century saw fewer processions across the village fields with cross, banners, and bells to drive off evil spirits and to bless the crops. In the Limousin, where in 1876 many peasants still reckoned their age according to ostensions—great septennial processions with scores of villages in their entirety parading behind relics, drums, and banners—the emotional content gradually seeped away, and the penitents in their colorful costumes disappeared; and new religious groups that borrowed nothing from the old traditions meant little to the popular public. Politically inspired prohibitions keeping religious processions off the streets separated folklore and pious celebrations, hastening the decline of both.[43]

Local pilgrimages of the popular sort leveled off or declined. Some were domesticated into the Marian cult. Others were suppressed because they gave rise to scandalous practices, as when Morvan women seeking a cure for barrenness too often found it in adjacent woods; or because they always brought disorders, like the wrestlers' *pardon* of Saint Cadou at Gouesnac'h (Finistère) that never failed to end in fights and brawls. The mercantile activities that had grown around traditional devotions killed them, like trees stifled by ivy. Easter Sunday processions had to be given up in some places because the streets and squares were too crowded with stalls and carrousels. Tourists and sightseers helped to keep observances alive as pure pageantry, but finally, "when everyone wants to watch the procession, there is no one left to take part in it." Between the wars, automobiles denied the roads to those pilgrimages traditionally made on horseback, and the enclosure of fields discouraged them. In 1939 the *Courier du Finistère* noted that the traditional procession stopped at the wires barring access to the ancient chapel of Saint-Roch at Landeleau. "What is the use in destroying the grass of a field to enter a building in ruins and without a roof?"[44] No such reasoning could have been accepted half a century earlier.

Yet phosphates, chemical fertilizers, and schooling had spelled the beginning of the end. In 1893, a drought year in Bourbonnais when many men were having masses said for their emaciated cattle (which died anyway), the priest reproached Henry Norre, a self-taught man who farmed not far from Cérilly, for not attending church. "I haven't got the time," he answered. "And really,

I haven't got much confidence in your remedies for the beasts. My remedies are better; you can check." Daniel Halévy quotes another story about Norre. This time the farmer returned from the railway station with a cartful of fertilizer and met the priest. "What are you carting there?" "Chemicals." "But that is very bad; they burn the soil!" "Monsieur le curé," said Norre, "I've tried everything. I've had masses said and got no profit from them. I've bought chemicals and they worked. I'll stick to the better merchandise."[45] It was the requiem of nineteenth-century religion.

Chapter Twenty

THE PRIESTS AND THE PEOPLE

A corpse was going sadly
To its rest under the loam.
A priest was going gladly
To bury it quick and go home.

SO SANG LA FONTAINE with his usual feeling for popular realities. We cannot be certain what kind of religion it was that decayed. But we can tell that the declining role of its representatives was fairly wide and welcome. Sympathy for men of the cloth was either lukewarm or downright bitter. The "good priest," charitable and kindly, whom we occasionally encounter in nineteenth-century novels, has found no place in popular lore, which provides no proverbs in praise of the clergy, but dozens that criticize its members. If your son is clever, advised one Corrèze proverb, make him a mason; if he is nasty make him a priest.[1] Many Basque proverbs make reference to money-grubbing priests; and there is a story that Avarice, having killed a man, sought sanctuary in a church and has not come out since.*

Most friction in the countryside stemmed from and turned about monetary concerns. The First Estate was no exception to the general rule. Priests were in an impossible position. Until the separation of church and state, their salaries began at 450 francs and doubled in a lifetime. Together with other perquisites and surplice fees, a priest perhaps made 1,000 or 1,200 francs a year. If he wanted to eat, dress, and live up to his station, he had to scramble desperately for every penny.[2] This created difficult situations, for peasants held the representatives of an unworldly faith guilty of a distinctly worldly rapaciousness, and priests felt that they were rendering essential services that should be paid for. Both sides were right, but their relationship was only too often a demeaning one. In country villages, the prefect of Yonne reported under the Consulate, "no money . . . no baptism, no marriage, not even extreme unction,

---

* Georges Hérelle, *Etudes sur le théâtre basque*, p. 166. Paul Sébillot quotes other sayings from different parts: "Be wary of a woman's front, a mule's rear, a priest on all sides"; "Clean house, neither priest nor pigeon. Peaceful house, neither woman nor chaplain." But none doubted that it took a certain talent to be a priest, and few that the clerical condition was an enviable one: "L'om es hurous, / Un jour quan l'om se marida, / Huets jours quan l'om tua lou lard, / Toujours quan l'om es curé." (*Le Folk-lore de France*, 4: 231–39.)

even less any kind of funeral dirge; one haggles as in the marketplace; it is at this price or not at all." No wonder that in Saintonge (and probably elsewhere), the people held that the big bell of the church rang out "Doune! Doune! Doune!" (Give! Give! Give!).[3]

The priest often appears as tyrant or exploiter, manipulating his monopoly of the essential rites of passage. Thus, at Bouan (Ariège) the gendarmes reported that he expected gifts or refused the holy sacraments and would not attend the dying, however poor they were, unless he was first paid nine francs. Nine francs in 1862 was a great deal of money! What little success Protestantism had in the countryside at mid-century reflected the peasants' attempts to escape from the high fees exacted by some priests. In Yonne, Ariège, the Limousin, we hear that "the popular classes" were turned away by clerical demands for money. Protestantism was cheap. A novel about the Limousin countryside (written by a priest) records frequent grumbles about the cost of masses, burials, and other services. A Protestant sympathizer remarks that the Protestant minister provides his parishioners a bench to sit on and a stove to warm the chapel, advantages that one did not find in the Catholic church.[4]

The priest in many—perhaps most—rural communities received contributions in kind that people identified with the tithes supposedly abolished by the Revolution. This seems to have been the case in much of western France, and was still practiced in parts of Anjou, Poitou and Gâtine as late as 1888. In the southeast the catechism used in the diocese of Annecy in 1876 incorporated the duty to pay tithes as the seventh commandment—a passage that the Republicans did not fail to use as anticlerical propaganda.[5] But even without such payments, clerical fees jarred. The masses said to lay ghosts or cast off spells laid on animals were costly. So was the occasional dispensation that was needed, say, to marry a cousin. And there was now an alternative authority to sanction occasions that had once been ruled by the Church alone. Country people were slow to avail themselves of this, but friction with ecclesiastical authority could now lead to a break and recourse to the civil power. Squabbles over fees and other differences could produce ugly incidents, like the one at Massat (Ariège), where the priest simply refused to marry a local man when the whole wedding party was in church, at which bride and groom stalked off, saying that they would do without him. A dispute of this sort, which could lead to civil marriage and hence, at death, to the refusal of Christian burial, might snowball into a village cause. One instance of the refusing of burial rites to a villager at Bourganeuf (Creuse) provoked serious local disturbances in 1841 and discredited the priest responsible for the trouble.[6]

Death and funeral ceremonies were a constant source of friction, and inspired demonstrations against incumbents accused of discriminating between rich and poor. There was resentment against priests who charged a fee for the use of the pall (three francs at Soutein, Ariège), which meant that the poor had to go without. In Périgord sextons and priests levied a toll on corpses passing through their parish, a practice that led to considerable ill-feeling. At Saint-André-le-Gaz (Isère) we hear that excessive burial fees had led to "open war" and, by the 1880's, to the widespread abandonment of a religion embodied in a violent and resented priest. Hostility was not likely to have been made so manifest as this in small communities before the 1880's, but it led to explosions when opportunity afforded, as at Lambesc, a fairly large bourg in Bouches-du-Rhône, in 1850.[7]

Places in church cost money, seats and stalls had to be paid for, and there were frequent incidents between the sexton and the priest on one hand and local people trying to get in free—or to bring their own chairs to church. I am convinced that the amount of disaffection this alone caused was immense. The right to carry the statues and the banners of the saints in annual processions was normally auctioned off: 40–50 francs for Saint Radegunda, 15–20 francs for Saint Marien, one franc for a banner. A child's mastery of the catechism was measured (or alleged to be) by the gifts he brought to the priest and the number of candles his parents contributed. A child who was first in his catechism, and who should thus have been in the first rank in the communion parade, was relegated to fourth or fifth place, with predictable results for his and his parents' attitude. Grudges grew, rancor and hostilities festered, which when the time was right would help alienate men and their families from an institution they no longer needed to treat with caution.[8]

What was the role of politics in all this? In a direct sense, relatively minor; indirectly, vast. In a pastoral letter of 1875 the bishop of Limoges attributed the general weakening of faith (or we might better say the open exhibition of people's true feelings) to straightforward political causes: "the public events of 1870 and 1871, the September revolution, ... the Commune, secret societies, the ever more general reading of the newspapers, the agitations caused by the frequency of elections." Whatever else this meant, it was a token that the Church was deeply involved in politics. As all historians say and as contemporaries experienced, the Church was the core and the inspiration of organized resistance to the Republic that emerged after May 16, 1877. Particularly at the provincial level, ecclesiastical influence led the Bonapartist or royalist opposition into what was in effect a clerical party, eventually to be joined by conservative Republicans as well. In these circumstances Republicanism and anticlericalism were one, hence Gambetta's "Clericalism, there's the enemy!" Religion, declared the conservative biographer of the conservative and royalist provincial poet Arsène Vermenouze, "religion was the bond that bound the conservatives." And Louis de Vogüé confirms this: If you went to mass, you couldn't really be a Republican. If you were a Republican, you fought against priests, nuns, and superstitions.[9]

It is true that certain economic or class rivalries found expression in religious terms, as they did in political ones: active adherence to a confession, as to a political faction, because of frictions of a worldly sort; or, as in Gard or Haute-Loire, simply because of historical memories going back to the Wars of Religion.[10] It is also true that in some places priests were agents or supporters of revolutionary social change. The priest of the Left is not a twentieth-century phenomenon only. Social extraction, Christian doctrine, or merely the human sympathies of men particularly close to human tribulations produced a fair number of hostile critics of the existing order, easily accused of Socialism. Priests were denounced for inciting servants to disobey their masters and not to work on holidays in order to attend church services; for having canticles sung to the tune of "La Marseillaise"; for speaking ill of the rich and of employers; for "stoking the fires of antagonism between the poor and the better off." But this only encouraged anticlericalism among respectable property owners like the notary in Zola's *Germinal,* who "at dessert . . . took a resolute free-thinking line" because the local priest sided with the miserable striking miners. The notary was, in his own view anyway, a man of the Left, against the Church that had betrayed him and the cause of property.[11]

A law of July 12, 1880, abrogated the legislation of 1814 forbidding work on Sundays and certain holidays. The previous law had been respected largely in the breach; but a conjunction of anticlericals and employers had wrought the new one, partly to spite the priests. Before it was repealed in 1906, this law helped provoke endless friction between conscientious clerics and the social groups most likely to furnish them support. But if the activities of pious or social-minded priests, even their politics after the 1890's, turned some conservatives or royalists against them, they did not endear them to Republicans. The gulf had been dug too wide. By 1899, as the *Revue du clergé français* admitted, in the public eye the clergy stood for backwardness, reaction, and conservatism.[12]

As long as belief in the supernatural mission of the Church endured, the Church was not too closely identified with any particular section of the faithful. But in the nineteenth century skepticism was increasing, just at the time when the Church's close association with the upper classes and their views became more evident.* The Church no longer symbolized the unity of all, but stood for the domination of one particular faction. Faith in the declining Church was linked to a political stance that was also declining; both lost from the connection.

The long-drawn-out struggle between the clerical party and the Republican regime forced people to take sides constantly in the most obvious terms: attending church, abstaining from processions, choosing their children's

* In 1829 Monsignor de Quélen proposed in a sermon at Notre Dame: "Non seulement Jésus-Christ était fils de Dieu, mais encore il était de très bonne maison du coté de sa mère, et il y a d'excellentes raisons de voir en lui l'héritier légitime du trône de Judas [*sic*]." (Quoted by Jean Meyer in Jean Delumeau, ed., *Histoire de la Bretagne,* p. 443.)

schools. After 1879 official reports hailed the increasing tendency to give up religious practice as a measure of growing support for the regime. In December 1879 the prefect of Cantal welcomed the disappointing level of attendance at the celebration of the feast of the Immaculate Conception: "The public saw in it an endeavor hostile to the government and has generally refused to associate itself with this." The old unanimities, already battered, were being further sapped by official pressure. Fear and deference, which had worked in favor of religious convention, began to work against it. Those who wanted to stand well with the authorities kept away. Those who wanted to conform now had to choose between different kinds of conformity. And the voice of authority, so powerful in its effects on certain communities "used to passive obedience, accustomed to direction from above," spoke with unexampled violence against the "degradation" and "besotting nature" of holding "absurd" religious beliefs.[13]

"Absurd" beliefs could be enlisted on either side. In 1885 at Saint-Laurent-sur-Gorre (Haute-Vienne) the priest complied with the regulation prohibiting the ringing of bells in storms. The villagers resented his decision. The Radical municipal council spread the story that the new regulation was the work of priests, bishops, and nobles, who hoped that poor people would be ruined by storms no longer averted by the bells. Finally, the anticlerical municipal council overrode the prefect, directed the church bells to be rung in storms, and scored a point with the villagers.[14]

This sort of thing helps remind us what rural politics were about, and stresses the level at which debate was carried on.* It is important to remember this as a simple truth when weighing anticlerical arguments, lest the basis of their appeal be misinterpreted. They were rational, but they were pitched in terms designed to move people with interests and a state of mind far removed from the intellectual urban ken. Thus reference to papal interference in French politics is said to have contributed to the Republicans' successes in 1877. Gambetta asked the peasants if they would want their sons sent to get themselves killed to put the Pope back on his throne. Was this an argument that clericalism had gone too far, as André Latreille and René Rémond make it out to be, or simply an appeal to the French peasants' known reluctance to lend their sons for anything but gain?†

The notorious struggle between priest and teacher falls into the same cate-

---

* In the Abbé Labrune's novel, *Mystères des campagnes*, the village priest points out to peasants who are considering having an infant baptized by the Protestant minister that his rival wears spectacles. "Does he really?" (Argument whether he does or not.) Then: "If he wears spectacles, I don't want him to touch my child," says the father. (P. 233.)

† *Histoire du catholicisme*, 3: 413. It was in fact widely believed that the Pope aspired to the French throne, and that his ambitions had only been thwarted by the Emperor's sending troops to Rome. But readiness to believe the worst of the Pope was based on an earlier and bitter prejudice sparked or spurred by the demonetization of the papal one-franc piece, which had circulated interchangeably with the French franc until the 1850's. (See Philip G. Hamerton, *Round My House*, pp. 213–15.)

gory. *Frères ennemis*, their discord stemmed less from undeniable ideological differences than from their contest for authority. Priest and teacher were both local notables, their position based not on material wealth but on the possession of esoteric knowledge and the key role they played in communal affairs. Their social extraction was roughly similar: brighter (or physically weaker) sons of small artisans and peasant farmers, promoted by schooling. "Qui langue a, à Rome va," they said in Tarn-et-Garonne. Both represented official culture, especially in their command and use of French. To be sure, we have seen that priests often taught or preached in patois in order to reach and hold members of their congregations. Even so, for centuries they had been the only men with learning in their parish, and they were instrumental in the penetration of French.[15]

The language of prayer, when it was not Latin, was French. One spoke French to gents of the upper classes; it followed that one used it when addressing God or saints. In Languedoc, for instance, the Catholic church began to use French in the fifteenth century, presenting most of its homilies in that language and sending missionaries out to preach in French. By the nineteenth century, these tendencies had grown stronger. Most of the bishops, like prefects, came from outside their diocese. They had no understanding and little sympathy for popular religious practices that the Church generally associated with paganism or folklore, or a mixture of both. Students were prohibited from speaking patois in seminaries, as in normal schools. The teaching orders were notoriously opposed to local dialects, and most of all the Jesuits, inventors of the infamous "symbols" borne in evidence of linguistic lapses. It comes as no surprise to hear a Breton nationalist criticizing them as well-meaning strangers only interested in the spread of French.[16]

Challenged by the teacher, whom he was accustomed to treat as an underling, and by the teacher's wares, the priest began to take a different view of things. Where before priests had patronized what learning had been available in the village, now many suspected it because it could lead to "bad books." Their stress on the learning of the catechism clashed with the teacher's interest in other subjects, which were gradually recognized as more relevant to current needs. Catechism clashed with the school certificate, and the latter won. A peasant quoted by Gaston Méry in 1907 explained: "We compare what the teacher gives us with what the priest can give. Well, he gives us more. It's the teacher that has taught us how to read, and that is useful in life. He has taught us how to reckon and that is even more useful... and then that is not all. If we need advice for our taxes, for our business, we just go to see him. He's got books and papers about farming, about fertilizer."[17] The things one could see, the things one could touch, were taking over; and the school rode forward on their tide. The peasant's need had shifted from consolation to advice on concrete matters; and on this level, at this time at least, the presbytery could not keep up with the school.

With the school looming as an increasingly dangerous competitor, language took on a new role in the priest-versus-teacher struggle. The priest was cast or cast himself as a defender of local speech; first, simply to oppose the teacher's French, but also because it helped preserve the faithful from subversion. Yet, though he played the reactionary in this struggle and was frequently accused of "the abuse" of using Basque, Breton, or other dialects in religious instruction, catechism, and preaching, reports indicate that most priests complied with official requirements—and thus with the historical tradition of their Church.[18]

The struggle between church and school at the village level was thus cultural only in a subordinate sense. Agencies that had operated jointly and in a similar direction became rivals and had to adopt the weapons that lay at hand. As for the political struggle, it was—as we have seen in other politics— concrete and personalized. The creation of lay schools led to incidents that inevitably snowballed. In Pyrénées-Orientales priests would not admit children from the secular schools to church events; mayors retaliated by prohibiting church processions. In Haute-Vienne mayors proposed to prohibit processions because priests used them to pressure parents not to send their children to secular schools. In Ariège some mayors prohibited processions "solely to avoid clashes," others because there might be trouble from "fathers hurt in their pride because of the preference shown to children of congregational schools." We hear of priests who used their influence to get a tenant's lease changed or revoked; who saw that work was given or taken away; who made a weapon of bread orders for the needy; and who baldly discriminated against the children of unregenerate parents in catechism or church. We hear of the tolling of the death knell for those who sent their children to lay school; and of a priest who refused the sacraments to a schoolteacher's mother.[19] This does not sound too new, and one dares to think that the anticlerical side did not disdain similar methods. What matters is the resentment that the struggle bred and the lasting dissensions it created.*

Religious pageants and processions, among the rare events that brightened the otherwise dreary days, were the first to suffer. Teachers perhaps pursued traditional observances with particular ruthlessness in their zeal to "uproot superstition." Republican officials banned or obstructed them as part of their anticlerical campaigns. Priests themselves, only marginally sympathetic, abandoned them as "medieval" or defended them merely as political issues. Meanwhile, the traditional songs sung at devotional feasts were replaced by militant canticles designed for the circumstances: "Sauvons Dieu et la France!" or

---

* Bérenger-Féraud remarks that though many processions in Provence fell victim to politics around 1877, they were already in decline and would probably have died out unassisted (*Réminiscences populaires en Provence*, p. 343). We should give some thought also to the statement (in Theodore Zeldin, *Conflicts in French Society*, pp. 142–44) that many parish priests were driven to the verge of madness by friction with the local people and the local councils, sparked less by ideological disagreement than by the struggle for power.

"Nous Voulons Dieu, car les Impies Contre Lui Se Sont Soulevés." This meant that even where traditional ceremonies endured, parts of tradition were lost—this time from the inside.[20]

Thus clerical or anticlerical politics affected the popular mind indirectly. They helped to sap tradition and disintegrate practices that had been part of life for centuries. But political arguments as the cities knew them would not and could not engage the countryside until the country mind had shifted to the wavelength of the city. This would take a long time. Meanwhile, the existence, the pervasiveness, the vigilance of politico-religious conflicts discredited what had long been undisputed and advanced alternative attitudes. As the century ended, a portion of clerical opinion recognized the counterproductive effect of political involvement.[21] My own belief is that pettier factors, more closely linked with the personality of the priest and his relations with the community, contributed at least as much to calling him into question.

We have seen that straitened means condemned the priests to rapacity. There was less excuse for their authoritarianism. The best historian of the French priesthood in the nineteenth century, Father Joseph Brugerette, has attributed the unpopularity of priests to their "absolutist and retrograde ideas," which in his view ran counter to the ideals of greater social and political independence that were gaining ground.[22] My own view is that the tendency toward independence, itself a product of novel possibilities, did not suggest rebellion against the priest or a complete break with him; it simply made it possible. Like the stern schoolteacher, the authoritarian priest was the product of an authoritarian family in an authoritarian society. They would all be challenged in due course, when opportunity offered. The priest's immediate problem was not that he was too absolutist, but that he was less retrograde than the villagers he sought to direct. Venality lost friends, but attempted reform lost more.

There has been some discussion whether the "Jansenism" of many graduates of nineteenth-century seminaries contributed to what has been called de-Christianization—itself a misleading term if it suggests more than the abandoning of church rituals. As early as 1828 an old Yonne priest, trained before the Revolution, had criticized his younger colleagues: "The young reformers of humankind flatly refuse absolution to all but girls who do not dance and lads who never go to taverns... and in this way they avoid the trouble of confessions." Doubtful about this view, Latreille and Rémond remark that after all this was no more than "a certain moral rigorism or harshness, ... frequent in that clerical generation."[23] Yet moral rigorism should not be underrated when its effects touched every aspect of popular observance and turned the priest into a killjoy—a resident and interfering Mrs. Grundy.

The consoling cleric undoubtedly existed, but when we meet the priest he is always saying no. No drinking on the Sabbath, or in periods when a mass is being said, or while processions pass. No Sunday morning markets. Too many pigs—disgusting animals; people feast on them when they should be fasting. The fishermen work on Sundays, the priests persuade fish merchants not to buy fish on that day. The reactions were expectable. At Usclades (Ardèche), the priest entered the local tavern to silence "certain songs," but had to retreat under a barrage of insults, followed by snowballs! In a village nearby the priest ran out of church to put an end to a noisy farandole troubling the evening prayers, broke the drum with his fist, and barely escaped lynching. Men were becoming less willing to accept this kind of interference, and even less willing to admit the priest's right to interfere in their private lives.[24]

The practice of coitus interruptus, which was apparently spreading, led to vexation and acrimony. We know that in 1840 the bishop of Le Mans had been troubled by the number of young husbands showing themselves eager to avoid conception, though not intercourse. Questioned and condemned by their confessors, more and more of these, growing weary of ecclesiastical pressures, were keeping away from the communion table or abandoning religious practice altogether.* We have no way of knowing whether the bishop's concerns reflected rural practices, or only urban ones. The picture grows clearer, however, by 1867, when Redemptorist missionaries in the Somme reported that parish after parish was "ravaged by onanism." The men reproved for this vice refused to mend their ways and "live far from the sacraments." There and elsewhere, husbands evinced a growing resentment toward confessors who wrung every last detail of intimate practice from their wives. There had always been some objection, and this grew through the century, to confessors prying into private affairs—the profits of merchants, the small peculations of traders, the indiscretions of untoward talk or reading. Now, confession was attacked as an interference in marital relations, "probing the conjugal bed," and an invasion of privacy that excited minors to debauchery by suggesting notions they would not themselves have thought of. We can well understand why the occasional crime or deviation by a member of the clergy was greeted with acrid delight, even though as a rule embezzlement, sexual assault, indecent exposure, visits to brothels, and other lapses were de-

* To the bishop's request for guidance, Rome replied that while the husband does indeed commit a sin by spilling his seed "outside the receptacle," the wife, for her part, could submit passively to such practices without committing the sin. E. Le Roy Ladurie, who cites the case, remarks that this subtle distinction would become the basis of French theological and confessional practice, hence of the country's religious dichotomy: men = sinners, and as such are excluded or self-excluded; women = resigned, innocent, and passive, and remain within the Church. (*Le Territoire de l'historien*, Paris, 1973, pp. 314-15.) This division could be complicated or reinforced by priests' attempts to use their hold on believing wives in order to influence the political behavior of their spouses. In 1885 the priest of Payssas (Ardèche) exhorted the village women to make their husbands vote for the conservative electoral list "under pain of mortal sin" for wives who did not carry out instructions. In 1897 we hear about a man of Finistère who refused to follow his wife's electoral counsel and who "since that time could have no intercourse with her as a result of clerical proscription." (Alexandre Pilenco, *Moeurs du suffrage universel*, Paris, 1930, pp. 193-200.) See also Claude Mesliand, "Contribution à l'étude de l'anticléricalisme à Pertuis de 1871 à 1914," *Annales de sociologie des religions*, 1960, pp. 49-62.

cently hidden from view. "The priest is the law, prohibition, forbiddance," wrote the Abbé Larichesse of Cantal in an 1865 study of confession. Familiar with claims that people avoided church because its doctrines ignored human passions, he did not see laxity as a valid remedy. No wonder that, by 1883, we find the public prosecutor at Grenoble noting that the reserve and mistrust with which the peasants of Isère treated their priests was "a form of self-defense" against the clergy's attempts to trespass on their freedom of conscience in newly reserved domains like family affairs and politics. An article in a clerical review published in the last year of the century summed it all up: "The clergy is unpopular. To men of the people the priest is by definition a hostile being."[25] It was in this guise that many priests worked hard to saw off the branch on which they sat.

"Modern" religion extolled new cults (the Virgin, the Blessed Heart of Jesus, the Holy Sacrament) over familiar ones, and sought to purify practice. The clergy had always shown a certain hostility to popular rejoicing as essentially pagan; feasting was gross, libertine, leading to violence and keeping peasants away from church services.[26] Unable to eliminate such feasts, the Church incorporated them but did not cease to treat them with suspicion. Around mid-century the hierarchy set about purification. Balazuc, in Ardèche, boasted a Confrérie de Saint-Antoine (better known as the Fraternity of the Cow, because its members killed one every year and distributed its meat to the poor). In 1845 the priest found the fraternal banquets were too washed down with wine and suppressed the confrérie. His action set off a riot, but it was final in Balazuc and representative of a wider trend. Religious · congregations and fraternities, especially penitents, had lost sight of their original purpose, which was to aid the poor, bury the indigent, honor their members in death. They had become social and drinking societies—*blancs le matin et gris le soir*, they said in Velay—or political clubs, their chief public function restricted to marching in processions wearing colorful, awesome robes and hoods. "This form of devotion no longer corresponded to the mentality of the population," commented a canon. Certainly not to the mentality of reforming clergymen. Far gone in their worldly ways, the penitents were reformed to death and left to expire slowly in the first two decades of the Third Republic. They were replaced with associations specifically dedicated to prayer and to pious works. The result was a setback on both sides: the new associations, which the clergy sponsored, sometimes wilted or died; meanwhile, the old groups, abandoned by the clergy, withered badly also. "In a few years," wrote Edward Harrison Barker in 1893, "there will be no Blue Penitents at Figeac. As the old members of the confraternity die, there are no postulants to fill their places. Already they feel, when they put on their 'sacks,' that they are masquerading, and that the eye of ridicule is upon them."[27]

The same was true for the whole popular cult of relics, processions, ostensions, rogations, statues, rocks, caves, and healing springs, successively routed out as excrescences. Branches or stones that women grated or ground up against barrenness were done away with wherever this could be achieved. At Allanches (Cantal) one of the major local feasts—Saint John's, in midsummer—waned during the 1830's when local priests ceased to take part in "ceremonies outside religious worship" and restricted themselves to purely religious ceremonies. About the same time in Gers the miraculous fountain of Saint John the Baptist at Nougarolet was put out of commission by a priest intent on scotching superstition, who simply filled its basin in. In 1845 the rector of Ploemeur (Morbihan) had the village menhir torn down—one of the magic stones that peasants crowned with flowers, anointed with butter, or slipped money to. All over Brittany the ancient megaliths became "forbidden" or "accursed" stones.[28]

Still, stubborn beliefs and practices survived even without clerical participation or endorsement. A song from Barjols (Var) affirms it:[29]

L'evesque ès vèngu,	The bishop's come,
La capelo, la capelo.	O the chapel, O the chapel.
L'evesque ès vèngu,	The bishop's come,
La capelo n'a fondu.	The chapel he has torn down.
Naoustré festaren	We'll feast
Sant Antoni, Sant Antoni,	Saint Anthony, Saint Anthony,
Naoustré festaren	We'll feast
Sant Antoni quand voudren.	Saint Anthony when we please.

In 1865 a Nièvre country priest decried "the multitude of vain superstitions" rampant among his Morvandiaux. About the same time, another priest in the Saumurois was denouncing the rain-making rite of dipping a processional cross in a magic fountain and throwing in some wine while calling on the fountain's patron saint, "you give us water, we give you wine!" The clergy, he insisted, should try to "suppress [the usage] as superstitious, and this despite popular complaints." In 1879 the rector of Tredarzec (Côtes-du-Nord) demolished the chief shrine to Saint Yves, center of a local cult the Church disapproved of, the shrine of Saint-Ives-de-la-Vérité. It had no effect. A few years later a man said to have been condemned by the avenging saint was dead, and his alleged murderer acquitted. A new priest assigned to Breuilaufa (Haute-Vienne) in 1880 tried to put an end to the traditional practice of ringing the church bells on All Hallows eve and throughout the morning of All Souls. He locked the church doors, but the indignant peasants threatened to break them down, crying "that no one could prevent them from ringing for their dead." A few years later another Limousin village rose to defend its right to ring the church bells in a storm.[30] Other popular customs put up a solid fight. In Cantal just before Easter the shepherds made the rounds of local farms, singing old songs appropriate to the occasion and collecting bits of food, eggs, and a few coins. "The clergy was hostile" to this "immemorial custom," the *réveillers,* perhaps because "the rusticity of the Evangelists [whom the shepherds portrayed] and of their songs appeared unworthy of religion." The custom survived none the less, at least to the 1890's. And menhirs continued to be worshiped despite ecclesiastic execrations. In 1896 the menhir at Plouguernevel (Côtes-du-Nord) was crowned by a cross, and an accompanying tablet promised 40 days' indulgence for every Pater and Ave that the faithful said.[31] The Church continued to join what it could not lick.

One thing it sought to lick—and with a determination that cost it even greater popular sympathies—was the festival and the vulgar rejoicing that accompanied it. In Morbihan a local man of letters expressed regret in 1863 that priests, who once, far from condemning dancing, had given it tacit approval by coming to watch and applaud, had become rigorous and reproving. The permissive priest of yore was gone. For the new, stern curé, popular feasting went on for far too long. It kept a man from work not only while it lasted, but while he painfully recuperated in its aftermath. In any case, as the Oc ditty had it, "There is no feast without a morrow."[32] A feastday was likely to run into two or three, its participants carried away by the unaccustomed respite. What was much worse was the abandoned behavior: the unchaste dress of women and lewdness of the men, the return home at dawn, the drunkenness and debauchery without measure. Civilization meant measure, limits; but preternatural wildness kept breaking through. Savagery was too near the surface, too lightly chained, not to cast off its bonds. There lay the danger of those "lascivious dances" and the tunes that ushered in pagan violent moods.[33]

Father Labrune in his Limousin village preached and campaigned against them. Reprehensible passions, unbridled license, obscene cries, offended chastity, concubinage, and illegitimate children—all sprang from his flock's frenzied attachment to dancing. In Burgundy, too, the mid-nineteenth century saw a grand clerical offensive against dances and bals. The archbishop of Sens fulminated "against the deplorable abuses that reign in the countryside and that arise from dances and from public *bals.*" One village priest in Yonne called for a state of siege in his commune of 376 souls, where "all the young ...crowded in the same hall (*at night!*) give themselves over passionately to dances of a revolting obscenity."[34]

Priests often refused communion, even at Easter, to girls who went dancing and sometimes to their parents as well; but when, in 1858, the Minister of the Interior showed concern over the bishop of Tarbes's pronouncement of an excommunication of all persons "indulging in the pleasures of dance," the prefect of Hautes-Pyrénées reassured him: it was part of a clerical campaign against low necklines. Ladies had to be made to promise not to pass on décolleté dresses to servants and maids "lest these be tempted to dress above their station and develop tastes that lead to many vices."[35] So sauce for one sort of goose was not meant for any other sort. Like dresses, dances permissible at one level of the social ladder were inappropriate when exhibited on lower rungs. It is true that the proprieties were in greater danger, but moral rigorism was also easier to exercise.*

Dancing, in any case, competed with the contemplation and the prayer that should command Sundays—the day of the Lord. "Today Sunday does not belong to the Lord, but to dancing," sighed *La Semaine religieuse* of Montpellier in 1877. But Sunday brought for most the only intermission in hard labor. They wanted to enjoy it as they could, and there was a widespread custom that after mass or vespers people danced. Priests denounced this, and also railed against the reels and jigs that joined on saints' feastdays and pilgrimages. They tended to react to local fiddlers as if they were unclean sinners. We hear of one in Vernajoul (Ariège) who made a scene when the minstrels scheduled to play during the afternoon's celebrations of the Emperor's Day, August 15, escorted the mayor to church service in the morning. The report of the incident cites "his well-known feelings against music, dancing, etc." We hear about another priest, at Soutein (Ariège) who clashed with the mayor for licensing a public dance on the occasion of the local feast in 1884. The curé denounced it as immoral.[36]

A folklorist of the 1880's expressed regret at the oversensitivity of priests and warned that when these diversions held on pilgrimage days ended, the pilgrimages would end too. He was not fundamentally wrong. Pilgrimages endured, but when they were no longer part of popular rejoicings they represented only a religion from which the life had been drained away. Moreover, the danger to such institutions of the Church was all the greater because the Church was becoming more dispensable. Around 1900 the priest of Morette (Isère) refused absolution to a girl unless she promised to give up dancing. "If you don't want to give it, keep it!" answered the girl.[37]

The Church's firm base in popular need was declining, the framework it provided for social activity became less essential as more activities went on outside its purview, yet it persisted in restricting those that did. Far from sustaining "retrograde" ideas, the priest seems to have collaborated with the schoolteacher to stamp them out. The scorn that teachers showed for rustic superstitions was often shared by priests, who were increasingly reluctant to take part in magic rites decried by the official culture. The peasants "are very stick-in-the-mud and want essentially to keep their ancient practices"—shades of the village schoolteachers' decrying of routine! Reformist priests, on the other hand, were bent on renovation. Even familiar statues were sacrificed for posher urban plaster, and at Landivisiau (Finistère) in 1906 an English

---

* Jean-Marie Vianney, curé of Ars, was the only priest who managed to extirpate dancing and taverns in the whole of his parish. To this day there are no dances at Ars, and the young go to neighboring communes for their fun (whereas in other areas many balls are organized by the priest or the Catholic youth groups).

traveler noted so many old saints for sale for a few francs that one could have furnished a Breton paradise.[38]

The growing division between the Church and its public thus took two turns. Many among the hierarchy and clergy, fearing the modern world, cut themselves off from the cultivated classes, from the working class, and from what Brugerette called a society taken with independence.[39] Many (sometimes the same) also disapproved of antiquated and semi-pagan forms of popular piety and worship: the colorful rituals of urban fraternities, the laxity attached to public ceremonial and festivities, the unregenerate magic practices. Yet the attachment of the popular masses to ancient things that the Church wanted to leave behind was even greater than their attachment to the Church. Eliminating the practices helped to estrange the people.*

Archaic societies envisage their existence and survival as being dependent on exchanges between the world of the living and the world of the dead, the latter contributing to the fertility and renewal of the former. In France, as elsewhere, exchanges of this kind were symbolized by seasonal ceremonies that had been taken over by the Church, which also infiltrated or adopted the social organization that supported them: generational groups and fraternities. The great satisfying dramas that marked the rhythm of the seasons were reinforced by religious ceremonial. As supernatural interpretations crumbled under the impact of materialism, and even more before the puritanical expurgations of the clergy, the basis for the belief itself, where simple minds made simple associations, also crumbled. Removing the religious content of the natural magic also took a good deal of magic out of religion. The churchmen did not realize the danger of such reforms. Hard-pressed by contemporary criticism of superstitions, identical with long-held reservations of their own, they considered the tree of the Church too strong to be hurt by pulling off the ivy. Yet when the ivy had been pulled away, the tree was left alone and isolated. Over and over, the struggle over practices it disapproved of left the Church mistress of an emptied field.

In the years before the First World War, as a priest was to note, "in towns [people] awaken to our ideas [while] our rural peasants become ever more pagan." Cardinal de Cabrières also bewailed the rural population's "absolute and almost scornful indifference." The Catholic revival that has been much talked about, the "consoling growth of the eucharistic movement," the "religious and patriotic renaissance of Catholicism" around the turn of the century (Rémond and Latreille date it from 1885 to 1914), was an intellectual and

---

* Emile Durkheim has defined religion as a society based on certain beliefs and practices that are held in common by all believers and that are traditional, hence obligatory. The stronger and the more numerous these beliefs and practices the more integrated the religion and the greater its ability to preserve its cohesion and that of the believing group. "The detail of dogmas and rites is secondary," he says. "The essential is that they should be such as to keep up a collective life of sufficient intensity." (Le Suicide, 1969 ed., p. 173.)

middle-class affair.[40] From the words of an exultant priest, it is apparent that the nocturnal adoration, the fraternities of the Blessed Sacrament, the general communions of men and of the young, were a class phenomenon, since all the cases cited refer to schoolboys, for many of whom, as Baudrillart suggests, religion had become a kind of sport.*

In fact, fewer and fewer men were being drawn to the priesthood. Their numbers dwindled steadily through the last quarter of the century, even under the Moral Order of the 1870's. Bishops had been complaining about the paucity of religious vocations since 1815, but their cries became sharper after 1871, when seminaries began to appear alarmingly empty: 34 students at Nîmes in 1875 against 80 before the war, 53 at Reims in 1878 against 100 earlier, and 90 at Verdun in 1874 against 150. "Vocations diminish in a frightening manner," lamented the bishop of Tours in 1877. In 1876 seminaries (*grands séminaires*) had 12,166 students, in 1880, only 8,400. The number of ordinations reached their nineteenth-century peak of 1,753 in the year 1868, then declined rapidly until 1877, when they roughly stabilized at about 1,580. They fell from 1,518 in 1904 to 1,014 in 1909 and 704 in 1914. In 1904 there were still 13.5 secular priests for every 10,000 Frenchmen—1:739. In 1913 there were only 12—1:832. By 1929 the ratio stood near 1:1,000.[41] By all accounts, these men, well-trained in pious practices, were ill-prepared to meet the challenges of the rising world or answer its criticisms. "The clergy on the whole dislikes the times it lives in, hence cannot heal them." An English observer well acquainted with the French was struck by the ignorance of village priests. This is confirmed by the impressions of outstanding priests like Alfred Loisy and Georges Frémont: mental laziness accompanied by "unbearable smugness."[42]

The catastrophic drop in numbers was due in some measure to practical considerations that dried recruitment up. The military law of 1889 made seminarians liable for military service, in part with the deliberate purpose of discouraging clerical recruitment. Its effects were relatively negligible, however, since the most likely alternative, attending normal school, was little better; after all, apprentice teachers also served one year.† The separation of church and state was a more serious matter. The priest's prestige was seriously affected. "These gentlemen must have done something to be treated like this by the government," was one conclusion young men drew. Another, more mundane, was that priests were poorer and the priesthood a less desirable career.[43]

---

* Abbé Bellamy, *Les Effets de la communion* (Paris, 1900), especially pp. 48ff; Henri Baudrillart, *Les Populations agricoles*, 3: 38. It is true that some impressive statistics were claimed for the Crusade of the Rosary, which ended shortly before 1914. Over 100,000,000 rosaries (it was reported) were said for the salvation of France. But the rosary is a mechanical form of prayer and does not necessarily reflect a high degree of religious feeling in the practitioner.

† Still, Father Frémont in Nice noted on December 16, 1906, that of 54 students only 25 were left: "Les autres sont partis au régiment, sur l'ordre du Ministre de la Guerre" (Joseph Brugerette, *Le Prêtre français*, 3: 29).

Church authorities were the first to agree. Some expected that one-third of the priesthood would be left to starve. Many old priests sought to resign from a living that no longer provided them with a living, and some bishops, worried by the gaps threatening in many parishes, tried to compel them to stay in their posts. By 1908 in the Versailles diocese there were but 500 active parish priests to serve three-quarters of a million souls (and Versailles was a desirable area). Other priests girded themselves to earn some money. An alliance of worker-priests was organized and published a journal, *Le Trait d'union,* to help members in the trades they had chosen to pursue—carpentry, book-binding, watchmaking, embroidery, printing, cattle-raising, commercial farming. It also advertised remedies like the fragrant lozenges "excellent at burials." The alliance encouraged other priests to take up sidelines, as indicated by the title of its secretary's brochure, *Métiers possibles du prêtre de demain.* In 1901 a special review was founded to help with the "Recrutement sacerdotal."[44]

Above all, Holy Orders ceased to seem an honorable and secure career. Parental tenderness, opined the bishop of Reims, turned young people away from an uncertain profession. "It's only human wisdom." By 1910 the average number of incoming seminarians had fallen 50 percent. A survey shows very sharp drops in enrollment by 1910, four years after the Separation: from 85 to 20 at Ajaccio, from 100 to 53 at Angoulême, from 45 to 23 at Avignon, from 254 to 162 at Cambrai, from 70 to 24 at Langres, from 12 to 0 at Moutiers, from 65 to 30 at Nice, from 200 to 130 at Rodez, from 57 to 15 at Sens, from 40 to 16 at Tulle, from 69 to 39 at Valence, and so on. Some children were discouraged by their schooling; after all, now authoritative voices told them there was no God, at least not the God of the priest: "J'sons bin obligé d'an crère." And simmering resentments, fed by the propaganda of enlightenment, were breaking surface: "We bear the priest a grudge because, when we were small, he made us believe in hell, in the devil, in all those things that made us afraid. When we grew up we understood he had got us all excited about nothing, and it rankles."[45] Above all, the integrative functions once performed exclusively by religious institutions were now performed by numerous secondary groupings (clubs, associations, parties). Church ritual—designed to control situations and modify experience—was being thrust aside by new techniques. The priest who had once directed was relegated at best to a confirming role. And even this lost much of its importance as village society became less homogeneous.

Paradoxically enough, this development was reflected in what was happening to the dead. The dead, as we have seen, had a role to play in ancient tradition; and though the Church added its own content to the old forms, it had accommodated the beliefs in the revitalizing agency of the dead. In the nineteenth century two things were to affect this. For one thing, sanitary and hygienic considerations, along with innovations in mortuary practices, pushed cemeteries from the parish center to nonpopulated areas.* Corpses dressed in a simple shirt or wrapped in a winding sheet had decayed rapidly and permitted a turnover in burial plots that kept up with parish needs. The greater prosperity and the desire to keep up with the bourgeois Joneses introduced elaborate coffins; villagers no longer were content with a few roughly finished planks crudely nailed together, but insisted on polished monuments, preferably upholstered and adorned with gilt. Their occupants lived up to their surroundings: a better shroud, the best clothes, a pillow, prayerbook, and rosary, and a supply of holy medals. By 1913 we find a widow at Châteauponsac (Haute-Vienne) describing the pomp with which her husband was laid to rest: fitted out in his wedding jacket over a new shirt, with his cane, his snuffbox full of fresh tobacco, a shroud of the best quality and a new woolen blanket, his hat beside him and under his head a feather bolster well plumped out.[46]

Investments of this order demanded a durable resting place. Graves came to be bought or to be leased for longer periods. Poor Yorick could no longer be disinterred after a few years that his grave might receive another's bones. Increasingly luxurious tombs helped to differentiate the dead and mark their social standing. The second half of the century saw more and more cemeteries move from the center to the outskirts, a process whose suggestive overtones went beyond class divisions.

Until cemeteries moved out of the village, churchgoers would stop and say a prayer over a relative's tomb. On Sundays churchyards had been the chief meeting-place. Before and after mass, groups formed to talk and to live together but also with the dead, before whose tomb one knelt. Now the removal of the dead reflected the accelerated dismissal of a past that also grew increasingly remote. It also reflected doubt about survival and another world. Testaments, once concerned in part with the dead person's future, prescribing masses, prayers, restitutions for the salvation of their souls, now concentrated on terrestrial property and its transmission.[47]

Traditional rites were waning. Throughout much of France a dead person had routinely been provided with a coin, a throwback to pagan times, when this was meant to pay his fare across the River Styx: in 1871 the mother of a dead girl, asked why she closed her daughter's hand over a sou, answered, "To let her have some fun in paradise." In many places the straw or straw mattress of the deathbed used to be burned. Beds with box mattresses made this costly, and the old custom disappeared. In Bourbonnais, until the 1890's local women made a profession of laying out the dead and guarding them for a small fee and "all that is on the bed at the time of dying."[48] Here, too,

---

* We could do with more information on cemeteries, from the cholera epidemic of 1832, which led to the opening of new ones, to the attacks on clericalism, which included an attempt to strip cemeteries of their religious character and provided one more bone of contention for the angry 1880's and 1890's.

more elaborate beds and bedding made costs too high and abolished another practice. Death shifted from public mourning to more private grief. Wailing and lamenting had long remained social affairs; the professional mourners who shrieked and tore their hair during ritual dirges represented the communal grief at a struggle with death that was always doomed to defeat, the only opportunity to show a more general despair over a condition in which one never wins. Yet even this popular ritual faded away as conditions bettered. Grief that had been displayed in public came to be kept in the family. Professional mourners seem to have persisted to the turn of the century, but we hear that the custom was greeted with derision in Lorraine in 1889. Just as professional orators over a tomb declined as schooling provided more fashionably stereotyped phrases.[49]

The dead remained important, and All Souls Day, their feast, brought into church even those who did not set foot in it at any other time. But the bishop of Limoges knew well what this betokened when he accused his flock in 1862: "The cult of the saints and of the dead is still the outstanding trait of your character." The cult of the dead may be the starting point of organized religion; but that religion need not be Christian. The cult of the dead may even be a substitute for the cult of a particular god. "The more a civilization eliminates God, the more it practices the cult of the dead," a student of the question has said.[50] In fact, it can do without either. And without their representatives.

PART III

CHANGE AND ASSIMILATION

Chapter Twenty-one

THE WAY OF ALL FEASTS

Il serait bien difficile de faire cesser les anciennes coutumes; il
faut laisser au peuple quelque sorte de divertissements qui con-
tribuent beaucoup à leur faire oublier leurs peines.
—LIEUTENANT DU ROI EN LANGUEDOC

Mais quelqu'un troubla la fête...
—LA FONTAINE

WE HAVE SURVEYED the agencies of change at work. Now it is time to look
at some direct effects of their conjunction. Since we have just left the realm of
religion, as good a place as any to start is with a related one—that of feasts.

It is not every day that there's a feast, says the French proverb; but at one
time, almost every other day was a feast—*fête, assemblée, ballade, frairie,
vogue, apport, rapport, préveil,* or *riotée*—in some place or for some trade.
The diversity of land, crops, weather, and interests made for vast variety, in
details and in dates. Thus in Savoy, where every valley lived under different
conditions, rituals and celebrations similar in kind differed in nature from
village to village. On the other hand, we have seen that saints venerated in
many communities might perform differing functions. Saint George, honored
widely through the country, had special significance in Lorraine, where the
Moselle River was subject to winter freezes. His processions celebrated the
reopening of river traffic. Everywhere, however, feasts carried religious overtones: *ducasse* in the north (from *dédicace*), *pardon* in Brittany (from the
indulgences attached to a pilgrimage), *bénéiçon* or *bénichon* in the Jura
and Vosges (from benediction); *roumavage, romerage,* or *roumeyrage* (from
roumieu, the pilgrim who went to Rome); *voto,* or *boto,* for the votive saints'
feasts of the southwest, *kermesse* from the Flemish *kerk-misse.*

Even the profane terms relate to saints' festivals, for no rejoicing, jubilee,
or merrymaking would have arisen without supernatural sanction. And everywhere great feasts shared a magic character: the ashes of the Christmas log
or of the midsummer pyre were prophylactic, destroyed vermin,* ensured
fertility; the reed or fern blessed on Palm Sunday preserved from fire or
lightning. Carnival, especially, marked the return of active life after the

---

* In fact they do. In wine country Saint John's feast was used as a signal to destroy all com-
bustible waste, refuge of diverse parasites. Those vine-stock bundles that had not been removed
from the vineyards by June went into Saint John's bonfire (*Enquête sur ... l'agriculture,* Marne).

enforced pause of winter, the resumption of productive labor, the beginning of a new year in the calendar of the fields.* The ceremonies performed on such occasions were considered crucial to the welfare of the community and its members. In Mazières-en-Gâtine at about mid-century feasting and dancing during Carnival went on for three days, a teacher recalled, but they were not devoid of purpose: "One danced chiefly in the bakehouses, in front of the oven door, in order to have hemp." In Sologne, one danced on the compost heap, so that the chickens should prosper.[1] In the Norman bocage a fire feast celebrated with torches endured to the last quarter of the century, designed to rid the fields of moles and field mice. In lower Berry, around Issoudun, firebrands (*brandons*) were flourished through the fields on the first Sunday of Lent to aid the winter wheat and save the crops from blight and weeds. The original firebrands had been made of corn cockles, thistles, and mullein, the noxious plants they were meant to eliminate. Midsummer fires (among other things) brought marriage and fertility. Almost everywhere the lass who jumped over the embers expected to find a husband before the year was out; and the men and women who did so sought fertility for themselves or their property.[2]

Naturally enough, especially when fertility was concerned, the festivities were highly convivial. There was more and better food than usual. And there was also generally a fair, a tradition that continued in many places even during the Revolutionary period when patron saints' feasts and pilgrimages were banned.[3] Benoît Malon remembered how the September feast at Prétieux in Forez meant mutton, pie, and wine, sous for the children to buy little sugared dolls, the intoxicating music of two bugles and a drum, lads all dressed up parading past on horses with beribboned girls riding pillion, a horse race with rich prizes, and dancing into the night.[4]

There were regions, like Rouergue and Quercy, where feasts were exceedingly rare. "The monotony of a life of work and deprivation is troubled only once a year at the patron saint's feast...lasting two days," reported a Lot teacher in 1881. "The young, deprived of amusements during the whole year...dance even more than they eat." The same was true of Pierre Besson's village in Cantal. People had neither the time nor the means for such affairs. The patron saint's feast was about the only real festivity of the year, with lots of food and wine, though "for lack of habit, one got tippled at once." Further to the south a different attitude made the censorious feel there was no day

* Hence also a time for purification rites. In Sologne, Bernard Edeine tells us, the women struck the household beds with spindles enjoining the vermin (and evil) within to "go to the neighbor's house!" They also swept the house out backwards, then carried the muck to the neighbor's doorstep. (*La Sologne*, 2: 803, 805.) As ever, evil cannot just be made to vanish; it must be expelled at another's expense. But the rite described cannot have been carried out without some opposition. In a general sense, it is well to remember the words of Claude Durand: "As a matter of fact, this death of Carnival, of Lent, or of Winter, constitutes a double sacrificial negation. Most of the time it is a question of the 'death of Death,' of the fertilizing power of death, of the power of life that rests in death." (*Les Structures anthropologiques de l'imaginaire*, Paris, n.d. [1965?], p. 332.)

without procession or *farandole*. "One has to pray or one has to shout, one has to sing or one has to dance." In little towns along the Rhône the fire companies drilled on Sundays and marched past to the sound of martial music, "creating new festivals for the inhabitants."[5]

Above all, the annual feast, with its parade, horses, costumes, band or bands, ringing church bells, cannon shots, gunfire, and exploding crackers and fireworks, was the high point of the small town's year—"focus of personal emulation and point of honor of civic pride" for rich and poor, as in the Carnival of Rio today. Villagers streamed in from roundabout to see the procession, splendid as an army with banners, to join in the rich mix of religion and profanity, to drink, eat, and dance and combine business with pleasure.[6] Not even the suspension of Church festivals during the Revolution could stop this. In Osséja and in a great many other places, the dances in the village square continued to be held on Saint Peter's day without the customary mass beforehand: the magic, social, and economic functions embodied in the festival were too great to drop. As Paul-Louis Courier wrote in 1822, in his *Petition for Villagers Who Are Prevented from Dancing,* feasts were not just for fun: "Many a cow is sold that hadn't been sold at the fair," and many a marriage made.[7]

But Courier was pleading for a festival that was being stifled. His *Petition* was a solitary shot fired to defend the inarticulate. The heavy artillery was ranged on the other side: festivals (as we have seen in the previous chapter) were sources of disorder, of moral laxity, indulging superstition and heathenish debauchery; they disrupted production, encouraging people to waste their time drinking and dancing when they should be at work. Viewed from every angle of the dominant urban culture, these affairs were better done away with. This took some doing; but it succeeded in the end. The local bourgeoisie drew back from having anything to do with such anomalous vulgar pastimes, thus curtailing their splendor and depriving them of the unquestioned status that they once enjoyed. Politically troubled times led to the real or imaginary linking of traditional rejoicing and political protest or subversive activity. Government and police officials, foreign to the localities they administered, found noisy popular practices particularly threatening, in part because they were unfamiliar, in part because they could always degenerate into less innocuous demonstrations. In any case, the margin between the two was narrow and uncertain. As Maurice Agulhon points out, manifestations of almost every kind incorporated a traditional ritual (rough music or the farandole), and this could easily be made to serve for, or turn into, a political demonstration. The forces of order also frowned on the discharging of sundry firearms to celebrate christenings, wedding parties, processions, and festivals. This indiscriminate use of arms, which the administration preferred to reserve to itself, had to be repressed by fines and prison sentences.[8]

In the process, administration and police clashed not only with local custom, but with local authorities, for whom such customs were commonplace and in no wise shocking. Typical of such encounters was the storm that broke out at Vézelay in December 1853 over a local tradition called a *garçonnade*. "Every time a marriage is celebrated between a young lady of the town and a young man from outside the locality," explained the local justice of the peace, "it is the habit of young men of the working class to gather, armed with rifles, in order to offer the bride and groom a compliment, which they accompany by discharging their weapons. This is what they call rendering honor to the married couple." In fact, the matter was probably more complicated. A noisy salute to newlyweds was pretty standard, and generally involved a payment to the young men who rendered such homage. But beyond this, a "fine" was levied against an alien spouse for appropriating one of the local girls. One cannot tell how much of this was still remembered in urban Vézelay, whose "bourgeoisie," in the words of a report written some months before, seemed "to have preserved, like the town it lives in, the character and physiognomy of an earlier age." At any rate, the justice of the peace's report continued:

Hallowing this immemorial usage, 14 young men of Vézelay gathered the fifteenth inst. on the occasion of Mademoiselle Reuch's marriage and, armed with rifles, marched behind their drums, between 7 and 8 in the evening, to the Reuch house to accompany the intended to the civil ceremony. The corporal of gendarmes came around 10 P.M. to report the happenings, since these constituted a nocturnal disorder that troubled the tranquility of the population and, at the same time, a breach of a decree of the municipal police prohibiting the use of firearms in town.

I told the corporal about the custom mentioned above, which if it is no excuse is at least an extenuating circumstance, and invited him to show indulgence. But the corporal informed me that these young men were all dressed in uniforms of the National Guard, which none of them had the right to wear, and that they claimed to have permission from the mayor, who supposedly discussed the matter with the police superintendent but failed to inform him [the corporal], military chief of the locality specially charged with the maintenance of public order and the repression of all violations thereof.

On the following day the religious ceremony took place in the morning, the guard of honor still present and functioning. Around noon they could be seen going down the main street, drum before. They had retained the uniforms but had laid aside their arms to carry a barrel of wine (one of them sitting astride it), pies, bread, and other goodies—"a grotesque march," opined the justice of the peace, who crossed their path. Yet as a local man he was prepared to be tolerant, and invoked ancient usage and the innocent intentions of the accused to beg the imperial prosecutor's indulgence on their behalf. The police chief also pleaded for indulgence: "I have asked several inhabitants and all have said that it has always been thus." The mayor himself had provided the uniforms out of a stock of old ones that had been stored at the town hall, and the license he had delivered on December 1 read "as has been the custom since time immemorial without the least harm." In later correspondence, the mayor would tell the prefect that garçonnades went back "from mayor to mayor to the mid-seventeenth century," and that for his part he had issued permits for such affairs only the previous year with no questions asked.

The authorities, however, proved unrelenting. The mayor was responsible for the gendarme's embarrassment, and for impairing his authority, answered the sub-prefect. "No custom, no precedents should or could give you the right to permit young men to don, contrary to article 259 of the Penal Code, uniforms of the National Guard and, for the purpose of private celebrations, to organize for two days a noisy and armed company." Tradition was no excuse, nor was the traditional hierarchy. The mayor complained that the gendarme was being shown preference over him. "I cannot imagine a comparison between a corporal and myself. And yet in whose favor is the decision going ... ? [His] is a German head, as incapable of understanding the sense of a police regulation as of speaking French or acting as a Frenchman." The gendarme corporal was called Schoettel, and one assumes from the name that he was Alsatian. But he was the representative of national authorities against local ones: an iron pot banging against old clay crocks. Within a few days, the mayor and his assistants resigned, as did Doctor Reuch, the bride's father, who was a member of the Yonne sanitary council and of several other departmental bodies. The prefect accepted their resignations. Nothing was left of the bitter dispute except a thick file of correspondence.[9]

Police and safety regulations forged ahead. The use of fireworks was codified and restrained. Pistols were introduced that were able to fire only blanks. Law and order enforced with solicitude gnawed away at the festive rioting of centuries. But on April 25, 1905, the mayor of Cheny (Yonne) still found it necessary to publish the following *arrêté*:

Whereas the custom that young men have of firing shots in order to render honor on the occasion of a marriage or some other ceremony (the custom generally called *billarde*) may be dangerous for others and for themselves ... ; whereas this custom, which is perfectly praiseworthy and bears witness to good intentions, may advantageously be replaced by offering flowers, reciting compliments, etc., be it ordered: ... *Billardes* are prohibited in the commune of Cheny.[10]

The public forms of entertainment also increasingly disturbed humanitarians. Not all events were as innocuous as the wildly popular one at Prats (Pyrénées-Orientales) in which blindfolded men armed with sabers slashed at large sausages hung along the village street. Most festivals included a "torture," whether in fact or in effigy. "No good feast without a torture," as Louise Michel noted about her native Haute-Marne.[11] One might burn a human dummy of, say, King Herod or even stones, but live animals were more satisfying: cats, rats, foxes, snakes, or toads.* The list suggests the original symbolic purpose of eliminating evil (cats or toads, familiars of witches), or noxious beings (rodents or predatory animals). But the sadistic excitement may have survived the prophylactic intent. A law of 1850 prohibiting cruelty to animals put an end to such practices, but not it seems to gory and cruel games.

Everyone knows about cockfighting, which legislation has still not stamped out. But trussed-up birds were used in games of skill or chance: bound to a branch or mast to be shot at, or killed by throwing stones, or slashed at by mounted or blindfolded men. In the eighteenth century, around Sacy in Yonne, the men would buy a goat, tether it, then throw cudgels or stones until they battered it to death. The carcass would be roasted and devoured, with the successful killer absolved from sharing in the cost. Such fun is no longer heard of in the nineteenth century, but geese remained a popular target for similar sport, still practiced as part of the July 14 festivities in a number of places. At Saint-Florentin (Yonne) the proceedings were opened by the mayor, *ceint de son écharpe*, surrounded by the municipal council, whose members presumably helped him cast the first stone. In Lower Vivarais, though rifle shoots were organized until 1914 with sheep as targets, the favorite game was the *tir au poulet*. The unfortunate chicken was bound by one leg in a hole in the ground, or hung from a tree. Competitors who paid for each throw threw stones at it. The man whose stone finally despatched the bird won the pot. Though banned, the game was still being played at Vans and at Malarce (Ardèche) in 1939.†

The most original form of this sport seems to have been devised by Allier mariners, who strung a goose by its legs from a rope across the river, then flung themselves at it from the prow of a rowboat. If a man managed to grab it by the neck as he was falling into the water, his crew was likely to be showered with the poor goose's blood, but they had won the bird. Games of this sort endured to the end of the century. We hear of them in Auvergne,

---

* Arnold Van Gennep, *Manuel de folklore français*, 1.4: 1852–62. Less deadly activities still shocked progressive minds. At Vouzon (Loir-et-Cher) at Carnival time the wool carders rang the church bell, threw a manikin in carder costume from the steeple, and then burned it. Bernard Edeine tells us that in 1855 the priest tried to prevent this, but the mayor's *adjoint* had the church opened by a locksmith and, the priest reported, "la folie s'est faite comme par le passé" (*La Sologne*, 2: 803).

† On Yonne, see M. C. Moiset, "Usages, croyances, traditions, superstitions," in *Bulletin de la Société des Sciences ... de l'Yonne*, 1888, pp. 104–6; on Ardèche, Pierre Charrié, *Folklore du Bas-Vivarais*, p. 279. Of course, animals like plants also served a symbolic purpose. Thus, Charrié tells us, in certain hamlets near Lamastre a faggot of firewood was placed at the door of a new bride. Sometimes the pyre that she lit was surmounted by a perch to whose top was tied a cock, symbol of infidelity, which was left to burn alive (*Folklore du Haut-Vivarais*, p. 55). See also Alfred Reh, "Les Joutes strasbourgeoises ou le Gaenselspiel," *Nouvelle revue des traditions populaires*, 1950, pp. 174–89, which makes clear that a live bird continued to be used through the German occupation, and that the practice was abandoned only after the First World War.

in Lorraine, in Franche-Comté. No doubt the people had all the fun they could.[12]

Games were not games to peasants, especially when they were competitive. Even horse races, an ancient feature of many feasts in Brittany and other regions, gave rise to troubles and fights that led to their suppression.* This was the truer when it came to the various ballgames roughly resembling rugby or hurling that were widely played by village or hamlet teams. From Brittany to Picardy *soule* (*choule*) or variants thereof survived to the end of the century, and in a few places even later, despite numerous attempts to prohibit it. The popularity of the game is still reflected in numerous family names from Brittany to Artois (e.g., Chouleur, Chollet, Le Cholleux, Le Choulloux, Le Solleux), in place names (e.g., the Solle valley in the forest of Fontainebleau), and in linguistic usages (e.g., the Norman term for setting a dog on someone— *chouler un chien contre*). The game was seasonal, played only from Carnival through the months of Lent, which suggests it was not a simple entertainment (however bloody). Of course, it reflected communal rivalries and perpetuated them by creating new frictions. A game of soule went on for many hours, and ended with numerous players injured, and often some dead. It is no wonder the authorities disapproved of it and did their best to end it. And they succeeded on the whole. In northwestern Orne, at Bellou-en-Houlme, where the annual game (played with a bran-stuffed leather ball weighing some 12 lbs) involved several hundred players and as many as 6,000 onlookers drawn by the bloody reputation of the show, it took four brigades of gendarmes to stop play on Mardi Gras in 1851. The game was played out by stealth the following Sunday and for a few years more, but the need for secrecy drained it of fun. It was given up, like its counterpart at Saint-Pierre-d'Entremont nearby, also abandoned in the 1850's only after a heavy show of force.[13]

One way or another, feasts and disturbances were one. Significantly, in Allier one term for feasts was *riotée*. After all, that was part of their purpose: to alter the even rhythm of everyday life and thus refresh it. But the boisterous horseplay, the discharge of pent-up energies, as the prefect of Hautes-Pyrénées deplored, made for "excesses often harmful to health and nearly

---

* In Bourbonnais, too, horse races were an ancient custom, recalled by the Whitmonday *chevau-fug* (a hobbyhorse-like race) of Montluçon and especially by the *fêtes baladoires* of country parishes, which the authorities had long tried to legislate out of existence because of the troubles and brawls that always ensued. The races at La Ronde, where a King of the Race was elected, were finally suppressed in 1870; but a horse fair, which had grown up around the race, continued at Chambérat until 1908. (Francis Pérot, *Le Folklore bourbonnais*, p. 53.) We have to remember the high fertility value of the horse, hence not only of horse races but of horse-dances with their magic disguises (*chevau-fug* above, *chevau-frus* in Provence, *călăraşi* in Romania) and all kinds of related rites. Fernand Benoît tells us that all along the Rhône valley, in Dauphiné and Ardèche, at Carnival time the youths carry horsetails. They also pretend to hammer horseshoes on the girls and to unshoe them with pliers—a symbolic fertility rite reflected in the saying *a toumba un ferre* ("she's lost a horseshoe") and the verb *sferra* (to have a child). Hence Alphonse Daudet's remark about his *Arlésienne* who had "perdu un fer ou deux en route." (*La Provence*, p. 329.)

always to good behavior," which only too often became "the occasion of public disturbances." There was the rub. And what was true in the Pyrenees at the beginning of the nineteenth century remained true all over rural France pretty well to the beginning of the twentieth.[14]

Rejoicing included fighting. The intoxication of a brief respite and sometimes of drink kindled high spirits higher. Teasing turned to tussles, contention to affrays. Those who were used to this took it for granted. In 1774 an Argonne priest described a local ceremony after which "one goes to make merry, to dance, to fight, etc." He argued for abolition of the ceremony but not of the forms of fun that followed. After all, battles between village youths were often ritual, though no less bloody for it. The fights at fairs and festivals, like the exchange of taunts or competition in sports, were probably degenerate heirs of half-forgotten communal conflicts, local wars, or long-drawn-out legal proceedings over pasture, timber, water, or meadow rights. In 1862 Jules Michelet recalled that villages used to fight without knowing the reasons for it, but added that it was still being done in places that were a bit out of the way. This seems to be confirmed by the mayor of Osséja, in Cerdagne, who took great care at every village celebration to keep potential contenders separate, assuming that "the division existing between the young men of this commune must necessarily give rise to fights."[15]

After mid-century most references to this matter rejoiced that bloody affrays were things of the past, yet qualified the statement to show that they still survived. This seems to have been the case in Basses-Pyrénées, where the joint efforts of Church and legal authorities had by 1858 only incompletely stifled the traditional fights. Or in Aubrac, where the very popular pilgrimage to the Lake of Saint Andéol was finally abolished in 1867 after a particularly bloody bout. The clergy had long sought this end; only police action achieved it. As usual, clerical opposition by itself tended to be ineffective when popular interests were at stake. The Breton pardon of Saint Hervé, held on the border between Vannetais and Cornouaille, involved a bloody ritual struggle for the saint's banner, possession of which ensured a rich crop of buckwheat that year. The battle always left many wounded, often seriously and sometimes mortally. A priest attempted to suspend the procession in order to avoid such bloodshed but found, as a Finistère chronicler explained, that "Bretons obey their priests blindly only when these show themselves the slaves of ancient beliefs." Invading the sacristy, the peasants took the banner and forced the priest, bound to a chair, to attend the ceremony and the ensuing battle.[16]

There is some evidence to suggest that, as in the case of all traditions, the older generation in many villages played a not insignificant part in maintaining traditional feuds. We come across complaints that when the young "of diverse parties" proposed to hold joint meetings to organize the local feasts, the opposition came from the older generation: "Old age does not soften the violent mood the older age groups retain from their past." This past was their revolutionary experience and the settling of scores consequent to it. Time would help allay such factors, at least by killing off those directly involved. But we know that memories were long and potent at the village level, long enough to let a candidate win a parliamentary election in the Jura in 1902 by pointing out that his rival's uncle had a hand in trying Republicans after December 2, 1851.[17]

It may be that the collective memory became diluted when the school poured new suggestions into it. It may be that village-to-village feuds waned as military service created bonds, or at least common references, that stretched beyond the limits of the parish and lasted after the uniform was put aside. It may even be, as Charles Tilly has suggested, that collective violence was nationalized and thus removed to a less immediate plane.[18] There certainly was more adequate police enforcement, and as the century progressed—especially in its second half—fighting became less a communal and more of a personal enterprise.*

In 1875 Maurice Bastié recalled the bloody brawls that inevitably marked the votive feasts of villages in Tarn. He rejoiced that the "barbarian usage" had by then disappeared. It had not quite. Evidence from Brittany and from the Pyrenees suggests there had been transference, that serious clashes continued to occur, but within the structure of modern institutions—in political rivalry or conscript drafts.[19] But public violence and gang fights can hardly be cited today as evidence of archaism. What matters is their context and their causes: by the end of the century these showed the impress and used the terminology of the modern world.

One usage that came under heavy fire, as a military observer of 1863 put it, was "the mad, noisy glee" of Carnival: "In these days of mirth and of abandon, the villagers' spirits take flight; grotesque disguises, charivaris, songs excite the jollity of some, the legitimate irritation of others; hence they not only awaken the imagination of rural poets but often give rise to quarrels and dangerous brawls."[20]

All sense that Carnival, which in those days ran all the way from Epiphany to Ash Wednesday, had a particular function seems to have been lost from sight. The revivifying and purifying purposes of ribald ceremonial, ignored by the upper classes, came to be largely forgotten by the participants too. The links that the masks periodically reforged between the dead and the living, the prophylactic magic of the fires and their scattered ashes, the sympathetic magic of disguises and play-acting, the symbolic expiation of Carnival himself, carrying the community's sins into the flames, turned into a season of pranks, practical jokes, and foolery. Yet even these could be fraught with

---

* Jean Vartier tells us that around Gérardmer, in Vosges, when the farm lads were invited to a *grande veillée* they did not agree right off unless they were told *"et peu, on s'bettrai"*—and then, we'll have a fight. (*La Vie quotidienne*, p. 90; I am indebted to Michael Marrus for this reference.)

menace. The dispassionate account of the military observer gives all the clues we need to understand why anything with even the least taint of traditional ritual and rejoicing was cause for official unease.[21]

Disguises, rough music, satirical songs and verses potentially subversive and critical of village notables, carried the seeds of trouble.* Processions and counter-processions could easily clash, as they occasionally did at Pouilly-sur-Loire, where a group of young men held a procession on Ash Wednesday to mock and guy the Penitents; the youths, wearing white shirts and cotton bonnets with straw sticking out so as to almost hide the face, carried chains and chamberpots filled with wine to quaff from, and whipped one another around the town to the indignation of the more devout. Even in small villages opposing groups would organize rival dances, donning red or white bonnets to indicate their allegiances, and masked men would fall to fighting egged on by their womenfolk. Alternatively and just as serious, one hears about "disguises intended to injure the honor and reputation of the mayor and priest." The guilty parties were severely punished.[22]

The possibility of political content was particularly feared by the authorities. Close watch was kept; allusions to political and social themes, or expressions of criticism and opposition were quickly suppressed. The final judgment of bloated Carnival, condemned to die as Lent took over, afforded a convenient opening to condemn the rich, "living insults to peasant soberness," if indeed it did not give rise to more explicit political statements.[23] In Brie Carnival included a "trial of the Marquis and the Marquise." In Var, we hear of the political sensations it could cause.† The political tensions of the 1850's produced a rich crop of such breaches for the authorities to deal with. At Mauzé (Deux-Sèvres), a French-speaking bourg in a patoisant countryside, we hear of a procession in which the centerpiece was a young peasant who sym-

---

* Note that the popular license, scandalous songs, and shouted obscenities shocked and upset the respectable classes in town or bourg, rather than in the countryside proper; but the disguises, often using dress of the opposite sex, were particularly shocking to the priests. In the *Revue des traditions populaires*, 1919, pp. 40–41, Paul Saintyves printed an Upper Breton ronde in which the girls of Paimpont forest come to seek absolution for having gone dancing in boys' breeches, and are denied it by the angry priest:

> J'avons couru les danses
> En habit de garçons . . .
> J'avions bien des culottes
> Mais point de cotillons . . .
> Allez-vous-en, les filles
> Pour vous point de pardon.

In the song, the girls do not heed the priest; in practice, too, the travesties continued "dans certaines campagnes."

† In 1871 in many Brie villages the figures carried around were those of the Marquis and Marquise Bismarck. Meanwhile, in Franche-Comté young people passed through the streets at Carnival singing satirical songs, "made up for the occasion," to ridicule members of the upper classes who had been involved in some scandal during the year (Charles Beauquier, *Traditions populaires*, p. 29). On Brie, see *Bulletin folklorique de l'Ile-de-France*, 1939, p. 25; on Var, see Maurice Agulhon, *La République au village*, pp. 411–15.

bolized Liberty in Chains and repeatedly sang the rebellious "Chant des Vignerons." At Volonne (Basses-Alpes) the priest became the subject of an "immoral and irreligious" masquerade, whose organizers ended in court. In several places the military, obsessed with secret societies sending each other signals after the manner of James Fenimore Cooper's Mohicans, put out fires lit in honor of the occasion. At Bray (Somme) the mayor prohibited masks after sundown, and the gendarmerie intervened when unruly youths gathered "to sing and cause disorder." The population seemed ready to defy the rule until cowed into silence by a show of force. Two brigades of gendarmes and one company of infantry sent from nearby Peronne "produced a very good effect."[24]

The Empire disappeared, but the suspicion of popular festivities did not. In February 1877 we hear that during a farandole at Arles-sur-Tech (Pyrénées-Orientales) a fight between Republicans and Legitimists was only narrowly averted when the gendarmerie intervened. The same tension threatened the Carnival of 1878, with opposing parties seeking to hold separate dances.[25] Politics was shattering the communion of the great seasonal ceremonies. National issues and national divisions complicated local ones and helped to emphasize them.

They also interfered with them in another way. Since the Revolution, festivals had been recognized as useful didactic instruments to create desirable attitudes.* The constitution of 1791 decreed the establishment of national festivals "to preserve the memory of the French Revolution, maintain fraternity between citizens, and bind them to the constitution, the fatherland and the laws." The expression of enthusiasm, however artificial, would create enthusiasm—engender or reinforce adherence to a regime or creed. To this end, official feasts competed with traditional ones, which they eventually helped to stifle. The Revolution's successors had followed the example it set: August 25 under Louis XVIII, November 4 under Charles X, and May 1 under Louis Philippe were dedicated to the King.

Archives reveal very serious efforts to *create* feasts where there had been none before. Mayors and municipal councils were required to organize celebrations and to report on their success. Work was prohibited. There were to be festive illuminations, bells, fireworks, dancing, religious services, and the distribution of alms. The files are crowded with near-illiterate reports that testify to much humble effort, to great poverty, and to little success—in part because when resources were limited, the villagers husbanded what they had for the traditional feasts.

---

* The notion was not new, only its systematic application. Thus, in Lorraine, the *fête des Rois* had been celebrated with special pomp since the fifteenth century in honor of Duke René's victory over Charles the Bold of Burgundy on Jan. 5, 1477. This celebration was suppressed under the French occupation in the seventeenth century, reestablished by Leopold of Austria, again suppressed between 1702 and 1714 while Louis XIV's troops occupied the country, and finally abolished in 1737 by Stanislas Leszczynski.

Subsidies provided by the prefect or by rich citizens could usually produce a corporal's guard of indigents to cheer the King's name after a distribution of bread or a barrel of wine had snared a public, but the poorer the parish the less likely it was to see such funds. At Aspres in Pyrénées-Orientales, "L'assistance na pas été autant nombreuse que l'inspiration de la fete devoient nous faire espérér malgré que nous les abons exciter." While at Saint-Hipolite (*sic*), "Jai fait publié par le Crieur public la veille dans toute la Commune que personne ne pouvait travaillé messieurs les avitans de la commune ont violé la loi une grande partie."[26]

Peasants were reluctant to give up work for these new festivals in general, and balked especially at the November date chosen by Charles X, when the cold and rains limited the possibilities of enjoyment, and there was apt to be winter sowing or other duties that could not be put off.[27] This was even truer of October 6, the day of national mourning for the execution of Louis XVI, when there was not even the promise of dancing to mitigate the nuisance of enforced idleness. That feast went out with the Bourbons, and Louis Philippe had the good fortune to have his saint's day fall on the first of May, which had long-standing popular associations. Because of the coincidence with May Day, maypoles could be presented as symbols of loyalty and honor to the King. Even then, the celebration was sometimes shifted to the nearest Sunday in the knowledge that no one would attend on a weekday. Thus in the Pyrénées-Orientales in 1841. That same year the sub-prefect of Saint-Flour, in Cantal, reporting on the solemnities and rejoicings in his town, added: "As for the rural communes, it is impossible to get anything done, especially on a weekday."[28]

Still, as a result of steady pressure from the prefect, the rural communes of Cantal were beginning to accept the first of May by the end of the reign, especially when the date also saw the dispensing of charity to the poor, who never failed to express proper gratitude.* Yet none of these fabricated feasts were given time to pass into local custom: nine years for Louis XVIII's, five for Charles X's, and seventeen for Louis Philippe's were too little. Then came the celebrations that welcomed the Second Republic in 1848. Alain Corbin sees these as the last occasions in the Limousin when folklore and political life interpenetrated in a truly spontaneous manner. In Forez Benoît Malon recalled the March Sunday when the village planted a tree of liberty, with two free tubs of wine placed in the village square, and free white bread and cheese for all the children. Malon and his little brother got half a glass of wine and "highly excited, we followed the two drummers who marched back and forth

---

* As the mayor of Nieudan duly noted, reporting the events of May 1, 1847: "Etant sortis de léglise Nous avons deménde aux proprietaires ésés, de donnér quelque chose aux pauvrés pour leur faire Celebrer la faite de St. Philipe, Nous avons ramasse 8ofr15c que nous avons distribué aux pauvres de la Commune ils ont desiute tous Crie vive Louis Philipe, vive louis philipe Notre bon roi, et avons terminé ainsi la faite du roi." (Archives Départementales, Cantal 43 M2.)

from one end of the village to the other, followed by enthusiasts crying 'Long live the Republic!' "[29]

Yet the old habits endured. In November 1848, for the promulgation of the new constitution, informal reports did not suffice; there had to be official *procès-verbaux*. The constitution rated a feast of its own, and a law of 1849 established commemorative ceremonies for the Revolution in February and a feast of the Republic on May 4. There was scant time to celebrate before the Second Empire replaced them with a new feast on August 15. This had the advantage of falling on the feast of the Assumption of the Holy Virgin, and was enforced with the regime's customary efficiency. By then, more numerous public employees, together with the founding of schools that could marshal children to join in, ensured greater participation. Thus by 1852 at Saint-Hippolyte (Pyrénées-Orientales), where a generation before the mayor could hardly scrawl out his reports and the village could hold no service for lack of a priest, we find a school, a flag, a village policeman who could carry it, a cantonnier, and a mayor whose rhetoric had a distinctly poetic cast.[30]

But the heyday of civic ceremonial came only in the 1880's. The year 1879 opened the Republic of republicans. Jules Grévy became president. The public powers returned from Versailles to Paris. "La Marseillaise" became the national anthem. In 1880 July 14 was made the national feast, but it too took time to gain acceptance. In some part this was the work of opponents of the Republic, like the many priests who refused to ring their bells or let the tricolor fly from their church towers.[31] But the chief problem was, as in other cases, the awkwardness of the season, a time when peasants worked particularly hard and were tired out. Proof, if any proof is needed, of the politicians' ignorance of (or indifference to) what was appropriate at harvest time. In some cases the fête was shifted to the nearest Sunday; in many more permission was sought to do the same.[32] What success there was depended on local political orientation, especially where notables were concerned and while the celebration remained, as it had been at its invention, a "feast of the bourgeois."[33] In many places, the situation must have been like that at Blond (Haute-Vienne), described in a report of 1882:

Je vous répond a votre l'etre et linstituteur avais mis un drapou ainsi que son adjoin qui en avais mis un a sa croisé aveque un écris ou il yavais vive la republique liberté egalité et fraternité et bien y i luminé. . . .

au burau de tabaque il yavais un drapau ainci au bureau de la poste un drapau votre frere avait mis des chandelles a leurs croissé des bougis bruler sur le mur de vans la mairie mais pas de drapau a la mairie.

des geunes gens se sont procurer de la poudre et ont fais partir quelques caux de essepion de petit canon.[34]

It seems quite probable that, despite the efforts of a century, many small communes of the 1880's (like Orcines in Puy-de-Dôme) had never known such public celebrations. Most of them seem to have found the occasion unimportant, if not a downright nuisance, and the small costs involved an imposition. The prefect had a small fund available for subsidies, but this did not go far. Most of the costs had to be borne by the parish, that is, by its citizens. This inevitably caused a tug-of-war between the traditional local feast and the new national festival. Political considerations complicated matters, with the enemies of the Republic backing the old celebration and its friends opposing it, if only by implication.[35] As for the schoolmaster, hostility to obsolete ways and the partisans of superstition very often seemed to him only consistent with his patriotic attachment to the Republic, the fatherland, and the Fourteenth of July.*

By 1889, when the Republic celebrated the hundredth anniversary of the Revolution, officially sponsored feasting had progressed in scale and content. Banquets had become an essential part of festivities, illuminations were no longer the exception but the rule, and popular initiative could even intervene to start impromptu dances. Then came the 1890's and the Ralliement, which meant that *"réacs"* who had so long abstained from governmental feasts made it a point to join them. And July 14 itself "becomes ever more part of custom," so that as the sub-prefect of Riom was pleased to note, "many small rural communities celebrated on the day itself instead of putting it off to the following Sunday."[36]

One casualty of the competition between festivals, in which July 14 emerged the clear winner, was the religious procession of the Church. There is a direct relationship between the official abolition of such processions and the official sponsorship of rival festivities, with one Republican municipality after another banning the religious celebrations, and with the government withholding the soldiers who lent color to the event and often drew a significant crowd on their own account. Gustave Hervé, who grew up in Brest, remembered how, after 1881, "it was no longer the Corpus Christi procession that attracted everyone's attention ... but rather the Fourteenth of July with its elaborate parade." By the mid-1890's this effect had reached smallish market towns, like Billom (Puy-de-Dôme), where in 1896 the once all-important summer processions passed almost unnoticed. It was July 14, "now accepted by all, even reactionaries," that had taken their place.[37]

But if the great ceremonies of the Church declined, so too did humbler local feasts and rites.† We hear of this already under the July Monarchy.

---

* In an article in the *Revue pédagogique*, December 15, 1901, Henry Martin, school inspector at Bourg-en-Bresse, described the schools' contributions to the celebrations that marked the annexation of Franche-Comté to France, and delighted in "this ceremony that makes the school stand out and shows to the simple population of the countryside that a manifestation embellished by poetry and music can move and charm without having any religious character."

† Or rather say more precisely, the *popular* ceremonies declined. Meanwhile, new ceremonies, primarily official ones such as *vins d'honneur*, inaugurations, and school prize-givings became increasingly frequent. But they too tapered off after a time, and even at their peak they seldom involved the community as a whole.

Dissensions between the authorities and the Church, great keeper of traditional ceremonial; the occasional rebelliousness of firemen or national guard, balking at supplying the martial or musical element for small-town parades; the division of a society that attended things together and that began to separate into factions—all contributed to make common festivities less common and less attractive. Here too the rivalry with official feasts was an uneven struggle. In many cases local schools had been dismissed on the occasion of a particular feast (as was done for the feast of Saint Nicholas in Lorraine and Bourbonnais). This ceased to be countenanced in 1855, so that official holidays should have all the advantages on their side. Successful leaders of Provençal *bravades* gained too much political capital for the authorities to look on them with a friendly eye. In any case, there were few men left ready to ruin themselves to gain local kudos. The last bravade at Draguignan was celebrated in 1860. The rites of May, like those of Carnival, could lend themselves to slanderous allusions that had to be discouraged by the courts. Other local customs ended in drinking bouts followed by battles royal. The *chevau-fug* of Montluçon were finally forbidden in 1869. The pyres lit on Saint John's eve (June 23) or at Saint Peter's (June 29) carried the danger of fire and also frequently gave rise to disturbances. In addition they reflected political divisions, one party taking them over, the other opposing them. At Arles-sur-Tech (Pyrénées-Orientales) in 1878 the Legitimists alone danced at Saint John's feast. The Republicans stayed away. The village pyre did not survive much longer.[38]

The causes of decay were many, the decay itself was evident. Belief in the beneficial function of popular ceremonies was fading. The control of the environment by technical means was gradually improving. Assumptions to the contrary were losing ground to rival conformities carried by the elementary school books—and the penny press. July 14 represented progress and a new kind of hope. It was not so much that technical progress solved many problems of the past or that new problems did not crop up in consequence. It was rather that men who had been taught to seek mystical causes and magic solutions for their problems now learned to tackle them by different means or, just as important, to put their faith instead in progress and the promise of a better life to come. The science and technology that made magic redundant also erased the memories that told people why certain rites made sense. Seasonal rites survived, but without any perceived usefulness, hence without meaning. They became games for children, and were tolerated—when they did not bother the adult world too much—chiefly as entertainment.

The relegation of serious observances to the status of children's games is one of the most striking indications of what Max Weber called the disenchantment of the world. The rationalization of a universe in which effect could be expected to follow cause advanced apace. And the enchanted parts were set aside for children.

In 1860 an army officer saw May queens collecting money in Isère and noted: "In past times it was adults who thus made a spectacle of themselves. ... Today only little girls continue the tradition." At one time the May queens had been nubile lasses collecting gifts and money for their dowries. But now this had become absurd and was left to children. Fifteen years earlier in that department another officer had noted that many a mountain parish elected a king and a queen of May, who would rule over the rituals of the day seated on a throne. Then, as the century wore on, the kings, or *abbés de la jeunesse*, disappeared. By 1860 almost all were gone. The children who were now elected to play the queen of May and her retainers continued the wasted rite by collecting money to spend on "buying dainties."[39]

Soon it would sink even lower and be left to the children of the poor. The same was true about the many occasions, at New Year or Epiphany, or during Carnival, depending on the area, when throughout France young men had toured the villages, often in disguise, singing traditional ditties and collecting gifts—smoked meats, dried fruits, eggs, money—to end in a feast at the local inn. First their disguises became simpler. Then the gifts became increasingly symbolic. André Varagnac suggests that as diet improved and meat in particular began to be considered a staple, such gifts in kind no longer promised an exceptional banquet, and were abandoned as a matter of popular judgment and of the recipients' pride. In any case, by the turn of the century we hear that such door-to-door rounds had been left to children. In Upper Vivarais, where masks and masquerades had been common practice for adults and "youth," the custom was increasingly abandoned after 1870 until in 1914 "it was quite discredited and regarded as an amusement for children." In Franche-Comté, "rare exceptions apart, it is only children, especially those of the poor, who go around collecting gifts today." Similarly, at Cleebourg (Bas-Rhin) it was only poor children who went around collecting what in the 1930's came to be looked on as alms.[40]

The trees, branches, or maypoles that had been set up in the village square, or in front of the house of the most recently married couple, or before the homes of all the village girls, lost their ancient significance as symbols of fertility or of the authority of the village; even, in time, their significance as a sign of social approval or disapproval. By the end of the century we hear that in Franche-Comté village youths, instead of placing a branch in front of the house of each girl, now "find a collective token easier and less costly," and put a single maypole in the village square—with an empty bottle on top. It is true, the observer adds, that the forest administration strenuously protested the enormous damage visited on forests as a result of the old practice. But one cannot help thinking that such opposition must have existed earlier. Now, it provided the rationalization for an abandonment that reflected an exhaustion of belief. All that was left was a hallowed memory of fun and perhaps profit, so that in many places youths did not even offer tokens to the maidens of their choice, but gave them "vulgarly to the municipal authorities or to the officers of the fire company ... with a view to the gastronomic rejoicings that will follow."[41]

So the May Day symbols endured, but the memory of their significance faded. The various references to them suggest decline. In Meuse they "still exist in a good few places" in 1890; in Vosges they "tend to disappear toward the end of the century"; in Nivernais they were "general to 1914, then found sporadically"; in Franche-Comté they were "discriminating before 1914, became routine thereafter."[42]

This was the case with many practices. The shepherds' feasts of Mâconnais, once celebrated by "adolescents between fifteen and twenty," became a children's frolic.[43] And toleration for childish pranks was itself receding. In 1880 at Abbeville, the children still went about the streets at Easter time banging with the small hammers they used in church on Maundy Thursday and singing an old refrain in honor of Saint Stephen. By 1885 the custom was obsolete, "following a municipal regulation."[*] Midsummer pyres, great fertility rites, their virtue remembered in the original sense of the English word bonfire, had been fed with wood collected by village youths from all the inhabitants. Then the collecting chore was relegated to the children. Householders began to refuse to contribute. The necessary wood was sometimes obtained by pilfering. Ritual thefts, well accepted in the first half of the century, came to be seen as trespass and spoliation. There were complaints and fights. At Crécy-en-Brie (Seine-et-Marne) toward 1860–70 the theft of wood for the fire by children gave rise to "numerous lawsuits." Municipal authorities intervened, prohibiting the collections. At Brioude these had stopped altogether by the 1880's, leaving only the custom of children offering flowers to their parents on that day. Midsummer pyres continued to be lit in Haute-Loire at the turn of the century, but only children now danced around the flames. In Morvan, too, where around 1890–1900 the children built the bonfire for the "fire and dance of torches" on the first Sunday in Lent, an old woman in her seventies who came to secure a firebrand to guard her against storms explained that in her time this was not done by children but by men and women—a serious rite with words and steps and purpose.[44]

All over France, it seems, bonfires receded with the century. In the Ardennes they seem to have waned under the Second Empire, and attempts to revive them in the 1890's did not meet much success. At Château-Thierry they disappeared in the 1870's. By 1885 in Eure-et-Loir, where a few years before bonfires blazed widely, "the custom is being lost." Similarly, by the mid-1890's there were almost none in Saintonge, though in the 1870's every village had had its "new fire." Once common throughout Dauphiné, bonfires by the mid-

---

[*] Dieudonné Dergny, *Images, coutumes et croyances*, 1: 326. There must have been political overtones to this new rule, applied just at a time when municipality and church were at daggers-drawn.

1880's seem to have lighted mostly the mountain villages. In Charente-Maritime they were "pretty rare" by the end of the century.[45] The prestige attached to the lighting of bonfires declined or disappeared or became a bone of political contention. The King once lit the fire on the Place de Grève. In 1854 the sub-prefect of Saint-Flour was honored as the representative of the Emperor and given precedence in lighting the bonfire there on August 15.*

Squire, priest, mayor, oldest inhabitant, or president of the youth group, the first person to light the local bonfire reflected the values obtaining in his community. By the 1880's we hear that in Oise the clergy were keeping away, and the fires were now lit by children—a bad sign, as we know. In Creuse and Corrèze, where pyres were becoming rarer, they were once lit by local notables, now by "local people"—a vague term that seems to indicate lower prestige. In Lozère the priests no longer lit the village pyres and now recommended that their congregations avoid ceremonies devoid of religious character. The mayors took over the ceremony around 1885 and lit the bonfire to the sound of "Long live the Republic! Long live the mayor!" And there was dancing around the pyre with patois songs and "La Marseillaise." At Clessé (Haute-Saône), "formerly men organized this bonfire [the bordes, on the first Sunday in Lent], then the young men, then children alone were left to gather the faggots and the thorns; finally the old custom disappeared around 1910."[46]

There is plenty of evidence that bonfires, May Day offerings, and other observances endured into our century and indeed can still be found here and there. What matters is that their original associations have long since been forgotten. Prescriptions and ceremonials with a legitimacy of their own became dispensable, which meant that they could be jostled about, dismissed, or abrogated as convenience decreed. A striking illustration of this process appears in the fate of a ritual that long obtained in a village slightly west of the Argonne forest, Mesnil-en-Hurlus in northeastern Marne. On the first Sunday in Lent, day of torchlight feasts, the man most recently married in the village had to contribute a cartwheel (in good condition). This was carried to the top of a hill and made to roll down until broken, and the pieces were then distributed for good luck. Here was a fertility rite, possibly anterior to Christianity, directed to generation, fecundity, and plenty. In the vineyard country of Moselle such wheels (often set alight) frequently crashed through the vines and caused serious damage, but the vineyard owners accepted the destruction on the grounds of public (that is, magic) utility. At Hurlus, how-

---

* Archives Départementales, Cantal 43 M3 (St.-Flour, Aug. 16, 1854). The account suggests that the mayor of the town normally set the first torch. Interestingly, the cholera epidemic that hit Toulon in 1884 saw the resumption of bonfires that had only recently been discontinued. The excuse was that fires drove out miasmas and purified bad air, but in fact they appear to have been reinstituted simply because people took great pleasure in them. The fires were tended and maintained over a period of several weeks. All this time the Navy provided material for an especially big bonfire on the quay. (Bérenger-Féraud, *Réminiscences populaires sur la Provence*, pp. 138–39.)

ever, as early as the Second Empire a local landowner, irate at the damage the wheel caused to his crops and hedges, had sought to prevent its passage. The issue was brought before the justice of the peace at nearby Ville-sur-Tourbe, who found for the villagers, and the practice continued. Then came the Franco-Prussian War, and the swathes it cut seem to have discouraged weddings. At any rate, no marriage took place between 1869 and 1876. This meant that the man married last, in 1869, was forced to provide a fresh wheel every year for seven years in a row. The eighth year he finally refused to do so, and thus the custom lapsed.[47] What had been unthinkable at mid-century could be accepted by 1876. The war had upset the long-established continuity—and there are frequent references to other customs lapsing at this time. But could the war have wrought such permanent change if the custom had not been on the way out already and belief crumbling, as the earlier protest suggests?

Utility had shifted to another plane. Young Bretons who had once taken ashes from the festival bonfires to improve their fields began to have recourse to fertilizer. In Vosges, where Midsummer bonfires were closely associated with cowherds and cattle pasturage, the fires declined in the late 1880's. Pasture was giving way to cultivated land; there were fewer cattle and fewer cowherds, and the police prohibitions of the 1850's based on the threat of fire could finally be enforced. In Languedoc by 1891 only children still believed that the water of the local stream changed to wine and the pebbles to bread at midnight on Saint John's Eve. At La Coquille (Dordogne), Saint John had long been especially honored by shepherds as their patron. Each year on June 24 they had brought gifts of sheepskins, fleeces, and as many as 40 or 50 lambs to the church dedicated to him. But around 1900 "the faithful no longer gave lambs to the priest; they also ceased to give him wool when it reached a profitable price."[48] Their faith decayed as possibilities of marketing increased, a twofold development that seems to have been brought about by improvements in local communications.

Having lost their unifying magic sense, ceremonies like Carnival and Midsummer bonfires were briefly infused with new meaning by politics. But the power of politics shook them to pieces, and the forces of "enlightened" criticism were of no mind to repair them. Priests had already hammered at superstitions; now teachers too attacked the disorder and the irrational aspects of Carnival, Yule logs, lighted firebrands, and bonfires, and rejoiced as these declined or disappeared.[49] In Vivarais Carnival disappeared in bigger centers and only survived on the upper heights. In Lauragais in 1891 Carnival was decaying; only vestiges of its past splendor were left. "Carnival is on its way down," reported one teacher in 1899. "People find it ridiculous to rig themselves out in cast-off clothes and put on false faces."[50]

Yet in the end the same urban forces that had stifled Carnival and other popular cults revived them when the blood had drained out of them. Even as village teachers rejoiced in the disappearance of absurd practices, they were reappearing as urban entertainment. A historian of popular festivals in Paris has noted that the processions of Carnival and Mid-Lent Sunday would be replaced by publicity floats and artificial distractions. The procession of the fatted ox, suppressed in Marseilles in 1853 and in Paris itself since the Prussian war, was reestablished "to the delight of the rubbernecks" of 1891.[51] At Nice the old communal fertility rites of maying were transmuted into flower festivals; and the May queens were revived as Rose queens to become focal points for local celebrations. In 1895 a perpetual endowment at Pessac (Gironde) established the Rose Queen's feast, which was still the town's chief festival in 1970. In Ardèche "only the votive feast still keeps its attraction, but only by imitating those of towns." At the romerage of Saint-Jeannet (Alpes-Maritimes) in 1909, the traditional pyre was replaced by store-bought fireworks and homemade tents by better marquees bought in Nice; the fife and drums gave way to an eight-piece band; and interest in the traditional games was plainly fading. Even the Carnival disguises that had been abandoned to children were taken up again in imitation of the city folks' new passion for masked balls. Having succeeded in suppressing popular rituals, the urban culture assimilated and regurgitated them as seemingly original products of its own. By that time they were no longer fêtes, just shows. Only suggestively garbled memories remained. By 1957 Laurence Wylie in his Vaucluse village would hear about the Midsummer festival: "There was a game that consisted of jumping over the bonfire, because it was said that whoever got across would not be bothered by fleas."[52]

This evolution was perfectly natural. Traditions tend to be immemorial because memory is short. There is every indication that traditions are subject to change like everything else, and, of course, subject to outside influences. Feasts had generally been treated in a fairly practical manner. In Brie most pilgrimage feasts were seasonal, grouped into two periods: in spring before the haying and in late summer after the harvest and before winter closed in. In Marche, on the other hand, one of the most popular saints for feasting was Saint Anthony because his day fell in January when the masons were back from Paris. When a patron saint's day coincided with awkward periods, the fête was sooner or later moved to a more convenient day, such as the nearest Sunday or the anniversary of another saint. In Haute-Marne, between the Meuse and Saône rivers, parishes whose patron saint was Saint Stephen had long avoided the awkward problem of a date, December 26, that falls between Christmas and New Year by celebrating their patron instead in mid-September, after the harvest and before the grapes have ripened. Likewise at Brouenne (Meuse), the votive feast of Saint Hilary (January 13), following close on New Year and Epiphany, received only cursory attention. The real feast was la petite fête—Saint Martin's on November 11, which lasted for three days. The hot summer months as a rule did not afford much time for feasting.[53]

That was the problem with the national festival for Louis on August 25, as with July 14. And one great Morvan feast, the *fête du Beuvray*, held on an otherwise barren mountain the first Wednesday in May, died out when it was shifted to July in the last part of the century.[54]

Carnival and Lent fitted the calendar well. During the one, plants lay dormant, "so youth could devote many days to pleasure," as we hear in the Pyrenees; during the other, reserves were running out, and only a few vegetables were left over from winter stores. As Joseph Cressot has noted, the frugality of the Lenten fast was prescribed by the situation. Recalling his youth in the 1880's in southeastern Champagne, he writes: "Nothing ... but the last cabbages pulled out of their frozen straw, leeks, turnips, potatoes. It was the heyday of herrings"—one a day for an adult, half for a child. So, fasts as well as feasts tended to be preserved by traditional conditions as long as these conditions lasted. When they outlasted conditions, it was in a new sense— "without religious spirit, but by tradition, which is close to it," as an informant put it in describing the feast of Saint Vincent at Gouaix (Seine-et-Marne).[55] Holy days had turned into leisure time.

Conditions counted less, of course, as they became less specifically local and more homogenized. One aspect of this was that certain local traditions spread to new areas: Saint Nicholas's day, native to the north and northeast, was the most important of the December feasts in Lorraine and the Jura but was ignored in most of the rest of France as an occasion for popular celebration. This feast would be spread by literature and publicity toward the end of the nineteenth century, when it became fairly general. About the same time December 6 was being displaced in its native habitat by an interloper—the Alsatian Christmas tree, carrying Christmas with it. The Yule log, part of most Christmas celebrations, gradually gave way to fir trees, while local practices were left to be forgotten.[56]

Protestants and public schools, recognized agents of modernity, were the chief diffusers of the Christmas tree. At Lantenne, in Doubs, the Christmas tree, unknown before, was introduced by a schoolteacher, abandoned, then taken up again, again at school, probably after the First World War, as the occasion for an annual celebration and distribution of toys. In Ardèche the Protestants came first; at Salavas their church sported a tree in 1891, and a few years later we hear of another tree at a Protestant-owned factory at Viviers. Secondary schools followed suit at Vans and elsewhere. By 1903 the Catholics set out to imitate their adversaries. The French Catholic Women's League began to organize Christmas trees in all parishes of the Vivarais, complete with the toy distributions that provided one of their main attractions. After 1918, when every primary school tried to have its own tree, the coming of Father Christmas added the last touch to a typical tale of urban penetration.[57]

Communal and historic feasts declined to extinction; and once-public celebrations became increasingly private. Christmas, New Year, and Twelfth

Night turned into family affairs. So did the sacred events of life: baptisms, first communions, and marriages became private ceremonies, ultimately most of all big meals. Eating and drinking had been a great aspect of feasting; now they swallowed the whole sense of the term.[58] There were no holy days left to celebrate, only holidays—free time—to enjoy not as collective communion but as evasion. Traditional feasts had fixed people in their milieu; modern holidays dispersed them, allowed them to escape the life of everyday and the traditional framework. There was no more call for renewal ceremonies that glorified time (the seasons), work (the harvest), or the community through its patron saint. The redistribution of goods managed through the ritual collections was more efficiently (and more stringently) managed by the state. The opportunities for courting were no longer restricted to a few village dances a year. The compensating festive hierarchies that paralleled the established social structure could now be found in sports, trade unions, political parties. The license and change in norms afforded by festivals became meaningless when license became the norm. The teaching and the transmission of traditions became a function of the schools. Urban society could do without festivals, even official ones. Seen in the context of traditional village life, it *was* a festival.

Chapter Twenty-two

CHARIVARIS

Ainsi donc le charivari, qui primitivement était un châtiment
infligé spontanément par le peuple à ceux dont le mariage blessait
les usages reçus et constituait un défi à la morale publique, est
devenu un amusement pour les villages.

—HENRI LALOU

MANY MAY MOURN the passing of traditional celebrations like Carnival. But
few today, and possibly few people of the time, would want to shed a tear for
a more somber aspect of Carnival that we have only hinted at so far: the ridicule and punishment of those who had contravened the rules of village society.
Social censorship of this order was another thing that modern society could
and would dispense with. The state had laws, police, gendarmes, magistrates.
There was no need for, and eventually no room for, unofficial justiciaries to
visit society's wrath on those who "sinned" against it. Yet this form of rough
justice endured into the twentieth century.

A transgressor was still tried and burned in effigy at Carnival in small bourgs
of the Charentes shortly before 1914, or promenaded facing a donkey's tail,
as apparently still happened in Champagne and the Ardennes at the turn of
the century. In Bourbonnais "they would smear his face with honey and with
feathers, put an old basket or nightcap on his head, place a distaff in his hand,
and drive him through the town or village sitting on a donkey with his face
looking to the back." There would be a public trial, there would be satirical
songs, and finally a manikin would be executed. If the guilty party had taken
to his heels, his nearest neighbor would be seized instead for having failed
to intervene and mend the situation. The memory of the practice survived in
the remark Lorrainers made about a wife-dominated household: "Le voisin
ira sur l'âne!"[1] This seems unfair from a modern viewpoint, to which, in any
case, matters of this sort appear strictly private. But in village communities
where everything was known to everyone, and where public opinion was the
chief (or sole) agency of social discipline, transgressions were seen as dis-
solving forces (much as the publicity of the Kinsey report had the effect of
rendering many secret practices licit). With everyone affected by everyone's
behavior, everyone was responsible for everyone else. Perhaps unfairly but
quite logically, the nearest neighbor was the first justiciary. If he failed, he

could be chastised by those, primarily the young men, who shouldered the punitive duties of the village.

Most often those duties were exercised by means of the charivari—*colliourari* in Ariège, *calibari* in Lot, *tocsin* in Vosges, *tracassin* in Ain, *caribari* in Corrèze and Aveyron, *caroviou* in Var—rough music, mock serenade (quoth the dictionary), a vast discordant uproar, the clashing of pots and pans, ringing of cowbells, rasping of rattles, blowing of horns, shouting of jibes and jeers, or actual singing of songs composed for the occasion. Generally, though not always, the performance would take place at night, the dark adding its inherent menace to the frightening din, and the harassment could sometimes go on for months—a wearing experience for the strongest victims, and for their neighbors too.*

The most frequent inspiration of charivaris was marriage outside the accepted norms: a widow or a widower remarrying too soon after the spouse's death, an older man or woman wedding a partner judged too young, notorious partners in adultery marrying after the spouse's death, or a man marrying into the community from an alien village who thus poached on the preserves of the village youth. This is not very surprising, since matters of property were of great importance, and marriage or remarriage played a great part therein. The remarriage of widows and widowers was common, especially when the death rate was high: 18.7 percent of all marriages performed at Vraiville (Eure) between 1850 and 1950.[2] What mattered more was to protect the children of the first marriage and the interests of rightful heirs. It also mattered that accepted decencies should be respected, that the dead should be treated with deference and decorum, that widows should not rewed with unseemly haste. The choice of marriageable partners in societies that were largely endogamous was normally restricted. A stranger marrying into such communities deprived the local young; and so did an older man, who might also be presumed to enjoy an unfair advantage as being better off than his younger rivals.

Hints of immorality or ridicule (as in the case of age differences) made such matters worse, because they affected the honor of the village. Those whose behavior cast ridicule on their community had to be paid in shame. And often, in fact, the rough justice of the charivaris addressed itself less to morality than to honor: punishing cuckolds rather than adulterers. Public ridicule concentrated on males so unfortunate as to fail the dictates of honor by letting themselves be beaten or cuckolded, on young girls of dubious reputation, and on adulterous couples whose dalliance came to light.† Most other transgressions

---

* The last recorded charivari at Etelfay (Somme) took place in 1906. It had gone on for two months before it culminated at Mardi Gras with a march-past of manikins that were finally burned in great pomp beside the railroad tracks just when the evening train was passing. The local gendarmes watched, intervening only after 9 P.M. when the caterwauling threatened the communal rest. (Jacqueline Picoche, *Un Vocabulaire picard d'autrefois*, p. 71.)

† In certain villages a list of *cornards* was drawn up and circulated annually on Saint Joseph's day, March 19. (See Charles Perron, *Proverbes de la Franche-Comté*, p. 122; Perron, *Broye-les-*

could be bought off. The young who charivaried also determined the amount of the fine that could prevent the rough music or secure its ending. In villages of Hautes-Pyrénées, strangers coming to marry or to settle in the community were subject to payment of "a right of entry," without which they got a charivari.[3] But almost everywhere, as we have seen, neighbors and especially the village young organized "barrages" on the way to church, which held wedding parties up to playful ransom and which could easily degenerate into resentful raucousness if the expected tip or fine was not forthcoming. At Saint-Jeannet (Alpes-Maritimes), all marrying couples had to pay a tax to the *abbot* of the local youth. The tax was based on the estimated fortune of the couple and was levied at a higher rate in the case of remarriages. Refusal to pay led to a charivari; generous payments to bonfires, volleys of shots, and serenades in the couple's honor.*

So things could be simple and quite pleasant, if one paid. The alternative was humiliation at Carnival or in a charivari organized to strike at an offender while the fire was hot. The public jibing at Carnival was doubtless painful, but from all accounts the charivari was rather frightening; and in any case, intolerable from the point of view of public authorities beginning to assert themselves at the expense of more ancient bodies. In Var a village mayor expressed indignation as early as 1821: "Disorders worthy of times of ignorance and barbarism" should be brought to an end. One had to prove "to those who, despite the efforts of the authorities, think they can do what they like with impunity under the pretext of an established usage, that one cannot hold people who remarry up for ransom."[4] Our good mayor has summed everything up: the practice linked to "ignorance and barbarism," hence condemned by progress; the efforts of new "authorities" to supplant the old; the stress on the rule of law (one can no longer do just as one liked); the denunciation of traditional fines as sheer blackmail. So there were now some persons unwilling to accept the assumptions on which the charivari was based. And it seems that this point of view allied with police hostility to disturbances of the peace drove rough music back, especially in large urban centers.[5] J.-A. Delpon noted that the charivari was beginning to disappear in the towns of Lot in 1831. At Saint-Jeannet, then in Var, it was prohibited in 1838. Yet, as at Vézelay, the more local the local authorities were and the less inhibited by the presence of limbs of the law, the more likely they were to support the practice, or at least close

---

Pesmes.) In the mid-1880's the widowed tenant farmer of the Séveyrac estate near Bozouls (Aveyron) had his lease canceled following a charivari that had denounced his housekeeper for sleeping with him (*L'Aubrac*, 2: 181).

*J.-E. Mallaussène, *Saint-Jeannet*, p. 23. Compare events at Vézelay in 1853. See also Paul Fortier-Beaulieu, *Mariages et noces campagnardes dans les pays ayant formé le département de la Loire* (Paris, 1945), pp. 236–42. Note that on the western border of Loire marriages provided the occasion for charivaris designed to revive family feuds that sometimes went back generations and might have started up over such diverse things as a suicide, the loss of a sow, or a boundary dispute. This was known as reproaching ("Faire des reproches").

their eyes to it.[6] Thus at Daumazan (Ariège) the marriage of the notary's servant girl, alleged to have been tampered with by her master, led to a charivari in 1844 whose participants ended in police court. Even so, "troubles" continued there, but both gendarmes and local authorities were sympathetic and minimized whatever infraction of the law there was. Under the Empire the village was run on a tighter rein; and in December 1861 the new mayor prohibited all songs and satirical noise-making after 8 P.M. as a disturbance of the peace: the provocations of songs and countersongs, each growing more insulting than the last, made for disorder and violence.[7]

It is worth remembering that not all the objects of charivaris took them lying down. A good many replied in kind or even fired at their raucous tormentors. Of course, the nature of charivaris was to isolate their prey and make the victim helpless to retaliate. But even isolated men armed with determination and a good shotgun could cause some damage. This was all the truer when politics figured in.[8]

Charivaris were a very forcible form of criticism: they could be directed as much against an offending notable as a local drunk or a chronic debtor.* It is hardly surprising that they were also connected with politics. In October 1819 a charivari organized by the anticlerical bourgeois of Brest forced the bishop of Quimper to put an end to the mission preached there by Jesuits. Similar tumults greeted the return of another mission in 1826. At Mas-d'Azil (Ariège) a political charivari in November 1830 was raised to repay a man accused of having used similar methods himself in 1815. At Moulins (Allier) in 1832 we hear of two: one against the bishop, the other against a local deputy, Monsieur de Schonen, "considered too devoted to King Louis Philippe." About this same time the "bourgeois" of the small bourg of Montpezat (Ardèche) were organizing Legitimist charivaris that worried the gendarmes. In 1833 the Minister of the Interior wrote to the prefect of Ariège to warn him against a proposed "outrage against our civilization," grotesque parodies of the disorders the government had recently repressed. A Republican society (*Aide-toi*) was apparently plotting to charivari all deputies. Prefects were to be on their guard and to use all means to prevent this. I have found no further trace of the alleged plot, but it suggests the propaganda possibilities of charivaris, with the government well aware of them—and of how they could be turned into political demonstrations.[9]

In February 1834 Auxerre Republicans charivaried the mayor so effectively that the armed forces had to intervene. The following February (again the Carnival!) another Yonne town, Tonnerre, reported similar trouble. The sub-prefect complained that in the rural communes Shrovetide was being used as an excuse for songs that turned to politics. But most of the evidence

---

* Their participatory counterpart, the donkey ride, was also inflicted on a variety of miscreants who had offended against other than sexual interdictions. At Angely (Yonne) thieves and pilferers were "mounted"; elsewhere the ride was forced on outsiders who flouted community custom by working on local feastdays or by trying to join in a village dance (M. C. Moiset, "Usages, croyances, traditions, superstitions . . . ," *Bulletin de la Société des Sciences . . . de l'Yonne*, 1888, pp. 20–22).

refers to Tonnerre itself: one hears of a lot of songs, both personal and political (after all, the two were almost identical) being bandied about between February 18 and February 23, and of floats that were politically allusive. On February 24 the mayor forbade the use of drums between 6 P.M. and 8 P.M., hoping to discourage the raucous demonstrations that had marched to them. But the crowd marched without drum or float, and worse still, singing "La Marseillaise." The police superintendent could not disperse them; the national guard refused to intervene because all the inhabitants knew each other. Rather than send for troops, the authorities decided to sit it out and wait for the end of Carnival.[10]

The February Revolution of 1848 and the elections that followed also involved charivaris, though in what numbers one cannot tell. We hear of one at Strasbourg directed against an unpopular conservative deputy, Renouard de Bussière; of others at Belley (Ain) against Adolphe d'Angeville, author of the pioneering *Essai sur la statistique de la population française*, denounced as Malthusian in town and countryside, "the worst of insults in the Jura of 1848."[11] The sparseness of the evidence could reflect the rarity of the usage. Yet it may be that such conventional forms of attack were not thought to deserve a mention.

Noticeably, the political charivaris were largely restricted to towns with a political public. In smaller places even "political" tumults remained on familiar ground. At Arfeuilles (Allier) in 1828 a charivari was raised against the superior of the little seminary who had fired a teacher the students liked; at Cusset, in the same department, a charivari attacked the new justice of the peace in 1832. At Cunlhat (Puy-de-Dôme) a big charivari turned against the collector of taxes and the local doctor, accused of having used their influence on behalf of an unpopular candidate to the General Council of the department. Only at Bretenoux, a smallish bourg in northeast Lot, do we hear of a truly political case in which a "representative of the people," Monsieur de Saint-Priest, had been charivaried and the local authorities had done nothing about it. But this was 1849, and Bretenoux is only a couple of miles from the castle of Castelnau. Political sentiment must have run strong and one-sided.[12]

This is almost the last political charivari I have found. Unless we count one that never came off. This involved Jules Favre, the Republican barrister, who while in Morlaix to plead a case in August 1866 was spared the ordeal when a local magistrate prevented a charivari from being organized against him. The religious struggles of the turn of the century provided a revival, notably in Allier, where anticlericalism was strong and where in the years after 1877 roadside crosses were often broken and priests publicly insulted. Songs against priests were much appreciated, and some charivaris took place in front of village churches, as occurred at Dommerat, not far from Commentry, during Lent in 1884. On the other hand, straightforwardly social charivaris continued. In January 1853 the corporal of gendarmes at Belley (Ain) reported a considerable charivari in one village in which about 100 persons of both sexes gathered to harass the widow Gauthier. The gendarmes intervened to disperse the crowd, arrested one man, and then had trouble when the rest of the crowd sought to free him, but "force est resté [*sic*] à la loi." In March of the same year the army commander at Lyon wrote about a charivari at Saint-Martin (Loire), not far from Montbrison, "on the occasion of a widower who married a young girl," in which the *charivariseurs* continued their racket even after they had been paid 20 francs. Worse still, the mayor had supported them against the helpless gendarmes. The issue went as far as the Minister of the Interior, with the mayor arguing that the gendarmes were making unnecessary trouble.[13]

But the Empire would not tolerate unlawful assemblies that often ended tragically, as in Gers where near Lombez, in August 1853, a married man accused of having left a girl in the family way was stabbed with an awl and died after a charivari degenerated into a brawl. Still less, one supposes, would the state countenance scofflaws who, more than just defying the minions of the law, aimed their barbs directly at them. At Limoges, attempts to round up local prostitutes in 1857 failed because the women ran away from the hospital where they were confined and if they were further harassed, set off charivaris that got sympathetic support from the nearby barracks.[14]

One suspects that police efforts helped to stifle the custom in a good few places. At Foix and at Saint-Girons the *cour cornuélo* operated through the 1840's, sentencing errant couples to public ridicule. A Limousin folklorist seems to think that the last charivaris at Tulle occurred in the 1850's but adds (after the First World War) that "in the countryside they are ever more rare," which suggests that where police forces were distant and local autonomy strong, the tradition endured. In the Basque country, wrote an observer in 1857, the police had tried to repress "these traditional games that had become too licentious" for 15 or 20 years. But without success. The traditional game survived until after the Great War, with popular approval. At Agos-Vidalos (Hautes-Pyrénées) a bridegroom who refused the "honors" proffered for his wedding and—what was worse—would not pay for them became the object of a charivari in 1858. Others occurred at Argelès, against widowers who remarried and against a man-beating wife (1861); at Lau, where the objection was not specified; and at Tilhouse, not far from Lannemezan.[15]

Local Basque poets (*koblakari*) would often improvise charivari serenades to some traditional tune, and these would be taken up by the assembled crowd or sung around the village. But songs in local dialect especially composed for the occasion were a particular feature of the charivari: we hear of them in Ardèche and Lauragais, where names of the more notorious songsters survived well past their death.* They were no doubt as bawdy as the charivaresque farces performed at Carnival, which raised cries of indecency, obscenity, gross impropriety. Rape, birth, and castration were enacted on stage and commented

---

* As in the case of a ropemaker from Villefranche (Haute-Garonne) who devised rhymes for a fee for people of the surrounding countryside. His wit and his wide audience seem to have made him feared and influential (P. Fagot, *Folklore du Lauragais*, pp. 147–49).

on in the rudest language. This would not do. The offending plays were banned. The young were forced to camouflage their farces within acceptable mystery plays or tragi-comedies that could get by the censors far away at the prefecture. Hence the authorities were able to aver that such gross farces were dead (sub-prefect of Mauléon, 1903), while they carried on sub rosa. Still, it does seem, as the evidence thins out or its tone changes, that custom slipped into prankishness, while essence seeped away. By 1891 the charivari songs of Lauragais had "lost their primitive flavor for us who do not understand their particular references." And no new songs or poets rose to take their place.[16]

In a charivari at Baume (Ardèche) in the 1860's, whose organizers were condemned to fines and prison sentences, the object of their attention could have bought them off for a sétier of wine (21 liters). The man who recalled this in the 1880's was glad that "such bizarre and unpardonable customs disappear from day to day; the lights of instruction ... teach all to respect the liberty of their fellows."[17] And, right enough, the schools taught that charivaris were improper. As the first-year civics text adopted in the 1880's warned: "Those who make a charivari (confused noise of pans, cauldrons, whistles, and shouts) at somebody's door with an offensive purpose are punished with a fine up to 15 francs and even with prison sentences."[18] Primarily what one finds by this time are survivals that have taken refuge in the countryside.[19] The last charivaris at Nanteuil (Seine-et-Marne) occurred in 1870; at Villiers-sur-Morin about a decade later. At Prades (Pyrénées-Orientales) in 1896 we hear: "charivari at a widow's who was about to marry for a second time. The mayor himself kept order." At Châteaulin in 1901 the local priest, "very unpopular in a religious town," planned a procession that would prevent the Mardi Gras fun. The local youth decided to follow the religious procession in disguise and organized a charivari. The police and the mayor persuaded the priest to give up his plan. In the Bourbonnais uplands the homemade bullhorn called the *bourloir*, made out of local beechwood, was still used for charivaris in 1908; and Varagnac was to witness a charivari in 1943 just a few miles from Montauban against a widow who had remarried.[20]

In effect, like bonfires, like Carnivals of which they had so often been a part, charivaris survived here and there, resurfaced now and then. In Angoumois, where as in Quercy charivaris could be heard of through the Second World War, there were places where the long intervals between sporadic revivals made all assume the charivari was dead. There were other places where it had been abandoned in the early 1900's and where its memory was dying or already dead because few children had heard about it from their parents. In Loire many villages still mounted charivaris in the 1930's but many others reported their disappearance with the turn of the century or the First World War. Most revealing, however, at Charlieu, a cantonal township in the department's northeast where charivaris were still to be heard, "now those who make them hide themselves."[21]

The practice of promenading misdoers on a donkey had declined in the same way: remoter, more isolated areas persisting in it the longest, so that the Ardennes, Poitou, parts of the Meuse valley still knew the *asoade* (or whatever) in the 1880's. Some of the last specific references to beaten husbands thus held up to scorn come from small, remote places: Grand-Brassac (Dordogne) in 1880, a hamlet near Aumagne (Charente) in 1901. In Sologne by the last quarter of the nineteenth century, *cornards* were no longer publicly humiliated in bigger bourgs like Souesmes or Mennetou-sur-Cher. More isolated communities, like Saint-Viatre and Selles-Saint-Denis, kept the donkeys busy until 1914 but, as at Villeny, "it was only for fun." The spontaneous popular castigation of untoward breaches of usage or morality had become simply sport for the villagers.[22] The carcass of charivaris remained. But it was disemboweled.

Chapter Twenty-three

MARKETS AND FAIRS

Grace is given of God, but knowledge is bought in the market.
—ARTHUR HUGH CLOUGH

THE EVOLUTION OF sociability in the countryside can be studied—and it should be studied, for here we can afford only passing attention—in two other domains: that of the public marketplace, and that of the semiprivate but highly communal veillée.

Markets and fairs were major cogs in the wheels of the old economy, turntables of essential exchanges, mostly within a limited local context. Markets were frequent, at least weekly, and there one sold and bought items of everyday necessity—for the most part food. Fairs were periodic and offered a wider choice of goods—apparel, cattle, tools, and household utensils—as well as entertainment. All rural societies included fairly large numbers of landless peasants and varying numbers of artisans or forest folk, or both, who had to buy some or all of their food, albeit from their neighbors.

Like the traditional seasonal migrations, the markets played their part in maintaining archaic institutions by permitting their clientele to make ends meet. Poor people bought and sold small quantities, and so had to market frequently. In a society of the ancient model the marketplace replaces non-existent shops and provides what people in towns have learned to take for granted: the opportunity to procure what one needs or wants.

The frequency of markets grew, however, when burghers, their numbers growing and their standards rising after the 1830's, began to buy their butter, cheese, milk, and eggs fresh to improve their daily diet. Peasant women began to sell poultry or dairy products in the market weekly instead of five or six times a year, and the novel cash income gradually turned them also into purchasers in the marketplace for luxuries once homemade or done without: shoes, kerchiefs, umbrellas, smocks, salt fish and butcher's meat. Industrial products penetrated the rural world and rural industry declined, as we have seen. But the cash to buy garments or metal plowshares, scythe blades or baker's bread at the fair, was earned in the market. And the fair itself grew as cattle-raising developed, providing a new focus of interest and resources that made fairs busier, more numerous, and more significant in both economic and social terms.

The fair had had its own importance before this happened or began to happen. While industry was localized and communications rare and mediocre, the fairs held in little towns were indispensable centers of exchange. They could be very small indeed, like the one held at Songy in Marne, which nevertheless raised the town out of the class of surrounding villages, made it seem an important bourg, and brought local business to life.[1] After all, the nearest sizable town, the sub-prefecture at Vitry, was six leagues away, a considerable enterprise over the bad roads of the mid-nineteenth century. But where fairs were few or lacking because of isolation, as in the Morvan, inhabitants did not hesitate to go a long way to a famous fair and feast like the annual fair on the first Wednesday in May that covered the otherwise barren Mount Beuvray (at the extreme limit of Saône-et-Loire and Nièvre) with tents, stands, beasts, and improvised dramshops, and attracted thousands. Also popular were the lowland fairs, where Morvandiaux could exchange their cattle for apparel, leather, tools, candles, whatever they might need, or highland Ariégeois their wool for grain.[2] Better roads after mid-century would bring an orgy of trade—comparatively speaking at least, when one remembers previous conditions. The trade went with civilization and was explicitly so perceived; witness the Tarn-et-Garonne saying about a poor southwestern village, Monbéqui, not far from the Garonne: "A Mountbéqui, soun mau civilisats. N'au pas ni fièro ni mercat" (At Monbéqui they are not civilized. They have neither fair nor market).[3]

Every small town, aware of the activity and gain a fair could bring, wanted one of its own; and imperial decrees in 1852 and 1864 simplified the process of obtaining permission to establish one or add to those already in existence. Yet there seems to have been no great explosion of new fairs in more backward areas under the Second Empire, but on the contrary a very moderate increase compared with the growth that had taken place since the 1820's and the boom that followed the mid-1870's. Of Puy-de-Dôme's 172 annual fairs in 1903, 44 were said to have existed from time immemorial, 21 had been set up before 1850, and 14 dated from between 1851 and 1870. Then came a flood: 39 new fairs in 1871–80, 21 more in 1881–90, and another 33 in 1891–1903.[4] The coincidence with the building of secondary roads seems quite apparent.

Yet though more roads meant more trade, and more trade more fairs, more fairs also meant less trade for each.* Not quite, of course, because the cattle

---

* See Frédéric La Guyader in Olivier Perrin and Alex Bouet, *Breiz Izel*, p. 184, noting, in 1914, that the vast multiplication of fairs since the 1830's had made for smaller attendance at each and the decline of even the most glorious. Other factors probably contributed to the general decline, notably the tendency of dealers to buy directly from the farm and the accessibility of retail shops.

trade was rising in importance. Still, by the 1870's observers who saw that the popularity of fairs was inverse to the facility of communications noted that in the lowlands railways made the fairs decline.[5] In the late 1870's and the 1880's fairs continued to be regional events in the mountain regions of Ardèche. But by 1889 Port-Dieu (Corrèze), an important entrepôt since the bridging of the Dordogne in 1845 to connect Corrèze and Puy-de-Dôme, was feeling the impact. The trade of its 14 annual fairs (twice as many as in the eighteenth century) was described as "slight." And at Céret (Pyrénées-Orientales) both the fair and the fête of 1896 showed disappointing results.[6]

As long as roads were bad, a few miles could make a difference. Once they were improved, a bigger center nearby could kill a small one. In Cantal the bourg of Jussac, whose fairs had been well known for wool and cattle, could not survive the pull of Aurillac, only some six miles south. Other centers declined because they were ill-placed in relation to new roads, like Rochegoude and Besse, or to railroads, like Maillargues dethroned by Allanche and Condat by Riom-es-Montagne, and even, finally, Moissac when the new bourg of Neussargues became a railway junction. In western Ardèche old-established fairs like Saint-Etienne-de-Lugdarès, in a closed valley, and Loubaresse, once a crossroads of mule-trains, declined, while Langogne benefited from its position on a new railway line. In Ariège, too, with trains passing the Pyrenees to both the east and the west, the lively mule trade of mid-century wasted away and the region's fairs with it. Even those fairs that had prospered found retail trade beginning to destroy their purpose. By 1916 Edouard Herriot described their economic function as antiquated and out of date. By the 1920's the automobile would make this even truer. Small market towns had become shopping centers, and things that used to be bought once a year in bulk could be picked up as the need arose, on the occasion of the weekly visit to the market.[7]

But none of this really mattered, because one of the major functions of the market and fair was social. In Béarn, indeed, one said of an uncouth person who could not be trusted in company that "he's not for the fair." And, while the economic functions of the marketplace fluctuated, its social role continued to increase. Neither self-sufficiency nor other shopping facilities deterred people from attending a market that gathered in the neighborhood to exchange news even more than goods.[8] The inland Bretons, who hardly ever traveled otherwise, did not hesitate to spend part of the year on the road because of a desperate need—"their malady"—that drove them to attend fairs even when they had nothing to buy or sell. In Finistère during the July Monarchy farm servants contracted not only for wages, but also for so many days off a year to attend markets or fairs. And Elie Reynier says the same about Vivarais: "The market is the social and sociable life of rural people dispersed throughout the countryside." Fairs were feasts (*feriae*). Most of them coincided with religious occasions: Whitsun and Trinity Sunday in June, Assumption in

August, but especially the feasts of Saint John (June 24), Saint James (July 24), Saint Bartholomew (August 24), Saint Matthew (September 21), Saints Simon and June (October 28), Saints Martin and Andrew in November.[9]

One of the elements of every feast was that it attracted merchants. Aigues-mortes actually called its festival *la foire*, the fair; and many festivals were known as *apport* or *rapport*, that is to say, the place where one brought something, hence a market. By modern times the two were inextricably intertwined. "One never saw a fair without a feast," a peasant from Brie was quoted as saying in 1939.[10] The motives for attendance were equally mixed. Still, the stands of itinerant peddlers were above all a show, and beside them were the stands, tents, cabins, or open-air pitches of showmen and strolling players: "charlatans, magicians, musicians and singers, bohemians and gamblers," wrote the police superintendent of Mirande (Gers) in 1876. Patent remedies were sold by the heirs of the great Cabotin to a patter accompanied by cymbals, clarinets, or trumpets; teeth were pulled, unbreakable chains were broken, swords swallowed, and flames breathed out. There were sellers of images, almanacs, and broadsheets. There were specialists who spelled out and explained ballads before they sold them. There was much drink, and there was dancing. In Auvergne and Rouergue today "the old fairs" are the ones where a person dances; and the old-fashioned fair like the old pilgrimage combined religious ceremony and marketing with a marriage mart.[11]

Some fairs were devoted to this latter purpose, notably the marriage fairs at Périzé (Finistère), Challans (Vendée), and Saint-Didier-sous-Rochefort (Loire). But there were many foires des jeunes or des jeunesses where young people came to meet, mix, and court, to break out of the narrow endogamy of village society. Indeed, several sayings warned against letting girls frequent too many markets or fairs, for, as in Gascony:

> Hilhe qui galope lous marcats,
> Nou damoure goayre chens pecats.

In this case, as in others, the fair provided the chief or only opportunity for contact with the external world.[12]

This is what peasants appreciated, this and the opportunity to find out things, pick up information, meet acquaintances from beyond the village, look at new doings, relax, get drunk.* In 1874 the artists of Epinal were turning out colored pictures that showed that fairs were fun. By 1882 in the Montagne Noire of the southwest "fairs are no longer . . . meeting-places for those who have commodities to buy or sell. They are as much gatherings for entertainment as for business or trade." Most of those who went were attracted not by the prospect of making a deal but by curiosity, "the desire to spend the day sauntering about." For Auvergnats fairs were a holiday.[13] By the eve of

---

* They still do, even though the economic role of fairs has largely waned.

the war, just when economists were telling us that the economic function of fairs was waning or had waned, they seem to have been at the height of their vogue in hitherto isolated regions. In Gascony the peasants, "bored with monotonous and solitary tasks," had taken up buying and selling cattle because it gave them a chance to get away from routine labor and an excuse to attend fairs, meet people, enjoy the fun of trading, which was like gambling for them. In some villages about one-third of the population was involved in the new pastime, though it brought little or no economic profit. In the Limousin, too, peasants developed a passion for fairs; any pretext to get to one served, even driving a few sheep that one meant to drive back home come evening time. "There is even a sort of shame about not going."[14]

This was quite true, though there was more to it. Southwestern peasants had raised no cattle until the bourgeois landowners for whom they sharecropped sold off their properties. As the estates began to be broken up in the last third of the century and their lands fell into peasants' hands, small landowners, enjoying a new sense of dignity, shifted from corn bread to the wheaten bread that had been a privilege of the upper classes. For the same reasons, they began to breed and trade in cattle. It is true that with the owners gone more farmers needed their own draft animals. But above all, dealing in cattle had been a favorite speculation of the former owners.[15] Buoyed by his new dignity as his own master, the peasant would take over the old privilege, which brought with it a certain sense of leisure, though not revenues, since accounts suggest that Gascon breeding methods were mediocre. The profit that he sought was a social one.

How far was this perceived? Moralistic observers of the 1880's like Henri Baudrillart and Alexandre Layet have commented on and deplored the new delight in socializing.* A Limousin priest, however, reviewed the development in a more sensible light. The fairs, wrote Père Gorse in 1895, were a new factor in the peasant's life. They were the subject that interested him most—what theaters or horse races were for city folk. The peasant honored all fair days within a radius of about 30 miles and discriminated among their specialties. He looked for any pretext to go: selling a rabbit or a dozen eggs, or buying shoes when the village shoemaker lived next door. The truth was that he simply wanted to talk to people and to know how things were going. Economists criticized this: the peasants should waste less time, work more, drink and gallivant less. But Gorse saw the fair as a well-earned respite and, also, as a source of emulation.[16]

It may well be that fairs did inspire the imitation of urban ways and roles just at the time when peasants were ready to follow them. Contact with city

---

* The attitude should be familiar to the reader. In 1859 the General Council of Rhône refused all applications for new fairs with the argument that for country people fairs were simply occasions for idleness and dissipation, drawing them away from their work and nearly always ending in disorder and debauchery (Gilbert Garrier, *Paysans du Beaujolais*, 1: 340).

folk had resulted chiefly in distrust. Exchange had been restricted to the commercial plane, and the city man was inevitably a slicker, greedy and hard. Now there are indications that there was more to it. There is the comment of an agronomist in 1884, who felt that Limousin peasants learned to handle French much better at fairs than in school. There is the thought that the peasant had the material means and the physical opportunity to take it a bit more easy. Drink itself, for which so many reproached the peasants, was an urban luxury. So was consciously or unconsciously wasting time, or having time to waste, or chatting on any day but Sunday. And so was having novelties to talk about: "One can talk about [the fair] for a week, and then talk about the next," remarked G.-M. Coissac in 1913. But even critics admitted that the peasants were learning about commodity and cattle prices, and that they had learned to meet glib traders on pretty equal terms. The market was not only a place to trade but also an attitude, a frame of mind, and this was a novel acquisition for most rural folk.[17]

Chapter Twenty-four

VEILLEES

Après le souper, on veille encore une heure ou deux en teillant
du chanvre, chacun dit sa chanson à son tour.
— JEAN-JACQUES ROUSSEAU

Veillée, *n.f.* Time from supper to bedtime, evening (in company);
sitting up to work, etc. in company.
— CASSELL'S FRENCH-ENGLISH DICTIONARY

THROUGHOUT MOST OF rural France the winter evenings were long and
cold and lonely. Fires had to be husbanded; candles and rushlights too.
Everything cost too much. Adequate heat and light were almost unthinkable.
During the frigid winter months in Mâconnais women, when they had finished their housework, went into the stables for the *veillées du jour*. The men
would join them there, and the midday meal was often taken in the stable
because the house was too cold. The evening meal necessitated a fire, but
where fuel was short, people made the briefest possible use of the fire. So after
the *soupe* they hastened to curl up in a pallet, in the dark, sharing the animal
heat of one or several neighbors, presumably asleep; or took refuge in the
stable; or repaired to any other place where they could find a little warmth.

In places like Treigny in Yonne, where pottery was the main industry, most
of the local people warmed themselves in winter by the heat of the kilns and
"thus dispensed with making fires at home." The justice of the peace in 1852
reported considerable crowds "à la veillée" every evening. In parts of Marne
veillées were held in wine cellars, which being of chalk kept in the warmth.
Artisans who worked late into the night, perhaps because of different tasks
during the daytime, needed a light, as carpenters and shoemakers did. Around
them there might form a chatting circle, which sometimes turned into a
chambrée. But most evening gatherings were to be found in barns or sheep-
folds or stables, where the warmth of animals was more important than the
sharp odors of manure.[1]

Whether in house or stable, neighbors or friends gathered on winter evenings, once or twice a week, or even every day. Meeting in turn at one place
after another, three to six families or more thus saved on heat and light, using
only one family's resources at a time. It was not only firewood that mattered,
but lighting. In the mountains of Provence, where the rustic *caleu*, a wick
burning in walnut oil, continued to be used to the end of the century, partici-

pants of veillées shared lighting costs.[2] In Languedoc, when the veillée began, the mistress of the house put out her own tallow candle and lit a communal one whose price was shared by all who attended.*

Veillées began as the fall labors dwindled—sometimes around All Saints, more often after Saint Martin's (November 11)—and tended to end in March or around Easter, when the spring's sowing came. Their span reflected the natural order: as days grew longer, veillées grew shorter, and the women used one distaff less in their spinning. Hence the proverb "By Carnival day, a spindle put away" (*A carmentrant, eune fusée sous le banc*). As this suggests, the practical aspect of evening gatherings went beyond need, to production. According to the region, women spun, knitted, embroidered, or tatted; men dressed hemp, plaited baskets, or repaired their implements. The women, generally charged with more meticulous work requiring better light, got the best seats at veillées, close to the fire or the *lumignon*, though they often ate their meals standing up while serving their menfolk. The men generally sat far from the fire, in the near-darkness. Fruit was stoned, nuts shelled or chestnuts blanched, apples peeled for the preparation of a local wine or for making jam. In Upper Brittany alone, Paul Sébillot has distinguished, by activity, five different sorts of veillées in operation in 1880: spinning (*filouas* or *filanderies*), hemp-twisting (*erusseries de chanvre*), apple-cooking (*cuisseries de pommé*), night laundering (*lessives de nuit*), and *veillonas*, especially devoted to fun and dancing.[3]

Music and fun were a feature of most veillées; just as all evidence confirms that a major attraction was the opportunity for courtship and flirtation between lads and girls. The number of songs and games specifically involved with these courtship customs is vast. At Saille-les-Bains (Loire), the nut-shelling began by rushlight around 5 in the afternoon, went on till 10 or so, when salt bread and buckwheat cakes were served, the empty shells were gathered up, and the young people danced to the accompaniment of a hurdy-gurdy, a singer, or (later) an accordion. This pattern was roughly followed in most such gatherings; and in another Loire village, Saint-Martin-d'Estréaux, not far from Lapalisse, we hear that in 1910 four-fifths of all marriages were born out of veillées.[4]

But veillées also had a didactic function—generally informal. Traditional skills were learned by participation. Traditional wisdom was learned in the same way. The talk was full of allusions to the past: the time of the lords, of the Revolution, of the wolves and how they disappeared. The oral culture perpetuated itself by the tales told, the pious legends, the teachings about the supernatural realm, the explanations of nature and of life, the precepts that applied to every sort of situation and that were contained in the formulas, songs, and proverbs repeated over and over again in these amorphous schools.

---

* But no more than half of the communal candle could be used at a meeting, so a knitting needle was thrust through it to divide it in half. When the needle fell, the veillée was over (René Nelli, *Languedoc*, p. 103).

In Lorraine, where Louis Marin has argued that the veillée had a peculiar educational purpose, the winter meetings turned around traditional tales and fables and on the commentary they inevitably provoked—a kind of public reflection on experience and tradition, and a communion with the past. These ancient village institutions were going strong in the 1880's. The growth of industry, the influx of workingmen of outside origin, the flow of material novelties into the countryside—and schools of course—would finish them off. By 1900 half the parishes of the Lorraine plateau had given up veillées. Many of the rest had given up reciting the traditional tales, hence had shed their role in the transmission of oral traditions.[5]

The competition of the schools was much too strong. In Breton gallo country, where by the 1880's veillées seem to have been less frequent than in the past, we hear that the old tales were being replaced by stories from the schoolbooks—often told by the children. The modern wisdom was the preserve of youth, not age. But the people of education and involved in education in the rural areas had never liked veillées. Schoolteachers felt their influence was pernicious. Rude language was used; there were lewd stories and sometimes lewder songs. In any case there were better things for the young to do. "Instead of gadding about to veillées uttering cries that make one doubt whether they are men or wild beasts," grumbled one teacher in Tarn in 1861, "they could go and read a book." And in a survey of the previous year, teachers in a wide range of departments—Aveyron, Ardèche, Ain, Saône-et-Loire, Nièvre, Bas-Rhin—expressed the hope that libraries might counter the mischief done in veillées.[6]

It was not so much that veillées were rude as that they were unenlightened. It is true that one feared moral laxity in gatherings "where all sexes and all ages are admitted." Priests hotly objected to the moral promiscuity of the sexes crowded together at night, and to what ensued: "revolting dances, unbecoming puns and double entendres, dangerous discourse." They would "brand and prohibit them from the pulpit" in Ariège; and local reformers denounced these "gravely objectionable gatherings ... with their corruption, lewd jokes, and songs." Unfortunately, "young village girls enjoy the greatest liberty," and it was to be feared that "they take advantage of it on their way home." In Brittany, observed Sébillot, the clergy "by dint of preaching has forced the disappearance [of veillées] just as it has suppressed dancing."[7]

Still, moral objections were not new. Intellectual objections, supported by the schools, had greater force. A report on the state of the schools in Ariège in 1868 makes clear that what was regarded as "a deadly deep-rooted" evil was the filling of young heads with "tales full of superstitious terrors." No wonder that the priests and teachers were not admitted to Lorraine veillées. They were seen as critics of old customs and of traditional tales, working to annihilate them and to root out the mentality they perpetuated.[8]

Conditions were working for the critics. By the turn of the century, veillées were wasting away. Their productive functions were affected one by one.

Spinning declined as a contribution to the household budget. We hear of this first under the Second Empire, but obviously the decline took time to affect isolated regions. Hemp ceased to be an important crop; and chestnuts played less of a part in diet, as did nuts in providing oil. In a survey of 12 Roannais villages that at one time apparently had veillées about every other day during the winter season, two reported that they had been abandoned by 1900, another that they had declined about that time (only old maids still went), and a fourth that men had stopped dressing hemp about 1907 and even dancing had ceased in 1914. Four villages in all saw 1914 as putting paid to these activities; and in another, such social gatherings were infrequent after that date, falling off from three times a week to three times a year. In the seven villages where veillées survived, they were kept alive for the dancing (no work was mentioned), or by the continued patronage of a few people who would not give them up, or as a place for the old to meet. In most cases their ending was ascribed to concrete developments: the end of hand embroidery, of nut-shelling, of hemp-dressing. The same is true of Savoy, where veillées stopped once the market for walnut oil disappeared and the trees were cut for rifle stocks and furniture.[9]

The veillée appears to have declined well before the end of the century in some areas. In the Ardennes reports from schoolteachers suggest it waned during the 1880's. In Upper Brittany by 1880 the considerations of safety, which had led peasants to live close to one another, were no longer so pressing, and the distances between more isolated farms inhibited large gatherings. Meanwhile, improved roads gave more people access to other types of social activities in the bourg. Either way, veillées suffered. In Bresse, where in the 1870's all the inhabitants of certain hamlets had gathered for veillées, coming if need be by boat, by 1894 only the people in the poorest parts, untouched by prosperity, still kept up the custom.[10] There, as in Mâconnais and Bouches-du-Rhône, the major purpose of such gatherings seems to have been to find warmth and company in a stable. When homes became more comfortable and inns or cafés became available in villages, veillées lost their practical purpose.

Now their format could be adapted to more novel enterprises, subversive of the world they represented. When, in 1905, a Socialist or Socialist-inspired study group was formed at Cuisery (Saône-et-Loire), a large rural bourg only a few miles east of Tournus, the pattern it adopted was that of the veillée. There were songs and moral tales; there were the sketch-playlets called *saynètes*, such as the one about John, a poor peasant in love with Jane, whose wealthier parents refuse to entertain his suit. We do not know the impact of these notions (clearly related to the proximity of the proud old town that boasted Greuze and Albert Thibaudet among its sons). But we do know that all proceedings were suspended from spring to fall, just as the veillées had been when fieldwork called.[11]

Meanwhile, where life remained hard, and especially where local crops continued to provide a task for winter evenings, veillées carried on. In Cantal we hear of them at least to the end of the century. In Gers, to the north of Auch, poor sharecropper country where the diet remained deficient to the Second World War, veillées—"where one played belote or knitted while shelling and picking corn and eating potatoes and chestnuts baked in ashes"—began to disappear only after 1945. By contrast, by 1890 "the time of long veillées [was] past" for villagers south of Sedan; and in Vexin (where velocipedes appeared in *villages*) the veillées were withering: "only about ten persons," "the conversation apathetic," "rare remarks." There was some women's gossip, but not even much of that because the men were listening; the women preferred to guard their tongues until they could exchange confidences among themselves at the washhouse.[12]

Common tasks and need provided a concrete excuse for social gatherings, and so did the lack of alternatives. When these motives waned so did veillées. The young left for the café, especially as bicycles became available. The balance of ages broke down. Without the young, the evenings became duller, and the old people who continued the circles tended to spend most of their time at cards, especially when artisanal tasks like ropemaking or basketweaving became less profitable as commercial products got cheaper. At Maillane in the mid-nineteenth century the peasants had gathered on winter evenings to work and warm themselves in the stable; by 1906 they went to play billiards or cards in a café. Even in Finistère, where veillées had been relatively short because of the need to economize fuel, by 1914 we see the servants hastening off to their own quarters while the master looks through the local paper or reads a chapter of the lives of the Breton saints. It seems that light and heat now permitted this. The interesting thing is that many traditional gatherings lingered on, like certain rites, until a war precipitated their end—either in 1870–71 or in 1914–18.[13]

It is clear from the changed composition of the surviving veillées that their integrative functions no longer held. The classic veillée had gathered a group of different ages; now young and old tended to part company. The gatherings had been larger and had been based on locality rather than social class. This changed too. As early as 1869 we hear that in Vosges veillées were splitting up on social lines. As "civilization" spread, Xavier Thiriat tells us, tablecloths made their appearance, wine was served instead of the cheaper local brews, and festive spreads of meat, salad, and cakes replaced the rye bread and cheese of yore. As a result families that were unable to match the standards of their richer neighbors drank and played cards at separate veillées.[14]

The veillées of the new model were simply get-togethers, unconstrained by the conditions and necessities that had ruled the old. In Bourbonnais the men played cards, the women knitted or sewed. The same thing in Rouergue. In Allier, where men had occupied themselves in making the baskets they used in sowing (*saneaux*), wood or metal baskets were now bought in shops, and the veillée was devoted to reading, correspondence, and playing cards. In Franche-Comté husbands read novels while their wives sewed (the women would take up spinning again in the Second World War). Emile Guillaumin, for one, had little regret at the passing of the veillées or at the passing of the folklore that had been served in them. It had been only cover for, if not the inspiration of, chronic anxiety, suspicion, and uneasiness. Now, wrote Guillaumin in 1936, the world held less violence, less savagery.[15] The superstitions that the veillée sustained and quickened were no longer appropriate.

Chapter Twenty-five

THE ORAL WISDOM

In the beginning was the Word.
—JOHN 1:1

WITH THE PASSING of the veillées there died one of the great institutions for the transmission of knowledge acquired by word of mouth. In the veillées there had been much talk, the voicing of personal memories, the recitation of tales, saws, and witty sayings. The degree to which this went on seems to have varied from region to region. Peasants in general do not appear to have been very articulate. But whether they tended to be taciturn and sober, as in the Landes or Beauce, or expansive and ebullient, as in Languedoc, peasants everywhere relied heavily in their everyday speech on an established fund of locutions that could take the place of general ideas. Like old Père Martin in Ernest Lavisse's widely used elementary school text, *L'Année préparatoire d'instruction morale*, the peasants talked largely in proverbs, *dictons*, common sayings—ready-made expressions of wisdom or comment. Proverbs, wrote Père Gorse, "there's the peasant's creed, the learning he has ripened and assimilated to the innermost recesses of his soul.... All his thought is in them, and beyond that he thinks no more."[1] We should do well to heed this.

Like memories preserved by word of mouth, an oral culture is almost by definition subject to change and evanescent. The formulas it elaborates are almost the only windows we have to look into its soul. At this stage in our observations what they reveal to us will not be very new, but if these formulations are valid evidence, they make still clearer the kind of world that we have left behind.

The philosophy of life was stoic: "When the man can't cross by the bridge, he will cross through the water"; "When we have nothing left, we shall have nothing to lose." The realism was harsh: "A scalded cat fears even the cold water"; "The weakling cheats, the strong commands." After all, someone had to give the orders: "Many masters means no master." The song of the turning mill wheels was "I'll do unto you as you do unto me." In any case, "Someone else's trouble is a dream." There were no illusions: "One has to do anything to eat." And especially when it came to money: "To get his hands on the purse, a man will even marry a bear." Trust was in short supply: "If one knew what goes on at night, one would have iron doors"; "You plant in vain if you don't enclose"; "Who comes from afar can lie more easily"; "It is easier to catch a rabbit than a liar"; and "If you pay anything in advance, you're paying your tormentor." But even one's closest kin could let one down, so "Don't strip yourself before you are in bed"; "Who gives his goods away before he dies deserves to suffer." And in any case, "He who complains lasts longest."[2]

One didn't give secrets away: "Don't shout too loudly, for bushes have ears." Or trust in men's discretion either, for "A man would rather swallow his teeth than his tongue." The land was worth what the man was worth, but there was no justice: "The man who works gets the straw, the one who doesn't gets the wheat." And the peaceful inherited only trouble: "Pretend you're a sheep, the wolf will eat you up." It was no use pushing too hard: "You'll surely have enough land to cover you one day." But there was no sympathy for the idle: "Spin, Adeline, if you want clothes on your back"; "Lazybones would like to eat marrow but bewails his trouble in cracking the bone." No room for nostalgia either: "All yesteryears are good"; "Every tree has its shadow." And if "It's always fair weather for someone," most peasants probably added an under-the-breath "but not for me." There was scant room for affection: "Dead wife, new hat"; "Sorrow for a dead wife last as far as the door." As for a child, "Better load him down than fill him up."

Wisdom lay in economy: "Undress Saint Peter to dress Saint Paul." And in prudence: "Don't count the eggs in a chicken's arse"; "After the fair, we'll count the cowpats"; "Always keep a pear for thirst." Wisdom also lay in knowing one's place: "Swineherd in this world, swineherd in the next"; "Don't pretend you know better than the priest"; "Don't fart higher than your arse"; "Don't be vain like a flea under a velvet coat"; "Youth, don't raise your head; it is a sign of pride; do like the ear of corn: when it is ripe it hangs its head." Keep out of sight: "One's only happy in one's hole." Above all, keep away from the powerful: "Who thrusts himself among the legs of the great risks being trampled." And from lawmen: "A willow for shelter, a bailiff for friend, one is fast without friend and without shelter." Be close with your money—"You choke if you pay out to get a profit"—better do without.

Excellent advice most of it, for survival in a world full of dangers. No wonder the Basque proverb said, "Old words, wise words."

So, proverbs are compact ideological statements—much matter decocted in a few words, according to the definition of a seventeenth-century worthy. They reveal traditional experience, define the rules and structure that society sets for individuals, fashion their mentalities, and help them construct their identities. They sketch out a world-view within accessible limits. The bourgeois refers in his saying to the splendors of the Bay of Naples, but the countryman has more accessible images of grandeur: "Who hasn't seen Auch cathedral and the belltower of Rodez has seen naught," says the southwestern saw. And closer still to home: "Between Tudet and La Chapelle [Tarn-et-Garonne] there is more money than in England"; or, "At Mountbégui the people haven't even the earth to make a pot."[3] Finally, proverbs regulate most people's elementary relations—not only with their fellow men, but with their land and work.

This is where the English notion that proverbs incorporate one man's wit and all men's wisdom reveals itself as coined by an urban mind. The wisdom proverbs carry is not universally valid, and does not aim at generality. The monitory proverb provides specific counsel grown out of local conditions. "Year of wind, year of naught," says the Franc-Comtois, referring to the sudden gusts of dry wind from the south betokening drought. The Franc-Comtois also despises the northwest wind that blows in the springtime, which he calls prickle-blossom (*l'air de pique-blanches*) because it causes late frosts that kill the plum blossoms before the fruit has had a chance to set. Hence the old proverb that refers to Paris, which lies in the same direction:[4]

> Neither good wind nor good people
> Have ever come from those whereabouts.

This would not make sense in central or western France. On the other hand, the Poitou adage advising that nuts are ripe for picking at Saint Magdalen's (July 22) would have no meaning in Franche-Comté, where nuts do not ripen until September. In Morvan the advice for spring sowing is very precise: you have to sow your barley by Saint George's day (April 23); by Saint Mark's (April 25) it will be too late. But this is good for barley and for the latitude (and altitude) of a north-central plateau. It does not apply farther south, any more than another Morvan dicton: "February rain is as good as manure, March rain isn't worth a fox's piss." In Gers they tend to be even more discriminating: "The ox wants rain [for hay and straw], the pig wants dryness [for the wheat he gets]." In the Limousin pigs would eat acorns, and cattle graze on grass. And few outside the appropriate countryside would understand "Year of beechnut, year of famine; year of acorns, year of naught," which recalls the difficult times when, in the east, people ate the food of trees that they disdained when things went well. In Ardèche the west wind that blows from the rugged uplands of Velay bringing fine rain and often hailstorms is perceived as coming from Pradelles in Haute-Loire (just across the border), hence *lou pradellentcho*.[5] Similarly, in Gers, where the dominant winds come from the west and bring rain, rural dwellings faced east and turned blind walls to the windy side. For Gascon peasants east is the front (*le devant*), west is the rear. On the other hand, the *vent d'autan*, hot and dry, blows from the east or southeast; hence the old proverb that

> The East wind goes to see its father [ocean],
> Will return in tears [rain].*

Traditional sayings are local, and their meaning is often lost unless one knows the associations that brought them into being. Thus, in Auvergne, spring coincides not with the swallow, but with the cuckoo:

A brillaou introu.	April arrives.
Cucu chantou.	Cuckoo sings.
Sounailles marlou.	Bells tinkle.

The cuckoo's song signals the release of cattle from their winter quarters; their bells celebrate their return to fresh grass and sunshine. Less romantically, the comparison of an unkempt girl with a resin candle made sense only where people were familiar with the messy dripping ways of such candles— Lauragais, Minervois, Agenais, and other southwestern regions. In Bourbonnais "Like godfather, like godson" refers not to some moral influence, but to the fact that grandfathers were normally selected to act as their grandchildren's godfathers.[6]

Practical advice for the Franc-Comtois farmer was based on common sense, which may not be as common as the term suggests. Sow wheat below and plant vines above. Sow wheat in damp ground and barley in dry (Plutarch had said as much). If you want good turnips sow them in July. On the other hand, do not ever sow winter wheat after Saint Clement's (November 23); this must have referred to emergencies, since the fall sowing was proverbially related to the feastday of Saint Denis (October 9). Everything was couched in rhyme and related to familiar benchmarks, which made the counsels easier to remember:[7]

---

* In Provence, too, the *bise*, the good breeze that blows from west or northwest is the wind from behind [the house]: *vent de darrèr*. Jean Poueigh cites similar locutions in parts of Languedoc, where "sea" or "mountain" may stand for south: "Mari clar e cers escur, es de plèjo à cop segur," or "mountagno claro, Bourdèu [Bordeaux] escur, plèjo per sigur." The wind is commonly said to blow from, or in relation to, a familiar local landmark: Canigou in Pyrénées-Orientales, Maguelonne in Hérault, Arbizon or Montaut in Hautes-Pyrénées, Marcou in the Lower Cévennes. (*Le Folklore des pays d'Oc*, pp. 52–58.) Similarly, the position of the sun determined various place-names: at Miradoux (Gers) the sun rose above the spot called Le Point du Jour; at Pavie (Gers) it rose over the mill of Hébus (Phoebus); and Bigourdans knew it was noon when the sun stood above the Pic du Midi de Bigorre. (Henri Polge, *Nouveaux mélanges de philologie et d'ethnographie gersoise*, Auch, 1960, p. 108.) Lucienne Roubin tells us that in the villages of Upper Provence the highest point struck by the sun at noon and visible to the men working in the fields as to the womenfolk close to their houses became the midday line or the midday stroke, *barre dúou miedjóu* ("Ordonnance toponymique en montagne provençale," in *L'Homme, hier et aujourd'hui*, Paris, 1974, p. 477).

Ai lai Saint-Jouset
Sanne tas pouets [peas].

Ai lai Saint-Pancrâ
Sanne las chenevâ [hemp].

Ai lai Saint-Aubin
Sanne das pois, t'en airé bin [you'll have aplenty].

Ai lai Saint-Denys
Darrère vouguâsson du pays [last sowing].

Qui veut bon navet
Le sème en juillet.

Passe la Saint-Clément
Ne sème plus de froment.

A la Sainte-Catherine
Tout bois prend racine.[8]

They were remembered so well that the proverbs survived the reality. Thus the saying has it that if it rains on Saint Médard's day (June 8) the rain will go on for 40 days. This could have had a semblance of sense before the Gregorian calendar reform of 1582, when that day fell around what is now mid-June, a time when the weather varies little. It makes less sense at the beginning of the month, when the weather is still notoriously unstable. A more striking example is to be found in a whole series of sayings about the length of days, according to which by Saint Lucy's (December 13) the day begins to grow a tiny bit—by a flea's step in most versions. This was quite correct before 1582, when the feastday fell after the winter solstice, but makes no sense by the modern calendar, since days are still growing short on December 13. Yet these sayings continue to be repeated—even in the *Petit Larousse*.[9]

Authentic peasant art was very limited. The printed images that flooded the countryside and that we shall shortly meet were an urban art, just as the oral story was a rural one. But the peasant's verbal imagery was very rich indeed, expressed in language that was full of humor and lyricism. Thus in Livradois sickles were called *volants* (flyers) because in use they flew and turned in flashes. Pastures in the Vendée bocage were *mouchoirs à boeufs*. The small winegrowers of the Marne valley west of Epernay called the absentee owners from the Reims "mountain" they worked for *cossiers*, after the beans (*cosses*) that grew between the vines and provided the workmen's staple diet. In fall the gangs of grape-pickers who descended like a horde on the vineyards were *les hordons*. In Nièvre a man was no more afraid of something than a lawyer is of an écu; and something was made or done on purpose just as dogs are made for the express purpose of biting people. In Ille-et-Vilaine an active person was one who did not put both feet in the same sabot, and a cow drifting away from the herd mowed violets (*faucher la violette*).

Popular Breton speech was (and is) full of picturesque metaphors: hard water that wears hard on linen "has teeth"; waves are "the roof of the sea"; the sun is the great butter-robber because it melts it; a man swelled up with pride is "stretched like a ship's sail"; and one who lives by his wits "lives off his nails." "The sun is past his threshold" indicates that a person is dead or out-of-date. One flings oneself on or seizes something or someone avidly "like misery upon poor people." As for a man who will agree with anybody, or modulate his song to anything, he is of the wood that flutes are made of. He can play any tune you like.

In Franche-Comté a similar locution described those who are easily satisfied: they are of the wood pitchforks are made of. Pitchforks are also used to spread things out—generally manure—in fairly large quantities, so to say that it is easier to spend than to save, one said, "What comes with a rake, goes with a pitchfork." Since weavers were proverbially poor, a skinny person was thin as a weaver's dog. And since roadworkers were reputed to take it easy, something could be as rare as the sweat of a *cantonnier*. A frail or gim-crack structure—building or marriage—fell apart like a castle built of corn-husks. The cornmeal cakes known as *god* or *gaudes* had to be stirred a long time; so restless tossing about in bed became "to stir the *god*." Similarly, *farter*, a term that means rubbing or wearing down by friction as dressers did to hemp, came to mean wearing the sheets to threads by tossing about in bed.[10]

The ready-made imagery of the language would be recruited into service in the musical dialogues between groups of girls and lads at veillées, feasts, and other occasions; in the alternate couplets (like the Basque *koblak*) im-provised and sung by poets (koblakari) trying to best each other; or in the almost ritual exchanges of japes and droll insults chanted or shouted by shep-herds from one mountainside to another. All these, of course, also helped further enrich the store of locutions. So did in-jokes drawn from local stories. One old favorite concerns some men who were being lowered down a well on a rope. The man above shouts down that he can hold on no longer, and back comes the helpful advice: "Spit on your hands!" Another praised the wise old man who, alone in the whole village, managed not to slip and spill his water when going up the muddy slope that led from the well. Why? He was the only one who had the sense to set down his full buckets before he slipped.[11]

There were a great many tales to tell. Some were grounded in historical events. In Burgundian Chalonnais the memories of the imperial raids of the seventeenth century persisted; the same in Bresse, where in the early 1900's children had grown up praying to the Virgin every evening for protection against the Kaiserlicks of Captain Lacuzon. Elsewhere it was the Swedes of the Thirty Years War who fed the legends. In Mâconnais, which was spared the ordeal of invasion until the Allied occupation of 1815, the fairly benevolent presence of the Austrian troops seems to have left traumatic memories, so that in folktales the Austrians replaced even Saracens as the prototypes of past conquerors, and vestiges of ancient monuments were often attributed to the Austrians.[12] Historical memories of another sort were perpetuated in the tales of old people, like the grandfather of Léon Côte in Bourbonnais, who "did not know the name of the masters who through his long life, nearly centenary, had governed France; but could recite without fail the redoubtable winters, when the black bread . . . was rare, when the snowdrifts blocked the low doors, when one stayed in bed for days . . . to save the meager provender."*

Historical experience and social tensions could also be transmuted into fables and fairytales. The fact that few such tales are available now in their original patois makes their analysis somewhat similar to reconstructing pterodactyls from a few bones: the glint in their eyes is missing. We know at any rate that old tales were generally adapted to the peasants' world. Cinderella, who in the Perrault version is the daughter of a gentleman, appears in oral tales as a peasant girl: she spins wool and guards sheep. It is while engaged in this last humble task that she encounters fairies, who give her clothes and shoes—not to go dancing but to attend mass—and it is at church that she meets the prince.† Similarly, in the literary version of "Beauty and the Beast," Beauty is the daughter of a merchant, but in all oral versions she is of much lowlier extraction: her father is a woodcutter, a gardener, a winegrower, or an unskilled laborer, according to the region. Even the kings of many fairytales sound more like prosperous farmers than monarchs: they hire their own servants, go out to meet a shepherd, or set off to the fair asking their daughters if they want anything brought back. One Breton story, more sophisticated than most, has a peasant lad winning his princess, thanks to a fairy's help, despite the bad faith and intrigues of the court around her. In the end, however, the couple return to live in the youth's village, where they are happier than in the royal palace because "kings are surrounded by a crowd of parasites, all lazy and lying."[13]

Every striking feature in nature was explained by a tale. Jays had once been blue all over but lost their splendid plumage because one of their ilk had revealed the place where Jesus was hiding under a sheaf of corn. Mineral sources were generally the results of the fairies' intervention. Individual forests, rocks, and caves had their own legends, chiefly of terrible combats in which all the fighters seem to finish dead (a memory of the peasants who issued forth after the men-at-arms had done their bloody work), of wicked lords and innocent shepherdesses raped, of noble hunters and their band condemned

---

* *En montagne bourbonnaise*, pp. 32, 36. Guy de Maupassant, writing on his travels in Brittany, observed: "Le paysan vous parle des aventures accomplies quinze siècles plus tôt comme si elles dataient d'hier, comme si son père ou son grand-père les avait vues" (*Oeuvres*, 1: 255).

† It seems that those oral versions that derive from Perrault restore the heroine to the fields.

forever to roam as a *chasse maligne*.* Gargantua and Pantagruel appear in
popular legends, but equally often one encounters local heroes like Morvan's
John-of-the-Bear and his two companions, Wring-Oak and The-One-Who-
Turns-Windmills-by-Blowing-with-His-Behind.†

The peasant hero may be very strong, but he is just as often humorous and
cunning. Violence seems to be left to the specialists: innkeepers who murder
travelers (travel is never safe), but mostly nobles. These last, as villains, could
be replaced in some tellings by Satan, just as he could be replaced by a rich
farmer, a big landowner, or a nobleman. Fictional dangers gave way before
real oppressors, oppressors took on symbolic evil form; the peasant's fantasies
gave him a yearned-for chance to triumph over either. Many a tale presents
the devil attempting to exploit some rustic clown he takes to be stupid, entic-
ing the "bumpkin" into contracts, deals, or farming experiments for his own
gain—very like the alien bourgeois or lord of the manor must have looked in
the cottager's eye.[14]

Escape into myth or fable provided a substitute for impossible action, the
possibility of projecting hatreds and resentments, of rejecting fears, of situat-
ing misery, toil, and terror in some other world where they could be mastered
by magic means or simply by fictional fulfillment. Thus, the medieval romance
of the four Aymon brothers, translated into Breton in the sixteenth century,
became no longer the tale of four knights resisting a prince (Charlemagne),
but the story of rebel shepherds who assert their independence ("We have no
master, because we are the strongest") and who articulate the peasant's own
hatred of the nobles.‡

True Breton stories, insists F. M. Déguignet, a peasant himself, are easy to
recognize by the theme of an encounter between peasant and lord, or peasant
and devil, the enemy always finally balked by the peasant's cunning or by the
intervention of a priest. This last could sometimes lead to dire results, as can
be seen from a tale told in Lower Brittany to help explain the origin of the
potato blight that ravaged the Quimper region in the late 1840's. A would-be
wizard of Finistère had gone to the devil's fair at Gourin (Morbihan) and
bought a black cat to help him in his contrivances. The cat, of course, was the
devil, and only a powerful exorcism would rid the land of it. A priest finally

* Abbé M. M. Gorse, *Au pays bas de Limosin*, p. 26; Francis Pérot, *Folklore bourbonnais*,
pp. 7–14. The tales of the chasse could be updated simply by adding new means of transport.
Thus Claude Seignolle quotes the warning of an old man of Montazeau (Dordogne), who cau-
tioned his listeners to beware not only of the howling pack of "King David's hunt," but also of
the "fiery train" that followed the hunt—four or five carriages passing through the sky, full of
damned souls and pulled by the devil himself (*Les Evangiles du diable*, Paris, 1967, p. 324).

† Jean Drouillet, *Folklore du Nivernais*, 4: 25. This last theme appears in a great many folktales in which the poor revenge themselves against the rich by means of farts (see Raymond
Doussinet, *Les Travaux*, p. 485).

‡ But nobles got no worse than the peasant who preyed on his fellows. Many popular tales
denounce the debtor turned usurer, the miserable oppressed man who becomes an oppressor in his
turn (see Cénac-Moncaut, *Littérature populaire de Gascogne*, chap. 1).

managed to cast the cat out in 1845, but before vanishing it let off a fart so powerful that it knocked over the exorcist and turned all potato leaves black throughout the region.

The starvation and misery of the hungry 1840's had to be explained. The poor blamed the rich who engrossed, forestalled, and starved them; the rich blamed the poor who had made songs against the potatoes they had to eat too often for lack of other things, and had thus provoked God's wrath. Finally, all agreed to blame the devil, which may have helped ease the social conflict.[15]

The folk imagination at work in the political and economic realm can be seen in some of the stories born in the Third Republic. In 1889 it was said that General Boulanger had met Don Carlos (the Legitimist) and Mandrin (the bandit) in a cave at Balme in Dauphiné. In 1898, when grain was dear, the story circulated that Jews had bought up large quantities, loaded them on ships, and ordered them dumped into the sea. In 1906 word spread through Côtes-du-Nord that dead monks and nuns had come to seek members of the persecuted religious orders and hide them away in caves until things got better. In all these stories traditional motifs are intertwined in typical fashion with fact. But by this time the popular press was supplementing the popular imagination, and the extraordinary fin-de-siècle fantasies of Leo Taxil suggest that contemporary folklore had become predominantly urban.[16]

By that time, too, traditional rhyming proverbs had been forgotten in a great many places. Everyone now, wrote a collector of the proverbs of Franche-Comté in 1876, can afford printed calendars that show the phases of the moon and indicate the appropriate times for sowing, planting, and other operations. Such a development was slower to come elsewhere, but even in the wild Morvan we hear that at Fléty (Nièvre) in 1911 "the present generation doesn't know the sayings that used to rule all life."[17] The present generation was school-educated, and school taught universally accepted proverbs, preferably forged in urban circumstances. The peculiar institutions designed to transmit the manners, tales, and wisdom of the village, like the *piats-bans* and the *couarails d'enfants* of Lorraine, where children soaked up the lore of local artisans and other assorted elders through traditional fables, collapsed and disappeared with the schools' coming in the 1880's. One more support of the oral tradition fell with them.[18]

Proverbs were still used to inculcate a view of life and of right and wrong, but the view was an altogether different one. They taught deferred gratification—"what is put off is not lost"—something no peasant would have accepted, and rightly. They taught that everyone is free to choose his tastes and colors, which went against communal judgment; and that all professions are good ("there is no stupid trade"), when every man knew that some were better than others; and that days follow each other but all are different. They taught that time is money and credit valuable; that all that is new is fine;

that simply to will something is to achieve it (one succeeds if one really wants to); and that values and ways of life are relative: other times, other ways. The peasant might have said "other places, other ways," but he would have known that only his own ways were right.

Conventional wisdom now respected the proprieties. No saw would be acceptable to the new order that expressed ancient wisdom in uncouth terms.* The dominant class still thought that only a fool would try to fart higher than his arse, but that sort of language now was relegated only to the essays of Montaigne—when not expurgated. And nothing could be accepted save in French. Which made for many exclusions. And memories were short. In any case, the old were no longer by definition wise, and old words were wise words no longer.

* In 1919 Emmanuel Labat wrote: "La littérature non écrite du village est morte" (*L'Ame paysanne*, p. 58). Was there a relation between the death of the oral tradition and that of the local speech in which the old tales had been told? The two declined together.

Chapter Twenty-six

FLED IS THAT MUSIC

Adieu! Adieu! thy plaintive anthem fades
Past the near meadows, over the still stream,
Up the hill-side; and now 'tis buried deep
In the next valley-glades:
Was it a vision, or a waking dream?
Fled is that music:—Do I wake or sleep?
—KEATS

AT A TIME WHEN light was bad, occasions for entertainment few, public performances outside church or fair strictly limited, music—homemade—and dance played a crucial role in the peasant's life.

Music was mostly song: the songs of shepherd or of shepherdess, of workers in fields or walkers on the road, of beggars at the door, or weavers at the loom, or women spinning; the melody to which a tale was told, ballad of a memorable event or Breton *gwerz* or Basque improvisation; the opening challenges in tavern-drinkers' brawls; the warp and woof of dancing.

Sung dialogues engaged farmers or shepherds miles apart. Wives recognized their men returning home at eventide by their song. Old people remember that "as soon as we were two on the road we began to sing."[1] During the cholera epidemic of 1833 the Breton peasants, on whom official circulars and posters were wasted, heeded a song that advised them of the precautions they should take: eat little fruit and mix vinegar with the drinking water. Beggars carried the ballads from village to hamlet to farm—and possibly the germs of cholera as well. In October 1870, when the prefect of Finistère sent out mobilization orders for the militia reserves, his circular included "a detail of some importance: let those militiamen who play the *musette* or *biniou* [bagpipes] be sure to bring their instruments. They will receive extra pay."[2]

A Romanian student of the *doină* has found numerous folksongs dealing with misery, exploitation, taxes, gendarmes, conscription, hunger, usury, oppression, and the endless suffering of peasants whose abiding bitterness could scarcely be contained:[3]

> They lead us like oxen,
> They shear us like sheep.

This sort of song, less a patch for grief than a fan to stir and articulate social resentments, seems very rare indeed where I have looked in France. Pierre

Laroche cites an example from Lauragais, where, as in many parts, interference with hunting rights sparked more resentment than any political issue.
There, a song about poaching, which was the only way most poorer men
could get near other meat than from their own slaughtered pigs, remarks
bitterly:[4]

> What would the gentry do
> If they couldn't lean on the poor?
> They'd have to do some work themselves,
> They wouldn't be so stiff and fat.

Scriveners, too, come in for their share of comment, as in the Breton song
about the *gars faraud* (the toffed-up bumpkin), which ends wishing him a
diet of bedbugs:[5]

> J'voudrai bin qu'tous les procourus
> N'mangeaient que des punaises,
> Les pau'p'tits labouroux comm'ma
> N'en seraient que pus à lous aise.

Finally, George Sand seems to have heard two fretful songs that Berrichons
had apparently forgotten by 1900 or so:[6]

> Je maudis le sergent,
> Qui prend, qui pille le paysan,
> Qui prend, qui pille
> Jamais ne rend.

> Dites-moi, donc, ma mère,
> Où les Français en sont?
> Ils sont dans la misère,
> Toujours comme ils étions.

This is little enough to go on. Above all, though, when this sort of thing
shows up, peasants may sing it but, as often as not, they have not created it.
Real peasant songs, it seems, are not plaints of deprivation, since what we
call deprivation was taken as the norm, but expressions of experience in the
everyday context of life, especially the aural landscape of herding, plowing,
and reaping and the amorphous noises of man and bird and beast: moans and
hollers, sighings, cries and groans and titters find consummation in rhythm
and melody.

"When the plowman sings, the plow goes well." Much singing was functional. One of its common purposes was to urge oxen on under the yoke.
Brioler or *hôler* in Berry, *bouarer* in Vendée, *arander* in Poitou, *kioler* in
Morvan, was (is?) considered a rare art when done well. Those who had
the knack were prized and long remembered, and farmhands who possessed
the skill were hired away rather like outstanding cooks in bourgeois households. Songs were also sometimes used to set the pace for mowing and harvesting. The men and women working sang individually, and mostly when

they interrupted work. But in the Pyrenees we hear of women who were hired at harvest time to sing the old *segaïres* songs. They did not work, but simply followed the line of reapers, singing to give them rhythm and heart.[7]

The harvest songs might be about a local legend, like that of Jeanne d'Oymet, seduced and left behind by a king's son; or humorous, or semireligious. They also referred to the work itself. In Lot "the nightingale sings on my spine" referred to the stiffness in the back and limbs of those who made their way bent almost double to cut with the sickle *"bas e round,"* low and regular. But as in this instance, many work songs were actually after-work songs. A respondent to a folklore survey noted that in Corrèze threshers' songs appeared more often in books than in barns, because threshing was hard work and raised enough dust to discourage even the jolliest of workers.[8] So the *flagel* was more often heard when men were drinking or winnowing grain.

Hard work where you need your breath does not encourage singing.[9] Which may be why we hear about women singing at home for fun where they had no field tasks, while not too far away where they were "slaves of the earth" they were silent. It is also why so many songs are attributed to shepherds and artisans. Breton weavers, who often worked in their clients' homes and carried their frame from farm to farm, had a whole repertory; their primitive looms produced "a strangely jerky sound," a staccato of violent clangs and clashes as the blocks drove the shuttle through the warp that was translated into a staccato song, "Tric Trac de Olu!" Blacksmiths, also known as iron-thumpers, had similarly rhythmic songs:[10]

> Dingdong, the fire's strong,
> Come on hammer, bong bong bong!

But, again, a smith or farrier needs his breath, and anyway, his work often required his full attention. I am inclined to doubt the authenticity of work songs connected with such things as rowing or pile-driving, however apt their rhythm.* It is the more routine, repetitive tasks, like hauling cable and counting the salt-cod catch, that lend themselves to singing and to creating songs. Hence the great Breton song factory, "where there's as much singing as in all the rest of Brittany," was the flax country of Trégorrois. It was the girls and women spinning out the yarn who sang as they went about their work and passed on the songs. Similarly in the Ardennes, it was the women spinning who contributed most heavily to the fund of songs, singing "interminable, tearful melodies (bought from the ballad peddler) about the life of men who await death in jail, or how a mother suddenly recognizes the child the gypsies stole."[11] Here, as in many other cases, it is hard to tell how much was incorporated from outside and how much improvised.

Improvisation, in any case, is an imitation: of existing forms, of models

---

* When Poncy, the Lyon mason, dedicated his book of songs to George Sand, he explained that they had never been sung on the job because workers' songs were made up after work, by the fire or over a drink.

taken from familiar ballads. And the songs traditionally improvised at wedding feasts, whether by a local person with a reputation for it or by all guests contributing a verse in turn, must have clung fairly close to hackneyed, reassuring rhythms.[12] Local songsmiths as such seem to have been quite rare, witness the reputation of those we occasionally hear about and the rarity of their imprint on a song. Peasants, who frequently put their names or initials on a plate or lintel, mantelpiece, cross, or stick of furniture, seem to have left scarcely a trace on a composition. One of the only two cases I have come across is this announcement by a lyricist from Bournezeau (Vendée):

> Who has composed this melody?
> It's me, good fellow Eclaircy,
> Eating fat pumpkins at Badiole's mill,
> Served by goodwife Chalais with a will.*

Just because so many improvisations were evanescent, it is a pleasure to revivify and to preserve the scene, and give Eclaircy and goodwife Chalais, not forgetting the pumpkin, a small niche in history.

Little is left of this sort of thing. What we do have, thanks to nineteenth-century folklorists, are pastorals and carols. The former should not be confused with such urban patriotic patoisant imitations as the Limoges poet Joseph Foucaud's "Song for a Shepherdess":[13]

> Long live French youth!
> They do everything well.
> Whether fighting or dancing,
> You've never seen their like!

Unlike this sort of nonsense, which no self-respecting shepherdess would have thought of uttering to her sheep, the real *pastourelles* that people sang when guarding herds or shucking corn of an evening are miniature eclogues, and usually turned on the encounter of a gent and a shepherdess. Revealingly enough, the encounter often goes badly for the gent, who is fooled or made a fool by the cunning lass: an inversion of roles that provided fantasized revenge for frustrated yearnings, and for the scorn country wenches could plausibly expect from a city swain. Just as revealing, the dialogue form nearly always had the gent speaking French and the lass answering in local dialect, as in this example, "La Bargieira et lou monsur," in which the country girl speaks Limousin and the monsieur French:[14]

---

* Sylvain Trébucq, *La Chanson populaire en Vendée*, p. 20. This manner of signature also appears in a song that a master mason of Embrun (Hautes-Alpes) composed in support of his candidate in the elections of 1846: "Qui a composé la chanson? / C'est Derbezon, maître maçon, / Un jour, étant à l'Isère, / Plantant des pommes de terre. / Vive Allier! Vive Allier! / Sera toujours le premier!" (Isère is a quarter or neighborhood of the little town of Embrun.) Curiously, a local lawyer who supported the opposing candidate answered this with a song in patois. (Henry Thivot, *Vie Publique dans les Hautes-Alpes*, pp. 41–42.)

> Adieu, la bergère!
> Adusias, monsur!
> Que fais-tu solette
> Dans ce bois obscur?
> Fiale ma counoulha,
> Garde mous moutons.

The same mixture of tongues is found in noëls. After all, one spoke French to one's superiors when one could. It was natural to use it in addressing God or saints. One also dressed for the occasion, as a Morvan noël makes clear:[15]

> Let's don our fancy outfits,
> For it's a festive day,
> To worship the new baby
> A-lying in the hay.
> To go there all bemucked,
> Would surely not be good.
> Us'll adore our master,
> An' muckiness is rude!

Fancy clothes, fancy speech.

In one noël of Lower Quercy the shepherds hastening to Bethlehem stop to pick up Jean Frances, the only man in the village who speaks French, because you cannot speak to God in patois. Otherwise, however, such songs treat the holy characters in a familiar vein. One of the shepherds in a noël from Allier inquires if Saint Joseph was not jealous when he learned about Mary's pregnancy. Another, in a Corrèze song, fears that since Mary is a virgin she must lack milk for Jesus, and so brings some along. In Gascony the angel who wakes the shepherds speaks French, and they cannot understand what he is telling them. He is asked to speak so that he can be understood, and turns to Gascon to tell them that they are fortunate to hear the news he brings. His hearers doubt it—"A happy fate is never our lot; it's not meant for poor shepherds"—but they dutifully go off to Bethlehem. When they finally reach the stable, however, Saint Joseph will not open the door because he is afraid of strangers. They ask him to glance through the dormer window at the passport the angel gave them: "You've come to the wrong address," says Saint Joseph. "I'm just a poor artisan [*un praoube mestériaou*], who doesn't know how to read."[16]

A great many noëls were printed, but these were of urban origin, as can be seen from the tradesmen's carol reproduced by Geneviève Bollème in which doctors, goldsmiths, and printers are among those to offer gifts, and bakers are enjoined to obey police regulations and to give honest measure. Homemade noëls drew on what could be had locally, and were likely to josh neighbors, local notables, and possibly innkeepers, never allowed to forget that they had refused haven to travelers in need. A Vendée noël sends shepherds and farmers to Bethlehem, but also weavers and *sergetiers* bearing gifts of canvas and worsted. Merchants proffer cabbage, turnips, onions, and chicory for the family stew—more likely fare than the delicacies of urban carols. When the gifts have been presented, the shepherd (endowed with the songsmith's name—Perrin Moréa) prays to the Infant Jesus:[17]

> O dainty child, for your mother's sake,
> Save us from misery's ache,
> From poll tax and salt tax.

Noëls may be the place where we find the common people's claims expressed most openly, and where their hopes and aches are most clearly articulated, as in this noël of 1770, sung in a small country parish of Bourbonnais:

> We'll see the war come to an end;
> Here are the good times coming back.
> See the God born to us
> To disarm the wild beasts.
> We shall be masters in our homes,
> Nor fear anything anymore.*

It may simply be that more noëls survived because of their seasonal reemployment and their interest to folklorists. At any rate, though the traditional groups that went round singing them were gradually driven out of cities (as from Moulins in 1866), the noëls went on being sung in original versions at least to the end of the century.[18]

Like the noëls, but more deliberately, some popular songs addressed themselves to social, economic, and, finally, political issues. When not the work of seminarians, priests, or middle-class balladeers, these were generally written by urban artisans. It was a priest who wrote the notorious "Que forâ-tu paubro Jonou?"[19]

> What will you do, poor Jenny?
> There's not a lad to be found.
> They're all for the army bound.
> The hunchback, the crocked, and the old
> Are all you can get if you're bold!

It was a journeyman carpenter on a *tour de France* in the mid-century who wrote a popular clog song ("Les Esclops") in Cévenol patois. And it was two stocking weavers from Languedô, "*de la classe de mil huit cent di*," who composed another song bound for fame:[20]

---

* Francis Pérot, *Folklore bourbonnais*, p. 115. Compare this with the text of a prophecy of 1673, during the Dutch War: "Enfin la Paix succédant à la guerre / Va donner à chacun un grand contentement. / Un prince triomphant, bening [*sic*] et débonnaire, / De son Pays accablé finira le tourment." (Geneviève Bollème, *Les Almanacs populaires*, p. 82.)

The Préfet and Monsieur le Maire
Are a pretty jolly pair.
They run the draft with easy breath,
To send us singing to our death.

We also hear about a local songster at Neuzonville (Ardennes), a twenty-four-year-old locksmith named Demoulin, who met with other smiths in a particular tavern where they sang and danced—and also (reported the gendarmerie) sang subversive songs written by Demoulin. This was 1850, and when the little gang marched through Neuzonville wearing red bonnets (the Phrygian caps of the Revolution) and singing Demoulin's songs, they clashed with the police and were brought to court.[21] But Neuzonville was a large market town, and *compagnons*—journeymen members of trade guilds—had a tradition of making up songs, which seldom echoed out into the countryside. There, they were more likely to sing the doubtfully translatable:[22]

The National Guard	La garde nationale
Are a lot of petticoats.	Sanesont que des jupons.
They've marched through the mountains,	Ont été par les montagnes.
And they've stolen all the groats.	Ont volé les sousissons.

The years after 1848 would send the tide of subversive songs into rural areas, but even in the most authentic of them, Claude Durand's "Chant des Vignerons" of 1850, the writer was influenced by Victor Hugo's verse.* Durand, though mayor of his Deux-Sèvres village, was at least a man of the land himself. The best-known and most frequently quoted of the revolutionary covey was written by a drifting urban poetaster, Pierre Dupont:[23]

Oh! quand viendra la belle,
Voilà des mille et des cent ans,
Que Jean Guêtré t'appelle
République des paysans?

Of course political agitation when literacy was minimal had frequent recourse to songs and to recitation. The list of agitators arrested in Gironde after December 2, 1851, included two workers who, like Demoulin in the Ardennes, had produced "bad verse": Pierre Vigier, who had been a cooper but now worked at devising political songs and verses, and Elie Boizac, a baker at Pian-sur-Garonne, who "writes bad verse and believes himself fated to exalted destinies. Hence malcontent."[24] Men like these wrote in French, and their products were as true to the popular mind as a gendarme's report. Others, more sophisticated, hoped to reach the patoisant peasantry by writing in local speech. Pierre Laroche cites one song of the sort from Lauragais, "Bibo la Républico!," but its allusions to distant politics and its support of

---

* So would Marcelin Albert be, half a century later.

Armand Barbès, relatively unknown in the southwest even after May 1848, may have made it even more impenetrable than propaganda in French.[25]

Eugène Pottier, father of "L'Internationale," pretended that the Second Empire had frozen popular songs:[26]

> Articulated by the cold,
> Words have frozen harder than they were of old.
> No more Assemblies (even patois-bound).
> It's snowing everywhere: words without sound.

But this referred only to the political products of urban chansonniers, and even their work was still to be found on the roads in 1854, when the police in Yonne reported they had confiscated several subversive broadsheets; and when in the Morvan "La Morvandelle" mocked the two-bit Caesar who had put down liberty. One reacts skeptically to the report of "a patriotic song of spontaneous and popular origin" in Yonne that welcomed the increase of the draft for the Crimea. But one can well believe that Isaac Maurin, a shoemaker in Gard who was sentenced to jail for six days, was guilty of writing a patois song "arousing hatred and scorn of citizens against each other" and setting the poor against the rich. "La Morvandelle," with its schooled prosody, could not match the native tang and raciness of ditties made up in the countryside by Republican shoemakers who sang about

> L'gros Napoléon,
> Sur sa gros ch'vaux blancs.

Or, in 1879, after the death of the Crown Prince:

> Prisonnier à Sedan,
> Revendant à Sedan
> Revendant aux Allemands
> La France et ses enfants.
> Il faut applaudir les zoulous
> Qui viennent de poignarder Loulou.

Elsewhere, in 1869, when the banker Isaac Pereire lost the hotly disputed election at Limoux, an old Limoux Carnival song was refurbished to run, roughly, very roughly:

> They have bunged up your behind,
> Poor Perera, poor Perera.
> They have bunged up your behind,
> Poor Perera, it's not kind.

The song was still being sung in the Aude wine country after the Second World War to taunt losers in local elections.[27]

The Third Republic had its own full share of spontaneous political songs. At Veslud (Aisne) in 1876, when the big landowners decided to enclose their lands with wire and thus deprive fellow villagers of common pasture, the great ensuing trial between *piquets* and *truands* evoked satirical songs. At Sauvetat, in Guyenne, the years between 1885 and 1890 were one long battle between the partisans of the priest and the mayor. The secularist clan used patois songs, written or adapted for the circumstances and sung in the village square as political ammunition. In Ariège at Gestiès political songs were made up and sung at the Carnival in 1894, and two years later, at Capoulet, the mayor was accused of putting the youth up to preparing such songs for the local feastday, August 2. In 1904, when vineyard workers struck at Beaufort in Minervois, one owner clashed with the pickets: "They make him a song in which they call him *iron head*."[28] Making up songs as arguments in a conflict continued to be done until after the First World War. The charivariseurs also knew well that there is no more memorable way of getting at your opponent.

Like Eugène Pottier, Maurice Agulhon has suggested that the popular tradition in songs and other old forms was hurt by the marriage of politics and folklore, which led the government to move against them.[29] What we call folklore had always reflected local politics. When local politics became national, the government began to meddle; the agents of authority turned against village songsters, farandoles, Carnivals, and the like, quite willing to lose the baby with the bathwater.

But the marriage with politics itself affected folklore. Songs were among the first things to feel the influence of the outside world and, in most cases it seems, to welcome it. Popular music is popular not in terms of its origins, but in terms of who accepts what. We have already seen noëls and pastorals incorporating the more elegant French, if only to ridicule it. And it appears that other traditional dialect songs, like the New Year's *guillouné* of Gascony ("au gui l'an neuf"), were altered by sixteenth- or seventeenth-century *francimans*—Frenchified Gascons—who had to make themselves understood by French officials in order to get a tip.[30] More important than such forfeitures, though, is the fact that songs traveled. Given the relative paucity of local sources in the countryside, there was need for constant replenishment, and contributions from outside were readily accepted. Ballads and songs were eagerly learned and even bought at fairs, or from itinerant peddlers. Most of them were drawn from vaudevilles and older operas. And most of them were urban creations. But there were others, too. George Sand tells of a minstrel from around La Châtre in Berry who told her he went every year to look for new dance themes among the woodcutters of Bourbonnais because they were the greatest composers in the world.[31] In 1854, at the time of the Crimean War, a workers' singing society in Nord featured a homemade song about a lad who tries to kiss a girl and receives a good beating for his pains:

> Ah! te t'in souviendras, Nicolas,
> D'avoir bayé Thrinette!

The refrain fitted the political situation. It became the war song that all conscripts of Nord sang when they went off to battle. Within a few years it could be found in Normandy, with patriotic lyrics:[32]

> Ah! tu t'en souviendras, Nicolas,
> Du combat de Sinope!

Many of the ballads that the weavers and spinners sang were in French or at least came from outside the parish. This too was bound to introduce strange themes and notions. Even within Brittany, the tailors and sabotiers, itinerant beggars and rag-and-bone men who carried the songs out of Trégorrois must have carried them to regions where the speech was different and perhaps the rhythms, too. No wonder French could appear as a lingua franca.

Finally, though most rural music was song, the best (that is, the most expensive) music was instrumental. Instrumental societies, modeled on the bands that accompanied Army units until the organization of regimental bands in 1860, were founded as early as the eighteenth century to play wind, wood, and brass. By mid-century every small town that could had its own band for special occasions; but such displays remained, in the words of the subprefect of Céret in 1894, "a rare diversion in the rural communes." Instruments were expensive; learning to play was hard; failing a substantial number of inhabitants one couldn't hope to get far beyond fife and drum. Yet the bands (and the cafés) of small towns spread city tastes in music well outside their borders. Local and itinerant players were expected to conform, and found that they were hired and paid accordingly when there was a choice. They tried to follow fashion. And those who played for their own amusement tried to follow them. By the 1880's or 1890's the goatherds around La Garde-Freinet (Var), with their homemade flutes, "imitated perfectly the real musicians they heard at village fêtes. They played polka, mazurka, and quadrille tunes."[33]

Bagpipes and flutes and hurdy-gurdys went with particular melodies. As they were replaced by more fashionable instruments—accordion and brasses— the chants and dances they had accompanied (as in Vendée) also went by the board. Perhaps they would have gone anyway, for country people sought the city's music even before they sought its speech. When a self-taught villager in southern Puy-de-Dôme put together, in a homemade notebook, a selection of songs he had collected before 1848, what he hoarded was not native lore, but the songs and poems most typical of the official culture: "Noble espérance, De notre enfance"; and "Un ange au radieux visage, Penché sur le bord d'un berceau."[34]

The more alien the language, the greater its prestige. Everyone spoke patois, grumbled a musical folklorist in the 1890's about the people of Lower Poitou, but when they made verses and songs they set this aside. "It is the townsmen, it is *mossieu noutr' mâétre*, whose language they try to imitate." The moment the peasant thought he was good enough, he wanted to sing in French. Music-hall jingles were his idea of good music. He tried to imitate them or expected his local minstrels to do the job for him. As for patois songs, it was the literate city folk who looked to them for inspiration. What Charles Nisard called *la muse foraine* was interested only in Paris wares.[35] The desire for novelty, coupled with the prestige of city life and activities, made songs one of the great avenues by which the national language penetrated the alien country-side.*

The most spectacular case in point is "La Marseillaise." Born at Strasbourg as the battle song of the Army of the Rhine on April 25, 1792, the new composition was given its first official airing in the salon of that city's mayor the next evening, then was played by the National Guard band that Sunday, April 29, and sung by the Lyon volunteers of the First Rhône-and-Loire Battalion, who paraded on the Strasbourg *place d'Armes*. It was printed within a few days, and by May 17 we hear of its being sung at Montpellier. Within a few days a delegate of the Constitutional (that is, Girondist) Society of Montpellier had carried it to Marseille, where on May 22 he sang it, arousing great enthusiasm, at the end of a Constitutional banquet. The very next day the song was printed in the local press. More important, it was also printed on a separate broadsheet, several copies of which were given to each of the volunteers of the Marseille Battalion, then being raised with some difficulty. Because they sang the song constantly and distributed copies of it on their march to Paris, which took all of July, the song became known as the hymn or the air of the Marseillais.[36]

This raises an intriguing question: who sang "La Marseillaise"? Or more precisely, how was it that these young recruits so readily sang the song in French? In 1792, by all accounts, French was as foreign to most Provençaux as it is to Senegalese today—perhaps rather more so. The ordinary people of Marseille understood enough French to get by in affairs of business and other day-to-day transactions, but seldom spoke the language. This suggests that the volunteers who, we know, were led by young men of the upper classes—hence bilingual—included a good few whose trade edged toward French: ex-soldiers, journalists, artisans, and dockworkers. A writer of the 1840's claimed that the corps of volunteers consisted of only a few true Marseillais among a rabble of foreign elements; and though he is a hostile witness, one

* On this process, see Terence Ranger, *Dance and Society in Eastern Africa* (Berkeley, Calif., 1975), especially p. 129. In this book Ranger traces the history of a dance style called *beni*, which had developed on the coast of East Africa in places like Mombasa and Dar-es-Salaam. As beni penetrated into the back country of the interior, it carried with it the aura of Swahili civilization. It was danced to songs whose words were in Swahili, it came from the great Swahili urban centers, and as a local informant told Ranger, "People who could sing in such a dance were esteemed very highly as Swahili, even though his or her spoken Swahili was very poor."

could reasonably suppose that there would be numbers of outsiders in a great port, that many of them would be politically available, that some would be glad to find work, even in the army, and that they understood at least some French. In any case, this mixture of "rude men of the people" and young men of the upper classes, using "foreign speech mingled with swear words," captured the popular imagination along their way. They also sang Rouget de Lisle's hymn, to which they had added a refrain in Provençal:

> Marcheu, trou de Diou.
> Marcheu, pétard de Diou.
> Leis émigras, noum de Diou.
> N'avouran ges de bouen Diou
> Qué leis curé monar et vieou.

But obviously what was remembered and learned wherever they passed was the words in French.[37]

By autumn the hymn created in the far northeast and disseminated first from the south, and only then from Paris, was sung throughout France— "by all the troops and by the children," specified a report of October 28, thus naming the chief agents of its penetration. Within a very short while we hear about the first counteruse of the exciting tune: a version in Vendean dialect sung by the insurgents of the west. Many would follow. The paradox was that the new hymn was linked to a city whose people did not speak French, or, in the case of many, feel that they were French.[38] But even those who did not speak French could sing it, and singing endowed them with the gift of tongues. We hear about a political riot at Tarascon in 1850, where it was said the Reds cried out ferociously while singing "La Marseillaise." The song even helped the singers pick up an elementary knowledge of the national language, perhaps encouraged them to learn more of it. At any rate, though banned by the Second Empire, "La Marseillaise" never disappeared. A workers' song of 1853, which has the journeymen off for a Monday's drinking in the country, has them settling down to sing as they quaff:

> And if one of us should know it,
> Let him sing "La Marseillaise"!

In 1858, in the wake of Félix Orsini's attempt against the life of Napoleon III, we hear that the song caused an incident when sung in a rural commune of the Pyrenees.[39] It was only a little later that the young Arsène Vermenouze learned to play the trumpet for the sake of the tune. In 1879 the Republicans reinstated it as the national anthem—and *that*, by the 1890's, it had fully become. The warlike patriotic song of a political faction had in the end become the song of all, carrying not only the language of its lyrics but a potent national sentiment. "One sings 'La Marseillaise' for its words, of course," said Maurice Barrès in 1902, "but [especially] for the mass of emotions that it stirs in our subconscious!"[40] Could anything but a song have wrought so much? There were, of course, many other songs in French besides "La Marseillaise," and some were immensely popular, notably those of Pierre-Jean de Béranger in the 1830's. François Mazuy, writing in Marseille in 1854, emphasized the impact these and other French songs had in spreading the national language. So national integration, among other things, involved a war of songs. Before educated men turned to collecting popular songs, like butterflies on pins and just as dead, they pursued them with their ire. Songs went with dances, and their goings-on, like those of the veillées with which both were frequently associated, were steadfastly denounced throughout the century as coarse, improper, bawdy, lewd, spurring immodesty in girls and lust in men. Certainly some of the lyrics that have come down to us must have made respectable ears burn. A rather mild example comes from Châteauneuf, in Saintonge, where they danced a very fast reel called "Le Bal de Suzon" or "Bal de Pête la Veille":

> Suzon est encor'q'une enfant
> Qui fait tout c'que sa mère lui défend.
> Quand elle se fâche, elle lui répète:
> Pête! Pête! Pête! Pête!
> Quand elle se fâche, elle lui répète:
> Pête! Pête! Pête! Pête!
> Pête, veille, en attendant.[41]

Like many of his well-intentioned ilk, Xavier Thiriat, writing about the Vosges in the late 1860's, stressed the vulgar character of native songs as opposed to "those coming from big cities and written in our time," which he found "well inspired and true expressions of noble sentiments."[42] Such feelings were the stronger among professional carriers of civilization and literacy: the teachers.* Songs, like other forms of popular culture, were best shed, and the sooner the better. "All one hears in our countryside," grumbled one would-be reformer in 1860, were "coarse and impure songs...trivial melodies...obscene and demoralizing lyrics." The local youth going to veillées, grumbled a minister in the Pyrenees, made the valleys ring with their powerful discordant voices, "entuning warlike and erotic songs, which happily they do not always understand." These could be replaced by edifying hymns to God and nature; perhaps the schools could wean them from their bad ways. A teacher agreed: the songs that would improve morals, refine feelings, ennoble the spirit, develop intellect, were completely unknown. Schoolteachers (wrote Paul Bordes) had to realize that it was their duty, nay their mission, to propagate such songs.[43] They did.

---

* Consider this remark in Charles Robert, *Plaintes et voeux présentés par les instituteurs publics en 1861*, p. 104: "Que dire de ces chansons obscènes ou à double sens vendues les jours de foire sur la place publique de la ville voisine et importées au village quelquefois par les pères de famille eux-mêmes pour y faire lire leurs enfants. Elles sont chantées le soir à la veillée et commentées sans réserve devant les jeunes filles."

In 1864 a school inspector in the department of Aude proudly reported that "the lewd songs that wounded even the least modest ears have been replaced by the religious and patriotic choirs of numerous *orphéons* [choral societies] due to schools and the initiative of teachers." Under the Republic, such virtuous but isolated efforts turned into nationwide campaigns. Jules Simon, Minister of Public Instruction in 1872, had been struck by the vulgar airs and stupid lyrics of the songs workers or peasants sang when they got together. He sought to remedy this, namely by distributing songbooks for use in schools, and making singing lessons an important part of the elementary school curriculum. In these songbooks, which followed German models, were concentrated songs that were plainly designed to inculcate a sense of the fatherland, of civilization, and of moral ideals. So effective was this program that by the mid-1880's we begin to hear the hills echoing no longer with lewd ditties but with the songs of Paul Déroulède yelled out by enthusiastic schoolboys. Songs learned at school, noted a gratified Félix Pécaut in 1894, were beginning to replace among adult youth "the bad songs that have been too current in France."[44]

The schools had an important collaborator—the orphéon, which was often in fact conducted by the teacher. To Amédée Reuchsel, one of the great apostles of the singing creed, there was no more socially useful profession than that of choirmaster. Singing together had great moral and intellectual value, "provided popular singing can be raised from mere musical stuttering to a level of artistic expression that reflects the refinements and the progress of musical taste."[45]

Orphéons and more typically working-class singing societies began to appear in Paris and in Nord during the Restoration and spread through the rest of France after the 1850's. About 1,000 such groups were founded during the nineteenth century, but few proved really lasting, and fewer still got close to the rural level. Reuchsel found only 58 orphéons that were founded before 1880 still going in 1906; 15 of these were in the north, 8 in Paris or the Paris suburbs, 5 in Lyon, 3 in Toulouse, 17 in other departmental capitals, and the remaining 10 in fairly important provincial towns.[46] (See Map 20.) A similar impression is left by an examination of the Associations file of Pyrénées-Orientales, which shows that every choir in the department was in either a cantonal or a district town. Most, moreover, dated from the 1890's; the earliest listed was founded in 1886. Such singing groups were instruments of the official culture.* Even in Nîmes, Marseille, and Montpellier, where

* True, Michelle Perrot indicates the role of local singing groups in the program of meetings held by striking workers or in putting on shows to raise strike funds. But I would argue that this was part, at least, of a process of "negative integration" in the cultural life of the wider nation. The more so, since such programs usually began with "La Marseillaise" and ended with the "Chant du Départ." (*Ouvriers en Grève,* 2: 529.) More typical in my view was the situation at Douai (Nord), where in the 1870's the posh Société Chorale was rivaled by an orphéon whose singers belonged to the "popular classes" and whose performances were found "rather laughable"

Map 20. Orphéons (choral societies) dating from 1821–1880 extant in 1906.
SOURCE: Amédée Reuchsel, *L'Education musicale populaire: L'Art du chef d'orphéon* (Paris, 1906), pp. 139–41.

workingmen had separate societies and sang works in local dialect of their own devising, they avoided public performances of "songs in the vulgar tongue." When Louis Napoleon visited Aix-en-Provence in 1852, attempts to organize a performance of Provençal songs for his benefit failed. The

by upper-class cognoscenti. Nevertheless, the orphéonistes competed against other singing societies in neighboring towns, and when they won, the great bell of the city tolled for their triumph. The victorious singers reentered their town in a triumphal procession, and flowers were thrown at the open carriages in which they proceeded, behind a band, to the town hall, where they were fêted at a *vin d'honneur*. (Madame Camescasse, *Souvenirs*, pp. 83–85.) This sounds like very positive integration indeed in the rituals of the official culture.

choirs sang fragments from operas and comic operas, and original songs in French by local composers.[47] Cultural snobbery, or refusal to play an exotic role? The result was the same.

In the countryside, however, all this took much longer. Not that resistance was deliberate; it hung on communications, facilities, and restricted means. Traditional songs went with poverty and isolation, and depended heavily on the survival of traditional carriers of song. As the activities of these carriers declined, country songs, like country veillées, gave way. In 1873 we hear that beggars had become few in Forez and Velay, and that they no longer sang while begging. In Brittany in the 1880's minstrels and bards were being pressed back by the "civilization" attendant on roads and railways, and traditional songs were receding before city ones. Fiddlers and bagpipers added more and more music hall pieces to their repertory. At country weddings, remarked a folklorist in 1881, one seldom heard anything but sentimental love songs that had been fashionable in towns a score of years before. Not all who sang them understood what they said. We hear about a Provençal five-year-old who learned by heart a French ballad, which he sang over and over to his father's pride, and in which he was almost letter perfect, though he did not understand a word of it and could not have said what any of it meant.[48] But the eventual outcome of the new tendency was predictable.

In the late 1880's peddlers, sabotiers, and rag-and-bone men were thinning out fast, and native poetry and song waned with them. Flax and homemade linen gave way to factory-made goods, fewer songs were spun along with flax, and by 1905 we hear that the last bastions of Breton songs—Tréguier, Lannion, Morlaix, Guingamp—have fallen to French. In Lot local dialect songs were still sung at harvest time and Carnival in the 1880's but were otherwise going out, perhaps as a direct result of greater material comfort.[49]

The old conscript songs faded out, too. Many had been in local dialect; others, in French, had referred to conditions of military service that changed after 1889. Around 1900 observers noted the disappearance of these traditional tunes and their replacement by songs on more general themes, such as drinking, with no local flavor or particular character of their own. Albert Dauzat considered that patois songs disappeared in Auvergne and were replaced by French ones by the end of the century. Julien Tiersot, who worked in the Alps and in Dauphiné about that time, could not find a single song in once-isolated Bourg-d'Oisans that was truly popular. In roughly the same period, Francis Pérot noted the rapid disappearance of popular and native melodies in Bourbonnais.[50]

Everywhere it seems that itinerant singers and musicians who went from fête to fête had forgotten the old songs and verses. In any case, the young, school-taught, despised them. "No one knows old country songs or sees the old local dances. . . . The eternal trumpet repeats the same musical tunes everywhere, and the city slippers of the peasant girls shuffle in the same slow waltz."

Café-concerts, once the preserve of wealthier places, made their appearance in lesser towns. Peasants started attending them, now that they had the means, and brought the new saws home. Greater exposure to this "high-class" singing, backed up sometimes by a gramophone, began to affect the singing at the feasts. Tillage songs and banquet songs, henceforth in French (at least in basically French-speaking areas), reflected the repertory of the *café-concert.* Standards of singing rose, but voices did not improve; so fear of ridicule began to hamstring those who had never hesitated to start up a tune. Specialization took another step, and, in due course, the habit of singing itself declined as professionalism and technology took over.[51]

But though I believe singing did truly decline in the general and evolutionary sense, and especially with the advent of radio between the wars, the process was surely a slow and patchy one. Allegations that people were singing less than of yore go back at least to the beginning of the nineteenth century, and seem simply a way of saying that things were not what they used to be in the speaker's youth. France differed in its many corners, as we know. Where songs and singing were anchored in local ways, they endured a long time—as in Brittany. When President Carnot was murdered in 1894, a ballad appeared—the "Gwerz ar Président Carnot"—to mark the event; another, in 1896, detailed a drunken murder at Locquenolé (Finistère). As late as 1961 an anonymous Breton composed a gwerz called "Emgann Montroulez" (the Battle of Morlaix) to tell the story of the great artichoke war in which the peasants clashed with the sub-prefect.[52]

As the report of a song-gathering mission intimated as early as 1883, the Breton bards were getting old and dying out. But Frances Gostling still encountered them in Finistère in 1906:

At the pardon on Trinity Sunday, the ragged bards assemble at Rumengol from far and near. I recall one of them sitting with his wife behind a stall piled high with leaflet songs. The couple were singing with all their might to a group of young peasants who, having bought the words, were thus learning the tunes traditionally, as they had probably been handed down for many a generation.... The young folks wanted tunes ... to sing to those songs with which the pockets of their sky-blue jackets were already bulging.

Here are the familiar figures peddling their own songs wherever crowds assembled, often by way of printed broadsheets prepared at their dictation; and it is true that they are old. Yet Yann Brekilien quotes a number of younger songmakers who were active at the turn of the century and before the First World War.[53] The school that taught the Bretons French also taught them how to read and write. Thereafter, the songmaking tradition could bear fruit on paper, the singing public could actually read the words. What changed was less the bent to singing than the subject of the songs, hence their cultural baggage. There is no evidence that other parts of France still produced songs *spontaneously* to mark the exploits of political encounters or the appointment of new Prime Ministers. But the very use of such themes suggests that a once-isolated land had joined the community of other Frenchmen.*

A similar development, in which national forms and themes penetrated native ones, seems to have occurred in dancing. Simple to learn, rhythmic sometimes to the point of binding participants in a common spell, traditional dancing was a fundamentally collective enterprise. Every dancer attended on every other one, did what everyone did in a jogging communion where all were part of the same mass and lived the same experience. In traditional dances, every dancer carried by the joint enterprise is freed of personal initiative, responsibility, even self-consciousness, released into the sort of physical and psychic euphoria that makes dancing such a special pleasure. A dancing that heartens and thrills and stimulates, fascinates and inspirits, can serve multiple functions: magic, as at Carnival to ensure a good crop of flax or on May eve to placate the fairies; religious, to honor saints and their feasts; ceremonial, as at marriages; utilitarian, as a way of pounding the loam of a threshing floor; above all, perhaps, recreational.[54]

Hard physical work demands relief, not, it appears, in relaxation but in contrasting agitation; and dancing throughout the nineteenth century had the reputation of providing such relief. Dancing broke weariness—*cassait la fatigue*—and most backbreaking toil tended to strike a balance with a dance. Industrial workers relaxed by dancing tirelessly on Sundays and, sometimes, immediately after their work. This was even more striking in the countryside, partly perhaps because of the sensible tendency (followed in veillées) to combine the useful and the pleasant whenever possible. Harvesting, threshing, and pulling up or trampling crops, all gave rise to dances and to fêtes. These have been studied most thoroughly in Brittany by Jean-Michel Guilcher, and I have drawn most of my instances from his work. But though Brittany is richer in traditional dances than most regions, the examples to be found there seem fairly representative of a world where hard work and hard play went together.

In those parts of Brittany where several villages got together come September to pull each other's beets, there would be dancing at night two or three times a week. These autumn *arrachages*, now gone, are still remembered as the season of "night feasts." Perhaps the simple gathering of unwontedly large numbers produced a festive mood comparable to that of a fair or feast. This was most obvious during the grain harvest, which saw the hardest and most

* Raymond Doussinet mentions a violently anti-British ballad in connection with the Boer War that circulated in the Charentes at the turn of the century (*Les Travaux et les jeux*, p. 497). Likewise in back-country Var song-sellers hawked ballads about the Russo-Japanese and Turko-Italian wars, the sinking of the *Titanic*, various famous local crimes, and the like. Comments Léon Sénéquier: "Ainsi, par ce moyen, la jeunesse des coins les plus réculés pouvait chanter ce qui se chantait dans les villes quelques semaines auparavant" (*Connaissance de La Garde-Freinet*, p. 67).

prolonged labor of the year. This enterprise also brought together untoward numbers of workers. Not only did it culminate in harvest feasts, but the gangs of itinerant harvesters seem to have followed each day's toil with boisterous dancing. We even hear of troops of women laborers who came down from Flanders to work around Dunkirk at harvest time toward the end of the Second Empire and who, their labor ended, every evening "give themselves over to almost fantastic and prolonged dances, despite the fatigues of the day; they rigorously exclude any man from their sport." This last was indeed a "peculiar trait," as J. A. Barral has put it, and suggests the therapeutic aspect of such play.[55]

Most of the time, dancing was an integral part of the courting ritual; witness the many places where engaged or married couples simply did not join in the dance. At most veillées the elders watched while the young danced. Breton yarn-and-spinning parties seem to have been reserved for the single young. In a Languedoc village we hear that the village feast was largely viewed as an opportunity to bring out marriageable lads and lasses, and was the function where most of the older villagers had found their spouse. "Those engaged and the young married couples do not dance. They have already found."[56]

Yet dancing was also fun, and Bretons found ingenious ways of linking fun and labor. Threshing the grain was followed by dancing; but the winnowing process was itself a collective dance—the *amblendadeg*, in which participants, barefoot or wearing unstudded sabots, trampled the *sarrasin* (buckwheat) to free it of the last bits of rind still clinging to the kernel. So were the *fest al leur nevez*, in which a new threshing floor was pounded down, and similar dances held to level out an earthen floor for a new house. This sort of thing was hard work, and the expression *poania da zansal*—to toil at dancing—reflects it. But it had its uses, and it would endure as long as buckwheat was the principal grain and bare earth the only flooring.[57]

People with limited means who danced a good deal, and often spontaneously, had to provide their own cadence. One Pyrenean mayor in 1838 complained that he could not hold a dance on the anniversary of the July Revolution because he could not find musicians. Most people seem to have done without musicians for a good while longer. At Ligardes (Gers) the dancing song (*cansoun dansadero*) was replaced by instruments during the July Monarchy: first fife and tambourine, then hurdy-gurdy or violin. But Ligardes, though hardly urban, was the chief bourg of a canton, and smaller places presumably waited longer.[58]

In Vendée the violin was beginning to be heard in the little town of Beauvoir-sur-Mer in 1868, but in the surrounding areas "the peasants remain true to their ancient habit of dancing *rondes* while singing." In the Basque country village lads learned their dance steps on the threshing floor of evenings, with one youth singing or whistling appropriate songs while the dancing master put his students through their paces. This only waned in the twentieth century. In any case one, two, or three itinerant musicians served a fairly large area and were sometimes unavailable because several functions coincided. Some regions—Trégor, Léon—appear to have had no instruments (outside the towns) until the appearance of the accordion. In others the owners of such instruments as there were—bagpipes, fifes, fiddles, or oboe-type woodwinds like the *bombarde* of Morbihan—performed only for a fee. Feasts with musicians had greater prestige, but a good many weddings relied on invited or hired singers, and people had no less fun. It is hard to tell, but I am inclined to think that vocal accompaniment, ranging upward from a simple tra-la-la, was pretty much the rule for peasant dances other than substantial marriages and important feasts until quite late in the century. *Sonneurs* and *ménétriers* continued to be rare until the 1890's, and their passing through a village still an event that gathered crowds.[59]

Dancing was simple and simple to learn. Complex traditional forms, like those of some Basque dances, called for special training. But most local repertory was limited, and the same movements recurred over and over. Children saw the local dances endlessly repeated, assimilated them, copied and imitated the steps, and were gradually permitted to join in. Initiation was easy, and novices did not stand out much, since the traditional dances were collective, danced in the round (*branle* or *ronde*) or in two facing lines (*bourrée*). The dancers held hands or clasped their neighbors' shoulder or waist, repeating the same moves and steps, which soon became an almost automatic motion. Guilcher has noted the predominance of the use of the closed circle, facing inward, capable of admitting an unlimited number of dancers and also of excluding the rest of the world. The steps and rhythms used in the circle were generally simple: the common gesture of one local group reinforcing its unity as much as or more than church attendance, and also differentiating it from other groups. Like a circle, a chain was capable of taking any number of dancers, even up to a thousand, as sometimes happened in those Breton marriages in which every guest but the destitute paid for his share, and the dance became practically one with the community.[60]

All this persisted through most of the nineteenth century (and into our time in rural parts of Brittany or the Landes). When, in the late 1880's and the early 1890's, Trébucq scoured the Vendée, "mounted on [his] swift bicycle," he still found lads and lasses dancing jigs in the round, "singing and gesticulating with irresistible animation." About the same time, an English wayfarer described the loud, stomping bourrées he watched at a Lozère village inn, danced to the accompaniment of singing and whistling.* But the tradi-

---

* Sylvain Trébucq, *La Chanson populaire et la vie rurale*, 1: 8; Edward Barker, *Wandering by Southern Waters*, pp. 284–87. But Barker noted that the only females who participated were the maidservants. "In these villages and small towns the girls are kept out of harm's way." Furthermore, "the priests wherever they have influence ... set their faces strongly against dancing by the two sexes."

tional collective jigs and shuffles encountered growing competition from the modern style of dancing in pairs. At Lille and Nancy under the Second Empire young people were still joining hands in collective song-dances in the streets. But gradually adults were leaving these to adolescents, and they in turn began to leave them to children. In Gers the beaten earth that had been good enough for the old hops had to give way to parquet flooring and to the relative constraints of dancing indoors. Local roundelays were being overborne by "wanton" waltzes, polkas, and schottisches. The dancers had learned the steps from soldiers who returned from military service under the July Monarchy, and "nearly all the young people would have thought to lose face if they had not followed their lessons." In Morvan it was young men returning from Paris in the 1870's who introduced new dances that in due course replaced the square dance and the jig. In Lot by 1880 all that one knew was "ballroom dances," especially quadrilles. In Doubs by 1889 even "pretty quadrilles" were going out, replaced by waltzes, polkas, and mazurkas. In Corrèze in 1893 the bourrée had almost been forgotten, and the *montagnarde* was far less popular than it used to be. People preferred quadrilles, polkas, waltzes, and schottisches. In Lorraine "the dances of city people" took over in the 1880's. Children were being taught to perform traditional local dances for their quaintness, but if at some wedding or feast a group began to perform a traditional dance, people would crowd around and watch as if it were a curiosity.[61]

In Lauragais, too, by 1891 "old dances disappear progressively and most already survive only as memories." In the Upper Limousin bourrées survived as oddities; everyone was said to dance waltzes and polkas. In the villages of the Creuse valley even the waltz declined; at the conscript dances of 1913 couples danced polkas and schottisches to the pumping of accordions. In Basque villages dance companies declined after the turn of the century. The young were losing interest in traditional dances, and there was less prestige in performing them. As a result, the old Basque masquerades decayed. Portions were dropped or abridged, and poor dancers or even non-dancers were enrolled for lack of any choice in a vicious circle that inevitably led to withering.[62]

As people began to travel about more, strangers from the outside were more and more likely to be found at what had once been closed communal dances,* and this too affected the repertory. In Dauphiné the traditional rigadoon, danced either to a fiddle or to a simple song, began to share the honors at local dances with more citified forms toward the end of the century, partly, we are told, so strangers could also dance and join in local affairs. Old instruments—bagpipes, or fife and drum—gave way to louder brasses, which helped

---

* At Branches (Yonne) in the old days a stranger who dared attend the village bal was set faceback astride a donkey with the animal's tail between his teeth, to be led for several turns around the dancing area, and then was forced to stand drinks for his tormentors. (M. C. Moiset, "Usages, croyances, traditions," pp. 21–22.)

to eliminate old dancing songs as well. In Auvergne and the Limousin in the 1890's "fiddles and brass supplant the bagpipe and the simple song." By the end of the century, the hurdy-gurdy had been displaced by the accordion, "henceforth the obligatory accompaniment at feasts and dances."[63] The musical repertory necessarily changed; the door to urban influences was opened wider still.*

Those influences led to the founding of numerous rural musical societies in the 1880's and thereafter, which gave regular concerts and "family dances" where young people met, courted, and danced as they once had at veillées. For a smallish village like Changy in Roannais, without many alternatives, the musical society, which was founded in 1891 and lasted into the 1930's, provided an indispensable service. The more indispensable because as veillées declined so did the convenient custom of lads and lasses courting in fields and pastures, which were increasingly enclosed by 1900. Concurrently, the number of dances rose. The formal, organized bals for marriages or feasts could not alone provide adequate social opportunities once veillées disappeared. Young people began to organize informal dances in some barn or in the backroom of a bistro. They also organized dancing societies, which if one can judge by the case of Pyrénées-Orientales were a major preoccupation of the young people for miles around. There they played such an essential role that even traditional feuds gave way before them. In 1896 the mayor of Baixas expressed his delight that youth groups, reconciled around the dancing society, had given up the brawls that turned public places into battlegrounds. In 1900 the youth groups of Céret signed what amounted to a formal treaty, regulating the operations of the dancing society (founded in 1897) and specifying when different bands would be allowed to play. Céret is a district town; Baixas, Thuir, and Bompas are large market towns and administrative centers of their canton. But the bicycle (and its precursors) made them accessible to country lads, and in the decade before 1914 more and more farm boys came to own bicycles.[64]

At the same time, the rise of the new dances helped widen the gulf between generations. On the eve of the First World War a Limousin folklorist noted that the bourrée was danced only by mature persons, the young disdaining it. It also helped widen the gulf between the traditional and urbanized elements in the countryside. Peasants who had danced a great deal at local veillées and feasts found themselves embarrassed and often ill-at-ease before the newfangled (and ever-growing number of) urban dances. They danced them

* The disappearance of once-familiar instruments produced strange etymological effects. In Sologne the popular urban ceremony of the procession of the *boeuf gras* during Carnival had been taken up by a good many rural bourgs. At Yvoy-le-Marron, a village of Loir-et-Cher, the fatted ox had been paraded around to the accompaniment of a hurdy-gurdy and came to be called the *boeuf viellé*. By the turn of the century, with the *vielle* abandoned and forgotten, the term had lost its sense, and people now used the incomprehensible *boeuf violet*. (Bernard Edeine, *La Sologne*, 2: 799.)

badly, if at all, and they perceived more strongly than ever their inferiority to urban standards, even those adhered to by their more affluent neighbors.[65] In any case, much of the original point of dancing had by the turn of the century drained away. Once upon a time dancing had reconciled the public and private, rite and relief, the affirmation of group unity and the expression of individual personality. Now all the public ritual aspects of dancing began to lose their force, the collective character disappeared, and the sport became simply a form of personal gratification taken in company.

Most important, perhaps, the functional aspects of dancing had been seeping away. People had danced on certain pilgrimages, in certain processions, in or outside the church—as David once danced before the Ark of the Covenant. The *tripettes* of Provence, a sort of jig designed to drive out the falling sickness (*mal caduc*), were still being danced around Manosque in the 1890's. One danced around the bread oven, around the hearth, between the vines. Participants and observers understood the homeopathic virtues of leaps and bounds designed to make the crops grow high, of mimicry that simulated work gestures: sowing or reaping or pressing the grapes. At Saint-Marcel-d'Ardèche, on the patron saint's day, in barren mid-January, the villagers put up a mast topped with a bunch of evergreen and danced around it, singing:[66]

> Plantaren la frigoulo et jamaï blan-bé l'arabara.
> Faren la farandoula et la mountagne flourira!

Sympathetic magic or exorcism, dancing had a powerful share in it.

Then fertilizer came in, and rat poison, agronomy, medicine—and schools, of course—and this sort of dancing lost its practical sense: it became simply a show, for fun. The local dances no longer had a function to perform; and so they could be abandoned more easily, since (their functional purpose abandoned or rejected) they compared badly with their modern competitors. What had been an accessory, mere dancing, took over from the original purpose, which was gradually forgotten. And at that stage city dances were clearly better. They always had been "better" and more desirable, but they had also been relatively inaccessible. When all could find access to the instruments that played their music and to the parquet floors that facilitated their steps, all could agree that this was progress—especially the girls!

With the suspension of most festivities for four and often five years during the war of 1914, the young ceased to learn such traditional dances as were still to be found. Veterans returned to their village bringing new "American" dances, and these soon became the new crazes of the young. Traditional dances survived fitfully among the aged, but they were old, just as polkas and mazurkas were now "old."[67] No longer a social rite, dancing turned into simple amusement.

Chapter Twenty-seven

LE PAPIER QUI PARLE

I love a ballad in print, a-life, for then we are sure they are true.
—SHAKESPEARE

WE COME NOW to an obvious question affecting popular culture, and one of the most difficult, despite the attention it has received: when and how reading matter affected the common man. The printing press stands at the entrance of the modern world as dragons guard the gateway of a temple. But who, in nineteenth-century France, had access to the temple of the printing press? The answer is, surprisingly many people, for one need not read to enjoy its products. Yet printing was an urban art par excellence; it disseminated texts, images, ideas, that had been formulated by urban minds. Like printed songs, these often became popular in terms of their acceptance. They were not necessarily so by birth.

Books are the obvious representatives of printed culture, and the most obvious inhabitants of the town. By the Restoration books could be bought in general stores, at the grocer's, or from old-clothes merchants and second-hand-furniture men, all of whom often sold primers, calendars, almanacs, and prayerbooks, and some of whom also lent them.[1] There were few public libraries and they were little used. When, under the Restoration, the prefect of Nièvre borrowed the keys to the library at Nevers, he kept them for a year and even then was asked to return them only because "a second inquirer had appeared." When and where libraries began to be frequented, as at Lille, they remained the preserve of cultivated men and local scholars, a kind of sanctuary where *blouses* and sabots would have been looked on askance.[2] Reading rooms run for profit were even more inaccessible, not only in terms of cost, but also in purely physical terms, since like the bookshops, they were all located in better parts of town. Beginning in the 1820's various initiatives were launched to produce "good" books—Christian, moralizing, frequently saccharine—and these works were widely distributed by philanthropists and by the clergy. Serious efforts were made to get them into the hands of men, and sometimes even women, of the working class. But the scanty evidence suggests that they reached mostly the middle class and those aspiring to join it. The poorer inhabitants of urban centers, assuming that they could read, lacked the privacy in which to read a book, the light by which to read it, and most probably also the time and energy to attempt it.[3]

This only really changed with the 1860's, when "popular libraries" in bigger industrial towns battled for the opportunity to capture the popular mind; when rival lending libraries, some "Red," some Catholic, clashed in political struggles that reveal the existence of a working-class reading public; and when the authorities in small provincial towns reported the spontaneous founding of "savings societies" for collective subscriptions to newspapers. But once again, practically all the evidence and all the figures concerning this ill-documented field apply to urban centers.[4] By 1890 there were 11 "popular libraries" serving the 758 communes of the Limousin. School libraries, of course, were far more numerous—333 in 1877 for 396 public schools—but even they lent out only an average of 30 books a year until the 1880's.[5]

The Second Empire witnessed a revolution in printing processes that made it possible to produce books on thinner paper and in smaller type, developments that greatly diminished their bulk, hence their cost, and encouraged competition to sell them more cheaply. Even so, novels, children's books, and other "respectable" works selling at a price equivalent to one or two days' wages were not aimed at the working class, but at the small bourgeoisie. Charles Nisard, whose *History of Popular Books*, published in 1854 and re-edited a decade later, remains our richest source, was impressed by the growing thirst for printed matter, which permitted publishers to get rid of their unsold stocks. In 1853 some nine million books seem to have been distributed yearly. But when we hear about the go-ahead workingmen buying books —Agricol Perdiguier or Pierre Gilland—what they purchased were the street vendors' products, "little booklets at 30 centimes, spread out on walls or on the parapet of bridges: abridgements of Robinson Crusoe, Telemachus, Paul and Virginia, Bayard's life," or Aesop's fables.[6] The workers' tastes in reading material presumably lagged behind those of the more widely read bourgeois. They read much the same books that the peasants read, but fewer peasants read any books at all.

An imperial prefect of Nièvre once remarked that if books were strewn on the roads, no one would pick them up. And at that, he seems to have been thinking not of the peasants, but of the bourgeoisie.[7] Could it have been because peasants not only did not read books, but simply did not read? In 1860–61, as part of a contest set up by the Ministry of Education, thousands of schoolteachers responded to questions concerning local reading habits. A study of 1,207 of these responses, the cream of those received, reveals (expectably) that reading was extremely rare (13 positive observations), and that the reading of novels was almost nonexistent. What evidence of interest there is comes primarily from the north and northeast, the Paris region, Côte-d'Or, and Bouches-du-Rhône. But a report from Eure-et-Loir gives us a clue: "No one reads in the countryside, and bad books get there more than good ones." So perhaps no one read, but there were books. Only they were bad: "bad books swarm in the countryside" (Ardennes); "immoral serials" (Somme); "almanacs—a collection of tales as absurd as they are insignificant" (Loiret); "cheap serials...poison our countryside" (Seine-et-Oise); "only the Almanac" (Eure, Seine-Inférieure, Moselle); "frivolous and pernicious books" (Yonne); "almanacs and songbooks" (Aveyron); "those who know how to read own a missal, the almanac, sometimes the tale of the four Aymon brothers" (Dordogne).[8] And so it goes.

Other snippets of evidence are gleaned from routine official sources. "Right now," a teacher of Saône-et-Loire reported in 1864, "one doesn't read at all in the countryside, neither good books nor bad." The same for the Pas-de-Calais, apart from a little during the winter period of veillées. In 1866 the mayor of Senez (Basses-Alpes) responded to an inquiry on reading tastes in his area: "I have the honor to tell you that one doesn't read in the commune." The prefect of Seine-et-Marne, confronted with the same problem, found the situation perplexing: "The number of our country people who like to read is so small that it is quite difficult to understand their taste." We have already glimpsed this taste, but it was obviously not what it should have been. What the people liked and what they should get were, on the whole, different things. This can be seen in the works housed in school libraries. Practically unused and as good as nonexistent when the 1860's opened, school libraries numbered 4,800 by 1866 and 14,395 by 1870. In that same five-year period their loan rate rose fivefold. A good deal of that increased use, however, probably most of it, reflected urban readership. In the countryside, as a report from Morbihan explained in 1866, only schoolchildren borrowed books. Otherwise, "the books lack readers even more than the readers lack books." For one thing—reports from Finistère, Côtes-du-Nord, and Corsica confirm it—most people did not know French, and of those who did, half at least did not know how to read.[9] But then, why should they have bothered?

An elementary school inspector from Aix explained in 1864: "The country people who turned to the teacher to obtain these books [from school libraries] are...very alike to children; hence the books that are meant for children suit them perfectly."[10]

For children or adults, then, school libraries offered sound knowledge and indoctrination into the new world's ways. The mayor of Senez, when he had reported that no one in his area read, had volunteered the thought that if people did read, they would like books of stories. The prefect of Seine-et-Marne had pointed out the enormous popularity of the "little press"—*Journal de la Semaine, du Dimanche, du Jeudi*—with its tales and news and gory or sentimental serials. But this was too debased. Book lists submitted by teachers or departmental groups for their libraries consisted above all of agricultural, scientific, and historical works. Could that kind of fare be why books lacked readers; why in 1866, two years after the school library of Ocagnano (Corsica) had received a fine collection of (French) books, their pages were still uncut; why in 1878 the educational inspector reported from Allier that the work of school libraries "progressed slowly" when the figures he gave showed that readership had actually fallen?[11] The books were of no interest to the local people.

We shall see that by this time things were beginning to change, and it is precisely the change that interests us. But change from what? We have already heard what reading matter the peasant liked, and the authorities kept a wary eye on it. At the very beginning of the nineteenth century, we hear about those "small writings ... that are the library of the poor and the first books of childhood": almanacs, calendars, yearbooks, chapbooks, collections of tales and stories, songs, prophecies, canticles, ballads, accounts of recent events and judgments of criminal courts, primers, and the *Croix de Dieu*.[12] By the July Monarchy "demagogic books" were joining these in being hawked through the countryside: accounts of trials and songs with political overtones, speeches attributed to leaders of the Great Revolution, Republican catechisms, and so on.[13]

As for those who distributed them, we have already encountered one of the principal figures—the itinerant peddler with his backpack, sometimes accompanied by a little monkey, displaying his wares at fairs, on the farm threshold, or in the village square. His pack always contained prints, tracts, chapbooks —sometimes in the false bottom of a box. There were, besides, professional ballad singers, sometimes doubling as beggars, with their stock of flysheets; and rag-pickers who took a hand in the same trade. There was a peculiar breed of saint exhibitors, men who trod the roads with their "saint" in a small cupboard on their backs. Some were Italians, with a wax doll in a glass case dressed in finery and surrounded by artificial flowers; and many were charlatans who represented their figurine to be whatever saint was venerated in the locality where they stopped, and sold color prints and pious objects—chaplets, medals—made holy by simple contact with it.[14] There were men from Chamagne, the Lorraine village where Claude Gelée the painter had been born. Chamagnon families left their village every autumn, the man carrying a small chest on his back that opened into a triptych. The center panel showed the Virgin or the Crucifixion, and one of the flanking panels held a picture of Saint Hubert. The wife and children carried merchandise. In villages the triptych was displayed on a table, and while the man commented on its pictures, the family sold the medals, chaplets, tracts, and images in their stock. Such entrepreneurs were generally known as *montreurs*.* In

---

* Augustin Dubois, *Les Anciens Livres de colportage*, p. 2. The parish registers of Chamagne show that some 3,000 passports were issued to peddlers between 1850 and 1870. See also Jean Vartier, *La Vie quotidienne en Lorraine*, chap. 6.

Burgundy, where the cult of Saint Reine was widespread, there traveled around *le montrou de sainte Reine*, who opened the panels of his Gothic-shaped reliquary after singing a long ballad about the saint. Once he had attracted a crowd, he turned to his real business—peddling small pictures of saints, battles of the Empire, Tom Thumb, Cinderella, and Little Red Riding Hood.[15]

In a study of popular imagery we find reproduced the patter used by a montreur of Saint Hubert in 1866, which gives a good idea of the approach:

See here the great Saint Philomenar who was a great saint, that there is no such great miracles that the great Philomenar hasn't done. See here the child Jesus who was born at Bethsalem, who was the son of the great all-powerful God, who redeemed us of our sins, who died on the cross for us, that there is no such great miracles that the child Jesus hasn't done. See here the great Saint Reine, that the pagans massacred who was a great saint. See here the great Saint Peter, who has the keys to paradise, hence that our Lord gave to him, that there is no such great miracles that the great Saint Peter hasn't done. See here the good father of Martincourt [Mattaincourt, in Vosges] who's healed all sorts of ills, that there is no such great miracles that the good father hasn't done. See here the great Saint Hubert, who was the greatest of all hunters. He was hunting in Arden forest when our Lord appeared to him a great day of Good Friday, hence that each and every one must evoke against plague, accident, thunder, and mad dogs. Hence that each and every one shall be kept safe forever and will go straight to heaven if he wears on him the medal of the great Saint Hubert, that there is no such great miracles that the great Saint Hubert hasn't done.[16]

We may laugh at the level of this approach, but it sold the crowd, and especially, it appears, when the pictures being peddled portrayed saints or Biblical scenes. Three-quarters of the pictures that survive today are religious. This may be because they were treated with more respect than others. Many were pinned or pasted inside a chest lid or cupboard door to become the centerpiece of a small, personal altar; others were attached under the lids of boxes containing money or something else considered rare and precious, like letters. Yet such pictures were also commonly pinned or sewn to hat or clothes (which could hardly have contributed to their preservation), or nailed to a wall, a bedboard, or the mantelpiece, or put up in the stable. The saints provided personalized protection—for self, for home, for precious objects, for the cattle. Guardian images, *images de preservation*, were everywhere, and so was the Crucifixion, reminder that the peasant's difficult life was nothing when compared with the Passion of Christ.[17] There was even a Saint Napoleon, printed in 1842 and reprinted in 1869, representing "under a rather unexpected aspect," as an official commented, the image of Napoleon surrounded by flowers and by female saints playing the harp.*

---

* Archives Départementales, Vosges 9 bis M17 (Apr. 1874). A prolonged search under the First Empire had uncovered a Saint Neopolis or Neopolas, martyred in Alexandria under Diocle-

So popular were religious images that in popular parlance all printed pictures became "saints" or "saint sheets." A child got a centime to go and buy a saint even if the picture he bought represented a war scene or a fable. "What saint do you want?" asked the peddler. "I want animals," answered the child. He could have asked for battles; or for the soldiers' uniforms that helped recruit volunteers for the army; or for the Wandering Jew; or for Lustucru, the legendary blacksmith who cut off women's heads and forged them new ones; or for Saint Fainéante (Saint Idle), which was supposed to warn against the evils of idleness but actually publicized its pleasures.[18] Other hot-selling items were *Goodman Misery*, who had trapped death itself in his magic pear tree; *The Great Devil Money*, patron of financiers; *The World Turned Upside Down*; *The Art of Dying Well*, with demons thronging around a deathbed, lusting for one more soul; and *Credit Is Dead*, with droll illustrations of all those who killed him. Taste was eclectic and the image-decorated house appears in many prints, as in contemporary novels. Balzac, with his usual eye for truth, tells us of the darkened walls whose only ornament consisted of those illuminated images in blue, red, and green that show the death of credit, the Passion of Jesus Christ, the grenadiers of the imperial guard.[19]

That was just on the eve of the great tide of cheap, popular images about to sweep over France during the July Monarchy and the Second Empire, and generally associated with Epinal in the Vosges, where by 1842 the firm of J.-C. Pellerin alone turned out 875,000 prints a year. Pellerin and another Epinal firm between them are estimated to have produced 17,000,000 such pictures under the Second Empire. Some 40 other printers were active during that time, and pieces of their work were still to be found on the market at the beginning of the twentieth century.[20] But printers and engravers were urban professionals; their models and themes were taken from the towns; even figures of peasants and their accessories of life, when they appear, seem to have derived from urban models.[21] This had always been so, and most of the traditional depictions that issued from a press reflected urban attitudes of one sort or another. But images of earlier days had grown familiar, had had the time to percolate into the rural world and be accepted by it. Contemporary differences in speech or garb or values were another matter. Like *Mrs. Miniver* projected before an audience of Afghans, such pictures could add the spice of exoticism, but the distance between two very different ways of life limited the appeal of many of the images in the countryside.

Some of these prints were inspired by melodramas or operettas. One favorite depicted *La Fille de Madame Angot*. Others dwelt on exemplary themes, with sinners meeting a deserved punishment at the end. Two in this class were

---

tian. A slight adjustment and the fortunate martyr became Saint Napoleon, whose feast, established by an imperial decree of February 19, 1806, was celebrated on August 15—the same day as the feast of the Assumption.

The Catastrophes and Tragic End of the Child-Who-Touches-Everything (1863) and Pellerin's *Two Apprentices* (1864), which was inspired by Hogarth's *Industry and Idleness*, a secular version of Saint Idle's story. Like certain other series of the late 1860's, all rather reminiscent in costume and scenery of the Countess of Ségur's children's novels, these were above all destined for children of the middling and petty bourgeoisie. Other prints of a political nature, like those concerning the grotesque hunchback Monsieur Mayeux, were very popular even among the workers, especially those of Paris, but never caught on in rural areas. The peasants clung to their traditional images and moralities as long as both lasted. Even in 1874 Epinal turned out two different prints to show virtue rewarded. One, urban, had the abandoned bride making her family rich by trade. The other, on the theme of the grasshopper and the ant, showed careful, hard-working Martha being repaid with a proposal of marriage: "Miss Martha my name is Bigarreau. I have my mill that brings me 1,000 *écus* a year. I offer you my hand and my mill." Virtue deserved and brought reward; but the aspirations, values, and possibilities of town and countryside continued to differ into the first decade of the Third Republic.[22]

Whatever the message or presentation, there is little question of the popularity and impact of the form itself. These pictures were the great bibles of the little people. Studied long and attentively by men, women, and especially wondering children who had little else to distract or appeal to them, they left a powerful imprint on people's minds. Anatole France has testified how much he owed to the *images d'Epinal*. Charles Péguy's work is interwoven with it. *The Great Devil Money* shows what he describes in *L'Argent* (1913) as the capitalist bourgeoisie infecting the people: every class, especially commoners, groveling to gather gold coins distributed by the devil. *The Burial of Marlborough* sets off a long discussion of historical analyses in *Clio II*. The images of Saint Joan, so popular in Orléans, inspired Péguy's worship. He even, in an optimistic moment, compared his life to an *image d'Epinal*: "He was little, he worked well, ... he went to school ... and rose in the world."[23] If this was the effect these pictures had on Péguy, what of the semiliterate people who were their major public? They reinforced the common man's hatred of money power; made known the figure of the Jew, unknown in the flesh in most parts of France; reflected the hopeless hopes of misery; stressed the accepted morality of work; and preached traditional virtues, usually along with traditional resignation.

Then came the images of the modern world. Current events and propaganda of every kind began to take over. Even as early as 1848 the government distributed General Cavaignac's picture by the tens of thousands. The following regime did as much for Napoleon III and his family. Pretenders under the Third Republic—Prince Victor Bonaparte, the Comte de Paris, General Boulanger—followed suit. Battles, catastrophes, or notorious figures like Garibaldi were all illustrated in color plates; and in 1899 a print entitled *True and Authentic History of Panama, Jr.* was circulating in Haute-Vienne, a satire of President Emile Loubet under attack as a supporter of Dreyfus.[24] Often such "occasional" prints came accompanied by a ballad that explained the sensational or terrifying event depicted. At this point, traditional and current sensationalism merged in a popular literature especially partial to bloody crimes, fabulous stories, and other daunting things that made the flesh creep like today's horror films—the *canard*.

Canards and *occasionnels*—the former folio sheets, the latter smaller pages— have been dated back to the fifteenth century and the invention of printing. How the *canard* came by its name is uncertain—perhaps from the imperial eagle on Napoleon's battle bulletins. At any rate the term soon came to designate an absurd story addressed to a credulous public. That may be why Balzac in the 1840's wrongly supposed that the newspaper had killed *canards*. Partially right for Paris, he was quite wrong so far as concerned the rural areas, where they circulated by the tens of thousands to the end of the century and sometimes beyond.

Not necessarily sensationalist, *canards* illustrated and discussed news items, carried useful tips (how to make currant syrup or heal the cramps), and provided calendars. Yet they are best remembered for their accounts of curious events and strange beasts, real or imaginary: pirates abducting maidens; the ravages of the great African Terrorifer on Monomotapa's shores; the arrival of an orangutan at the Jardin des Plantes; assassination attempts against the throne; the raising of the obelisk on the Place de la Concorde; wars in distant parts; great fires or mine disasters; the birth or death of princes; wolves devouring children; dogs loyal to their masters to the death; floods; miracles; love or madness, or often as not the two combined, with lovers losing their minds and putting a violent end to life; new railways and their unbridled speed, or better still, a railway engine under heavy steam when a corpse is discovered in a passenger's trunk. Progress, sensationalism, and sanctimoniousness went hand in hand as often as they could—quite happily in the case of comets, when broadsheet legends could rejoice that no one still believed all the ancient humbug, and at the same time recite most of it.[25]

Above all, the *canard* carried events into places where nothing ever seemed to happen, asserting the extraordinary where routine reigned. It spoke to the illiterate or barely literate, as can be seen from titles that are not only lurid, but written to be spoken rather than simply read. Its raw material was timeless: stories and themes were periodically revived, like that of parents who murder their own child without knowing it, a theme that Albert Camus was to use in his *Malentendu*, and that *canards* never exhausted through several centuries. *Canards* did not seek to be up-to-date, but were satisfied to be thrilling; wrote not of the actual but of the sensational. They did attempt to invest news items with some plausibility by giving lots of circumstantial evidence, details of weapons, blows, and wounds. "Horrible murder committed Monday, July 16, in the Rue Traversine upon two persons, one of whom was pierced by eleven blows from a paring knife, while the other had the artery of his right arm cut with a knife." Yet detail can drown out fact. As Jean-Pierre Séguin, a devoted student of the art, has pointed out, *canards* give the month and even the hour of some event, but seldom the year it happened. By way of illustration, he presents one undated *canard* that reads: "Arrest of the priest, La Collonge, vicar of Sainte-Marie, near Beaune, department of Côte-d'Or, accused of having murdered his mistress, who had mothered several of his children, of having cut her into pieces, and of having thrown them into the parish pond, where women found them while doing their laundry." Under this, a large woodcut shows two gendarmes arresting a cheery-looking cleric standing beside a body of water in which one can see a woman's head and hair afloat and, a little farther back, one of her legs. Details and ballad follow.[26]

Priests of course provided particularly succulent morsels, but an attentive reading of *canards* reveals many of the problems, resentments, and prejudices of their readers: greed for the money that middle-class victims of crime have carried or concealed; the suspicion of all strangers and of travelers, who have good cause to fear for their lives themselves; the reluctance to get involved in other people's business (dogs are better than men in giving aid); the venting of collective fury on some victim; the murder of children by parents and of parents by children; gang rapes; innocence condemned and sometimes saved; the unexpectedness of soldiers actually returning home from service; the terror of mad dogs, foxes, or wolves from whose bite until 1885 there was no cure except for the intervention of Saint Hubert; the danger of lonely places. Most country crimes took place in the mountains and woods; but from these accounts the roads and inns were no safer. Above all, fear, fear, fear: of brigands, thieves, rape, fire, hail, floods, rabies, epidemics, violence of all sorts. Were *canards* foils for the regular course of existence, the welcomed contrast of the extraordinary; or do we read a different note in a discussion of Halley's comet in a *canard* of 1835? "It would be pretty ridiculous for men who live quietly in the midst of so many ills constantly menacing them to worry about events as improbable as the destruction of the earth by a comet!"

Worry or no, the incredible tales of *canards* were accepted, skeptically perhaps, but in a context of general ignorance. As a *canard* of 1843 remarked: "What they say in Paris is nothing to what they say in the provinces." There, the huckster's rod pointed out the deliciously lurid details, the ballad was sung, the broadsheet was bought and nailed to the wall at home, "and this simple five-centime sheet terrified all who read it."[27]

But the peddler's pack contained other reading matter: religious works, canticles, psalters, lives of the saints; real books of history or practical advice;

collections of model letters; and, of course, the poisonous writings that we have heard denounced, *The Language of Flowers, The Ladies' Oracle, The Lovers' Catechism, The Key of Dreams,* and other suggestive publications. Above all, it carried the small volumes of what was generally described as the Bibliothèque bleue, smallish, badly printed and barely legible on coarse paper, often unpaginated, and roughly bound in the same bluish paper that was used to wrap sugarloaves. At mid-century these little booklets, with their fables, legends, tales of knightly valor, and, most of all, almanacs, sold at a rate of about 9,000,000 a year. Fairy stories, often taken from folklore and recast in print, were served up in new forms with familiar aspects. Knightly tales had an eager and devoted public.[28] Between 1818 and 1850 some 10,000 copies of the Breton-language version of *The Lay of the Aymon Brothers,* 527 pages long, were sold in the countryside of Lower Brittany.*

But the core of a book collection—particularly if the collection numbered only one—was the almanac. Joseph Cressot has enumerated his peasant grandfather's books, gathered in the decades that ran from Louis Philippe to Sadi Carnot. Most of them are almanacs: big ones, *Almanac des familles, du pèlerin, Le Messager boiteux, Le Bon Laboureur;* small ones, *Almanac du paysan, du vigneron, de la maison rustique;* and the *Bavard* and *Mathieu de la Drôme,* with their calendars, zodiacs, phases of the moon, tasks for the month, collections of proverbs and jokes, recipes, and occasional pictures.[29] Molière's Monsieur Jourdain asks his master to teach him how to read, but he does not want to read just anything, he wants to read the almanac so he will know when there is a moon and when there is none. Behind the satire lurks the reality: the almanac is the simple man's treasury of knowledge. Almanacs were for the poor, for those who had little time, for those with empty purses, for the most modest class that read little, remarks Geneviève Bollème. But in fact one did not need to read in order to tap the secrets of such books; one could still gaze at them, consult them for their signs, whose code was more easily learned than the alphabet, and saved troubling with the latter. No wonder that the men of Plozévet walked to Quimper and back, a 50-km hike in all, just to buy an almanac; that in some places the word came to be used as a synonym for a book (or great book: "le bon Yeu inscrit tout sus soun armanat," they said in Saintonge) or in revealing locutions. Liars in Saintonge were "menteurs coume in'armanat," while Auvergnats ridiculed a loquacious prattler as "bougre d'almanach."[30] The jest, however, cannot conceal a cer-

---

* Yann Brekilien, *Vie quotidienne des paysans en Bretagne,* pp. 91ff. André Burguière, who confirms this, also quotes an old tailor of the Quimpérois who remembered that "in the old days a house without the *Bouhez ar zent* [Book of Saints] was not a very honorable house" (*Bretons de Plozévet,* p. 153). The Bretons also had their own variant of the Wandering Jew—Boudedeo— and composed a host of songs about his perambulations, including an encounter with Goodman Misery. A gwerz on that subject was published at Morlaix as late as 1886 (Champfleury, *Histoire de l'imagerie populaire,* 2d ed., Paris, 1886, p. 71). All this raises intriguing questions about the alleged illiteracy of Breton peasants, whose apparently widespread ability to read Breton did not count as learning in official eyes.

tain appreciation. Books had an intrinsic power; they were magic objects passed from father to son for generations as a treasured possession. Their rarity added to their prestige. "Books have an incredible authority in the peasant's eyes," reported a teacher from Haut-Rhin in 1861. "They are infallible!"* And the book par excellence was the almanac.

In the mid-nineteenth century "15 million Frenchmen learned the history of their country and its laws, the world's great events, the progress of their sciences, their duties, and their rights only through the almanac." Emile de Girardin exaggerated a little, but as a great press magnate he was in a position to know. So were Jules Michelet, Edgar Quinet, and Emile Littré, all of whom sought to reach the people through little almanacs of their own, but without success. The traditional almanacs had won the peasants' hearts. They bought them the moment they appeared, even if they had to borrow the money; they exchanged them among themselves or hired them at a sou a go from an enterprising peddler, and so might have read up to 10 a year. "These little books," reported a teacher from the relatively enlightened Vosges, "are so often exchanged, read, and reread that one can no longer make out the title on the cover."[31] The teacher added that they were no longer read for their predictions: the peasants did not believe these anymore in 1861.† That is as it may be. For me, part of their attraction may be found in a story from the Second World War about the fate of an old copy of the *New York Herald Tribune* in Nazi Germany. Someone had bought it for three bottles of cognac from a Swedish sailor whose ship had berthed in Kiel. "The paper made its way through at least a hundred or more pairs of hands who could neither read nor write, and hardly spoke English. Yet in their hearts they knew that this language ultimately contained a secret and powerful weapon."[32]

Almanacs had their practical uses, but also a talismanic quality; they opened the door to knowledge, traditionally the preserve of the privileged, the urban, the rich. Deprived of books as they were deprived of other material goods, and hence of knowledge, the poor "of the most modest class that reads little" were isolated, cut off from useful things. The almanac provided this. How far was it perceived as a bridge to "culture"? At first, the jumble of information it provided must have made as much sense as a beachcomber's trove. The character of the older popular culture was confusion: the categories were not distinct, chronology was irrelevant, fact and fancy, wonders, and fables mixed

---

* *Bulletin de la Société Franklin*, 4 (1872): 109. Sanford Kanter quotes the remarks of a member of the Commission de l'Instruction Primaire (Archives Nationales, C3129, Jan. 19, 1872) to the effect that Charente peasants had "a sort of superstitious fear of education" and felt that "to teach their children to read would be to turn them into sorcerers" ("Defeat 1871," p. 116). And Philip G. Hamerton wrote of an intelligent young Burgundian peasant who, having no idea of printing, assumed a book was some sort of beautiful manuscript (*Round My House*, p. 278).

† In 1903 we find Henri-Adolphe Labourasse repeating that the almanac had lost much of its credibility (*Anciens us*, p. 184). There must have been a lot of credibility if this still had to be said 40 years later!

together on an equal footing. But gradually urban values took hold. Modern science was first of all about categories. Modern life affirmed that categories were meaningful. Bollème's study of almanacs shows how in the nineteenth century the qualifying terms used in their titles came to emphasize veracity, truth, and genuineness; also size and quantity. As in the official world, fact mattered, at least in the affirmation; and quantity was seen as an aspect of quality. Terms like French (which had appeared timidly in the eighteenth century) and National also gained ground; and—homage to a new sense of modernity and fashion—a number of almanac titles imitated newspapers, with names like *Le National, Le Temps, Le Nouvelliste,* and *Le Courier.*[33] Time was trickling into the domain of the timeless; official knowledge came in with a rush through schools. Schools, books, the spreading skill of reading, were making knowledge accessible, less of a mystery and less rare. The almanac continued to exist, but divested of magic power and prestige. Furthermore, like the veillée, it had combined use and pleasure. The former ebbed as science and its more reliable advice took over. Pleasure remained for some, but separate from use; as in modern life where leisure and work, play and gainful employment, became distinct categories. Defunctionalized, desanctified, the almanac would become a book like any other.

The images and printed matter of the countryside had been the same as those of city folk. A gap had grown between the two as the fare offered the latter became less naive and more up-to-date. This is what marked country reading through much of the nineteenth century, until the gap narrowed and finally, in the twentieth century, vanished. Only a few years after the nineteenth century passed the halfway mark, Nisard, noting the survival of legendary tales in the countryside, was already pronouncing their death sentence. And official inquiries of the 1860's bore him out, showing that they were beginning to disappear, along with those who had hawked them. *Le Figaro* carried an article in its June 28, 1884, issue on Chinese news sheets, which it identified as curious specimens of primitive information.[34] An instance and clear proof of how little the urban literate classes knew about what went on beyond their ken. Not only in small towns and in rural areas, but in Paris itself, many Frenchmen knew no other source of information than news sheets similar to those of the Chinese. But they were becoming hard to find.

A file from Vosges in the 1870's shows a notable change of material in the peddler's pack. He still hawked such things as lives of the saints and accounts of bandits' exploits, but the traditional *canards* had turned to news—*nouvelles intéressantes* of alleged recent crimes. One tract, though still with a portrait of an astrologer on the cover, turns out to offer *Family Readings,* providing a truly "edifying collection" (as the title claims) in commendation of bravery, honor, and devotion to duty. And finally, there was *War Stories: The French Campaign,* detailing some battles of 1870. Traditional fantasy was giving way to contemporary news and to an urban standard of morality. By the 1880's officialdom, which heretofore had interfered mostly for political reasons, began to ban "false or exaggerated" news reports, and headlines screaming of an explosion in Parliament, the suicide of Sarah Bernhardt or of Louise Michel, a catastrophe in some mine.[35] Morality now included greater accuracy.

By then, newspapers were taking over the sensationalist functions of *canards*. The *Petit Journal*, splendid value for one sou, was a sort of *News of the World*: birth of quadruplets, bride gives birth a few hours after wedding, American abandons his bride and goes off with her dowry, sub-prefect falls off his horse. There was easy-to-understand coverage of happenings in Paris and the provinces that lent itself to comment and discussion around the kitchen table, news from abroad (sales of Cuban slaves, the chaining of Russian conscripts), court chronicles (elopements, confidence tricks, vendettas, crimes of passion), accounts of shows, debts, bankruptcies, current market prices (cattle, grain, etc.). One could not ask for more. Yet after 1890 the *Petit Journal's* illustrated supplement (eight pages, five centimes) offered vast front- and back-page illustrations in most glorious color, each with long explanations in print, a much better value than a *canard* or saint sheet. But the Supplement's debt to these is reflected in the subjects that it illustrated—current events (war or entente cordiale) and sometimes public figures, but especially catastrophes, shipwrecks, mining disasters, an automobile attacked by wolves, bloody riots, children defending a shop against *apaches*, a farmer's wife attacked by gypsies, a gamekeeper buried alive by poachers, the gamut of popular taste brought up-to-date.

No wonder the image industry, declining for some time, fell off irremediably in the 1890's. Though as late as the 1880's numbers of women in Bourbonnais were still buying these pictures, after the turn of the century no one bothered; in any case shops handed them out free as an advertising gimmick.* Broadsheets were going out. One of their last heroes would be the mass murderer Tropmann, executed in January 1870. In 1888 Paul Sébillot noted that

---

* Francis Pérot, *Folklore bourbonnais*, p. 108. Of course by then posters were plastered on every street. Indeed, already in 1889 we find the Remiremont municipal council alarmed about the effects of the horrifying or indecent posters seen about (French soldiers decapitated by Chinese; a rapist about to assault his victim, advertising Zola's *La Bête Humaine*)—"provocations that no one can avoid, and that attract the schoolboys more than the classics do" (Archives Départementales, Vosges 9 bis M26, Dec. 1889). The first two exhibitions devoted specifically to posters were in fact held that very year. In 1896 the League for the Uplifting of the Masses, going further than the protest of the Remiremont city fathers, put up large posters of Puvis de Chavannes' *Life of Saint Genevieve* in order to counter the influence of Toulouse-Lautrec's indecent works. But the poster would not be stopped. As Ernest Maindron wrote in his *Les Affiches illustrées* (Paris, 1886), "The museum is in the street, and this is only a beginning" (see Bibliothèque Nationale, *Cinq siècles d'affiches illustrées françaises*, Paris, 1953). Note that posters were not the only new source of public imagery. In this same period the Post Office was beginning to distribute the decorative calendars that were to become a part of every humble home; and firms selling seed, fertilizer, and agricultural equipment were following suit. I know of no study of the role such calendars played in bridging the gap between popular and academic taste.

images and *canards* survived in Lower Brittany (always, to be sure, with Breton captions!). But in Upper Brittany they were scarce; the broadsheets once found everywhere in Finistère or Côtes-du-Nord were now almost non-existent (one could read newspapers). When a notorious woman prisoner, Hélène Jégada, was tried at Rennes and a local printer sought to cash in with a broadsheet, he knew his public well enough to cut costs by using the plate of an advertisement for toothache to portray her. In Bourbonnais the last local criminal to elicit a broadsheet was Madame Achet, at Chantelles, near Moulins in 1891. Tropmann and the assassinated magistrate Antoine Fualdès went on selling: a photograph taken between 1900 and 1914 shows a *marchand de complaintes* singing such wares before his unfolded canvas. Frédéric Le Guyader assures us that in 1914 the type remained a fixture of the Breton fairs, where images also continued to be sold. Yet when in 1911 we are told that these items had become objects of interest for artists and amateurs, we know that their survival was anachronistic and exceptional.[36] Like noble shepherdesses at Versailles, the intellectuals took up *canards* and the Bibliothèque bleue as sources of inspiration. "The people," now pretty well all the people, preferred the papers and their color supplements.

The contents of the peddler's pack changed, then vanished like the peddler himself. It is hard to tell if these wares preceded him into oblivion; but as a general pattern the improved roads and means of transportation that encouraged the growth of peddling activities soon also resulted in more numerous stores, including bookstores; and in the penetration of Paris print into hitherto printless regions. Already in 1866 a report on the subject concluded that the peddler book trade was disappearing "bit by bit under the impact of the facilities the book trade manages to set up in the smallest localities."[37] That seems premature. A map drawn up by Alain Corbin shows that the number of bookstores in his three Limousin departments increased as follows between 1851 and 1879: Creuse, from 15 to 36; Haute-Vienne, from 20 to 47; and Corrèze, from 13 to 19. Either way, this is not many outlets for departments whose population in 1863 ran between 270,000 (Creuse) and 320,000 (Haute-Vienne). Since, as we might expect, bookstores were heavily concentrated in the prefectures, the other parts of the departments had few indeed. Corrèze has 289 communes and 30 cantons. Half its booksellers were concentrated in Brive and Tulle, and all the rest were divided among only five other localities. In Haute-Vienne, with 205 communes and 29 cantons, 12 of the 20 bookstores in 1851 were in Limoges, and 21 of 47 in 1879; the number of other places served rose from five to seven in 28 years. Creuse, home of numerous migrants, improved the most. In 1851 six localities were served outside the prefecture at Guéret; by 1879 the number had risen to 14. This was still only slightly better than one *chef-lieu de canton* in two, but better by a good piece than Corrèze and Haute-Vienne, where only about one in every four could boast a bookseller.[38] We have to bear this sort of situation in mind when reading about the impact of settled booksellers on peddlers and peddlers' wares in rural areas, for we have seen that many parts of France lived in conditions not very different from those of the Limousin.*

Yet all the evidence indicates that book peddling was a dying trade. The prefects' replies to the inquiries of the Ministry of the Interior in 1866 make this clear. In Gers 27 permits were delivered to hawkers from outside the department in 1865, but only nine in the first six months of 1866. Dordogne, Landes, Cantal, Isère, Allier, Loire, Puy-de-Dôme, Manche, Orne, the Alps, Seine-Inférieure, Indre, Saône-et-Loire, Creuse, Vosges, and Côtes-du-Nord show the same pattern. We find a clue to this phenomenon in the response from Côtes-du-Nord, quoting the report of the police superintendent of Saint-Brieuc to the effect that almost no novels had been sold in the past years, something the peddlers blamed on the great number of little newspapers publishing serials. The peddlers sold a good part of their wares in little towns. With the appearance of the *Petit Journal* in 1863, they began to lose their public. In Loir-et-Cher we hear of the disastrous competition of cheap illustrated papers: in Loiret the peasants read almanacs, the city readership "illustrated publications at five and ten centimes."[39]

The country public for printed matter had always been limited. Now, with no urban sales to make their enterprise worthwhile, fewer and fewer peddlers would bother to exploit that market. Significantly, in Cantal, the lists of books authorized for peddling shrank concurrently with the inquiry of 1866 (the permits granted by the Third Republic would only authorize the sale of newspapers). Book peddlers were being driven out of the towns into a countryside that did not provide an adequate market except for almanacs.† This may well be why those who trafficked in the traditional wares lost interest in their surviving clientele and instead of attempting to compete with the new, more attractive forms, preferred to dispose of their existing stocks and turn entirely to proven profitable lines: almanacs, schoolbooks, and books for prize-giving. It was a vicious circle. "Those buying books from peddlers," reported the prefect of Eure-et-Loir in 1866, "belong to the less enlightened and poorest classes; not infrequently they are illiterate or nearly so." They got what they could afford. When they could afford better, they would turn elsewhere. Consider the collection held by a Catholic farmer Daniel Halévy visited in Bour-

---

* But note that some publishers sent salesmen out into the countryside to sell their books. This is mentioned as a novelty in 1866 in Saône-et-Loire and Loire, to which the Maison Conrad of Saint-Etienne dispatched two traveling salesmen every month, who offered the novels of Dumas, Sue, Paul de Kock, and other writers in serialized installments. Their sales were substantial, we are told. (Archives Nationales, F[17]9146.)

† The number of tracts and pamphlets sold in Haute-Vienne fell sharply, from 129,663 in 1863 to 28,693 in 1864, and the sales dwindled to almost nothing by the end of the decade. On the other hand, the numbers of almanacs edited and stamped at Limoges indicate that sales in this domain continued to be impressive: 318,730 in 1872, 516,075 in 1877, nearly 4,000,000 over the period 1872–79 (Alain Corbin, "Limousins migrants," pp. 510–12).

bonnais in the early 1900's. On his bookshelf (one!) there stood *The Lay of the Aymon Brothers*; a work by Edouard Drumont (probably his turgid and vitriolic anti-Semitic pamphlet *La France juive*); the Bible (bought from a Protestant peddler); and a small pile of tracts of the liberal Catholic Sillon. He was, to be sure, a man of property and of some social standing, and even then, "very much above the average" of his sort. Still, even the average had been inspired to new tastes by modern and attractive schoolbooks and by the wares of towns.[40]

Of course, all this affected only the peddler's sales of printed matter, and even that relative to the continued isolation of his customers. Around the 1880's and 1890's peddling as such declined, not only because the development of the local trade and shops made it unprofitable, but because fewer men needed a subsidiary source of income. Most could buy land; many found steady jobs or sources of income near home; some (as we have seen) set up as shopkeepers, others as small farmers. There were still peddlers on the roads, but they were fewer, and by the 1890's we find them with their backpacks and their uncertain trade only where isolation still obstinately persisted: in the Causses, in Aude, Ariège and other parts of the Pyrenees, in the Landes, in the Loire valley (whence they disappeared about 1905).[41] By then, the press had fully assumed its role of conducting social electricity to the whole of the nation. This was a change not only from the day of Chateaubriand, who coined the phrase, but from mid-century when, in the words of the public prosecutor at Aix, "the people of the countryside and even those of the towns read papers little; when they read them, they don't understand them." Opinions and evidence tend to be contradictory, but I am inclined to agree. Certainly printed matter trickled or flowed through the countryside, but the spoken word was what made an impact. We hear about agitators trying to drive their speeches home by leaving pamphlets behind in taverns or scattered on the roads, an enterprise that returned them nothing, for the men who would willingly enough listen to arguments carried *viva voce* could not read and thus had no idea what was in the subversive tracts.[42]

By the 1860's literacy had improved, but in the countryside newspapers continued to be scarce. In all of Ariège, with a population of 252,000 in 1865, the total circulation of daily newspapers was 1,200; in Corrèze in 1867 "there are no newspapers in the villages." Official or unofficial comments and reports refer largely to the public of little towns. Village notables may have received a paper by mail or perhaps brought one home from town, like the mayor of Pouldergat (Finistère) in 1864, who returned from Quimper with a paper that all the municipal councilmen discussed. The newspaper was still, like the white bread brought home from fairs, a rare urban delicacy, preserve of the privileged few.[43]

When the *Petit Journal* appeared in 1863, there were a great many places where no one quite knew what a newspaper was or had any idea that this might be purchased like any other item on the open market. Its sales soon soared, especially since the government looked on it with favor, as a welcome diversion from political concerns.[44] In well-off farm households the *Petit Journal* might be read aloud on the doorstep in summer, or around the table on wintry nights by the light of a lamp or chaleu. But it appears that "the popular masses" were scarcely touched by it. In all of Corrèze, Creuse, and Haute-Vienne apparently only 171 copies were sold during the entire first quarter of 1876. As Félix Pécaut remarked in 1879, "The people learn to read; they do not read as yet, even in the departments that statistics call enlightened." But newspapers were beginning to "seek out [the common man], even in his village."[45]

Only a trickle still. In the Limousin the number of copies of newspapers in circulation rose from 6,154 in 1869 to 8,185 in 1876. The rise was due to the appearance of local papers, whose circulation tripled after the Prussian war and would increase further after 1880. They were read largely for their local news and only came to life at election time. As the low circulation figures readily show, newspapers continued to be read mainly by the artisans and shopkeepers of small towns and the notables and municipal councilmen in villages.[46]

What happened later is reflected in two reports that date ten years apart. In 1878 the police superintendent at Rivesaltes (Pyrénées-Orientales) declared that the press had no influence on local people's minds. In 1888 the chronicler of a Corrèze village noted that the peasants were buying newspapers at the fair and bringing them back to be read aloud by the best reader at the veillée. The author was concerned about the effect this had on peasants' minds. He was not alone. The police began to take notice, as is indicated by hitherto unheard-of comments in their reports. "Much read by the peasant," remarked the police superintendent of Aurillac in 1896 about *L'Avenir du Cantal*, which with a circulation of 2,300 three times a week sold more copies than all the Cantal press in 1877. He could have said as much about the 4,300 copies of *La Croix du Cantal* that priests and sextons distributed through the countryside each week.[47]

By 1903 in a country bourg in Upper Brittany—Guipel, in Ille-et-Vilaine—with a population of about 1,500, 15 persons were buying a daily paper, and there were a great many more who, on Sunday, bought one of four local newspapers or the *Petit Journal* or the *Petit Parisien*. In Hérault by 1907 almost every commune received newspapers. In some communes it was still only the priest, the notables, and the public employees who read them, and in most the peasants read them only irregularly. But the habit spread rapidly between 1907 and 1914. Thus at Pérols, a village of about 1,000 in the coastal plain of Hérault, 120 persons read newspapers in 1907, 214 in 1914. In rural Puy-de-Dôme newspapers had barely existed in the 1890's; by 1906 or so they wielded considerable influence. News of current events penetrated to the far corners of the mountains, to be discussed and wondered at: the explosion that killed so many on the battleship *Iéna,* a Paris strike of electricians and the menace of a strike by food workers, the death of Marcelin Berthelot, the chemist, and the revelations of the private papers of the papal nuncio.[48] Sensational news no doubt, and likely to catch the eye. But note that now the eye was there, ready to be caught; and that the print, which it now deciphered fairly readily, made it familiar with events on a national scale.

Such novelties helped drive out traditional topics of conversation. There was no more need for the news-spreaders (beggars, tailors) who went from farm to farm carrying the gossip of a region and snippets from the outside world. There was less room for folktales. At Guipel, in 1903, "the taste for newspapers creates serious competition for legends and traditional stories. It expels them from thought and from conversation." In Gascony (wrote Emmanuel Labat in 1910) peasant conversations used to turn on local events, gossip, and news. To be sure, peasants now talked about the weather and crops as they always had, but they also discussed politics and prices. What interested them now was the news newspapers brought them from afar: events in Morocco, trials and scandals, *apaches* and crime, flying machines. The village chronicle seemed petty compared with that of Paris; the storytellers who had livened the veillées had disappeared; old stories now had to be sought in books. When this sort of literature disappeared, added Labat, the very fact of its disappearance undoubtedly *meant* something.[49] An insipid remark, apparently, and yet not without sense.

What could it mean, when content in some ways remained unchanged— the same sensationalism, a very similar superficial logic, many familiar themes? Yet the scale had changed, the locus of the action had broadened or else been clearly sited in the town; and the very accessibility of the new urban culture, now easier to reach and to comprehend, made it more seductive. This meant in part that from concrete local concerns the peasant mind was turning to ones it shared with other Frenchmen. Newspapers established a unanimity of readership in which regional peculiarities no longer counted. As with the schools, as with politics, the press advanced both the process of homogenization and the level of abstract thought. The cultural tradition reflected in the press leaned to generalities, favored national or universal themes over local, specific ones. This in due course rubbed off on the readers' thinking. It rubbed off on the readers' language, too. Not only did the papers hasten the spread of French; they brought a whole vocabulary that reinforced but also supplemented the one learned in the schools. On the whole, the French vocabulary of the lower classes in the 1880's was too limited for any really sensible discussion of current affairs or current politics. In 1883 even Socialist propaganda "written in a very clear style" recommended the use of a dictionary. As for the people in agricultural areas, "the number of words they can understand is very restricted."[50]

Newspaper style was simple enough to be accessible. As with almanacs, one could at need make out words one did not understand by reference to their context or to illustrations. Gradually, the newspaper readers' vocabulary grew; and by the mid-1890's Pécaut, who 15 years before had grumbled that even when people knew how to read they did not, was now troubled that they were reading the wrong things (again). "New and strange educators" competed with the schools, but actually represented the same party: that of modernity. "*Le Petit Parisien* is the Holy Scripture of the countryside," declared a Catholic in 1913.[51] We know that the King James Version molded the English language. Here were unauthorized versions, rued by Church and school, that played an unstudied part in molding the speech of the French, and their minds as well.

Chapter Twenty-eight

WRING OUT THE OLD

Ring out the old, ring in the new,
Ring happy bells, across the snow!
The year is going, let him go;
Ring out the false, ring in the true.
—TENNYSON

"You are old, Father William," the young man said,
"And your hair has become very white;
And yet you incessantly stand on your head—
Do you think, at your age, it is right?"
—LEWIS CARROLL

"CONTINUITY HAS broken down," wrote Jules Méline about the changing world around him. "No longer an evolution, it is a true revolution that is taking place and that pursues its way." Looking back at those years, the folklorist André Varagnac claimed that France in the last quarter of the nineteenth century underwent a veritable *crise de civilisation*.[1] Traditional attitudes and traditional practices crumbled, but they had done so before. What mattered after 1880 was that they were not replaced by new ones spun out of the experience of local community. The decay and abandonment of words, ceremonies, and patterns of behavior were scarcely new. What was new and startling, said Varagnac, was the absence of homemade replacements: the death of tradition itself.

Varagnac was right. Some French peasants even today sow at the new moon and prune trees at the waning moon; but a general statement need be right only in a general way. The end of the century saw the wholesale destruction of traditional ways. It is no coincidence, surely, that this period saw a great spurt of interest in folklore studies. Serious folklore research began only in 1870, and one of France's great folklorists, Paul Delarue, has called 1879–1914 its golden age. Most of the great journals devoted to such research were founded in that period: the *Revue celtique* and the *Revue des langues romanes* in 1870, *Romania* in 1872, *Mélusine* in 1877. Others of importance lived only within its span: *La Tradition* (1887–1907), the *Revue du traditionnisme français et étranger* (1898–1914), and Paul Sébillot's *Revue des traditions populaires* (1888–1919), which lived and died with him.

The 1880's also saw the founding of the special folklore collections that in due course led to the Musée d'Ethnographie and the Musée des Arts et Traditions Populaires.[2] The research carried out by Sébillot revealed the possibilities of a whole new field. In 1895 the Society for National Ethnography and Popular Arts began to study not just the literary folklore that had been the sole interest of the romantics, but popular art, objects and techniques as well. Peasants were studied as a vanishing breed; their culture was dissected and their sentimental value grew. From George Sand to Maurice Barrès, writers took up the noble peasant as an earlier century had taken up the noble savage. Sets of picture postcards featured scenes that had scarcely been worth notice shortly before: thatched cottages, farmers pitching hay, harvest feasts, peasants in regional costumes.[3]

But for all who rued the loss of olden ways and sought to record and preserve their memory, many others rejoiced at their passing and did all they could to speed it. Speaking at Cahors in 1894, Senator Jean Macé, moving spirit of the prestigious Ligue de l'Enseignement, expressed the prevailing view with vigor: "Let every dying day carry away with it the remains, the debris, of the dead beliefs."[4] And every day did; certainly every year. No longer did the sower beginning on his field first throw a handful of seed in the air, "Voilà pour Le Bon Dieu," another into the hedge, "Voilà pour les rats, rates, et ravons," and only then one on the ground, "Voici pour moi!" No longer at Pierrecourt and at Blangy-sur-Bresle, between Dieppe and Abbeville, did the man whose grapes ripened first give a bunch to the church to be placed in the Virgin's hand; nor did this custom survive for the first bunch of hemp and flax in the countryside around Quiberon. The proximate causes were different—Phylloxera at Pierrecourt, political conflict at Quiberon—but the underlying causes were the same. The customs had outlived their time. At Audierne, in Brittany, where certain brutal but colorful initiation ceremonies for cabin boys were abandoned at the turn of the century, "a wave of strangers and tourists" was blamed, but the same sentence conceded that the locality had "lost its former cohesion."[5]

In Loire a whole host of courting and marriage customs died out. Courting in the fields (*bergerer*, or *aller à la bergère*) ceased as fewer and fewer girls went out to tend sheep or cattle, and especially when fields began to be enclosed. The ritual of hiding the bride-to-be, to be searched out by the groom and his friends, abducted, and forced prettily off to church, was abandoned at Noailly when a girl stifled to death in a cupboard in 1885; but the custom had long since ended at Saint-Germain-l'Espinasse, a larger and less isolated village nearby, where it seems to have been dropped as early as 1870. Exactly the same was true of *pétarades* (the firing off of guns); they were discontinued at Saint-Germain weddings in 1870, but lasted another 15 years at Noailly. In both Noailly and Saint-Germain a simpler, less socially objectionable wedding custom lasted longer: the bride was presented with a broom, a distaff, or some seed to sow as a reminder of her duty to work. This practice survived into the early twentieth century, when brides began to find it debasing. In Beauce, where brides were presented with a distaff right in church, a southern girl who married into a family of Auneau (Eure-et-Loir) in 1896 was the first to refuse to accept it.[6] Some fairly crude customs lasted surprisingly long—instances of couvade, for example, in which fathers take to their beds on the morrow of childbirth, being reported in Morvan as late as 1905—but they were increasingly seen as grotesque.[7]

Changing crops, tools, and conditions also affected customs. Veillées, as we know, died out in part because people could afford to light and heat their own homes. Cash and machines put an end to customary payments in kind—like the eleventh bale of every harvest worker. After about 1900 we hear that employers actually preferred to pay to have work done. In Alsace, Aube, and other parts of France, where a newly married couple had been yoked to a plow in a ritual of fertility and of labor, the custom disappeared as new-style, heavier plows were introduced.[8] In Mâconnais, where before the Phylloxera every possible bit of land had been planted to grapes, dead leaves and heather were gathered by groups of peasants in the winter to be used for stable litter and bedding; this custom, *la feuillée*, was given up at the turn of the century as more balanced farming and better transportation made more suitable materials available. Patent medicines and chemists' wares replaced traditional herbs and remedies. Old people in Vaucluse told Laurence Wylie in 1957 that they had known the old remedies but now "when we are ill we go to the doctor."[9]

As flax and hemp ceased to be cultivated on any scale, the songs connected with them ceased to be sung, and other worksongs followed them into oblivion. The singing, drinking, and dancing that had accompanied the threshing of grain survived the advent of mechanical threshing machines (*manèges*) turned by oxen or horses (around the 1880's in Upper Brittany), but died out when power-driven threshing machines (*batteries à la mécanique*) spread in the late 1890's.[10] Harvest feasts, once universal, disappeared. "When everything was done, it was a relief and people celebrated. Today it is all done fast and with less fatigue." Hence no more feasts accompanying the return of the last loaded cart, no more rejoicings around the last sheaf of wheat, no celebratory bouquet presented to the farmer's wife, no more *pare-scéye, parsoie, gerbaude, raboule*.[11]

The skills involved with such practices were lost with them: how to tie a wheatsheaf, how to plait the straw dolls that were presented to the farmwife or the straw torches used in some ceremonies ("plaiting them was a whole art, neither too pliant nor too tight"), how to build in drystone or adobe, how to thatch a roof. Men had learned immemorial, customary, repetitive gestures: digging, sowing, cutting with sickle or scythe, sharpening, carrying, stacking, threshing, work as instinctive and skilled in its way as the artisans' *tours de main*. They had to learn new gestures appropriate to new ways and new instruments, and to unlearn old ones now deemed uncouth, like spitting and chewing tobacco.

New gestures, new conventions, took their place: riding a bicycle, rolling cigarettes, winding a watch or consulting it. Dressing and undressing with any frequency are very recent habits.[12] Looking into a mirror is another one. So is washing, especially washing one's hair. The art of skiing was learned by mountain folk in the 1890's and early 1900's. In 1899 an officer of the alpine corps presented the priest of Val d'Isère with a pair of skis. Soon the people of the surrounding hamlets learned to make their own in local wood: larch, birch, ash. By 1913 every family attending Sunday mass had a particular part of the church wall where it stacked its skis.[13]

Practices changed, traditions changed with them. National ceremonies appeared whose recurrence made them traditional. Some, like the Emperor's feast, did not have time to become established; others, like the Fourteenth of July, are vigorous still. Within less than a century after 1870 all civic ceremonies in France had a national, not a local, character. At a more private level, festive practices evolved in the same way; white dresses at marriage, gifts at Easter time, Christmas trees, became very quickly immemorial ways, though dating in most places less than a century back.[14] The "traditions" of the twentieth century are newer than most people think.

The best-known instance of the birth of a new tradition is found in conscription ceremonies. Beginning probably with the draft lotteries for militia service in the eighteenth century, conscription grew in importance during the revolutionary and imperial wars and settled into custom along with long-term service during the nineteenth century. The term conscript was used from infancy to indicate men born in the same year, hence bound together in a special fellowship ("He is my conscript" was equivalent to but stronger than the bourgeoisie's "We went to school together"). Ceremonies developed, first, as we have seen, efforts to secure "good numbers" by divination, talismans, and village sorcery; then processions, parades, and battles against gangs from other villages.[15] When the draft lottery ended, the ceremonies went on. Conscripts continued to make their rounds for gifts and toasts, continued to hold their dances and their banquets. Their parades now took them to the medical examination at the induction center or to the railway station. Induction became less of a burden, a "good number" less of a blessing, but the rites of conscription were well established. Indeed, instead of dying with universal military service, they put out new shoots: they incorporated *conscrites*, girl-friends of the same age group.

"In the past, military service lasted so long that no one thought of marriage," remarked a Loire villager toward the end of the century. "Now the conscripts go to see their *conscrites*." In the old days, explained another, "the day of the draft lottery, the conscripts chose a tavern and made good cheer with their fathers, the mayor, and the rural constable. No one paid attention to *conscrites*. Since 1893, they've been inviting their *conscrites* to dances." In the old days conscripts presented brioches to municipal councilmen (Cherrier, 1880), or to the priest or the mayor (Ambierle, Saint-Haon); by 1895, 1897, 1898, depending on the locality, they were presenting their brioches to their conscrites.[16] It took a few years for people's minds to change or for ideas to travel; but a shorter period of military service, by allowing young men to make marriage plans, made the new custom seem more natural than the old.

A changed attitude to symbols led to still other changes. Traditionally conscripts' last days of freedom included a visit to the town brothel. They arrived there as a group, with the village flag in the van, and no one saw any harm in a ceremony appropriate to induction into the ranks of adult men. In 1891, however, the conscripts of Bray-sur-Seine were stopped at the brothel door by the village constable, who threatened to confiscate the flag rather than allow it to be carried into such a place. The constable won the ensuing argument. Despite the conscripts' strong resentment at having, as it were, to strike their colors, the flag and its bearer had to wait outside.[17] National symbolism by now was stronger than any other.

Should the persistence of conscription ceremonies, and especially the invention of conscrites, lead us to qualify Varagnac's assertion that traditions were dying? Scarcely, for these ceremonies dated back no further than the early part of the century, and had been perpetuated largely as convenient occasions for conviviality. Their persistence should remind us, rather, that rites are functional. They serve particular interests. When such interests disappear or fade, or when men see a better way of serving them, the rites may persist as long as they are no bother—especially if they provide some fun. But they are no longer taken seriously as ritual, and thus give way easily before even modest opposition or disappear forever when a crisis leads to their seemingly temporary suspension.

Leaving personal experience aside, the role of wars in dealing the coup de grâce to lingering customs is quite remarkable. Contemporary observers noted this development without comment or simply attributed it directly to the catastrophe. But war was less a cause of change than a precipitant of changes already under way.[18] Edgar Morin makes precisely this point when he writes that in the parish of Plodémet "the war of 1914 accelerated and amplified most of the processes set off in 1880–1900." Like the Great Revolution in peasant parlance, the Great War became a symbolic dividing line between what once was and what is, so that informants in a survey used terms like *jadis* and *avant la guerre* interchangeably. Yet wars are not watersheds for customs, but difficult times in which people are forced to focus on essential matters and come to see things differently. Many festive customs were necessarily suspended by the Great War. In the countryside, mourning was almost as universal as hardship: two years for parents, one for siblings. There were few pigs to slaughter, no festive family meals, no public festivities. And after the war there was the great influenza epidemic. By 1919 the old customs were no longer part of people's lives. Some were restored to their prewar prominence, but many were quietly forgotten.[19]

Even the war of 1870–71, we have already seen, made significant inroads into the old way of life. Campaigns were relatively short by twentieth-century standards, and casualties much lighter, but an important area of the north-east—from Belfort to the Doubs and the Jura, and west from Haute-Saône to Aube and all parts north of the Ardennes—remained under German occupation until at least the end of 1872 and in some cases until August 1873. This scarcely made for a festive mood. At any rate, many folklorists see here the "1789 of our popular traditions," and there is some evidence to bear them out.[20] In the wine country of Marne the *fête du cochelet*, in which the grape-pickers brought the last bunch of grapes to the vineyard owner, ended with the war. At Delle, near Belfort, Midsummer fires did not survive three years of German occupation.[21] In Orne, occupied till the spring of 1871, certain villages never resumed their traditional bonfires. At Saint-Germain-l'Espinasse (Loire), as we have seen, some of the more boisterous marriage customs were given up in 1870. Along the Oise valley, in Aisne, hemp and flax production fell disastrously under the occupation and never recovered; neither did the festive activities connected with it, which died out in 1890. We have heard how the Prussian war brought an end to an ancient fertility rite at Le Mesnil, in Marne. Most of these instances occurred where the war made its impact felt; in any case they are not particularly numerous. The war of 1914–18 was different. As Father Garneret described it for Franche-Comté, it was "the bloody break that struck our villages such a blow: 20 dead for 300 inhabitants and all the customs shattered."[22]

Precisely those isolated regions where customs had resisted longest bear out Garneret's words. In Vivarais the Great War was "a true break in the warp of history." In Loire a long list of customs ended with 1914: charivaris in a number of places, veillées, the fir trees that were raised to flank the threshold of the newly married. Even dowries allegedly lost some of their importance. In Aveyron after 1918 only children lit "small" Midsummer fires; the same or none at all in Gard, Périgord, Sarladais, Diois, Quercy, and, rather expectably, Argonne. In Aisne and the Pas-de-Calais harvest customs ended with the war; more surprisingly, the same thing happened in Puy-de-Dôme. In Marne many practices lapsed: *feux de brandons*, the November hiring of servants for the year (*louée de Saint-Martin*), various marketing and dietary customs, many Midsummer fires. But much the same practices lapsed in the Puy area and in Bourbonnais. The bands of harvesters were now in uniform. The seasonal hirings-out were suspended, and with them the festivities, the songs, the dances. In Forez there were no able-bodied men to carry the saints' statues in processions; they were never carried again. The disguises worn at Mardi Gras disappeared. The custom of ringing the bells all through Allhallows Eve was abandoned.[23]

The map of extinct fires runs from the Ardennes to the Landes and Cantal. Carnival died where it had survived in Forez, Auvergne, the Limousin. Old rites like the election of an Abbot of Youth or a King of Clerks, which had lingered in Provence, disappeared. So did the *chambrettes*, bled of their membership. We need not continue. The quake was terrifying, and the old one-horse shay collapsed in all its parts. "Now fêtes are finished," declared the people of Lantenne, "we shall see no more fêtes." They would. Fêtes were in fact held again there after some years, but they were different—they were all for fun.[24] The ritual had been dying and now it was gone.

For national integration, the war was an immense step forward. Destructive to lingering anachronisms, it at the same time hastened the advent of all the transmutations we have seen taking shape. Ways of speaking, eating, and thinking, which had been changing rapidly in any event, were thrown into a blender and made to change faster still. Time had something to do with this: the effects would have been more superficial if the war had been as short as the war of 1870–71. The refugees from German-invaded regions, parked in villages inland, began by living apart but ultimately were obliged by circumstances to interact with the villagers. Language difficulties alone must have been severe. A northern miner, in his recent memoirs, tells how he had to "relearn French" when he was sent for a lung operation to an Aveyron clinic where no one could understand the *chtimi* he spoke.[25] Evacuees of urban or industrial background were particularly alien, but even farming families were foreigners outside their pays. Still, farmers were short-handed; the displaced were in need of means and services; the war went on and on. Whatever people felt about each other, cultural integration forged ahead.

All this was even truer of the soldiers. The hazards of war carried them all over a country they had recently learned about from books, forced them to "relearn French" in order to communicate with comrades and civilians, opened a door on unknown worlds, milieus, ways of life. Along with the hard life of the front there was an unfamiliar abundance; wine, coffee, and meat at every meal taught the survivors habits they would not easily unlearn. "Il est resté un pauvre homme," wrote Michel Augé-Laribé about the average peasant, until the 1914 war "lui a fait voir du pays."[26] Basic economic conditions kept him in their grip even when the war was over, and only another war really put paid to stubborn survivals.* But the French peasant was never

---

* Some students place the watershed between old and new attitudes in 1939–42. Gustave Thibon so dates the transition in Vivarais, as Placide Rambaud does for Maurienne (see Thibon, "Un Exemple d'émiettement humain," pp. 50–51; and Rambaud, *Economie et sociologie de la montagne*, p. 172). Arnold Van Gennep makes a similar remark (*Manuel de Folklore*, 1.4: 1579). Much of this turned on the serious food shortages of 1940–45, which put an end, among other things, to long and gargantuan marriage feasts. In Mâconnais, Emile Violet tells us, the public marriage dance disappeared in 1939. The village community that mandated that all celebrations be open to every member had disintegrated earlier, when "the rich" no longer conformed to its customs. But such failures to conform had been punished by charivaris. The war excused the inexcusable. (*Les Veillées en commun*, p. 2.)

again the "pauvre homme" that he had been before. For him, as Joseph Pasquet has said of Morvan, today began in 1914.[27]

Many grieved over the death of yesterday, but few who grieved were peasants. Thatched cottages and log cabins are picturesque from the outside; living in them is another matter. Old folk in the Breton commune investigated by Morin had no fond remembrance of the old days. For them as for the Republican reformers of the Third Republic, the past was a time of misery and barbarism, the present a time of unexampled comfort and security, of machines and schooling and services, of all the wonders that are translated as civilization. Morin quotes a seventy-year-old man: "A hundred years ago, this place, ah, yes, it was really wild, full of savages. People were not civilized. They fought and a lot were thieves. People tried to sleep with their neighbors' wives. We weren't educated people, we didn't know how to read, we didn't know how to write, there was no school. Now we are civilized; people know at least how to read and write, all of them. Before there was misery; now we are well off." Roger Thabault says much the same thing about the people of Mazières in 1914: "All, even the poorest, had a lively sense... of immense material progress. They had an equally lively sense of great social progress, of limitless evolution toward more liberty and more equality, thanks to the vote."[28]

This helps explain the extraordinary difference between the intellectual despair and decadence of the fin-de-siècle elite and the optimism, hope, and sense of progress so evident among the masses. To be sure, elite intellectuals and reformers had seen that the new panaceas—democracy, education—did not bring the betterment they had once seemed to promise. But the elite classes were also affected by breakdowns in the old system that they saw or sensed, and that they sought desperately to avert against the will of those directly involved. "The world we have lost" was no loss to those who had lived in it, or so at least the evidence suggests.

Indeed, was what had gone truly lost, or had it been discarded? Store-bought goods, city styles, baker's bread, were considered superior and probably were. The music, songs, and dances of the city were preferred. To be sure, there was a good deal of coming and going about the process, so that idealized medieval pastourelles could turn into more or less popular shepherd songs that would be taken up in a later period by aristocrats playing at what they took to be vulgar ways; and folktales done over by Charles Perrault or the Comtesse d'Aulnoy could be borrowed back, as we have seen, for use in some veillée.* Nurses and maids from the countryside brought rural ballads

* For a splendid illustration of the borrowing process at work, consider the story Jean-Michel Guilcher tells of a religious pastoral that was still performed in Lower Brittany in the first third of the twentieth century. Moving back through time, he traced its derivation to a late-eighteenth- or early-nineteenth-century work in *trégorrois* dialect, inspired by a slightly older publication in *vannetais* dialect; this in turn was based on a "pastoral play" published in French in the early

into town kitchens and nurseries, where the young of the upper classes learned them.[29] But most of the current flowed outward from the city. The codes and ways of the upper classes were seen as better and deliberately imitated by the rest. Servants and artisans imitated the bourgeois; peasants imitated servants and artisans. The crux was not contact but opportunity.

Why had contact alone not carried things further? Even secluded communities, after all, had contacts with the world around them, including the urban world, throughout our period and long before. Apparently isolated bastions—the Pyrenees, the Limousin, Auvergne, even Brittany—were crossed by travelers (sometimes in large groups) and touched by all sorts of influences. Peasants in those regions knew about events, techniques, languages, social changes, but viewed them naturally in terms of their own interests— that is, in terms of a particular economic base and social form. It was not that the world passed them by, but rather that they accepted only what they could recognize as suitable until such time as economic and social development made a wholesale acceptance seem sensible.

Since for a long time they recognized few changes indeed as suitable, the peasant masses were widely regarded as passive, stubborn, and stupid.* Yet we can see now that their narrow vision was the vision of frightened men in desperate circumstances; that the village was a lifeboat striving to keep afloat in heavy seas, its culture a combination of discipline and reassurance designed to keep its occupants alive. Insecurity was the rule, existence consistently marginal. Tradition, routine, vigorous adherence to the family and the community—and to their rules—alone made existence possible. The village was an association for mutual aid.[30] Lands, pastures, and ovens were generally ruled in common; dates for sowing and harvesting were set for one and all. Since all had to pull together, no deviance could be tolerated.†

---

eighteenth century at Caen, then at Rennes and Nantes, which was based on still older forms going back to the New Testament mystery plays still alive in sixteenth-century France. ("Conservation et renouvellement dans la culture paysanne ancienne de Basse-Bretagne," *Arts et traditions populaires*, 1967, pp. 1–18.)

* More apt is the suggestive observation of Philip G. Hamerton that the peasants he saw were at once full of intelligence and unbelievably ignorant, their intelligence operating in one sphere and shutting out everything outside it (*Round My House*, pp. 228, 229).

† We have seen that this included both public and private behavior. Conformity was a major virtue: "O faut venter du vent qui vente," they said in Saintonge, where *orighinau* was the supreme insult thrown at a nonconformist neighbor (Raymond Doussinet, *Le Paysan santongeais*, pp. 305, 382). The slightest difference could provoke resentment; relations between neighbors or kin were dominated by envy and the fear of arousing it. Even marriage songs recognized this: "Lous nous espous qu'au espousat, / Au despieyt dous qui an mau parlat. / S'abèu crebat tous lous yelous, / Qu'auren crebat tous sounque nous. / S'abèu crebat aques matin, / Qu'en auré crebat binte cinq." (C. Daugé, *Le Mariage et la famille en Gascogne*, pp. 88–89.) Presumably one more reason why so many country men, and women even more, seized the opportunity to leave their village for the town. What sociologists regard as the alienations of urban living must have appeared as emancipation to them.

In such circumstances, innovation was almost inconceivable. Routine ruled: the structural balance attained by a long process of trial and error, reinforced by isolation and physical circumstances. At Tarascon (Ariège) in 1852, "the agricultural population thinks present agricultural methods have reached their peak of development and must not be set aside, being the fruit of long experience." Wisdom was doing things the way they always had been done, the way they were supposed to be done. "If you do as your neighbor does, you do neither ill nor well," advises a proverb of Franche-Comté. To the peasant, routine connoted not mindless labor but precious experience, what had worked and hence would work again, the accumulated wisdom without which life could not be maintained. For the Landais farmer, wrote Jean Ricard in 1911, the past was "a guarantee of the present; in freeing himself from it he would fear to compromise the future."[31]

Ricard and other modernizers found this incomprehensible. "Bent under a yoke of habit," read an 1831 report, the peasant "wants to live as his father lived, less out of respect for the ancients than from a blind suspicion of anything new."[32] Yet the suspicion was not necessarily blind. Practices and techniques that peasants fought to preserve may have hampered general progress, but were of vital importance to themselves. The conflict was not between changing techniques and backward minds, let alone between progress and obstinate reaction; it was between two kinds of interests, the peasant's being no more inherently blind than the capitalist's. In the short run, which was all most peasants could afford, there is no reason why they should have welcomed innovations that harmed their interests. Self-sacrifice would have been the greater blindness.

This short-run rationale was often explicit. "Our alimentary needs," read a report from Cabannes (Ariège) in 1852 about a proposed improvement in cattle-raising methods, "prevent us from attempting anything of this sort, let alone turning the fields to pasture." Economic interest suggested one thing; want and reality opposed it. The narrower the margin, the less the chance of experiment. Only the rich took chances—or the irresponsible. Few understood this. Thus a prefect of the Second Empire could write of "the poor peasant without instruction, without reserves, without the necessary forethought to apply the great improving ideas and to await their results."[33] Peasants knew better. Their forethought told them that without reserves they would not live to see the results of the most wonderful innovations. If they wanted to stay alive, they had to work with what they had.*

A book published in 1865 by a woman landowner in central France caviled against *petite culture*, the smallish farms (up to 20 acres, hence not so very

---

* In the long run, this caution became a habit that reinforced a natural wariness and negativism. Even when traditional crops or methods could safely, perhaps profitably, be abandoned to give new ones a trial, "the experiment is a risk, and few dare to risk loss in some bold enterprise whose failure is awaited by their scoffing neighbors" (Comte de Neufbourg, *Paysans*, p. 18).

small!) that "encourage the peasants' love of routine and repugnance to progress."[34] But what options did they have? Within a few lines it becomes clear that they lacked the capital to make improvements or take risks. Parcelization had its drawbacks, but for the peasants it was parcels or nothing. And of course they had no access to credit, bar usury. They were not mindless, let alone idle; they were realistic, and their reality was the lack of money.

Where capital was lacking, innovations made little progress. To the French peasant a new technique could prove itself only by experience; and experiments were necessarily left to outsiders with the time, the means, and "modern" views of the virtues of novelty. There might have been more agricultural improvements if more land had been in the hands of owners with adequate capital, but then France would have been quite a different country. In any case, would the peasants have fared better? Christiane Marcilhacy quotes a teacher in Zola's *Earth* (1887) apostrophizing the peasants of Beauce: "You hope to fight with your two-cent tools, ... you who know nothing, who want nothing, who stew in your routine."[35] But as Marcilhacy shows, many a big tenant farmer came to grief when his improvements failed to pay off, and peasant routine often survived where modern initiative went under.

Many peasants, says the Comte de Neufbourg in a book full of good sense and quite ignored, "live from day to day, and routine foresees things for them. We should not mock or destroy this routine: it would be missed, it is their wisdom." Subsistence farming—raising a bit of everything and making one's own bread and clothing—was a matter not of blind routine but of calculated necessity: "When one buys one's bread there is never any money left." Routine, concludes Daniel Faucher, is "the precious fruit of experience, a treasury of wisdom"; the peasant abandons it "only when assured that he can do so without damage."[36] And that, as we have seen, is what happened.*

Traditional communities continued to operate in the traditional manner as long as conditions retained their traditional shape: low productivity, market fluctuations beyond the producer's control, a low rate of savings, little surplus. What surplus the peasant could accumulate was taken from him in taxes or usurious interest, spent on church buildings and feasts, or invested in land. But land did not increase total production until capital investment in improvements became both possible and thinkable. And this did not happen until

---

* Lucien Gachon, "L'Arrondissement d'Ambert," in Jacques Fauvet and Henri Mendras, *Les Paysans et la politique*, pp. 393–96. Mendras tells how the agriculture of the canton of Sauve (Gard) passed from polyculture to specialization. There the peasants had practiced a mixed farming that was well adapted to autarky and little cash until late in the eighteenth century, when rising taxes and manorial dues forced them to find a way of raising cash. They added mulberry trees to their store of crops and began to raise and sell silkworms, a course they had previously resisted but now saw as the most economical and convenient way out of their current pass. This change gradually introduced them to the market economy. A nineteenth-century crisis in the silk market led to a new adaptation, this time to the vine. With that, they had to give up their traditional polyculture altogether, but the mulberry had smoothed the way for the change-over, especially as far as mentalities were concerned. (*Esprit*, June 1955, p. 919.)

the market became an accessible reality, that is, until the expanding communications network brought it within reach. Economic growth could then proceed at a faster pace, and producers could literally change their minds about what they were doing and to what end. Road and rail were the decisive factors in this change. Schools shaped and accelerated it.

The very rhythm of life and work changed. People's bodies had operated at a pace set by the heart and lungs. Working songs, walking songs, after-working songs had imitated the rhythm of the work. Plowmen had worked to the rhythm of horses or oxen. Hoers would take a bite out of a hunk of bread, throw it ahead of them, hoe their way up to it, and bite and throw again. Threshers' songs reproduced the rhythm of the flails:[37]

> Pas par pas, haut, bas,
> Lous flagels s'arrest oun pas.

Machines, by divorcing labor and rhythm, cut popular songs off from lived experience, opening the way to urban tunes unrelated to the rhythms of labor.

Along with the rhythm of work the whole rhythm of life changed. Labor became steadier, casual interruptions for rest fewer. Even the land got less rest. The French word for fallow, *jachère,* derives from the Latin *iacere,* "to rest"; and peasant logic accorded this right to the land as to themselves.[38] Old practice bore out the sense of such reasoning; new practice made it out-of-date.

The very use of terms like out-of-date reflects a viewpoint alien to the traditional order. In a world highly dependent on natural conditions, seasonal and liturgical rhythms governed people's sense of time. Every situation had its earlier precedent, equivalent, or analogy. It was in the past that people sought lessons for the present: not new lessons but old ones that were never out-of-date. Past and present were not two but one: a continuum of time lived, not a series of units measured by the clock. A feast or a fire, a harvest good or bad, a family event, lived on in memory and served as a more natural point of reference than the calendar. Songs and tales about events a century old evoked powerful emotions.[39] Proximity in time was relative, almost unimportant.

Traditional time had no fixed units of measure; there was not even a break between work and leisure. Even the loss of time (comings and goings, pauses, waiting) passed largely unnoticed because integrated in routine and unquestioned. We have seen, for example, that land was often counted in the units of man or animal time it took to work it: not a fixed measure but one relative to conditions. Conditions also determined the value of time: it was cheap, very cheap, when everything else was scarce. A woman would walk from her village to the market, 35 km each way, to sell her dozen eggs at 14 sous rather than 12; would wait the day out in any kind of weather to sell her butter at 20 sous rather than 19.[40] A late-nineteenth-century postcard showing a peasant "Off to the Market" in a two-wheeled donkey cart sums things up:[41]

> Two pretty good leagues away,
> Won't take but half a day.
> I'll sell the butter whatever they utter,
> Today, tomorrow, or the next day's okay.

A few peasants had watches and displayed them with pride. But even to them a watch was "a horse in the stable," useless when one could refer to cockcrows, to the stars, to the sun's touching this or that rock or tree, or to one's own shadow. As with watches, so with the calendar. The calendar year meant nothing, the rhythm of seasons everything. In Auvergne the basic division was between winter, from All Souls to Saint George's day (November 1–April 23), and summer, when beasts could sleep out of doors. In Franche-Comté, summer was divided not into months but into "times": the time for going outdoors (*patchi fou,* going out), essentially spring; the times for haying and for harvesting. In the late autumn and winter, there were "times" for sewing and for *vieillin* (veillées).[42]

In the French language, *temps* refers to both weather and duration: two concepts to us but not to the peasant whose longer hours of work came in the fair weather of the summer. To the farmer, time is work; life is work; work brings subsistence and independence. In the city, time and work have another meaning: productivity, surplus, profit, comfort, leisure. In late-nineteenth-century France these two notions of time clashed, and one disappeared.* No other outcome was possible. The new world of markets and of schools worked only on its kind of time; and the difference was fundamental. Old skills based on watching and imitating what one's elders did, old forms of intuition learned from the wise or simply discovered in oneself, gave way before the new techniques and practices of rationality. Success was achieved not by harder work, greater strength, or inspired guessing, but by superior reasoning. The new process was rational ("we do this because"), quantitative ("this way we turn out that much more"), abstract ("these are the rules"). Internalized rhythms of labor were replaced by learned skills and norms. A man who thinks his work is no worse, certainly, than one who does not; but he is certainly different.

Just as the schools and the skills they taught created a new breed of children, so the machines when they came introduced a different relationship between

---

* Compare Pierre Bourdieu and Abdelmalek Sayad, *Le Déracinement*, p. 157. As time became a measurable quantity, it could then be "lost": a notion unknown to an economy that gave little thought to "fully employed" or "wasted" time. Labor, no longer diffuse, turned into a commodity that could be—indeed, should be—quantified in terms of time. One could mouth saws like "time is money" until the cows came home: they made no sense as long as the one seemed endless and the other hardly real. Time only made sense when money made sense; and money was a part of modern technology that, we have seen, was only adopted late. By the time Bachelin wrote *Le Serviteur* (published in 1918, but composed on the eve of war), he had figured out that his father worked 12 minutes to earn five centimes, thus he had to work 24 minutes for a glass of red wine and two hours for a 50-centime packet of tobacco. "C'est une grande force dans la vie que d'avoir, comme étalon de ses besoins et de ses désirs, le prix d'une heure de son propre travail" (pp. 151–52). I think such standards and awareness were new.

man and nature. The earth lost its sacredness, the gods their divinity, magic its power. Machines were not a bad thing: they replaced animals or men doing the work of animals. But they destroyed men's harmony with their world by rendering their hard-won skills and movements useless. The peasant's skilled hand was as little needed in the new world as his patois. Marx relates workers' alienation fundamentally to the question of who actually owned the means of production; but the alienation of the rural worker, where it occurred, lay less in being deprived of property than in the discontinuity between his body and his work. The results of work done by machine could be observed, but the sense of control and the pleasures of craftsmanship were gone. Traditionally work was a way of life, not just a way of earning a living. Man at work was almost the whole of man. The man with a machine was only half a working unit, and in productivity terms the less important half.[43]

Peasants did not keep accounts. What they did with their time was determined not by the market but by family needs, and working any harder than most people did was probably impossible anyway. The universal view was that of an old winegrower in Mâconnais: "When a man works as hard as he can, he must earn enough to feed himself and keep his family alive. That is justice."*

Only around 1900-1905, wrote an Aveyron observer, did peasants there begin to grasp "the notions of productivity and the use of time."[44] Only about then did many see at last that subsistence farming, far from the road to a glorious autonomy, was the essence of futility and self-exploitation. Like the nineteenth-century factory worker before him, the twentieth-century peasant came to see work in a new light: no longer for subsistence but for pay. The logic of a money economy took over. One result was that since all work was expected to produce cash revenue in proportion to the effort involved, a lot of work was seen as no longer worth doing.[45] Where work had once encompassed a multitude of undertakings—weeding, mending enclosures or buildings or tools, pruning or cutting trees, protecting young shoots against cattle, splitting firewood, making rope or baskets—it was now judged by the norms of salaried labor. Tasks that did not yield ready returns in cash were considered not work but pottering, like going around the fields to look them over. Modern people paid others to do them or let them go undone.

Most of all this is neither good nor bad. It is. It happened. It is the essence of what happened in France between 1870 and 1914.

* V. Dupont, *Quand Eve filait*, p. 9. This confirms what we know already, that official values shaded imperceptibly into local ones. The work ethic had been part of official morality and religion since the seventeenth century, of common sense as far back as the mind can go. It did not take Guizot or the teaching of the schools to spread it. Thrift, forethought, self-help, were no strangers to the peasant. Only their possibilities were severely limited. Peasants knew all about deferred gratification. Only there was so little gratification to defer that it left scarcely a mark on statistics. What changed in the nineteenth century, and the more so as the century moved on, were the limits of possibility, hence the applicability of values known but relatively irrelevant before that time, a matter of degree.

Chapter Twenty-nine

CULTURES AND CIVILIZATION

Every countryman who has learned to read renounces the countryside in his heart.
—JOSEPH ROUX

The colonist only ends his work of breaking in the native when
the latter admits loud and clear the supremacy of the white man's
values.
—FRANTZ FANON

THE FAMOUS hexagon can itself be seen as a colonial empire shaped over the centuries: a complex of territories conquered, annexed, and integrated in a political and administrative whole, many of them with strongly developed national or regional personalities, some of them with traditions that were specifically un- or anti-French. A partial roll call serves as a reminder: in the thirteenth century, Languedoc and parts of the center; in the fifteenth, Aquitaine and Provence; in the sixteenth, Brittany; in the seventeenth, Navarre, Béarn, Pays Basque, Roussillon and Cerdagne, parts of Alsace and French Flanders, Franche-Comté; in the eighteenth, the Duchy of Lorraine, Corsica, the papal Comtat-Venaissin; in the nineteenth, Savoy and Nice.[1] By 1870 this had produced a political entity called France—kingdom or empire or republic—an entity formed by conquest and by political or administrative decisions formulated in (or near) Paris. The modern view of the nation as a body of people united according to their own will and having certain attributes in common (not least history) was at best dubiously applicable to the France of 1870.

Just after the First World War, Marcel Mauss pondered the difference between peoples or empires and nations. A people or an empire he saw as loosely integrated and governed by an extrinsic central power. A nation, by contrast, was "a materially and morally integrated society" characterized by the "relative moral, mental, and cultural unity of its inhabitants, who consciously support the state and its laws." It is clear that France around 1870 did not conform to Mauss's model of a nation. It was neither morally nor materially integrated; what unity it had was less cultural than administrative. Many of its inhabitants, moreover, were indifferent to the state and its laws, and many others rejected them altogether. "A country," says Karl Deutsch, "is as large as the interdependence it perceives."[2] By that standard the hexagon shrivels away.

The question here is not political: political conflict about the nature of the state and who shall rule it reflects a higher degree of integration than our outlying populations had attained. The question turns rather on "the wide complementarity of social communication" that for Deutsch makes a people one. Outside the urban centers, over much of France there was no "common history to be experienced as common," no "community of complementary habits," little interdependency furthered by the division of labor in the production of goods and services, and only limited "channels of social communication and economic intercourse." If by "society" we mean a group of people who have learned to work together, French society was limited indeed.[3]

Despite evidence to the contrary, inhabitants of the hexagon in 1870 generally knew themselves to be French subjects, but to many this status was no more than an abstraction. The people of whole regions felt little identity with the state or with people of other regions. Before this changed, before the inhabitants of France could come to feel a significant community, they had to share significant experiences with each other. Roads, railroads, schools, markets, military service, and the circulation of money, goods, and printed matter provided those experiences, swept away old commitments, instilled a national view of things in regional minds, and confirmed the power of that view by offering advancement to those who adopted it.* The national ideology was still diffuse and amorphous around the middle of the nineteenth century. French culture became truly national only in the last years of the century.

We are talking about the process of acculturation: the civilization of the French by urban France, the disintegration of local cultures by modernity and their absorption into the dominant civilization of Paris and the schools. Left largely to their own devices until their promotion to citizenship, the un-assimilated rural masses had to be integrated into the dominant culture as they had been integrated into an administrative entity. What happened was akin to colonization, and may be easier to understand if one bears that in mind.

"Conquest is a necessary stage on the road to nationalism," wrote a student of the subject in 1901. A nation cannot or should not conquer "major peoples," but "to bring into a larger unity groups without a clear cultural identity, to draw in, to enrich, to enlighten the uninstructed tribal mind, this is the civilizing mission we cannot renounce."[4] Many of the themes of national integration, and of colonialism too, are to be found in this brief statement: conquered peoples are not peoples, have no culture of their own; they can only benefit from the enrichment and enlightenment the civilizer brings. We must ask now whether this colonial image can be applied to France.

---

* Compare Karl Deutsch, *Nationalism and Social Communication*, p. 92: "Group assimilation can only be further accelerated by reducing or destroying the competing information recalled from the unassimilated past, and by reducing or repressing the unassimilated responses to which it would give rise in the present.... However, assimilation can be accelerated very greatly by increasing the rate of new experiences from society."

The simplest answer comes from French sources. In Franche-Comté in the twentieth century, it was remembered that people had for many years had themselves buried facedown as a protest against that region's annexation by France.[5] The fact need not be true; the memory and the claim are significant. Current references to French conquest are found mainly in the south and in the west, where they are confused by present-day political issues. Yet, ambiguous as they are, the hearing they find suggests the reality behind them. The strain must have been intense when the forces of order—army, gendarmes, judges (except justices of the peace), and police—came from outside, and when the normal friction between police and natives was rendered more acute by linguistic differences. Order imposed by men of different code and speech, somebody else's order, is not easily distinguished from foreign conquest. In the southwest, wrote M. F. Pariset in 1867, union with France "was suffered, not accepted. The fusion was accomplished slowly and against the will."[6] Forty years later, when Ernest Ferroul, the Socialist mayor of Narbonne, charged that the barons of the north were invading the Midi as in the olden days of the Albigeois, *Le Figaro* warned its readers: "Make no mistake, this is a country to be reconquered, as in the days of Simon de Montfort."[7] Education —by politics as by schools—was inculcating a new allusiveness. Together with such symbolic literary figures as Tartarin and, later, Bécassine, historical allusions like these reinforced a view of the provincial population as childlike, backward, garrulous, unenterprising natives of underdeveloped lands.[8]

Throughout the century the overseas colonies provided comparisons for certain parts of France. In 1843 Adolphe Blanqui compared the people of France's Alpine provinces to those of Kabylia and the Marquesas, and the comparison was several times repeated in official reports and in print: 1853, 1857, 1865.[9] The natives and the customs of rural France, their superstitions and their oddities, were studied and described only too often with uncomprehending condescension. Their ways seemed shallow and devoid of reason, their reasonings were ignored. Native communities were despoiled of their rights (forest code, pasture, commons, fishing and hunting rights) in the name of progress, of freedom, of productivity, and of a common good that made no sense to those in whose name it was proclaimed. Because the forces of order ignored and scorned the logic of the societies they administered, "because this ignorance and contempt were the very essence of their action, the men responsible for this policy could not estimate its disastrous consequences." These words of Pierre Bourdieu and Abdelmalek Sayad, writing about colonial administration, apply quite well to rural France through the nineteenth century.[10]

In the forests of the Pyrenees, and notably in Ariège, people took up arms against police and administrators who were "newcomers to the region and ignorant of our rights, our needs, and the local situation," alleging that they

were "crushing the local people" with their corrupt exactions. Native re-
bellions kept flaring up; as late as 1900 "all the mountain resounded to the din
of horns and savage calls."[11] In Corsica, an utterly foreign land whose inhabitants did not aspire to independence but prized their autonomy in matters
close to home, "the locals would have nothing to do with 'continentals.'"
By the First World War the island was no better assimilated to France than
Gévaudan had been a century before. A despairing report of November 1917
tells us that bandits, deserters, and defaulting recruits were more numerous
than gendarmes—"the only people one can count on, more or less."[12]

If Corsica provides too easy an argument, take the Landes, which in 1826
was called "our African Sahara: a desert where the Gallic cock could only
sharpen his spurs." A Restoration writer described the Landes as "a trackless
desert where one needs a compass to find one's way," inhabited by a "people
alien to civilization." A writer of the 1830's compared the region to the wastes
of Kamchatka and Libya, and even Michelet wrote about the idiots of the
Landes. Travelers, army officers, and officials all used the same language:
vastes solitudes, immenses solitudes. The natives, if mentioned at all, were a
subject of pity. Settlements were *colonies*, isolated and sparse. The "empty
wastes" were waiting to be "claimed for civilization," i.e. developed for economic exploitation.[13]

And developed they were by engineers like François-Hilaire Chambrelent,
who undertook drainage and planting of pines at his own expense in 1849–55
before the law of 1857 forced communes to follow his example. Since parishes
were poor, the law permitted them to raise funds for the improvements they
had to make by selling off portions of their commons: a perfect instance of
a colonial law that forced the natives either to use their lands productively
or to cede them to those who would. The results proved advantageous not
just to outside capitalists but to the Landais, who had long suffered grievously
from pellagra and debilitating fevers in this poorest corner of France.

The developers' intentions were good, even if they were also profitable to
some of those who formulated them. Profit in any case was part of good intentions, as was the good conscience of men who—in the way of men—
ignored values other than their own. Balzac had deplored the waste of land
in unprofitable commons. "Many of these lands could produce immensely,
enough to feed whole villages. But they belong to mulish communities that
refuse to sell them to speculators, preferring to keep them as pasture for a
few score cows."[14] That those few score cows (in the Landes, sheep) were
the very essence of a functioning economy and an established way of life
made no difference to Balzac or the speculators. History, as usual, was written by the victors.

Ardouin-Dumazet, visiting the Landes at the turn of the century, claimed
that the new generations appreciated the change: better nutrition, better

health, longer life expectancy. But he admitted that the old remained hostile to the developers. Nor did the colonial references cease with the improvement of the region's economy. As late as 1910 or 1911 Jean Ricard could describe the settlements of resin-tappers established by turpentine companies north of Arcachon as resembling "in some African land, a gathering of huts grouped in the shadow of the Republic's flag." And yet, surprisingly, "we are in France."[15]

To be in France meant to be ruled by French officials. In Savoy, where friction between the French administration and the natives was intense, it was said that French officials "arrived there as for a tour of duty in the colonies." In 1864 a writer in the *Revue des deux mondes* compared Savoy to Ireland.[16] People in other regions made even more explicit comparisons. "They are sending colonists to faraway lands to cultivate the desert," complained a Breton, "and the desert is here!" "They are building railway lines in Africa," wrote the *Revue du Limousin* in 1862. "If only they would treat us like Arabs!" An agricultural review took up the cry: "There is in the heart of France a region to be colonized that asks only to be accorded the same working conditions...as the colonies."[17]

Equally explicit references were made to the development of Sologne. "Here it is clearly a question of colonization," wrote Ardouin-Dumazet in 1890; Sologne's developers were as enthusiastic about their work as Algeria's. A little later, at Salbris (Loir-et-Cher): "There is an interesting parallel between the present colonization of Tunisia and the development work going on in Sologne. In Tunisia, as in Sologne, the capitalists have played an important part." Still, "everything considered...the colonization of Sologne is the more marvelous."[18]

The greatest colonial opportunities, of course, were offered by Brittany. After its forced union with France in the sixteenth century, Brittany's towns were invaded by Frenchmen who overbore or replaced the native merchants and Frenchified the people they employed or otherwise influenced. Royal ports like Lorient and Brest were garrison towns in foreign territory, and the term colony was frequently employed to describe them.[19]

As we have seen, things in Brittany had changed only slightly by the 1880's. In 1891 France's inspector general of education, Carré, published an article in the *Revue pédagogique* "on teaching the first elements of French to the natives of our colonies and the countries subject to our protectorate." The article advocated the *méthode maternelle*—no more translation, but direct learning of French as in the Berlitz schools today. More interesting, it was a recasting of an article published three years earlier in the same journal "on teaching the first elements of French in the schools of Lower Brittany." The method was reasonable; the problems were identical. Another educator, in a speech delivered at Algiers in 1891, praised Carré's method for being "as applicable to little Flemings, little Basques, little Bretons, as to little Arabs and little Berbers." By 1894 Carré's method was being used in primary schools in Lower Brittany, Flanders, Corsica, and the Basque country. Attacked that year as unsuitable for teaching French to natives of Algeria and Tunisia, it was defended by one of Carré's students, Abel Poitrineau, then inspector at Rennes, on the basis of his experience in Brittany.[20] The debate was logical, the logic inescapable.

But the similarity between Brittany and French colonies overseas went deeper still. Between 1840 and 1938, 600,000 hectares—one-fifth of the peninsula's territory—was converted from waste to plowland. In a 1946 study Jean Chombart de Lauwe described this effort as "a true colonizing enterprise,"[21] and a glance at one of its heroes, Jules Rieffel, bears him out. Born in Alsace in 1806, Rieffel went to Lorraine to study agriculture under the great agronomist Mathieu de Dombasle. Graduated in 1828, he decided to seek an agronomist's fortune in Egypt; but before taking off he visited his master's family in Brittany. During his visit there, Rieffel met a Nantes shipowner named Haentjens who had just bought a domain called Grandjouan. Rieffel was persuaded to shift his sights, and under his direction Grandjouan became first a model farm, then a distinguished agricultural school.

In short, two central performers in the agricultural development of Brittany were an ambitious Alsatian for whom a Breton domain appeared an acceptable alternative to Egypt, and a Flemish shipmaster turned estate owner who provided capital of urban and international origin. What could be more typical of a colonizing enterprise? Chombart de Lauwe put it in a nutshell: "The clearing of the moors was made possible by an abundance of labor, the availability of capital, the initiative of a team of agronomists, and the discovery of new techniques."* All but the first were foreign.

In a book of 1914 Camille Le Mercier d'Erm compared Brittany to such other oppressed and vanquished nations as Ireland, Bohemia, Finland, and Poland. Le Mercier d'Erm and his friends represented mostly themselves; far more Bretons would have preferred full membership in the French commonwealth.[22] But each aspiration in its own way reflects a sense of incomplete integration, and that is what concerns us here.

Let us now try another tack and see how well Frantz Fanon's *The Wretched*

---

* Jean Chombart de Lauwe, *Bretagne et pays de la Garonne*, pp. 27, 131. Bretons also provided a good deal of the cheap immigrant labor much as the immigrants from less-developed countries do today. See notably Abbé Elie Gautier, *Emigration Bretonne*, and the advertisement he quotes, p. 99, which was printed in the *Progrès de Briey* and reprinted in *La Paroisse bretonne* (Paris, Sept. 1909): "Je préviens MM les cultivateurs que courant janvier j'irais chercher quelques wagons de domestiques en Bretagne.... Ils seront débarqués tous sur la place de la gare à Longuyon, où chacun pourra choisir le sujet qui lui plaira le mieux." This is not to say that Bretons were alone in this regard. Quite the contrary! See André Armengaud, *Les Populations de l'est-Aquitain*, p. 252. Cheap native labor was traditionally despised. See also Martin Nadaud, *Mémoires de Léonard*, especially p. 54, concerning the insults Creuse masons had to endure during their migrations and on the *chantiers* where they worked.

of the Earth—one of the great denunciations of colonialism—applies to the conditions we have described. The following passages, some of them conflated rather than uninterrupted quotations, are representative:

Underdeveloped regions, absence of infrastructure, a world without doctors, without engineers, without administrators.

Cultural alienation, as colonialism tries to force the natives to give up their unenlightened ways, [to believe that] it was colonialism that came to lighten their darkness.*

Colonial domination disrupts the cultural life of a conquered people (death of the aboriginal society, cultural lethargy). New legal relations are introduced by the occupying power. Intellectuals seek to acquire the occupying power's culture.

The customs of the colonized people, their traditions, their myths—above all, their myths—are the very sign of [their] poverty of spirit and of their constitutional depravity.

Colonialism turns to the past of the oppressed people, and distorts, disfigures, and destroys it, devaluing precolonial history. It is the colonist who makes history: "This land, it is we who made it."†

The more brutal aspects of the occupying power's presence may perfectly well disappear, [bartered for] a less blatant but more complete enslavement.

The native bourgeoisie, which has wholeheartedly adopted the ways of thinking characteristic of the occupying country, becomes a spokesman for the colonial culture, as does the intellectual, who soaks it up greedily.[23]

The violence so prominent in Fanon's pages was rare in nineteenth-century France, perhaps because risings capable of seriously threatening the state were a thing of the past. Given time and skins of the same color, assimilation worked. But otherwise Fanon's account of the colonial experience is an apt description of what happened in the Landes and Corrèze. In France as in Algeria, the destruction of what Fanon called national culture, and what I would call local or regional culture, was systematically pursued. Insofar as it persisted, it was plagued by inertia and growing isolation. "There is a shriveling around an ever more shrunken core, ever more inert, ever more hollow." After a while, says Fanon, native creativity ebbs and what is left is

---

* Friedrich Engels, for whom the French conquest of Algeria was "fortunate . . . for the progress of civilization," would agree with this view: "After all, the modern *bourgeois*, with civilization, industry, order, and at least relative enlightenment following him, is preferable to the feudal lord or to the marauding robber" (quoted in Shlomo Avineri, ed., *Karl Marx on Colonialism*, New York, 1968, p. 43).

† "Hell is being deprived of history," Morvan Lebesque would write (*Comment peut-on être Breton?*, p. 43). See also Frantz Fanon, *Les Damnés*, p. 40: *monde sur de lui* ("a world of statues: the statue of the general who carried out the conquest, the statue of the engineer who built the bridge; a world that is sure of itself"). And note the battles waged around statues under the Third Republic: in 1903 Combes dedicated the statue of Renan opposite Tréguier cathedral; in 1932 the monument at Rennes celebrating Brittany's incorporation into France was bombed on the fourth centennial of that occasion.

"rigid, sedimentary, petrified."[24] Local reality and local culture wane together. So it was in nineteenth-century France.

And yet ... Taken as generalizations such accounts as Fanon's seem to me to underrate the choice and the autonomy of the colonized. Neither Bourdieu and Sayad, nor Fanon, nor our own observations suggest that the traditional societies were inert to start with. It seems to follow that they gave way to force, were vanquished by superior powers and "colonized" against their will. Is this what really happened? Not in France.

There, as we have seen, traditional culture was itself a mass of assimilations, the traditional way of life a series of adjustments to physical circumstance. Change is always awkward, but the changes modernity brought were often emancipations, and were frequently recognized as such. Old ways died unlamented. New goods created new needs; but even deprivation was measured at a higher level. And the old remembered. New ways that had once seemed objectionable were now deliberately pursued and assimilated—not by a fawning "bourgeoisie" or self-indulgent "intellectuals," as in Fanon's account, but by people of all sorts who had been exposed to such ways and acquired a taste for them. Perhaps this should make us think twice about "colonialism" in underdeveloped countries, which also reflects regional inequalities in development. It certainly qualifies the meaning of colonization as an internal process.

Development is not an equivocal term. It means only one thing: greater production of material goods and greater accessibility of material advantages to all. And that is what development brings, whatever disillusions may follow in its wake. The notion of underdevelopment has been criticized because it takes as its norm for underdeveloped societies the economy and culture of quite different societies.[25] Yet few underdeveloped societies live so isolated from developed societies as to be ignorant of their advantages. By the nine- teenth century the broadening scope of social and economic relations could well allow development and underdevelopment to be perceived objectively as rungs on the same ladder.

Thus, when we describe a given society as underdeveloped, we say not what the society is but what it is not. We describe what it is lacking: means of pro- duction, levels of productivity, forms of culture, life-styles, attitudes. In the present study, we have examined what may be called underdevelopment in nineteenth-century France. We have seen that the positive aspects and institu- tions of the underdeveloped regions were ways of coming to terms with want and insecurity. Custom and inertia made for their survival, opportunity for their abandonment. Perhaps the currently accepted views of colonialism need some qualification in this light; perhaps the unfashionable fin-de-siècle views of "progress" deserve another look. Or is the colonization of underdeveloped regions acceptable internally but unacceptable beyond the colonizer's home- land? What is a homeland? Something that time, accident, and opportunity have allowed to be hammered into shape and be accepted as a political entity: India, China, Mexico, the United States, the Soviet Union, the United Kingdom.

Let us now return to France and stay there. Conquest and colonization created it, as they did other realms, and the process was completed in the nineteenth century. What was the critical period? I have argued for the two score years on either side of 1900. Other arguments have been made, sometimes quite forcefully, for other periods. The more or less accepted view of the Great Revolution as a watershed cannot be ignored, bolstered as it has been by recent work on the profound changes affecting French family and sexual behavior long before 1870. Laurence Wylie and other sociologists have dwelt on the 1950's, when tractors, cars, and television sets hastened the cultural homogenization of slow-changing villages. One can make a similar case for the mid-nineteenth century, revolving around 1848 and the coming of the railways. Every such argument, including mine, is plausible; none is overwhelming.

Nor need one be. History, says Fernand Braudel, is the sum of all possible histories. The question to ask is not whether an argument is right enough to exclude all others, but *how* right it is, how much it tells us that we did not know. In these pages we have seen profound changes in productivity and diet shift portions of rural France away from the verge of catastrophe, from primitive want to needs that are more familiar.[26] We have seen national unity painfully forged at a later date than is generally supposed. We have seen cultural homogenization following economic integration, itself achieved after much effort and pain. We have seen that certain parts of France impressed their values and techniques (sometimes deliberately) on other parts, altering their way of life. We have seen that this process proceeded slowly and unevenly, far more so than most accounts of the nineteenth century suggest. We have seen, in short, the nation not as a given reality but as a work-in-progress, a model of something at once to be built and to be treated for political reasons as already in existence.

My argument has not been that the early years of the Third Republic were *the* time of transition from the traditional to the modern world in great portions of rural France, but rather that they were *one* such time—as important as any other, more important than most. To make this point, I have tried to show not only that many things changed during the period, but that they changed faster or more significantly than they had done before that period or would do after it.

I submit that this has been shown. Between 1880 and 1910 fundamental changes took place on at least three fronts. Roads and railroads brought hitherto remote and inaccessible regions into easy contact with the markets and lifeways of the modern world. Schooling taught hitherto indifferent millions the language of the dominant culture, and its values as well, among them patriotism. And military service drove these lessons home. The forces of modernization affected different areas different ways at different times.* But after the changes described in this book had taken place, variations in language and behavior were significantly less and the ascendancy of modernity was significantly greater. The regions of France were vastly more alike in 1910 than they had been before Jules Ferry, before Charles Freycinet, before Jules Rieffel.

In 1836 Adolphe d'Angeville concluded the introduction of his pioneer statistical essay with the observation, anticipating Disraeli, that there were two nations in France, divided by the now familiar imaginary line running from Saint-Malo to Geneva. North of that line peasants were fewer but taller, better fed, better schooled, and housed in homes lit by more windows. Their vices tended to be those of the new society (suicide, illegitimacy), their crimes to be against property rather than persons. They were relatively easy to recruit for army service and relatively quick to pay their taxes, as befits citizens of a modern nation. In the south people were shorter, worse fed, and worse housed. They were violent in both crime and politics, hostile to taxes, and slow to accept conscription. Roads in the south were thinner on the ground. Land was less productive, and the tools and methods of working it were less developed.[27]

This geographical division was in effect the division between urban and rural France—better still, between the poor, backward countryside and the areas of France, rural or not, that were to some degree permeated by the values of the modern world. As a Tulle newspaper put it in 1849, the peasants of Nord were like bourgeois, the peasants of Corrèze like beggars. That was the distinction that had to end if the real France was to be the France of political rhetoric. And we have seen it ending. In the event, more and more peasants of Corrèze became like bourgeois, too, in exactly the sense that the writer of 1849 had meant.†

* Common sense and the evidence I have seen suggest that the various regions succumbed to civilization roughly in relation to their exposure to urban—and especially Parisian—influence and to the degree of such influence, the facility, hence the scale, of migration, the proximity of railroads, and so on. Yet even here there is no watertight rule: the Limousin, closer to Paris, was opened to its influence later than Provence, which of course not only benefited from the traditional Rhône valley link and earlier railway connections, but was more urbanized. Still, why did the men of faraway Ardèche migrate to Paris in greater numbers than those of Nièvre or Orne? (See L. M. Goreux, "Les Migrations agricoles," p. 365.) Explanations can be found, of course; but they encumber any general rule with numerous exceptions. The point about generalizations is that they are only generally true, at best.

† The two Frances d'Angeville evoked still jostled each other as the nineteenth century ended; but their differences had been attenuated. Deficiencies in diet were less remarkable. After 1880 the children of the south grew taller. After 1900 southern conscripts began to close the gap between themselves and the tall men of the north. By then they had already caught up with the north in literacy. And though fertility among married couples (one indication of a change in mentality) tended to decline later in departments south of the line, the proportion of women getting married increased in the south almost as fast as in the north. (See Etienne Van de Walle, *The Female Population of France*, especially pp. 178, 184.)

But something even more important than that was happening, something that did not happen in 1789 or 1848 or 1950, a change that represents in retrospect the great cultural event of the time: the end of a profound division of the mind.

From the Middle Ages to the seventeenth century, high and low cultures agreed on the fundamental interpretation of the world and of life. Literacy or illiteracy made little difference to people's understanding of the condition of man, his purpose and his means. Knowledge varied in degree but not in kind. In the seventeenth century things changed. Natural science and rationalism with its particular logic created a separate culture of the literate, while the illiterate clung to the old ways. The relative cultural unity of Western society was dissolved, and people henceforth lived in two different worlds of the mind.

Coherent religious theories of life that had been accepted by most educated members of the community became survivals—superstitions—no longer compatible with the scientific principles of the time. Correspondences and analogies that made sense in one system seemed childish and futile to the other. What had been common sense was forsaken by those who pursued higher wisdom, and became the province of those who regulated their existence by the seasons and the stars. Deprived of the support of elite thought, popular belief broke into a thousand subsystems unintegrated into a comprehensive view of the world. Popular wisdom was bitsy—a collection of recipes, ceremonies, rituals—and popular religion was little more. Yet both were crucial, providing believers with things people badly need: explanations, a sense of control, reassurance, a framework for individual and social activities. From the cultivated point of view, popular culture was a morass of deprivation and ignorance. So was it from the point of view of its own most gifted spirits, those who yearned in vain for truths this culture could not teach them. Much popular magic and religion—and some rejection of both—reflected a persistent quest for just such truths.

After about 1650, then, the culture of the elite and that of the rural masses went their separate ways. (The urban masses were quicker to assimilate rationalistic ideas, as befitted their place in the capitalist scheme of things.) When, after about 1800, the gap began to narrow, it was thanks in large part to the rural world's increasing intercourse with the urban world. But material circumstances were crucial: increasingly effective control of the environment opened the door to urban views suggested by like experience. The more sophisticated people of the city believed, and in time demonstrated to the satisfaction of more and more peasants, that the world could be explained without evoking magic or supernatural intervention. The rural convert to rationalism could throw away his ragbag of traditional contrivances, dodges in an unequal battle just to stay alive, with the heady conviction that, far from being a helpless witness of natural processes, he was himself an agent of change.

At best, most people approached change hesitantly and experienced its effects with great ambivalence. But once they had drunk of its fountain, there was no turning back. The pattern of nineteenth-century belief continued to be, as Jacob Burckhardt said, "rationalism for the few and magic for the many."[28] Yet, by the end of the century, the nature of the magic, and the authority on which it was accepted, had profoundly changed. People still took their cultural norms and assumptions from others; but popular and elite culture had come together again.

APPENDIX

Use of French Language Among the General Population and in the Public Schools, 1863

Department and number of communes	Non-French-speaking communes		French-speaking communes		Language of instruction			Schoolchildren (ages 7–13)		
	No.	Population	No.	Population	Schools using idiom or patois only	Schools using idiom or patois and French	Schools using French only	Unable to speak or write French	Able to speak but unable to write French	Able to speak and write French
Ain—450	5	1,029	445	368,738			809	3,731	15,594	21,137
Aisne—836			836	564,597			1,215		24,511	32,102
Allier—317			317	356,432			472		17,535	24,549
Alpes (Basses-)—254	244	122,206	10	24,162			495	2,525	5,364	6,588
Alpes (Hautes-)—189			189	125,100			623	579	4,052	9,856
Alpes-Maritimes—146	87	126,524	59	68,054		5	352	11,318	4,180	4,954
Ardèche—339	181	167,245	158	221,284		66	712	5,846	27,999	11,049
Ardennes—478			478	329,111			747		8,479	25,662
Ariège—336	332	229,676	4	22,174			415	13,676	8,263	4,461
Aube—446			446	262,785			588		6,242	18,691
Aude—434	430	229,487	4	54,119			626	6,180	8,801	13,842
Aveyron—282	282	396,025					1,204	9,681	19,606	19,366
Bouches-du-Rhône—106			106	507,112			638	5,257	32,349	13,583
Calvados—767			767	480,992			989		13,299	29,650
Cantal—259			259	240,523			649	3,123	12,458	9,991
Charente—428	102	91,568	326	287,513			657	3,717	12,981	18,675
Charente-Inférieure—479			479	481,060			835	226	27,001	28,035
Cher—290			290	323,393			407		25,882	16,315
Corrèze—286	211	218,839	75	91,279			463	16,520	9,352	9,647
Corsica—353	353	252,889			448		68	19,082	5,598	6,721
Côte-d'Or—717			717	384,140			1,006		16,671	21,136
Côtes-du-Nord—382	178	301,610	204	327,066		299	368	19,913	38,296	28,861

Department										
Creuse—261			261	270,055			424	1,938	13,455	13,996
Dordogne—582			582	501,687			762	16,234	13,108	18,140
Doubs—639	210	86,129	639	296,580			929	5,644	14,616	17,818
Drôme—366			156	240,255			760		20,274	8,550
Eure—700			700	398,661			748		27,335	8,324
Eure-et-Loir—426			426	290,455	373		552		5,250	24,724
Finistère—284	272	506,956	12	120,348	33		128	29,683	23,814	18,615
Gard—348			348	422,107			919	242	24,523	19,422
Garonne (Haute-)—578	547	298,012	31	186,069			957	7,766	23,359	16,738
Gers—466	466	298,931	547	667,193			747	7,124	7,126	9,757
Gironde—547	324	276,095	7	133,296			1,152	9,729	16,846	34,004
Hérault—331			350	584,930			976	11,828	11,500	19,500
Ille-et-Vilaine—350			245	270,054			732		46,095	19,329
Indre—245			281	323,572			350		12,544	16,986
Indre-et-Loire—281			233	286,613			441		8,296	21,496
Isère—550	317	291,135	583	298,053			1,229	12,722	25,049	24,425
Jura—583	307	232,894	24	67,945			932	16	8,068	24,155
Landes—331			298	269,029			512	25,670	5,315	2,147
Loir-et-Cher—298			320	517,603			433		11,968	17,140
Loire—320	235	218,940	25	86,581			706	4,176	47,523	10,789
Loire (Haute-)—260			208	580,207			502		5,695	14,193
Loire-Inférieure—208			349	352,757			628	13,566	29,298	37,844
Loiret—349	290	223,385	25	72,157			614		8,555	34,225
Lot—315			192	244,324			631	17,079	7,476	5,805
Lot-et-Garonne—316	124	87,741	193	137,367			572	4,482	7,134	21,456
Lozère—193			376	526,012			849	3,893	7,234	3,762
Maine-et-Loire—376			644	591,421			768		23,270	31,032
Manche—644			667	385,498			1,217		27,118	32,636
Marne—667			550	254,413			950		8,446	30,123
Marne (Haute-)—550			274	375,163			796		6,512	19,064
Mayenne—274			637	381,903			541		10,083	29,338
Meurthe—714	77	46,740				170	1,040	2,451	1,652	39,417

APPENDIX (continued)

Use of French Language Among the General Population and in the Public Schools, 1863

Department and number of communes	Non-French-speaking communes No.	Population	French-speaking communes No.	Population	Language of instruction			Schoolchildren (ages 7–13)		
					Schools using idiom or patois only	Schools using idiom or patois and French	Schools using French only	Unable to speak or write French	Able to speak but unable to write French	Able to speak and write French
Meuse—587	109	251,809	587	305,540		181	939	20,457	234	30,305
Morbihan—237	245	179,782	128	234,695		504	268	14,565	22,901	11,055
Moselle—629			384	266,675			644		400	40,657
Nièvre—314			314	332,814			458		22,298	18,966
Nord—660	83	112,935	577	1,190,445		146	1,345	3,800	68,316	84,587
Oise—700			700	401,417			967		4,206	42,338
Orne—511			511	423,350			738		26,468	13,236
Pas-de-Calais—903			903	724,338			1,381		52,936	29,196
Puy-de-Dôme—443	420	466,455	23	109,954	14		947	8,581	37,760	21,333
Pyrénées (Basses-)—559	292	199,329	267	237,299		48	875	11,158	22,396	22,276
Pyrénées (Hautes-)—479	462	185,615	17	54,564			781	7,259	3,992	10,431
Pyrénées-Orientales—230			230	181,763	45		373	8,406	6,757	5,059
Rhin (Bas-)—542	437	290,565	105	287,009		513	614	29,730	13,214	39,138
Rhin (Haut-)—490	203	258,456	287	257,346		685	216	12,968	11,752	49,402
Rhône—258			258	662,493			866	2,423	25,656	33,513
Saône (Haute-)—583			583	317,183			1,037		259	29,676
Saône-et-Loire—583			583	582,137			979		41,409	27,191
Sarthe—389			389	466,155			679		11,353	36,550
Savoie—325			325	275,039			973		20,631	14,392
Savoie (Haute-)—309			309	267,496			621	5,605	6,539	18,898
Seine—70			70	1,953,660			1,647	4,000	10,000	159,124
Seine-Inférieure—759			759	789,988			1,323		62,710	19,082

Department										
Seine-et-Marne—527			527	352,312			767		12,401	26,950
Seine-et-Oise—684			684	513,073			1,056		1,820	49,663
Sèvres (Deux-)—355			355	328,817			573		23,047	13,176
Somme—832			832	572,646			1,321		20,172	35,841
Tarn—316	306	270,278	10	83,355			665	5,582	5,384	27,716
Tarn-et-Garonne—193			193	232,551			388	892	6,428	13,343
Var—143	143	315,526					463	8,290	7,328	11,869
Vaucluse—149			149	268,255			387	3,524	5,707	19,606
Vendée—298			298	395,695			554		43,319	2,278
Vienne—296			296	322,028			476		15,790	19,288
Vienne (Haute-)—200	105	190,146	95	129,449			412	3,715	13,773	12,007
Vosges—548	2	1,106	546	414,379			1,033	1,756	9,863	32,808
Yonne—483			483	370,305			737			39,059
TOTAL—37,510	8,381	7,426,058	29,129	29,956,167	92	3,438	65,338	448,328	1,490,269	2,079,830

SOURCE: Archives Nationales, F17* 3160, manuscript Ministère de l'instruction publique, 1863: "Statistique. Etats divers."
NOTE: French was not in general use in any of the communes of 4 of the 89 departments, was not in use in more than half the communes of 20 others, and was not in use in a significant proportion of another 6. In 2 other departments, though the bulk of the communes were French-speaking, sizable areas still were not.

NOTES

NOTES

Complete authors' names, titles, and publication data for works cited in short form are given in the Bibliography, pp. 573–96. On the works cited in full in these Notes, the place of publication is Paris unless otherwise noted. I have used the following abbreviations in the citations:

AD	Archives Départementales
AEP	Archives de l'Enseignement Primaire
AG	Archives Administratives de la Guerre. Service Historique de l'Armée
AN	Archives Nationales
Atlas	*Atlas folklorique de la France*, Archives of the Musée des Arts et Traditions Populaires, "Enquête," 1944
ATP	Manuscript surveys of the Musée des Arts et Traditions Populaires
BFI	*Bulletin folklorique de l'Ile-de-France*
BFS	*Bulletin de la Société Franklin*, 4 (1872)
EA	"Enquête sur les formes anciennes de l'agriculture," 1937, Archives of the Musée des Arts et Traditions Populaires
HE	Monographies d'instituteurs, Archives de l'Enseignement Primaire
JO	*Journal Officiel*
MATP	Archives of the Musée des Arts et Traditions Populaires
MR	Mémoires et reconnaissances files, Archives du Ministère de la Guerre
RDM	*Revue des deux mondes*
RGA	*Revue de géographie alpine*
VA	Varagnac archives, including Moisson/St. Jean (manuscript surveys of the Musée des Arts et Traditions Populaires)

Introduction

1. See André Siegfried's preface to Thabault, *Mon village*, p. 7.

2. Varagnac, pp. 58–59.

3. Wright, pp. v, vi.

4. AN, *Etat sommaire des versements faits aux Archives Nationales par les ministères et les administrations. Supplément*, 3.2 (1957), 8: "La comparaison est saisissante entre l'absence quasi totale de documents pour la période 1880–1914 et l'extraordinaire richesse de versements effectués après 1936." See also AN, "Ministère de la Justice, Division

criminelle, Correspondance 1870–1887," manuscript introduction dated summer 1938: "Il semble, à moins qu'un ensemble de documents que j'ignore vienne remplacer ces dossiers détruits de la division criminelle, qu'il sera impossible à l'historien d'écrire la vie journalière de la Troisième République en France entre les années 1870 et 1890."

5. "Fin-de-Siècle: The Third Republic Makes a Modern Nation," in Mathé Allain and Glenn R. Conrad, eds., *France and North America: Over Three Hundred Years of Dialogue* (Lafayette, La., 1973).

Chapter One

Epigraph. "Avertissement" to *Petites garnisons, Cahiers de la quinzaine,* 5.12 (1904): 9.

1. Balzac, *La Comédie humaine,* 8 (1969): 35; AD, Ariège Pe 45 (July 30, 1831); Thuillier, "Pour une histoire," p. 257; all military quotations are drawn from AG, MR 2281.

2. Haussmann, 1: 104.

3. EA, Landes.

4. Feret, 1: especially p. 310.

5. AG, MR 1228 (1843), MR 1234 (1843), MR 1207 (1857).

6. Joseph Roux, p. 147.

7. AG, MR 1300 (Hte.-Vienne, 1822), MR 1236 (Morbihan, 1822), MR 1231 (Landes, 1843), MR 2281 (Loire-Inf., 1850); Souvestre, *Derniers paysans,* 2: 84.

8. Romieu, p. 319.

9. AD, Vaucluse, M 11–45 (Apt, Feb. 15, 1850); *Courrier de la Drôme,* Dec. 18, 1851; Vigier, 2: 152ff, 278, 335; David, p. 15.

10. AD, Finistère, 10 U 7 (1867, 1886).

11. AG, MR 2281 (Nièvre, 1862); Bois, *Paysans* (1960 ed.), pp. 68–69, quoting a primary school inspector's report of 1873.

12. AN, F[17] 9259 (Côtes-du-Nord). See also Lagarde, p. 19.

13. Trébucq, *Chanson populaire en Vendée,* p. 99; Trébucq, *Chanson populaire et la vie rurale,* 1: 233. AG, MR 1218 (1825), contains a report concerning the area of St.-Pons and St.-Amand (Hérault) that gives a rather ironic account of local customs as odd as those of savages. In AD, Pyrs.-Ors., 3Mi 224, the commissaire spécial at St. Laurent refers (Feb. 11, 1896) to "ces contrées à demi-sauvages," inhabited by besotted populations.

14. Ardouin-Dumazet, 28: 252–53.

15. See Agulhon, *1848,* p. 120. Yet none of the court records on rural arrondissements that I have examined shows any prosecution under this law up to 1906.

16. Marcilhacy, "Emile Zola," p. 583.

17. Merley, p. 247.

18. Elisa Chevalier, p. 274; AG, MR 1274 (1857).

19. Léon Gambetta, *Discours et plaidoyers politiques,* 2 (1881): 22, 29.

20. AN, F[17] 9269 Morbihan, (insp. gén., June 8, 1880); *Instruction primaire,* 1: especially p. 805; Trébucq, *Chanson populaire en Vendée,* p. 30.

21. Combes and Combes, p. 41.

22. Stendhal, *Vie de Henri Brulard,* quoted in François, pp. 769–70; Flaubert, 1: 285.

23. Bardoux, p. 228; Déribier Du Châtelet, pp. 180, 182.

24. David, pp. 15–16, 20–22; Bonnemère, 2: 352.

25. AG, MR 2281 (Le Mans, 1861; Bourges, 1862), MR 2262 (1873).

26. Fage, *Autour de la mort,* p. 4; Ardouin-Dumazet, 34: 335; Mauriac, p. 34.

27. On Parisians, especially of the lower and working classes, despising countrymen, see René Bonnet, *Enfance,* pp. 24ff: "péquenot," "bouseux," "encore un qui n'a pas été baptisé à Notre Dame," etc.

28. Le Gallo, 1: 62–65; *La Croix des Côtes-du-Nord,* Dec. 23, 1894.

29. *Encyclopédie*, 6 (1756): 527, under "Fermier"; Bois, *Paysans* (1960 ed.), pp. 298, 301.

30. Mme. Clément-Hennery, *Promenades dans l'arrondissement d'Avesnes* (1828), quoted in Van Gennep, *Folklore de Flandre*, 1: 14; Demolins, *Supériorité*, p. 226.

31. Mandrou, 1975 ed., p. 177; Nelli, p. 33. The *Progrès libéral* of Toulouse noted the custom as late as 1878. See Jalby, p. 17. Others used the notion of race in a similar context. See Audiganne, *Populations*, 2: 49; and Méline, p. 218.

32. Esnault, *Imagination*, pp. 100–102; Garneret, p. 89; Bodard, pp. 27–28; David, p. 13; Betham-Edwards, *France*, 1: 164.

33. Esnault, *Imagination*, pp. 284–85. Local speech often assimilated middle-class arrogance and Parisian pretensions. On Picardy, see Picoche, p. 77. In Saintonge they said of an uppity parvenu(e): "On dirait que son thiu é d'la ville de Paris!" (Doussinet, *Le Paysan*, p. 441.)

34. AD, Ariège 5M3 (July 5, 1856); Souvestre, *Derniers paysans*, 1: 133.

35. Halbwachs, "Genre de vie," pp. 439–55. Just as revealing, in the 163 pages of Redfield's *Peasant Society and Culture*, there are copious references to Islamic, Asian, African, and Latin American societies and cultures but scarcely any remarks about Europe.

36. Thus in 1901 one survey, among many, could speak of "almost all our youth." Eugène Montfort, "Les Tendances de la jeunesse française au XXe siècle," *La Revue*, June 15, 1901, pp. 581–609.

37. Haussmann, 1: vii.

38. Blanqui, "Tableau," 28: 9–13, and 30: 1.

39. *Ibid.*, 30: 1; Bonnemère, 2: 355. See Lavergne, *Agriculture*, p. 416, for confirmation of the prediction ten years later.

40. Gambetta, *Discours* (cited in note 19 above), 4: 317–30.

41. Baudrillart, 3: 389.

42. Lavergne, *Agriculture*, p. 416.

43. Jules Brame (Nord) in *Moniteur universel*, June 19, 1861, pp. 928–29.

44. Jeanton, *Légende*, pp. 72–73; Cobb, *Police*, p. 297.

45. Cénac-Moncaut, *Littérature*, pp. 309, 312; Cénac-Moncaut, *Conte populaire*.

46. *Evocations*, Oct. 1965, pp. 22–24.

47. Souvestre, *Derniers Bretons* (1843 ed.), p. 118.

48. *Le Patriote savoisien* (Chambéry), Sept. 9, 1870, quoted in Lovie, p. 493.

49. Corbin, pp. 1087, 1106.

50. *Ibid.*, pp. 678–79; Vigier, 2: 164, 312–13.

51. (London) *Times Literary Supplement*, May 4, 1973, p. 490.

52. AN, F¹ᶜ V Loiret 6 (conseil gén., Aug. 1840); *L'Echo du Cantal*, May 31, 1856.

53. Gorse, pp. 37, 45; Robert Sabatier, p. 249; Doniol, *Patois*, pp. 107–8; Trébucq, *Chanson populaire en Vendée*, p. 240.

54. Ardouin-Dumazet, 28: 166–67; Perrin and Bouet, pp. 386–87; Vazeilles, 2: 6; Rouchon, 1: 84, and 2: 113; Gorse, p. 125.

55. Decoux-Lagoutte, p. 36; Coissac, p. 238; Marius Vazeilles, *Bulletin de la Société des Lettres, Sciences et Arts de la Corrèze*, 1956, p. 12.

56. AG, MR 1282 (Puy-de-Dôme, 1850); AD, Ariège 5M3 (1850).

57. See Blanqui, "Tableau," 30: 5, claiming that over one million lived at this level of destitution in the mid-19th century; AD, Yonne III M¹ 131 (July 7, 1849); and Lafayette, "Paysages," p. 538.

58. AD, Pyrs.-Ors. 3M1 246 (1888). The bourrée is from Poueigh, *Chanson populaires*, 1: 203: "Bido d'un pastou/ Bido régalado/ Le maiti léitou/ La neit, la calhado."

59. J.-A. Delpon, 1: 199.

60. Malon, p. 100.

61. Chaix, p. 274; Malon, p. 100; Trébucq, *Chanson populaire en Vendée*, p. 244; Pérot, p. 231.

62. Durand-Vangarou, 1 (1963): 337, and 2 (1964): 284, 312; Ardouin-Dumazet, 29: 242. See also Violet, *Clessé*, p. 114 (Mâconnais); Vidalenc, *Peuple des campagnes*, p. 99 (Châteauroux); Maupassant, 1: 264–65 (Lower Brittany); and Pasquet, p. 135 (Morvan).

63. Leproux, *Médecine*, p. 30; AD, Finistère 4M (Aug. 29, 1872).

64. See especially AN, BB 1935 and 1936; AD, Pyrs.-Ors. 3Mi 246 (Apr. 29, 1889); Lovie, p. 314; and Polge, *Matériaux*, p. 22.

65. AN, BB30 370 (Agen, Jan. 6, 1862).

66. *Revue de Gascogne*, 1884, quoted in Polge, *Matériaux*, p. 22: "Qui de palhe ague cobert, goarde que lo foec no s'y day de près."

67. Bonnemère, 2: 392–93; Buffet, *Bretagne*, p. 38. Even before machines, the introduction of scythes, which close-cropped the fields, and of rakes left little stubble suitable for thatch, as the Minister of Agriculture observed about Picardy in 1869. At the same time, a number of departments offered subsidies designed to encourage the replacement of thatch (Degrully, p. lxxxi).

68. Michel Chevalier, p. 669; Fourcassié, pp. 63–64; Ardouin-Dumazet, 40: 21.

69. Perron, *Proverbes*, p. 22; *Barbizier*, 1950, p. 376; Francus, *Midi de l'Ardèche*, p. 233.

70. Cobb, *Police*, pp. 317–18; AN, BB 24 327–47; AD, Yonne III M¹ 114 (préf., Nov. 7, 1839); AN, BB 24 327–47 (préf. Indre, 1848), Fⁱᶜ III Ariège 7 (sous-préf. St.-Girons, Dec. 27, 1853), Fⁱᶜ III Loiret 12 (1856–68), BB 30 371 (Angers, July 18, 1854).

71. Blanchard, p. 190; Lavergne, *Agriculture*, p. 102; J. A. Barral, *Agriculture de la Haute-Vienne*, p. viii.

72. AN, BB 18 1766, 1769, 1775 (Toulouse, Mar.–Aug. 1868).

73. Bunle, p. 84.

74. Michel, p. 226, quoted in Thomas, p. 21.

75. Perron, *Proverbes*, p. 66; Charrié, *Bas-Vivarais*, p. 246.

76. Juge, pp. 139, 150; Renard, *Philippe*; Francus, *Voyage Fantaisiste*, 2: 36.

77. Garneret, pp. 25, 30; Esnault, *Imagination*, p. 195. See the images in Méraville, p. 337: "batailler contre la terre," "lutter la vie," "on lutte la misère," etc.

78. AN, Fⁱᶜ III Hte.-Vienne 11 (préf. Hte.-Vienne, Sept. 30, 1858). On mediocrity, see the quote of Nicolas-François Cochard, administrator and historian of the First Empire, in Savigné, p. 12. "La loi divine du travail" was invoked by the Marquis de Beaucourt, president of the Société Bibliographique et des Publications Populaires, at the society's congress of Nov. 1890, supported by an impressive quotation from Monsignor Dupanloup (*Congrès*, 1890, p. 12).

79. AG, MR 1218 (Hérault, 1825); Labrune, p. 295; Bardoux, p. 231.

80. AD, Yonne III M¹ 234 (comm. de police St.-Florentin, Aug. 30, 1865); AN, BB 30 373 (proc. gén. Besançon, July 13, 1866); Boscary, pp. 214–17, quoting comm. de police of Aubin (Aveyron), 1866; Bastié, 2: 152; AD, Pyrs.-Ors. 3 Mi 224 (comm. spécial St.-Laurent, June 30, 1895).

81. HE II, Cesse (Meuse), 1899; Labourasse; AD, Vosges 11 T 18 (Damas-aux-Bois).

82. Baudrillart, 3: 120.

83. Lafayette, "Paysages," p. 549; Théron, p. 498.

Chapter Two

Epigraph. *Essays: of Superstition.*

1. Lavisse, *Année préparatoire*, pp. 41ff.

2. Côte, p. 54.

3. Littré, p. 13; Leproux, *Médecine*, pp. 30–35 (spells as protection); Ardouin-Dumazet, 30: 147 (Roquefort); Pérot, pp. 34, 141 (hunter's guns, marcous).

4. Lapaire, pp. 11–12; Déribier Du Châtelet, 2: 126; Drouillet, 4: 15–16, 31, 62–63. On the fate of the dead priests, see also Sébillot, *Folk-lore*, 4: 175.

5. Séguin, *Canards du siècle passé*, fig. 11; Van Gennep, "Cycle préhivernal," p. 19; Moiset, pp. 128–29. In George Sand's Berry, too, "wolves" or werewolves could be a cover for marauding gangs wearing wolfskins (Vincent, pp. 246–47).

6. Barral, *Agriculture de la Haute-Vienne*, p. 747; Marcelle Mourgues, "Mérimée à Cannes," *Provence historique*, July 1956, p. 194; Brekilien, p. 226; Hertz, pp. 186–87.

7. Duclos, 1: 24; Jalby, pp. 116, 119 ("S'érou pas las pooüs, los ritous crébarien de fan"); Dieudonné, 1: 103–6; Déribier Du Châtelet, 2: 126.

8. Souvestre, *Derniers paysans*, 1: 28; Brekilien, p. 241; *Petit journal*, June 1863; Claude Seignolle, *Les Evangiles du diable* (1967), p. 194; Pérot, pp. 122–23.

9. Jalby, p. 270; Bouteiller, *Sorciers*, p. 153.

10. Labrune, pp. 363ff; Marcilhacy, *Diocèse du XIXe siècle*, p. 127; Pérot, pp. 25, 104.

11. Drouillet, 4: especially p. 140; AN, F¹⁷ 9267 (Lozère, 1881).

12. Leproux, *Médecine*, pp. 48–49; Barker, *Summers*, p. 241; Feret, 1: 321–22.

13. Buffet, *Bretagne*, p. 44; Fage, *Fontaines*, p. 5.

14. Polge, *Quelques légendes*, pp. 71–81.

15. Polge, *Etudes et documents* (n.d.), 2: 57; Francus, *Valgorge*, pp. 46–47; Pérot, p. 9.

16. Pérot, p. 40; Violet, *Autrefois*, p. 39; Barker, *Summers*, p. 241; Polge, *Quelques légendes*, p. 76.

17. Fage, *Autour de la mort*, pp. 11–12.

Chapter Three

Epigraph. *Paradise Lost.*

1. Brochon, *Chanson française*, 2: 110–12: "Bravant la routine et sa haine, / Dans sa valeur puisant son droit, / La mesure républicaine / A détroné le pied de roi."

2. AD, Cantal, *Répertoire de la série T*, 1: 61; AN, F¹ᶜ III Ariège 7 (July 25, 1855).

3. AD, Vosges 11 T 19 (instituteur Docelles); Bois, *Paysans* (1971 ed.), p. 227; EA, Bassigny (Hte.-Marne); Ricard, p. 54; Haudricourt and Delamarre, especially p. 415.

4. Mazon, p. 45.

5. AD, Gironde, ser. U., Tribunal de Bazas, Police correctionnelle; AN, F¹⁷ 10757 (Bas-Rhin, 1861).

6. AN, F¹¹ 2734 (*Enquête agricole*, 1867, p. 321), F¹¹ 2727 (*Enquête agricole*, 1866, "Résumé des voeux émis dans les commissions départementales").

7. AG, MR 1212 (Isère, 1843), MR 2267 (1874); Pujos (Castelnau); Buffet, *Haute-Bretagne*, p. 148; Baudrillart, 3: 421; Gorse, pp. 42–43.

8. Reynier, *Histoire*, 3: 151; Pérot, *Folklore*, pp. 155–56; Gorse, pp. 42–43.

9. J. A. Barral, *Agriculture de la Haute-Vienne*, p. 75.

10. Hubscher, p. 365.

11. Perrin and Bouet, p. 90; Collot, p. 10; Dussourd, p. 57; Lejeune, 2: 210–11.

12. Machenaud, p. 51.

13. Clément Brun, p. 57 (Savoy); Cénac-Moncaut, *Colporteur*, pp. 10–11 (southwest); Duchatellier, *Agriculture*, pp. 190–91 (Lower Brittany); Le Guyader, p. 12 (Quimper); Anthony, pp. 73–75 (Breton denominations).

14. Alfred Giron, p. 43; Barker, *Wandering*, p. 119; Gorse, p. 276.

15. AD, Puy-de-Dôme M.04478 (comm. de police, Brassac, July 26, 1896) and M.04469 (sous-préf., Riom, Sept. 25, 1896); Ardouin-Dumazet, 32: 209; Valaux, p. 77; Gagnon, 2: 260; Chataigneau, p. 426; Bourdieu, "Célibat," p. 55.

16. Gadrat, p. 130; AN, F¹⁷ 10757 (Ariège, Jan. 1861), BB¹⁸ 1462 (proc. gén. Limoges, July 12, 1848); Thiriat, *Agriculture*, pp. 10–11; Audiganne, "Métayage," p. 643; AD, Finistère 4M355 (Landerneau, June 6, 1870); Roger Brunet, p. 201.

17. Norre, p. 9; Ajalbert, *En Auvergne*, p. 77.

18. Maspétiol, p. 153; Combes and Combes, pp. 174, 175 (St.-Gaudens, southwest); AG, MR 1223 (Millas, Thuir, etc., Pyrs.-Ors., 1837); Bailly, p. 29 (Brie); Foville, *Enquête*, 1: 147 (Bresse); Mazon, pp. 33–34 (muleteers); Ardouin-Dumazet, 28: 166 (Corrèze); G.-Michel Coissac, "Les Artisans de village," *Le Limousin de Paris*, Oct. 15, 1912.

19. Armengaud, *Populations*, p. 90; Bachelin, *Serviteur*, p. 69; *Evocations*, 1963, pp. 79–83 (cash wages in Lower Dauphiné became routine after 1918); *L'Aubrac*, 2: 97; Foville, *Enquête*, 1: 147; Ricard, pp. 63–64; Brekilien, p. 78.

20. Nelli, pp. 171–72; AN, BB 30 370 (Agen, July 28, 1856); Passama, p. 52.

21. Lavigne, p. 375; AG, MR 1195 (Hte.-Saône) quoted in Vidalenc, *Peuple des campagnes*, p. 138; Octave Mirbeau quoted by Jean Longuet, *La Raison*, June 1908, p. 5.

22. Francus, *Midi de l'Ardèche*, p. 245: "Qui tire de l'argent/est content. / Il peut payer / Il faut s'en tenir près."

23. Gorse, p. 27.

24. Corbin, pp. 205–7; Francus, *Valgorge*, p. 252.

25. Marcilhacy, *Diocèse du XIXe siècle*, pp. 138–40; Lavigne, p. 375; "Etat de la question des caisses d'épargne en France," *Journal des économistes*, July 1874, pp. 9–10; Bigo, pp. 207–8.

26. Portal, pp. 307–10.

27. Brochon, *Chanson sociale*, p. 67.

28. Girard, *Politique*, pp. 230–31; Corbin, pp. 205–21 *passim*; J. A. Barral, *Situation*, p. 54; AD, Hte.-Vienne M 101 (June 1909).

29. AN, F[ie] III Corrèze 3 (sous-préf. Brive, 1852); AG, MR 1300 (Hte.-Vienne, 1845); AN, F[ie] III Basses-Alpes (Apr. 15, 1856); Pariset, *Lauragais*, p. 187.

30. On working-class anti-Semitism, see Edmund Silberner, "Socialists and the Jewish Question, 1800–1914," manuscript in my possession, as well as Professor Silberner's numerous publications. See also a Ministry of the Interior circular of Mar. 21, 1848 (AD, Yonne III M[1] 116), reacting to the attacks on Jews after the February revolution. The worker-poets of mid-century readily identified banker and usurer with Jew. See Poncy, p. xvii (addressing his patron George Sand) and p. 70. The anti-Semitism of rural and urban Alsace is well documented. See Audiganne, *Populations*, 1: 157; Betham-Edwards, *France*, 1: 248; and above all Paul Leuilliot, "L'Usure judaïque en Alsace," *Annales historiques de la Révolution française*, 1930, pp. 231–50; Leuilliot, *L'Alsace au début du XIXe siècle* (3 vols., 1959–60); and F. L'Huillier's chapters in Dollinger, pp. 395–468.

31. See AD, Hte.-Vienne M 741 (sous-préf. St.-Yrieix, May 20, 1848), on the priest of Ladignac, who had 20 or 30 debtors in the commune and was owed at least 50,000 francs.

32. Demolins, *Comment élever enfants*, p. 2; Garneret, p. 7.

33. Thuillier, "Pour une histoire," p. 261.

34. Bigo, p. 59. See also Corbin, p. 202.

Chapter Four

Epigraph. *Du pouvoir* (Paris, 1947).

1. Labat, *En Gascogne*, p. 8 (originally printed in *RDM*, Aug. 1, 1910, p. 637). See also G. H. Bousquet, "Quelques remarques sur l'évolution de l'économie domestique en France depuis Louis-Philippe," *Revue d'histoire économique et sociale*, 1967, pp. 509–38.

2. Saint-Just quoted in C.-J. Gignoux, *Saint-Just* (1947), pp. 231–32; AG, MR 1282 (1827); Blanqui, "Tableau," 30: 3–5; AD, Yonne VIII M[4]5 (Feb. 10, 1847). Just how cut off some areas were may be seen from the opening lines of a marriage contract signed in Aveyron in the last years of the July Monarchy: "Du 14 janvier 1846. Napoléon par la grâce de Dieu et la volonté nationale, Empereur des Français, à tous présents et à venir. Salut. Par devant Me Jean Victor Auguste G., notaire royal à la résidence de

Saint-Chély d'aubrac." *L'Aubrac*, 3: 309, quotes this without comment. One may compare it with a note in the *Wall Street Journal* of Aug. 8, 1975: "Economy-minded Democratic Gov. Dukakis of Massachusetts still uses stationery bearing the name of his Republican predecessor."

3. Bonnemère, 2: 375; Hudry-Ménos, p. 635; Pariset, *Lauragais*, p. 44.

4. Railroads killed almost as many vineyards as the Phylloxera—those of Brie, among others, where under the July Monarchy the vine had reigned around Meaux. See Bailly, p. 15.

5. Meynier, *A travers le Massif Central*, p. 362; Gachon, *Commune*, p. 143; René Dumont, p. 187. Fauvet and Mendras, map 8, p. 33, shows that autarky still survived in large parts of Aveyron, Cher, Corrèze, Dordogne, Loire-Inf., Mayenne, Morbihan, Basses- and Htes.-Pyrénées, Sarthe, and Vendée. See also maps 10 and 11 on p. 34.

6. AG, MR 1282 (1827).

7. Robert Redfield, "Primitive Merchants of Guatemala," *Quarterly Journal of Inter-American Relations*, 1939, pp. 42–56; Irwin Sanders, *Balkan Village* (Lexington, Ky., 1949), pp. 105–6.

8. AN, Dordogne F⁹177 (préf. to Min. de Guerre, Mar. 4, 1830); Gadrat, p. 127; Morère, "Revolution de 1848," p. 61. On Nièvre and Allier, see AG, MR 1278 (1841); on Vendée, Cavoleau, pp. 92, 639; on Lozère and Aveyron, AG, MR 1274 (ca. 1836); and on Oléron, AG, MR 1233 (1847). See also, on Beaulieu, AG, MR 1228 (1843): *Itinéraire de Bayonne à Tulle*, a fascinating document. Beaulieu-sur-Dordogne was chef-lieu of its canton of Corrèze. Its population in 1973 was 1,794.

9. Roubin, p. 105. "Better fart in company than die alone," they said in Lower Vivarais; and it was well not to attract the disapproval of one's neighbors for, as another proverb had it, "Mal vu, moitié pendu." (Charrié, *Bas-Vivarais*, p. 245.)

10. Ricard, p. 84 (Landes); Laurentin, 1: 51 (Lourdes); Guillaumin, *Appui de la Manche*, p. 73 (about the period 1903–5).

11. AG, MR 1234 (1822), MR 1274 (1857), MR 2275 (1877); Trébucq, *Chanson populaire et la vie rurale*, 1: 51.

12. AG, MR 1282 (1827).

13. AG, MR 1274 (1836), MR 1278 (Nièvre, 1840); Lafayette, "Paysages," p. 537; AG, MR 1274 (1826); Rocal, p. 269.

14. AG, MR 2267 (1873), MR 2275 (1877); Barker, *Wandering*, pp. 173–74; Trébucq, *Chanson populaire et la vie rurale*, 1: 51.

15. Mireur, 5: 280.

16. See, for examples among many, Jean Caziot, *La Valeur de la terre en France* (1914), p. 299; H. Germouty's introduction to the 1912 ed. of Nadaud, pp. 11–12; and C.-F. Ramuz, *Salutation paysanne* (1929), p. 22. Administrative and cultural divisions were far from similar, and the pays reflected the latter. Thus, until the Revolution Aigurande in Indre belonged to Berry and the bishopric of Bourges though it was administratively linked to the Marche; but some of its outlying villages belonged to the Marche and the bishopric of Limoges. As a result, until the late 19th century the inhabitants of the lower part of town (Berry) called the upper town La Marche.

17. Poueigh, *Folklore*, p. 11: Cado terro sa guerro; / Cado pais soun bist; / Cado bilatge soun lengatge; / Cado parsa soun parla; / Cado maison sa faiçon. (Chaque terre sa guerre; / Chaque pays son aspect; / Chaque village son langage; / Chaque lieu son parler; / Chaque maison sa façon.)

18. Gorse, p. 210.

19. Armengaud, *Populations*, p. 12; AN, F¹⁷9261 (Finistère, 1880), F¹⁷9269 (Morbihan, 1880); Le Lannou, 2: 409; Buffet, *Haute-Bretagne*, p. 20.

20. Renard, *Mots*, pp. 22–25; Dauzat, *Glossaire*, p. 18.

21. AN, F¹⁷ 9265 (Loire-Inf., May 4, 1880).

22. Audiganne, *Populations*, 2: 99–100.

23. Gachon, *Auvergne*, p. 145; Wylie, *Chanzeaux*, p. 16; *Barbizier*, 1950, p. 357; Francus, *Voyage fantaisiste*, 2: 465.

24. Michel Chevalier, "La Vallée de Campan et la République d'Andorre," *RDM*, 1837, no. 4, pp. 618–42, quoted in M. Chevalier, p. 659; Perrin and Bouet, p. 185; Valaux, p. 67; Norre, p. 7.

25. Hérelle, *Etudes*, especially pp. 70–71. See also Assier, 3d ed., pp. 231–40.

26. Esnault, *Imagination*, p. 151; Jeanton, *Légende*, p. 32; Norre, p. 7. In Bourbonnais the term *arcandier*, derived from *marcandier* (peddler), means vagabond, thief, good-for-nothing, like its needy and thievish prototype (see R. Brunet, p. 15).

27. Gorse, p. 210; Van Gennep in preface to Seignolle. See also Gadrat, p. 126.

28. Michel Chevalier, p. 176.

29. Norre, p. 7; Seignolle, pp. 33–34.

30. Guillaumin, *Panorama*, p. 60; Roubin, p. 164; Gorse, p. 286; *Barbizier*, 1950, p. 357; Hérelle, *Etudes*, pp. 165–66; Belbèze, p. 30.

31. Berthout, p. 23.

Chapter Five

Epigraph. "Justice, my friend, is like spiderwebs. It only catches little flies, the oxfly breaks the web."

1. Blanqui, "Tableau," 30: 14; Juge, p. 128; AG, MR 1300 (Hte.-Vienne, 1843); Leproux, *Dévotions*, p. 5.

2. Leproux, *Dévotions*, p. 5; Bougeatre, p. 17; Esnault, *Imagination*, pp. 227–28; Jeanton, *Légende*, p. 88.

3. Blanqui, "Tableau," 30: 14; Sébillot, *Littérature*: Les huissiers sont des fripons, / Les avocats sont des liche-plats, / Les procureurs sont des voleurs.

4. Labrune, pp. 267–78. Nor, of course, were they unaware that "judges excuse the wine and hang the bottle." As another proverb had it, "It always rains upon the soaked" (Béteille, pp. 36, 177).

5. AG, MR 2267 (Ille-et-Vilaine, 1875); Belbèze, p. 108.

6. AG, ser. G8 (correspondance générale).

7. A. M. Guerry de Champneuf, *Essai sur la statistique morale de la France* (1833), p. 39; Levasseur, 2: 455; Gabriel Tarde, p. 69.

8. Levasseur, 2: 456; Szabo, pp. 39–40.

9. Davidovitch, pp. 45–47; Levasseur, 2: 443, 450; Robert Vouin and Jacques Léauté, *Droit pénal et criminologie* (1956), pp. 45–47. Compare A. Q. Lodhi and Charles Tilly, "Urbanization, Crime and Collective Violence in 19th-Century France," *American Journal of Sociology*, 1973, pp. 296–318. Unfortunately, their data are confined to major crimes. For some explanations of statistical tides, see M. Perrot, "Délinquance et système pénitentiaire en France au XIXe siècle," *Annales: E. S. C.*, 1975, especially p. 72.

10. See Corbin, pp. 110–11; and AD, Gers M 2799 (gendarmes Nogaro, Sept. 3, 1875).

11. Perrin and Bouet, pp. 198–200; Séguin, *Canards du siècle passé*, p. 43; Michel Chevalier, p. 611. For a striking illustration, in this connection, see the etching by Auguste Lepère entitled *Pilleurs et épaves* (undated but probably made in the 1860's or 1870's) in Gabriel P. Weisberg, ed., *Social Concern and the Worker* (Utah Museum of Fine Arts, 1973), no. 37, p. 86.

12. AN, F¹¹712, préf. Nantes, quoted by Cobb, *Police*, p. 305. Folktales show little trace of sympathy for such outlaws; most reflect dread and fear of their vengeance. Only execution could deliver the peasants of their depredations, and this, in most stories, was carried out by gendarmes, who cut off the bandit's head or burned him alive. See Marie-

Aymée Méraville, *Contes populaires de l'Auvergne* (1970), pp. 75–79 and especially pp. 116–21.

13. AN, F⁷12850 (Bastia, Jan. 31, 1896, Calvi, Feb. 6, 1896, Corte, Feb. 5, 1896, Sartène, Jan. 5, 1908, and *passim*).

14. AD, Yonne III M²²17 (sous-préf. Joigny, Apr. 17, 1855); Flaubert, 1: 308. Dubief, p. 251, writing in 1911, asserted that there were no police forces worth speaking of in the countryside.

15. Gabriel Tarde, p. 98; Davidovitch, pp. 41–42. But when, as in 1870–71, police manpower was siphoned off for wartime tasks, the number of *délits constatés* fell off markedly. Note that by 1885 the number of police (14,886) and gendarmes (20,874) stood at about the level that was to obtain to the eve of the war (A. Lacassagne, *Peine de mort et criminalité*, 1908, p. 68).

16. Henri Polge, personal communication to author, Nov. 27, 1973 (Basque clergy); A.-E. de Saintes, *Michel, le jeune chevrier* (the cited novel); AG, MR 1221 (1835), MR 1223 (1837).

17. AD, Gers M 2237 (comm. de police, Lombez, Dec. 10, 1876), reporting that contraband matches were widely available, and that with the end of home searches people were buying more than ever. See also AD, Puy-de-Dôme M 04476 (sous-préf. Thiers, July 27, 1890). The civil court files of Ste.-Menehould show prosecutions as late as 1885 for contraband tobacco, as late as 1888 for the possession of contraband matches, and as late as 1908 for the smuggling and illegal sale of matches (AD, Marne, 11 U 912 and 915).

18. J.-A. Delpon, 1: 204; AD, Lot 7 M 10 (which bulges with reports of such brawls between rival villages, 1816–47); Malaussène, p. 13.

19. AD, Finistère 4 M 322 (Mar. 2–14, 1866).

20. AD, Puy-de-Dôme M 04478 (1896; 1897), Pyrs.-Ors. 3 Mi 246 (1889–91); *Le Finistère*, Jan. 11, 1890 (for what this is worth, of three court cases reported in this issue, one was for theft and the others for rape, one involving a minor); AN, F⁷12849; and F⁷12850 (the Corsican files). Francus, *Vivarais*, p. 180, has a suggestive comment about the once-famous cutlery of Montpezat (Ardèche): "L'adoucissement des moeurs parait avoir beaucoup nui au commerce des couteaux." But not in the adjacent mountains.

21. AD, Finistère 10 U 7/39. One might add to this Yves Castan's remarks about the 18th-century Gascon's "propensity to suspicion, to fear, even to panic" on the slightest provocation. The trip home from a fair at nightfall, often in a drunken state, was frequently an occasion of great misapprehension and panic fears that turned into unpremeditated violence. See André Abbiateci et al., *Crimes et criminalité en France sous l'Ancien Régime* (1971), p. 168.

22. AD, Gers M 2172 (sous-préf. Lombez, Jan. 19, 1872), Cantal 42 M2 (July 22, 1861), Gers M 2799 (comm. de police Lectoure, Mar. 16, 1875), Marne 11 U 842 (tribunal civil Ste.-Menehould); *Le Roussillon*, Apr. 17, 1891.

23. Morère, *Notes*, p. 3.

24. AD, Finistère 4 M 351 (sous-préf. Châteaulin, June 9, 1853), Ariège 5 M 53¹ and 5 M 53² (1830–31 to 1846).

25. On troubles over forests, see Polge, *Mon vieil Auch*, p. 52; Deffontaines, *Homme et forêt*, p. 103; Louis Clarenc, "Le Code de 1827 et les troubles forestiers dans les Pyrénées centrales," *Annales du Midi*, 1965, pp. 293–317; AD, Yonne III M¹141 (May 19, 1848), M²²16 (Nov. 8, 1852); and AN, BB 30371 (Angers, Aug. 25, 1851). On the Demoiselles and their imitators, see Morère, *Notes*, p. 5; Michel Chevalier, especially pp. 357, 720–26; L. Gaillard, *Montagnes de Massat* (Toulouse, 1900); AN, BB¹⁸1460 (proc. gén. Toulouse, to Min. Justice, Apr. 4, 1848); and AD, Pyrs.-Ors. 3 Mi 163 (sous-préf. Prades, June 14, 1879). The song is cited by Michel Chevalier, p. 720.

26. AD, Basses-Pyrs. (tribunal St.-Palais, police correctionnelle). See also *L'Aubrac*, 2:

27, 99. Perrot, "Délinquance" (cited in note 9, above), p. 72, provides useful clarifications and tells us that whereas between 1831 and 1835 the yearly average of délits forestiers was around 135,000, by 1910 such offenses numbered only 1,798.

27. AD, Gironde, ser. U (tribunal Bazas, police correctionnelle); AD, Finistère, ser. U (tribunal Châteaulin, police correctionnelle).

28. *Ibid.*

29. *Ibid.*: 19 in 1856, 25 in 1880, and 52 in 1906 (while hunting offenses fell in almost the same proportion). The same is true at St.-Palais (Basses-Pyrs.): 25 in 1856, 49 in 1880, and 73 in 1905. But there infractions of the hunting laws declined later than in Finistère: 19 in 1856, 50 in 1880, and 34 in 1905. More than other categories of evidence, court and police records demand less an analysis of the raw statistics than a careful reading of what the *internal* evidence may reveal.

30. Gautier, *Siècle d'indigence*, p. 32.

31. Dupeux, p. 159; AN, C 956: "Enquête sur le travail agricole et industriel (décrêt du 25 Mai 1848)," Loir-et-Cher; AD, Cantal 110 M1 (Jan. 22, 1847).

32. Armengaud, *Populations*, p. 157.

33. On Montmerle, see Gagnon, 2: 294–95. On chronic begging, see Jollivet, 3: 27; Valaux, p. 273; Baudrillart, 1: 629; *Bulletin de la Société d'Emulation des Côtes-du-Nord*, 1875, p. 29; and *L'Aubrac*, 2: 185–86. In Aubrac, as elsewhere, beggar tramps seem to have followed a regular circuit. Some landowners reimbursed their tenants for the aid they provided.

34. AN, BB 30 371 Angers (comm. de police Beaupréau, June 28, 1865); Guilcher, *Tradition*, pp. 34–35; Mignot, p. 26; P. Mayer, pp. 10–12; AD, Finistère 4M (Douarnenez, July 31, 1889, Sept. 6, 1890, May 1891; Pont l'Abbé, Oct. 24, 1889); Lovie, pp. 302–3.

35. AD, Gers M 2799 (comm. de police Mirande, Oct. 15, 1876).

36. Méline, p. 82 and especially p. 214; Dubief, p. 20.

37. AD, Finistère 10 U 7/57 (tribunal correctionnel Châteaulin, May 6, 1886); AD, Cantal 50 M1 (series of circulars beginning in the Second Empire and running through 1901). See also AD, Cantal 40 M 11 (Apr. 1889). As late as 1911, according to Dubief, peasants were still reluctant to denounce beggars for fear of reprisals (pp. 241–42, 246–47).

38. Foville, *Enquête*, 1: 137.

39. Levasseur, 2: 443; AD, Marne 11 U 842 (tribunal civil Ste.-Menehould), Basses-Pyrs. (tribunal St.-Palais, police correctionnelle).

40. The latter could also perform a useful function by ridding communities of troublesome or unwanted members. See AD, Finistère 4M (Riec, near Pont-Aven, Dec. 31, 1900). The law of Dec. 7, 1874, sought to end the parents' freedom to hand their children over to professional beggars or itinerant mountebanks, but the practice evidently continued. See Dubief, p. 125.

41. Habasque, 1: 289–90; Souvestre, *Derniers Bretons*, pp. 21, 22.

42. Arbos, p. 203; Hamelle, p. 626.

Chapter Six

Epigraph. *Au bas pays de Limosin*, p. 8.

1. *Instruction primaire.*

2. Leroux, p. 18; *Instruction primaire*, 1; AEP, 4, Clamecy (Nièvre), report for 1882–83; AD, Cantal, manuscript: "Département du Cantal: Statistique numérique présentant la décomposition par canton du chiffre des conscrits de la classe de 1864 sous le rapport du langage."

3. AN, F17 9271 (Basses-Pyrs., 1877; Pyrs.-Ors., 1875).

4. HE II (Pas-de-Calais).

5. *Instruction primaire*, 2: 993–94 (Tarn-et-Garonne); 2: 72 (Lozère).

6. Coornaert, pp. 164–65; Dauzat, *Patois*, p. 27.

7. A. Brun, *Langue*, p. 74; A. Brun, *Recherches*, especially pp. 435–36.

8. Grégoire, report read to the Convention, 16 Prairial, year II (May 1794), quoted by Dauzat, *Patois*, pp. 27ff, and by Gazier, pp. 290ff.

9. A. Brun, *Recherches*, pp. 473ff; G. Arnaud, *Histoire de la Révolution dans le département de l'Ariège* (Toulouse, 1904), pp. 47–48; Francisque Mège, "Les Populations de l'Auvergne au début de 1789," *Bulletin historique et scientifique de l'Auvergne*, 1905, p. 124 (see also pp. 121–22); Gazier, especially p. 280, where at least one of Grégoire's correspondents answered in such bad French that some of his phrases seem unintelligible. See also Hyslop, especially p. 48.

10. Gazier, p. 5.

11. A. Brun, *Parlers régionaux*, p. 111; Gazier, p. 5; Paul Sérant, *La France des Minorités* (1965), p. 30; A. Brun, *Langue*, pp. 96–97. See also Cobb, *Police*, p. 336.

12. AEP, 4 (Dec. 7, 1834).

13. Pécaut, *Rapports*, p. 71; Sarcey quoted by Maspétiol, p. 294; Baudrillart, 3: 7; Mazuy, p. xv; A. Brun, *Parlers régionaux*, pp. 115–16; Monzie's circular of Aug. 14, 1925, quoted by Hayes, pp. 311–12.

14. Raoul de la Grasserie, *Etude scientifique sur l'Argot* (1907), p. 1; Louis Legrand, *L'Enseignement du français à l'école élémentaire* (1966), p. 39.

15. Van Gennep, *Décadence*, p. 14.

16. Gérard; Labrune, p. 57; AD, Cantal 39 M 9 (sous-préf. St.-Flour, Oct. 24, 1867).

17. Polge, personal communication to author, Nov. 27, 1973; AD, Gers M 2799 (comm. de police Gimaut, Sept. 26, 1875). For an example of the use of an untranslatable term, see, in the Gers file cited above, commissaire de police Lectoure, Mar. 16, 1875. Vidalenc, *Peuple des villes*, p. 49, mentions that in Rhône officers on half-pay acted as interpreters of Auvergnat in local courts.

18. AD, Finistère 10 U 7/23 (Châteaulin, 1856) (interpreters); *Instruction primaire*, 2: 950 (on Htes.-Pyrénées, where one *often* hears witnesses give evidence in patois, occasionally translating some word for the benefit of judge or jurors); Baudrillart, 3: 361 (Ariège); Le Blond (Midi).

19. Officers: AG, MR 1300 (Hte.-Vienne, 1824), MR 1236 (Morbihan, 1827), MR 1274 (Lot-et-Garonne, 1826), MR 1231 (Gironde, Landes, 1844), MR 1228 (Basses-Pyrs., 1856). Doctors: AD Ariège 8 M 28 (1854); Armengaud, *Populations*, p. 328.

20. AG, MR 1274 (Cantal, Lozère, 1844); Armengaud, *Populations*, p. 429; David, p. 220; Duclos, 1: 141.

21. AG, MR 2262 (Azay-le-Rideau, 1874), MR 2270 (Htes.-Pyrs., 1877), MR 2284 (Montpellier, 1860; Périgueux, 1877); L. Favre, *Parabole de l'enfant prodigue en divers dialectes, patois de la France* (1879); Maupassant, 1: 264.

22. AN, F¹⁷9275 (Tarn, 1875; insp. gén., 1877; Deux-Sèvres, 1881); F¹⁷9277 (Vienne, Hte.-Vienne, insp. gén., 1879, 1881); AD, Hte.-Vienne 4 M 85 (police report, Jan. 13, 1910).

23. Pécaut, *Rapports*, pp. 45 (Lot-et-Garonne), 58 (Basses-Pyrs.); Buisson, 1.2: 730, 1650. Note that when, at the end of 1883, Nietzsche took lodgings in the old city of Nice (or Nizza, as he always called it), all the workers and clerks in his neighborhood spoke Italian.

24. Malègue, *Guide de touriste*; Baudrillart, 3: 577; AD, Ariège 5 M 105 (maire Orgeix, Apr. 25, 1887).

25. Laurentin, 1: 153.

26. Dauzat, *Patois*, p. 32; AD, Puy-de-Dôme F 0275 (1899); Gorse, pp. 11–12.

27. Betham-Edwards, *France*, 1: 6, 345; Ajalbert, *En Auvergne*, p. 67; Barker, *Wayfaring*, p. 35; Baudrillart, 3: 333; Barker, *Wandering*, p. 56.

28. Desormaux, pp. 254–55; Bloch, pp. 4–7. Maurice Robert, in his edition of Léon Dhéralde's *Dictionnaire de la langue limousine* (Limoges, 1968), 1: xliii, quotes this comment: "Et si on faisait un congrès de langue d'oc. Hé Di! Millé Dious! Pecaïré! Mais pour que chacun des délégués comprenne, il faudrait que les orateurs s'expriment en français."

29. Duclos, 1: 141; André Martinet, *L'Express*, Mar. 24–30, 1969, p. 43 (on the linguistic effects of war, to which may be added the testimony of Picoche, p. x); P. Barral, *Département de l'Isère*, p. 71; Bloch, pp. 4–7. Simin Palay's Béarnais comedy of 1927, *Lou Franchiman*, presents just such a situation, in which the village young are sorely tempted by the national language and "feel ashamed of those at home . . . bound to speak mangled French." (See Gaston Guillaume, *Le Théâtre Gascon*, 1941, pp. 95–99.) An old proverb of Béarn warned: "Qu'auera maü per lous Bernès quoun lous hilhs parlent francès" (It'll go badly for the Béarnais when their sons speak French). Quoted in G. B. de Lagrèze, *La Société et les moeurs en Béarn* (Pau, 1886), p. 347.

30. Violet, *Clessé*, p. 128; Dauzat, *Patois*, p. 33; Laborde, p. 357; P. Barral, *Département de l'Isère*, p. 71; Léon Deries, *L'Institutrice au pays normand* (Saint-Lô, 1899), p. 4.

31. Bardoux, p. 239.

32. Mazuy, pp. 75–76; A. Brun, *Français*, pp. 12–13; A. Brun, *Parlers régionaux*, pp. 8–9.

33. Alphonse Roche, p. xviii. Two score years later, 10,000 copies of the *Armana* were printed.

34. Beslay, p. 97.

35. A. J. Rance, "L'Académie d'Arles," *Revue de Marseille et de Provence*, Nov. 1888, p. 486; Louis Gaillardie, *Dans les rues de Toulouse* (Toulouse, 1898); Poueigh, *Folklore*, p. 190; Malaussène; Dauzat, *Patois*.

36. Clough, pp. 276–78; Coornaert, pp. 266–67 (p. 287: in 1857 the mairies of Bailleul and Cassel still made out birth and death certificates in Latin). *Instruction primaire*, 1: 64, referred to the same problem in the Corsican context: everyone used Corsican, even the schools until 1862; but because *actes de l'état civil* were now being drawn up in French, the language was slowly spreading.

37. Coornaert, pp. 306–7.

38. Mayeur, *Abbé Lemire*, p. 15; Baudrillart, 2: 277.

39. Coornaert, pp. 323, 324.

40. Duchatellier, *Agriculture*, p. 181; P. M. F. Pitre-Chevallier, *La Bretagne ancienne et moderne* (1845), p. 648, quoted by Le Gallo, 2: 402; Flaubert, 1: 314, and again p. 326.

41. Prefect Finistère, 1881, quoted by Le Gallo, 1: 61; AD, Finistère 4M (préf., Oct. 1879); *Revue pédagogique*, Oct. 15, 1892, p. 376, Mar. 15, 1894, p. 217.

42. *Revue pédagogique*, Oct. 15, 1892, p. 376, Mar. 15, 1894, p. 217; Perrin and Bouet.

43. Drouart, p. 24.

44. Gostling, pp. 34, 109, 137; D. A. G. Trégoat, *L'Immigration bretonne à Paris* (1900), p. 9; Le Bourhis, p. 9; Bonneff and Bonneff, *Classe*, p. 197.

45. Bonneff and Bonneff, *Classe*, p. 197; Lebesque, p. 117.

46. Baudrillart, 1: 424–26.

47. *La Langue bretonne*.

48. A. Brun, *Langue*, p. 9: "La plume et l'encrier appellent le français."

49. Dauzat, "Breton," p. 227; Dauzat, *Glossaire*, p. 10.

50. *Instruction primaire*, 1: 129; Boillot, *Français*.

51. Morvan: Baudiau, 1: 52–53; Forestier, *Yonne*, 1: 373. Burgundy and Champagne: AG, MR 2264 (Côte-d'Or, 1875), MR 2268 (Marne, 1877). Poitou: L. Buffières, *Géographie communale . . . du département des Deux-Sèvres* (Niort, 1875), p. 48. Beauce and Perche: Société Archéologique de l'Eure-et-Loir, 1868 survey, manuscript no. 21 in Biblio-

thèque Municipale, Chartres, quoted by Giret, p. 17. Marche: Corbin, pp. 448ff. Moulins: Pérot, p. 119. See also HE II concerning the Argonne.

52. Renan quoted by Jacques Monfrin, in François, p. 773; HE II (St.-Chély, Ste.-Enimie in Lozère, 1888); Ardouin-Dumazet, 31: 183; Wylie, *Village*, p. 297.

53. AD, Cantal 39 M 9 (Oct. 24, 1867).

54. Forestier, *Yonne*, 1: 203; AG, MR 1274 (Lot, 1844); J. Sabbatier, p. 132; Marouzeau, pp. 102–3; Doussinet, p. 77.

55. Arnold Van Gennep, *Revue des idées*, June 15, 1911, pp. 8ff; Coissac, pp. 188–89.

56. Hérelle, *Etudes*, p. 152.

57. AG, MR 1218 (Hérault, 1828); Ariane de Felice, "Contes traditionnels des vanniers de Mayun (Loire-Inf.)," *Nouvelle revue des traditions populaires*, 1950, p. 456.

58. Polge, "Gascon," p. 150.

59. Fortier-Beaulieu, p. 647.

60. Berthout, p. 135; Perdiguier, p. 32.

61. A. Brun, *Parlers régionaux*, pp. 115ff; Paul Mariéton's introduction to Joseph Roux, p. 11; Pariset, *Lauragais*, p. 13. Ardèche, Allier, Limousin examples: Reynier and Abrial, p. 9; Darnaud, p. 31. Oblates: Corbin, p. 995. Bilingual sermons: Polge, "Gascon," p. 152.

62. Polge, "Gascon," pp. 148, 152 (citing *La Semaine religieuse de l'archidiocèse d'Auch*, 1901, pp. 401, 423).

63. Dauzat, "Breton," pp. 273–78.

64. Scorn of patois: Leroux, p. 1; Marouzeau, p. 29. Women's role: R. Thévenelle, *Revue pédagogique*, Dec. 15, 1891, p. 536; André Guilcher, "L'Habitat rural à Plouvien," *Bulletin de la Société Archéologique du Finistère*, 1948, pp. 36–39; Dauzat, "Breton." Officer's remark: AG, MR 1218 (1824).

65. Garneret, pp. 8–9; A. Brun, *Parlers régionaux*, pp. 132–35.

66. Dauzat, *Essais*, pp. 2–4.

67. Séguy, pp. 7–8; A. Brun, *Parlers régionaux*, pp. 135ff; A. Brun, *Français*, p. 17; Dauzat, *Patois*, pp. 33ff. Simin Palay's *Franchiman* (see note 29, above) is a caricature of a widespread type, speaking an incongruous mixture of Gascon and French: "Puis après, bous sabez, faut aboir des magnières des gens dé comme il faut. Et j'en connais pas guères qu'ils soient, comme on dit, un quelqu'un distingué. Moi, bous sabez, je fus dé tire arremarqué." In the popular stories of Saintonge, a well-known figure is Chanfroésit, whose name derives from *chanfroéser*: to speak French incorrectly and in an affected manner. Thus, Chanfroésit takes his leave: "Et aghréghez mes civilizations accélérées" (Doussinet, *Les Travaux*, p. 333).

68. On Vosges and Meuse, respectively, see Bloch, p. 125, and Labourasse, pp. 19–20.

69. Paul Cornu, "Les Parlers nivernais," *Cahiers du Centre*, 5.54 (July 1913), pp. 31–35.

70. Polge, personal communication to author, Nov. 27, 1973. Compare Redfield, p. 48, on the Yucatan, where maize in the field has one name and maize for sale in the market has another.

71. Lefebvre, *Vallée*, p. 219.

72. Dauzat, *Patois*, pp. 49–53.

73. Doniol, *Patois*, p. 52; Brekilien, p. 77. See also C. Bally, p. 83; Dauzat, *Défense*, p. 79; and F. Marullaz, *Hommes et choses de Morzine* (Thonon, 1912), pp. 216–17.

74. As does the old usage cited by Littré: *parleüre*.

75. J. Sabbatier, pp. 1–5. For references to the same point in Landes and Yonne, see Ricard, p. 98, and Lizerand, p. 55, respectively.

76. Francus, *Valgorge*, p. 16; Duneton, pp. 90–94. Deutsch, p. 62, observes: "Silences are eloquent. Without silences there is no speech." Marouzeau, pp. 30–36, claims that the Limousin peasant had no word for love, just factual descriptions; and Baudrillart, 3: 422, points out that, lacking an equivalent for the French *respect*, the peasant of Tarn used

the word for fear, so that a child was taught to fear his father. Yet Dhéralde (cited in note 28, above), 2: 278, lists *omour, omouroucha,* and *omouron,* as well as *respe.*

77. Duneton, pp. 84–85; Mendras, "Sociologie," p. 323.

78. Labat, *Ame,* p. 178.

79. Duneton, pp. 185, 194; Labat, *Ame,* p. 179; Bonheur, *République,* p. 32; Sénéquier, pp. 186ff; Charles de Tourtoulon, *Des Dialectes et de leur classification* (1890); Beaulaygue, p. 6. Hence the importance of familiarity with this other, outside culture and its frame of reference; something that a peddler or army veteran might acquire, but a wise old villager might not, and that the new generation might in changing circumstances possess in greater degree than the old.

80. Duneton, pp. 101–2. Duneton notes that French has only four terms for certain cooking utensils compared with 10 in Corrèze speech (pp. 105–6, 201). Dhéralde (see note 28), 2: 283, lists 47 local names under the word bird (*oseu*).

81. Gorse, pp. 8–9.

Chapter Seven

Epigraph. *Lettres sur l'histoire de France.*

1. Taine, preface to Vol. 1 of *Les Origines de la Révolution en France* (1875).

2. Lavisse, *Livret d'histoire: Année du certificat d'études,* pp. 13, 19; Lavisse (with Thalamas), *Opuscule,* pp. 28–29.

3. Albert Soboul, "The French Revolution in Contemporary World History," University of California, Los Angeles, Departmental Colloquy, photocopy, Apr. 1973, p. 4. See also, for example, Albert Mathiez, *La Révolution française* (1939), 1: 69.

4. Benda, pp. 11, 74, 76, 91–92. See also Pierre Fougeyrollas, *La Conscience politique dans la France contemporaine* (1963), p. 316.

5. Dupront in François, pp. 1440, 1442.

6. AG, MR 2153 (1860) around Clermont and Riom. At just this time the Abbé Féraud was writing about the men of Fours (Basses-Alpes) being forced "to abandon their patrie" to seek elsewhere the means that its soil could not provide (p. 409). See also Dupront in François, p. 1442. Vidalenc tells us that in Lyon Auvergnats and other immigrant *horsains* were treated as foreigners, and that during the hard times of 1848 natives "energetically" called for their expulsion (*Peuple des villes,* p. 49).

7. Hayes, pp. 3–5, 15.

8. Blanqui, *Déboisement,* p. 21; Angus B. Reach, *Claret and Olives: From the Garonne to the Rhone* (London, 1870), p. 59; Renan quoted by Benda, pp. 7–8.

9. Marc Bloch, *Annales,* Mar. 31, 1934, p. 180.

10. Juge, p. 116; Arthur Young, *Travels During the Years 1787, 1788 and 1789* (London, 1792), pp. 146–47.

11. A. Brun, *Introduction,* p. 58; Grégoire, *Papiers,* St.-Calais (Sarthe), Ambérieux (Ain); Cobb, *Police,* pp. 307, 313, 315. See also Hyslop, pp. 62, 185, 186, 190.

12. A. Brun, *Introduction,* pp. 110ff.

13. AN, $F^{17}9262$ (Oct. 1880); Barrès, 6: 294, 295; Labourasse, p. 86.

14. Coissac, p. 423; Deffontaines, *Hommes et travaux,* p. 400; Labat quoted by Paul Masson, *La Provence au 18e siècle* (Aix, 1935), 1: xxix; Mazuy, pp. 181, 224–25; Henri Vienne, *Esquisses historiques: Promenades dans Toulon ancien et moderne* (Toulon, 1841), quoted by Agulhon, *Ville ouvrière,* p. 48.

15. AG, MR 2280 (Bouches-du-Rhône, 1859, 1862).

16. Hertz, p. 116.

17. AG, MR 1228 (St.-Jean-Pied-de-Port, 1846): Pécaut, *Rapports,* p. 52, repeated almost word for word by Buisson, 1.2: 2507; AG, MR 1223 (Pertus, 1844): Alphonse Roche, p. 49.

18. Joseph Roux, p. 183; Aimé Giron, p. 45; Coornaert, p. 324. Boulanger won the election.

19. Paul Sérant, *La France des minorités* (1965), p. 103; AN F^{17}9262 (Oct. 1880); Hyslop, p. 314.

20. Marlin, *Opinion*, pp. 7–8; Lovie, p. 495.

21. Gobineau, pp. 145, 150–54, 161; George Sand, "Journal," *Revue politique et par-lementaire*, 1870, pp. 593, 596, 608; Reynier, *Histoire*, 3: 308; Corbin, pp. 1349–51; Kanter, *passim*. For confirmation, see Gabriel Monod's recollections of his war service with a field ambulance: *Allemands et Français* (1872). Of the *francs-tireurs*: "bandits, terreur du paysan qu'ils pillaient, battaient et ne défendaient pas" (p. 109). Of the peasants of Beauce: "Démoralisés et égoistes, ils étaient incapables de s'imposer un sacrifice pour nos soldats ou nos blessés, tandis que la peur et l'intérêt en faisaient souvent les alliés des Allemands." An officer operating in the east during October 1870 gives further details. At Belverne (Haute-Saône) "la population ... n'a pas pour nous de grandes sympathies. Au fond, son plus grand désir est que nous nous en allions pour laisser les Allemands arriver en paix, et je crois qu'on ne peut, ici, se fier à personne.... Mais comme il est pénible de se considérer, en France, comme en pays ennemi." A few days later, in the region of Baume-les-Dames (Doubs), "en général nos reconnaissances sont assez mal reçues par les populations." In one village a French patrol saw the people running to greet it with food and gifts, only to turn away when they realized that the men were not Prussians. (Comminges, pp. 245, 255–56.)

22. Gobineau, especially pp. 39–40; Flaubert (Apr. 29, 1871) quoted by Guillemin, p. 285; Barrès, 13: 88 (Nancy); Mignot, pp. 6ff (Bar-sur-Seine); Sébillot, *Folk-lore*, 4: 403.

23. On Savoy, see AN, BB 30 390 (proc. gén. Chambéry). See also Lovie, chs. 7 and 8, especially p. 429 (Lt.-Col. Borson's report of July 1864 to Maréchal Randon, Archives de l'Armée, 3G1); pp. 542–45 (on Gambetta); and pp. 560, 569 (on 1873 and 1874, respectively). The same is probably true of Nice, also only joined to France in 1860, also treated as a colony in the period following annexation, its natives backward and despised, according to Jacques Basso, *Les Elections législatives dans le département des Alpes-Maritimes de 1860 à 1939* (1968), pp. 79–80. The prefect, aware of local resentment, referred to it repeatedly; and notably in a report of 1869 in which he spoke of the suspicion the annexed population felt for "l'élément français," then crossed this out to write "l'élément nouveau." In Nice, too, there seem to have been troubles in 1870–71. (See Basso, pp. 87, 118–27.)

24. Rambaud and Vincienne, p. 34.

25. Le Roy Ladurie, pp. 25–26, 70, 80–81. This commitment seems confirmed by *Annuaire du Doubs* (Besançon, 1843), p. 153, which reveals that on Jan. 1, 1841, the Doubs had 57 *insoumis*, compared with 400 in Loire, 684 in Cantal, 736 in Haute-Saône, and 1,309 in Basses-Pyrénées. On Ariège's legendary proclivity to draft evasion, see Gadrat, p. 130.

26. AG, G^{8}1 (1853), G^{8}183 (Pyrenees, 1874–76), MR 2283 (Ponts-de-Cé, 1859), 2280 (Corsica, 1860; Hérault, 1862), 2284 (Allier, 1864).

27. AG, MR 1268 (Loiret, 1828), 2277 (Brie, 1860), 2280 (Béziers [Hérault], 1862; Nice, 1869), 2262 (Puy-de-Dôme, 1873), 2284, 2261 (Gironde, 1873).

28. AG, MR 2262 (Hte.-Vienne, 1873; Indre valley [Indre-et-Loire], 1873), 2261 (Hérault, 1874), 2270 (Gard and Vaucluse, 1877). See also MR 2284 (Hte.-Vienne, 1876), predicting that one could expect "passive obedience [of the population of Isle and Aixe] as long as one was strong enough to impose it; but it would be useless to expect any spontaneous help in critical circumstances."

29. Francus, *Midi de l'Ardèche*, pp. 177–78.

30. The information in this paragraph and following ones is drawn from three works by Paul Sébillot, *Folk-lore*, 4: 370–73, 379, 401, *Notes sur les traditions* (Naples, 1888), p. 11, and *La Bohème galante* (1873), p. 73; and from Bérenger-Féraud, *Réminiscences*, p. iv.

31. Jean Adhémar in Bibliothèque Nationale, comp., *La Légende napoléonienne* (1969); Sébillot, *Folk-lore*, 4: 394ff.

32. Bodley, *Cardinal Manning*, p. 185; *Le Figaro*, Feb. 3, 1907; Meynier, "Deux hameaux," p. 370; Maurice Huet, *Sabres de bois, Fusils de paille!!!* (1905), pp. 70–71.

33. Fleurent, p. 325; V. Dupont, p. 118; Belbèze, p. 108; Jean Yole, *Le Malaise paysan* (1929), p. 264; AD, Puy-de-Dôme M 0127 (May 3, 1843); Pécaut, *Etudes*, p. 26; Dupront in François, p. 1465; Gambetta, speaking at Le Havre in April 1872, quoted by Gontard, *Oeuvre*, p. 5.

34. AD, Finistère 44 J 3.

35. AN, F^{17}9277 (Hte.-Vienne). The volumes of the Domrémy visitors' book are in AD, Vosges. But again, see *Le Figaro*, Feb. 3, 1907: among the recruits surveyed in 1906, precisely half had not heard of Jeanne d'Arc. A smaller proportion, very likely, than would have been found in earlier decades.

36. Bouteiller, of course, is Barrès's bête noire. See *Les Déracinés* in Barrès, 3: 202.

37. Carlton J. H. Hayes, *Essays on Nationalism* (New York, 1926), p. 5.

38. Alexandre Sanguinetti, quoted in *Le Figaro*, Nov. 12, 1968.

39. E. J. Hobsbawm, "From Social History to the History of Society," *Historical Studies* (New York, 1972), p. 23.

40. Van Gennep, *Décadence*, pp. 4–5: "Vivre, c'est envahir." This is more than social Darwinism. Say rather social Bergsonism!

Chapter Eight

Epigraph. *En province.*

1. See Table 3 in Georges Dupeux, *Le Société française, 1789–1960* (1964), p. 20. One may add that when the Second Empire ended, fewer than one soul in four lived in a town of 5,000 or more; 38.4 percent in 1911.

2. See Zeldin, *France*, 1: 105–6; and Mayeur, *Débuts*, pp. 58–59. Pinchemel, *Géographie*, 1: 192, offers different figures.

3. Compare the French census figures for 1866 and 1896 broken down in *L'Economiste français*, Jan. 4, 1902.

4. AD, Creuse M 0710 (Dec. 20, 1873). As noted in EA, Morbihan, p. 11, many products were not covered in the statistics, partly because they were used in the home or in barter, partly because peasants tended to hide what they grew for fear of the tax collector. For plausible criticisms of the restricted scope of the Agricultural Survey of 1866–67, see Dr. L. Vacher, *L'Enquête agricole dans le département de la Corrèze* (Brive, 1874).

5. Labrousse in Fernand Braudel and Ernest Labrousse, *Histoire économique et sociale de la France, 1660–1789* (1970), p. 739; Jacques Bujault cited by Vidalenc, *Peuple des campagnes*, p. 348; officer cited *ibid.*, p. 355.

6. Redfield, p. 27; Corbin, p. 33 (comparative tables of the weight of slaughtered cattle) and p. 30 (chief crops, 1840–52); E. Muret de Bort, "L'Agriculture ancienne et la nouvelle en Limousin," *Agriculture du centre*, 1866, pp. 40ff.

7. Compare Soboul, *Question*, p. 57, with AG, MR 2267 (Aisne, 1875) and 2268 (Marne, 1877); Corbin, pp. 36–38; Norre, pp. 4–5; Augé-Laribé, *Politique*, p. 104; and Lovie, p. 170.

8. Corbin, p. 607.

9. Elicio Colin, "L'Evolution de l'économie rurale au pays de Porzay de 1815 à 1930,"

Bulletin de la Société Archéologique du Finistère, 1947, pp. 61ff; EA, Côtes-du-Nord, p. 11; EA, Lozère; AD, Puy-de-Dôme M 04478 (Brassac, Mar. 7, 1897); Ricard, p. 59; Bombal, p. 514 (Hte.-Dordogne); EA, Basses-Alpes, pp. 25–27 (Valensole). Mesliand, p. 135, places the Vaucluse peasant's shift from a subsistence to a consumer economy in the 1900–1930 period.

10. Pérot, p. 206; Doussinet, *Les Travaux,* pp. 196, 342. Similar names can be found in most parts of France: witness Malemoisson, Malijai, or Maljasset (*male jacet*) in Basses-Alpes, which also boasts a hamlet named Infernet (Little hell); Féraud, pp. 225, 256, 376, 418.

11. Daniel Faucher, *Evolution récente du genre de vie dans les campagnes françaises* (1953, offprint).

12. Michel Chevalier, pp. 142, 146; AD, Marne 11 U 843.

13. EA, Allier 37, p. 7, Corrèze 37, 1: 4; Deffontaines, *Homme et forêt,* p. 33 (who adds that change was fastest where the landowners actively intervened). See Musset, *Bas-Maine,* pp. 336–37, on Mayenne, where the amount of fallow fell from 90,350 hectares in 1852 to 75,457 in 1862 and to a negligible 23,607 in 1892. Some gave up the practice entirely; others first reduced the fallow period from two years to one. But "slowly farmers cease[d] to let their lands rest."

14. Corbin, pp. 387, 568. Again, the point is how much all this varied over time. Vidalenc, *Peuple des campagnes,* p. 346, tells us that for all practical purposes fallow disappeared in Upper Normandy around 1850, but persisted after that in some parts of the region. As for common pasture, this could still be found in the Ile-de-France until the 1890's.

15. Théron de Montaugé, p. 605; Barral quoted by Corbin, p. 585; Corbin, p. 583. Garneret, p. 36, tells us that at Lantenne old leases indicate four carts of manure were used per *journal.* By the 1950's this had grown to 8–12 carts for wheat, 15–20 for beets or potatoes.

16. AG, MR 1180 (Moselle, 1838); Corbin, pp. 33, 602. Compare Stendhal, 3: 128.

17. On Mayenne, see Musset, *Bas-Maine,* pp. 307, 352–53; and Bodard de la Jacopière, *Chroniques craonnaises* (Le Mans, 1871), p. 31.

18. Hérault, p. 180 (Vendée); Suret-Canale, p. 303; Buffet, *Haute-Bretagne,* p. 117; Lullin de Châteauvieux, *Voyages agronomiques* (1843), 2: 444.

19. Ardouin-Dumazet, 27: 280–81.

20. Cordier, p. 34; Sion, p. 349; EA, Dordogne, Seine-Inférieure.

21. Much of the information in this discussion is based on EA, *passim.* See also Gachon, *Brousse-Montboissier,* p. 43; F. Benoît, *Provence,* p. 160 (Provençal saying); F. Benoît, *Histoire,* p. 28; Lovie, pp. 168–69; and R. Brunet, p. 195. Colin (cited in note 9 above) finds the wooden plow still in use side by side with iron plows in Finistère around 1870–71, with the brabant first appearing in 1901.

22. EA, Indre-et-Loire.

23. Perrin and Bouet, pp. 137, 145; F. Benoît, *Histoire,* pp. 46–48 (in 1858 the Agricultural Society of Aveyron brought in harvesters from Tarn to encourage the use of the scythe in Aveyron); EA, Gard, Indre, Hte.-Marne, and others; Michel Chevalier, p. 693; Soboul, *Communauté,* p. 306.

24. Vazeilles, 2: 9; Abel Chatelain, "La Lente Progression de la faux," *Annales: E. S. C.,* 1956, pp. 495–99; EA, Gers. Note that at one time using a scythe on grain was regarded as a desecration (Henri Polge, personal communication). See also F. Benoît, *Histoire,* pp. 46–48.

25. EA, Aveyron and *passim.*

26. J. A. Barral, *Agriculture du Nord,* p. 50; R. Brunet, p. 196; Foville, *Enquête,* 2: 318; *Evocations,* 1963, pp. 79–83.

27. See F. Benoît, *Histoire*, p. 23; H. Chobaut, "L'Industrie des fourches de Sauve," *Mémoires de l'Académie de Nîmes*, 1926–27 (Nîmes, 1927), p. 109; and the judicious remarks of Leroi-Gourhan, *Milieu*, pp. 383–86.

28. EA, Meurthe-et-Moselle 37, pp. 6–7; Perrin and Bouet, p. 149.

29. Thabault, *Mon village*, pp. 95, 99, 155, 156, 158; Haudricourt and Delamarre, pp. 420–22.

30. Cuisenier, pp. 91–92.

31. On the structure of fields and how that bears on society and mentalities, see Marc Bloch, *Les Caractères originaux de l'histoire rurale française* (Oslo, 1931); and Jules Sion's review "Une Histoire agraire de la France," *Revue de synthèse*, Mar. 1932.

32. EA, Côtes-du-Nord.

33. Hudry-Ménos, p. 605; Corbin, pp. 30, 35; AN, F^{1c} III, Hte.-Vienne 8 (sous-préf. Rochechouart, Dec. 29, 1858); EA, Tarn, Nièvre; Thibon, p. 40; AD, Pyrs.-Ors., Sept. 30, 1895.

34. Valaux, p. 137; Vidalenc, *Peuple des campagnes*, p. 341; P. Mayer, pp. 4–5; J. A. Barral, *Situation*, p. 29 (investment in land brought 2–3% return, in cattle 8–10%). Barral's book *Agriculture de la Haute-Vienne*, based on visits and surveys of the 1870's, shows the critical role of capital, scientific enterprise, and rational accounting methods (themselves inspired by and based on capital) in developing and improving land. The average peasant stood no chance in that league. For further details, see Giovanni Hoyois, *Sociologie rurale* (1968), p. 37; and E. Affre, *De l'histoire et de l'évolution de la race bovine limousine* (1926).

35. J. A. Barral, *Agriculture du Nord*, 2: viii.

36. See AN, C 3372 (1884 report of prof. of agriculture, Limoges); and Corbin, pp. 607, 608. For specific examples, see *La Réforme sociale*, 1885, p. 466; Betham-Edwards, *France*, 1: 63–64; Ardouin-Dumazet, 34: 5; and R. Dumont in *Bulletin de la Société Française d'Economie Rurale*, July 1954, p. 22.

37. Serge Bonnet, *Sociologie*, pp. 29–30, 32; Longy, *Canton*, pp. 111–12; EA, Côtes-du-Nord, Creuse, Ille-et-Vilaine.

38. Foville, *France*, 2: 93; EA, Calvados, Jura; Le Guen, pp. 476–77.

Chapter Nine

Epigraph. *Vie et opinions de M. Frédéric Thomas Graindorge* (1959 ed.), 2: 274.

1. Charrié, *Bas-Vivarais*, p. 240.

2. Garneret, pp. 198, 242; Perron, *Proverbes*, p. 60. See also Jalby, p. 198.

3. S. Tardieu, *Vie domestique*, p. 119; AD, Ariège 5M3 (Jan. 31, 1862).

4. Merley, pp. 236–37; AD, Hte.-Loire P5907–13 (1881), P5853 (1851).

5. Garneret, p. 200; Théron de Montaugé, pp. 81–82, 433; J.-A. Delpon, 1: 194–96; Bonnemère, 2: 481.

6. Souvestre, *Derniers Bretons* (1854 ed.), 2: 147; Malon, p. 104; Chaix, p. 274; Clément Compayré, *Guide du voyageur dans le département du Tarn* (Albi, 1852), quoted in Armengaud, *Populations*, p. 151.

7. Lapaire, p. 7; Drouillet, 2: 77; Lafayette, p. 538; Thuillier, *Aspects*, p. 70. For the full text of the report, see Bourgoing, especially p. 403.

8. AG, MR 2280, 2281, 2284; J.-A. Delpon, 1: 194. Decoux-Lagoutte remarked, in 1888, that if the laborers of Treignac seemed soft, this was due to their poor diet, and that once the workingman had meat and wine he would be stronger (p. 55).

9. Plessis, p. 133; Corbin, p. 81.

10. AG, MR 2262 (1874); Francus, *Valgorge*, pp. 113–14; Violet, *Clessé*, p. 114. According to AG, MR 2284 (Hte.-Vienne, 1876), the area of Aixe and Isle, southwest of

Limoges, was more prosperous and its peasants better fed than other parts of the depart-ment. Yet even there the peasants ate almost no meat, but lived largely on rye bread, corncakes, potatoes, and chestnuts. As for Gascony, "Ail e pan, repech dou paysan," asserts the proverb (Daugé, p. 231).

11. AD, Vosges, 11T17; Gautier, *Dure Existence*, pp. 92–96; AD, Puy-de-Dôme F 0274 ("Monographie de l'Instituteur de Miremont en Combrailles," 1899).

12. Ardouin-Dumazet, 34: 115.

13. Le Bourhis, p. 69; Jules Renard, *Le Matin*, Nov. 21, 1908. According to Jules Sion, p. 457, the diet of the rural population in wealthier Normandy in 1909 had not changed much since 1863; it included a bit more alcohol, but no more meat. The daily fare con-sisted of potato stew, pickled herring, cheese, and watered cider. Thuillier, *Aspects*, p. 60, refers to a farm foreman around 1890 who had meat only on Sundays and used cheese to season his standard fare of potatoes, because cheese was cheaper than butter. Compare Cressot, p. 56, noting that there was little cream because a pound of butter could be sold for 12 sous.

14. Féraud, p. 145; Doussinet, *Paysan*, p. 210.

15. Gorse, pp. 92–95.

16. *Ibid.*, pp. 92–95; Juge, p. 15; Sébillot, *Coutumes*, p. 341; Mignot, pp. 25–26; Bogros, p. 184. On peasants selling all they can, see AG, MR 1198 (Doubs, 1835); Picamilh, 1: 311; Max. Sorre, "La Géographie de l'alimentation," *Annales de géographie*, 1952, p. 192; and Vazeilles, 2: 1–4.

17. AD, Ariège Mh 72 (1845); Garneret, p. 206; Michel Chevalier, pp. 214–15. Com-mon usage attests to the links between bread and all aspects of life. Decent people were "des bonnes pâtes," peevish or surly ones were "mal cuits," those who felt unwell were "cuits en blanc"; and a time of worry was "long like a day without bread" (Méraville, p. 292).

18. Layet, p. 166; Drouillet, 2: 77; Charrié, *Bas-Vivarais*, p. 316; Betham-Edwards, *France*, 1: 109.

19. Blanqui, "Déboisement," p. 17; René Bonnet, *Enfance*, p. 103; Van Gennep, *Folk-lore des Hautes-Alpes*, 2: 313; Deffontaines, *Homme et forêt*, pp. 79–80; Esnault, *Imagi-nation*, p. 137; Foville, *Enquête*, 1: xxxiii; Coissac, p. 214; Perron, *Proverbes*, p. 60. See also the Gascon comment that "he who can't cut it can't earn it"—presumably not strong enough for either! (Jalby, p. 199.)

20. Turlier, p. 248; Besson, pp. 67–69; Decoux-Lagoutte, p. 22; Garneret, p. 293.

21. See Corbin, pp. 607ff, on the peasants' attachment to a diet composed essentially of starches.

22. Perrin and Bouet, p. 171; Poueigh, *Folklore*, p. 35: "En boune maisou pâ dur e lègne sègue." In the west, where barley bread remained the basic diet to the 1890's, the saying persists, "grossier comme du pain d'orge."

23. Thiriat, *Vallée de Cleurie*, p. 299; Decoux-Lagoutte, p. 22; Thuillier, "Alimenta-tion," p. 1178; Foville, *Enquête*, 1: 159; Le Guyader, p. 140. Around the First World War, old men in Berry, one of the breadbaskets of France, remembered the heavy, clayey barley bread they had eaten as "so black that today a dog wouldn't have it" (Vin-cent, p. 137).

24. Perron, *Franc-Comtois*, p. 193; EA, Dordogne; AN, F¹cIII Ardèche II (Tournon, Dec. 30, 1858), F¹cIII Creuse 8 (Boussac, Aubusson, 1859); Corbin, p. 67; Pérot, p. 180.

25. Hérault, p. 200: 20 percent of the budget in 1850, 10 percent in 1900, 9 percent in 1913, 4.4 percent in 1957. And as bread consumed less of the budget it became less sacred. Compare Dauphin and Pézerat in *Annales: E. S. C.*, 1975, p. 547: In 1856 bread provided 86 percent of the caloric intake of a southwestern peasant family.

26. Deffontaines, *Homme et forêt*, p. 50; AG, MR 1234 (1822), 1218 (1844); Maspétiol, p. 146; R. Brunet, p. 199 (indicating that in Comminges the chestnut was still the poor man's winter bread in 1886).

27. Bozon, *Histoire*, p. 216; Ardouin-Dumazet, 28: 92–94; EA, Savoie; L.-A. Fabre, *La Restauration des montagnes* (Bordeaux, 1907), pp. 55ff. According to Fabre, an official survey in 1902 found that 39,000 ha. of forest land, with some four million trees between 40 and 100 years old, had disappeared in the preceding 10 years; 91,000 ha. of chestnuts alone were swept away between 1882 and 1907.

28. Garneret, p. 173; Pasquet, p. 24; Boillot, *Traditions*, p. 88.

29. Gérard, p. 7 (Vosges); Poueigh, *Folklore*, p. 34 (Pyrenees); d'Assier, pp. 37–38, 165; Perron, *Proverbes*, p. 60. Eating was also recognized as costly. In Auvergne a ruined man was said to have eaten his domain (Méraville, p. 291).

30. Poueigh, *Folklore*, p. 205; Baudrillart, 3: 608; Corbin, p. 69; Dr. de Wachter quoted in J. J. Hémardinquer, "Le Porc familial," *Annales: E. S. C.*, 1970, pp. 1745–59.

31. Le Bourhis, pp. 68–69; René Dumont, p. 465; Besson, p. 69; Sébillot, *Coutumes*, pp. 327–28. Until 1900 milk was the principal source of protein in the rural center and west.

32. Perrin and Bouet, pp. 437–40. In the last third of the 19th century roast chicken appeared: "an innovation that clashed with Breton customs," comments Le Guyader.

33. J. A. Barral, *Agriculture de la Haute-Vienne*, p. 681; AD, Hte.-Vienne 1 Z 105 (Bessines, Mar. 24, 1861); Thiriat, *Vallée de Cleurie*, p. 298; Machenaud, pp. 55–56; Cressot, p. 45. At Saint-Saud (Dordogne, pop. 3,000), itinerant butchers sold about 10 kg of meat a week in 1900 (Rocal, p. 159).

34. AG, MR 1180 (1842); Théron de Montaugé, p. 448. Théron adds that the peasants used a coarser flour.

35. *Statistique agricole de la France. Résultats généraux de l'enquête décennale de 1882*, p. 263; Jean Claudian in François, pp. 181–82. See also J. A. Barral, *Agriculture du Nord*, 2: 28; Lovie, p. 315; Romieu, p. 333; and Bonneff and Bonneff, *Vie*, pp. 11, 29–30.

36. Bastié, 2: 160; Corbin, p. 78.

37. Jean Claudian in François, pp. 181–82; Doussinet, *Paysan*, p. 203.

38. Labat, *Ame*, p. 221 (the article in which this story first appeared was published in 1913); Le Lannou, 2: 66–67.

39. Fortier-Beaulieu, pp. 304, 354. See also Franchet, p. 111; and Pourrat, p. 184.

40. Gorse, p. 165; Buffet, *Bretagne*, pp. 152–53; Reynier, *Pays*, 1: 150; Ardouin-Dumazet, 36: 119–20; Belbèze, pp. 77–78; Renard, *Nos Frères*, pp. 18, 21.

41. Labat, *Ame*, p. 222; E. Le Roy Ladurie, "L'Aménorrhée de famine," *Annales: E. S. C.*, 1969, pp. 1589–1601.

42. Morin; Blanqui, "Tableau," 30: 5; Combes and Combes, pp. 245–46; Perrin and Bouet, p. 79; Du Camp, p. 357; L. Lavault, "Châtillon-en-Bazois," *Cahiers du Centre*, Aug. 1909, p. 16.

43. Buffet, *Haute-Bretagne*, p. 127; René Dumont, pp. 399–400; Roger Dion, *Val de Loire* (Tours, 1933), p. 622; Dion, "Géographie humaine rétrospective," *Cahiers internationaux de sociologie*, 1949, p. 8; AD, Hte.-Vienne 1 Z 105 (Bessines, Mar. 24, 1861).

44. On drinking and the social role of the tavern, see Théron de Montaugé, pp. 82–83; AD, Ariège 5 M 3 (Pamiers 1857); AD, Yonne III M^{1}117 (1849), M^{1}119 (1851), M^{1}233 (1862); Audiganne, *Populations*, 1: 30; Brochon, *Chanson française*, introduction, vol. 1; and Poncy, pp. 236–37.

45. AD, Pyrs.-Ors. 3Mi 163 (Prades, June 14, 1879); Poueigh, *Folklore*, p. 88.

46. Fauvet and Mendras, p. 396; Théron de Montaugé, p. 449; Thiriat, *Vallée de*

Cleurie, pp. 298–99; AG, MR 2262 (1874); Besson, pp. 67, 69; Boscary, pp. 224–25; Ricard, p. 101.

47. Pourrat, p. 192.

Chapter Ten

Epigraph. *The Georgics of Virgil*, tr. John Dryden (1697), Book 2.

1. Amussat, p. 263.

2. Aguilhon, pp. 34–35; AD, Pyrs.-Ors. 3M1 224 (Rivesaltes, Jan. 8, 1896); AG, MR 2281 (Moulins, 1860); Thuillier, *Aspects*, pp. 56–57; Baudrillart, 2: 203.

3. AG, MR 2262 (Limousin, 1874); Francus, *Valgorge*, p. 346.

4. Corbin, pp. 99–100; Perron, *Broye-les-Pesmes*, p. 65; S. Tardieu, *Vie domestique*, pp. 148–51; Machenaud, p. 61; Coissac, pp. 211–12.

5. Drouillet, 4: 163; Ardouin-Dumazet, 32: 84; Pradier, p. 85; V. Dupont, p. 140.

6. AN, F^{17}9253 (May 1877); Charles Dumont, p. 20; Romieu, p. 332. Mme. Romieu noted further, "Soldat, il [the peasant] acquiert au régiment des habitudes de propreté qu'il ne conserve pas longtemps." Doussinet, *Paysan*, p. 368: "We peasants work up a good sweat; it cleans the body."

7. Francus, *Voyage humoristique*, p. 154; Francus, *Voyage fantaisiste*, 1: 40.

8. Doniol, *Patois*, pp. 64–65. Killing a cockroach was considered unlucky (Charrié, *Bas-Vivarais*, p. 173).

9. Ardouin-Dumazet, 28: 290; Perron, *Broye-les-Pesmes*, p. 65; Coissac, pp. 211–12.

10. J.-P. Aron in Le Roy Ladurie, p. 228; Th.-C. Delamare, *La Vie à bon marché* (1854), pp. 304–5; Amussat, p. 257.

11. Cobb, *Reactions*, especially p. 67.

12. Chaix, pp. 274–76.

13. AG, MR 2277 (Isère, 1860); Dr. Darnis, *Etudes sur le goitre et le crétinisme dans le Tarn-et-Garonne* (Montauban, 1869); Charles Chopinet, "Etude sur le goitre et le rectalisme dans les Pyrénées Centrales," *Revue du Comminges*, 1892, pp. 1–33; Michel Chevalier, p. 671.

14. Morère, *Notes*, pp. 8–12; AD, Yonne V M^{11}7 (Epidémies, 1831–46); Forestier, *Yonne*, 2: 197–204; Corbin, p. 129; Turlier, 1: 247–48, who states that at Lusigny, in Sologne (pop. 1,150) 60 died in 1865 and 59 in 1866, mostly of fevers; AD, Hte.-Vienne M 1047 (1877); Perron, *Proverbes*, p. 60.

15. Belbèze, pp. 30, 35–61, 76, 92ff; Francus, *Voyage fantaisiste*, 2: 10; Corbin, 6: xxxviii. In the thirteenth century, already, Albert the Great had found occasion in discussing impotence to remark that this evil spell "is found especially among peasants" (Flandrin, p. 86).

16. *Tradition*, pp. 248–51; Hamerton, *Round My House*, p. 249; L. A. Mouret, *Des erreurs populaires en médecine* (Le Puy, 1872), quoted in Rouchon, 2: 211; *Le National*, Feb. 1879, quoted in *ibid.*, p. 220.

17. Francus, *Voyage fantaisiste*, 1: 88; AD, Hte.-Vienne 4 Z 6 (St.-Yrieix, July 6, 1889); Yonne V M^{18}1 (Aug. 16, 1841).

18. AD, Yonne V M^{18}1 (May 13, 1808). For confirmation, see Vincent, p. 210, on the peasant's fatalism about illness: "He does not want to thwart destiny."

19. Thuillier, *Aspects*, p. 71, quoting a report of 1851; P. Bidault, *Les Superstitions médicales du Morvan* (1899); Le Guen, p. 465 (Côtes-du-Nord). See also AG, MR 2267 (Isère, 1875); and Hamerton, *Round My House*, pp. 251–53.

20. A. Lesaëge, *L'Homme, la vie et la mort dans le Nord au XXe siècle* (Lille, 1972), p. 118.

21. Francus, *Midi de l'Ardèche*, p. 212.

22. AG, MR 1233 (Charente-Inf., 1844); Monot, *Mortalité*, pp. 45–47. On the supposed hygienic advantages of country over town and the peasants' acceptance of this urban myth, see Burguière, p. 76.

23. Barker, *Wandering*, p. 118.

24. Longy, *Canton*, p. 39.

25. Leproux, *Médecine*, pp. 30–32. See also Thuillier, *Aspects*, p. 80; and Francus, *Voyage humoristique*, pp. 231–32.

26. Gadrat, p. 128; Combes and Combes, pp. 100–101. Same note in Maine; see Musset, *Bas-Maine*, pp. 395–96. See also "Essai sur l'agriculture du département de la Mayenne en Mars 1852," *Bulletin de la Société de l'Industrie de la Mayenne*, 1853, pp. 133–41.

27. Vazeille, 1:4.

28. Dainville, p. 155.

29. Amussat, p. 32; Perron, *Broye-les-Pesmes*, p. 65; Bougeatre, p. 21.

30. AD, Yonne III M¹207 (Tonnerre, Mar. 20, 1852). Vincent, writing about George Sand's Berry during the same period, confirms this; see p. 127.

31. Blanqui, "Tableau," 28:17.

32. Fauvet and Mendras, p. 396. See also the essays of Pierre Chaunu and Gabriel Désert in *Le Bâtiment: Enquête d'histoire économique* (1971).

33. In some areas the basic structure of houses became lighter, and traditional tile then became simply impossible. On architectural changes, see Drouillet, 2:31; Valaux, p. 135; and Polge, *Matériaux*, p. 27.

34. Sion, p. 470.

35. AG, MR 2284 (Vienne, 1877); Drouillet, 2:27; Foville, *Enquête*, 1:xxx; Valaux, pp. 137–40. The very poor, of course, continued for a long time to dwell in cottages that were like foul dungeons. See Sion, pp. 474–75, remarking that there had been little noticeable progress in Normandy in 1909.

36. René Dumont, p. 222; Drouillet, 2:27; Polge, *Matériaux*, p. 42; Francus, *Valgorge*, p. 215.

37. AD, Puy-de-Dôme F 0275 (Vic-le-Comte, 1899); Foville, *Enquête*, 1:xii, xxxix; Jeanton, *Habitation rustique*, pp. 88–92; Ardouin-Dumazet, 27:45.

38. Jeanton, *Habitation paysanne*, p. 71; Jeanton, *Habitation rustique*, pp. 47–48; Foville, *Enquête*, 1:138. For a report of the same usage in Normandy, see Sion, p. 473.

39. Bougeatre, p. 31; Doussinet, *Paysan*, p. 348; Poueigh, *Folklore*, p. 31.

40. Bougeatre, p. 31; *Atlas*, Allier, pp. 791–92; Fortier-Beaulieu, p. 54; S. Tardieu, *Vie domestique*, p. 158; Passama, p. 107 (Minervois); Colin, p. 72 (Brittany; but his comments suggest how few must have been affected at this early date); Foville, *France*, 2:213 (Lorraine).

41. Camescasse, p. 112; Halévy, p. 35.

42. The 1848 survey quoted in Vigier, 2:128; AG, MR 1236 (Morbihan, 1827); Doussinet, *Paysan*, p. 368; AD, Cantal 87 M1 (ref. Mauriac, 1864); Francus, *Voyage fantaisiste*, 2:40. Edeine, 1:254, tells the story of the Solognot landlord of the 1870's who visited one of his tenants and was so moved by the state of the dirt floor that he offered to put flagstones in. "Mais nout'e maît'e," answered the peasant, "alle est carr'lée la chamb'e, la tarre que vous voyez n'on la rapporte anvec les sabots, quand qu'i y en a trop, j'lenlevue anvec la bêche." (But master, the place *is* flagged. The earth you see, we bring it in on our sabots. When there's too much, I remove it with the spade.)

43. Perrin and Bouet, p. 25 (Brittany); Marin, *Veillées*, p. 14 (Moselle); Ricard, p. 55 (Landes); *Conseils hygiéniques aux cultivateurs des campagnes, par un maire de campagne* (1850).

44. Aguilhon, pp. 33ff; MATP, manuscript 44.294. "Enventair de la veuve Drouet: La cremaillere; La pincette Et la barre de feut; Un chandelier, 2 mauvaise chaise; Une

table Et une huche, une comode; 3 aciette Et 3 coeuilliere Et 2 fourchette; Un plat plat et une potte; 9 mauviaze chemize, de 3 corcet, 3 mauvaize robe; un corps avec sa robe, un Bois de Lit avec ces ridos; 2 couverture, une de Lit Et une de dos; Un lit de plume et un traversin; 3 drapts; Et un amuvais sac de toille." (Capitalization and spelling are faithfully reproduced, but the punctuation has been changed in order to run-in this list.)

45. Besson, p. 55 (Auvergne, cowherd); Dainville, p. 160 (all other areas). At Ligardes (Gers), as in Besson's Cantal, possession of a clock (or for that matter of an umbrella) indicated solid comfort, if not riches (Donnedevie, pp. 110–11).

46. Cordier, p. 34; Perrin and Bouet, p. 14; Colin, p. 74; Drouillet, 2: 177; Buffet, *Haute-Bretagne*, p. 185; Boillot, *Traditions*; Thuillier, "Pour une histoire," p. 251; Lizerand, p. 55; Drouillet, 2: 64; Lejeune, 1: *passim*; Costérisant, p. 4. Note that soldiers did not get personal mess tins until 1885. As for sitting to eat, this is what Daugé writes of the southwest (p. 228): "Rarement on se met à table, excepté en ville et dans les bourgades. Manger sur le poing, même à la maison, est un vieil usage de Gascogne. Un couteau à bec recourbé [*lou piquepan*] sert de fourchette."

47. Frantz Bonnet, *En Compagnie de Charles Péguy* (Mâcon, 1956), pp. 9, 11.

48. Nelli, pp. 94–103; Drouillet, 2: 52.

49. Bougeatre, pp. 21–23, 27; Drouillet, 2: 52; Fortier-Beaulieu, p. 385, 536; Perrin and Bouet, pp. 25–27; S. Tardieu, *Vie domestique*, pp. 5–6.

50. Bachelin, *Village*, pp. 15–16.

51. According to S. Tardieu, *Vie domestique*, pp. 217–18, inventories of Mâconnais houses show little change between 1710 and 1810, rapid change from the 1850's on, especially in 1870–90. See also Vazeilles, 1: 3.

52. S. Tardieu, *Vie domestique*, pp. 74–75.

53. Labourasse, pp. 13–14. In places like Plozévet (Fin.) domestic comfort represented by coal stoves, woolen mattresses, and even matches came only after the First World War (Burguière, pp. 160–61).

54. See Thiriat, *Vallée de Cleurie*; and Bogros, pp. 112–20.

Chapter Eleven

1. On donnages continuing in 1888, see Labourasse, pp. 103–5. On this and much else, see Edward Shorter, *The Making of the Modern Family* (New York, 1975), a mine of information, unfortunately published after my manuscript was in press.

2. H. Mendras, "Sociologie du milieu rural," in Georges Gurvitch, ed., *Traité de sociologie* (1958), p. 322; Franchet, p. 25.

3. Perron, *Proverbes*, p. 53. Many sayings testify to the importance of wealth. "Beauty, you can't eat or drink it," they said in Gascony; and "however ugly she be, a lass'll find a mate if she has money." True, "money doesn't make happy marriages; however, it helps a lot." As for looks, "the pretty girl's the one who works and earns." (Daugé, pp. 22, 23, 48.) Beauty is often equated with plumpness (attesting to means) or to sturdiness (promising hardiness at work): "Flesh goes well with bones"; "A little fat under the skin makes girls as pretty as a pin"; "Let God just make me big and fat. (Pretty and pink, I'll see to that!)" (Flandrin, p. 132.)

4. Trébucq, *Chanson populaire et la vie rurale*, 1: 4; Trébucq, *Chanson populaire en Vendée*, p. 46.

5. Houillier, p. 65; Gorse, p. 7.

6. Rambaud, *Economie*, pp. 178–80. Rates of change varied from place to place, but the general tendency was the same. At Plozévet (Fin.) 61.5% of those born before 1850 had married endogamously but only 54.1% of those born after 1850 (Burguière, p. 43).

7. MATP, manuscript 54.294 (Hérault and the southwest). Again a host of proverbs. "He who marries far away either betrays or will betray"; "He who marries far away

does so 'cause there's no other way"; "Women and melons can't be known from afar" (Daugé, pp. 30–31). And from Flandrin, pp. 139–40: "Build with local stone"; "One is stronger on one's home ground"; "In a strange country the cows beat the oxen"; "Who takes the neighbor's daughter knows what's wrong with her."

8. Perron, *Broye-les-Pesmes*, pp. 48–49; Seignolle, p. 34. See also Suzanne Blandy, *La Dernière Chanson* (1880), pp. 23–24, about the resentment in the village of Uchizy in Mâconnais over the marriage of a local girl to a man of Bresse, on the other side of the Saône.

9. Van Gennep, *Folklore du Dauphiné*, 2: 630; Bérenger-Féraud, *Réminiscences*, p. 193; Ségalen, p. 98.

10. Bougeatre, p. 19; Perron, *Broye-les-Pesmes*, pp. 50–51.

11. Corbin, p. 136; *Barbizier*, 1950, p. 376; Bonnemère, 2: 428.

12. Dainville, p. 159; Gorse, pp. 177, 178 and chap. 7 *passim*. See also *Semaine religieuse de l'Archidiocèse d'Auch*, Oct. 1, 1898 (brought to my attention by Henri Polge), in which the archdiocese is reminded that in choirs the soprano roles should be sung by young boys.

13. Bladé, p. 437. For more examples, see Daugé, pp. 120, 125–26, 140. As for folk wisdom on how women were best treated, the evidence is consistent: "Women want to be beaten"; "Hit your wife, she'll listen to you"; "Women and omelets are never beaten enough"; "Women and laundry need a good beating"; "The silent woman's never beaten"; "Who wants to hit his wife will never lack excuses"; "There is no reason like the stick"; "Bad horse the spur, bad woman the stick." (*Ibid.*, pp. 121, 143–44.) Marriage songs hinted at what was to come. "She weeps and she's right / The state of a lass is bright. / The state of a lass is a treat. / The state of a wife is [*delete*]." Or, the saying on presenting the bride to the groom on their wedding-day: "Aqui que l'as, tan la boulès! Ne-n hessis pas estroulhe-pès" (Here's the one you wanted so much! Don't use her as a doormat). Or, the mother-in-law's greeting to welcome her *bru* into the house: "Espie, nobie, p'ous cantous. T'y balheran cots de bastous!" (Look well into the corners, bride. That's where you'll be beaten with a stick!) (*Ibid.*, pp. 16, 71, 97.) The general merriment must have been a little strained.

14. Gorse, chap. 7 *passim* (Corrèze); Bonnemère, 2: 425–27 (western France); Aimé Giron, p. 130 (Velay); R. J. Bernard, "L'Alimentation paysanne au XVIIIe siècle," *Annales: E. S. C.*, 1968, p. 1454 (Lozère); Violet, *Clessé*, p. 114 (Mâconnais); Laborde, p. 362 (Limousin).

15. Laborde, pp. 358–59; Micheline Baulant, "Démographie et structure familiale au XVIIe siècle," *Annales: E. S. C.*, 1972, pp. 960–61.

16. AN, F^{17}10757 (Ariège); Gadrat, p. 131; Laborde, p. 359; Coissac, p. 179. But see Perrin and Bouet, p. 280, where Le Guyader disagrees: by 1914 the woman had come to look like the boss!

17. Coissac, p. 179; Garneret, pp. 293, 310; Bogros, p. 44.

18. Laborde, p. 359; Ogès and Déguignet; Labourasse, p. 176. As for the war of the sexes, many competitive rituals suggest an adversary relationship and a competition for power. Before the altar, the groom sought to stand or kneel on the bride's shawl or skirt, while she crooked her finger to prevent the wedding ring from sliding past the first knuckle. On entering their new home, the young couple struggled to see who could first grab a pair of pants and who would be left holding the menial broomstick. References to such practices can be found in every work of folklore.

19. *Petit Journal*, Jan. 1, 1900, supplement no. 459; AD, Finistère 10 U 7 39.

20. According to Betham-Edwards, in Côtes-du-Nord, where the Iceland fisheries were based, the women had sole charge of the household affairs; the men when at home did nothing. Moreover, it was the housewife who invested the money from the season's catch.

(*France*, 2: 171.) But see Corbin, *passim*, for the migrant male's very active role in running the household's business.

21. E. Brouard, *Histoire de France racontée à l'aide des tableaux* (1882), p. 54. Educational and social promotion was (dimly) reflected in the law of December 7, 1879, which permitted women over 21 to act as witnesses to wills and other public or private documents.

22. Coissac, p. 178; J. H. Ricard, "La Vie paysanne d'août 1914 à octobre 1915," *Revue politique et parlementaire*, Dec. 1915, pp. 358–73; EA, Lot (directeur des services agricoles).

23. AD, Vosges 11 T 18 (1899); Belbèze, p. 67.

24. Dr. Deguiral, "Considérations sur la démographie pyrénéenne," *Annales de la Fédération Pyrénéenne de l'Economie Montagnarde*, 1944, pp. 59–72; Michel Chevalier, p. 747; Garneret, p. 62; Charrié, *Bas-Vivarais*, p. 176. In Franche-Comté the term for this was "faire des lièvres." Across the Rhône, in Vivarais, they called it "faire des loups."

25. Romieu, pp. 340–42.

26. Lapaire, pp. 26ff. He added: "Le bourgeois met des formes à son impatience." Hence, perhaps, the proverb quoted by Charrié, *Bas-Vivarais*, p. 246: "To believe in an heir's tears, you must be mad."

27. Rocal, p. 30; Daugé, p. 49.

28. Franchet, pp. 143–46; Bonnemère, 2: 359–60; Bernard, pp. 48–49; Thuillier, *Aspects*, p. 70. Thuillier has more recently illustrated this further from the 1844 memoir of Adolphe de Bourgoing in his *Economie et société nivernaises au début du XIXe siècle* (1974), pp. 205, 403.

29. Théron de Montaugé, p. 441; Deffontaines, *Hommes et travaux*, pp. 98–105; Renard, *Philippe* (unpaginated). Note the Gascon proverb: "The first inheritance of the married man is the child" (Daugé, p. 47).

30. Gorse, pp. 23, 187–88; Decoux-Lagoutte, p. 38; Charles Dumont, p. 40.

31. Pariset, *Lauragais*, p. 90 (who notes that by the 1880's and 1890's this changed); Fortier-Beaulieu, pp. 669, 685. Another informant said: "It is a sign of glory to have children before getting married" (Perrin and Bouet, p. 451).

32. Ariès, *Histoire* (1948 ed.), pp. 495ff; Thuillier, *Aspects*, p. 78. The development is referred to in one way or another in George Sand, *La Mare au diable* (1845); Claude Tillier, *Mon Oncle Benjamin* (1900); Henri Bachelin, *Juliette la Jolie* (1913); and many other works. Burguière, p. 67, tells us that the people of Plozévet, like the rest of the Bas Bretons, did not limit births before the end of the nineteenth century, with the result that there was a marked fall in the decade after 1904. On the diversity of magic practices to which wives had recourse in the hope of inhibiting their husbands' reproductive powers, see Georges Rocal, *Les Vieilles coutumes dévotieuses et magiques du Périgord* (Toulouse, 1922), pp. 44–45.

33. This discussion is based on tables in Etienne Van de Walle, *The Female Population of France in the Nineteenth Century* (Princeton, N.J., 1974). I owe much thanks to my friend Lutz Berkner for guiding me through the complexities of demographic lore.

34. "Fertility and Family Structure in France," Institute for Advanced Study, Princeton, N.J., 1972, pp. 30–31.

35. AN, BB 30 370 (Agen, Oct. 7, 1863).

36. AD, Ariège 5M3 (Apr. 5, 1856), Yonne V M^{11}1 (35), 1826–27; Forestier, *Yonne*, 1: 341; Hugo, 1: 77 (also notes the frequent inverse ratio between infanticide and illegitimacy); Corbin, p. 703; Ministère de l'Intérieur, *Enquête générale ouverte en 1860 dans les 86 départements de l'Empire: Rapport de la commission instituée le 10 oct. 1861* (1862).

37. Léon-Petit, p. 1; Monot, *Mortalité*, pp. 21–27; Thuillier, *Aspects*, p. 82.

38. Monot, *Mortalité*, pp. 43–48. For hair-raising details on the practice and effects of wet-nursing, a readily accessible source is Shorter (cited in note 1, above), pp. 175–81.

39. Paul Gemaehling in Friedmann, pp. 335–49 (notably, the maps on pp. 336–37, 339, and 345); René Dumont, pp. 438–39. Concerning general celibacy rates, Flandrin, p. 67, contributes some illuminating figures: of men between 18 and 59, 38% were unmarried in 1851, 27% in 1936; of women between 15 and 49, 44% were unmarried in 1851, 29% in 1936.

40. Garrier, 1: 68; Desprès, pp. 136ff; Le Guen, p. 465; Perron, *Proverbes*, p. 53; Sébillot, *Coutumes*, pp. 88–89. At Chaponost many girls married after building a kitty as domestic servants in town. No wonder that the Auvergnat proverb averred that old meat makes good soup. Or, as in the Provençal variant, "Old hen, good stock!" (Flandrin, p. 134.)

41. Quoted by Dominique Julia, "Sur les moeurs périgourdines," *Annales de démographie historique*, 1971, pp. 417–20. See also Zeldin, *Conflicts*.

42. Armengaud, "Débuts," pp. 172–73; Théron de Montaugé, p. 441 (and p. 636 for the *Survey* of 1866); Lavigne, pp. 372–73. See also Gachon, *Auvergne*, pp. 316–17.

43. Belbèze, p. 222; Dr. Mirc, "Les Points de dégénérescence nerveuse en Agenais," *Revue de l'Agenais*, 1924, p. 119; Deffontaines, *Hommes et travaux*, p. 104.

44. Trébucq, *Chanson populaire en Vendée*, pp. 240–44.

45. Pujos (Francoulès and Pradine); AD, Vosges 11 T 19 (Domptail, 1888); AD, Puy-de-Dôme F 0274 (Miremont, 1899), F 0275 (Vic-le-Comte, 1899), F 0276 (Yronde and Buron, 1899).

46. Labat, *Gascogne*, pp. 100–103.

47. Rambaud, *Economie*, p. 177; Ségalen, p. 83.

48. Ségalen, pp. 100, 122.

49. A. Berthaud, *Du respect de l'autorité* (Poitiers, 1896); Jacques Porcher, "La Famille bourgeoise: Les Pères et les fils," *Revue bleue*, 1897, pp. 2–8; Francus, *Valgorge*, p. 262; *Recueil agronomique du Tarn*, 1855, quoted in Armengaud, *Populations*, p. 295.

50. Labat, *Ame*, pp. 115–17.

51. Buffet, *Bretagne*, p. 13; Semaines Sociales de France, comp. *La Crise de l'autorité* (Lyon, 1925), especially p. 173.

52. See Labourasse, pp. 59–60 (for Mogeville); Bonnamour, pp. 229–30 (for this rebellion against "the yoke of family structures" in the Morvan); Corbin, p. 372; and G. Clément-Simon, *Limousin, caractère et moeurs* (Limoges, 1890), pp. 8–9 (at the time he wrote, a local proverb still insisted that the chimney must keep smoking—"chal que lou fournel fume"—and newlyweds attended a requiem mass the day after their wedding for the dead of both families).

53. Pariset, *Lauragais*, pp. 128ff; Pariset, *Montagne Noire*, pp. 164ff; EA, Tarn-et-Garonne.

54. Sauzet, pp. 230–38; EA, Puy-de-Dôme.

55. J. Munaret, *Du médecin de campagne et de ses malades* (1837), p. 127.

56. Bernard, pp. 43, 51; Labat, *Ame*, p. 141.

57. Chataigneau, p. 427.

58. See Arsène Dumont, *La Natalité à Saint-Pierre-de-Clairac (Lot-et-Garonne)* (1901), pp. 14–16, noting that profit was now expected not from production but from inheritance.

59. Quoted in Delacroix, p. 200.

Chapter Twelve

Epigraph. AN, BB 30 370.

1. AN, F^ie III Loiret 7. See also Marcilhacy, *Diocèse 1849–78*, pp. 344, 346.

2. Le Roy, *Jacquou*, p. 51.

3. Young, pp. 12, 16, 58, and many other references; Meynier, *A travers le Massif Central*, pp. 21ff; Gachon, *Limagnes du Sud*, p. 289; Lavisse, *Souvenirs*, p. 28; Thabault, *Mon village*, pp. 48–49. And in Musset, *Bas-Maine*, p. 426: "Le village évite la route." Similarly, Garrier, 1: 223: through the first half of the nineteenth century, the highway from Lyon to Saint-Etienne "traverse un milieu rural qui lui reste étranger." A couple of miles from it, the parishes of the countryside "restent isolées et repliées sur elles-mêmes."

4. Cavaillès, p. 207. See also Deffontaines, *Hommes et travaux*, p. 390; and Say, 1: 1049–56.

5. Camescasse, p. 182.

6. Meynier, *A travers le Massif Central*, pp. 21–27; Girard, *Politique*, pp. 230–31; Jules Brame in *Moniteur universel*, June 19, 1861, pp. 928–29; Romieu, pp. 266–67.

7. Bozon, *Industrie*, especially p. 219; Marcel Gautier, pp. 96ff; Charles Biermann, "La Circulation en pays de montagne," *Annales de géographie*, 1913, p. 271.

8. Marcel Gautier, p. 301. Transport activities are still estimated to take half the farmer's time today.

9. Caralp-Landon, p. 24, noting that in 1875 "c'est sur un ensemble de petits parcours que circule le tonnage relativement important."

10. M. de Vogüé, p. 922.

11. Haussmann, 1: 67; Armengaud, *Populations*, p. 128; Mignot, pp. 3–31; Pariset, *Lauragais*, p. 7; A. Cournot, *Souvenirs, 1760–1860* (1913), p. 16.

12. AD, Cantal IT 809 (223), July 3, 1880; R. Brunet, p. 205; Labourasse, p. 21; Barnett Bruce Singer, "Pillar of the Republic: The Village Schoolmaster in Brittany, 1880–1914" (Ph.D. diss., University of Washington, 1971), p. 116.

13. Bougeatre, p. 139; Ardouin-Dumazet, 14: 172.

14. AD, Lot 5M38(1); Perrin and Bouet, p. 131; Romieu, pp. 266–67; Pujos (Castelnau, Lot); AD, Pyrs.-Ors. 3M1 224 (St.-Laurent-de-Cerdans, Oct. 31, 1895). Conditions similar to those bewailed by the prefect of Rhône in 1818: "Partout où leur sol a quelque valeur, il est envahi; chaque année la charrue morcelle la voie publique; les haies marchent... les cimetières mêmes ne sont pas respectés; la cupidité des riverains envahit aussi bien les tombes que les chemins qui y conduisent" (Garrier, 1: 219).

15. AD, Yonne III M⁵8 (Dec. 1830); AG, MR 2261 (Hte.-Garonne, 1873); Pujos (Lamadeleine, Lot); Mazières, 1: 315, 318; René Chatreix, *Monographie de la Commune de Saint-Maurice-la-Souterraine* (Guéret, 1938), p. 115.

16. AN, Fⁱᵉ III Ardèche 11; AD, Puy-de-Dôme, M 04478 (Brassac, 1896); Merley, pp. 24–28; AD, Cantal 110 M1; Marcel Lachiver, *Histoire de Meulan* (1965), p. 359.

17. Labrousse; Lugnier, pp. 102, 106; Charrié, *Haut-Vivarais*, p. 213; Michel Chevalier, p. 980; AG, MR 1223 (Pyrs.-Ors., 1840, 1841), 1218 (Gard, 1844).

18. Bozon, *Histoire*, p. 184; Francus, *Valgorge*, p. 457; Francus, *Voyage fantaisiste*, p. 283; Higonnet, p. 168; Michel Chevalier, p. 620; Philippe Arbos, "Les Communications dans les Alpes françaises," *Annales de géographie*, 1919, pp. 161–76; Armengaud, *Populations*, pp. 126–27. Machenaud, p. 36, reports that at Ardillères, southeast of La Rochelle, the roads were no better at mid-century than before the Revolution. In the 1850's one could get about only on horseback or on foot. In 1903 the General Council of Charente-Maritime still described the Aunis as "completely deprived from the point of view of transport."

19. Francus, *Midi de l'Ardèche*, p. 240: "Per lou pois d'en bas, lou bat. Per lou pois d'accol, lou saccol."

20. Poueigh, *Folklore*, p. 38: "De tout chiffon, un tortillon."

21. Reynier, *Pays*, vol. 2, quoted in Nelli, p. 51; Charrié, *Bas-Vivarais*, pp. 294, 300; AN, C 945 (Canton d'Ax), quoted in Armengaud, *Populations*, p. 154; AN, BB 30 370 (Aix, July 11, 1865); Boissier, p. 68.

22. Baudrillart, 3: 556–57; Boissier, p. 103; "Tron, tron, tron, moun'âne, vè z'Auré; / Fauto d'âne, l'anan de pè. / Hi pouhi! Que demô yrau â la sâ. / Hi cavalo! Que demô yrau à la grâno. / Hi chava! Que demô yrau airon vi."

23. Mazon, pp. 7, 37, 99, 101; Drouillet, 2: 215.

24. Arbos, "Les Communications," cited in note 18, above, p. 174.

25. Foville, *France*, 2: 141. On Aveyron, see Boscary, pp. 56–57.

26. Romieu, p. 281; Fustier, pp. 244–45; Toutain, *Transports*, p. 259; J. B. Proudhon, *Réformes à opérer dans l'exploitation des chemins de fer*, 1868 ed., p. 56; Théron de Montaugé, pp. 601–2; AN, $F^{11}2734$ (*Enquête agricole*, 1867), p. 156.

27. See Chambre Consultative des Arts et Manufactures de Nevers, *Rapport à M. le Préfet sur l'industrie et le commerce dans le département de la Nièvre* (Nevers, 1858), p. 6; Lovie, pp. 584–85; Francus, *Midi de l'Ardèche*, pp. 257–58; and Longy, *Canton*, p. 29.

28. Durand, p. 121; Marcel Gautier, p. 214; Colin, pp. 19, 78.

29. Valaux, p. 294; Lavergne, *Economie rurale*, p. 434.

30. Valaux, p. 295; Ardouin-Dumazet, 53: 25; Conseil Général de la Loire-Inférieure, quoted in *Les Aspects sociaux de la vie rurale* (1958), p. 194.

31. Cavaillès, pp. 281–82, 562–63, 574.

32. *L'Ariégeois*, June 22, June 29, 1861; Michel Chevalier, pp. 967ff; L.-S. Fugairon, *Topographie médicale du canton d'Ax* (1888); Coornaert, p. 301; A. Tardieu, *Auvergne*, p. 1. Corbin, p. 159: "De 1860 à 1880, le Limousin reste peu concerné par l'édification des réseaux ferroviaires." But see AD, Hte.-Vienne M 1454, where in 1861 the prefect could not predict the markets for the grain trade during the year to come because of the extent to which traditional marketing patterns had been disrupted by the new Limoges-Périgueux line. Still, this was a main line, and Corbin's judgment, based on exhaustive research, is still valid.

33. Considère, 3: 83–84, 87. Considère's articles are well worth rereading.

34. See Isaac Péreire, *La Question des chemins de fer* (1879), pp. 185–90; Cavaillès, p. 276; and Viple, p. 13.

35. Fustier, p. 256; Gachon, *Limagnes du Sud*, p. 436; Wolkowitch, pp. 99, 104; G. Chabot, *La Côtière orientale de la Dombe et l'influence de Lyon* (1927), pp. 44, 46.

36. Chatelain, "Problèmes"; Pinchemel, *Géographie*, 1: 163; Chabirand, pp. 204–5, 226, 229.

37. Wolkowitch, p. 100.

38. Between 1910 and 1913 a viaduct was built over the Gartempe permitting communication between the Lower Marche and the Limousin and in the same period an electric tramway began operating between St.-Sulpice-les-Feuilles, in the far northeast corner of Haute-Vienne, and Limoges—one of those "lignes à intérêt secondaire mais en fait capitales pour nos campagnes isolées." For 40 years thereafter, six times a day, the little train carried people back and forth through the once silent vales. (Peygnaud, p. 147.)

39. F. Grenier, *L'Industrie dans le Cantal* (Saint-Flour, 1836); Meynier, *A Travers le Massif Central*, p. 37; M. D. Glenat, "La Vie dans les Coulmes," *RGA*, 1921, pp. 135–58, and especially p. 149; Georges Jorré, "L'Etablissement des routes dans le massif du Vercors," *ibid.*, pp. 229–84 (especially p. 230, quoting AD, Drôme o 331/1). Louis Cortès, *L'Oisans* (1926), pp. 277–80, provides a list of roads built in that area; most were built in the 1880's and 1890's, but none predated 1881.

40. Sauvan, pp. 524, 542, 544, 593–94; EA, Drôme.

41. Bonnemère, pp. 375, 386; Reynier, "Voies de communications," pp. 202–5; Francus, *Valgorge*, pp. 30–34. See also Lizerand, p. 56; and Hudry-Ménos, p. 619.

42. See Pujos (Craissac and *passim*); Pariset, *Montagne Noire*, pp. 156, 158 (Cabrespine).

43. Ardouin-Dumazet, 35: 188 (Brousse); Boscary, p. 157.

44. René Dumont, p. 94; Baudrillart, 3: 121; Boscary, p. 158; Lesourd and Gérard, 1: 268–69; Le Lannou, 2: 28–29; P. Barral, *Départemente de l'Isère*, pp. 65ff.

45. Cited in Francus, *Valgorge*, p. 39.

46. M. Blanchard, *Géographie des chemins de fer* (1942), pp. 58–60. Compare Wolkowitch, p. 71.

47. Marion, 6: 13; Gonjo, p. 49; Augé-Laribé, *Politique*, p. 53; AD, Cantal 40 M 11 (Mauriac, Dec. 30, 1879): "L'arrondissement attend avec une impatience fébrile le chemin de fer projeté." See the figures in Raymonde Caralp, "L'Evolution de l'exploitation ferroviaire en France," *Annales de géographie*, 1951, pp. 321–36 (especially p. 321); and René Clozier, *Géographie de la circulation* (1963), 1: 201–3.

48. Lavallée, *RDM*, Mar. 1882, quoted in Marion, 6: 14; Toutain, *Transports,* pp. 187–88; Romieu, pp. 270–72.

49. Blanchard, especially p. 43.

50. *Ibid.,* p. 127, and pp. 130–31, quoting Maxime Baragnon, *Le Monopole du PLM et la navigation du Rhône* (Nîmes, 1871); AN, BB 30 370 (Aix, Oct. 15, 1850).

51. Achard, pp. 47, 237; Merley, pp. 144–45; AD, Hte.-Loire P 5907 (1881).

52. Demolins et al., *Populations*, pp. 7, 55; Paul Cornu, *Grèves de flotteurs sur l'Yonne* (Nevers, 1911), p. 43; Ardouin-Dumazet, 27: 18–19.

53. Armengaud, *Populations*, p. 226; Bombal, pp. 67–71, 391–92; J. Maffre, "Le Transport du bois par flottage sur l'Aude," *Folklore-Aude*, Dec. 1941. According to Lebeau, p. 324, in 1872, 137 Ain rafts still carried fir from Jura to Lyon, and this traffic ended only after the First World War. The old mariner's statement is cited by Auguste Mahaut in two works: *Le Progrès de la Nièvre*, Feb. 20, 1900, and *L'Idée de la Loire navigable combattue* (Nantes, 1905), p. 19. For confirmation, see Thibon, p. 41.

54. Markovitch, pp. 81–84.

55. Suret-Canale, p. 295; Sion, pp. 317, 321; AD, Vosges 11 T 18 (1889).

56. Dauzat, *Village*, p. 115.

57. Lovie, pp. 189–93.

58. Cholvy, pp. 64–66; Moscovici, p. 29.

59. AD, Hte.-Vienne M 101 (July 1909), Yonne III M^{1}234 (Sept., Oct. 1865); Ardouin-Dumazet, 36: 20; J. A. Barral, *Agriculture du Nord*, 1: 12; Corbin, pp. 45–50; Cousteix, p. 27.

60. AD, Hte.-Loire 20 M 30 (sous-préf. Brioude, 1872); Merley, p. 240; AD, Puy-de-Dôme, M 04469 (sous-préf. Thiers, Oct. 21, 1894). See also AD, Puy-de-Dôme, M 04478 (comm. Brassac, Feb. 28, 1897): "Les ouvriers des mines des Companies du Gros Ménil et de Commentry Fourchambault chômont toujours le Lundi; mais la majeure partie des ouvriers étant propriétaires ou locataires de quelques parcelles de terrain ils utilisent leur journée libre y compris la demi-journée du Dimanche pour s'occuper dans les champs."

61. Deffontaines, *Homme et forêt, passim.*

62. AD, Hte.-Vienne M 118; AN, BB 30 374 (Bordeaux, 1865); Ardouin-Dumazet, 29: 227–28.

63. Bozon, *Histoire*, p. 217; Armengaud, "Fin des forges," p. 66; Suret-Canale, pp. 298–99, 331; Delumeau, pp. 412–13, 469.

64. AD, Vosges 11 T 18 (instituteur Le Clerjus, 1899).

65. *L'Encyclopédie* (1753), 3: 548–52; Boissier, especially pp. 77, 90; AG, MR 2264

(Isère, 1875); Pérot, pp. 74–75; F. Gex, "La Clouterie en Bauges," *RGA*, 1933, especially p. 194.

66. Corbin, p. 638; AD, Puy-de-Dôme F 0275 (Vic-le-Comte, 1889); AD, Pyrs.-Ors. 3Mɪ 224 (St.-Laurent-de-Cerdans, Oct. 1895); AD, Cantal 40 M ɪɪ (prés. Chambre de Commerce Aurillac, May 1909). See also Gex, "Clouterie," cited in note 65, above, pp. 175–220; and Veyret-Verner, "L'Ouvrier paysan dans les Alpes françaises," *Mélanges . . . Bénévent*, pp. 183–91.

67. Emile Bériès, *Elémens d'une nouvelle législation des chemins vicinaux* (1831), p. 43; Capot-Rey, p. 262; M. Blanchard, "Les Voies ferrées de l'Hérault," *Bulletin de la Société Languedocienne de Géographie*, 1922, pp. 141–78; Achard, pp. 30–31.

68. Maspétiol, p. 344; Blanchard, *Essais*, p. 221; Garavel, p. 64.

69. Gachon, *Limagnes du Sud*, p. 370; Mazon, pp. 27–28.

70. Malon, p. 103.

71. Loua, *France*. Toutain, in *Transports*, p. 13, places the jump between 1866 and 1914, when he feels the saturation point was reached.

72. Corbin, p. 183; Boscary, pp. 162–63; *Mélanges . . . Bénévent*, p. 203; Levasseur, 2: 509.

73. Labat, *Gascogne*, p. 648.

74. Bigo, p. 56; Cénac-Moncaut, *Colporteur*, pp. 10–11; Esnault, *Imagination*, p. 191.

75. Armengaud, *Populations*, p. 211; AN Fⁱᵉ III Tarn 7 (July, Oct. 1859), Fⁱᵉ III Ariège 7 (July 1859); Pelicier, p. 6; Portal, p. 448.

76. See, e.g., Cavaillès, p. 166.

77. Quoted in Marcel Gautier, p. 196.

78. R. L. Stevenson, *Vailima Letters* (New York, 1896), 2: 275.

Chapter Thirteen

Epigraph. *The Cherry Orchard*, Act 4, in Anton Chekhov, *Plays* (Penguin Books, n.d.), p. 39.

1. Markovitch, pp. 85–87. Under the Second Empire France had 1.350 million employers and some 1 million workers: less than 1 employee per establishment. The 1876 census shows 1,516,650 and 2,952,297 persons engaged in "industry" and "artisanate," respectively (*ibid.*). The "industrial population" of Haute-Loire, according to the 1881 census, consisted of 9,340 entrepreneurs and 9,806 workers (Merley, p. 241). Loiret had 48.2% entrepreneurs and 51.8% workers engaged in industry in 1906; by 1911 the proportion had changed to 41% and 59% and by 1921 to 38.6% and 61.4% (A. Montuenga, *Aspects de la vie économique et sociale du Loiret pendant la guerre, 1914–1918*, mémoire de maîtrise, Faculté des Lettres, Tours, 1969, pp. 160–61).

2. See Corbin, p. 402.

3. See Maspétiol, p. 153.

4. AD, Pyrs.-Ors., Fêtes #8 (Aug. 26, 1861); Lejeune, 2.3: 7.

5. Garneret, p. 135; Donnadieu (Agenais and Tarn-et-Garonne); Bladé, pp. 138, 141, 611; Poueigh, *Folklore*, pp. 158–62. See also AD, Pyrs.-Ors. 3Mɪ 223 (Perthus, Sept. 25, 1878).

6. Fortier-Beaulieu, p. 670 and *passim*. Compare Agulhon, *Vie sociale*, p. 304, stating that the artisans (blacksmith, apothecary, linen-weaver) played the role of the elite in small villages where there was no bourgeoisie.

7. Thabault, *Mon village*, pp. 50, 106, 170; Renard, *Oeuvres*, 2: 395.

8. Thibon, p. 46; J. A. Barral, *Agriculture du Nord*, 2: 7, 173–75; Cressot, p. 101; R. Brunet, p. 209; Duclos, 1: 21.

9. Violet, *Autrefois*, pp. 8–12; Nelli, p. 157; Fage, *Autour du mariage*, p. 19. In Sologne,

Edeine, 2: 977–79, lists other *métiers*, among them collectors of pine cones, of cowpats (and other dung), above all of leeches. These last, who sometimes died from loss of blood, disappeared in the 1870's when doctors ceased to employ leeches (1: 477). Charrié, *Bas-Vivarais*, p. 323, finds only 2 or 3 cendrousos still operating in the 1880's: collecting ashes from farm to farm, selling them on Saturdays in Aubenas market and, with the proceeds, buying butter, which they sold in turn at Villeneuve-de-Berg, 17 km away. True *pieds-poudreux*!

10. Poueigh, *Folklore*, p. 162; Rouchon, 1: 55; Perrin and Bouet, pp. 166, 173; Colin, p. 77; Souvestre, *Derniers Bretons*, pp. 42, 43; Renard, *Oeuvres*, 2: 290.

11. Cressot, p. 89; Lucien Febvre, "Une Enquête: La Forge de village," *Annales*, 1935, pp. 603–14. Note that at Mazières in 1886 there were 9 smiths working in 4 smithies; 20 years later there were only 4, in 2 shops (Thabault, *Mon village*, p. 170).

12. Gautier, *Dure existence*, p. 28; Meynier, *A travers le Massif Central*, p. 366; BFI, 1942, p. 15; Dauzat, *Village*, p. 93.

13. Cressot, p. 89; Poueigh, *Folklore*, pp. 168–69: "Ensemble comme sabot et bride," "Carnaval au sabot débridé," "Bavard—gueule comme un sabot."

14. Francus, *Voyage fantaisiste*, 2: 290; Thabault, *Mon village*, pp. 168–69.

15. Pinchemel, *Structures*, pp. 136–37; Thabault, *Mon village*, pp. 168–69.

16. Snuff: Perrin and Bouet, p. 338. Umbrellas: Donnedevie, pp. 110–11; Théron de Montaugé, p. 453. Smoking, Cressot, p. 115; Paul Sébillot, *Le Tabac* (1893), pp. 3, 13. Thuillier, "Pour une histoire," p. 261, remarks that around 1900 Nièvre used some 55 tons of snuff.

17. Garneret, p. 213; Clément Brun, p. 15.

18. André Mabille de Poncheville, *Jeunesse de Péguy* (1943), p. 21.

19. *Revue de folklore français*, 1942, pp. 106–7; Drouillet, 1: 117; Desforges, p. 23; Michel Chevalier, p. 657; *Un Village et son terroir*, p. 37.

20. Michel Chevalier, p. 657; Fortier-Beaulieu, pp. 201, 218, 269, 299.

21. Boscary, pp. 202, 228, 230.

22. See Corbin's remarks on this variation and the examples he gives, p. 97.

23. Le Roy, *Moulin*, pp. 11–12; Bonneff and Bonneff, *Classe*, p. 67; Combes and Combes, pp. 149, 151, 154, 157, 161; Gustave Flaubert, *Bouvard and Pécuchet* (New York, 1954), p. 44; AG, MR 2153 (Morbihan, 1861), where men were just beginning to wear smocks.

24. Besson, p. 37; A. Tardieu, *Auvergne*, p. 5.

25. Nadaud, 2: 88; Dauzat, *Village*, p. 140.

26. Decoux-Lagoutte, pp. 20–21; AD, Puy-de-Dôme F 0274 and F 0276 (1899).

27. Ardouin-Dumazet, 34: 28; Fortier-Beaulieu, p. 706.

28. *Congrès des sociétés savantes de Provence*, 1906 (Marseille, 1907), pp. 601–8.

29. Dubreuil-Chambardel, pp. 158–59, 161; Reynier, *Pays*, 2: 191.

30. Fortier-Beaulieu, especially pp. 5, 22, 23, 599; Suzanne Tardieu, *Revue de synthèse*, 1957, pp. 360–61; Bourdieu and Bourdieu, "Paysan," p. 165.

Chapter Fourteen

Epigraph. *Round My House*, p. 116. Hamerton adds: "The noblesse and the bourgeoisie, on the other hand, have very similar customs, at least when their pecuniary circumstances are nearly alike."

1. Guillaumin, *C.-L. Philippe*, pp. 9–10; Blanqui, "Tableau," 28: 18.

2. Pariset, *Lauragais*, p. 151; AN, F^{17} 9275 (Deux-Sèvres, 1882); Ardouin-Dumazet, 34: 256; AN, F^{ic} III Ardèche 11 (Oct. 7, 1856).

3. Ardouin-Dumazet, 28: 21, 23.

4. *Ibid.*, 34: 256, 259; Pariset, *Lauragais*, p. 150; Monteils-Pons, p. 77 (Florac); Allaux, pp. 17, 26 (there was no slaughterhouse at Pamiers, of course!); AD, Corrèze M 717 (1874; Tulle); Reynier, *Histoire*, 3: 219 (Privas).

5. Agulhon, *Vie sociale*, pp. 35–36; Roubin, p. 38; E.-J. Savigné, *Lettres d'un touriste* (Vienne, 1876); *Rapport sur l'assainissement de la ville de Pamiers* (Pamiers, 1867), pp. 8ff.

6. AG, MR 1218 (Hérault, 1828), MR 1228 (*Itinéraire de Bayonne à Tulle*, 1843); Annet Reboul, *Moeurs de l'Ardèche au XIXe siècle* (Valence, 1849), p. 120.

7. Reynier, *Histoire*, 3: 219; Hugo, 2: 172; Lejeune, 2.2: 488ff; Ardouin-Dumazet, 31: 6; Bastié, 2: 158–59; Mireur, 1: 72 (from *Le Var*, May 30–July 4, 1897).

8. Challaye, p. 15. See also Mallet, pp. 32–33; and Juge, pp. 20–21.

9. Michaud, pp. 238–39; Challaye, pp. 18ff; Louis A.-M. de Vogüé, p. 323; AD, Pyrs.-Ors. 3M1 163 (Céret, 1879).

10. AD, Gers M 2799 (Vic-Fézensac, Apr. 7, 1874); Ardouin-Dumazet, 29: 238. On stations, see also Bertaut, p. 5.

11. AN, F^{17}9271 (Pyrs.-Ors., 1875); Beslay, pp. 85–88.

12. Louis A.-M. de Vogüé, p. 323.

13. Reynier, *Pays*, 2: 301; AN, BB 30 396 (Bordeaux); Mireur, 2: 270–74, 353.

14. Bastié, 2: 151; Buffet, *Haute-Bretagne*, p. 110; Labat, *Gascogne*, p. 636.

15. Cited in Rougeron, *Département de l'Allier*, 43; Lafarge, p. 222.

16. Foville, *France*, 1: 51, and 2: 57, 60; AD, Lot 37 (E. Delrieu manuscript on Cahors); AG, MR 2267 (Ille-et-Vilaine, 1874); Monteils-Pons, pp. 24–25; Febvre in "Le Travail et les techniques," p. 23. See also Archives Municipales de Limoges, *Tableau récapitulatif du récensement de 1881.*

17. Labat, *Gascogne*, p. 641.

18. *Ibid.*, pp. 636, 643ff.

19. Garrier, 1: 285; Mistral, p. 19.

20. Challaye, p. 24; Labrousse in Friedmann, p. 19.

21. Armengaud, *Populations*, pp. 282ff; Théron de Montaugé, p. 534; Pariset, *Montagne Noire*, p. 181; AN, BB 30 388 (Toulouse, 1859); Gachon, *Commune*, p. 161.

22. Armengaud, *Populations*, pp. 290–91; Labat, *Gascogne*, p. 649.

Chapter Fifteen

Epigraph. *Les Paysans*, p. 37.

1. Agulhon, *République*, p. 289.

2. *Les Blouses.* See also the historical foreword to the 1957 ed. by Jean Dautry.

3. Blanqui, *Déboisement*, pp. 34–35; Souvestre, *Derniers Bretons*, p. 14; Assier, intro. to 2d ed.

4. Dupeux, p. 147; AN, BB 30 374 (Bordeaux, 1864).

5. AD, Puy-de-Dôme M 0116 (sous-préf. Issoire, 1841), Ariège 5 M 3 (Sept. 1866; see also Apr., May 1865), Gers M 1326 (sous-préf. Lombez, 1867), Cantal 39M9 (Murat, Nov. 1866, July 1867; Mauriac, Dec. 1866, Apr., May 1867), Vosges 8M23 (comm. de police Epinal, Nov. 1869); AN BB 30 371 (Angers, Apr. 1866), BB 30 390 (Limoges, 1867).

6. AD, Cantal 39M9 (Murat, Dec. 1866; Mauriac, May–June 1867), Gers M 2237 (Plaisance, Dec. 1875; Lectoure, May 1877); AG, G^{8}180 (Bayonne, 1873), G^{8}182 (Bordeaux, 1875), G^{8}184 (Bordeaux, 1877). See also AN, BB 30 390 (Agen, 1868; Colmar, 1870).

7. AD, Pyrs.-Ors. 3M1 163 (préf., Dec. 1894), 3M1 226 (comm. de gendarmes Perthus, May 1898), 3M1 224 (Bourg-Madame, Oct. 1896), Ariège 5M 72^1 (sous-préf. Pamiers, June 1905).

8. Karl Marx and Friedrich Engels, *Selected Works* (Moscow, 1951), 1: 302, 303.

9. Pariset, *Lauragais*, pp. 87–89.

10. Marouzeau, pp. 14–15; Pierre Bourdieu, "Stratégies matrimoniales," *Annales: E. S. C.*, 1972, p. 1110.

11. *Le Vingt-quatre février*, May 3, 1849, cited in Bouillon, p. 89, where the prosecutor's statement also appears.

12. Perrin and Bouet, pp. 369–72; Bernard, pp. 39–41; Corbin, pp. 405, 415; Ségalen, pp. 75, 79; AD, Yonne III M¹178 (Chablis, Nov. 1852); Labrune, pp. 11–18; Vigier, 2: 51. See also, on Anjou and Jura, the observations of M. Eizner and M. Cristin, "Premières hypothèses comparatives sur trois monographies," *Revue française de sociologie*, 1965, pp. 55–73.

13. See Louis Clarenc, "Riches et pauvres dans le conflit forestier des Pyrénées centrales," *Annales du Midi*, 1967, pp. 307–15; and Corbin, p. 669. See also Loubère, especially p. 1032, who finds one-dimensional explanations of peasant votes, such as Soboul's economic thesis ("Question"), "too general and schematic; peasant reactions were far more complex." The variety of local conditions, resulting in distinctly different orientations and interests, made for a greater disparity in behavior than can usually be accommodated by any single interpretation.

14. R. Brunet, p. 222; Raymond Williams, *The Long Revolution* (New York, 1961), p. 136.

15. Cobb, *Reactions*, p. 125.

16. Labat, *Gascogne*, p. 638; Corbin, p. 814; Albert Soboul, "Survivances 'féodales' dans la société rurale française au 19e siècle," *Annales: E. S. C.*, 1968, pp. 965–86.

17. J.-A. Delpon, 1: 213; Corbin, p. 659; AD, Ariège 5M 531 (maire Saurat, Apr. 21, 1834; comm. de police St.-Girons, May 1837; sous-préf. St.-Girons, May 1837); Anny de Pons, "En glanant parmi les archives judiciaires," *Cerca*, 1960, pp. 324–33; AD, Hte.-Vienne M740 (sous-préf. Bellac, Jan. 1847).

18. AD, Creuse U0357 (tax collector Ajain); Haussmann, 1: 255–56; AD, Finistère, 4M 322 (sous-préf. Morlaix, July 1848); Duchatellier, *Agriculture*, p. 205. See also M. de Vogüé, p. 922: at the end of the Second Empire, the older Pagels had no idea who ruled France. (They also refused paper money, having lost confidence in it since its depreciation in 1848.)

19. Vigier, 2: 255.

20. Hamerton, *Round My House*, p. 233: "The peasant . . . really remembers nothing of the past but its evils . . . *corvée* . . . wars of religion."

21. Batisto Bonnet, p. 307; Doussinet, *Paysan santongeais*, p. 335; Jeanton, *Légende*, p. 66; Rocal, pp. 131–32.

22. Bernard, p. 8; Palmade, p. 86; P. Féral, "Le Problème de la dîme," *BSAG*, 1949, pp. 238–54; C. Cadéot, "L'Evolution du métayage dans le Lectourois," *BSAG*, 1951, pp. 29–36; AG, G⁸180 (Nov. 1873); AD, Lot 5M 37(1) (Figeac, Oct. 1873). Similarly, Hamerton tells us the Burgundian peasants believed that Henri V would reestablish the old corvées (*Round My House*, p. 228). Corbin, pp. 1374–76, shows the vast contrast between the cities of the Limousin, which were sympathetic to the Commune, and the countryside, where the tensions of spring 1871 sparked fresh fear that the Ancien Régime might be restored, along with tithes and privileges for the clergy and aristocracy.

23. See the reports in AN, BB¹⁸1767 (May–June 1868); and *Le Courrier de la Vienne et des Deux-Sèvres*, June 5, 1868. This is reminiscent of the Grande Peur of 1846, whose outbreak in Morvan is chronicled by Guy Thuillier, *Economie et société nivernaises au début du XIXe siècle* (1974), pp. 99–103. The drought that summer gave rise to widespread fear of "metteurs de feu." "Both ignorant and credulous," as the prefect put it, the peasants directed their suspicions against nobles and priests—the latter already accused of having caused the potato blight of 1845 and now charged with protecting criminal firebugs by turning them into dogs when they were in danger of arrest. On the collec-

tion of tithes and other offerings in kind, see J. Magraw in Zeldin, *Conflicts*, pp. 209–10, including the Comte de Chambord's specific denial of 1874 that the Bourbon restoration meant the reestablishment of tithes.

24. Ardouin-Dumazet, 29: 242ff; André Armengaud, "Sur l'opinion politique toulousaine en août 1870," *Annales: E. S. C.*, 1954, pp. 106–7.

25. Armengaud, as cited in preceding note.

26. Mireur, 6: 237–38; Agulhon in Baratier, p. 466; AD, Yonne III M¹121 (curé Coulangeron, Mar. 1848), III M¹128 (Sept. 1848), III M¹136 (préf., May 1849); AN, BB 30 370 (Agen, Dec. 1849); AD, Lot 6M9 (Figeac, July 1848). In Hautes-Alpes, too, most of the troubles of 1848 were connected with forest guards. See Thivot, pp. 66–68, and AN, BB 30 360 (5) (proc. gén. Grenoble, Mar. 19, 1848), quoted by Thivot, concerning "the unenlightened inhabitants of our countryside," and especially the mountainous parts of Drôme, Isère, and Hautes-Alpes.

27. AN, BB 30 396 (file on events subsequent to Dec. 2, 1851); AD, Yonne III M¹159 (prisoner's letter to préf., Mar. 1852: "On m'a mit dans une sosiété, donc que j'ai toujours pensé que c'était une sosiété de bienfaisance.... Une fois que vous m'orez mis en liberté, sy jamais vous entendez dire quelque chose de moi, tranché moi la tete, je le mériterait"); Reynier, *Histoire*, pp. 267–69, 270; Vigier, 2: 312–13, 314; Ténot, *Province*, pp. 116–18. Another aspect of the "secret societies" appears in a report of the public prosecutor at Grenoble, who in Jan. 1852 noted that the oath taken on joining such societies included the obligation to defend the Catholic faith, and that many young men had taken to arms in the belief that they were doing so. "Par une ignorante et stupide obéissance à un serment prêté, ils n'en suivirent que la lettre, tandis que les meneurs se réservaient d'en appliquer l'esprit," which stood not for religion but for "socialism." (Quoted in Thivot, p. 103.)

28. Reynier, *Histoire*, p. 270; Corbin, pp. 1210, 1212, 1216; AN, BB 30 401 (Limoges), BB 30 396 (Bordeaux, Agen, Limoges).

29. Ténot, *Province*, pp. 135, 160–61; Vigier, 2: 88, 200–205, 216–24; Soboul, "Question," p. 52. The mountain people were hardly unique in their narrow outlook. The Languedocians too lacked the "awareness that allowed them to translate specific grievances into political action." No wonder that "their action still resembled that of 18th-century peasants." It would take the new experiences that the late 19th century brought to turn them into something else. (See Loubère, especially p. 1030.)

30. AD, Yonne III M¹207 (Courgis, Jan. 19, 1852).

31. Ténot, *Suffrage*, pp. 8–9; Corbin, p. 564.

32. Noted by George Sand, as cited by Georges Duveau in preface to Nadaud, *Mémoires de Léonard* (1948 ed.), p. 39.

33. Bois, *Paysans* (1971 ed.), pp. 120–21, 130.

34. AD, Gers M 2237 (Plaisance, Jan. 1876); Palmade in Girard, *Elections*, p. 197; *La République*, Apr. 15, 1878.

35. M. Faucheux in Girard, *Elections*, pp. 149–62; Beslay, p. 64; Hugonnier, p. 53; Reynier, *Pays*, p. 125. Thibon, p. 52: "On est blanc ou rouge pour des raisons de famille, de sympathie, d'intérêt: les réflexions et les aspirations politiques ne jouent là qu'un maigre role." L. Gachon in Fauvet and Mendras, p. 409: "Mon père était rouge parce qu'il était cantonnier. Mon grand-père maternel ... était rouge pour des sévices qu'un parent à lui, enseignant, avait subi au temps de Badinguet." See also Burguière, pp. 100, 217.

36. AD, Pyrs.-Ors. 3M1 163 (préf., Dec. 3, 1889); Perron, *Broye-les-Pesmes*, pp. 79–80. See also the remarks of the public prosecutor at Grenoble (Jan. 9, 1850), quoted by Thivot, p. 95. So far as he was concerned, the Hautes-Alpes remained outside all national party politics. Elections were struggles between private interests and interest groups, and electoral struggles were the more heated because "there is never any ques-

tion of real political issues, whatever the banner under which either side chooses to take its positions."

37. AD, Lot 6M9 (June 21, July 12, 1848), Yonne III M¹276 (Mar. 26, 1853).

38. AD, Vosges 8M23 (sous-préf. Mirecourt, Oct. 1869; préf., Jan. 1870); AN, BB 30 390 (Agen, July 1870). See also préf. Loir-et-Cher, 1856, quoted in Dupeux, pp. 429–33; AN, F¹ᶜIII 7 Loiret (Pithiviers, Apr. 1853, June 1857, Sept. 1858); AD, Yonne III M¹232 (sous-préf. Sens, Jan. 1861); AD, Ariège 5M 53² (juge de paix Labastide-de-Séron, June 1865); AD, Gers M 1326 (sous-préf. Mirande, Jan. 23, 1867; préf., Jan. 25, 1867); and AN, BB 30 370 (Aix, Oct. 1867). Writes Le Guen, p. 481: "Dans ce milieu, les hommes se distinguent plus par leur tempérament que par leur idéologie."

39. Hence the subversive influence of commercial travelers when they appeared: "couriers of demagogy" (AN, BB 30 370, Jan. 4, 1859).

40. AD, Gers M 2237 (Plaisance, Jan. 1876).

41. AD, Puy-de-Dôme M 04474 (préf., Aug. 1907). See also AD, Gers M 1326 (Nogaro, July 17, 1869); Coissac, *Mon Limousin*, p. 172; AD, Tarn IV M²65 (préf., Feb. 1872); and AD, Pyrs.-Ors. 3M1 163 (préf., Jan. 1892). A good expression of this point of view was formulated in 1863 by the mayor of Bains (Hte.-Loire), who urged the voters of his little parish to vote as he told them, because then "when the mayor solicits for the parish, for you and your children, the deputy's influence will secure the favors or aids from the government" (Pilenco, p. 95).

42. AN, F¹ᵇII Ardèche 4 (Aubenas, Mar. 1874); AD, Pyrs.-Ors. 3M1 223 (Bourg-Madame, Nov. 1876, Mar. 1882; see also Prats-de-Mollo, Dec. 1876), 3M1 163 (préf., Jan. 1892) (the whole 3M1 224 file contains communications insisting on the exclusive importance of local issues, not "political" ones!); AD, Vosges 8bisM30 (Rambervillers, Sept. 1887); AD, Cantal 40M 11 (St.-Flour, 1889); AD, Puy-de-Dôme M 04475 (Billom, Dec. 1890), M 0162 (Riom, Mar. 1892), M 04469 (Thiers, Aug. 1896; Issoire, Jan. 1897); AD, Lot 5M37 (1) (Gourdon, June 1897); Belbèze, p. 98.

43. Agulhon, *République*, pp. 265–66. At Plozévet (Fin.), also, the "red" party led by the Le Bail family represented the claims and aspirations of the less well off; but also and often neighborhood feuds (and sheer violence) under the cover of Republicanism and anticlericalism (Burguière, p. 217).

44. Mendras, "Sociologie," p. 322.

45. AD, Pyrs.-Ors. 3M1 163 (July 1889).

46. Hugonnier, pp. 45–50, 64; Guichonnet, pp. 74–76.

47. Viple, p. 293; Bozon, *Histoire*, p. 245.

48. AD, Pyrs.-Ors. 3M1 223 (Céret, Dec. 1876).

49. Baudrillart, 3: 422; Anne D. Sedgewick, *A Childhood in Brittany Eighty Years Ago* (Boston, 1927), p. 21. The peasants of Saint-Lary (Hte.-Garonne) maintained a feudal relationship with their local lord through the middle of the century. "Malheur à qui ne lui parlait pas chapeau bas!" remembered his son. "Un revers de canne avait bientôt fait voler le couvre-chef récalcitrant. A cette époque, ces façons ètaient supportées tout naturellement." (Comminges, pp. 6–7.) On the same point, see J. Suret-Canale, "L'Etat économique et social de la Mayenne au milieu du XIXe siècle," *Revue d'histoire économique et sociale*, 1958, p. 310. For a portrait of a true village autocrat, Joseph-Antoine Fournier, mayor of Ceillac (Htes.-Alpes) for over half a century from the Restoration into the Second Empire, see Thivot, pp. 60–64, and Polydore Delafont, "Un Village des Hautes-Alpes," *Revue du Dauphiné*, 1938, p. 3. Fournier allowed neither bill collectors nor tax collectors to set foot in his parish, married and judged his subjects himself, exiled sinners against the local code, and ruled without contest until his death.

50. Chaix, p. 283; EA, Calvados, quoting *Mémoires de la Société d'Agriculture de Caen*, 1836; AD, Yonne III M¹228 (juge de paix Auxerre, Oct. 1857); AN, F¹¹2734 (*Enquête*

agricole, 3d rev., Dec. 1867), p. 60, and F¹¹2725, *Enquête agricole* (answers to question-naire, Aisne); Bastié, 2: 170.

51. Théron de Montaugé, pp. 646, 648.

52. Garneret, p. 134; Valaux, p. 68; P. Mayer, pp. 6–7; Francus, *Rivière d'Ardèche*, p. 59.

53. Bastié, 2: 149–50. See also Pinchemel, *Structures*, p. 87; Gachon, *Brousse-Montbois-sier*, p. 80; and Buffet, *Haute-Bretagne*, p. 113, on the decay of the interdependence in work and services, whose breakdown spurred that of traditional personal relations.

54. Lapaire, pp. 32–33; Houillier, p. 65. In Nièrre, donkeys were sometimes Cabinet Ministers (René Dumont, *Agronomie de la faim*, 1974, p. 23).

55. L. Fardet, *Géographie du département du Loiret* (Orléans, 1926), p. 20 (quoted words); Wylie, *Chanzeaux*, p. 81; Rougeron, *Département de l'Allier*, especially p. 53; AD, Ariège 5M3 (Oct. 1865), Yonne III M¹234 (Joigny, Oct. 1865). Tarn deputy Bernard Lavergne in Chamber, 1887, quoted in Maspétiol, p. 367: "It's the rural bourgeoisie that decides the elections in the countryside."

56. Francus, *Voyage humoristique*, p. 69; Abbé Meyraux, "La Bastide de Cazères-sur-Adour," *Bulletin de la Société de Borda*, 1894, quoted in *BSAG*, 1969, p. 487; V. Dupont; Demolins, *Supériorité*, pp. 234–35. See Emile Combes, *Mon Ministère* (1956), p. 5, for such a dynasty of country doctors.

57. Louis A.-M. de Vogüé, pp. 129, 139, 326–28. Italics mine.

58. Audiganne, *Populations*, 1: 41, 66; 2: 199; Louis A.-M. de Vogüé, pp. 328–29.

59. Rougeron, *Personnel*, p. 9.

60. AD, Hte.-Vienne M132 (sous-préf. Rochechouart, 1857); Corbin, p. 1625; AD, Yonne III M¹127 (Tonnerre, May 1851).

61. Ténot, *Suffrage*, *passim* and introduction: "absolute political ignorance." See also Bernard, p. 8. For the peasant, said Jules Ferry, "comme le railway [la liberté] lui est indifférente. Elle ne le gêne pas, et il ignore encore qu'elle peut lui servir" ("La Lutte électorale en 1863," *Discours et opinions*, 1893, 1: 48).

62. On this point, see Corbin, pp. 1140ff. See also Christian, p. 165: "Power in isolated communities accrues to those who are the brokers with the outside world."

63. Armengaud, *Populations*, p. 351; AD, Hte.-Garonne 4M61 (Mar. 1848); Beslay, p. 46; AD, Vosges 8M25 (Sept.-Oct. 1878), Pyrs.-Ors. 3M1 163 (June, Aug. 1879); Massé, p. 39; AD, Cantal 40 M 11 (Aurillac, Nov. 1879, St.-Flour, Jan. 1880).

64. Beslay, p. 111.

65. AN, F¹ᶜIII Ardèche 11 (Jan. 1859), BB 30 371 (Angers, Oct. 1860); AD, Yonne III M¹230 (Tonnerre, Sens, July 1859), M¹233 (Feb.-June 1862).

66. AD, Pyrs.-Ors. 3M1 136 (Aug. 1891). But for evidence of rural indifference, see AN, F¹ᶜIII 1125 Allier (Jan. 1918), and F¹ᶜIII 1125 Privas, Ardèche (Jan. 1918). Most recently, in the Santongeais saying of 1940, a time when men were back from the army and sales were good: "War can go on; we've all we need" (Doussinet, *Paysan*, p. 444).

67. AN, BB 30 388 (Toulouse, July 1856), BB 30 370 (Aix, Mar. 1852), F¹ᶜIII Hte.-Garonne 9 (Apr. 1859). Hence perhaps one reason for the role of drink in elections, when alcohol consumption showed a meteoric rise. On this point, see Pilenco, pp. 217–22, who calculated, *inter alia*, that in the electoral district of Montreuil (Pas-de-Calais), dur-ing the two months preceding the elections of 1902, the 4,000-odd voters increased their *normal* intake by over 19,000 liters of pure alcohol—about 500 additional shots of *eau-de-vie* per voter.

68. AN, BB 30 390 (Chambéry, July 1870); AD, Lot 6M9 (Cazals, May 1848); Beslay, p. 47. See also AD, Yonne III M⁴13 (July 1849).

69. Beslay, p. 67.

70. Corbin, pp. 534–37, 951–52; AD, Vosges 8M44, 8M46.

71. AD, Pyrs.-Ors. (Associations); Donnedevie, p. 277; Sénéquier, pp. 104ff.

72. Bougeatre, p. 196; Vigier, 2: 185; Roubin, pp. 58, 90–91.

73. Beslay, pp. 98–99; Roubin, p. 135.

74. Lancelot, pp. xiii, 249; Masseport, p. 86.

75. Note in Lancelot, pp. 198–202, and in Dupeux (quoted in Lancelot, p. 200) various other factors in abstention: topography, weather, distance from parish center, distance from the road itself.

76. Dupeux, p. 389; Lancelot, pp. 188–89; Serge Bonnet, *Sociologie*, p. 256. See also *Journal Officiel* (Chambre), 1912, p. 2004, quoted by Pilenco, p. 292: "Il apparaît que l'arrondissement de Sartène, très arriéré, où les abstentions sont très nombreuses, ne possède pas dans son ensemble une éducation politique digne de citoyens capables de pratiquer le suffrage universel en toute liberté et en toute indépendance." But then Sartène is in Corsica!

77. Rougeron, *Conseil général*, p. 14; AD, Finistère 4M (Châteaulin, 1889); P. Barral, *Département de l'Isère*, pp. 521–22; Rougeron, *Département de l'Allier*, p. 12. As the mayor of La Fouillouse (Loire) had said in 1898: "On arrive toujours à tout savoir" (Pilenco, p. 265; see also his discussion of open voting, pp. 259–71).

78. AD, Vosges 8M23 (St.-Dié, Oct. 1869, Neufchâteau, Mar., Apr. 1873); Rougeron, *Département de l'Allier*, pp. 8–11; Bougeatre, p. 175; AD, Lot 6M13 (Figeac, Sept. 1878).

79. P. Barral, *Agrariens*, p. 40; AD, Cantal 40 M 11 (Mauriac, Oct. 1879; Aurillac, Nov. 1879), Gers M 2237 (Lectoure, Feb. 1876); Daniel Halévy, *La République des Ducs*, 1937, p. 370; Gambetta quoted in René Rémond, *La Vie politique en France*, 1969, 2: 346; Francus, *Valgorge*, p. vi.

80. AD, Pyrs.-Ors. 3M1 163 (Sept. 1889); L. Gachon in Fauvet and Mendras, p. 411.

81. AD, Gers M 2799 (Mirande, July 1888), Puy-de-Dôme (Esprit public, 1890's *passim*), Ariège 2M5 and 5M72^1. See also L. Gachon in Fauvet and Mendras, p. 429.

82. Assier, 3d ed., pp. 238–40.

83. Hamelle, pp. 635–45; *Le Semeur* (St.-Flour), June 29, 1907; AD, Cantal 40 M 11.

84. Garneret, p. 172: At Lantenne, near Besançon, "electoral fever rose to the greatest pitch round 1905, and when the soldiers of 1914–18 returned," just when local and national experience coincided. See also Corbin, pp. 1148–49.

Chapter Sixteen

My chapter title derives from Placide Rambaud and Monique Vincienne, *Les Transformations d'une société rurale: La Maurienne*, chapter 4: "L'Emigration, industrie des pays pauvres."

Epigraph. "Rondel de l'adieu."

1. Abel Poitrineau, *Revue d'histoire moderne*, 1962; Bonnamour, pp. 218–19.

2. Foville, *Enquête*, especially 1: xxxiii.

3. AD, Yonne VI M^{1}2 (juge de paix Coulanges-la-Vineuse, 1832); Chatelain, "Problèmes," p. 12.

4. Fel, p. 145.

5. Garneret, p. 118.

6. Clément, p. 481.

7. Abbé Margot-Duclot, "L'Emigration des Hauts-Alpins," *La Réforme sociale*, 1905, pp. 763–85 (p. 777).

8. Servat, pp. 131–32; Michel Chevalier, p. 737; Plessis, p. 146. See also A. de Lavergne, *Rapport présenté au nom de la commission chargée de visiter les exploitations rurales de l'Ariège* (Foix, 1875), p. 13.

9. Baudrillart, 3: 446; Gachon, *Limagnes du Sud*, pp. 413–15.

10. See J. Corcelle, *Les Emigrants du Bugey* (Belley, 1912); and the remarks of Lebeau,

pp. 311–12, who quotes a ditty of Jura migrants: "Early to rise and late to bed, / That's how one picks up *gros sous*, / *Ecus*, white [silver] coins, / To return home purse full and do up the house."

11. Corbin, pp. 236–37, 259, 264; AD, Creuse M 0472 (1857); Clément, pp. 489–90; Peygnaud, p. 214. In the 1850's the commune of Saint-Pardoux (Creuse), pop. about 1,400 (in 1962, 711), issued between 113 and 148 passports for the yearly departures; in most years they were granted to over 10% of the total population, which must have covered almost all able-bodied males.

12. Pierre Vinçard, *Les Ouvriers de Paris* (1850), p. 38.

13. Corbin, p. 1239; Hertz, p. 113; Ajalbert, *Mémoires*, pp. 13, 36.

14. Corbin, p. 284; AD, Creuse M 0471 (juge de paix Ahun, 1874); Maurice Halbwachs, *La Classe ouvrière et les niveaux de vie* (1913), p. 38. In general and expectably, Halbwachs' opening chapters on peasants are less realistic and more theoretical than the main body of the work, which focuses on the urban working class.

15. Drouillet, 2: 218–19; Ardouin-Dumazet, 1: 34; AG, MR 1278 (Morvan, 1842); Brochon, *Chanson française*, 2: 73; AD, Yonne III M¹226 (Avallon, Mar. 1853); Demolins et al., *Populations forestières*, pp. 8–13; Bonnamour, pp. 218–19.

16. Monot, *Industrie*, especially pp. 29, 32, 34; AD, Yonne III M¹231 (Avallon, Mar. 1860). Monot uses statistics for 1858–64 covering Montsauche and northeastern Nièvre: pop. 14,133, births 2,884, number of nursing mothers leaving for Paris, 1,897 (i.e., two-thirds).

17. Ardouin-Dumazet, 1: 30–42; Drouillet, 2: 63.

18. Nadaud, *Mémoires de Léonard* (1912 ed.), p. 47. See also *Enquête agricole*, Hte.-Vienne, p. 158, quoted in Corbin, p. 252; and Boscary, p. 179.

19. Paul Roux, p. 6; Foville, *Transformations*, pp. 395–406; Paul Deschanel, *J. O. Chambre*, July 10, 1897, p. 1937.

20. P. Barral, *Département de l'Isère*, p. 113; Le Guen, p. 466. Brittany's net outmigration rose from an annual average of 8,000 in 1831–51 to 116,000 in 1851–72; the figure stabilized at 126,000 in 1872–91, and then soared again, to average 206,000 in 1891–1911.

21. Guilcher, "Vue," p. 9; *Bulletin de la Solidarité Aveyronnaise*, Feb. 1910, p. 9, Feb. 1912, p. 48; Chataigneau, p. 437; E. Potet, *Annales de géographie*, 1912, pp. 265–68; Deffontaines, *Hommes et travaux*, pp. 116–19.

22. On much of this, see Camille Valaux, *La Réforme sociale*, 1909, p. 350, quoted in Gautier, *Emigration*, p. 14.

23. Clément, p. 485; *Bulletin de la Solidarité Aveyronnaise*, Feb. 1912, p. 48, Dec. 1913, p. 42; Guillaumin, *Paysans*, pp. 119–20; Deffontaines, *Hommes et travaux*, p. 409; Fortier-Beaulieu, p. 265. Bourdieu and Sayed, p. 94: "En Kabylie, l'émigration vers la France qui, jusqu'à une date récente, avait pour fonction première de donner à la communauté paysanne les moyens de se perpétuer, change de signification et devient elle-même sa propre fin.... Occasion de rompre avec l'agriculture et la communauté,... occasion de s'émanciper de l'autorité familiale."

24. The couplet is from Ogès and Déguignet, p. 115: "A baone eo beuzet Ker-Is, Ne neuz ker ebet evel Paris." The rest of the paragraph is based on Bozon, *Vie*, p. 454; Marouzeau, especially p. 19 on Masrouzaud (Creuse); Serge Bonnet, *Sociologie*, p. 46; EA, Meuse, 1937; Adolphe Meyer, *Promenade sur le chemin de fer de Marseille à Toulon* (1859), p. 13; and *Des causes et des effets du dépeuplement des campagnes par M. M...* (1866), pp. 4–5, 7.

25. Méline, p. 110; Pécaut, *Quinze ans*, pp. 70–74.

26. Jules Vallès in *L'Evènement*, 1866, quoted in Rouchon, 2: 132 (peasants' sons "ont moins peur d'être soldats, parce que les casernes sont dans les villes"); Sion, p. 457; Norre, especially p. 97.

27. Georges Davy in Friedmann, p. 37; Belbèze, pp. 51, 69, 141 ("depuis des siècles, le paysan méprise sa condition"); Duneton, p. 195; Compère-Morel in *Compte-rendu du Congrès SFIO de 1909*, quoted in Gratton, *Paysan*, p. 71; Combe, p. 177. The list of factors is based on the chapter headings in Deghilage, *Dépopulation*.

28. Goreux, pp. 330–31; AD, Yonne III M¹231 (Tonnerre, May 1860); Daniel Zolla, "La Condition du travailleur rural," *Revue des français*, 1912, pp. 163–69; Foville, *France*, 2: 227.

29. Both quotes are from Chatelain, "Migrants," p. 15.

30. *L'Aubrac*, 4: 215. The rest of this paragraph is drawn primarily from AN, BB 30 378 (Dec. 1849, May 1850); Corbin, p. 1133; René Chatreix, *Monographie de la commune de Saint-Maurice-la-Souterraine* (Guéret, 1938), pp. 110–11; *Mémoires de la Société des Sciences . . . de la Creuse*, 1938–40, p. 172 (most people ate from the same bowl, but emigrants' homes were the first to adopt plates); Boscary, pp. 186–87; and Ajalbert, *En Auvergne*, p. 32. See also AD, Yonne III M¹231 (Avallon, Jan. 1860): "Poursuites contre Margue, maire de Provency, ancien valet de chambre à Paris, qui est venu importer dans l'Avallonais des vices jusque là inconnus dans ce pays." Similarly, Henri Bachelin, *Les Sports aux champs* (Nevers, 1911), pp. 38–39, tells the story of an "ancien valet de chambre qui est revenu manger au village ses économies amassées sou par sou," who is the first to tell his compatriots about the velocipede, and in due course to bring one to the village.

31. Deghilage, *Dépopulation*, p. 69.

32. AD, Puy-de-Dôme, *Rapports d'inspection générale, 1881*; AD, Cantal IT 993 (insp. primaire Murat, Mar. 1909); Longy, *Port-Dieu*, p. 75; AN, F¹⁷ 9277 (Hte.-Vienne, 1872).

33. Le Saux, p. 22.

34. Chatelain, "Migrants," p. 7, exaggerates the "swift proletarization" of workers from these areas (compare Corbin's prudent conclusions, p. 1076 and *passim*). But migrants clearly were (as the authorities complained) carriers of urban ideas and freedoms, more so in some areas than others, depending on the nature of their milieu (e.g., having less impact in the conservatively religious Auvergne than in the Limousin).

35. AD, Creuse M 038 (juge de paix Chambon to préf., June 1857); Corbin, p. 1266; AN, F¹ᵇ II Corrèze 7 (préf., Feb. 1874), about the little town of Bort; Chatelain, "Migrants," p. 15, quoting *Moniteur du Puy-de-Dôme*, Jan. 13, 1871; Chanoine Trilouillier, *Rapport sur l'émigration cantalienne* (Congrès diocésain d'Aurillac, 1908), pp. 1–39; Ardouin-Dumazet, 28: 193.

36. Hugonnier, pp. 60–61; Germouty, p. 450.

37. Cholvy, pp. 42–44; Goreux, p. 331; Pinchemel, *Géographie*, 1: 181.

38. See in Lancelot, p. 45, a map of those who were absent from their places of residence when the 1891 census was taken, showing 25% or more absentees in the Massif Central, Côtes-du-Nord, Ariège, and parts of the southeast against a national average of about 17%.

39. AD, Creuse M 0472 (1857); Corbin, pp. 286–88; Agulhon, *République*, p. 172.

Chapter Seventeen

Epigraph. Contrasting themes in Robert Jalby, *Le Folklore de Languedoc*.

1. The material in this paragraph is drawn from Schnapper, pp. 70, 137; and Peygnaud, p. 137.

2. Burguière, p. 90; AN, BB 30 371 (Angers, Jan. 1866); Hérault, p. 227.

3. AD, Vosges 8M23 (Feb. 1872), Puy-de-Dôme M 04476 (Feb. 1890). To be precise, substitution (except between relatives, to the 4th degree) had been abolished by a law of 1855. But it had effectively been replaced by the possibility of purchasing "exoneration" from military service for a fee of 2,500 francs paid directly to the army authorities.

4. Belbèze, p. 62.

5. AN, BB 30 370 (Agen, July 1854, Jan. 1855, July 1859), BB 30 371 (Angers, Jan. 1866, July 1867), BB 30 390 (Rennes and Montpellier, 1867), BB 30 370 (Aix, Apr. 1867 and *passim*).

6. AN, BB 30 375 (Mar. 1868), quoted in Lovie, p. 449; AN, BB 30 373 (Besançon, Jan. 1866, Apr. 1868).

7. Cobb, *Police*, p. 99; AG, MR 1218 (Hérault); AD, Cantal IT 832 (June 1832); AG, MR 1269 (1839), MR 1228 (1840); AD, Ariège 5M3 (St.-Girons, 1856, 1857); AG, MR 2283 (1859, 1860), MR 2275 (1860, Eure-et-Loir, Ille-et-Vilaine; 1877, Seine-Inf.); Hérault, p. 227.

8. AG, MR 1274 (Lozère, 1844; see another report from Mende in 1845 to the effect that these people looked on desertion as a glory); Pons, *Cerca*, 1960, p. 326; Lovie, p. 268. In Poitou, where in times of want people ate *garobe*, a bread made of black vetch grown for the pigeons' winter feed, some families in the early nineteenth century deliberately fed their sons on it so that they would grow up stunted and unfit for service (*Tradition*, p. 81).

9. Pérot, p. 44.

10. AG, MR 2261 (Basque country, 1873; Landes, 1874), MR 2267 (Ille-et-Vilaine, 1876), MR 2270 (Gers, 1876; Hte.-Garonne, 1876, 1877), MR 2275 (Sarthe, 1878); AD, Pyrs.-Ors. 3M1 163 (Sept. 1879); Pérot, pp. 10, 44; Sébillot, *Coutumes*, pp. 82–83. Interestingly, national conscription made for the nationalization of the magic practices designed to secure a good number. Thivot, p. 328, comments that "all these means, once particular to a given province, had gradually spread throughout the country, brought in most often in our department [Htes.-Alpes] by peddlers."

11. See the copious file in AD, Vosges 23 Z 13 (July 1913). Perhaps anti-militaristic propaganda drew less on the new internationalism than on the old distastes. See, for instance, Gaston Couté's song "Les Conscrits," in Brochon, *Chanson sociale*, pp. 97–100, which reflects the clear difference between the old, native anti-militarism and the new fin-de-siècle brand, which was, if anything, elitist and anti-populist.

12. Cénac-Moncaut, *Jérôme La Friche*, pp. 25–26; Garneret, p. 329; Père Toine in *Cahiers des amis de Jacquou*, 1939, p. 9.

13. AG, MR 1218 (Hérault, 1825), MR 1228 (Landes, 1843), MR 2277 (Rhône, 1859), MR 2281 (Allier, 1860), MR 2283 (Côtes-du-Nord, 1860), MR 2283 (Deux-Sèvres, 1862).

14. See AG, G^{8}2, throughout the Second Empire.

15. Hamerton, *Round My House*, pp. 91–99.

16. Durkheim, p. 259, for example, points out that the rate of military suicide, whose high incidence had attracted attention, declined from 630 per million in 1862 to 280 per million in 1890. Military mentality, like military society, was becoming part of the national way of life. On the changed relations between the common people and their new Republican army, see Michelle Perrot, 2: 633, 696–98.

17. Henry Leyret, *En plein faubourg: Moeurs ouvrières* (1895), pp. 87, 88; Esnault, *Imagination*, 101; Duchatellier, *Condition*, p. 6; Captain Fanet, *Les Fêtes régimentaires* (1895).

18. F. Brunot, 10: 965; Esnault, *Imagination*, p. 101; H. Serrant, *Le Service du recrutement de 1789 à nos jours* (1935), p. 80. Reynier, *Privas*, p. 183: "Les Ardéchois qui faisaient leur service militaire à Privas . . . n'apportaient ou n'apprenaient pas grande chose de neuf. Un rôle bien plus efficace a été joué par la guerre de 1914–18, qui les a sortis et envoyés dans le nord et le nord-est."

19. On events in the Midi, see especially Le Blond, pp. 73, 88, 132.

20. AN, F^{17}9262, *Rapport sur les trois départements bretons*, Oct. 1880.

21. Voisin, p. 19; Ajalbert, *En Auvergne*, pp. 168–69; F. Brunot, 10: 983.

22. AG, MR 1282 (Puy-de-Dôme, 1827), MR 1300 (Hte.-Vienne, 1845); N. Sales in

Comparative Studies, 1968, p. 268. See Stendhal, 2: 479: "Those from poor areas change completely in six weeks. [They are simply amazed] at getting meat every day."

23. M. V. Parron, *Notice sur l'aptitude militaire en France suivie d'un essai de statistique militaire de la Haute-Loire* (Le Puy, 1868), p. 16. See also Taine, pp. 130, 191.

24. AG, G⁸177 (Blois, May 1871), G⁸179 (Le Mans, June 1872); Besson, p. 85.

25. Hubert Lyautey, "Du rôle social de l'officier dans le service universel," *RDM*, April 15, 1891; General Brécart, "Le Rôle social de l'officier," *Revue des jeunes*, July 1938; Eugène-Melchoir de Vogüé, *Remarques sur l'Exposition du Centenaire* (1889), (containing some of the ideas that inspired Lyautey); and Henri Rollet, *L'Action sociale des catholiques en France, 1871–1901* (1947), pp. 26, 328–29.

26. Gautier, *Siècle d'indigence*, pp. 144–46. Another change in life-style at the local level was commented on by an observer from the western fenlands. In a book describing the peculiar local practice among the rural young of couples' engaging in heavy public petting, Marcel Baudoin surmised that if this practice was beginning to decline, it was because the young men, "instruits par le service militaire, éprouvent désormais une sorte de fausse honte à se conduire comme leurs ancêtres" (*Le Maraichinage: Coutume du pays de Mont (Vendée)*, 1906, p. 117).

27. Guillaumin, *Panorama*, p. 21; General Lamoricière in *Moniteur universel*, Oct. 21, 1848, quoted by N. Sales, in *Comparative Studies*, 1968, p. 282; AN, BB 30 388 (Jan. 8, 1867); Ardouin-Dumazet, *Les Petites Industries rurales* (1912), pp. 16–17.

28. *La Réforme sociale*, 1909, p. 147; HE, instituteur of Soye (Doubs), 1899.

Chapter Eighteen

Epigraph. "La Victoire sociale" (1909).

1. AD, Yonne 3 T 1 (1810).

2. AD, Yonne 10 T 1 (Noyers, Aug. 1803).

3. AEP, 4 (Mar. 12, 1828); AD, Cantal IT 252 (1833, 1850, 1913), Eure-et-Loir, *Rapports d'inspection primaire*, 1837, IIT b 1; Giret, pp. 29, 34, 35, 38.

4. From Ernest Lavisse's speech at the opening of a new school at Nouvion, published in *Revue pédagogique*, July 15, 1891, pp. 1–9. See the same journal, Apr. 15, 1892, p. 327, for evidence that this was still the case in the late 1880's in the mountains of the southeast, around Puget-Théniers, where some schools had neither seats nor a stove.

5. AN, F¹⁷10757 (Commentry, Allier, 1861).

6. Balzac, *Les Paysans* (1844), chap. 3; Boudard; Singer, p. 18; Giret, p. 37.

7. Arnaud, p. 14.

8. AD, Yonne III M²²26 (Oct. 1853); Pierrard, p. 133, citing the letter of the rector of Lille to the prefect, Apr. 1829 (AD, Nord T 68/5); Ogès, *Instruction*, p. 81; Arnaud, pp. 15–20; primary inspector reports of 1836 and 1837 from the Dreux and Chartres areas, cited in Giret, pp. 42, 44; Cressot, p. 127.

9. Besson, p. 39; Jean-Louis Blanchon, *Palau de Cerdanya* (Palau, 1971), p. 37; Labrousse.

10. *Instruction primaire*, 1: 85; Tanneau, pp. 222–23; Gilland, p. 113; Borsendorff, p. 35. See also the school inspectors' reports of the 1870's cited by Zind, pp. 134–35.

11. *Instruction primaire*, 1: 97; AN, F¹⁷9253 (Privas, May 1877); Gazier, p. 119.

12. *Instruction primaire*, 1: 99, 127, 237, 247, 258, 366; priest quoted in *Annales de démographie historique*, 1971, p. 418.

13. Villemereux, *Rapport sur la situation de l'instruction primaire dans le département du Loiret* (Orleans, 1856), p. 23; AN, F¹⁷9265 (Hte.-Loire, July 1882).

14. AN, F¹⁷9265 (Hte.-Loire, Oct. 1881), F¹⁷9269 (Morbihan, Dec. 1880); Ardouin-Dumazet, 34: 125. See also Boudard; and Giret, p. 50. If one is to believe Robert Sabatier (p. 245), some béates were still alive and revered in Haute-Loire in the 1930's.

15. As a school inspector reported in 1871, "On n'est pas encore convaincu dans le Finistère de la nécessité de l'éducation des filles" (quoted in Burguière, p. 288).

16. Buisson, 1.2: 1317 (and *Rapports d'inspection générale*, 1881). Corrèze, declared the school inspection reports around 1860, was only "médiocrement civilisée."

17. See Ministère de l'Instruction publique, *Rapport à S. M. l'Empereur sur l'état de l'enseignement primaire pendant l'année 1863* (1865), especially pp. 89–92 (Victor Duruy's report); Ministère de l'Instruction publique, *Statistique de l'enseignement primaire, 1867–77* (1878); AN, F¹⁷9262 (Oct. 1880); and Augé-Laribé, *Politique*, p. 123.

18. Charles Portal, "L'Instruction primaire dans le Tarn au 19e siècle," *Revue du département du Tarn*, 1906, pp. 1–23.

19. Marion, 6: 21–25, 225; Mayeur, *Débuts*, p. 61.

20. See Buisson, 2: 1317, article "Illettrés." See also Ministère de l'instruction publique, *Résumés des états de situation de l'enseignement primaire, 1889–90* (1892), table 19bis; *Résumés, 1894–95* (1896), table 22 for percentage of brides able to sign their marriage certificate; *Résumés, 1888–89* (1890), tables 20bis and 21bis for married couples able to sign in 1886; *Résumés, 1885–86* (1887), table 22 for conscript literacy in 1885; and *Résumés, 1889–90* (1892), and *1894–95* (1896), tables 18bis and 20 for conscript literacy in 1889 and 1894, respectively. North of the line lay 32 departments with 13 million inhabitants and 740,846 schoolchildren (roughly 57,000 per million inhabitants). South of it were 54 departments with 18 million inhabitants and 375,931 schoolchildren (under 21,000 per million). See Charles Dupin, *Effects de l'enseignement populaire* (1826).

21. Pujos (Trespoux-Rassiels, 1881); AD, Finistère 4M (Châteaulin, Jan. 1901). See also Corbin, 3: 438.

22. AEP, 1 (insp. primaire, Bar-sur-Seine, Jan. 1873); Pécaut, *Etudes*, p. 23.

23. Giret, p. 69; AD, Vosges 11 T 17 (1889); Kanter, p. 116 (Hte.-Loire); Merley, pp. 246–47 (local official); *Instruction primaire*, 1: 475 (Allier); AN, F¹⁷10757 (Plassay, Charente-Inf.); Besson, pp. 9, 11 (Cantal); Darnaud, p. 19 (Ariège); Rocal, p. 310 (illiterate conscripts).

24. Compare these official statistics with AN, F¹⁷9271 (Basses-Pyr., 1877). See also *Instruction primaire*, especially on Ardèche, Rhône, Ain, Loire, Hérault, Aude, and Gard.

25. Pariset, *Lauragais*, p. 39.

26. Bonaventure Berger et al., *Manuel d'examen pour le volontariat d'un an* (1875), p. 46; Buisson, 2: 1499. Compare Léaud and Glay, p. 153, quoting Octave Gréard, vice-rector of the Academy of Paris in 1882: "to teach French . . . is to strengthen national unity."

27. AN, F¹⁷9271 (Basses-Pyr., 1877), F¹⁷10757 (Châteauneuf-du-Rhône, Drôme, 1861), *Instruction primaire* (Vaucluse); AN, F¹⁷9259 (Dordogne, 1875), F¹⁷9271 (Basses-Pyr., 1874); G. Bruno, *Tour de France*, pp. 164–65.

28. AN, F¹⁷9262 (Hérault, 1875); Francus, *Vivarais*, p. 309; AN, F¹⁷9276 (Tarn-et-Garonne, 1873).

29. AG, MR 2154 (Hte.-Garonne, 1861); AN, F¹⁷9264 (Landes, 1875).

30. *Instruction primaire* (Loire).

31. AN, F¹⁷9276 (Tarn-et-Garonne, 1873, 1877), F¹⁷9271 (Puy-de-Dôme, 1877), F¹⁷9276 (Vaucluse, 1883); Longy, *Canton*, p. 47.

32. AN, F¹⁷9271 (Basses-Pyr., 1876); *Rapports d'inspection générale*, 1881 (Basses-Pyr.); Blanchon, *En Cerdagne*, p. 26; Beulaygue, pp. 4–5.

33. AN, F¹⁷9259 (insp. Côtes-du-Nord, arr. Guingamp, Sept. 1877), F¹⁷9262 (Oct. 1880); *Langue bretonne*, pp. 3, 5.

34. *Langue bretonne*, pp. 3, 5. On the *symbole*, see Blanchon, *En Cerdagne*, pp. 49, 58, 61, 62; Besson, p. 25; Coornaert, p. 304; Perrin and Bouet, pp. 122–23; Singer, p. 185; Lafont, p. 212, quoting Frédéric Mistral, *L'Aioli* (1894); Robert Sabatier, p. 243; and Duneton, p. 21 ("C'est arrivé à ma propre mère plusieurs fois entre 1908 et 1912").

35. AN, F^{17}9262 (see also F^{17}9259 for a very moving collection of letters about adult evening classes in Côtes-du-Nord); *Langue bretonne*, p. 6.

36. On the great backwardness of girls' schooling and its effect on local speech, see AN, F^{17}9265, F^{17}9262 (Hte.-Loire, Hérault, Brittany); and Giret, p. 26, quoting 1868 survey, manuscript no. 21 in Bibliothèque Municipale, Chartres. This was reflected in the availability of normal schools for men and women teachers. In 1869 there were 76 for men, and only 11 for women. By 1887 the gap had almost closed, with 90 schools for men, and 81 for women (Levasseur, 2: 495).

37. Buisson, 1: 105–6; Reynier and Abrial, pp. 8–9, 34.

38. AD, Cantal IT 848 (258), director's letters June 8, Oct. 25, 1836, Dec. 16, 1837; end-of-year reports, July 1875, May 19, 1877; AN, F^{17}9261 (Gard), Ecole Normale Primaire de Nîmes, 1872, F^{17}9267 (Lozère), Ecole Normale Primaire de Mende, 1872, 1881. In 1864, according to the rector, most *normaliens* of Bas-Rhin were "peasants foreign to our speech" (Dollinger, p. 428).

39. AN, F^{17}9271 (Basses-Pyrs., 1874, 1875), F^{17}9259 (Dordogne, 1875), F^{17}9264, Ecole Primaire de Dax (Landes), 1876, F^{17}9276, Ecole Normale Primaire d'Avignon (Vaucluse), 1876, F^{17}9271, Ecole Normale Primaire de Perpignan, 1878, Puy-de-Dôme, 1877; *Rapports d'inspection générale*, 1881 (Lot-et-Garonne; Basses-Pyrs.; Aveyron).

40. Rouchon, 2: 36; *Instruction primaire, passim*; *Rapports d'inspection générale*, 1881 (Gers; Ariège; Htes.-Pyrs.); AN, F^{17}9262 (Hérault, 1864), F^{17}9275 (Deux-Sèvres, 1882).

41. H. Denain, *Discours de distribution des prix dans une commune rurale* (Chartres, 1862), p. 6; Félix Pécaut, *Le Temps*, Aug. 4, 1872; Pécaut, *Etudes*, p. 55. On teachers' condition, see AN, F^{17}9271 (Puy-de-Dôme, 1877); Marcel Lachiver, *Documents d'histoire régionale* (1971), p. 35; Labourasse, p. 14; and Florent, p. 219. See also Clément Brun, p. 61 (peasants' appreciation of teacher's skills); and HE II, Lozère, 1888: Recoules, near Marvejols (teachers' devotion to Republic).

42. AN, F^{17}9253 (Htes.-Alpes, 1882), F^{17}9275 (Deux-Sèvres, 1882).

43. On teachers' pay, see Antoine Prost, pp. 143–44, 372, 380ff; Clément Brun, p. 57; Mignot, p. 45; Besson, p. 34; and Singer, p. 94. Serge Bonnet tells us that in Meurthe-et-Moselle at the turn of the century, teachers looked with some envy on the pay of other workers. In the village of Jouaville the teacher earned 1,200 francs a year, to which he added 100 francs for his *brévet complémentaire* and a further 125 francs for acting as secretary to the municipal council: a little under 4 francs a day. An unskilled factory worker made 3–4 francs a day, and in the bigger bourg of Joeuf 4–5 francs. A railroad worker earned 2.5 francs a day. A day laborer on a farm could expect 1.5 francs and his food. ("La vie ouvrière vue par les instituteurs en Meurthe-et-Moselle [1890–1900]," *Mouvement social*, 1965, p. 85.)

44. AD, Puy-de-Dôme F62, "Monographie de l'école normale," 1900 (manuscript).

45. AD, Yonne VII M^{1}2 (Apr. 1836); AN, F^{1c}III Ardèche 11 (Apr. 1860); AD, Ariège 5M3 (congratulatory addresses on the occasion of Napoleon III's marriage, Feb. 1853; sous-préf. St.-Girons, Apr. 1856); préf. Bas-Rhin, quoted in Dollinger, p. 427; AD, Pyrs.-Ors. 3M1 224 (comm. Bourg-Madame, Jan. 14, Jan. 30, 1896).

46. AD, Yonne III M^{1}234 (Joigny, Oct. 1865).

47. AD, Pyrs.-Ors. 3M1 224 (Bourg-Madame, Jan. 14, 1896), Pyrs.-Ors. 3M1 225 (Perthus, July 1897); Guichonnet, p. 48; Esnault, *Imagination*, p. 229. Other nicknames given to the teachers were "head-stuffer," *empeille-cabi* (Louis Bollé, *Histoire et folklore du Haut-Bugey*, Bellegarde, 1954, p. 106); and *rabat-joie* and *tape-la-gueille* (Doussinet, *Les Travaux*, p. 340).

48. AN, F^{17}10757 (1861); Pécaut, *Quinze ans*, p. 199; HE 12.922 (inst. Vestric, Gard, 1878); Bastié, 2: 153; *Instruction primaire* (Académie d'Aix).

49. Malègue, *Guide l'étranger*, p. 163; AD, Cantal IT 993 (Velzic, about 1900).

50. Armengaud, *Populations*, pp. 328–29; AN, F^{17}9277 (St.-Yrieix, Hte.-Vienne, 1872);

Ogès, *Instruction*, pp. 22–23; Chabirand, pp. 197–98; *Instruction primaire*, 1: 361, 418; AN, F^{17}9276 (Vendée, 1881), F^{17}9259 (Côtes-du-Nord, 1877).

51. For details on dispersed settlements, see Foville, *Enquête*, 2: 235; and AN, F^{17}9276 (Vendée, 1872, 1876, 1881), F^{17}9276 (Brittany, 1880). See also Derruau-Borniol, p. 48, on Creuse, whose 266 communes were divided into 6,000 hamlets. At Plozévet (Fin.) school attendance began to flourish only after the bourg had grown into an active center for its commune, its more numerous inhabitants providing the school with a larger and more regular clientele. Before 1875 school enrollment had varied between 85 and 139. In November 1891 we find 200 children enrolled and 164 actually attending. By February 1893, 194 were attending out of 252 enrolled. (See Burguière, pp. 276–77.)

52. Buisson, 1.2: 1650; AN, F^{17}9263 (Indre, 1880); Lefournier, pp. 889–90; Corbin, 3: 438; Giret, p. 65; AN, F^{17}9262 (Brittany, 1880).

53. AD, Cantal 970 (325) (Pléaux, Feb. 1839); AG, MR 1228 (Basses-Pyrs., 1844); Garneret, p. 327.

54. AN, F^{17}10757 (Aveyron, 1861); Pariset, *Lauragais*, p. 39; AD, Gers M 2799 (gendarmes Seissane, Feb. 1875); HE II (Billy, 1899); Pujos (Ste.-Alauzie, 1881); *L'Egalité*, Mar. 26, 1882, quoted in Mona Ozouf, *L'Ecole, l'église et la république* (1963), p. 89.

55. AG, MR 1198 (Auxonne, 1834; Pontarlier, 1835); *Instruction primaire*, 1: 119; AN, F^{17}9267 (Lozère, 1877); Léon Dériès, *Rapport sur la situation de l'instruction primaire dans la Manche* (St.-Lô, 1892); Corbin, 2: 108–9; AD, Cantal IT 993 (St.-Flour, Feb. 1900?; Mauriac, Feb. 1900), IT 951 (insp. d'académie, 1902?). See also Giret, p. 57.

56. AG, MR 1198 (Doubs, 1835); J.-L. Roche, 2: 15; *Instruction primaire*, 1: 361; AN, BB 30 374 (Bourges, Jan. 1866).

57. AN, F^{17}9276 (1876), F^{17}9264 (1878).

58. Ardouin-Dumazet, 28: 196.

59. Van Gennep, *Manuel*, 1: 191; Bois, "Dans l'Ouest," p. 361.

60. Antoine Prost, pp. 94–95.

61. Giret, p. 37; AN, F^{17}9277 (Hérault, Lozère, 1872).

62. AEP, 2; Tanneau, pp. 216–18; Ogès, *Instruction*, pp. 22–23.

63. AD, Cantal IT 322.

64. AN, F^{17}9265 (Loire-Inf., Dec. 1875); Bougeatre, p. 172; Tanneau, pp. 216–18.

65. M. E. Decoux-Lagoutte, *Notes historiques sur la commune de Trélissac* (Périgueux, 1900), p. 91; Georges Wurmser, *La République de Clemenceau* (1961), p. 64; J.-L. Roche, 2: 11; AN, F^{17}9265 (Loire-Inf., Dec. 1875), F^{17}10757 (Garrevagues, Tarn; Rienbach, Ariège); Darnaud, p. 29; *Instruction primaire*, 1: 190.

66. *Instruction primaire*, 1: 190 and *passim*.

67. AN, F^{17}9265 (Loire-Inf., Dec. 1875), F^{17}9276 (Vaucluse, 1883).

68. Ariès in François, p. 926; Lovie, p. 342; Cavoleau, p. 864.

69. Thabault, *Mon village*, p. 85; Corbin, p. 458.

70. Buisson, 1: 730; AN, F^{17}10757 (Rienbach, Ariège, 1861); Singer, p. 174.

71. Ogès, *Instruction*, p. 42.

72. Drouillet, 2: 183; MATP, manuscript 43.308 (1875), accounts from Ménez-Braz, near Concarneau; manuscript 43.309 (1878), accounts from Kerguido farm near Concarneau.

73. Buisson, 1: 615–16; Corbin, p. 438.

74. AN, F^{17}9263 (Isère, 1876). See also F^{17}9259 (Dordogne, 1875).

75. Thabault, *Mon village*, p. 140; Lavisse, *Première année d'instruction civique*, p. 8. See also Lavisse, *Année préparatoire*, pp. 116–19, stressing the regularity and security of such jobs. On this theme, see Servat, p. 135; AN, BB 30 373 (Besançon, Apr. 1866); the remarks of the survey of 1866, quoted in Lovie, pp. 289–90; *L'Aigle du Tarn*, Sept. 22, 1867, quoted in Armengaud, *Populations*, p. 297. On Soye and Seine, see HE (no number), Soye, 1899; and Méline, p. 199.

76. Pujos (Montat, Valroufié, Cézac, Pern); Buisson, 1.2: 1492; AN, F¹⁷9271 (Puy-de-Dôme, 1877); Pécaut, *Rapports*, p. 26; *Rapports d'inspection générale* (Dordogne). For an earlier period, compare Laurence Stone, "The Educational Revolution in England, 1560–1640," *Past and Present*, July 1964, p. 68; and Thabault, *Mon village*, p. 140.

77. D'Estienne de Saint-Jean, "Paysan métayer de la Basse-Provence," *Ouvriers des deux mondes* (1888), p. 189, and Foville, *Enquête*, 1: 231 (on Provençal peasants in 1862 and 1894); Passama, p. 122; teacher of Théméricourt (Seine-et-Oise), *Monographie de Théméricourt, 1899*, quoted in Marcel Lachiver, *Histoire de Meulan et de sa région* (Meulan, 1965), p. 331 (and p. 332 for Vigny, nearby); AD, Puy-de-Dôme M 04476 (Mont-Dore, June 1890).

78. B. B. Singer, "The Teacher as Notable in Brittany," unpub. manuscript, p. 13; Besson, p. 27.

79. Moureu, p. 18. See also Besson, p. 33.

80. *Devoirs*, pp. 185–86.

81. Alfred Giron, p. 6; *Instruction primaire*, 1: 537; AN, BB 30 370 (Aix, Jan., Feb. 1850); Ogès, *Instruction*, p. 143; AD, Hte.-Vienne 1Z 105 (Magnac-Laval, 1865); Pécaut, *Education*, p. 3; Coissac, p. 184; Guilcher, *Tradition*, p. 16; Boillot, *Français*, p. 93; Perrin and Bouet, p. 218; Blanchon, *En Cerdagne*, p. 27.

82. *Devoirs*, pp. 15, 25, 119; G. Bruno, *Francinet*, pp. 153–54; Ardouin-Dumazet, 34: 93. This last is a common note. See AD, Gers M 2278 (Aug. 6, 1889), for an official's awards speech: "Without the schools the people would regress to barbarism."

83. François Guizot, *Mémoires pour servir à l'histoire de mon temps* (1971 ed.), p. 200. The law of June 28, 1833, may be found in Octave Gréard, *La Legislation de l'instruction primaire depuis 1789 jusqu'à nos jours* (1874), vol. 1.

84. Anon., *Des besoins de l'instruction primaire dans une commune rurale* (1861), p. 5; AN, F¹⁷9376 (Tarn-et-Garonne, 1868–69); Lavisse, *Première année d'instruction civique*, pp. 46–47.

85. G. Bruno, *Francinet*, pp. 138–40; *Devoirs*, p. 193; Lavisse, *Petites histoires*, pp. 69–72; AD, Vosges 11 T 17 (Chermisey, 1889).

86. Deghilage, *Education*, pp. 36–38; G. Bruno, *Francinet*, pp. 60, 78–79; Lavisse, *Petites histoires*, p. 100. See also Jules Steeg, *Les Bienfaits du travail* (1893), p. 1; and Conférence faite à Ay, le 28 novembre, 1891, par A. E. André, Inspecteur de l'enseignement primaire à Reims, "L'Education morale et civique à l'école" (1892), especially p. 3.

87. Lavisse, *Petites histoires*, pp. 40, 65–68. Note that Lavisse himself was the worthy offspring of the owners of a shop called "Au petit bénéfice." All schools propagandized students on the virtues of savings. See *Devoirs*, p. 137 and *passim*: form letters and exercises spelling out the advantages of savings.

88. See Deutsch, p. 152; and Pécaut, *Etudes*, p. 149.

89. AN, F¹⁷10757 (Aumessas, 1861); Lavisse, "Enseignement," pp. 208–10; Pécaut, *Education*, pp. 22–23.

90. Lavisse, *Première année de l'instruction civique*, p. 108; *Devoirs*, pp. 128–30, 150. There could also be unexpected reactions. Asked about the duties of those who govern, one child answered that they "must carry out their functions wisely and not crush the people with taxes." The teacher intervened to explain that taxes were necessary and had to be paid for the country's honor and welfare.

91. See A. Armbruster, *Instruction civique* (1882), a sort of secular catechism for 7- to 9-year-olds, pp. 8, 10; AD, Gers M 2278, awards speech to the *écoles communales* of Masseube, Aug. 6, 1889; and Blanchon, *En Cerdagne*, pp. 25–26.

92. AN, F¹⁷9376 (Puy-de-Dôme, 1869), F¹⁷9264 (Loire, 1878); Pécaut, *Etudes*, pp. 278–80; Berger et al., *Manuel* (cited in note 26, above), p. 20; AN, F¹⁷9276 (Vendée, 1879); *Rapports d'inspection générale*, 1881, Hte.-Saône.

93. Lavisse, *Première année d'histoire de France*. See also Lavisse, "Enseignement."

94. *Instruction primaire*, 1: 125, 221, 247; *Rapports d'inspection générale*, 1881, Cher.

95. AN F¹⁷9276 (Tarn-et-Garonne, 1873, 1881), F¹⁷9252 (Allier, 1878?, 1880), F¹⁷9262 (Ille-et-Vilaine, 1880).

96. Deghilage, *Education*.

97. Buisson quoted in Ozouf and Ozouf, p. 7; Besson, pp. 31, 32.

98. See G. Bruno, *Tour de France*, pp. 162, 177, 193–94, 236–39, 247, 305, 308; and Dupuy, pp. 132, 136–45.

99. For an accepted but questionable view, see Isambert-Jamati, p. 122; and Alphonse Dupront in François, p. 1433. For a counterargument, see Dupuy, p. 147. On Lavisse, see his *Première année d'histoire de France*, p. 216.

100. Lavisse, *Petites histoires*, p. 89. Compare Ronald R. Dore, *Education in Tokugawa Japan* (Berkeley, Calif., 1965), p. 292: "What does widespread literacy do for a developing country? The man who has in childhood submitted to some process of disciplined and conscious learning is more likely to respond to further training."

101. Gustave Hervé quoted in O. Harmel, *La Bataille scolaire* (n.d.), pp. 18–19; Pécaut, *Education*, p. 21; Ozouf and Ozouf, p. 31.

102. Ariès in François, p. 951; C. Bally, p. 220; Thabault, *L'Enfant*, introduction.

103. AN, F¹⁷9259 (Côtes-du-Nord, 1880), F¹⁷9275 (Deux-Sèvres, 1881, canton Mazières); Pujos (Cremps); Beulaygue, pp. 5, 6; Ardouin-Dumazet, 14: 340; Isambert-Jamati, p. 166; F. Gourvil, *Quelques opinions sur les langues locales dans l'enseignement* (Morlaix, n.d.), especially pp. 11–16.

104. Léon Dériès, *Après quinze ans, 1882–1897* (Saint-Lô, 1897), p. 21.

105. See *Devoirs*, pp. 24–25, 48, for the growing familiarity with references and identities that could henceforth be used by press, politicians, and the like; and Duneton, p. 196, who remarks of migrants that they wanted to live among the people and in the landscape that had been held in their mind's eye since their schooldays.

106. V. Dupont, pp. 129–36; HE II (Ribennes, Lozère, 1888); Rougeron, *Département de l'Allier*, pp. 126–27; *Langue bretonne*, p. 7.

Chapter Nineteen

Epigraph. Father to son, in *Diable aux champs* (1855), 1865 ed., pp. 15–17.

1. Latreille and Rémond, 3: 423, 425, 427. School-attendance figures, pp. 436–37, provide another index of the preeminence of the Church. The first detailed elementary school statistics, for 1876–77, show 71,547 schools with 4,716,935 students, divided as follows: lay schools, 51,657, with 2,648, 562 students; church schools, 19,890, with 2,068,373 students. The great majority of the church schools were girls schools, most of the church schools for boys being situated in towns. But note that at that time 69,000 of all French schools were Catholic, completely dominated by religious authority.

2. See Esnault, *Imagination*, pp. 293–94.

3. *Barbizier*, 1950, pp. 388–91; Juge, p. 130.

4. Gorse, p. 43; J. Sabbatier, p. 213; Péguy, "Pierre," p. 1220.

5. Romieu, p. 271; Le Saux, p. 85; Bois, *Paysans* (1971 ed.), p. 307; Deffontaines, *Hommes et travaux*, pp. 87–88; Singer, p. 67; Labrune, p. 5.

6. Prieur de Sennely cited in Edeine, 2: 691; Péguy, "Pierre," p. 1220.

7. Bonnet and Santini, especially p. 144.

8. Hilaire, pp. 57–58.

9. AD, Yonne V 11–13 (1800–1828; containing many and repeated complaints and injunctions against the tendency of laymen to take over the functions of absent priests), AG, MR 1269 (Beauce, 1837). See also AD, Yonne III M¹ 47 (sous-préf. Sens, Nov. 1814).

10. Fernand Boulard, *Problèmes missionaires*, 1: 145–47; Jeanton, *Légende*, pp. 15ff, 70; Hilaire, p. 60; J.-A. Delpon, 1: 212.

11. Derruau-Borniol, p. 55; Le Saux, pp. 30, 31; P. Labrune, *L'Emigration* (Aubusson,

1869), especially p. 18; Cholvy, p. 327; AD, Cantal 40 M 11 (préf. Aurillac, Nov. 1879).

12. AN, F^{ic}III Loiret 12 (sous-préf. Pithiviers, June 1859). Even St. Jean-Baptiste Marie Vianney, who tried to stamp out all other sins throughout his parish during his 41 years at Ars (1818–59), could not fight against this breach of the Lord's will.

13. Marcilhacy, "Emile Zola," p. 580, quoting from the archives of the Missions in Beauce, 1861; AD, Yonne III M¹233 (Sens, Apr. 1862).

14. Le Saux, pp. 32–37, 54 (citing the bishop of Limoges); Corbin, pp. 907, 911; AD, Puy-de-Dôme M 04470 (Riom, Oct. 1906); Belbèze, p. 74.

15. Le Saux, p. 54; Latreille and Rémond, 3: 360; Cholvy, pp. 226–27, 229; Edeine, 2: 701; Ségalen, p. 48.

16. Boulard (cited in note 10, above), 1: 154; Le Saux, p. 38.

17. Dupront in François, pp. 526–27; Daniel; Edeine, 2: 703 (Sologne); N.-J. Chaline, "Une Image du diocèse de Rouen sous l'épiscopat de Mgr. de Croy," *Revue de l'histoire de l'église de France*, 1972, p. 66 (Normandy).

18. R. Brunet, p. 221.

19. Halévy, p. 65; R. Brunet, p. 221. See also Le Saux, p. 94 ("Catholicism and sorcery were indissolubly connected in the peasants' mind"); and Lecoeur, p. 66, in 1883 ("Prêtres et bergers sont tous sorciers, dit un vieux proverbe qui n'a pas cessé d'être vrai").

20. R. Brunet, p. 221; Beauquier, pp. 74–75; Baudiau, 1: 47; Charles Dumont, p. 25; Pérot, p. 18; Labourasse, p. 158. On malign priests, see Zind, p. 189, quoting reports of the rector of the Academy of Poitiers in 1858–59. At Boux (Bouëx, Charente), if hail ravaged the crops, "c'est le prêtre du lieu qui le fait tomber par vengeance." At Vouzan (Charente) an old woman saw her priest with her own eyes "sitting on a cloud, casting thunderbolts." "Et tout ceci se croit," wailed the rector. On priests conjuring away storms, throwing a shoe or bonnet at them, and saying special prayers, see also Bérenger-Féraud, *Réminiscences*, pp. 291–93.

21. Le Saux, p. 92, quotes the curé of Saint-Victurnien (Hte.-Vienne) as saying in 1925: "On redoute que le prêtre n'introduise avec lui la mort."

22. Perrin and Bouet, p. 110.

23. Malon, p. 17; Hilaire, p. 66; A. A. Milne, *Winnie-the-Pooh* (London, 1926), chap. 3: "In Which Pooh and Piglet Go Hunting and Nearly Catch a Woozle." Readers should bear in mind that, while Heffalumps appear well authenticated, Wizzles and Woozles have a more uncertain pedigree.

24. On saints batteurs, etc., see Leproux, *Dévotions*, pp. xvi–xix. In Saintonge children struck by a mysterious illness or stunted in their growth are said to be struck by the saints (eit'battut des saints). Doussinet, *Paysan*, p. 96. "Before you get to God, the saints will eat you up," declares a Romanian proverb. Humility before men suggests humility before saints. If one is less than nothing, saints are very potent indeed. The more a person thinks he is able to help himself, the less he thinks he needs saints.

25. Perrin and Bouet, p. 157; Labourasse, p. 65; Daniel. Laborde, p. 357, points out that in calling George Sand "la bonne dame de Nohant," the people around La Châtre were likening her to the Virgin Mary, who was so known in Berry.

26. Lapaire, pp. 16–17; Daniel; *Cinq siècles*, especially pp. xxi, 90. For more evidence, see Benoît, *La Provence*, pp. 275–77. Benoît makes very clear the role of local dialect in the varying attributions of saints. Thus, St. Aurélien (locally Aureille), bishop of Arles, could make the north wind (Auro) blow and keep rain from spoiling the crops. Around Salon the peasants sought the patronage of St. Blaise, protector of their wheat (Provençal, *blad*). While St. Eutropius (St. Tropes; St. Estròpi) could also respond to the appeal of cripples (estropiés).

27. Labourasse, p. 68 (Meuse); Charrié, *Bas-Vivarais*, p. 145 (Ardèche); Hertz, p. 138 (Alps). Many legends warn against attempting to rebuild cult chapels on a different site, and Charrié tells the story of Notre-Dame-de-l'Espérance at Pramaillet, near Saint-

Etienne-de-Boulogne (Ardèche), where in 1823 the crowds of pilgrims and their excessive junketing brought official interdiction of the cult. The statue was transferred to Saint-Etienne and the chapel left to collapse, but the pilgrims kept coming, rebuilt the ruins and the cult was finally reestablished in 1872. (*Bas-Vivarais*, pp. 110, 127.)

28. Fage, *Fontaines*, pp. 14–15; Abbé Cazauran, *Castelnau-d'Auzan* (Auch, 1893), pp. 45–47, 62–63; Daniel.

29. *BFI*, 1954, p. 618.

30. Dupront, pp. 110–11; Cordier, p. 35; Pérot, p. 17.

31. Gostling, pp. 229–31.

32. Van Gennep, *Manuel*, 1.4: 2096 (Morbihan); Dergny, 1: 352–56 (Picardy); AD, Puy-de-Dôme F 0274 (Miremont, arr. Riom).

33. Fage, *Fontaines*, p. 10; Benoît and Gagnière; Paul Sébillot, "Les Ex-voto," *Revue des traditions populaires*, 1906, especially p. 162; Berthout, p. 24.

34. HE 12.836 (inst. Urcerey, Territoire de Belfort, 1888); Jeanton, *Habitation paysanne*, p. 112; Collot, p. 5.

35. AG, MR 1234 (Vendée, 1840); Zeldin, *Conflicts*, p. 163.

36. AN, F^{ie}III Ardèche 11 (Bourg-St.-Andéol, Oct. 1862).

37. J. Sabbatier, pp. 6, 166.

38. Laurentin, 1: especially pp. 171, 172, 177.

39. Lasserre, especially pp. 14, 30; Laurentin, 1: 63, 235; Taine, pp. 173, 175. Meanwhile, there was an ebbtide in the fortunes of older pilgrimage sites as railroads made the more prestigious ones accessible. See Vartier, *Vie*, p. 37, on the decline of Notre-Dame-des-Ermites, in Lorraine; and the comments of Christian, pp. 47, 66.

40. Laurentin, 1: 20–21, 26; Mgr. Dupanloup in *Lettre sur les prophéties contemporaines* (1874), quoted in Mayeur, *Débuts*, p. 13.

41. Labrune, p. 135; *Revue de synthèse*, 1957, pp. 386–89. Notably, in response to a listener's remark that Christianity was decaying and "on retourne aux pensées paiennes," Gabriel Le Bras is quoted as saying, "On y reste!"

42. AD, Puy-de-Dôme F 0274 (Miremont, arr. Riom); Edeine, 2: 765; Georges Rocal, *Les Vieilles Coutumes dévotieuses et magiques du Périgord* (Toulouse, 1922), p. 119. Bellringing against calamities also began to be abandoned toward the end of the century as lightning rods and hail insurance made it increasingly dispensable.

43. Labourasse, p. 76; Donnedevie, pp. 168–69, 271; Corbin, pp. 967–68, citing *La Semaine religieuse du diocèse de Limoges*, Apr. 23, 1876, p. 263. See also vast files in AN, F^{7}12391, 12392, 12393, and 12393^{a}; and AD, Hte.-Vienne 4M 33 (Bellac, June 1897), 4M 137 (St.-Léonard, 1904, 1911).

44. Dupront, p. 112; Daniel.

45. Norre, p. 51; Halévy, pp. 66–67. Keith Thomas, *Religion and the Decline of Magic* (Harmondsworth, Eng., 1973 ed.), p. 792, suggests that fertilizers replaced fertility rites. But he says this about Tudor England. We find it happening in the days of Jean Jaurès.

Chapter Twenty

1. Gorse, p. 9.

2. Brugerette, 2: 53. But see Jean Meyer in Delumeau, p. 441, on how the Breton priests' relative comfort compared with the general population gave them a certain personal independence and social prestige. Their salary was supplemented by gifts in money and in kind and, often, by a plot of land. Of course, conditions in Brittany were not necessarily reproduced in other regions. Prejudices were self-reinforcing. The more devout the region, the better off the priest and the higher his social position; the less devout the region, the worse the priest's economic situation, and the weaker also his position in the socioeconomic pecking order.

3. AD, Yonne V7 (1800); Doussinet, *Travaux*, p. 345.

4. AD, Ariège 5M 53² (Bouan, 1862; Barjac), Yonne V 151 (Sens, 1845); Labrune, p. 76. See also Zind, p. 163.

5. Dergny, 2: 32; *Petit catéchisme du diocèse d'Annecy* (Annecy, 1876), p. 5; *BSAG*, 1959, pp. 349, 358.

6. R. Brunet, p. 221 (Blajan, Hte.-Garonne); AD, Ariège 5M3 (St.-Girons, Mar. 1857); René Boudard, "Un Tumulte à Bourganeuf," *Mémoires de la Société des Sciences . . . de la Creuse*, 1957, pp. 109–12.

7. AD, Ariège 3M 105 (Soutein, 1884); Le Roy, *Moulin*, p. 104; Zeldin, *Conflicts*, pp. 177–78; AN, BB30 370 (Aix, June 1850).

8. AD, Hte.-Vienne 4M 24 (St.-Laurent-sur-Gorre, May–June 1881); Norre, pp. 78–79; Besson, p. 12. For stories of priestly charity and privation, on the other hand, see Hamerton, *Round My House*, pp. 335–40.

9. Le Saux, p. 129 (citing bishop's pastoral); Massé, p. 43; Mazières, 1: 381; Louis A.-M. de Vogüé, pp. 336–37.

10. Audiganne, *Populations*, 2: 213. See also Stuart R. Schram, "Traditions religieuses et réalités politiques dans le département du Gard," *Christianisme social*, 1953, pp. 194–254. On the clash between the "White" religious processions and the "Red" male-voice choir in a Vaucluse commune under the reign of MacMahon, see Henry Meynard, *Lourmarin à la Belle Epoque* (Aix, 1968), pp. 150–59. A generation later, in northern Ardèche, the traditional enmity of Protestants and Catholics assumed acute forms at election time. See Pilenco, p. 235, on the operations of armed bands gathered by village priests, and the ritual burnings of mannikins (or live goats) during the elections of 1902.

11. Correspondence in AN, FicIII Loiret 12 (Apr. 1859); Gustave Delpon, *Ma confession* (Clermont, 1887), p. 17; Emile Zola, *Germinal*, Chap. 7, p. 1.

12. AD, Finistère 4M (Landerneau, Oct. 1897); Berthout, especially p. 125.

13. AD, Cantal 40 M11 (préf. Aurillac, Dec. 1897); Monteils-Pons, p. 38 (referring to Florac, Lozère). See also AD, Puy-de-Dôme M 04476 (sous-préf. Issoire, Aug. 1890). Compare Father Coubé, speaking at Lourdes in April 1901, contending that in the elections of 1902 "there would be only two candidates: Jesus Christ and Barabbas!" (Quoted in Guillemin, p. 387.)

14. Le Saux, p. 115.

15. On the social extraction of priests, see Cholvy, pp. 264–65; Jean Meyer in Delumeau, p. 440; Corbin, pp. 901, 1215; and Le Saux, p. 80 (quoting *Missions des oblats*). Charrié contrasts the higher social extraction of priests in the Ancien Régime with that of the nineteenth-century priests, who were "simple peasants" (*Bas-Vivarais*, pp. 147–48). Reminiscent of the priest of Rebets (Seine-Inf.), whom an episcopal visitation of the late 1820's found to be "tout paysan et ne sachant parler qu'en paysan" (N.-J. Chaline, "Une Image du diocèse de Rouen," *Revue de l'histoire de l'église de France*, 1972, p. 62).

16. Garneret, p. 288; Cholvy, pp. 422–23; *Langue bretonne*.

17. Gaston Méry, *Libre parole*, Sept. 1907, quoted in Brugerette, 3: 26.

18. AN, F17 9271 (Basses-Pyrs., 1880, 1881); AD, Finistère M4 (Pont-l'Abbé, Feb. 1903).

19. AD, Pyrs.-Ors. 3M1 163 (préf., June 1879), Hte.-Vienne 4M24 (May 1881), Ariège 3M 105 (St.-Girons, May 1888; Dun, Aug. 1889; Rabat, Aug. 1890; Camon, Dec. 1896). On the cited examples of priests' actions, see AD, Cantal II 252 (important report by inspecteur d'académie, "La Lutte contre l'école laïque," Feb. 1913); "Le Couronnement de la Vierge Noire," *Revue pédagogique*, Dec. 1894, pp. 502–8; and André Hallays in *Journal des débats*, Dec. 23, 1894.

20. Berthout, p. 129; Bernard Lambert, *Les Paysans dans la lutte des classes* (1970), p. 39; Dergny, 2: 91–92.

21. Berthout, pp. 26–27.

22. Brugerette, 2: 55.

23. Abbé Pierre Collon, letter of Sept. 17, 1828, quoted in H. Rouyer, *Annales de Bourgogne*, 1956, p. 268 (Collon was born in 1755); Latreille and Rémond, 3: 362. See also Hilaire, p. 67. But see Zeldin, *Conflicts*, pp. 28–29: In 1855 at Saint-Amand-en-Puisaye (Nièvre) the priest noted in his parish register that Jansenism lay behind the hostility shown him by his parishioners. The Auxerrois, where clerical Jansenism was strong, was also fertile ground for anticlericalism.

24. AD, Ariège 3M 105 (Brussac, June 1812); Hilaire, p. 61; AD, Finistère 4M (Douarnenez, Feb. 1901); Sahuc, pp. 129, 131.

25. Hilaire, p. 64; Edouard Demachy, *La Confession selon le rite catholique* (1898); Zeldin, *Conflicts*, pp. 28–29, 31, 174; Abbé A. M. Larichesse, *Etudes philosophiques et morales sur la confession* (1865). On clerical transgressions, see AN, F^{ie}III Loiret 12 (June 1868; Feb. 1868), F^{7}12387–88 (Carcassonne, Sept. 1896; Brive, June 1898; Brest, Feb. 1903; Montpellier, Mar. 1903); and Berthout, p. 22.

26. Zeldin, *Conflicts*, p. 194, gives a list of various places where priests attacked fêtes, dancing, and finery between 1854 and 1867, making themselves altogether unpopular and driving parishioners away from church attendance. See in this connection AD, Isère 52M35 (July 1857), relating that at Goncelin the priest tried to prohibit the local *fête baladoire*.

27. Charrié, *Bas-Vivarais*, p. 149 (Balazuc); Canon Parmet, "Les Confréries de pénitents à Bourganeuf," *Mémoires de la Société des Sciences . . . de la Creuse*, 1919–21, p. 84; Barker, *Wandering*, p. 116. For other material on penitents, see Corbin, pp. 951–52; Rouchon, 2.2: 162–63; and Malaussène, pp. 362–63.

28. Déribier Du Châtelet, 1: 26; Polge, *Quelques légendes*, pp. 26–43 (a whole series of healing fountains abandoned in Gers in the first half of the 19th century); Brekilien, pp. 245–46; Mourgues, pp. 38–39.

29. Mourgues, p. 35.

30. Baudiau, 1: 47; Bouteiller, *Médecine*, p. 88; Brekilien, p. 265; AD, Hte.-Vienne 4M24 (maire Breuilaufa to préf., Nov. 1880); Le Saux, p. 115 (St.-Laurent-sur-Gorre, 1885). For more on the clergy's struggle against "superstitious" devotions and peasant persistence in observing them, see Georges Rocal, *Les Vieilles Coutumes dévotieuses et magiques du Périgord* (Toulouse, 1922), pp. 211–20.

31. Besson, p. 59; Brekilien, p. 246.

32. C. P. d'Amezeul, *Légendes bretonnes* (1863), p. 91; Poueigh, *Folklore*, p. 202: "Hèste sans hestoù, / Non n'y a, nou!" (Fête sans lendemain, / Non, il n'y en a point!)

33. See Serge Bonnet, *Communion*, pp. 264–65.

34. Labrune, pp. 19–23; Forestier, "Loi," pp. 201–2.

35. Letter from Ministre des Cultes to prefect of Htes.-Pyrs., Mar. 1858, quoted in Laurentin, 1: 231.

36. *La Semaine religieuse du diocèse de Montpellier*, Aug. 4, Aug. 18, 1877; Cholvy, p. 362; AD, Ariège 5M 53^2 (Vernajoul, Aug. 1866), 3M 105 (Soutein, 1884). See also Garneret, p. 306, for endless injunctions and sermons against dancing and bals.

37. Dergny, 2: 224; Garavel, p. 88.

38. AEP, 2 (Anet, Eure-et-Loir, 1874); HE II (Lozère, 1888); AD, Hte.-Vienne 4M24 (Nov. 1880); Gostling, p. 94. The young priest to whom Angus Reach talked on the little train from Bordeaux to La Teste in the Landes on the eve of the Franco-Prussian War deplored superstition and placed his hopes in schooling: "The boys and girls we get to come to school are taught to laugh at the notion of their old grandmothers being witches, and in another generation or two there will be a great change" (p. 98). Henri Polge, who has read through *La Semaine religieuse de l'archidiocèse d'Auch* from the first number in 1872, finds that the clergy, avoiding appeals to the supernatural or to the Scriptures, used "very positive arguments, scientific or pseudoscientific," found their most effective

allies among the salaried workers, who were the most fallen away from the Church, and showed themselves highly "sensitive to the prestige of science, indeed of positivism." (Personal communication, Dec. 8, 1973.)

39. Brugerette, 2: 55.

40. Abbé Desgranges and Cardinal de Cabrières quoted in Latreille and Rémond, 3: 547.

41. Brugerette, 2: 43, 47 (Guillemin, pp. 374–75, gives much lower figures on the enrollment in seminaries: 4,000 in 1881, 3,311 in 1894); Latreille and Rémond, 3: 544 (and Guillemin, p. 310); Julien Potel, *Le Clergé français* (1967), p. 29.

42. Latreille and Rémond, 3: 428–29, 430; Betham-Edwards, *France*, 1: 327.

43. See Brugerette, 3: 26, 29.

44. *Ibid.*; Narfon, pp. 294–95.

45. Brugerette, 3: 30; *La Croix*, survey of Aug.-Oct. 1907; Brugerette, 3: 28; Agnès Siegfried, *L'Abbé Frémont* (1933), 2: 663; Gaston Méry, *Libre Parole*, Sept. 1907.

46. See Camescasse, p. 116; Longy, *Canton*; and Coissac, p. 275.

47. Mireur, 2: 252; Dr. Warin, *Notions sur l'hygiène des habitations rurales* (Metz, 1858), p. 30; Perrin and Bouet, pp. 114–15; Labourasse, p. 55; Rambaud, *Economie*, p. 173.

48. Longy, *Canton*, pp. 67–68; Thiriat, *Vallée*, p. 315; Pérot, p. 169. The straw of the deathbed had been burned (in Burgundy) or stacked in a far corner of a field until it turned to compost (Provence). Mattresses would make such customs impractical. See Joseph Benoît, *En Provence*, p. 146.

49. Dergny, 1: 215–23; Mauriac, p. 27; Labourasse, p. 52 (and pp. 49–50, 56 on wakes).

50. Le Saux, pp. 91 (quoting bishop), 92; Garneret, pp. 289–90; R. Cruse, *Témoignage chrétien*, Oct. 12, 1967, p. 21.

Chapter Twenty-one

Epigraph. The statement by the Royal Governor (a man of the 18th century but otherwise unidentified) is quoted by Yves Castan in André Abbiateci et al., *Crimes et criminalité en France sous l'Ancien Régime* (1971), pp. 174–75.

1. Teacher quoted by Varagnac, p. 50; Sologne in Edeine, 2: 811.

2. Marcel Mayer, *Anet en Ile-de-France* (Montligeon, 1946), pp. 225–27; Jules Lecoeur, *Esquisses* (1887), p. 151; R. Guignard in *Revue de folklore français*, 1934, p. 107.

3. Labourasse, p. 118. For confirmation, personal communication from Henri Polge, who doubts that traditional feasts suffered much even under the Terror. See also Budin, pp. 151–52. In 1793 at Miélan they were busy building a church, and at Urdin, they were casting a new bell. About the same time, Ivry-en-Montagne (Côte-d'Or) sought to have one of its two church bells replaced, and a third added *aux frais de la nation*. Edeine, 2: 894–96, also believes that certain local feasts and *assemblées* in Sologne whose dates coincide with the dates of certain patron saints or pilgrimages now forgotten are survivals of fairs that grew up around pilgrimages to "good saints."

4. Malon, p. 498.

5. Pujos (Boissières); Besson, p. 99; Gustave Delpon, p. 12; AG, MR 1212 (Romans, 1845).

6. Mireur, 5: 317. For details, see M. P. Boissonnade, *Les Fêtes de village en Poitou et Angoûmois au 18e siècle* (Ligugé, 1897), pp. 10–11; Juge, p. 124; and AD, Puy-de-Dôme F 0274.

7. Blanchon, *Vie*, p. 57; Paul-Louis Courier, *Oeuvres* (1845), p. 175 (reprint of his pamphlet of July 13, 1822).

8. Déribier Du Châtelet, 1: 23–24; Mazuy, pp. 157–58; Gustave Delpon; Agulhon, *République*, pp. 151, 409–15; AG, MR 1841 (Pyrs.-Ors., 1841); Van Gennep, *Manuel*, 1: 139; Fortier-Beaulieu, pp. 117, 796, 813. On the use of the *fête patronale* to serve political and

personal ends, see AD, Ariège 5M 53² (1862) about the goings-on at Daumazan, near Mas-d'Azil, where a defeated candidate entertained the people and organized a rival public dance—"with splendid illuminations"—in defiance of the mayor.

9. AD, Yonne III M¹276 (sous-préf. Avallon, Mar. 26, 1853), III M¹275 (1853); Forestier "Garçonnade," pp. 9–10.

10. Forestier, "Garçonnade," pp. 9–10.

11. AD, Pyrs.-Ors. Fêtes 4 (Prats, 1838); Thomas, p. 33.

12. Achard, p. 235; Bougeatre, especially p. 259; Labourasse, p. 94.

13. Marcel Hemery, "Le Jeu de la choule dans l'Oise," *BFI*, 1946, pp. 3–11, 22; Perrin and Bouet, pp. 93–96; Lecoeur, pp. 159, 161. Picoche, p. 83, tells us that choule is still remembered at Etelfay in Somme, and was still being played at Tricot nearby in 1969. But while the opposing teams seem traditional (married men against "youths"), the play does not sound as brutal as in the past.

14. Prefect of Htes.-Pyrs. quoted in Lefebvre, *Vallée*, p. 23.

15. Lallement, p. 35; Jules Michelet, *La Sorcière* (1964 ed.), p. 139; Blanchon, *Vie*, pp. 57–61.

16. Picamilh, 1: 310; Ardouin-Dumazet, 32: 175; Perrin and Bouet, pp. 249–52.

17. Mazoyer, p. 416; Henri Prost, p. 29.

18. Julien Casebonne, *Cinquante années de vie paysanne* (Pau, 1963), p. 22; Charles Tilly, "How Protest Modernized France, 1845–1855," Center for Advanced Study in Behavioral Sciences, 1969.

19. Bastié, 2: 152; AD, Ariège 3M 105 (Bompas, 1885; Carla de Roquefort, Apr., Aug. 1888; Gestiès, Oct. 1889; Cabannes, Sept. 1900); Perrin and Bouet, p. 188.

20. AG, MR 2282 (Seine-et-Marne, 1863).

21. Varagnac, pp. 83–111.

22. Drouillet, 1: 172–73; AD, Ariège 5M 53¹ (Mazères, Feb. 1831), Yonne III M¹114 (Mar. 1840). For examples of incidents seen as politically dangerous, see AG, G⁸1 (Feb. 16, 1853), and G⁸2 (Mar. 5, 1853), containing reports of the commanding officer of the Sixth Military Division at Strasbourg to the Minister of War.

23. "Mémoires du Père Toine, paysan périgourdin," *Cahiers des Amis de Jacquou le Croquant*, 1939, p. 8.

24. AN, BB30 364 (Niort, Feb. 1850); *Le Glaneur des Alpes*, Mar. 10, 1850, quoted in Vigier, 2: iii; AG, G⁸1 (Bray, Feb. 7, Feb. 9, 1853). See also AN, BB30 370 (Aix, Mar. 1850).

25. AD, Pyrs.-Ors. 3M1 223 (Arles, Feb. 28, 1877, Apr. 30, 1878).

26. See the voluminous and touching reports in AD, Pyrs.-Ors. Fêtes 2.

27. AD, Yonne III M³12 (maire Auxerre, Oct. 1, 1825; maire Pontigny, Nov. 15, 1829).

28. AD, Pyrs.-Ors. Fêtes 4 (Mosset, 1831; St.-Paul, 1841), Cantal 43 M2 (St.-Flour, May 4, 1841).

29. Corbin, p. 1004; Malon, p. 317.

30. AD, Cantal 43 M2, and 43 M3 *passim*; AD, Pyrs.-Ors. Fêtes 8 (1852–69).

31. AD, Hte.-Vienne 1M 212 (1880–82), Puy-de-Dôme M 0132 (1880–82). Le Gallo, 2: 355, quotes the letter of a naval surgeon, written in Brest, July 13, 1880: "On dansera le soir, après le feu d'artifice, toute la nuit, sur les places publiques éclairées: c'est vous dire assez que les honnêtes gens ne dormiront pas."

32. AD, Hte.-Vienne 1M 212 (St.-Bonnet, July 17, 1882, and many others). AD, Puy-de-Dôme M 0132, contains numerous petitions to transfer the fête to Sunday (notably, in 1881 to July 17).

33. AD, Puy-de-Dôme M 0132 (Royat, July 15, 1882; Ambert, July 15, 1882), Hte.-Vienne 1M 212 (Lacroisille, July 16, 1883).

34. AD, Hte.-Vienne 1M 212 (Blond, July 15, 1882).

35. On the initial attitudes of small villages to July 14, see AD, Puy-de-Dôme M 0132

(Orcines, June 17, 1885; July 1, 1886, begging for subsidies); and AD, Ariège 5M 105 (Orgeix, July 19, 1888). On the tension between the old festivals and the new, see AD, Gers M 2799 (L'Isle-Jourdain, Aug. 6, 1888; Gimont, July 7, 1888; Eauze, July 15, 1889).

36. AD, Cantal 43 M5, file on "Fêtes du Centenaire," May 5, 1889, and for a variety of ceremonies, 43 M6 (e.g., Aug. 1897, July 1910); Rougeron, *Département de l'Allier*, p. 67; AD, Pyrs.-Ors. M31 163 (Oct. 1, 1879), Finistère 4M (Douarnenez, Sept. 26, 1897), Puy-de-Dôme M 04469 (sous-préf. Riom, July 1896). There were feasts and counter-feasts. The Right tried to launch one for Jeanne d'Arc; for a typical report, see sous-préf. Mauriac in AD, Cantal 40 M 11 (Oct. 9, 1909). The anticlericalists sought to launch festivals of their own, like *les casse-croûte du Vendredi-dit-Saint*; see Viple, p. 64; and AD, Ariège 5 M 72¹ (Pamiers, July 1909). But in neither case was there any great success.

37. Rougeron, *Département de l'Allier*, p. 39; Michael Scher, "The Young Gustave Hervé" (Ph.D. diss., University of California, Los Angeles, 1972), p. 122; AD, Puy-de-Dôme M 04478 (Billom, 1896).

38. AD, Yonne III M³25 (dissension); Pérot, p. 85 (St. Nicholas); Mireur, 5: 328 (Draguignan); Gagnon, 2: 319–26; AD, Pyrs.-Ors. 3M1 223 (Arles-sur-Tech, July 2, 1878).

39. AG, MR 2277 (Isère, 1860), MR 1212 (Isère, 1845); Van Gennep, *Manuel*, 1: 1458, 1460, 1508. According to Charrié, in Ardèche and nearby, serious May queens had disappeared by 1840 and only children still enacted the rite, which had been an urban one there to begin with (*Haut-Vivarais*, pp. 93–94). Around 1890, however, E. H. Barker still found a "king of youth" being elected in the Albigeois, with the most recently married couple having to contribute a pail of wine to the proceedings. But Ambialet (Tarn), where Barker noted this, was a very small parish indeed (*Wandering by Southern Waters*, pp. 184–85).

40. Beauquier, pp. 1ff; Varagnac, p. 31; Charrié, *Haut-Vivarais*, p. 75; Van Gennep, *Manuel*, 1: 1513. Edeine, 2: 834, had the same impression of developments in Sologne. Carnival, pyres, and torchlight feasts had been ceremonies that interested the whole population of the village. They became a monopoly of the young (sometimes of a special group among them, like the conscripts), then were left to the children, before they finally disappeared altogether.

41. Beauquier, pp. 71, 72.

42. Van Gennep, *Manuel*, 1: 1558, 1560; Garneret, p. 297.

43. Van Gennep, "Cycle préhivernal," p. 53.

44. Van Gennep, *Manuel*, 1: 1798–99; Rouchon, 2.2: 193; Drouillet, 3: 138–39.

45. Van Gennep, *Manuel*, 1: 1751, 1764, 1791; Bertrand, pp. 117–19, 407–9.

46. Lallement, p. 35; Guillemot, pp. 160–61, 221; Varagnac, especially pp. 62–63; Violet, *Clessé*, p. 121. Pujos (Castelnau, Lot): in 1881 people still contributed their bundle, but the priest no longer blessed the bonfire.

47. Van Gennep, *Manuel*, 1: 1827; Bertrand, pp. 117–18; Guillemot, p. 161. Note that in 1883 Lecoeur referred to flaming wheels, but as practices with no contemporary relevance (pp. 225–26).

48. Buffet, *Bretagne*, p. 144; Thiriat, *Vallée*, pp. 324–25; Van Gennep, *Manuel*, 1: 2077.

49. See their monographs in the HE II series.

50. Fagot, p. 140; E. Rimbaud, *Saint-Jean-le-Centenier* (Vals, 1907), p. 49; Bougeatre, p. 257.

51. Vaultier, p. 87; L. G. Guerdan, *Un Ami oriental de Barrès* (1936), p. 51, quoting a note of Feb. 8, 1891.

52. Bozon, *Histoire*, p. 465; Malaussène, pp. 15–16; Van Gennep, "Cycle cérémonial," p. 436; Garneret, p. 294; Wylie, *Village*, p. 318.

53. See BFI, 1939, p. 24; Marouzeau, p. 111; Cressot, p. 228; HE II (Brouenne, Meuse, 1899); and Labourasse, p. 65. Sénéquier, p. 125, tells us that the bravade of La Garde-Freinet took place on the day of the Invitation de la Saints-Croix: "Ce jour ou plutôt cette

fête est comme Noël immuable et se situe le 3 du mois de mai, puis on la fit le premier dimanche de mai."(?)

54. André Dupin aîné, *Le Morvan* (1852), p. 42.

55. Hérelle, *Etudes*, pp. 24–25; Cressot, p. 145; André Souarnet in *BFI*, 1946, p. 12. See also Agulhon's remark (in *Ville ouvrière*, p. 115) that people cling to those customs they find rewarding and those festivities that suit them.

56. Van Gennep, *Manuel*, 1: 182–83; Gérard, p. 17.

57. Garneret, p. 293; Charrié, *Bas-Vivarais*, p. 73. Even the habit of placing Christmas presents in a sabot was an imitation of an urban practice.

58. EA, Landes. Note the popular meaning of "feasting," or *faire la nôce*.

Chapter Twenty-two

Epigraph. "Des charivaris," p. 499.

1. Varagnac, p. 103; Gagnon, 2: 335; Gérard, p. 8. In Lot we know that the *paillade* of husbands whose wives had contrived to beat them survived at least to 1831, because J.-A. Delpon mentions it in his *Statistique*, 1: 206–8. For historical background, see Natalie Zemon Davis, *Society and Culture in Early Modern France* (Stanford, Calif., 1975) especially chap. 4.

2. Ségalen, p. 66.

3. *Bulletin de la Société Académique des Hautes-Pyrénées*, 1861, pp. 471, 483.

4. Agulhon, *République*, p. 160. Note that the Church also condemned the charivari as a denigration of the sacrament of marriage.

5. But see *Le Petit Marseillais*, June 16, 1906, for an instance there.

6. J.-A. Delpon, 1: 207; Malaussène, p. 25; Lalou, pp. 498–99.

7. AD, Ariège 5M 53².

8. For examples, see Lalou, pp. 507–14; and Emile Pouvillon, "Les Antibel," *RDM*, May 1, 1892, pp. 5ff.

9. Le Gallo, 1: 46; AD, Ariège 5M 53¹ (Mas-d'Azil); Gagnon, 2: 336; Sahuc, p. 132; AD, Ariège 5M 54.

10. Forestier, *Yonne*, 2: 57ff.

11. Fernand L'Huillier in Dollinger, p. 414; Le Roy Ladurie in introduction to Angeville, p. xi.

12. Gagnon, 2: 336; AD, Puy-de-Dôme (Ambert gendarmes, Dec. 1836), Lot 6M9 (Apr. 1849).

13. *Bulletin de la Société Archéologique du Finistère*, 1962, p. 138; Viple, p. 59; AG, G⁸1 (Belley, Ain, Jan. 1853), G⁸2 (Comte de Castellane, Mar. 1853).

14. AD, Gers M 2172 (Lombez, Aug. 1853); Corbin, p. 134, citing AD, Hte.-Vienne 262 (1857).

15. Jalby, p. 145; Fage, *La Mort*, p. 16; François Michel, *Le Pays basque* (1857); *Bulletin de la Société Académique des Hautes-Pyrénées*, 1858–59, p. 25, and 1861, pp. 457, 471, 483.

16. Hérelle, *Théâtre rurale*, pp. 156–57, 161; Fagot, pp. 147–48.

17. Lucien Duc, *Mémoires d'un écolier* (1884), p. 81.

18. Lavisse, *Première année d'instruction civique*, p. 156.

19. At La Garde-Freinet, where a charivari was carried on for 3 to 12 months, the practice died out toward the end of the century, but persisted longest in the countryside (Sénéquier, pp. 82–83). Bérenger-Féraud, *Réminiscences*, pp. 209–10, tells us that in Provence, though suppressed by the police in towns, charivaris continued to be held in the villages late in the century. Nevertheless, in Loire they lasted to 1918 (Fortier-Beaulieu, pp. 16, 50), and in Mâconnais all the way to 1939 (Violet, *Veillées*, pp. 2ff).

20. Paul Bailly, p. 22; AD, Pyrs.-Ors. 3M1 224 (Prades, May 1896), Finistère 4M (Châ-

teaulin, Feb. 1901); Pérot, p. 23; Varagnac, p. 64. See also Charrié, *Haut-Vivarais*, p. 56.

21. Marc Leproux, "Contributions au folklore de l'Angoumois," *Nouvelle revue des traditions populaires*, 1950, pp. 435–41; Paul Fortier-Beaulieu, *Mariages et noces campagnardes dans les pays ayant formé le département de la Loire* (1945), p. 314.

22. P. Saintyves in *Revue des traditions populaires*, 1919, pp. 59–60; Marc Leproux, as cited in preceding note, pp. 440–41 (Aumagne); Georges Rocal, *Les Vieilles Coutumes dévotieuses et magiques du Périgord* (Toulouse, 1922), p. 31 (Grand-Brassac); Edeine, 2: 814–16 (Sologne); Lalou, p. 499.

Chapter Twenty-three

Epigraph. *The Bothie of Tober-na-Vuolich* (1848), part 4.

1. Franchet, p. 26. According to Bougeatre, p. 17, a village was recognized as a bourg when it had a market and fair.

2. Bozon, *Vie*, pp. 218–19. On fairs in Morvan, see Levainville, pp. 203–7 *passim*; and André Dupin aîné, *Le Morvan* (1852), p. 42.

3. Donnadieu.

4. AD, Puy-de-Dôme M 0893 ("Enquête de 1903").

5. One hears forest murmurs of this in Yonne by 1865. See AD, Yonne III M^{1}234 (sous-préf. Joigny, Aug., Oct. 1865); and Allix.

6. Francus, *Valgorge*, p. 352; Longy, *Port-Dieu*, pp. 5–10; AD, Pyrs.-Ors. 3M1 224 (Céret, Sept., Nov. 1896).

7. Durand, p. 297; Bozon, *Vie*, p. 470; Allix, p. 536, quoting Edouard Herriot, *RDM*, Apr. 15, 1916, pp. 758–87; Eugène Curet, "L'Industrie de la cordonnerie à Pertuis," *Congrès des Sociétés Savantes de Provence*, 1906 (Marseille, 1907), pp. 876–77. Pertuis had become the shopping center for all the southern slope of the Luberon. "Every Friday, twenty villages invade its public places, its inns, cafés, and shops. Weekly, its merchants thus receive the beneficial balm of the rural population and, thanks to what they make on Fridays, they smoke their pipes in peace the rest of the week."

8. Bourdieu, "Célibat," p. 101; F. Benoît, *Histoire de l'outillage*, p. 97.

9. Perrin and Bouet, p. 181; Reynier, *Pays*, 1: 149; *BFI*, 1939, p. 24.

10. Dauzat, *Patois*, p. 104; *BFI*, 1939, p. 24.

11. AD, Gers M 2799 (Mirande, Oct. 1876); Victor Fournel, *Les Spectacles populaires et les artistes des rues* (1863), p. 298; Perrin and Bouet, pp. 317–20; Guilcher, "Vue," pp. 38ff.

12. Flandrin, pp. 114–16; Fortier-Beaulieu, especially p. 549. On Gascony, see Daugé, p. 277 ("A girl who frequents markets does not remain without sins"); and on Languedoc, Fabre and Lacroix, p. 181.

13. AD, Vosges 9bis M26; Pariset, *Montagne Noire*, p. 239; Chaumeil, pp. 158–59.

14. Labat, *Gascogne*, p. 32; Coissac, pp. 239–40.

15. Jollivet and Mendras, 1: 183.

16. Gorse, pp. 282–83.

17. See Bois, *Paysans* (1971 ed.), p. 308; P. Mayer, p. 4; J. A. Barral, *Agriculture de la Haute-Vienne*, p. 759; Coissac, p. 240; and Redfield.

Chapter Twenty-four

Epigraph. *La Nouvelle Héloise*, part 5, letter 7.

1. S. Tardieu, *Vie domestique*, p. 156; AD, Yonne III M^{22}16 (Nov. 1852); Marne: personal communication from Mme. Hébert, 1973.

2. Roubin. In Forez "les voisins apportent leur bûche et leur huile, chacun sa part," reported Frédéric Noëlas in his *Légendes et traditions foréziennes* (Roanne, 1865), p. 319.

3. Garneret, p. 288; S. Tardieu, *Vie domestique*, pp. 155–56; Violet, *Clessé*, p. 114; Sébillot, *Littérature*, p. iv.

4. Fortier-Beaulieu, pp. 54, 70.

5. Marin, *Veillées*, especially p. 25; Marin, *Contes*, pp. 8, 30. See Le Roy, *Moulin*, for the story of the little tailor who read "La Ruche" and tried to educate the sharecroppers and cattlemen of Périgord at their veillées. But they would listen only to tales of the supernatural: *chasse-volante, loup garou, biche blanche*, etc.

6. Sébillot, *Littérature*, p. v; AN, F¹⁷10757 (Garrevagues, Tarn, 1861); Robert, "Lecture," pp. 106–8.

7. Forestier, "Loi," p. 202; Bordes, pp. 12–13; Sébillot, *Littérature*, p. v.

8. AN, F¹⁷9376, "Rapport sur la situation générale de l'enseignement primaire dans le département de l'Ariège en 1868"; Marin, *Veillées*, pp. 29–30. See also Mistral, p. 103.

9. Bonnemère, 2: 372; Fortier-Beaulieu; EA, Savoie.

10. HE 12.820 (Bulson, Ardennes); Sébillot, *Littérature*, p. 5; Foville, *Enquête*, 1: 150.

11. Madeleine Rébérioux, "Un Groupe de paysans socialistes," *Mouvement social*, 1966, especially p. 91.

12. Foville, *Enquête*, 2: 300; Jollivet and Mendras, 1: 137, 139; Bougeatre, pp. 147, 173.

13. Mistral, p. 103; Le Guyader, p. 224; Violet, *Veillées*, p. 2.

14. Fortier-Beaulieu, pp. 93, 196, 263; Thiriat, *Vallée*, pp. 330–31.

15. Gagnon, 2: 301; Jollivet and Mendras, 1: 127; EA, Allier, pp. 5–6; Garneret, p. 289; Guillaumin, *Panorama*, pp. 61–62.

Chapter Twenty-five

1. Lavisse, *Année préparatoire*, pp. 80–82; Gorse, pp. 14–15.

2. Examples in this paragraph and the following ones are culled from Gorse; Juge; Donnadieu; Hérelle, *Etudes*; Doussinet; and Alfred de Tarde.

3. Donnadieu.

4. Pujos (Laroque des Arcs); Perron, *Proverbes*, p. 2. See also Coissac, p. 313, on Creuse; and Musset, *Bas-Maine*, pp. 167–68, on the rustic calendar of Lower Maine.

5. Desforges, p. 18; EA, Gers; Perron, *Proverbes*, p. 22; Charrié, *Bas-Vivarais*, pp. 159–60.

6. Chaumeil, pp. 145–46; Fagot, p. 76 ("Madounai sélo, peto candelo..."); Pérot, p. 69.

7. Perron, *Proverbes*, pp. 44–45.

8. *Ibid.*

9. See ATP, manuscripts 43.86.6 (Charente) and 54.294 (Hérault); *Nouveau Petit Larousse* (1971), p. 834; Passama, pp. 47–48 (on traditional hiring practices persisting in Minervois however cumbersome); and Bogros, p. 163 (on Morvan children of the 1870's going round to gather eggs and other goodies at Carnival crying "Au guillanet"— "au gui, l'an neuf"—a survival of the old system in which the year began at Easter.

10. Delarue and Ténèze, 2: xxiv; Gachon, *Brousse-Montboissier*, p. 71; EA, Marne; Esnault, *Imagination*, pp. 57, 60, 69, 78, 200, 220, 224; Marc Leproux, MATP manuscript 43.115; Marie Drouart, "Petit dictionnaire pittoresque," MATP manuscript; Garneret, pp. 51, 71–72, 133, 157, 161.

11. Hérelle, *Etudes*, pp. 15–19; *Ethnographie*, 1966–67, p. 30.

12. Jeanton, *Légende*, pp. 73–79.

13. Delarue and Ténèze, 1: 44–45; Haudricourt and Delamarre, p. 414; Ogès and Déguignet, pp. 122–28.

14. Dévigne, pp. 29–30. On nobles and Satan, see the remarks of Parain, "Nouveau Mythe," p. 96. On the *Quatre fils Aymon*, see Souvestre, *Derniers Bretons* (1843 ed.), p. 271.

15. Ogès and Déguignet, p. 88.

16. Sébillot, *Folk-lore*, 4: 403, 404. On Taxil, see Eugen Weber, *Satan franc-maçon* (1964).

17. Perron, *Proverbes*, p. 56; Desforges, p. 18. See also Van Gennep, *Folklore de l'Auvergne*, p. 313; Delarue and Ténèze, 1: 46–47; Sébillot, *Littérature*, p. xi; and Labat, *Ame*, pp. 55–56.

18. On *couarails d'enfants* and *piats-bans* (*petits-bancs*, the little stools children brought to sit on while listening to their elders), see Marin, *Veillées*, p. 147; and especially Marin, *Contes*, pp. 7–8, 30, 129–33.

Chapter Twenty-six

Epigraph. "Ode to a Nightingale."

1. Guilcher, *Tradition*, p. 240; Trébucq, *Chanson populaire et la vie rurale*, 1: 53. No wonder many songs were simple one-part melodies in which anyone could join in impromptu.

2. Souvestre, *Derniers Bretons* (1843 ed.), pp. 145–46; Brekilien, p. 310.

3. See Ileana Vrancea, "Les Doinas roumaines," *La Pensée*, 1953, pp. 199–212.

4. Fagot, p. 250.

5. *Tradition en Poitou et Charentes*, p. 370.

6. Quoted in Vincent, p. 275.

7. Germain Laisnel de la Salle, *Souvenirs du vieux temps*, vol. 2: *Le Berry: Moeurs et Coutumes* (1902), cited in EA, Indre; Poueigh, *Folklore*, pp. 92, 106: "Quand lou bouie cànto, l'aràire vài ben!"

8. EA, Lot; EA, Corrèze.

9. Is this why we hear of so few real songs among the coastal mariners and rivermen of Languedoc? See Valaux, p. 83; Poueigh, *Folklore*, pp. 181–82.

10. Manceau, pp. 45–47; Buffet, *Haute-Bretagne*, pp. 148–49, 155.

11. Narcisse Quélien, *Chants et danses des Bretons* (1889), p. 18; Valaux, p. 83; Manceau, p. 47. On the length of ballads, see Doussinet, *Travaux*, p. 497: The "Complainte de Furet," a song about a murderer executed at Saintes in 1886 that was very popular in Saintonge, went on for 57 couplets.

12. On improvised songs, see Paul Sébillot, *Le Folk-lore. Littérature orale et ethnographie traditionnelle* (1913), p. 49; Garneret, p. 342; and Fortier-Beaulieu, p. 311.

13. Peygnaud, p. 57. Brekilien, p. 271, mentions that Breton love songs were generally the work of seminarians.

14. Gorse, pp. 140–41. See also Fagot, pp. 11, 23–25.

15. Marc Leproux, MATP manuscript 43.115.

16. E. Soleville, "Chants populaires du Bas-Quercy," *Bulletin archéologique et historique de la Société Archéologique de Tarn-et-Garonne*, 1889, pp. 7–9; Pérot, *Folklore*, p. 111; Coissac, especially p. 324; Cénac-Moncaut, *Littérature*, pp. 259–65.

17. Bollème, *Bibliothèque bleue*, pp. 232–35; Trébucq, *Chanson populaire en Vendée*, pp. 41–44. The original text of the last quotation is found in Trébucq, *Chanson populaire et la vie rurale*, 1: 166.

18. Pérot, p. 103; Gérard. At Gerardmer, old noëls were still sung in patois in the 1890's.

19. Peygnaud, p. 55.

20. Dauzat, *Village*, p. 162.

21. Brochon, *Chanson française*, 1: 27.

22. Monteil-Pons, in *Cerca*, 1960, p. 326.

23. AD, Yonne III M¹268 (Mar. 1854). AN, BB30 371 (Angers, June 1850), contains a triumphant letter from the public prosecutor at Rennes at his success (after two

acquittals) in securing a conviction for the singing of Dupont's song as a "délit d'attaque à la propriété."

24. AN, BB30 396 (Bordeaux, Jan. 1852).

25. Fagot, p. 252.

26. Brochon, *Chanson sociale*, p. 72.

27. AD, Yonne III M^{1}268 (Jan. 1854), M^{1}227 (Apr. 1854); Marc Leproux, MATP manuscript 43.115; Manceau, p. 52; Urbain Gibert, "La Partie des Meuniers ou le Carnaval de Limoux," *Annales de l'Institut d'Etudes Occitanes*, 1948, pp. 77–78: "Tau foutut un tap al tiol, / Paure Perera, paure Perera. / Tau foutut un tap al tiol, / Paure Perera per tojorn."

28. Jules Ferry, *L'Evolution économique de Veslud (Aisne)* (1946), p. 52; Abbé S. Solassol, *Le Revers de la médaille* (1895), pp. 30, 41, 67; AD, Ariège 5M 105 (Gestiès, 1894; Capoulet, 1896); Passama, p. 133.

29. Agulhon, *1848*, p. 109.

30. Cénac-Moncaut, *Littérature*, pp. 279–80.

31. *Cinq siècles*, p. 268; George Sand, *Les Maîtres Sonneurs* (1843). Similarly in *Consuelo*: "On dit chez nous [in Berry] que la musique pousse dans les bois," not only in Bourbonnais but, farther still, in Auvergne (quoted in Georges Roger, *Les Maîtres Sonneurs de George Sand*, 1954, p. 55).

32. André Desrousseaux, *Moeurs populaires de la Flandre française* (Lille, 1889), 1: 21–22.

33. Reuchsel, pp. 119–21; AD, Pyrs.-Ors. (Associations, sous-préf. Céret, 1894); Sénéquier, p. 163. Daugé, p. 102, tells us that in the Landes in the 1860's one had to pay 10–12 francs each for a bagpiper and flutist to play a wedding party to and from church, and to hire a violinist could cost as much as 40 francs. But that was for the rich, who sometimes even got a pianist, whose services were "très cher." In the Gascon countryside, where wedding parties had danced to the *vielle* (hurdy-gurdy), the *bouhe* (bagpipe), or the flute, by the twentieth century the accordion (and, more rarely, the violin) had taken over. In the Tarn, too, we hear that the clarinet and, after it, the accordion, spread through the countryside after 1900 (Jalby, p. 193).

34. Trébucq, *Chanson populaire et la vie rurale*, 1: 108; J.-L. Roche, p. 1. "Un Ange" was the product of Jean Reboul, a Provençal baker patronized by Lamartine, Alexandre Dumas père, and George Sand. For the imitative poetry of the self-educated, see the papers of Edgar Newman, notably "The Socialist Worker Poets of the Bourgeois Monarchy, 1830–1848" (unpublished manuscript); and Michel Ragon, *Histoire de la littérature prolétarienne en France*, 1974, especially chap. 2: "Socialisme romantique et littérature ouvrière au XIXe siècle."

35. Trébucq, *Chanson populaire en Vendée*, pp. 10–11; Nisard, *Des chansons*, 2: 2. See also Pottier, *Chants*, pp. 5, 22. Closer to Paris, and in the realm of Oïl, local songs seem to have disappeared earlier in the century. Gérard de Nerval, whose *Chansons et légendes du Valois* (1842) had a lot to say on the subject, was already complaining that the songs of his youth were seldom heard, and that journeymen, rivermen, washerwomen, and haymakers were more often repeating "les romances à la mode." See the whole passage in *Oeuvres complètes*, 1931, 1: 205–20. See also local details in *Congrès provincial de la Société Bibliographique et des Publications Populaires*, Mans, 1893 (1894), p. 494.

36. See Pierre Cavard, *L'Abbé Pessonneaux et la Marseillaise* (Vienne, 1954), pp. 135–36; and Alfred Chabaud, "La Marseillaise: Chant patriotique girondin," *Annales historiques de la Révolution française*, 1936, pp. 460–67. For a discussion of this evolution, see my essay "Who Sang the Marseillaise?" in Edward Gargan, ed., *Popular Culture in France* (Saratoga, 1976).

37. My account is based on Laurent Lautard, *Marseille depuis 1789 jusqu'en 1815, par*

un vieux Marseillais (1844), 1: 134; Jules Michelet, *Histoire de la Révolution française* (1869), 3: 238–39; Alphonse de Lamartine, *Histoire des Girondins* (1846), 1: xvi, para. sec. 26; Pollio and Marcel, especially pp. 104, 389, 392; and Mazuy (who cites the new refrain), pp. 29, 32, 33, 36.

38. Pollio and Marcel, pp. 87, 154; Sébillot, *Folk-lore de France*, 4: 387; F. Brunot, 9: 73.

39. AN, BB30 370 (Aix, Oct. 1850); "Un Lundi de liberté," in Eugène Baillet, *Chansons* (1867); AD, Ariège 5 M3 (Pamiers, Apr. 1858).

40. Maurice Barrès, *Scènes et doctrines du nationalisme* (1902), 1: 3. See AD, Finistère 4M (Pont-l'Abbé, June 1901), reporting that for the birthday of the director of the Catholic school a bonfire was lit in the schoolyard and the band played 4 pieces, ending with "La Marseillaise," which had to be repeated at the demand of a crowd that had gathered.

41. Raymond Doussinet, *Le Paysan santongeais*, p. 117: "Suzy's Dance," or "Fart, Ol' Woman, Fart." "Our Suzy's no more'n a kid. / Who does all her ma would forbid. / When ma becomes mad, / Suzy says 'That's too bad: / Just you fart! I'll not do what you bid.' "

42. Mazuy, pp. 39ff; Thiriat, *Vallée*, p. 381.

43. Bordes, p. 3; AN, F¹⁷10757 (Rienbach, Ariège, Jan. 1861).

44. *Instruction primaire*, 2: 37; Reuchsel, p. 91; Clément Brun, p. 93; Félix Pécaut, "Notes d'inspection," *Revue pédagogique*, Oct. 15, 1894, p. 307.

45. Reuchsel, pp. 1, 3.

46. *Ibid.*, pp. 119–21, 139–41.

47. Audiganne, *Populations*, 2: 152, 253.

48. Smith, p. 1; Quellien, *Chansons*, p. 34; Sébillot, *Littérature*, p. xi; Sénéquier, p. 198.

49. Valaux, p. 83; Pujos (St.-Paul, Labouffie).

50. Dauzat, *Village*, p. 161; Julien Tiersot, *Chansons populaires des Alpes françaises, Savoie, Dauphiné* (Grenoble, 1913); Pérot, p. 118. See also Van Gennep, *Folklore du Dauphiné*, 2: 582.

51. Fagot, p. 9; Dubreuil-Chambardel, p. 165; *Tradition en Poitou et Charentes*, pp. 356–57; *BFI*, Jan. 1946, p. 13.

52. Juge, p. 95; Brekilien, pp. 270, 283–84.

53. Quellien, *Rapport*; Gostling, p. 122; Brekilien, p. 270. See also Charles Le Goffic quoted in Brekilien, p. 283.

54. This paragraph is based largely on Guilcher, *Tradition*, p. 190.

55. *Ibid.*, pp. 17ff; J. A. Barral, *Agriculture du Nord*, 2: 424.

56. Jollivet and Mendras, 1: 159.

57. Guilcher, *Tradition*, pp. 18–21.

58. AD, Pyrs.-Ors. (Fêtes 4; Céret, 1838); Donnedevie, p. 125.

59. Edouard Gallet, *La Ville et la commune de Beauvoir-sur-Mer* (Nantes, 1868), pp. 73–74; Hérelle, *Etudes*, p. 26; Guilcher, *Tradition*, pp. 257, 309, 404; Lefebvre, *Vallée*, p. 23; AD, Pyrs.-Ors. (Associations, sous-préf. Céret, Mar. 1894). Fortier-Beaulieu, p. 134, mentions the village of St.-Forgeux-Lespinasse in Loire, where musicians had never been used at weddings. Once a wedding party brought one in from a nearby village: "Ceci n'avait jamais été vu et faisait rire tout le monde."

60. Guilcher, *Contredanse*, pp. 187–98.

61. Bogros, pp. 100–101; Pujos (Castelnau); HE 12.782 (Nommay, Doubs); Longy, *Canton*, p. 73; Marin, *Contes*, pp. 36–37.

62. Fagot, pp. 135–36; Hérelle, *Etudes*, p. 26.

63. Ajalbert, *En Auvergne*, p. 141; Ardouin-Dumazet, 28: 279; Grise, p. 9. See also Fage, *Autour du mariage*, p. 12; and Peygnaud, p. 16.

64. Fortier-Beaulieu, p. 110; Grenadou and Prévost, pp. 26, 37–40; AD, Pyrs.-Ors. (Associations); Halévy, p. 36.

65. Fage, *Autour du mariage*, p. 12; Bourdieu, "Célibat."

66. F. Benoît, *Provence*, pp. 321–25; Charrié, *Bas-Vivarais*, p. 139.

67. Guilcher, *Tradition*, p. 572; Grise, p. 10.

Chapter Twenty-seven

Epigraph. *The Winter's Tale*, act 4, sc. 3, line 262.

1. AD, Yonne 69 T2 (Tonnerre, Mar. 1825).

2. Thuillier, *Aspects*, p. 497; Pierre Pierrard, *La Vie ouvrière à Lille sous le Second Empire* (1965), pp. 267ff; Pierrard, *Lille et les Lillois* (1967), pp. 72–73.

3. Pierrard, as cited in preceding note; *BSF*, p. 222; Marquis de Fournes, *Rapport sur l'appui à donner à la propagande des bons écrits* (1873).

4. Roger Bellet, "Une Bataille culturelle, provinciale et nationale, à propos des bons auteurs pour bibliothèques populaires (Janvier–Juin 1867)," *Revue des sciences humaines*, 1969, pp. 453–73. Note, for example, that the savings and reading societies in Nièvre discussed in Thuillier, "Presse," p. 31, were in Cosne and Fourchambault, both centers of some size.

5. Corbin, pp. 472–74, 527. See also the story of Catholic attempts to reach the peasants through books, in *Congrès provincial de la Société Bibliographique, 1891* (Lyon, 1892), p. 11.

6. Nisard, *Histoire*; Brochon, *Livre de colportage*, pp. 86, 96–97.

7. Joseph Fiévée in 1815, quoted in Thuillier, *Aspects*, p. 497.

8. *BSF*, pp. 100–110.

9. *Instruction primaire*, 1: 728, 912; AN, $F^{17}9146$ (Senez, July 1866; Seine-et-Marne, 1866); *BSF*, p. 223; AN, $F^{17}9146$ (sous-préf. Bastia, July 1866).

10. *Instruction primaire* (Académie d'Aix-en-Provence).

11. Corbin, pp. 472–75; AN, $F^{17}9146$ *passim* (on Ocagnano, see July 1866), $F^{17}9252$ (Allier, 1878).

12. AD, Yonne 69 T1 and 71 T1 (circulars of Nov. 1810 and Dec. 1815).

13. AD, Yonne III M^1114 (Jan. 1839).

14. *Ibid.*, M^1233 (Tonnerre, Jan. 1862); Michel Chevalier, p. 684; Pérot, p. 160; Musset, "Genres," pp. 5–7; Leproux, *Dévotions*, p. xvii.

15. Collot, p. 9.

16. Mistler et al., *Epinal*, pp. 133–34.

17. See *Hommage à Gabriel Maignen: Canivets et images populaires* (Lyon, 1970); Mistler et al., *Epinal*, p. 16; and especially *Cinq siècles*, p. xxi. See also Jean Adhémar, *L'Imagerie populaire française* (1968); and P. L. Duchartre and R. Saulnier, *L'Imagerie populaire* (n.d.).

18. Marin, *Regards*, p. 170; Mistler et al., *Epinal*, pp. 64, 72. See also Paul Claudel, *Soulier de Satin* (act 4, sc. 1 and 2), for frequent mentions of "feuilles de Saints."

19. See *Cinq siècles*, p. 287 (*Chambre rustique*, 1852, with the Virgin and Napoleon nestling under the stairs); Paul Sébillot, *L'Imagerie populaire en Haute- et Basse-Bretagne* (1888), p. 5; and Balzac's *Peau de Chagrin* (1832). See also, two score years later, Angus Reach, p. 238: "I halted at a roadside auberge...and reaped my reward in the sight of a splendid cartoon suspended over the great fireplace, which represented, in a severe allegory, 'The Death of Credit Killed by Bad Payers.'"

20. J. M. Dumont in *Cinq siècles*, pp. 222, 258, 281–82.

21. Mistler et al., *Epinal*, p. 7; G. H. Rivière and Jean Adhémar in *Cinq siècles*, pp. xiv–xvii, xix.

22. Mignot, p. 5; Pérot, p. 108; Institut Français d'Ecosse, *Images populaires françaises*

(Edinburgh, 1960), especially pp. 9–10; *Cinq siècles*, pp. 92–93, 282; AD, Vosges 9bis M26 (1874).

23. See Bibliothèque Nationale, ed., *Charles Péguy* (1974), pp. 62–63, 154, 156, 158, 178, for good examples. See also Anatole France, *Le Vivre de mon ami* (1885), p. 162; and Emile Moselly, "Souvenirs sur Charles Péguy," in *Cahiers de l'Amitié Charles Péguy, 1966* (1968), pp. 80–81 (quoting a letter from Péguy to Maurice Barrès, 1910).

24. Institut Français d'Ecosse, *Images* (cited in note 22, above), pp. 16–18; AD, Vosges 9bis M17 (July–Aug. 1867), Hte.-Vienne 1M 191 (Limoges, Nov. 1899).

25. See the writings of Séguin, notably *Canards du siècle passé*; and R. Hélot, *Canards et canardiers en France, et principalement en Normandie* (1932).

26. References here and in the next paragraphs are to canards 52, 24, and 23 reproduced in Séguin, *Canards du siècle passé*; and to Séguin's remarks in "Canards de faits divers," pp. 33ff.

27. Pérot, p. 42.

28. AD, Cantal 49 M1 (lists of books and pamphlets); Corbin, pp. 507ff; *BSF*, p. 185; Bollème, *Bibliothèque bleue*, pp. 8–9, 12; Delarue and Ténèze, 1: 29.

29. Cressot, p. 129.

30. Bollème, *Bibliothèque bleue*, p. 20; Bollème, *Almanacs*, p. 34; Burguière, p. 153; Doussinet, *Travaux*, p. 446; Doussinet, *Paysan*, p. 411; Méraville, p. 310.

31. Girardin quoted in Dubois, pp. 25–26; *BSF*, pp. 108–10 (survey of 1861).

32. London *Times Literary Supplement*, May 25, 1973, p. 590.

33. Bollème, *Almanacs*, pp. 35–39.

34. See the remarks of Nisard, *Histoire*, 2: 494–95; and Séguin, *Canards du siècle passé*.

35. AD, Vosges 9bis M17; Séguin, "Canards de faits divers," p. 129; Archives de la Préfecture de Police, D B/198, Dec. 1884.

36. Paul Sébillot, *L'Imagerie populaire* (cited in note 19, above), pp. 5, 22; Pérot, p. 42; *Cinq siècles*, p. 287; Perrin and Bouet, pp. 368–84; Van Gennep, *Remarques*, p. 25. Little attention has been given to the canard's influence on the picture postcard, which appeared at this time. See Guyonnet, *Carte postale*; Guyonnet in *BFI*, 1948, pp. 14–16; and Roger Lecotté in *BFI*, 1954, p. 650.

37. *BSF*, p. 181; AN, F¹⁷9146 (préf. Cher, July 1866).

38. Corbin, p. 513.

39. See AN, F¹⁷9146, and AD, Cantal 49 M1, *passim*, for the national survey of 1866 discussed in this section. See also Darmon, p. 302.

40. AN, F¹⁷9146 (préf. Eure-et-Loir, 1866); Halévy, pp. 42–43.

41. Dubois, p. 3 (also on Sologne); R. Brunet, p. 213; Labourasse, p. 12; Charles Dumont, p. 46; AD, Ariège 6M59 (1901); Duclos, 1: 49–50; Ricard, pp. 83–84; Fortier-Beaulieu, p. 881.

42. AN, BB30 370 (Aix, Dec. 10, 1849; Feb. 14, 1850), BB30 396 (Bordeaux, a Jan. 1852 reference to J. P. Labro); the same file refers to one Boyer, called Migro, an edge-tool maker at Ste.-Marie-de-Frugère (Dordogne), age 38: "Demi lettré, abonné aux journaux socialistes, *en donnant lecture*" (my italics).

43. AD, Ariège 5M3 (Oct. 1865), Corrèze 164 T 4–5; Tanneau, p. 226. A number of references seem to trace the spread of newspaper reading in Yonne from insignificance (III M¹231, May 1860) to expansion throughout the countryside, where "all who can read a little" read the paper (III M¹234, May, July 1865). By local account, this group took in about a quarter of the rural population. But they could read aloud!

44. Séguin, *Canards du siècle passé*; AN, BB30 373 (Besançon, Apr. 1866).

45. Mazières, 1: 47; Corbin, pp. 531, 1407; Pécaut, *Etudes*, pp. 15, 16.

46. Corbin, pp. lxxi–lxxiv; compare pp. 1292, 1407. Burguière, p. 151, tells us that at

Plozévet only local newspapers were read until the First World War, when the *Petit Journal*, its illustrated supplement, and *Le Matin* made their "timid" appearance. On the small number of readers and the still-restricted reach, see AD, Cantal 40 M11 (Aurillac, May 1889); and AD, Puy-de-Dôme M 0162 (Thiers, Apr., May 1892), M 04478 (Brassac, Issoire, 1896), and M 04478 (La Bourboule, Apr. 1895). The slogan of the *Messager de la Manche* was "Peu de politique! Beaucoup de nouvelles!" (EA, Manche.)

47. AD, Pyrs.-Ors. 3M1 223 (comm. de police Rivesaltes, 1878); Decoux-Lagoutte, p. 53; AD, Cantal 40 M6.

48. Duine, p. 27; Cholvy, pp. 303–4; AD, Puy-de-Dôme M 04474 (Dec. 1906; Apr. 1907); compare AD, Puy-de-Dôme M 04478. It is hazardous but tempting to connect this wider distribution of national news with the "épidémies de grève" that Gabriel Tarde mentions in his *Essais* (1895), p. 15, "comme j'en ai vu s'ébaucher parmi des ouvriers meuliers du Périgord, qui voulaient simplement se mettre à la mode." We don't need to accept Tarde's explanation in order to find it suggestive.

49. Duine, p. 27; Labat, *En Gascogne*, pp. 651–54. See the remarks of Louis Chevalier, *Paysans*, p. 128; and Brochon, *Livre de colportage*, p. 98.

50. *Rapports d'inspection générale* (Doubs); *Le Cri du peuple*, Nov. 13, 1883, recommending Henri Brissac's brochure *Résumé populaire du socialisme*.

51. Félix Pécaut, "Notes d'inspection," *Revue pédagogique*, Oct. 1894, pp. 307–8; Pécaut, *Education*, p. 39; Thuillier, "Presse," p. 39.

Chapter Twenty-eight

Epigraph. *In Memoriam*, part CVI, stanza 2; *Alice's Adventures in Wonderland*, chap. 5, stanza 1.

1. Méline, p. 2; Varagnac, pp. 56–57. Also writing in 1905, an equally astute observer, Louis Marin, discerned "one of the gravest crises, perhaps the most grave, that French civilization has ever undergone." Changes were coming so fast that for "the first time . . . one sees all the customs unsettled . . . and it is in all the provinces that we see them unsettled one after the other, and so strongly that as a consequence the moral and economic life of the whole nation is unsettled in turn" ("Survivances," pp. 143–44).

2. The Société des Traditions Populaires was founded in 1885. According to Jeanton, *Mâconnais*, p. 5, just after the First World War "the elite of the local bourgeoisie" in Mâcon and Tournus discovered an interest in local traditions, costume, and folklore. The first local exhibition devoted to folklore took place in 1921. This is about the right *décalage* between Paris and the provinces!

3. See series like *Les Chansons de Jean Rameau illustrées*, edited at Bourges, with their attractive sepia photographs.

4. Félix Pécaut, *Critique religieuse* (1879), p. 31; Jean Macé quoted in *Bulletin de la Ligue de l'Enseignement*, 1894, p. 201.

5. Gautron du Coudray in *Le Nivernais*, Nov. 22, 1953; Dergny, 2: 7, 10–11; Van Gennep, *Manuel*, 1: 193.

6. Fortier-Beaulieu, pp. 2, 10, 14, 20, 27, 31, 379, 447 (Loire); Dauzat, *Village*, p. 147 (Beauce).

7. Van Gennep, *Manuel*, 1: 119. In Morvan, characteristically, churching continued until 1911. On couvades, see Fage, *Autour du mariage*, p. 18; Thuillier, "Pour une histoire," p. 255; Jalby, p. 18; and P. Cuzacq, *La Naissance, le mariage et le décès* (1902), p. 17.

8. Haudricourt and Delamarre, p. 450; VA, Moisson (Moselle, Somme, Pas-de-Calais).

9. Wylie, *Village*, p. 224.

10. Buffet, *Haute-Bretagne*, pp. 119–26.

11. VA, Moisson (especially Boulonnais, Aisne, Hte.-Loire).

12. Guillaumin, *Paysans*, p. 217; P. Mayer, p. 11; Hamp, *France*, p. 29; Jules Renard, *Philippe*, pp. 25–26. See also Thuillier, "Pour une histoire," very suggestive, like everything he writes.

13. Lefournier, p. 887.

14. VA, Moisson (Forez).

15. On conscripts, see Van Gennep, *Manuel*, 1: 213–23; Jeanton, *Mâconnais*, pp. 20–23; and Jeanton, *Travaux du Premier Congrès International de Folklore*, Paris, 1937 (Tours, 1938), pp. 245–47.

16. Fortier-Beaulieu, pp. 143–44, 175, 213, 231, 264, 313, 345; Fortier-Beaulieu, *Mariages et noces campagnardes dans les pays ayant formé le département de la Loire* (1945), pp. 40–43; Van Gennep, *Manuel*, 1: 221.

17. *La Feuille de Provins*, Jan. 30, 1891.

18. On the revelatory role of social catastrophes, see Maurice Halbwachs, *Les Cadres sociaux de la mémoire* (1952 ed.), chap. 7: "Les Classes sociales et leurs traditions." On wars, see Varagnac, pp. 59–63.

19. Morin, p. 50; Fortier-Beaulieu, especially p. 82; Garneret, p. 346.

20. Jeanton, *Légende*, p. 88; Pourrat, p. 189; Collot, p. 4.

21. EA, Marne; VA, St.-Jean / Moisson. Under the Empire the bonfire celebrations had been transferred from St. John's Eve to the Emperor's feast on Aug. 15, which must have contributed to their total disappearance.

22. Fortier-Beaulieu, p. 10; Guillemot, p. 22; Varagnac, p. 63; VA, Moisson; Abbé Jean Garneret, *L'Amour des gens* (1972), p. 253.

23. Bozon, *Vie rurale*, p. 465; Fortier-Beaulieu; VA, Moisson / St.-Jean; personal communication from Mme. Hubert (Marne). See also Edeine, 2: 824.

24. VA, Moisson; Roubin, pp. 115, 174–77; Garneret, *Village comtois*, p. 306.

25. J. H. Ricard, "La Vie paysanne d'août 1914 à octobre 1915," *Revue politique et parlementaire*, Dec. 1915, pp. 364–65; Maria Craipeau and Louis Lengrand, *Louis Lengrand, mineur du Nord* (1974), extracts in *L'Express*, May 20–26, 1974, p. 176.

26. Jeane Lhomme, *Economie et histoire* (Geneva, 1967), pp. 96–97; Augé-Laribé, *Politique*, p. 124.

27. Pasquet, p. 13.

28. Morin, p. 133 (see also pp. 45–49, 135); Thabault, *Mon village*, pp. 200–201.

29. Matoré, pp. 51, 88–90; Guilcher, *Contredanse*, p. 199; Nisard, *Histoire*, 1: 248; Gérard de Nerval, *Contes et légendes du Valois*, cited in Mandrou, p. 169.

30. Lefebvre, *Vallée*, p. 214.

31. Perron, *Broye-les-Pesmes*, pp. 54, 55; Michel Chevalier, p. 213. See also Leroi-Gourhan, *Milieu*, p. 457.

32. Ricard, p. 66; J.-A. Delpon, 1: 203.

33. Both quotations in this paragraph are from Michel Chevalier, pp. 689ff.

34. Romieu, p. 19. See Maurice Le Lannou, *Géographie de la Bretagne* (Rennes, 1952), 2: 200: "La trop célèbre routine du paysan de chez nous est moins une passivité de l'esprit et des énergies qu'un esclavage imposé par le manque d'argent."

35. Marcilhacy, "Emile Zola," pp. 578, 581.

36. Neufbourg, p. 9; Garavel, pp. 3, 8, 62; Daniel Faucher in *Journal de psychologie normale et pathologique*, 1948, p. 98.

37. EA, Lot. Compare Cuisenier, pp. 96–98; and Fanon, pp. 180–81: "Le contact du peuple avec la geste nouvelle suscite un nouveau rythme respiratoire."

38. Romieu, p. 111. "Of all progressive agricultural innovations, the suppression of fallow is the one most forcibly rejected by our farmers," wrote Mme. Romieu in 1865. Why? It was not laziness, but simply that "the peasant clings to the idea that ... everyone needs repose, beasts and people; why should the land be different from all the rest?"

39. Guillaumin, *Appui de la manche*, p. 75; Donatien Laurent, "Le Gwerz de Louis Le Ravallac," *Arts et traditions populaires*, 1967, p. 33.

40. Esnault, *Imagination*, p. 144; Gorse, pp. 259–60.

41. EA, Indre, no. 324. See also Ricard, p. 64.

42. Francus, *Midi de l'Ardèche*, p. 239; Chaumeil, p. 145; Marouzeau, p. 73; Perron, *Franc-Comtois*, p. 79.

43. See Gilbert Simondon, *Du mode d'existence des objets techniques* (1958), especially pp. 114–15.

44. EA, Aveyron. On the peasants' refusal to recognize concepts like profit and loss, or to keep accounts, and the deliberate avoidance of economic issues in order to live day by day, see *L'Aubrac*, 1: 267–74.

45. "When [the peasants] work solely for self-consumption," reported a priest from Savoy, "they feel as if they are destroying themselves, as if they are useless, as if they cannot make ends meet" (quoted in Maître, p. 23).

Chapter Twenty-nine

Epigraph. Roux, *Pensées*, p. 154; Fanon, *Les Damnés de la terre*, p. 35.

1. Compare Sicard, p. 26, talking of sociopolitical entities born of decolonization: "On se retrouve toujours en face d'un ensemble territorial élaboré de l'extérieur au gré des conquêtes, des décisions administratives ou politiques."

2. Marcel Mauss, notes of 1919–20, published posthumously as "La Nation," *L'Année sociologique*, 3d ser., 1953–54, pp. 7–68; Karl Deutsch, *Nationalism and Its Alternatives* (New York, 1969), p. 7.

3. The definition of society is from Ralph Linton, *The Science of Man in the World Crisis* (New York, 1945), p. 79. The rest of the quotes are from Deutsch, *Nationalism and Social Communication*, pp. 61, 70–71, 75.

4. Georges Valérie, *Notes sur le nationalisme français* (1901), p. 7.

5. Leproux, MATP manuscript 43.115.

6. Pariset, *Lauragais*, pp. 9–10. See also Souvestre, *Derniers Bretons* (1854 ed.), 2: 7.

7. R. Brunet in Wolff, p. 511; *Le Figaro*, June 19, 1907. See also Wolff himself, p. 7; and Jacques Ellul, *Métamorphose du bourgeois* (1967), p. 45, referring to "le Languedoc conquis à qui est imposé par le pouvoir le nom de France."

8. See Audiganne, *Populations*, 2: especially pp. 210, 258, on the picturesque naïveté of the Provençal; the primitive customs of Mazamet; the unique rudeness of the inhabitants of the Montagne Noire. Patrick Dumont, *La Petite Bourgeoisie vue à travers les contes quotidiens du Journal (1894–1895)* (1973), p. 71, remarks that the rural parts of France are presented as "des amériques peuplées de demi-civilisés."

9. See Charles de Ribbe, *La Provence au point de vue des bois . . .* (1875), p. 136; and de Ribbe, *Des incendies des forêts* (1865), p. 25. Even friendly observers thought of the simile. Thus, a Parisian lawyer who had befriended a group of Provençal shepherds could bring them to go on singing, because it made him feel as if he were "in some African caravan, among the Arabs" (Batisto Bonnet, p. 209).

10. Van Gennep, *Folklore de Flandre*, 1: especially p. 22 (quotations from the official survey of 1852); Arthur Dinaux, "Sobriquets de villages," *Archives du Nord de la France*, 1: 271. See also AG, MR 1218 (Hérault, 1825), MR 2281 (Loire, 1862); and Bourdieu and Sayad, p. 38.

11. Mayors of canton Quérigut (1843) and the official reports of 1850, 1859, quoted in Michel Chevalier, pp. 723–26; L. Gaillard, *Montagnes de Massat* (Toulouse, 1900), quoted in *ibid.*, p. 720.

12. AN, F⁷12849 (préf., Dec. 23, 1872; proc. gén. Bastia, May 18, 1874), F⁷12850 (1902, 1907, 1917); AG G⁸, correspondance générale, Corsica.

13. Ricard, p. 11, who also quotes Baron d'Haussez, *Etudes administratives sur les Landes* (Bordeaux, 1826), and Vicomte d'Yzarn Freissinet, *Coup d'oeil sur les Landes de Gascogne* (1837); Michelet in chap. 6 of the 17th century of his *Histoire de France*; AG, MR 1231 (Gironde, 1839); AN, F¹⁰2342 (Landes de Gascogne, May 1861).

14. Honoré de Balzac, *Le Curé de village* (1837), chap. 3. Compare Sicard, p. 53: the reconciliation of the legal structure with the ethnocultural whole that surrounds and supports it remains the great problem of nation-building.

15. Ardouin-Dumazet, 30: 34–35, 55, 120–22; Ricard, p. 80.

16. Lovie, pp. 378–79; *RDM*, June 1, 1864, pp. 631–32.

17. Perrin and Bouet, p. 267; V. Brenac, "Etude sur les conditions de travail agricole dans les parties montagneuses des trois départements de la Haute-Vienne, de la Creuse et de la Corrèze," *L'Agriculteur du Centre*, 1866; Gorse in *Revue du Limousin*, 1862, p. 297. Wolkowitch, p. 72, suggests that the appeal was heard. According to him, the lines—actually the secondary lines—built in the Massif Central express "the will of the masters of [France's national] economy to affirm a unified national market," suggestively contemporary to "their will of colonial expansion." Compare Fanon, p. 120: "The economy of the colony is always in complementary relationship to that [of the metropolis]."

18. Ardouin-Dumazet, 1: 98–99, 121.

19. "A new colony, most of whose inhabitants come from distant provinces," wrote the Minister of Marine in 1724; "a colony settled by seafaring people," wrote the Maritime Prefect to the First Consul in 1800; "a maritime colony, not a Breton town," echoed Emile Souvestre in 1841; "a maritime colony" peopled by "outsiders," noted a French traveler in 1859. See Le Gallo, 1: 37–39, 88–89; Souvestre, *Mémoires d'un sans-culotte Bas-Breton* (1841), 1: 304; and Ed. Valin, *Voyage en Bretagne-Finistère* (1859), p. 148.

20. *Revue pédagogique*, Mar. 15, 1888, Apr. 15, 1891, Feb. 15, 1894, Mar. 15, 1894.

21. Chombart de Lauwe, p. 115. See also Jean Meyer in Delumeau, pp. 420–21.

22. Le Mercier d'Erm, pp. 23–32; Louis Hémon, *Pour la langue bretonne* (Quimper, 1903), p. 2.

23. Fanon, pp. 72, 158, 177 (and 69), 33, 158 (and 40), 106, 116 (and 164).

24. *Ibid.*, p. 178.

25. See Cuisenier's very sensible remarks on this, especially p. 5.

26. Vincent, p. 141, around 1914, about Berry: "Si le paysan a conservé quelques anciennes coutumes, au point de vue de la nourriture son régime a complètement changé: la viande, le vin, le café, le sucre et les *douceurs* de toutes sortes, sont devenues les conditions ordinaires, et je dirais presque nécessaires, de son alimentation." The sea-change is immense!

27. Angeville, p. 16; and Le Roy Ladurie, introduction.

28. He said it about religion. See Keith Thomas, *Religion and the Decline of Magic* (London, 1973), p. 798.

BIBLIOGRAPHY

BIBLIOGRAPHY

Unless otherwise noted, the works listed below were published in Paris.

Achard, A. "Jumeaux et la batellerie de l'Allier," *Revue d'Auvergne*, 1917–21.

Aguilhon, J. J. Hyppolite. *Recherches sur les causes d'insalubrité de la commune de Saint-Ours.* 1856.

Agulhon, Maurice. *1848 ou l'apprentissage de la République.* 1973.

———. *La République au village.* 1970.

———. *La Vie sociale en Provence intérieure au lendemain de la Révolution.* 1970.

———. *Une Ville ouvrière au temps du Socialisme utopique: Toulon de 1815 à 1851.* 1970.

Ajalbert, Jean. *En Auvergne.* 1893.

———. *Mémoires en vrac: Au temps du symbolisme.* 1938.

Allary, L.-J. *Moulins depuis 50 ans, 1838–48.* Moulins, 1889.

———. *Moulins il y a 50 ans, 1831–36.* Moulins, 1886.

Allaux, Doctor. *Considérations hygiéniques sur la ville de Pamiers.* Pamiers, 1866.

Allix, André. "Les Foires," *La Géographie*, 1923.

Amussat, J.-Z. *Quelques considérations sur l'hygiène du peuple des campagnes.* 1849.

Angeville, Adolphe d'. *Essai sur la statistique de la population française.* 1836. Reprinted with an introduction by E. Le Roy Ladurie, 1969.

Anglade, Jean. *La Vie quotidienne dans le Massif Central au XIXe siècle.* 1971.

Anthony, R. "La Monnaie de compte en Bretagne," *Bulletin de la Société Archéologique du Finistère*, 1940.

Arbos, Philippe. "Evolution démographique et économique d'un village des Pyrénées méditerranéennes," in *Mélanges . . . Bénévent*, cited below.

Ardouin-Dumazet. *Voyage en France.* 54 vols. 1889–1910.

Ariès, Philippe. "Attitudes devant la vie et devant la mort du XVIIe au XIXe siècle," *Population*, 1949.

———. *Histoire des populations françaises.* 1948 and 1971 eds.

Armengaud, André. "Les Débuts de la dépopulation dans les campagnes toulousaines," *Annales: Economies, sociétés, civilisations*, 1951.

——. "La Fin des forges catalanes dans les Pyrénées ariégeoises," *Annales: Economies, sociétés, civilisations*, 1953.

——. *Les Populations de l'est-Aquitain au début de l'époque contemporaine, 1845–1871.* 1951.

Arnaud, F. *L'Instruction publique à Barcelonnette.* Digne, 1894.

Assier, Adolphe d'. *Aulus-les-Bains et ses environs.* 2d ed., Toulouse, 1873. 3d ed., Foix, 1884.

L'Aubrac: Etude ethnologique, linguistique, agronomique et économique d'un établissement humain. Centre national de la recherche scientifique. 4 vols. to date. 1970–73.

Audiganne, Armand. "Le Jura industriel," *Revue des deux mondes*, June 15, 1864.

——. "Le Métayage et la culture dans le Périgord," *Revue des deux mondes*, June 1, 1867.

——. *La Morale dans les campagnes.* 1869. Includes much of the material in the two articles cited above.

——. *Les Populations ouvrières et les industries de la France.* 2 vols. 1854–60.

——. *La Région du bas de la Loire.* 1869.

——. *Le Travail et les ouvriers sous la Troisième République.* 1873.

Augé-Laribé, Michel. *La Politique agricole de la France de 1880 à 1940.* 1950.

——. *Répertoire bibliographique d'économie rurale.* Montpellier, 1953.

Bachelin, Henri. *Le Serviteur.* 1918.

——. *Le Village.* 1919.

Baillet, Eugène. *De quelques ouvriers poètes.* 1898.

Bailly, Paul. "Aperçu sur les vins, vignes et vignerons de la région de Meaux," *Bulletin de la Société Littéraire et Historique de la Brie*, 1954. Based on the record book of a vineyardist who died in 1874.

Balandier, Georges. *Sens et puissance.* 1971.

——. *Sociologie des mutations.* 1970.

Bally, Charles. *Le Langage et la vie.* 1926.

Banfield, Edward C. *The Moral Basis of a Backward Society.* New York, 1967.

Baratier, Edouard, ed. *Histoire de la Provence.* Toulouse, 1969.

Barbizier. Annual almanac of Franc-Comtois lore, published by Abbé Jean Garneret of Lantenne (Doubs). 1950 vol.

Bardoux, M. "Des caractères et des moeurs des paysans au Bourbonnais," *Bulletin de la Société d'Emulation du Département de l'Allier*, May 1852.

Barker, Edward Harrison. *Summers in Guyenne.* London, 1894.

——. *Wandering by Southern Waters.* London, 1893.

——. *Wayfaring in France.* London, 1890.

Barral, J. A. *L'Agriculture de la Haute-Vienne.* 1884.

——. *L'Agriculture du Nord de la France.* 2 vols. 1867–70.

——. *Situation actuelle de l'agriculture en France.* 1866.

Barral, Pierre. *Les Agrariens français, de Méline à Pisani.* 1968.

——. *Le Département de l'Isère sous la Troisième République, 1870–1940.* 1962.

Barrès, Maurice. *L'Oeuvre de Maurice Barrès.* 20 vols. 1965–68.

Bastié, Maurice. *Description complète du département du Tarn.* 2 vols. Albi, 1875.

Baudiau, J. F. *Le Morvand.* Vol. 1. Nevers, 1865.

Baudrillart, Henri. *Les Populations agricoles de la France.* Vol. 1: *Normandie et*

Bretagne. 1885. Vol. 2: *Maine, Anjou,*... 1888. Vol. 3: *Populations du Midi*. 1893.

Beauquier, Charles. *Traditions populaires: Les Mois en Franche-Comté*. 1900.

Belbèze, Raymond. *La Neurasthénie rurale*. 1911.

Benda, Julien. *Esquisse d'une histoire des français dans leur volonté d'être une nation*. 1932.

Bénévent, Ernest. "La Vieille Economie provençale," *Revue de géographie alpine*, 1938.

Bénichou, Paul. *Nerval et la chanson folklorique*. 1970.

Bennassar, Bartolomé, and Joseph Goy. "Contribution à l'histoire de la consommation alimentaire," *Annales: Economies, sociétés, civilisations*, 1975.

Benoît, Fernand. *Histoire de l'outillage rural et artisanal*. 1947.

———. *La Provence et le Comtat Venaissin*. 1949.

Benoît, Fernand, and Sylvain Gagnière. *Pour une histoire de l'ex-voto*. N.d. [1950?]

Benoît, Joseph. *Confessions d'un prolétaire*. 1968. Originally published Lyon, 1871.

Bérenger-Féraud. *Réminiscences populaires sur la Provence*. 1885.

———. *Superstitions et survivances*. 2 vols. 1896.

Berger, Ida, ed. *Lettres d'institutrices rurales d'autrefois*. N.d.

Bernard, Léopold. *Les Idées révolutionnaires dans les campagnes du Bourbonnais*. Montluçon, 1911.

Bernot, L., and R. Blancard. *Nouville, un village français*. 1952.

Bertaut, Jules. *Ce qu'était la province française avant la guerre*. 1918.

Berthout, P. C. "Le Clergé français et le peuple à la fin du 19e siècle," *Revue du clergé français*, March 1 and March 15, 1899.

Bertrand, Alexandre. *Nos origines: La Religion des Gaulois*. 1897.

Beslay, François [Un Conservateur]. *Voyage aux pays rouges*. 1873.

Besson, Pierre. *Un Pâtre du Cantal*. 1914. The copy in Archives Départementales, Cantal, interleaved and heavily annotated by the author during the years 1940–44.

Béteille, Roger. *La Vie quotidienne en Rouergue avant 1914*. 1973.

Betham-Edwards, Margaret. *Anglo-French Reminiscences*. London, 1900.

———. *France of Today*. 2 vols. London, 1892–94.

Beulaygue, Paul. *L'Enseignement du français à l'école rurale*. Foix, 1897.

Bigo, Robert. *Les Banques françaises au cours du XIXe siècle*. 1947.

Birou, Alain. "Connaître une population rurale," *Economie et humanisme*, supplement July–Dec. 1957. An introduction to rural surveys and sociology.

Bladé, Jean-François. *Proverbes et devinettes populaires recueillis dans l'Armagnac et l'Agenais*. 1879.

Blanchard, Marcel. *Essais historiques sur les premiers chemins de fer du Midi languedocien*. Montpellier, 1935.

Blanchon, Jean-Louis. *En Cerdagne: Les Ecoles de la Belle époque*. Palau, 1973.

———. *Vie de l'ancienne vallée d'Osséja*. Toulouse, 1973.

Blanqui, Adolphe. *Du déboisement des montagnes*. 1848.

———. "Tableau des populations rurales en France en 1850," *Journal des économistes*, 28 (1851) and 30 (1851).

Bloch, Oscar. *La Pénétration du français dans les parlers des Vosges méridionales*. 1921.

Bodard, Lucien. *Plaisirs de l'hexagone.* 1971.

Bodley, J. E. C. *Cardinal Manning and Other Essays.* London, 1912.

———. *The Church in France.* London, 1906.

———. *France.* 2 vols. London, 1898.

Bogros, Edmond. *A travers le Morvan.* Château-Chinon, 1883.

Boillot, Félix. *Le Français régional de la Grand'Combe (Doubs).* 1929.

———. *Traditions populaires de Franche-Comté.* Hamburg, 1910.

Bois, Paul. "Dans l'Ouest: Politique et enseignement primaire," *Annales: Economies, sociétés, civilisations,* 1954.

———. *Paysans de l'Ouest.* 1960 ed. and abridged ed., 1971.

Boissier, Albert. "Essai sur l'histoire et l'industrie du clou forgé dans la région de Firminy," *Revue de folklore français,* 1941.

Bollème, Geneviève. *Les Almanacs populaires au XVIIe et XVIIIe siècle.* 1969.

———. *La Bibliothèque bleue.* 1971.

Bombal, Eusèbe. "La Haute Dordogne et ses gabariers," *Bulletin de la Société des Lettres de la Corrèze,* 1901.

Bonassies, Jules. *Les Spectacles forains et la Comédie française.* 1875.

Bonheur, Gaston. *Qui a cassé le vase de Soissons?* 1963.

———. *La République nous appelle.* 1965.

Bonnamour, Jacqueline. *Le Morvan: La Terre et les hommes.* 1966.

Bonneff, Léon, and Maurice Bonneff. *La Classe ouvrière.* 1912.

———. *Marchands de folie.* 1913.

———. *Les Métiers qui tuent.* 1900.

———. *La Vie tragique des travailleurs.* N.d. [1908?]

Bonnemère, Eugène. *Histoire des paysans.* 2 vols. 1856. Vol. 2 concerns the 19th century.

Bonnet, Batisto. *Vido d'enfant.* 1968.

Bonnet, René. *A l'école de la vie.* Nemours, 1945.

———. *Enfance limousine.* 1954.

Bonnet, Serge. *La Communion solennelle.* 1969.

———. *Sociologie politique et religieuse de la Lorraine.* 1972.

Bonnet, Serge, and Charles Santini. "Les Sauvages de Futeau: Verriers et bucherons d'Argonne au 18e et 19e siècles," *Mouvement social,* 1966.

Bordes, Paul. *De l'influence du chant choral sur les populations rurales.* Foix, 1860.

Borrel, Antoine. *Les Villages qui meurent.* 1932.

Borsendorff, Louis-André. *De l'instruction du pauvre: Tablettes d'un horloger.* 1884.

Boscary, Gabriel. *Evolution agricole et condition des cultivateurs de l'Aveyron pendant le XIXe siècle.* Montpellier, 1909.

Bouchard, Gérard. *Le Village immobile: Sennely-en-Sologne au XVIIIe siècle.* 1972.

Bouchey, Abbé Eugène. *Le Charbonnier dans les bois.* Besançon, 1969. Memoirs of the son of a charcoal-burner who had himself worked at the trade; written in 1874.

Boudard, René. "L'Enseignement primaire clandestin dans le département de la Creuse entre 1830 et 1880," *Mémoires de la Société des Sciences Naturelles et Archéologiques de la Creuse,* vol. 33.

Bougeatre, Eugène. *La Vie rurale dans le Mantois et le Vexin au XIXe siècle.* Meulan, 1971.

Bouillon, Jacques. "Les Démocrates socialistes aux élections de 1849," *Revue française de science politique,* 1956.

Boulard, Fernand. *Premiers itinéraires en sociologie religieuse.* 1954.

Bourdieu, Pierre. "Célibat et condition paysanne," *Etudes rurales,* 1962.

Bourdieu, Pierre, and M. C. Bourdieu. "Le Paysan et la photographie," *Revue française de sociologie,* 1965.

Bourdieu, Pierre, and Abdelmalek Sayad. *Le Déracinement.* 1964.

Bourgoing, Adolphe de. "Mémoire en faveur des travailleurs et indigents de la classe agricole des communes rurales de France, présenté aux Chambres et au pays par M. A. de Bourgoing, président du Comice agricole de l'arrondissement de Cosne" (Nevers, 1844), in Guy Thuillier, *Economie et société nivernaises au début du XIXe siècle.* 1974.

Bouteiller, Marcelle. *Médecine populaire d'hier et d'aujourd'hui.* 1966.

——. *Sorciers et jeteurs de sort.* 1958.

Bozon, Pierre. *Histoire du peuple vivarois.* Valence, 1966.

——. "L'Industrie du Seuil de Rives," *Revue de géographie alpine,* 1943.

——. *La Vie rurale en Vivarais.* 1961.

Braibant, Marcel. *Les Paysans d'aujourd'hui.* 1939. An anthology.

Brekilien, Yann. *Vie quotidienne des paysans en Bretagne au XIXe siècle.* 1966.

Brochon, Pierre. *La Chanson française.* 3 vols. 1956 and after.

——. *La Chanson sociale de Béranger à Brassens.* 1961.

——. *Le Livre de colportage en France depuis le XVIe siècle.* 1954.

Brugerette, J. *Le Prêtre français et la société contemporaine.* 3 vols. 1933–38.

Brun, Auguste. *Le Français de Marseille: Etude de parler régional.* Marseille, 1931.

——. *L'Introduction de la langue française en Béarn et en Roussillon.* 1923.

——. *La Langue française en Provence de Louis XIV au Félibrige.* Marseille, 1927.

——. *Parlers régionaux.* 1946.

——. *Recherches historiques sur l'introduction du français dans les provinces du Midi.* 1923.

Brun, Clément. *Trois plumes au chapeau.* Grenoble, 1950.

Brunet, Frantz. *Dictionnaire du parler bourbonnais.* 1964.

Brunet, Roger. "Les Campagnes commingeoises à la fin du 19e siècle," *Annales du Midi,* 1958.

Bruno, G. (Mme Alfred Fouillée). *Francinet: Principes généraux de la morale, de l'industrie, du commerce et de l'agriculture.* 1869.

——. *Le Tour de France par deux enfants.* 1877.

Brunot, Ferdinand. *Histoire de la langue française des origines à 1900.* Vols. 9 (1927) and 10 (1937).

Budin, Emile. *Mon village: Monographie de Ivry-en-Montagne.* Dijon, 1965.

Buffet, Henri-François. *En Bretagne morbihannaise.* 1947.

——. *En Haute-Bretagne.* 1954.

Buisson, Ferdinand, ed. *Dictionnaire de pédagogie et d'instruction primaire.* 3 vols. 1882–93.

Bunle, H. "Relation entre les variations des indices économiques et le mouvement des mariages," *Journal de la Société de Statistique de Paris*, 1911.

Burguière, André. *Bretons de Plozévet*. 1975.

Cambry, Jacques. *Voyage dans le Finistère*. Brest, 1835.

Camescasse, Madame. *Souvenirs: Douai au XIXe siècle*. 1924.

Camp, Maxime du. "Trois mois en Bretagne avec Flaubert," *Nouvelle revue de Bretagne*, 1947.

Capot-Rey, Robert. *Géographie de la circulation sur les continents*. 1946.

Caralp-Landon, R. *Les Chemins de fer dans le Massif Central*. 1959.

Carron, Marie-Antoinette. *L'Evolution économique d'une commune rurale au 19e et 20e siècle: Sainte-Feyre, Creuse*. 1954.

Castan, Yves. *Honnêteté et relations sociales en Languedoc, 1715–1780*. 1974.

Cavaillès, Henri. *La Route française*. 1946.

Cavoleau, J.-A. *Statistique ou description générale du département de la Vendée*. 1844.

Cénac-Moncaut, J.-E.-M. *Le Colporteur des Pyrénées*. 1866.

———. *Du conte populaire en Gascogne*. 1860.

———. *Jérôme Lafriche, ou le paysan gentilhomme*. 1859.

———. *Littérature populaire de la Gascogne*. 1868.

Chabirand, Raymond. *Amanlis: Histoire d'une paroisse rurale*. Rennes, 1968.

Chaix, B. *Préoccupations statistiques, géographiques, pittoresques, et synoptiques du département des Hautes-Alpes*. Grenoble, 1845.

Challaye, Félicien. *La France vue de Laval*. 1904.

Charrié, Pierre. *Le Folklore du Bas-Vivarais*. N.d. [1964?]

———. *Le Folklore du Haut-Vivarais*. 1968.

Chataigneau, Yves. "L'Emigration vendéenne," *Annales de géographie*, 1917. Based on the author's personal survey of 1913.

Chatelain, Abel. "Les Migrants temporaires et la propagation des idées révolution-naires en France au 19e siècle," *1848. Revue des révolutions contemporaines*, 1951.

———. "Les Migrations temporaires françaises au XIXe siècle," *Annales de Démographie historique* (1967), 1968.

———. "Problèmes de méthodes: Les Migrations de la population," *Revue économique*, 1963.

Chaumeil, Louis. "Travaux et jours d'un paysan auvergnat," *Annales de géographie*, 1939.

Chevalier, Elisa. *Guide pittoresque de la Nièvre*. 1857.

Chevalier, Louis. *Classes laborieuses et classes dangereuses*. 1958.

———. *La Formation de la population parisienne au XIXe siècle*. 1950.

———. *Les Paysans*. 1947.

Chevalier, Michel. *La Vie humaine dans les Pyrénées ariégeoises*. 1956.

Cholvy, Gérard. *Géographie religieuse de l'Hérault contemporain*. 1968.

Chombart de Lauwe, Jean. *Bretagne et pays de la Garonne: Evolution agricole comparée depuis un siècle*. 1946.

Christian, William A. *Person and God in a Spanish Valley*. New York, 1972.

Cinq siècles d'imagerie française. Archives of the Musée des Arts et Traditions Populaires, 1973.

Clément, Henry. "Etudes marchoises: L'Emigration," *Réforme sociale*, 1886.

Clough, Shepard B. *A History of the Flemish Movement in Belgium*. New York, 1930.

Cobb, Richard. *The Police and the People: French Popular Protest, 1789–1820*. London, 1970.

——. *Reactions to the French Revolution*. London, 1972.

Coissac, G.-Michel. *Mon Limousin*. 1913.

Colin, Elicio. "L'Evolution de l'économie rurale au pays de Porcay de 1815 à 1930," *Bulletin de la Société Archéologique du Finistère*, 1947.

Collot, Augustin. *De quelques anciennes traditions relatives au culte de Sainte-Reine en Côte-d'Or*. Dijon, 1949.

Combe, Paul. *Niveau de vie et progrès technique en France, 1860–1939*. 1956.

Combes, Anacharsis, and Hippolyte Combes. *Les Paysans français sous le rapport historique, économique, agricole, médical et administratif*. 1853.

Comminges, Comte de. *Souvenirs d'enfance et de régiment, 1831–1870-71*. 1910.

Congrès provincial de la Société Bibliographique et des Publications Populaires. 1890–1900.

Considère, A. "Utilité des chemins de fer d'intérêt local," *Annales des ponts et chaussées* (Mémoires et documents), 7th ser., 3 (1892), and 7 (1894).

Coornaert, Emile. *La Flandre française de langue flamande*. 1970.

Corbin, Alain. "Limousins migrants et Limousins sédentaires: Contribution à l'histoire de la région limousine au XIXe siècle (vers 1845–vers 1880)," Thèse de Doctorat d'Etat, University of Paris, 1973. A revised version of this work has been published under the title *Archaïsme et modernité en Limousin au XIXe siècle, 1845–1880*. 2 vols. 1975. My references are to the original dissertation.

Cordier, Claude. "La Vie en Bresse autrefois," *Visages de l'Ain*, July 1961.

Costérisant, O. *La Vie rurale fin de siècle dans la région de Brioude*. Clermont, 1945.

Côte, Léon. *En montagne bourbonnaise*. Saint-Etienne, 1958.

Cousteix, Pierre. "Le Mouvement ouvrier limousin de 1870 à 1939," *L'Actualité de l'histoire*, Dec. 1957.

Cressot, Joseph. *Le Pain au lièvre*. 1943.

Crubellier, Maurice. *Histoire culturelle de la France, XIXe–XXe siècle*. 1974.

Cuisenier, Jean. *L'Ansarine*. 1960.

Dainville, François de. "Taudis ruraux et psychologie paysanne," *Etudes*, Nov. 1945.

Daniel, Tanguy. "Pardons et pèlerinages: Diocèse de Quimper et Léon." Manuscript survey. Unpublished manuscript, 1968.

Darmon, Jean-Jacques. *Le Colportage de librairie en France sous le Second Empire*. 1972.

Darnaud, Firmin. *De l'instruction primaire: Appel aux Ariégeois par un maire de village*. Foix, 1866.

Daugé, Abbé C. *Le Mariage et la famille en Gascogne d'après les proverbes et les chansons*. 1916.

Dauzat, Albert. *Les Argots de métiers franco-provençaux*. 1917.

——. "Le Breton et le Français," *La Nature*, 1926.

——. *La Défense de la langue française*. 1912.

——. "Le Déplacement des frontières linguistiques du français de 1806 à nos jours," *La Nature*, 1927.

——. *Essais de géographie linguistique, nouvelle série*. 1938.

——. *Glossaire étymologique du patois de Vinzelles*. Montpellier, 1915.

——. *Les Patois*. 1927.

——. *Le Village et le paysan de France*. 1941.

David, Paul. *La Commune rurale*. Toulouse, 1863.

Davidovitch, André. "Criminalité et repression en France depuis un siècle (1851–1952)," *Revue française de sociologie*, 1961.

Decoux-Lagoutte, Edouard. *Canton de Treignac: Un Coin du Limousin en 1888*. Tulle, 1889.

Deffontaines, Pierre. *L'Homme et la forêt*. 1933.

——. *Les Hommes et leurs travaux dans les pays de la Moyenne-Garonne (Agenais, Bas Quercy)*. Lille, 1932.

Deghilage, Pierre. *La Dépopulation des campagnes*. 1900.

——. *L'Education sociale à l'école*. Montdidier, 1906.

Degrully, Paul. *Le Droit de glanage, grapillage, ratelage, chaumage et sarclage: Patrimoine des pauvres*. 1912.

Delacroix, Henri. *Le Langage et la pensée*. 2d ed. 1930.

Delafosse, Marcel, and Claude Laveau, "L'Evolution des marais salants dans l'Ouest de la France au 19e siècle," in Michel Mollat, ed., *Le Rôle du sel dans l'histoire*. 1968.

Delarue, Paul, and Marie-Louise Ténèze. *Le Conte populaire français*. 2 vols. 1957–64.

Delefortrie, Nicolas, and Janine Morice. *Les Revenus départementaux en 1864 et en 1954*. 1959.

Delpon, Gustave. *Clermont* [Hérault] *au XIXe siècle*. Lodève, 1878.

Delpon, J.-A. *Statistique du département du Lot*. 2 vols. 1831.

Delumeau, Jean, ed. *Histoire de la Bretagne*. Toulouse, 1969.

Demolins, Edmond. *Comment élever et établir nos enfants*. 1893.

——. *A quoi tient la supériorité des Anglo-Saxons?* 1897.

Demolins, Edmond, et al. *Les Populations forestières du centre de la France*. 1907.

Dergny, Dieudonné. *Images, coutumes et croyances, ou livre des choses curieuses*. 2 vols. 1971. Originally published Brionne, 1885–88.

Déribier Du Châtelet. *Dictionnaire statistique du département du Cantal*. 2 vols. Aurillac, 1852–53.

Derruau-Borniol, S. "Le Département de la Creuse: Structure sociale et évolution politique," *Revue française de science politique*, 1957.

Desforges, A. *La Vie dans un coin du Morvan*. Nevers, 1911.

Desormaux, J. "Enquête sur les parlers savoyards," *Revue savoisienne*, 1911.

Desprès, Armand. *La Prostitution en France*. 1883.

Deutsch, Karl. *Nationalism and Social Communication: An Inquiry into the Foundations of Nationality*. New York, 1953. Paperback, Cambridge, Mass., 1966.

Dévigne, Roger. *Le Légendaire de France*. 1942.

Devoirs d'écoliers français recueillis à l'exposition universelle de Paris, 1878. 1881.

Dieudonné, Christophe. *Statistique du département du Nord*. 3 vols. Douai, 1804.

Dollinger, Philippe, ed. *Histoire de l'Alsace*. Toulouse, 1970.

Doniol, Henry. *La Basse-Auvergne*. 1900. Originally published on the eve of the Revolution of 1848.

———. *Les Patois de la Basse-Auvergne*. Montpellier, 1877.

Donnadieu, S. "Proverbes recueillis en Tarn-et-Garonne." Archives of the Musée des Arts et Traditions Populaires, manuscript 49–70.

Donnedevie, Ch.-Bernard. *Histoire de la Commune de Ligardes*. Agen, 1926.

Doussinet, Raymond. *Le Paysan santongeais dans ses bots*. La Rochelle, 1963.

———. *Les Travaux et les jeux en vieille Saintonge*. La Rochelle, 1967.

Drouart, Marie. *L'Etat actuel du folklore en Haute-Bretagne*. Vitré, 1938.

Drouillet, Jean. *Folklore du Nivernais et du Morvan*. 5 vols. La Charité-sur-Loire, 1959–65.

Dubief, F. *La Question du vagabondage*. 1911.

Dubois, Augustin. *Les Anciens Livres de colportage en Sologne*. Romorantin, 1938.

Dubreuil-Chambardel, Louis. "Des patois, des costumes, des feux, etc.: Les Effets de la disparition des coutumes locales," *Réforme sociale*, 1905.

Duchatellier, A. M. *De la condition du fermier et de l'ouvrier agricole en Bretagne*. 1849.

———. [A. Du Chatelier]. *L'Agriculture et les classes agricoles de la Bretagne*. 1863.

Duché, Emile. *Le Crime d'incendie*. 1913.

Duclos, Jacques. *Mémoires*. Vol 1: *1896–1934*. 1968.

Duine, F. *Un Village de France*. Rennes, 1903.

Dumont, Charles. *Une Semaine dans les Causses*. Lons-le-Saunier, 1894.

Dumont, Jean-Marie. *Les Maîtres graveurs populaires, 1800–1850*. Epinal, 1965.

Dumont, René. *Voyages en France d'un agronome*. 1956.

Duneton, Claude. *Parler croquant*. 1973.

Dupeux, Georges. *Histoire sociale et politique du Loir-et-Cher*. 1962.

Dupont, V. *Quand Eve filait*. Rodez, 1957.

Dupront, Alphonse. "Tourisme et pèlerinage," *Communications*, 1967.

Dupuy, Aymé. "Les Livres de lecture de G. Bruno," *Revue d'histoire économique et sociale*, 1953.

Durand, Alfred. *La Vie rurale dans les massifs volcaniques des Dores, du Cezallier, du Cantal et de l'Aubrac*. Aurillac, 1945.

Durand-Vangarou, L. "Le Loup en Bretagne, 1773–1872," *Annales de Bretagne*, 2 parts, 1963, 1964.

Durkheim, Emile. *Le Suicide*. 1912 and 1969 eds.

Dussourd, Henriette. *Moulins d'hier*. Moulins, 1967.

Edeine, Bernard. *La Sologne*. 2 vols. 1974.

Esnault, Gaston. *L'Imagination populaire. Métaphores occidentales: Essai sur les valeurs imaginatives concrètes du français parlé en Basse-Bretagne*. 1925.

———. *Le Poilu tel qu'il se parle*. 1919.

Fabre, Daniel, and Jacques Lacroix. *La Vie quotidienne des paysans du Languedoc au XIXe siècle*. 1973.

Fabre, L.-A. *Etudes économiques et sociologiques dans les Hautes-Montagnes françaises*. 1912–17. Bound volume in University of California, Los Angeles, Research Library.

Fage, René. *Autour de la mort.* Limoges, 1927.

———. *Autour du mariage.* Limoges, 1922.

———. *Fontaines à chiffons et saints à rubans.* Tulle, 1920.

Fagot, P. [Pierre Laroche]. *Folklore du Lauraguais.* Albi, 1891.

Fanon, Frantz. *Les Damnés de la terre.* 1961.

Faucher, Daniel. "De quelques incidences en France de la révolution agricole du XVIIIe–XIXe siècle," in *Mélanges ... Bénévent,* cited below.

Fauvet, Jacques, and Henri Mendras. *Les Paysans et la politique dans la France contemporaine.* 1958.

Fel, André. *Les Hautes Terres du Massif Central.* 1962.

Féraud, J.-J.-M. *Histoire, géographie et statistique du département des Basses-Alpes.* Digne, 1861.

Feret, Edouard. *Statistique générale du département de la Gironde.* Vol. 1. 1878.

Flandrin, Jean-Louis. *Les Amours paysannes.* 1975.

Flaubert, Gustave. "Par les champs et par les grèves," in *Oeuvres complètes,* vol. 1: *Voyages.* 1948.

Fleurent, Joseph. "L'Idée de patrie en Alsace," *Revue politique et parlementaire,* 1907.

Fleury, Michel, and Pierre Valmary. "Les Progrès de l'instruction élémentaire de Louis XIV à Napoléon III d'après l'enquête de Louis Maggiolo (1877–1879)," *Population,* 1957.

Florent, André. *Labruyère, village de France.* 1936.

Forestier, Henri. "Une Garçonnade à Vézelay en 1853," *Pays de Bourgogne,* 1954.

———. "La Loi du 18 Novembre 1814 sur l'observation des dimanches et fêtes," *Annales de Bourgogne,* 1956.

———. *L'Yonne au 19e siècle.* 4 vols. Auxerre, 1959–67.

Fortier-Beaulieu, Paul. "Corpus du folklore du mariage dans le département de la Loire (Rive gauche)." Varagnac archives, manuscript dated 1936–37.

Fourcade, Jacques. *La République de la Province.* 1936.

Fourcassié, J. "Une Industrie pyrénéenne défunte: La Mendicité," *Annales de la Fondation Pyrénéenne d'Economie Montagnarde,* 1940–44.

Foville, Alfred de. *Enquête sur les conditions de l'habitation en France.* 2 vols. 1894.

———. *La France économique: Statistique raisonnée et comparative.* Vol. 1: *1887.* 1887. Vol. 2: *1889.* 1890.

———. *La Transformation des moyens de transport et ses conséquences économiques et sociales.* 1880.

Fox, Edward W. *History in Geographical Perspective: The Other France.* New York, 1971.

Franchet, Claude. *Les Trois Demoiselles Colas.* 1946.

François, Michel, ed. *La France et les français.* 1972.

Francus, Doctor [A. Mazon]. *Voyage autour de Privas.* Privas, 1882.

———. *Voyage autour de Valgorge.* Privas, 1879.

———. *Voyage aux pays volcaniques du Vivarais.* Privas, 1878.

———. *Voyage dans le midi de l'Ardèche.* Privas, 1884.

———. *Voyage fantaisiste et sérieux à travers l'Ardèche et la Haute-Loire.* 2 vols. Le Puy, 1894–95.

———. *Voyage humoristique, politique et philosophique au Mont-Pilat.* Lyon, 1890.

———. *Voyage le long de la rivière d'Ardèche.* Privas, 1885.

Friedmann, Georges, ed. *Villes et campagnes.* 1953.

Furet, François, and Wladimir Sachs. "La Croissance de l'alphabétisation en France (XVIIIe–XIXe siècle)," *Annales: Economies, sociétés, civilisations,* 1974.

Fustier, Pierre. *La Route.* 1968.

Gachon, Lucien. *L'Auvergne et le Velay.* 1948.

———. *Une Commune rurale d'Auvergne du XVIIIe au XXe siècle: Brousse-Montboissier.* Clermont, 1939.

———. *Les Limagnes du Sud et leurs bordures montagneuses.* Tours, 1939.

Gadrat, François. "La Vie du montagnard ariégeois au début du 19e siècle," *Bulletin périodique de la Société Ariégeoise des Sciences, Lettres et Arts,* 1924.

Gagnon, Camille. *Le Folklore bourbonnais.* 2 vols. Moulins, 1948–49.

Garavel, J. *Les Paysans de Morette.* 1948.

Garneret, Abbé Jean. *Un Village comtois. Lantenne: Ses coutumes, ses patois.* 1959.

Garrier, Gilbert. *Paysans du Beaujolais et du Lyonnais, 1800–1970.* 2 vols. Grenoble, 1973.

Gaulmier, Jean. *Terroirs.* 1932.

Gautier, Abbé Elie. *La Dure Existence des paysans et paysannes.* 1950.

———. *L'Emigration bretonne.* 1953.

———. *Un Siècle d'indigence.* 1950.

Gautier, Marcel. *Chemins et véhicules de nos campagnes.* Saint-Brieuc, 1971.

Gazier, A. *Lettres à Grégoire sur les patois, 1790–1794.* 1880.

Genoux, Claude. *Mémoires d'un enfant de la Savoie suivis de ses chansons.* 1870. Written in 1844.

Gérard, Albert. *Les Fêtes populaires dans les Vosges et en Lorraine.* Saint-Dié, 1896.

Germouty, H. "La Chanson des maçons de la Creuse et son auteur," *Mémoires de la Société des Sciences Naturelles et Archéologiques de la Creuse,* 1940.

Gilland, Pierre. *Les Conteurs ouvriers dédiés aux enfants des classes laborieuses.* 1849.

Giono, Jean. *Notes sur l'affaire Dominici.* 1955.

Girard, Louis. *Les Elections de 1869.* 1960.

———. *La Politique des travaux publics du Second Empire.* 1952.

Giret, Jean-Paul. *La Vie scolaire et les progrès de l'instruction populaire en Eure-et-Loir, 1833–1882.* Mémoire de maîtrise, 1973.

Giron, Aimé. *La Béate.* 1884.

Giron, Alfred. *Histoire d'une ferme.* 1880.

Gobineau, Arthur de. *Ce qui est arrivé à la France en 1870.* 1970.

Gonjo, Yasno. "Le Plan Freycinet 1878–1882: Un Aspect de la grande dépression économique en France," *Revue historique,* 1972.

Gontard, Maurice. *Les Ecoles primaires de la France bourgeoise, 1833–1875.* Toulouse, 1964.

———. *L'Oeuvre scolaire de la 3e République: L'Enseignement primaire en France de 1876 à 1914.* Toulouse, 1967.

Goreux, L. M. "Les Migrations agricoles en France depuis un siècle et leurs relations avec certains facteurs économiques," *Etudes et conjoncture*, 1956.

Gorse, Abbé M. M. *Au bas pays de Limosin*. 1896.

Gostling, Frances M. *The Bretons at Home*. London, 1909.

Gratton, Philippe. *Les Luttes de classe dans les campagnes*. 1971.

———. *Le Paysan français et l'agrarisme*. 1972.

Grégoire. *Papiers de Grégoire*. Bibliothèque Nationale. Cabinet des manuscrits. Fonds français. Nouvelles acquisitions, no. 2798.

Grenadou, Ephraim, and Alain Prévost. *Grenadou, paysan français*. 1966.

Grise, Auguste. *Coutumes du Trièves au XIXe siècle*. Grenoble, 1939.

Guépidor, François-Georges. *Petite bourse du travail de province: Etude de moeurs syndicalistes*. Orleans, 1909.

Guichonnet, Paul. "La Géographie et le tempérament politique dans les montagnes de la Haute-Savoie," *Revue de géographie alpine*, 1943.

Guilcher, Jean-Michel. *La Contredanse et le renouvellement de la danse française*. 1969.

———. *La Tradition populaire de danse en Basse-Bretagne*. 1963.

———. "Vue d'ensemble sur l'histoire de l'émigration en Auvergne et Rouergue." Archives of the Musée des Arts et Traditions Populaires, manuscript 66.6, dated 1965.

Guillaumin, Emile. *Charles-Louis Philippe, mon ami*. 1942.

———. *Dialogues bourbonnais*. Moulins, 1899.

———. *Panorama de l'évolution paysanne, 1875–1935*. 1936.

———. *Paysans par eux-mêmes*. 1953.

———. *Sur l'appui de la Manche (pensées au jour le jour)*. Moulins, 1949.

———. *La Vie d'un simple*. 1904.

Guillemin, Henri. *Histoire des catholiques français au XIXe siècle*. Geneva, 1947.

Guillemot, A. *Contes, légendes, vieilles coutumes de la Marne*. Châlons-sur-Marne, 1908.

Guyonnet, Georges. *La Carte-postale illustrée*. 1947.

Habasque, François-Marie. *Notions historiques, géographiques, statistiques et agronomiques sur le littoral des Côtes-du-Nord*. Vol. 1. Saint-Brieuc, 1832.

Halbwachs, Maurice. *Les Causes du suicide*. 1930.

———. "Genre de vie," *Revue d'économie politique*, 1939.

Halévy, Daniel. *Visites aux paysans du Centre*. 1921.

Hamelle, Paul. "La Crise viticole," *Annales des sciences politiques*, 1908.

Hamerton, Philip Gilbert. *France and England*. London, 1889.

———. *Round My House*. Boston, 1885. Written in 1875.

Hamp, Pierre. *L'Enquête*. 1920.

———. *La France, pays ouvrier*. 1916.

———. *Gens*. 1917.

Haudricourt, André, and M. J. B. Delamarre. *L'Homme et la charrue à travers le monde*. 1955.

Haussmann, Georges. *Mémoires du Baron Haussmann*. 3 vols. 1890–93.

Hayes, Carlton J. H. *France, a Nation of Patriots*. New York, 1930.

Hémardinquer, J. J. *Pour une histoire de l'alimentation*. 1970.

Hérault, Augustin. *Les Gas du bocage vendéen de 1760 à 1960*. Gizay, 1962.

Hérelle, Georges. *Etudes sur le théâtre basque.* 1925.

———. *Le Théâtre rural dans la région pyrénéenne.* 1923.

———. *Les Théâtres ruraux en France.* 1930.

Hertz, Robert. *Sociologie religieuse et folklore.* 1970. The study, published in 1928, was made before World War I, in which Hertz died.

Higonnet, Patrice. *Pont-de-Montvert: Social Structure and Politics in a French Village, 1700–1914.* Cambridge, Mass., 1971.

Hilaire, Yves-Marie. "La Pratique religieuse en France de 1815 à 1878," *L'Information historique,* 1963.

Houillier, François. "Les Travaux et les jours du paysan," *Etudes,* 1945.

Hubscher, Ronald-Henri. "Le Livre de compte de la famille Flahaut," *Revue d'histoire économique et sociale,* 1969.

Hudry-Ménos. "La Savoie depuis l'annexion," *Revue des deux mondes,* June 1, 1864.

Hugo, Abel. *La France pittoresque.* 3 vols. 1835.

Hugonnier, Simone. "Tempéraments politiques et géographie électorale ... Maurienne et Tarentaise," *Revue de géographie alpine,* 1954.

Hyslop, Beatrice. *French Nationalism in 1789 According to the General Cahiers.* New York, 1934.

Indy, J. d'. "Les Débuts du ski en Vivarais," *Revue du Vivarais,* 1953.

Instruction primaire. Etat de l'instruction primaire en 1864, d'après les rapports officiels des inspecteurs d'académie. 2 vols. 1866.

Isambert-Jamati, V. *Crises de la société, crises de l'enseignement.* 1970.

Jacquemin, André. *Epinal et l'imagerie populaire.* 1961.

Jalby, Robert. *Le Folklore de Languedoc.* 1971.

Jarré, Georges. "L'Etablissement des routes dans le massif du Vercors," *Revue de géographie alpine,* 1921.

Jeanton, Gabriel. *L'Habitation paysanne en Bresse.* Tournus, 1935.

———. *L'Habitation rustique au pays mâconnais.* Tournus, 1932.

———. *La Légende et l'histoire au pays mâconnais.* Mâcon, 1929.

———. *Le Mâconnais traditionaliste et populaire.* Mâcon, 1922.

Jollivet, Benjamin. *Les Côtes-du-Nord.* 4 vols. Guingamp, 1854–59.

Jollivet, M., and H. Mendras. *Les Collectivités rurales françaises.* Vol. 1. 1971.

Juge, J. J. *Changements survenus dans les moeurs des habitants de Limoges depuis une cinquantaine d'années.* 2d ed. Limoges, 1817.

Kanter, Sanford. "Defeat 1871: A Study in After-War," Ph.D. diss., University of California, Los Angeles, 1972.

Karnoouh, Claude. "La Démocratie impossible: Parenté et politique dans un village lorrain," *Etudes rurales,* 1973.

———. "L'Etranger, ou le faux inconnu," *Ethnologie française,* 1972.

Kindleberger, Charles P. *Economic Growth in France and Britain, 1851–1960.* Cambridge, Mass., 1964.

Labat, Emmanuel. *L'Ame paysanne.* 1919.

———. *En Gascogne.* Agen, 1911. Originally published in *Revue des deux mondes,* August, 1910.

Laborde, C. "La Civilité villageoise," *Mémoires de la Société des Sciences Naturelles et Archéologiques de la Creuse,* vol. 33.

Labourasse, H. *Anciens us, coutumes, légendes, superstitions, préjugés, etc., du département de la Meuse.* Bar-le-Duc, 1903. Largely based on teachers' monographs of 1889.

Labrousse, Pierre. "Trois ans d'école normale à Perpignan." Archives départementales, Pyrénées-Orientales, manuscript dated 1898, referring to 1845–48.

Labrune, Abbé P. *Mystères des campagnes.* Limoges, 1858. By a country priest.

Lafarge, Madame. *Mémoires de Marie Capelle, Veuve Lafarge.* 4 vols. 1841–43.

Lafayette, Charles Calemard de. "Esquisse des montagnes," *Annales de la Société d'Agriculture du Puy,* 1854.

———. "Les Paysages et les montagnards du Mézenc," *Annales de la Société d'Agriculture du Puy,* 1854.

Lafont, Robert. *La Révolution régionaliste.* 1967.

Lagarde, Louis de. *Nos paysans.* Aix, 1902.

Lallement, Louis. *Folklore et vieux souvenirs d'Argonne.* 1921.

Lalou, Henri. "Des charivaris et de leur repression dans le midi de la France," *Revue des Pyrénées,* 1904.

Lancelot, Alain. *L'Abstentionnisme électoral en France.* 1968.

La Langue bretonne et les écoles. Saint-Brieuc, 1895. Anonymous; signed X.

Lapaire, Hugues. "Le Paysan berrichon," *Cahiers du Centre,* 1913.

Larivière, Jean-Pierre. *L'Industrie à Limoges et dans la vallée limousine de la Vienne.* 1968.

Lasserre, Pierre. "Lourdes," *Revue géographique des Pyrénées et du Sud-Ouest,* 1930.

Latreille, André, and René Rémond. *Histoire du catholicisme en France.* Vol. 3: *La Période contemporaine.* 1962.

Laurentin, R. *Lourdes.* Vol. 1. 1957.

Lavergne, Léonce de. *L'Agriculture et la population.* 1865.

———. *De la population des arrondissements en 1846 et 1866.* 1868.

———. *Economie rurale de la France depuis 1789.* 4th ed., 1877.

Lavigne, Bertrand. *Histoire de Blagnac.* Toulouse, 1875.

Lavisse, Ernest. "L'Enseignement de l'histoire à l'école primaire," in *Questions d'enseignement national,* 1885.

———. *Livret d'histoire de France: Année du certificat d'études.* 1894.

———. *La Première Année d'histoire de France.* 1884.

———. *Souvenirs.* 1911.

——— [under pseud. Pierre Laloi]. *L'Année préparatoire d'instruction morale et d'instruction civique.* 1895.

———. *Petites histoires pour apprendre la vie.* 1887.

———. *La Première Année d'instruction civique.* 1880.

——— (with Thalamas). *Livret d'histoire de France: Opuscule du maître.* 1894.

Layet, Alexandre. *Hygiène et maladies des paysans.* 1882.

Léaud, Alexis, and Emile Glay. *L'Ecole primaire en France.* Vol. 2. 1934.

Lebeau, René. *La Vie rurale dans les montagnes du Jura méridional.* Lyon, 1955.

Lebesque, Morvan. *Comment peut-on être Breton?* 1970.

Le Blond, Maurice. *La Crise du Midi.* 1907.

Le Bourhis, Francis. *Etude sur la culture et les salaires en Haute-Cornouaille.* Rennes, 1908.

Lecoeur, Jules. *Esquisses du Bocage normand.* Condé-sur-Noireau, 1883.

Lefebvre, Henri. "Perspectives de la sociologie rurale," *Cahiers internationaux de sociologie,* 1953.

——. *La Vallée de Campan.* 1963.

Lefournier, Mathilde. "La Vie alpestre transformée par le ski," *Revue des deux mondes,* Oct. 20, 1935.

Le Gallo, Yves. *Brest et sa bourgeoisie sous la Monarchie de Juillet.* 2 vols. 1968.

Le Guen, Gilbert. "D'une révolution manquée à une révolution possible," Chap. 12 in Jean Delumeau, cited above.

Le Guyader, Frédéric. *See* Olivier Perrin and Alex Bouet, cited below.

Lejeune, Xavier-Edouard. "Les Etapes de la vie." 3 vols. University of California, Los Angeles, Library, manuscript. Covers 1843–1870's.

Le Lannou, Maurice. *Géographie de la Bretagne.* Vol. 2. Rennes, 1952.

Le Mercier d'Erm, Camille. *La Question bretonne: Les Origines du nationalisme breton.* Quimper, 1914.

Léon-Petit, Doctor. *Histoire d'une nourrice sur lieu.* 1893.

Leproux, Marc. *Dévotions et saints guérisseurs.* 1957.

——. *Médecine, magie et sorcellerie.* 1954.

Leroi-Gourhan, André. *L'Homme et la matière.* 1943.

——. *Milieu et techniques.* 1945.

Leroux, Alcide. *Du langage populaire dans le département de la Loire-Inférieure.* Saint-Brieuc, 1889.

Le Roy, Eugène. *Jacquou le Croquant.* 1899.

——. *Le Moulin du Frau: Histoire du meunier périgourdin Hélie Nogaret.* 1894.

Le Roy Ladurie, Emmanuel. *Anthropologie des conscrits français.* 1972.

Le Saux, Marguerite. *Approche d'une étude de la déchristianisation.* Mémoire de maîtrise, 1971.

Lesourd, Alain, and Claude Gérard. *Histoire économique: XIXe et XXe siècles.* 2 vols. 1963.

Levainville, J. *Le Morvan.* 1909.

Levasseur, Emile. *La Population française.* Vols. 2 and 3. 1891, 1892.

Lévy-Leboyer, Maurice. "La Croissance économique en France au XIXe siècle," *Annales: Economies, sociétés, civilisations,* 1968.

Littré, Emile. *Comment les mots changent de sens.* 1888.

Lizerand, Georges. *Un Siècle d'histoire d'une commune rurale: Vergigny.* 1951.

Longy, F. *Le Canton d'Eygurande.* Tulle, 1893.

——. *Port-Dieu et son prieuré.* Tulle, 1889.

Loua, Toussaint. *La France sociale et économique.* 1888.

——. *Les Grands Faits économiques et sociaux.* 1878.

Loubère, Léo. "The Emergence of the Extreme Left in Lower Languedoc, 1848–1851," *American Historical Review,* 1968.

Lovie, Jacques. *La Savoie dans la vie française de 1860 à 1875.* 1963.

Lugnier, Antoine. *Cinq siècles de vie paysanne à Roche-en-Forez (Loire), 1440–1940.* Saint-Etienne, 1962.

Lynch, Hannah. *French Life in Town and Country.* New York, 1905.

Machenaud, Roger. "Ardillères en Aunis." Archives of the Musée des Arts et Traditions Populaires, manuscript dated 1962.

Maggiolo, Louis. *Les Ecoles en Lorraine avant et après 1789.* 3d part. Nancy, 1891.

Maître, Jacques. *Les Prêtres ruraux.* 1967.

Malaussène, J.-E. *Saint-Jeannet (Alpes-Maritimes).* 1909.

Malègue, Hippolyte. *Eléments de statistique générale de département de la Haute-Loire.* 1872.

———. *Guide de l'étranger dans la Haute-Loire.* Le Puy, 1866.

———. *Guide du touriste dans la Haute-Loire.* Le Puy, 1886.

Mallet, Georges. *Mes souvenirs de la vie abbevilloise à la fin du XIXe siècle, 1875–1900.* Abbeville, 1950.

Malon, Benoît. "Fragment de mémoires," *Revue socialiste,* Jan.-July 1907. Only to the 1850's.

Manceau, Henri. *Gens et métiers d'autrefois.* Mézières, 1957.

Mandrou, Robert. *De la culture populaire au XVIIe et XVIIIe siècle.* 1964 and 1975 eds.

Marcilhacy, Christiane. *Le Diocèse d'Orléans au milieu du XIXe siècle.* 1964.

———. *Le Diocèse d'Orléans sous l'épiscopat de Mgr. Dupanloup, 1849–1878.* 1962.

———. "Emile Zola, historien des paysans beaucerons," *Annales: Economies, sociétés, civilisations,* 1957.

Marczevski, Jean, ed. *Le Produit de l'agriculture française de 1700 à 1958.* 1961.

Marin, Louis. *Les Contes traditionnels en Lorraine.* 1964.

———. *Regards sur la Lorraine.* 1966.

———. "Les Survivances dans les provinces françaises," *Réforme sociale,* 1905.

———. *Les Veillées lorraines.* 1946.

Marion, Marcel. *Histoire financière de la France.* Vol. 6: *1876–1914.* 1931.

Markovitch, T. J. *Le Revenu industriel et artisanal sous la Monarchie de Juillet et le Second Empire.* 1967.

Marlin, Roger. *L'Opinion franc-comtoise devant la guerre de Crimée.* 1957.

———. *La Presse du Doubs pendant la guerre de 1870–71.* Dôle, 1956.

Marouzeau, J. *Une Enfance.* 1937.

Maspétiol, Roland. *L'Ordre éternel des champs.* 1946.

Massé, Alfred. *Les Partis politiques dans la Nièvre: De 1871 à 1906.* Nevers, 1910.

Masseport, Jean. "Le Comportement politique du massif du Diois," *Revue de géographie alpine,* 1960.

Mathé, R. *Emile Guillaumin.* 1966.

Matoré, Georges. *Le Vocabulaire et la société sous Louis-Philippe.* Geneva, 1951.

Maupassant, Guy de. "En Bretagne," in *Oeuvres complètes,* Vol. 1. 1908. Originally published in *Nouvelle revue,* Jan. 1, 1884.

Mauriac, François. *La Province: Notes et maximes.* 1926.

Mauss, Marcel. "La Nation (notes)," *Année sociologique* (1953–54), 1956.

Mayer, Paul. "En pays normand." Archives of the Musée des Arts et Traditions Populaires, manuscript 43-6, dated 1905.

Mayeur, Jean-Marie. *L'Abbé Lemire.* 1968.

———. *Les Débuts de la Troisième République.* 1973.

Mazières, Jean. *Arsène Vermenouze (1850–1910) et la Haute-Auvergne de son temps.* 2 vols. 1965.

Mazon, A. *Les Muletiers du Vivarais, du Velay et du Gévaudan.* Puy-en-Velay, 1892.

Mazoyer, Louis. "Catégories d'age et groupes sociaux: Les Jeunes Générations françaises de 1830," *Annales: Economies, sociétés, civilisations,* 1938.

Mazuy, François. *Essai historique sur les moeurs et coutumes de Marseille au 19e siècle.* Marseille, 1854.

Mélanges Daniel Faucher: France méridionale et pays ibériques. Toulon, 1948.

Mélanges géographiques offerts au doyen Ernest Bénévent. Gap, 1954.

Méline, Jules. *Le Retour à la terre et la surproduction industrielle.* 1905.

Mendras, Henri. *La Fin des paysans.* 1967.

———. *Novis et Virgin.* 1953.

———. "Sociologie rurale," in Georges Gurvitch, ed., *Traité de sociologie.* Vol. I. 1956.

Méraville, Marie-Aymée. *Contes populaires de l'Auvergne suivis d'un mémoire sur la langue et le patois.* 1970.

Merley, Jean. *L'industrie en Haute-Loire de la fin de la monarchie de Juillet aux débuts de la Troisième République.* Lyon, 1972.

Mesliand, Claude. "Fortune paysanne dans le Vaucluse," *Annales: Economies, sociétés, civilisations,* 1967.

Meynier, André A. *A travers le Massif Central: Ségalas, Levézou, Châtaigneraie.* Aurillac, 1931.

———. "Deux hameaux limousins de 1906 à 1946," in *Mélanges Daniel Faucher,* cited above.

———. "Les Routes entre Aurillac et Mauriac," *Revue de la Haute-Auvergne,* 1933.

Michaud, René. *J'avais vingt ans: Un Jeune Ouvrier au début du siècle.* 1967.

Michel, Louise. *Mémoires.* 1886.

Michelet, Jules. *Le Peuple.* Lausanne, 1945.

Mignot, Cyprien-Hyacinthe. "Mémoires d'un instituteur rural de la région de Bar-sur-Seine." Archives of the Musée des Arts et Traditions Populaires, manuscript. Mignot lived from 1859 to 1939.

Mireur, Frédéric. *Les Rues de Draguignan et leurs maisons historiques.* 6 vols. Draguignan, 1921–24.

Mistler, Jean. *La Librairie Hachette de 1826 à nos jours.* 1964.

Mistler, Jean, François Blandez, and André Jacquemin. *Epinal et l'imagerie populaire.* 1961.

Mistral, Frédéric. *Mes origines: Mémoires et récits.* 1929. Originally published in 1906.

Moiset, M. C. "Les Usages, croyances, traditions, superstitions, etc., ayant existé autrefois ou existant encore dans les divers pays du département de l'Yonne," *Bulletin de la Société des Sciences Historiques et Naturelles de l'Yonne,* 1888.

Monot, C. *De la mortalité excessive des enfants.* 1872.

———. *De l'industrie des nourrices et de la mortalité des petits enfants.* 1867.

Montégut, Emile. "La Démocratie et la Révolution: Les Transformations de l'idée de patrie," *Revue des deux mondes,* Nov. 15, 1871.

Monteils-Pons, Doctor. *Florac au point de vue de l'hygiène et de la salubrité.* Montpellier, 1855.

Montusès, Ernest. "Le Député en blouse," *Cahiers du Centre,* 1913. The story of Christophe Thivrier.

Morère, Philippe. *Notes sur l'Ariège avant le régime démocratique: Le Paysan.* Foix, 1912.

———. "La Révolution de 1848 dans un pays forestier," *Bulletin périodique de la Société Ariégeoise des Sciences, Lettres et Arts,* 1922.

Morin, Edgar. *Commune en France: La Métamorphose de Plodémet.* 1967.

Morineau, Michel. "Y a-t-il eu une révolution agricole en France au XVIII siècle?" *Revue historique,* 1968.

Moscovici, Serge. *Reconversion industrielle et changements sociaux.* 1961.

Moureu, Charles. *De la petite à la grande patrie.* Toulouse, 1928.

Mourgues, Marcelle. *La Danse provençale.* Marseille, 1956.

Musset, R. *Le Bas-Maine.* 1917.

———. "Les Genres de vie anciens du Bocage normand," *Bulletin de l'Association des Géographes Français,* 1926.

Nadaud, Martin. *Discours et conférences de Martin Nadaud (1870–1878).* Vol. 2: *Six mois de préfecture . . .* Guéret, 1889.

———. *Mémoires de Léonard, ancien garçon maçon.* 1912.

Narfon, Julien de. *La Séparation de l'église et de l'état.* 1912.

Nauton, Pierre. *Atlas linguistique et ethnographique du Massif Central.* Vol. 4. 1963.

Nelli, René. *Languedoc, Comté de Foix, Roussillon.* 1958.

Neufbourg, Comte de. *Paysans.* 1945.

Nisard, Charles. *Des chansons populaires.* Vol. 2. 1867.

———. *Histoire des livres populaires et de la littérature de colportage.* 2 vols. 2d ed., 1864.

Niveaux de culture et groupes sociaux. Actes du colloque, 1966. 1967.

Nora, Pierre. "Ernest Lavisse. Son rôle dans la formation du sentiment national," *Revue historique,* 1962.

Norre, Henri. *Comment j'ai vaincu la misère.* 1944.

Noyon, N. *Statistique de département du Var.* Draguignan, 1846.

Ogès, Louis. *L'Agriculture dans le Finistère au milieu du XIXe siècle.* Brest, 1949.

———. *L'Instruction primaire dans le Finistère sous le régime de la loi Guizot, 1833–1850.* Quimper, 1935.

Ogès, Louis, and F. M. Déguignet. "Contes et légendes populaires de la Cornouaille bretonne," *Bulletin de la Société Archéologique du Finistère,* 1963.

Ozouf, Jacques, and Mona Ozouf. "Le Thème du patriotisme dans les manuels primaires," *Mouvement social,* 1964.

Palmade, Guy. "Le Département du Gers à la fin du Second Empire," *Bulletin de la Société Archéologique du Gers,* 1961.

Parain, Charles. "Une Falsification: L'Archéocivilisation," *La Pensée,* 1953.

———. "Un Nouveau Mythe: La Civilisation traditionnelle," *La Pensée,* 1949.

Pariset, M. F. *Economie rurale: Industrie, moeurs et usages de la Montagne Noire (Aude et Tarn).* 1882.

———. *Economie rurale: Moeurs et usages du Lauragais (Aude et Haute-Garonne).* 1867.

Pasquet, Joseph. *En Morvan: Souvenirs du bon vieux temps.* Château-Chinon, 1967.

Passama, Paul. *Condition des ouvriers viticoles dans le Minervois.* 1906.

Payne, Howard C. *The Police State of Louis Bonaparte.* Seattle, 1966.

Pécaut, Félix. *L'Education publique et la vie nationale.* 1897.

———. *Etudes au jour le jour sur l'éducation nationale.* 1879.

———. *Quinze ans d'éducation.* 1902.

———. *Rapports d'inspection générale sur l'Académie de Bordeaux.* 1880.

Péguy, Charles. *L'Argent.* 1913.

———. "Avertissement" to *Petites garnisons, Cahiers de la Quinzaine,* 5.12 (1904).

———. "Pierre: Commencement d'une vie bourgeoise," in *Oeuvres en prose, 1898–1908.* 1965.

Pelicier, Edouard. *Statistique de la télégraphie privée depuis son origine en France.* 1858.

Perdiguier, Agricol. *Mémoires d'un compagnon.* 1943.

Pergaud, Louis. *Les Rustiques.* 1921. Published posthumously; Pergaud died in 1916.

Peristiany, J.-G., ed. *Contributions to Mediterranean Sociology: Mediterranean Rural Communities and Social Change.* London, 1968.

Pérochon, Ernest. *L'Instituteur.* 1927.

Pérot, Francis. *Folklore bourbonnais.* 1908.

Perrin, Olivier, and Alex Bouet. *Breiz Izel ou la vie des Bretons dans l'Armorique.* New ed. with notes by Frédéric Le Guyader. Quimper, 1918. Originally published in 1835.

Perron, Charles. *Broye-les-Pesmes.* Besançon, 1889.

———. *Les Franc-Comtois.* Besançon, 1892.

———. *Proverbes de la Franche-Comté.* 1876.

Perrot, Michèle. *Les Ouvriers en grève: France 1871–1890.* 2 vols. 1974.

Peygnaud, Louis. *Le Bal des conscrits.* Aigurande, 1968.

Pic, M.-Xavier. *La Bête qui mangeait le monde en pays de Gévaudan.* Mende, 1968.

Picamilh, Charles de. *Statistique générale des Basses-Pyrénées.* 2 vols. Pau, 1858.

Picoche, Jacqueline. *Un Vocabulaire picard d'autrefois: Le Parler d'Etelfay (Somme).* Arras, 1969.

Pierrard, Pierre. "L'Enseignement primaire à Lille sous la Restauration," *Revue du Nord,* 1973.

Pilenco, Alexandre. *Les Moeurs du suffrage universel en France (1848–1928).* 1930.

Pinchemel, Philippe. *Géographie de la France.* 2 vols. 1964.

———. *Structures sociales et dépopulation rurale dans les campagnes picardes de 1836 à 1936.* 1957.

Pitié, Jean. *Exode rural et migrations intérieures en France.* Poitiers, 1971.

Plessis, Alain. *De la fête impériale au mur des fédérés.* 1973.

Poitrineau, Abel. "Aspects de l'émigration temporaire et saisonnière en Auvergne à la fin du XVIIIe siècle et au début du XIXe siècle," *Revue d'histoire moderne,* 1962.

Polge, Henri. "L'Artisanat dans le Gers sous le règne de Louis-Philippe," *Bulletin de la Société Archéologique du Gers,* 1969.

———. *De quelques légendes et traditions populaires dans la Gascogne gersoise.* Auch, 1957.

———. "Gascon et français," *Bulletin de la Société Archéologique du Gers*, 1953.

———. *Matériaux traditionnels de couverture et de construction dans le Sud-Ouest de la France*. Albi, n.d.

———. *Mon vieil Auch*. Auch, 1969.

Pollio, Joseph, and Adrien Marcel. *Le Bataillon du 10 août*. 1881.

Poncy, Charles. *La Chanson de chaque métier*. 1850. By a Lyon mason.

Portal, Charles. *Le Département du Tarn au XIXe siècle: Notes de statistique*. Albi, 1912.

Pottier, Eugène. *Chants révolutionnaires*. 1887. Preface by Henry Rochefort and Jules Vallès.

———. *Quel est le fou?* 1884. Preface by Gustave Nadaud.

Poueigh, Jean. *Chansons populaires des Pyrénées françaises*. 2 vols. 1926–33.

———. *Le Folklore des pays d'Oc*. 1952.

Pourrat, Henri. *L'Homme à la bêche*. 1941.

Pradier, Doctor. *Histoire statistique, médicale et administrative de la prostitution dans la ville de Clermont-Ferrand*. Clermont-Ferrand, 1854.

Prost, Antoine. *L'Enseignement en France, 1800–1967*. 1968.

Prost, Henri. *Charles Dumont et le Jura*. 1964.

Pujos, Inspector. "Recueil des monographies des communes de l'arrondissement de Cahors, rédigées par MM. les Instituteurs de cet arrondissement d'après les instructions et sous la direction de M. Pujos, Inspecteur primaire, 1880–1881." Archives Départementales, Lot, manuscript.

Quellien, N. *L'Argot des nomades en Basse-Bretagne*. 1886.

———. *Chansons et danses des Bretons*. 1889.

———. *Rapport sur une mission en Basse-Bretagne ayant pour objet d'y recueillir les mélodies populaires*. 1883.

Rambaud, Placide. *Economie et sociologie de la montagne*. 1962.

———. *Société rurale et urbanisation*. 1969.

Rambaud, Placide, and Monique Vincienne. *Les Transformations d'une société rurale: La Maurienne (1561–1962)*. 1964.

Rapports d'inspection générale sur la situation de l'enseignement primaire, 1879–1880. Ministère de l'Instruction publique, 1881.

Rascol, L. *L'Education populaire dans le Tarn, 1896–1899*. Albi, 1899.

Reach, Angus B. *Claret and Olives, from the Garonne to the Rhône*. London, 1870.

Redfield, Robert. *Peasant Society and Culture*. Chicago, 1956.

Renard, Jules. *Mots d'écrit*. Nevers, 1908.

———. *Nos frères farouches*. 1907.

———. *Oeuvres*. 2 vols. 1971.

———. *Les Philippe*. 1907. Unpaginated.

Renouard, Dominique. *Les Transports de marchandises par fer, route et eau depuis 1850*. 1960.

Résumés des états de situation de l'enseignement primaire. Ministère de l'Instruction publique, n.d.

Reuchsel, Amédée. *L'Education musicale populaire: L'Art du chef d'orphéon*. 1906.

Reynier, Elie. *Histoire de Privas*. Vol. 3: *1789–1950*. Privas, 1951.

———. *Le Pays de Vivarais*. Vols. 1 and 2. Valence, 1923, 1934.

———. "Voies de communication du plateau de Vernoux," *Revue du Vivarais,* 1952.

Reynier, Elie, and Louise Abrial. *Les Ecoles normales primaires de l'Ardèche.* Privas, 1945.

Ricard, J. H. *Au pays landais.* 1911.

Robert, Charles. *De l'ignorance des populations ouvrières et rurales de la France et des causes qui tendent à la perpétuer.* Montbéliard, 1863. Based on teachers' reports of 1860.

———. "Notes sur l'état de la lecture populaire en France et sur la situation des bibliothèques en 1866," *Bulletin de la Société Franklin,* 1872.

———. *Plaintes et voeux présentés par les instituteurs publics en 1861 sur la situation des maisons d'école.* 1864. Based on teachers' reports of 1860.

Rocal, Georges. *Croquants du Périgord.* Périgueux, 1934.

Roche, Alphonse V. *Provençal Regionalism.* Evanston, Ill., 1954.

Roche, Jean-Louis. "Carnets de lettres et de rapports à l'Inspecteur de l'Académie." Archives Départementales, Puy-de-Dôme, manuscript. The work of a nineteenth-century village schoolteacher (1827–71).

Rollet, Pierre. *La Vie quotidienne en Provence au temps de Mistral.* 1972.

Romeuf, Louis de. "La Crise viticole du Midi," *Revue politique et parlementaire,* 1909.

Romieu, Marie-Sincère. *Des paysans et de l'agriculture en France au XIXe siècle.* 1865.

Roubin, Lucienne. *Chambrettes des Provençaux.* 1970.

Rouchon, Ulysse. *La Vie paysanne dans la Haute-Loire.* 3 vols. Le Puy, 1933–38.

Rougeron, Georges. *Le Conseil général, 1871–1940.* Moulins, 1960. Rougeron was president of the Conseil général of Allier.

———. *Le Département de l'Allier sous la Troisième République.* Moulins, 1965.

———. *Le Personnel politique bourbonnais.* Moulins, 1969.

Roux, Joseph. *Pensées.* 1885. The reflections of a Corrèze country priest, published with an introduction by the Félibre Paul Mariéton.

Roux, Paul. *La Dépopulation des campagnes.* 1910.

Sabatier, Robert. *Les Noisettes sauvages.* 1974.

Sabbatier, J. *L'Affaire de La Salette.* 1857.

Sahuc, Régis. *Vent d'Usclades: Us et coutumes dans les montagnes de l'Ardèche.* Le Puy, 1966.

Sand, George. *Le Diable aux champs.* 1865.

Sarcey, Francisque. *Les Odeurs de Paris: Assainissement de la Seine.* 1882.

Savigné, E. J. *Moeurs, coutumes, habitudes (il y a plus d'un siècle).* Vienne, 1902.

Sauvan, M.-E. "L'Evolution économique du Haut-Diois," *Revue de géographie alpine,* 1921.

Sauzet, L. *Du métayage en Limousin.* 1897.

Schnapper, Bernard. *Le Remplacement militaire en France.* 1968.

Sébillot, Paul. *Coutumes populaires de la Haute-Bretagne.* 1886.

———. Le Folk-lore de France. Vol. 4: *Le Peuple et l'histoire.* 1907.

———. *Littérature orale de la Haute-Bretagne.* 1881.

———. *Les Travaux publics et les mines dans les traditions et les superstitions.* 1894.

Ségalen, Martine. *Nuptialité et alliance.* 1972.

Séguin, Jean-Pierre. "Les Canards de faits divers de petit format en France au XIXe siècle," *Arts et traditions populaires,* 1956.

——. *Canards du siècle passé.* 1969.

Séguy, Jean. *Le Français parlé à Toulouse.* Toulouse, 1950.

Seignolle, Claude. *En Sologne.* 1945.

Sénéquier, Léon. *Connaissance de La Garde-Freinet.* Draguignan, 1965.

Servat, J.-M. *Histoire de Massat.* Foix, 1936.

Sicard, Emile. "Essai d'analyse des éléments principaux des constructions nationales actuelles," *L'Année sociologique,* 1967.

Singer, Barnett Bruce. "Pillar of the Republic: The Village Schoolmaster in Brittany, 1880–1914," Ph.D. diss., University of Washington, 1971.

Sion, Jules. *Les Paysans de la Normandie orientale.* 1909.

Smith, Victor. "Chants des pauvres en Forez et en Velay," *Romania,* 1873.

Soboul, Albert. "La Communauté Rurale: Problèmes de base," *Revue de synthèse,* 1957.

——. "La Question paysanne en 1848," *La Pensée,* 1948.

Souvestre, Emile. *Les Derniers Bretons.* 1843 and 1854 eds. (The 1854 ed. is in 2 vols.) Originally published in 1836.

——. *Les Derniers Paysans.* 2 vols. Brussels, 1851.

Stendhal. *Mémoires d'un touriste.* 3 vols. 1932 ed.

Stewart, H. F., and Paul Desjardins. *French Patriotism in the Nineteenth Century (1814–1833).* Cambridge, Eng., 1923.

Suret-Canale, J. "L'Etat économique et social de la Mayenne au milieu du 19e siècle," *Revue d'histoire économique et sociale,* 1958.

Szabo, Denis. *Crimes et villes.* 1960.

Taine, Hippolyte. *Carnets de voyage: Notes sur la province, 1863–1865.* 1897.

Tanneau, Yves. "L'Instruction dans une commune de Cornouaille au 19e siècle: Pouldergat," *Bulletin de la Société Archéologique du Finistère,* 1972.

Tarde, Alfred de. *L'Esprit périgourdin et Eugène Le Roy.* Périgueux, 1921.

Tarde, Gabriel. *La Criminalité comparée.* 1910.

Tardieu, Ambroise. *L'Auvergne: Guide complet illustré.* Herment, 1886.

——. *Grand dictionnaire historique du département du Puy-de-Dôme.* Moulins, 1877.

Tardieu, Suzanne. *Meubles régionaux datés.* 1950.

——. *La Vie domestique dans le Mâconnais rural préindustriel.* 1964.

Ténot, Eugène. *La Province en Décembre 1851.* 2d ed. 1876.

——. *Le Suffrage universel et les paysans.* 1865.

Thabault, Roger. *L'Enfant et la langue écrite.* 1944.

——. *Mon village, 1848–1914.* 1944. Published in English as *Education and Social Change in a Village Community.* New York, 1972.

Théron de Montaugé, Louis. *L'Agriculture et les classes rurales dans le pays toulousain depuis le milieu du XVIIIe siècle.* 1869.

Thibon, Gustave. "Un Exemple d'émiettement humain et économique: L'Evolution du Bas-Vivarais depuis le Second Empire," *Economie et humanisme,* 1942.

Thierry, Augustin. *Lettres sur l'histoire de France.* 1827.

Thiriat, Xavier. *L'Agriculture dans les montagnes des Vosges.* 1866.

————. *La Vallée de Cleurie.* Remiremont, 1869.

Thivot, Henry. *La Vie publique dans les Hautes-Alpes vers le milieu du XIXe siècle.* La Tronche-Montfleury, 1971.

Thomas, Edith. *Louise Michel.* 1971.

Thompson, E. P. "Rough Music: Le Charivari anglais," *Annales: Economies, sociétés, civilisations,* 1972.

Thuillier, Guy. "L'Alimentation au Nivernais au XIXe siècle," *Annales: Economies, sociétés, civilisations,* 1965.

————. *Aspects de l'économie nivernaise au XIXe siècle.* 1966.

————. "Pour une histoire des gestes," *Annales: Economies, sociétés, civilisations,* 1973.

————. "La Presse nivernaise au XIXe siècle," *Annales de Bourgogne,* 1966.

Toubeau, Albert. "Le Prolétariat agricole depuis 1789, d'après les documents officiels," *La Philosophie positive,* 1882.

Toutain, J. C. *Le Produit de l'agriculture française de 1700 à 1958.* Vol. 2: *La Croissance.* 1961.

————. *Les Transports en France de 1830 à 1965.* 1967.

La Tradition en Poitou et Charentes. 1897.

"Le Travail et les techniques," *Journal de psychologie normale et pathologique,* 1948.

Trébucq, Sylvain. *La Chanson populaire en Vendée.* 1896.

————. *La Chanson populaire et la vie rurale des Pyrénées à la Vendée.* 2 vols. Bordeaux, 1912.

Trempé, Rolande. *Les Mineurs de Carmaux.* Vol. 1. 1971.

Tudesq, André-Jean. *Les Grands Notables en France.* 2 vols. 1964.

Turlier, Guy. "De quelques aspects de la vie humaine en Sologne bourbonnaise," *Notre Bourbonnais,* part 1, 1953.

Valaux, Camille. *La Basse-Bretagne: Etude de géographie humaine.* 1905.

Valdour, Jacques. *Ouvriers parisiens d'après-guerre: Observations vécues.* 1921.

Vallès, Jules. *Les Blouses.* 1957 ed.

Van de Walle, Etienne. *The Female Population of France in the Nineteenth Century.* Princeton, N.J., 1974.

Van Gennep, Arnold. "Le Cycle cérémonial du carnaval et du carême en Savoie," *Journal de psychologie,* 1925.

————. "Le Cycle préhivernal dans les croyances et coutumes populaires de la Savoie," *Revue d'ethnographie,* 1928.

————. *La Décadence et la persistance des patois.* 1911.

————. *Le Folklore de Flandre et du Hainaut français.* 2 vols. 1935–36.

————. *Le Folklore de l'Auvergne et du Velay.* 1942.

————. *Le Folklore des Hautes-Alpes.* 2 vols. 1946–48.

————. *Le Folklore du Dauphiné.* 2 vols. 1932–33.

————. *Manuel de folklore français contemporain.* 7 vols. 1943–.

————. *Remarques sur l'imagerie populaire.* 1911.

Varagnac, André. *Civilisation traditionnelle et genres de vie.* 1948.

Vartier, Jean. *Sabbat, juges et sorciers.* 1968.

————. *La Vie quotidienne en Lorraine au 19e siècle.* 1973.

Vasseur, Gaston. *Lexique serrurier du Vimeu.* Lille, 1950.

Vaultier, Roger. *Les Fêtes populaires à Paris.* 1946.

Vazeilles, Marius. *La Situation des paysans corréziens il y a un demi-siècle.* Tulle, 1955. Tirage à part, 2 brochures.

Vidal de la Blache, P. *Tableau de la géographie de la France.* 1911.

Vidalenc, Jean. *Le Peuple des campagnes.* 1969. This work and the next both cover the period 1815–48.

———. *Le Peuple des villes et des bourgs.* 1973.

Vigier, Philippe. *La Seconde République dans la région alpine.* 2 vols. 1963.

Un Village et son terroir: Minot en Châtillonnais. Musée des Arts et Traditions Populaires, 1973.

Villermé, H. *Tableau de l'état physique et moral des ouvriers et des employés dans les manufactures de coton, de laine et de soie.* 2 vols. 1840.

Vincent, Marie-Louise. *Le Berry dans l'oeuvre de George Sand.* 1919.

Violet, Emile. *Autrefois en Mâconnais.* Mâcon, 1930.

———. *Clessé.* Mâcon, 1929.

———. *Les Veillées en commun.* Mâcon, 1942.

Viple, Jean-François. *Sociologie politique de l'Allier.* 1967.

Vogüé, Louis A.-M. de. *Une Famille vivaroise (suite).* Reims, 1948.

Vogüé, Melchior de. "Notes sur le Bas-Vivarais," *Revue des deux mondes,* Oct. 15, 1892.

Voisin, Joseph. "Entre Loire et Allier," *Cahiers du Centre,* 1912.

Vovelle, Gaby, and Michel Vovelle. *Vision de la mort et de l'au-delà en Provence.* 1970.

Vovelle, Michel. *Piété baroque et déchristianisation en Provence au XVIIIe siècle.* 1973.

Vulpian, Alain de. "Physionomie agraire et orientation politique dans le département des Côtes-du-Nord, 1928–1946," *Revue française de science politique,* 1951.

Warner, Charles. *The Winegrowers of France and the Government Since 1875.* New York, 1960.

Wolff, Philippe, ed. *Histoire du Languedoc.* Toulouse, 1967.

Wolkowitch, Maurice. *L'Economie régionale des transports dans le Centre et le Centre-Ouest de la France.* 1960.

Wright, Gordon. *Rural Revolution in France.* Stanford, Calif., 1964.

Wylie, Laurence. *Chanzeaux, a Village in Anjou.* Cambridge, Mass., 1966.

———. *Village in the Vaucluse.* Cambridge, Mass., 1957.

Young, Arthur. *Travels in France During the Years 1787, 1788, 1789.* London, 1890.

Zeldin, Theodore. *Conflicts in French Society.* London, 1970.

———. *France, 1848–1945.* Vol. 1. London, 1973.

Zonabend, Françoise. "Les Morts et les vivants: Le Cimetière de Minot en Châtillonais," *Etudes rurales,* 1973.

INDEX

INDEX

MILES

0   50   100   200   300

Departments & Their Capitals